Africa and the Americas

Other titles in ABC-CLIO's

Transatlantic Relations Series

Britain and the Americas, by Will Kaufman and Heidi Slettedahl Macpherson
France and the Americas, by Bill Marshall, assisted by Cristina Johnston
Germany and the Americas, by Thomas Adam
Iberia and the Americas, by J. Michael Francis
Ireland and the Americas, by James P. Byrne, Philip Coleman, and Jason King

Africa and the Americas

Culture, Politics, and History

A Multidisciplinary Encyclopedia

VOLUME 1

EDITED BY

Richard M. Juang and Noelle Morrissette

Melissa Fullmer
Editorial Assistant

Transatlantic Relations Series

Will Kaufman, Series Editor

A B C ☰ C L I O

Santa Barbara, California   Denver, Colorado   Oxford, England

Copyright © 2008 by ABC-CLIO, Inc.

Library of Congress Cataloging-in-Publication Data
Africa and the Americas : culture, politics, and history : a multidisciplinary encyclopedia / edited by Richard M. Juang and Noelle Morrissette.
    p. cm. — (Translatlantic relations series)
3 v.
Includes bibliographical references and index.
ISBN-13: 978-1-85109-441-7 (hard copy : alk. paper)
ISBN-13: 978-1-85109-446-2 (ebook : alk. paper) 1. America—Relations—Africa—Encyclopedias. 2. Africa—Relations—America—Encyclopedias.

DT31.A43 2008
303.48'2706—dc22

                                        2007035154

12 11 10 09 08 10 9 8 7 6 5 4 3 2 1

Production Editor: *Kristine Swift*
Production Manager: *Don Schmidt*
Media Editor: *Jason Kniser*
Media Production Coordinator: *Ellen Brenna Dougherty*
Media Resources Manager: *Caroline Price*
File Management Coordinator: *Paula Gerard*

ABC-CLIO, Inc.
130 Cremona Drive, P.O. Box 1911
Santa Barbara, California 93116–1911

This book is also available on the World Wide Web as an ebook.
Visit www.abc-clio.com for details.

This book is printed on acid-free paper ∞

Manufactured in the United States of America

CONTENTS

SERIES EDITOR'S PREFACE

The transatlantic relationship has been one of the most dynamic of modern times. Since the great Age of Exploration in the fifteenth and sixteenth centuries, the encounters between the Old World and the New have determined the course of history, culture, and politics for billions of people. The destinies of Europe, Africa, North and South America, and all the islands in between have been intertwined to the extent that none of those areas can be said to exist in isolation. Out of these interconnections comes the concept of the "Atlantic World," which Alan Karras describes in his introductory essay to *Britain and the Americas* in this series: "By looking at the Atlantic World as a single unit, rather than relying upon more traditional national (such as Britain) or regional (such as North or South America) units of analysis, scholars have more nearly been able to re-create the experiences of those who lived in the past." This perspective attempts to redefine and respond to expanding (one might say "globalizing") pressures and new ways of perceiving interconnections—not only those rooted in history ("the past") but also those that are ongoing. Just one result of this conceptual redefinition has been the emergence of Transatlantic Studies as an area of inquiry in its own right, growing from the soil of separate area studies, whether European, North American, African, Caribbean, or Latin American. Students and scholars working in Transatlantic Studies are embarked on a new course of scholarship that places the transatlantic dynamic at its heart.

In this spirit, the Transatlantic Relations Series is devoted to transcending, or at least challenging, the boundaries of nation and region as well as of discipline: we are concerned in this series not only with history but also with culture and politics, race and economics, gender and migration; not only with the distant past but also with this morning. The aim, in a phrase, is to explore the myriad connections and interconnections of the Atlantic World. However, while the Atlantic World concept challenges the isolation of smaller, national perspectives, nations do continue to exist, with boundaries both physical and conceptual. Thus, this series acknowledges the intractability of the national and the regional while consistently focusing on the transcending movements—the connections and interconnections—that go beyond the national and the regional. Our mode of operation has been to build an approach to the Atlantic World through attention to the separate vectors between the nations and regions on both sides of the Atlantic. We do this through offering the six titles within the series so far commissioned, devoted, respectively, to Africa, Britain, France, Germany, Iberia, and Ireland in their engagements with the Americas. In each case, the transatlantic exchanges are those of all kinds: cultural, political, and historical, from the moment of first contact to the present day. With that organizing principle in mind, the object is to offer an accessible, precisely focused means of entry into the various portals of the Atlantic World.

Finally, a word about the origins of this series. In 1995, Professor Terry Rodenberg of Central Missouri State University invited scholars and teachers from eighteen universities on both sides of the Atlantic to establish an educational and scholarly institution devoted to encouraging a transatlantic perspective. The result was the founding of the Maastricht Center for Transatlantic Studies (MCTS), located in the Dutch city whose name, through its eponymous treaty, resonates with transnational associations. Since its foundation, MCTS has continued to bring together students and scholars from a host of worldwide locations to explore the intricate web of Atlantic connections across all disciplines: it has been a dynamic encounter between cultures and people striving to transcend the limitations of separate area and disciplinary studies. I am pleased to acknowledge the extent to which the Transatlantic Relations Series grows out of the discussions and approaches articulated at MCTS. Therefore, while the separate titles in the series will carry their own dedications, the series as a whole is dedicated with great respect to Terry Rodenberg and the students and scholars at Maastricht.

Will Kaufman
University of Central Lancashire
Maastricht Center for Transatlantic Studies

EDITOR'S PREFACE

The encylopedia of *Africa and the Americas* is part of the Transatlantic Relations Series and, like its counterparts, provides entries about the many past and present historical, political, and cultural relationships that tie both sides of the Atlantic Ocean. The first part of this preface offers a brief description of what you will find inside and how those materials are organized. The second part provides some ways to think about exploring the transatlantic world of Africa and the Americas for readers just starting to explore the topics found here.

In order to encompass the transatlantic world, this reference work contains four kinds of entries. Many of the entries in this encyclopedia deal directly with distinctively transatlantic topics, such as the slave trade, the plantation system, and reparations for slavery and colonialism. Others provide important contexts, such as the American civil rights movement, the fight for women's equality, and the history of colonialism, for understanding those connections. Still other entries offer a view of the African Diaspora in the Americas, its struggles, and its rich results, from the transfer of African knowledge into the Americas ("Technology Transfers") to the Harlem Renaissance. Finally, many entries explore and compare important processes that have a distinctive impact on Africa and the Americas, such as industrialization, environmentalism, HIV prevention, terrorism, and globalization. As a whole, these volumes offer a sense of the richness of the continents on both sides of the Atlantic and their long-standing connectedness.

The geographic scope alone of this project is vast: at 11,724 square miles (30,400 square kilometers), Africa is the second largest continent in the world, after Asia. North and South America are third and fourth, respectively. In light of the vast physical and historical area to be discussed, this encyclopedia seeks to cover the large transatlantic world in a variety of ways. Historically, we provide entries that run from the early days of transatlantic slaving voyages in the fifteenth century to the present day of post-independence Africa. Some entries have been included that will also help readers understand the contexts of precolonial Africa and pre-Columbian America. In terms of subjects, we have sought to cover history, culture, and politics in the broadest sense. You will find here many traditional entries about important people, places, and events, such as Bob Marley, South Africa, and World War II. You can also read about different religious and cultural beliefs, such as Islam and Santeria, as well as discover a useful overall demographic picture for the predominant faiths in Africa and the Americas ("Religion in Africa and the Americas,

Demography of"). At the same time, there are entries that many readers might not expect. These include ordinary objects and parts of life: "Rice in the African Diaspora," for example; "Hair"; and "Burial, African Practices in the Americas." Natural processes are included: "Evolution, Human," for example, and "Ecology." You will also find entries on complex economic, political, and social topics in such articles as "Microfinance"; "Cold War"; "Arms Trafficking"; "Health, Public"; "Agriculture, Sustainable"; and "Gay, Lesbian, Bisexual, and Transgender Movements, Africa and African Diasporic." This rich variety of entries will allow readers to think about Africa and the Americas from many different angles.

For readers seeking broad overviews of Africa and the Americas, this encyclopedia includes introductory essays. Each essay offers a way of envisioning the broad context of the transatlantic world of Africa and the Americas and provides brief references to key entries. For readers new to these aspects of Africa and the Americas, we encourage using these introductory essays as a springboard to future study.

The number of possible topics that could be included in a reference work such as this is enormous and grows daily. Because of this, you might find that we do not have a specific entry on the topic that you are looking for. For users of the electronic version of this encyclopedia, we recommend searching for key words related to what you need to find. It is likely that you will find some part of what you are looking for in a larger entry.

THE AFRICAN DIASPORA AND THE TRANSATLANTIC WORLD

In studying the transatlantic world of Africa and the Americas, it is vital to recognize the great diversity of the African continent, as well as of the Americas and the Caribbean. It is also important to keep in mind that the interactions and movements of peoples, cultures, and ideas that have occurred across the Atlantic since the fifteenth century have been both voluntary and forced. These transatlantic interchanges are a key part of the story of how the modern world was forged, not by any one nation alone, or even any one continent, but through continental and global networks of peoples and cultures: by the medieval African empires of Ghana, Mali, and Songhay through trade in gold, salt, and knowledge; through the spread of Islam in Europe, Africa, and the Americas; through capitalism and religious proselytizing in tandem with the rise of European nations vying for political and economic power through colonialism; through slave labor that fueled the early days of industrial economies; through the rebellion of enslaved and oppressed populations to defend their humanity and assert their right to political self-determination; and through the continued and persistent ties of black cultures to national and global politics, economics, and peoples.

The transformations brought about by the gradual development of a global economy were irrevocable for all involved, and it is critical to understand the consequences of the transatlantic slave trade and colonialism. While many benefits accrued to Europe and white settlers in the New World and Africa, the human cost was considerable. The greatest negative impact was suffered by the African societies that endured the transatlantic slave trade and the indigenous populations of the New World, both of whom experienced a catastrophic loss of population calculated in the millions. For the indigenous peoples of the New World, Spanish and Portuguese contact introduced a spate of diseases to which they had no immunity, resulting in the decimation of the indigenous population from Mexico to Brazil. Consequently, Spanish industries in the New World began to rely increasingly on the labor of enslaved Africans. Despite a higher immunity to common European diseases, however, the mortality rate for Africans in the Americas was still extremely high. Conservative estimates indicate that from ten to twenty million Africans died in holding pens and in the Middle Passage from African ports to plantations in the Americas. This estimate does not include the countless others who died in the forced marches from the interior to the slave ships. Mass enslavement, following the decimation of indigenous peoples in the Americas, was, in turn, a major part of the foundation of growing European and, later, U.S. strength on the world stage.

The colonialism that followed the growth of European power was the second large-scale transformation of transatlantic relations. Formalized by the Berlin West African Conference of 1885, the "scramble for Africa" saw the division of the continent into British, French, German, Belgian, Portuguese, Dutch, and Italian colonial territories. King Leopold II of Belgium described the continent as a "magnificent African cake" and the Berlin conference imposed boundaries without regard for preexisting cultural, ethnic, and linguistic regions. Furthermore, through a policy of "indirect rule," British colonial administrations constructed and maintained fictitious local "traditions" that set indigenous ethnic groups against each other, while France's policy of "direct rule" forbade indigenous cultural practices and languages and imposed French practices in their place. Today's complex political map of Africa is a consequence of European colonialism. Many of those colonial boundaries form the borders of contemporary independent African nations, even as cultures, languages, and religions still often cross those borders.

The transformation of Africa and the Americas through their global ties cannot be described exclusively through loss, however. Nor can the stark contemporary gap between the affluence of much of North America and the relative poverty of much of Africa be seen as simply "the way things always were." The ancient civilizations of Egypt, Nubia, and Ethiopia are important examples of black successes and more generally an attestation to the fact that preceding the legacy of enslavement, black peoples have had a history that is worthy of study. The ancient kingdoms and empires of Mali, Songhay, and Ghana are prominent examples of accomplishment that have become familiar only more recently to scholars of Africa and the African Diaspora. Both examples are important. Ancient Egypt, Nubia, and Ethiopia demonstrate that African dispersal occurred well before the slave trades of Eastern Africa and the transatlantic, and that in antiquity the spread of African culture and ideas influenced other regions and civilizations. The empires of Mali and Songhay facilitated the spread of Islam and founded a tradition of knowledge and learning, some of it written, as in the case of Timbuktu.

The student of the African Diaspora and of the transatlantic world more generally should be aware that Africans and African-descended peoples have taken an active role in determining their lives as a people, not only in the period of antiquity as leaders of civilization, but also in the modern era of enslavement and colonialism, as rebels and leaders in the cause of freedom and basic human dignity. Africans and African-descended people fought slavery and colonialism culturally, artistically, and politically as well as militarily. Individuals engaged in many kinds of rebellion against oppression: acts of resistance ranged from subversive acts such as stealing and running away for brief periods of time, to formally contesting slavery's legality and assisting abolitionists, to organized rebellion and revolt. The most famous of these revolts was, perhaps, the Haitian Revolution that resulted in the first independent black-led nation in the Americas. At a later time, African and Caribbean anticolonial movements, the U.S. civil rights and black nationalist movements, and the global movement for human rights would all influence each other.

Creative responses to domination and enslavement have extended beyond rebellion and revolution. African American literature was born out of the violence and racism to which its authors were subjected. For its earliest authors, African American literature was a response to the hypocrisy of nations who professed Christianity, European Enlightenment philosophies, and humanistic principles while owning slaves and profiting from slavery. Eighteenth-century authors used their writing as interventions in the ongoing debate about the humanity of black people relative to whites, a debate that did not consider that black persons themselves might take part in the conversation. Literature has a critical role historically and in this encyclopedia. Literacy was a tool to prove one's humanity and to dismantle the master's house using his own tools, as the critic Audre Lorde once put it, from its earliest forms (by, for example, Phillis Wheatley, Frederick Douglass, and Paul Lawrence Dunbar) to present-day works (by Charles Johnson, Toni Morrison, David Bradley, and Colson Whitehead, among many others).

In addition to engaging literacy and other values of the Western world, the African American literary tradition rests on prominent "nonliterary" forms of art in the black world, such as folklore, music, dance, and oral literature. These art forms have been essential to creating culturally specific worldviews in African societies and to re-imagining and adapting those views to the experience of New World slavery. African cultures have firm roots in oral tradition: the epic of Sundiata, celebrating the eponymous first ruler of the Mali Empire, is one such example and one of the oldest surviving epics, alongside Homer's *Iliad* and *Odyssey*. The spirituals, jazz, and blues are all New World musical responses to slavery and its aftermath, not transcendent of the experience but a way to survive it. Trickster figures from the Akan and other West African cultures were adapted to folklore in a New World setting, where animals play out master and slave roles. Folklore of "flying Africans" addressed the yearning for escape from slavery and the desire to return home. Dance was transformed: it became a cloak for the practice of martial arts in the case of Capoeira.

These cultural forms of expression have not always been appreciated as art. Until recently, colleges, universities, and secondary schools debated whether African American art, culture, and politics were legitimate subjects of study. Concomitant with the Civil Rights, Black Power, and Black Arts movements of the 1960s and 1970s, black activists confronted the cultural biases that undervalued not only these subjects but also the presence of black people in the educational system, as students and teachers. One result of this activism was the creation of Black Studies programs nationwide at many universities and colleges. Many of these programs continue to thrive and have helped to develop an understanding of concepts of race, supporting scholarship in the area of black studies as they have evolved in outlook to address a black world population. African and African American scholars have revised and reconfigured these approaches to address cultural exchanges between black peoples and other groups in a range of historical periods; to recover and revalue an African past of great civilizations; to understand the demography behind the black Diaspora; to understand how institutional policies shape the lives and aspirations of individuals; and to create an alternative canon of black authors' works. In short, all of the disciplines—history, art, literature, science, sociology, political science, religious studies, anthropology, agrarian studies—are brought to bear on studies of Africa and the African Diaspora: interdisciplinary approaches reveal the multifaceted nature of black experience.

In tracing the movements and dispersion of African and African-descended peoples throughout the world, it is important to consider the movement, both physical and intellectual, of black peoples back to the African continent in an effort to reconnect with a cultural homeland. African, Caribbean, and African American artists have engaged the idea of multifaceted black identity in a variety of ways, depending on background and circumstance as well as on the individual imagination of each. Significantly, their efforts to reconnect coincide with artistic "renaissances" such as the New Negro Renaissance, the Harlem Renaissance, and the Black Arts Movement, as well as with political movements in civil rights, Black Power, and independence. Early twentieth-century African American authors Langston Hughes and Arthur Schomburg used their written works to emphasize the value and importance of the African past in shaping a sense of contemporary African American life and art. Mid-twentieth-century African American visual artist Elizabeth Catlett engaged the idea of Afro-Mexican identity in her work. In the last years of his life, W. E. B. Du Bois renounced his American citizenship and became a citizen of Ghana. Black Panthers in flight from U.S. prosecution resettled in East African nations.

Many worldwide black intellectual movements have intervened in world culture and politics, creating positive concepts for black cultural identity and rejecting domination, such as "Négritude," "Pan-Africanism," "Noirisme," and "Black Power." In addition, a working critical and theoretical vocabulary has grown out of terms, some of which were coined by the thinkers of these movements, including "double consciousness," "Atlantic World," "black Atlantic," "transculturation," "postcolonialism," and "neocolonialism." These terms for the critical study of the African Diaspora originated in different decades, nations, and schools of thought, and demonstrate the active engagement with, and importance of, black communities around the world in understanding world history, politics, and culture.

Ultimately, while there is a shared experience of colonial domination and enslavement as part of black history around the world, there is also extraordinary diversity within the black community, and no one set of experiences is universal. Students of Africa and the African Diaspora in the Americas must consider the particular contexts of their subject, while also searching for the aspects of cultural retention, cultural transformation, and cultural innovation that define the relationship between Africa and the Americas.

Richard M. Juang and
Noelle Morrissette

References

Blassingame, John W., ed. *Slave Testimony: Two Centuries of Letters, Speeches, Interviews, and Autobiographies.* Baton Rouge: Louisiana State University Press, 1977.

Boahen, A. Adu. *African Perspectives on Colonialism.* Baltimore, MD: Johns Hopkins University Press, 1987.

Davies, Carol Boyce. *Black Women, Writing and Identity: Migrations of the Subject.* New York: Routledge, 1994.

Davies, Carol Boyce et al., eds. *The African Diaspora: African Origins and New World Identities.* Bloomington: Indiana University Press, 1999.

Genovese, Eugene. *From Rebellion to Revolution: Afro-American Slave Revolts in the Making of the Modern World.* Baton Rouge: Louisiana State University Press, 1979.

Gilroy, Paul. *The Black Atlantic: Modernity and Double Consciousness.* Cambridge, MA: Harvard University Press, 1993.

Gomez, Michael. *Reversing Sail: A History of the African Diaspora.* New York: Cambridge University Press, 2005.

Irele, F. Abiola. *The African Imagination: Literature in Africa and the Black Diaspora.* New York: Oxford University Press, 2001.

James, Winston. *Holding Aloft the Banner of Ethiopia: Caribbean Radicalism in Early Twentieth-Century America.* New York: Verso, 1998.

Lovejoy, Paul. *Transformations in Slavery.* New York: Cambridge University Press, 1983.

Miller, Christopher L. *Blank Darkness: Africanist Discourse in French.* Chicago: University of Chicago Press, 1985.

Mudimbe, V. Y. *The Invention of Africa: Gnosis, Philosophy, and the Order of Knowledge.* Bloomington: Indiana University Press, 1988.

Price, Richard, ed. *Maroon Societies: Rebel Slave Communities in the Americas.* Baltimore, MD: Johns Hopkins University Press, 1996.

TOPIC FINDER

COUNTRIES

Algeria
Angola
Antigua and Barbuda
Bahamas
Barbados
Benin, Republic of
Bermuda
Bolivia
Brazil
Britain: People of African
    Origin and Descent
Burkina Faso
Burundi
Cameroon
Canada (Africadian
    Culture)
Cape Verde
Central African Republic
Chad
Chile
Colombia
Comoros
Congo (Zaire), Democratic
    Republic of the
Cote D'Ivoire (Ivory Coast)
Cuba
Djibouti

Dominican Republic, The
Ecuador
Egypt
Equatorial Guinea
Eritrea
Ethiopia
Gabon, Republic of
Gambia, The
Ghana
Guinea
Guinea-Bissau
Guyana
Haiti
Jamaica
Kenya
Lesotho
Liberia
Libya
Madagascar
Malawi
Mali
Mauritania
Mauritius
Mexico
Morocco
Mozambique
Namibia
Nicaragua

Niger
Nigeria
Paraguay
Peru
Rwanda
Saint Kitts and Nevis
São Tomé e Príncipe
Senegal
Seychelles
Sierra Leone
Somalia
South Africa, History and
    Politics
Suriname
Swaziland
Tanzania
Togo
Trindad and Tobago
Tunisia
Uganda
Uraguay
Zambia
Zimbabwe

CULTURE AND FOLKLORE

Afrofuturism
Akan

Ananse
Ancestor Worship
Anthropology
Architecture
Architecture, Plantation
Art, African
Black Arts Movement
Black Athena
Black Classical Singers
Brazilian Carnival
Brazilian Culture
Burial Ground (New York City), African
Burial, African Practices in the Americas
Calypso
Candomblé
Caribbean Artists Movement
Carnival, Latin American
Castas Paintings
Ceddo
Cuban Music, African Influence in
Cuban Ritual Music, African Influence in
Drama, African American
English, African American Vernacular (AAVE)
Film (Africa)
Film (Caribbean)
Film (Latin America)
Film (North America)
Film (South America)
Film, Atlantic
Flying Africans
Folklore, African
Guinea Dance
Hair
Hip-Hop
Hip-Hop, Cuban
Hip-Hop, Women in
Imperial Germany, Black Entertainers in

Jazz and the Blues
Jazz, African
Kente cloth
Mexico (Afro-Mexican Identity)
Museums and Transatlantic Slavery
Music, African
Music, African Popular
Négritude
Nigeria, Drama in
Nigerian Traditional Dances
Notting Hill Carnival in London
Obeah
Ogun
Orisha
Oroonoko
Pageant, The African-American
Popular Music, American influences on African
Radio Marti
Reggae
Reggae, African
Soukous
Sundiata Keita (1202–1255) and Sundiata Epic
Television in Africa, American Influence on
Voodoo
Weimar Republic, Black Entertainers in the

CURRENT ISSUES

Agriculture, Sustainable
Arms Trafficking
Biotechnology
Cities
Coffee
Democracy, African
Democracy, Latin America

Diamonds
Diaspora
Diaspora, Demography of
EBONY
Ecology
Environmentalism
Ethnicity
Globalization
Green Revolution
Health, Public
HIV (Human Immunodeficiency Virus) and Prevention
Human Rights
Humanitarian Assistance
Immigration, United States
International Development
Jamaica, Women's Role in
Lost Boys of Sudan
Microfinance
Military Forces
Oil
Palm oil
Peacekeeping and Military Interventions
Reproductive Health and Family Planning in Africa, US Influence on
Restavek
Soccer
Socialism
Sudan—Darfur region
Technology Transfers
Terrorism
Trade Zones, African
Trade, Fair
Transculturation

FILM AND BROADCASTING

Ceddo
Film (Africa)
Film (Caribbean)

Avellaneda, Gertrudis
  Gómez de
Bakhita [Saint Josephine
  Bakhita]
Baraka, Amiri (Leroi Jones)
Barnet, Miguel
Bauzá, Mario
Bennett, Louise
Beyala, Calixthe
Blucke, Stephen
Blyden, Edward Wilmot
Brand, Dionne
Brathwaite, Kamau
Brindis de Salas, Virginia
Brooks, Gwendolyn
Brouwer, Leo
Brown, William
Bunche, Ralph
Cabral, Amilcar
Cabral, Cristina Rodriguez
Carver, George
  Washington
Casas, Bartolome de las
Castro Ruz, Fidel
Césaire, Aimé
Chamoiseau, Patrick
Chikaba [Venerable
  Therese Juliana of
  Saint Dominic]
Christophe, Henri
Clemente Walker, Roberto
Cliff, Michelle
Coetzee, J.M. (John
  Maxwell)
Columbus, Christopher
Condé, Maryse
Cruz, Celia
Cuffe, Captain Paul
Dabydeen, David
Dadié, Bernard Binlin
D'Aguiar, Fred
Dan Fodio, Uthman
Dangarembga, Tsitsi

Danticat, Edwidge
Dash, Julie
Delany, Martin Robinson
Dessalines, Jean Jacques
Diop, Cheikh Anta
Djebar, Assia
Doe, Samuel K.
Dongala, Emmanuel
  Boundzeki
Douglass, Frederick
Du Bois, W E B
Dutty, Boukman
Duvalier, François
Duvalier, Jean-Claude
Ekwensi, Cyprian Odiatu
  Duaka
Ellison, Ralph
Emecheta, Buchi
Equiano, Olaudah
Fanon, Frantz
Farrakhan, Louis
Fauset, Jessie
Gabriel
Garvey, Amy Jacques
Garvey, Marcus
Gates Jr., Henry Louis
Gilroy, Beryl Agatha née
  Answick
Glissant, Edourd
Goyemide, Etienne
Gronniosaw, Ukawsaw
Guillén, Nicolás
Haley, Alex
Hansberry, Lorraine
Head, Bessie
Hughes, Langston
Hurston, Zora Neale
Ike, Vincent
  Chukwuemeka
Imbuga, Francis D.
Jacobs, Harriet
James, C.L.R.
Johnson, Charles R.

Johnson, James Weldon
Johnson, Linton Kwesi
Jones, Claudia, née
  Cumberbatch
Juana Ines de la Cruz, Sor
Kaunda, Kenneth
Kincaid, Jamaica
King Jr, Martin Luther
Laing, Kojo
Lewis, Mary Edmonia
Locke, Alain
Lopes, Henry
Lorde, Audre
Louverture, Toussaint
  Bréda
Lumumba, Patrice
Mad Mullah (Mohammed
  bin Abdullah Hassan)
Malcolm X
Mandela, Nelson
Manzano, Juan Francisco
Marley, Robert Nesta (Bob)
Marrant, John
Marshall, Paule
Marson, Una
Martí, José
Mays, Willie Howard
McKay, Claude
Miller, Samuel T.
Mohammad, Warith Deen
Montaigne, Michel de
Moody, Harold
Morejón, Nancy
Morris, Mervyn
Morrison, Toni
Mullen, Harryette
Mutabaruka
N'Krumah, Kwame
Naipaul, V.S.
Nanny
Nwapa, Flora
O'Farrill, Arturo "Chico"
Okigbo, Christopher

CHRONOLOGY OF AFRICA AND THE AMERICAS

700   Advancement in transportation through the use of camels rather than horses permits long-distance travel over the Sahara Desert. The Sahel—a region of West Africa south of the Sahara—becomes established as an important area of trade connecting Africa, Europe, and Asia and a center of politics, culture, and religion as well. Three major empires—Ghana, Mali, and Songhay—develop from this hub. They are referred to collectively as the Sahelian kingdoms; all of them develop global connections within Africa and with Europe and Asia.

750–1200   Ghana Empire, dominated by the Soninke, a Mande-speaking people. It becomes known as "the land of gold" as the market intermediary of gold trade between the north and south. Its decline begins in 1075 with the invasion of the Almoravids, Berbers from the north.

1200–1500   Kingdom of Mali, covering most of West Africa. Sundiata, one of its greatest leaders, is praised for uniting the Malian Empire. Its decline begins in the 1400s, largely because of a succession of weak kings and the decentralization of its influence.

1350–1600   Songhay Kingdom, which existed under the Kingdom of Mali, begins to break away and establishes itself in 1350. Songhay was larger than Mali and was centered along the Niger River. The city of Timbuktu becomes a key center of Islamic learning and attracts scholars from around the world. The empire becomes so large it is hard to govern and falls because of a series of revolts.

1468   The Songhay Empire appears in the regions of present-day western Sudan and Mali, increasing in strength to reach its peak in the sixteenth century.

1482   Arrival of the Portuguese explorer Diogo Cam in the territory of the Kongo kingdom, which extends from the south of present-day Gabon to the northern parts of present-day Angola and east into the present-day Democratic Republic of the Congo's interior.

Portugal founds the slave fort Elmina, along with 13 to 15 others. Under British control, Elmina will become one of the largest forts in the transatlantic slave trade.

1492   Columbus's first voyage to the Americas, initiating the dramatic biological, cultural, and human exchange between

Africa, Europe, and the Americas known as the Columbian Exchange.

1510 The first African slaves arrive in Hispaniola, to work in mines and on plantations.

1519 The first Africans arrive in Mexico as explorers and servants during the conquest period of Spanish America's history, 1519–1540.

1526 The earliest documented rebellion of African slaves in the Western Hemisphere takes place at San Miguel de Guadeloupe; slaves rebel against the Spanish.

1534 The first Africans arrive in Uruguay with Pedro de Mendoza, a Spanish explorer of the River Plate.

1536 Diego de Almagro claims the region of present-day Chile for the Spanish crown, making it a colony of Spain. He brings the first blacks to Chile on this voyage, initiating the importation of slaves to supplement the indigenous labor force.

1538 Portuguese carve out the first sugar plantation in present-day Brazil.

1577 Sir Francis Drake sets sail on his legendary voyage of piracy and discovery through the Strait of Magellan, along the Pacific coast of South America, and north to Drake's Bay, beyond present-day San Francisco. He will claim the western American coast for England (as New Albion) and become the first Englishman (the second person after Ferdinand Magellan) to circumnavigate the globe.

1584 Sir Walter Raleigh dispatches an expedition to the coast of North Carolina. Upon learning of the fertility of the region from his captains' reports, he names it Virginia in honor of Elizabeth I, the Virgin Queen.

1595 Walter Raleigh attacks and plunders Trinidad in his search for El Dorado, the legendary City of Gold.

1596 Raleigh's *The Discovery of the Large and Bewtiful Empire of Guyana* inaugurates British travel and historical writing about the Caribbean.

1605 London colonists fail to establish settlements on Grenada and St. Lucia.

1606 James I grants a charter jointly to the Virginia Company of London and the Plymouth Company to establish a permanent settlement in the Chesapeake Bay region, prospect for gold, and seek out a waterway to the Orient.

1609 On behalf of the Dutch East India Company, Henry Hudson charts parts of the river subsequently named for him.

1612 Bermuda is formally established as England's second permanent colony in the Americas.

1616 Still searching for El Dorado, Sir Walter Raleigh angers King James I by attacking a Spanish settlement in present-day Guyana. The king will have Raleigh beheaded two years later.

English settlers attempting to settle Tobago are driven off the island by Carib attackers.

1617 Raleigh mounts his second marauding attack on Trinidad.

1619 Jamestown tobacco planters import the first Africans, sold as "indentured servants," to the American colonies.

Virginia's House of Burgesses first meets in July.

1620 Bermuda settlers establish self-government through an elected assembly, the second colonial parliament in the New World after the House of Burgesses.

Having steered off its original course, the former wine ship *Mayflower* briefly anchors off present-day Provincetown, Massachusetts, following a two-month voyage from Southampton, England. Anglican Separatists and non-Separatists on board the ship draw up the Mayflower Compact providing for the temporary government of the colony by "a civill body politick" and majority rule.

1621   The Dutch West India Company is founded to regulate trade to Africa and America—and to extend the Dutch war against Spain to the matters of access to raw goods, control of Caribbean colonies, and control of the transatlantic slave trade.

1624   The first English plantation settlement in the Caribbean is established at Sandy Bay, St. Kitts (St. Christopher). The French will arrive on the island one year later.

1625   The earl of Carlisle is granted a royal charter to colonize the Caribbean islands of Barbados, Montserrat, Nevis, and St. Kitts. The charter is later extended to include Anegada and the remaining Lesser Antilles.

Samuel Purchas's *Hakluytus Posthumus, or Purchas His Pilgrims,* condemns Spanish cruelty against the indigenous peoples of America and includes the Codex Mendoza, the first publication in England of a Mexican pictographic manuscript.

1626   Captain Maurice Thompson inaugurates English slavery in the Caribbean with the first shipment of African slaves to St. Kitts.

1627   England seizes Barbados from Spain, establishing its most profitable American colony in the seventeenth century.

England stakes its first claims to Dominica and St. Vincent.

1628   Anthony Hilton, fleeing from a murder plot on St. Kitts, establishes the first English settlement on Nevis.

1632   Antigua and Montserrat are settled by English adventurers. Following the success of Barbados, the colonies will thrive on sugar production facilitated by slave labor.

1634   The Netherlands Antilles begins as a Dutch colony under the government authority of the West India Company.

1638   English colonists plant their first successful settlement on St. Lucia in the Caribbean.

1639   A revolt on St. Kitts and Nevis occurs. The uprising of approximately sixty enslaved Africans sets a precedent for aggressive resistance to French New World slavery.

1641   Indigenous Carib wipe out the English settlement on St. Lucia.

1647   A group of religious refugees from Bermuda, the Eleutheran Adventurers, establish the Bahamas's first permanent English settlement.

1648   Dutch forces occupy the Caribbean islands of Anegada, Tortola, and Virgin Gorda, denying the English claim.

English religious dissenters from Bermuda begin to colonize the Bahamas.

1655   An English expedition under William Penn and Robert Venables captures Jamaica and the Cayman Islands from the Spanish—a poor substitute for the intended targets of Hispaniola and Cuba. Already populated by thousands of Maroons (escaped slaves), Jamaica will soon support the largest slave market in the Americas.

Swedes build their fort, Carolusburg, in what is present-day Ghana. It changes hands numerous times before the English gain control of it in 1664, renaming it Cape Coast Castle. It becomes the administrative center of England's African trade (under the Royal African Company) and is instrumental in creating England's Gold Coast Colony in the nineteenth century.

1660   The English crown's monopoly in slaving begins with the Royal Adventurers in Africa.

Virginia codifies the institutional legalities of slavery, supporting the colony's growing dependency on forced labor provided by the African slave trade. Declaring that baptism does not necessitate freedom, Virginia law will determine an individual's status as free or enslaved through matrilineal identification.

1661   Edward D'Oyley becomes English captain-general and governor-in-chief of Jamaica. Under D'Oyley, the island begins its long tradition as a haven for buccaneers who prey on Spanish ships sailing in and out of Port Royal. The colonial authorities will largely ignore the buccaneers because their activities distract the Spanish at a time when the English are in no position to protect the West Indies.

English settlers from Antigua colonize Barbuda.

1666   English forces drive the Dutch from Tortola and assume precarious control of the Virgin Islands. English occupation is not firmly consolidated until 1694.

1667   The Treaty of Breda is signed by England and the United Provinces of the Netherlands, formally ending the second Anglo-Dutch War. The Dutch formally recognize English control of New Netherlands.

The Bahamas are granted to the English proprietors of Carolina.

Antigua and Barbuda are formally colonized by Britain.

1670   The Treaty of Madrid grants England title to Jamaica.

The Virginia Slavery Act decrees that slaves baptized as Christians prior to importation are not liable to permanent enslavement. The act specifically addresses a growing debate concerning the morality and legality of enslaving fellow Christians.

1672   King James II's Royal African Company takes up the monopoly of the African slave trade, eventually leading to Jamaica's status as one of the largest slave markets in the world. With an enormous population of slave labor, the island will soon become the world's leading producer of sugar cane.

Rice comes to colonial America from Ghana. It is introduced to South Carolina shortly after its establishment as a colony.

1674   Slave importation is banned in Bermuda.

1676   A Quaker settlement is established in West New Jersey.

1678   Emigrants from Bermuda establish the first English settlements in the Turks and Caicos Islands. They engage in whaling and the production of timber and salt.

1680   African slaves are first brought to the coastal islands off Georgia and South Carolina from the West Indies.

1682   William Penn introduces Quakerism to America.

1685   French king Louis XIV promulgates the Code Noir in March. Its sixty articles set legal precepts on how slaves should be treated. The code, applied to French colonies in the Americas, is designed to ensure slave obedience and reduce the likelihood of revolts.

1688   Aphra Behn's *Oroonoko, or the Royal Slave* marks the starting point for a succession of plays and novels reflecting Britain's growing concern for social conditions amongst the slave societies in the Americas.

Irish Catholics fleeing religious persecution establish the first significant European settlement on Anguilla.

1689   King William's War begins, the first in a series of North American wars between England and France that will last over 125 years and include the seven-year period from 1756 to 1763 known as the French and Indian Wars. While the French are supported by Native American groups in Canada and Maine, the British (largely colonial troops) are supported by the Iroquois. Hostilities are mainly concentrated on the northern coast of North America and in the Upper Hudson-Upper St. Lawrence valleys; the British colonies on St. Kitts and Nevis are also embroiled.

1690   England claims the first recorded landing on the uninhabited Falkland Islands off the coast of Argentina.

1692   The English settlement of Port Royal, Jamaica, is destroyed by an earthquake.

1698   Five ships carrying 1,200 Scottish settlers land at Darien, on the Isthmus of Panama, in an ill-fated attempt to establish a Scottish colony (New Caledonia) in Latin America. After two years of severe hardship, illness, and attacks by the Spanish, the bankrupt colony is surrendered to Spain in 1700.

The Royal African Company's monopoly on the slave trade ends.

1703   The Methuen Treaty between Britain and Portugal grants commercial preference to British merchants in Brazil.

1708   Blacks now outnumber whites in Carolina.

1710   Boston merchants begin the importation of African slaves into Massachusetts.

1713   The Treaty of Utrecht ending the War of the Spanish Succession grants to Britain the *asiento,* the monopoly on importing slaves from Africa to the Spanish possessions in the Americas.

The Treaty also cedes to Britain the French territories of Acadia (the modern Canadian provinces of Prince Edward Island, New Brunswick, Cape Breton, and Nova Scotia). The cession does not stem the tide of French Catholic and Huguenot settlers.

The Treaty also cedes French St. Kitts to the British.

1717   The Bahamas become an official British colony.

1720   The first of the Maroon Wars erupts in Jamaica, where escaped slaves organize to fight white militia and secure land grants for settlement.

Old Calabar towns of Obutong and Aqua Akpa (also known as Duke Town) in present-day Nigeria become involved in the transatlantic slave trade. Between 1720 and 1830, 1 million slaves were taken from the port towns, mostly on British vessels.

1732   A group of philanthropists headed by General James Oglethorpe establish Georgia as a charity colony for London's poor and also as a barrier against French and Spanish settlement. Georgia's authoritarian government at Savannah will outlaw slavery, rum, and land sales. Initially focused on silk and wool, Georgia's economy will eventually turn to rice and cotton production facilitated by slave labor.

1733   The Molasses Act places duty on molasses obtained outside of Britain. The act is designed to ensure continued profitability for British-owned sugar plantations throughout the West Indies by placing prohibitive duties on the importation of sugar and molasses from outside of British possessions.

1739   The Stono Slave Rebellion commences in South Carolina with assaults upon plantations on the main road to Florida, where the Spanish have promised freedom to slave fugitives from the British territories. Nearly one hundred slaves participate in the rebellion under the leadership of a man named Jemmy. The local militia ruthlessly crushes the rebels, hanging the heads of executed slaves on landmark posts throughout the colony. New laws will be passed in South Carolina, Virginia, and Maryland that provide formal guidelines for the treatment of slaves.

The First Maroon War ends with Cudjoe's Treaty, authorizing the Maroons to develop autonomous communities in the hills of Jamaica's Cockpit Country. The Maroons guarantee the return of runaway slaves in exchange for security from British raids.

1750   Through the Treaty of Madrid, Spain buys back the *asiento*—the Atlantic slave trading monopoly—from Britain for £100,000.

The Company of Merchants Trading to Africa replaces the Royal African Company. It will facilitate the coastal slave trade during both the pinnacle and abolition of England's slave trade in West Africa.

1760   Tacky's Slave Revolt breaks out in Jamaica.

1762   A British invasion force arrives at Cojímar (15 miles east of Havana, Cuba) to challenge Spanish dominion; a ten-month British occupation of Havana follows. Britain also seizes the Spanish stronghold of Manila in the Philippines.

1763   The Treaty of Paris between France, Britain, and Spain ends the Seven Years' War (known as the French and Indian War in North America). France cedes to Britain all its territory east of the Mississippi River. Britain returns the key islands of the French West Indies but gains important Windward Islands such as Grenada and Dominica. Spain cedes Florida to Britain in order to secure the return of Havana. Britain is required to protect the Catholic institutions of the territories it acquires.

1764   Britain's Sugar Act (Revenue Act), an expanded version of the Molasses Act of 1733, introduces a three-cent tax on foreign refined sugar and places higher levies on non-British textiles, coffee, indigo, and wine. In addition, the act prohibits the importation of foreign rum and French wines.

The Colonial Currency Act is designed to prevent payment of debts in England with depreciated colonial currency; the measure creates a shortage of currency in the colonies.

1765   In British Guiana, settlers establish Burnaby's Code, a mode of democratic self-regulation that will continue until 1840. Meanwhile, slaves in the colony launch the first of three rebellions against their British enslavers.

1766   The first (temporary) British settlement is established on the Falkland Islands.

The Bahamas annex the Turks and Caicos Islands.

1767   Philadelphia becomes the largest city in the American colonies. Conflict arises, however, because Pennsylvania's grant encroaches on New York and Maryland territories. British surveyors Charles Mason and Jeremiah Dixon will resolve the issue by mapping the famed Mason-Dixon Line.

1770   A crowd of about 400 people attack a British guard post protecting the Boston customs office. Against the orders of his captain, a British soldier fires into the crowd, followed by others, resulting in the deaths of five people. American propagandists reconstruct the event as the "Boston Massacre."

In response to the Boston Massacre, the new ministry of Lord North repeals all the Townshend Duties except the tax on tea. Although the repeals initiate conciliatory gestures by colonial merchants, continued British pressure for colonial compliance results in further escalation of the conflict.

1772   In the Somerset case, the king's High Bench outlaws slavery in Britain. The decision guarantees emancipation to slaves who enter the British Isles, but does not apply to slaves held abroad in the British colonies.

A Narrative of the Most Remarkable Particulars in the Life of James Albert Ukawsaw Gronniosaw, an African Prince is published, the first slave narrative in English.

1773   In British Guiana, a five-month-long slave uprising is crushed by British military reinforcements from Jamaica.

1774   Fearful of the impact of war upon the West Indian economy, Jamaican planters petition King George III for reconciliation with the rebelling American colonists.

The Virgin Islands are officially established as a British colony.

1775   George III issues a royal proclamation formally declaring the American colonies to be in a state of rebellion.

1779   The British commander in the South, Sir Henry Clinton, issues the Philipsburg Proclamation declaring that all slaves captured while working for the American rebels would be treated as spoils of war and sold or distributed for the benefit of British soldiers. Slaves fleeing to the British army would be allowed to pursue any occupation they desired within the army.

1781   The slave ship *Zong* throws 132 living slaves into the sea to secure insurance money for "lost freight."

1782   Sir Joseph Banks, the royal botanical adviser, introduces nutmeg to Grenada. It will transform the economy following the collapse of the sugar industry.

1783   Birch Town is founded by Loyalist Stephen Blucke, a settlement of black Loyalists who are refugees from the War of Independence, in Nova Scotia.

1784   Admiral Horatio Nelson arrives in Antigua to oversee the development of the Royal Navy's West Indian base.

Black Loyalist immigrants to Nova Scotia now number 3,500.

1785   Venezuelan revolutionary Francisco de Miranda establishes a base in London, where much of the planning for the eventual independence of Latin America is carried out.

John Marrant's *A Narrative* is published, describing his spiritual journey and search for God. It is now considered a seminal African American text—an early example of the tradition of African American autobiography.

1786   The Committee for the Relief of the Black Poor is established in London on behalf of black Loyalist refugees from North America.

Britain acquires logging rights from Spain in what becomes British Honduras (Belize).

1787   The first transports of "Black Poor" set sail from Britain for West Africa, where their initial settlement will develop into the nation of Sierra Leone.

Quobna Ottobah Cugoano's *Thoughts and Sentiments on the Evil and Wicked Traffic of the Slavery and Commerce of the Human Species* is published in London.

In response to the U.S.'s Northwest Ordinance barring slavery from the territory comprising today's Illinois, Indiana, Michigan, Ohio, and Wisconsin, Parliament legislates the right of American slaveholders to emigrate to Canada.

1789   Olaudah Equiano's *The Interesting Narrative of the Life of Olaudah Equiano, or Gustavus Vassa, the African* is published in London.

1791   In May the French National Assembly decrees that colored people of free parents in Haiti will have legal equality with white landowners; the decree is reversed and rescinded in September 1791.

The rebellion of slaves in what will be called the Haitian Revolution begins.

The Sierra Leone Company is established as a joint-stock enterprise of British philanthropists, who effectively take over the failing colony of Sierra Leone.

1792   Nearly 1,200 disillusioned black Loyalists leave Nova Scotia for Sierra Leone, having encountered systematic discrimination and the loss of land and civil liberties in Canada.

1793   Upper Canada's *Act to prevent the further introduction of Slaves* challenges the importation of slaves from the United States into British North America.

Grenada is restored to Britain from the French.

1794   British forces invade St. Domingue to gain control of the French colony and reestablish slavery, two years into the slave rebellion that will give birth to the independent nation of Haiti in 1804.

1795   The Second Maroon War breaks out in Jamaica.

On Grenada, French African planter Julien Fedon launches a fifteen-month rebellion against British rule, aided by an alliance of "free colored" and slaves.

On St. Vincent, Victor Hugues launches a yearlong "black Carib" rebellion against the British, which will lead to the enforced exile of over 5,000 black Caribs from the island.

The West India Regiment, one of the earliest armies recruited in the Americas and composed of slaves, is formed. It is employed to police Britain's West Indian possessions but is also used in recently acquired areas of West Africa.

1796   In Britain's final serious attempt to take Puerto Rico from Spain, Admiral Sir Henry Harvey, General Ralph Abercromby, and 7,000 regulars are stopped by the Creole militia at San Juan. The British forces withdraw after thirteen days.

A British naval force captures Trinidad, belonging to the Audiencia of Venezuela, creating the first of many irritants to British-Venezuelan relations.

1799   Gabriel, enslaved property of Thomas Prosser, organizes a rebellion in Virginia. The goal is to approach the capital, Richmond, and take the governor, James Monroe, hostage, along with most other whites, in order to force the demands of slaves and free blacks for freedom and an equitable division of white property. His plan collapses because of poor weather and an informant's telling a white slave owner of the plot. Gabriel is hanged in 1800. It is estimated that between 500 and 600 slaves knew of the plan.

The state of New York passes the Gradual Manumission Act, which frees those slaves born after July 4, 1799, once they reached the age of twenty-eight (males) or twenty-five (females).

1800   Five hundred disillusioned Jamaican Maroons abandon Nova Scotia for Sierra Leone.

Black settler discontent in Sierra Leone leads to rebellion, which is quelled by the coincidental arrival of British soldiers accompanying the Maroons from Nova Scotia.

Gabriel Prosser leads a slave insurrection.

1802   Spain cedes Trinidad to Britain.

In January, Napoleon sends his brother-in-law, General Charles Leclerc, to Saint Domingue with a large fleet and 26,000 men to defeat the rebellion led by Toussaint Louverture.

1803   Jean Jacques Dessalines defeats French general Rochambeau on November 18,

1803 at the Battle of Vertieres, forcing Napoleon to abandon control of Haiti, to sell the vast territory of Louisiana in the present-day United States, and scrap his plans for extending the French Empire to the New World.

A slave rebellion breaks out in Montevideo, Uruguay. Almost two dozen enslaved and freed blacks conspire to leave the port city and settle on a small island in the River Yi. The settlement is attacked and defeated by the forces of the Spanish governor.

1804   In January, Haiti declares independence. Jean Jacques Dessalines is selected as its governor-for-life.

Uthman Dan Fodio, the first Sokoto Caliph, leads the Fulani jihad against the Hausa kingdoms, 1804–1810.

1805   A British prize court in the Bahamas rules that the U.S. merchant ship *Essex* was legally seized in 1799 for violation of maritime neutrality. American politicians view the ruling as part of an undeclared British war on American commerce.

1806   An unauthorized British force of nearly 2,000 occupies Buenos Aires, Argentina, in a bid to block both French designs and Spanish authority in Latin America.

A campaign by Creole militia under Santiago De Liniers to break the occupation of Buenos Aires ends with a British surrender.

1807   Having captured Montevideo, Uruguay, British forces again attack Buenos Aires. Again, a Creole counterattack forces a British retreat and capitulation.

British diplomats help to persuade the Portuguese royal family to flee a French invasion force and seek exile in Brazil. The Royal Navy escorts the Portuguese court from Lisbon to Brazil.

The Act for the Abolition of the Slave Trade is passed by Parliament, outlawing the slave trade among British subjects throughout the Empire. Following the adoption of this Act, the United States passess a law abolishing participation in the international slave trade that is finalized in January of the following year.

The African Institution, an antislavery group, is formed as a result of Britain's abolition of the slave trade.

Henri Christophe establishes a separate state in the north of newly independent Haiti in February; Alexandre Pétion declares himself president of the southern and western parts of the country in March.

1808   Britain's arch enemy, the French emperor Napoleon, seizes the Spanish crown, forcing Britain to reverse its ancient hostility to Spain. Now Britain props up Spanish colonial authority by refusing to support Creole secession and independence movements in Spanish America.

The Sierra Leone Company turns over the colony to the British government.

1810   Britain negotiates a preferential tariff advantage for exports to Brazil.

Simón Bolívar, the Latin American revolutionary leader, bases himself in London.

1811   The largest U.S. slave rebellion to date, subsequently called the Louisiana Rebellion, occurs. Led by a native of Haiti, at least 180 and possibly as many as 500 slaves march toward New Orleans, but federal troops quell the rebellion.

Paraguay achieves its independence from Spain.

1813   Beginning with Trinidad, slaves in the British Empire are systematically registered as a means of regulating the remaining internal Caribbean slave trade and to prevent smuggling.

1814 The Netherlands cedes three South American colonies—Berbice, Demerara, and Essequibo—to Britain at the close of the Napoleonic Wars.

France cedes St. Lucia, Tobago, and Dominica to Britain at the close of the Napoleonic Wars.

1816 The African Methodist Episcopal Church is officially established by Bishop Richard Allen.

The American Colonization Society (ACS) is formed.

1817 Chile's ports are opened following the overthrow of Spanish rule, in which the British Royal Navy under Admiral Thomas Cochrane participated.

1818 At Aix-la-Chapelle, the European powers agree actively to suppress the slave trade. The United States does not sign the agreement and refuses permission for British patrols to search for slaves on vessels flying the American flag. Consequently, slave traders of all nationalities take to flying the Stars and Stripes to avoid prosecution.

Chile achieves independence from Spain.

1819 Jamaican-born Robert Wedderburn opens a Unitarian church on Hopkins Street in Soho, London, using the church to advocate for democracy, general emancipation, and free speech.

1820 Paralyzed by a debilitating stroke, Henri Christophe, dictator of northern Haiti, kills himself (allegedly with a silver bullet) in order to escape the armed rebellion with which he is faced.

1821 In the war for Venezuelan independence from Spain, a British legion distinguishes itself for bravery at the Battle of Carabobo.

1822 Brazil wins independence from Portugal, assisted by British mercenaries and Royal Navy forces under Admiral Lord Thomas Cochrane. Britain formally recognizes Brazilian independence in January 1826.

Denmark Vesey conspires to take control of Charleston, Virginia, gathering somewhere between 600 and 900 supporters. The plan is leaked and Vesey, with others, is publicly hanged.

Liberia is established as a colony for freed American slaves by the American Colonization Society.

1823 U.S. president James Monroe enunciates the Monroe Doctrine in a message to Congress, declaring that the United States would not interfere in the affairs of Europe, nor would it seek to overturn existing European colonies in the Americas, but that it would vigorously resist any further European incursions into the Western Hemisphere.

Chile frees all of its slaves. It is the first Spanish American republic to do so.

1824 The Anglo-Argentine Treaty establishes a formal relationship of equality between British citizens and Argentines in Argentina, paving the way for expanded commercial relations.

British entrepreneurs arrive in the Mexican state of Hidalgo, beginning twenty-four years of ownership of the Real del Monte mining firm by the British Company of the Adventurers.

Captain Basil Hall's *Extracts from a Journal Written on the Coasts of Chile, Peru, and Mexico* is published.

1825 Frances Wright establishes the Nashoba community in Tennessee for the education and manumission of slaves.

Britain signs a treaty of commerce with Colombia.

The British-Venezuelan Treaty of Friendship and Commerce grants Britain most-favored-nation status and custom tariffs 5 percent lower than other countries.

On the heels of unprecedented speculative fever in Latin America (the Bubble Mania), the London stock market collapses, setting in train the great debt crises of the nineteenth century. By 1828, every Latin American country except Brazil will have defaulted on its loans to European banking houses, including the London-based Baring Brothers, Barclay Herring Richardson, and Rothschild.

1826   The Anglo-Brazilian Treaty designates the Atlantic slave trade as piracy, thus giving the Royal Navy the legal grounds to suppress it.

Britain signs a treaty of commerce with Mexico.

A Scottish colony is established at Topo, Venezuela; it will fail within the year due to the settlers' inability to adapt to the land and climate.

1827   Britain pays £250,000 to the United States in compensation for confiscated American "slave property" during the War of 1812.

1828   Mediation by the British envoy Lord Ponsonby ends a conflict between the Argentine Confederation and Brazil, creating an independent buffer state, Uruguay, that prevents the extension of Brazilian sovereignty to the River Plate while ensuring that Buenos Aires cannot control both banks of the river.

1829   The newly independent Mexican government formally abolishes chattel slavery.

1830   A Royal Navy squadron blockades the port of Callao near Lima, Peru, in order to enforce British trade rights.

1831   The former Dutch colonies of Berbice, Demerara, and Essequibo are consolidated into British Guiana.

Mary Prince's *The History of Mary Prince, A West Indian Slave Related by Herself* is published in London.

Samuel Sharpe leads the Christmas slave uprising in Jamaica. The rebellion rages for a month, ending in the executions of over 350 rebels.

In Nat Turner's Rebellion, the slave Nat Turner gathers from 60 to 80 men and plans to overtake the ammunition stores of Southampton, Virginia. Between 57 and 65 white people are killed; over 200 African Americans are killed in retaliation by whites, regardless of their involvement, and federal troops are sent in to quell the rebellion. Turner eludes capture for two months, but he is eventually publicly hanged. A lawyer for the state hears his confession and commits it to print.

1833   The American Anti-Slavery Society is founded on the heels of the New England Anti-Slavery Society. Both are modeled on the British Anti-Slavery Society (founded in 1823), with which links are established.

The British West Indian Emancipation Act (Colonial Slavery Abolition Act) is passed by Parliament, abolishing slavery throughout the British Empire effective the following year. The former slaves in the West Indies are left landless.

Colonial authorities establish the British Windward Islands Administration, comprised of Dominica, Grenada, St. Lucia, St. Vincent, and the Grenadines.

Rejecting Argentina's claims to the Falkland Islands after Spanish withdrawal, Britain reclaims the islands as a crown colony and British naval forces arrive to protect the seal fisheries located there.

1834   Antigua, Bermuda, and the Virgin Islands emancipate all slaves effective immediately, with no period of apprenticeship.

A period of apprenticeship (1834–1838), a transitional four-year period between slavery and its full abolition, begins for most of Britain's remaining slave-based colonies.

Britain signs a treaty of commerce with Venezuela.

1835 U.S. secretary of state John Forsyth reaffirms that the American government will not be bound by a European ban on slave trading.

The Male Revolt in Bahía, in present-day Brazil, involves African Muslims of many ethnicities (including Hausa) who band together in a failed attempt to overthrow the slave system.

1837 Britain signs a treaty of commerce with the Peru-Bolivian Confederation.

The Sokoto Caliphate is solidified, including regions of what is now Nigeria, Benin, Niger, and Cameroon.

1838 The emancipation of African slaves in British Guiana is completed.

The first indentured servants from India arrive on Trinidad.

Slavery is abolished in Jamaica.

1839 In its policing of the Atlantic slave trade, the Royal Navy begins searching and seizing Portuguese slave ships as well as the slave ships of other nations flying under the Portuguese flag.

1840 The World Anti-Slavery Convention in London refuses to recognize women delegates. Consequently, U.S. feminists Lucretia Mott and Elizabeth Cady Stanton, having met at the London convention, resolve to organize the first women's rights convention. It will be held at Seneca Falls, New York, in 1848.

Britain signs a treaty of commerce with Bolivia.

1841 Slaves onboard the *Creole,* sailing from Hampton Roads, Virginia, to New Orleans, seize control of the ship, killing one person, and demand to be taken to the nearest British colony. The *Creole* reaches Nassau, in the Bahamas, and Britain's refusal to arrest, extradite, or provide compensation for the slaves

exacerbates tensions with the United States for the next twelve years.

The British government engages German naturalist Robert Schomburgk to map the borders of British Guiana. His work is completed in 1844, drawing immediate protest from the Venezuelan government over the lands west of the Essequibo River. This marks the beginning of the Venezuela Boundary Dispute.

European powers (the Ottoman Empire and France) allow the Muhammad 'Ali dynasty of Egypt to be established. Its last ruler is King Farouk, who is dethroned and exiled in July 1952.

1842 The Webster-Ashburton Treaty establishes the current border of Maine and New Brunswick, grants the United States navigation rights on the St. John River, and provides for joint U.S.-British cooperation to suppress the Atlantic slave trade.

Following the Peruvian government's nationalization of the guano industry, the London merchant house of Antony Gibbs and Sons is awarded the sales monopoly for Britain. By the late 1850s, Gibbs will control much of the global guano market.

Britain signs a treaty of commerce with Uruguay.

The Paraguayan government issues a "free womb" law that provides for the emancipation of slaves when they reached adulthood. The free Afro-Paraguayan population experiences a growth spurt.

1845 A combined Anglo-French force lays a blockade of Buenos Aires in order to prevent Argentina's intervention in the Uruguayan civil war. The blockade continues until 1848.

Parliament passes the Aberdeen Bill authorizing the Royal Navy to pursue suspected slavers into Brazilian ports.

Numerous violations of Brazilian sovereignty result in bitter domestic resentment, but in 1850, Brazil finally outlaws the importation of slaves.

U.S. abolitionist Frederick Douglass's *Narrative of the Life of Frederick Douglass, Written by Himself,* is published. He travels to Ireland and Scotland, where he is enthusiastically received.

1846   Frederick Douglass travels to England, where he meets with leading British abolitionists including Ellen Richardson, Mary Estlin, Thomas Clarkson, and Julia Griffiths. They help convince Douglass to start a newspaper and raise the money to buy his freedom.

Parliament passes the Sugar Act that removes protective tariffs on sugar imports from outside the British Caribbean, dealing a heavy blow to Caribbean sugar producers.

Consolidating various abolitionist societies into a single nondenominational organization with the purpose of ending slavery, the American Missionary Association is founded. It will help found ten historically black colleges in the United States.

1847   Liberia gains independence from the American Colonization Society, making it Africa's oldest independent nation and the second oldest independent nation of black citizens (Haiti being the oldest).

1848   The Treaty of Guadalupe Hidalgo ends the Mexican-American War begun in 1846. Mexico loses two-fifths of its territory—most of the present-day U.S. Southwest. Previously, Britain encouraged Texas not to join the Union, attempted to improve Mexico-Texas relations, and agreed to construct and sell warships to Mexico for defense against the United States. Now the question is: "What will England say?"

In a bid to increase their influence on the Mosquito Coast, British settlers seize the port of San Juan del Norte and expel all Nicaraguan officials.

1849   Britain forces Nicaragua to sign a treaty recognizing British rights over the Miskito Indians and establishing a protectorate over their territory. In an attempt to counterbalance British influence in the region, Nicaragua and the United States sign the Hise and Squier treaties, which give the United States an exclusive right of way across the Isthmus of Panama and the right to fortify the route. In return, the United States promises to protect Nicaragua from other foreign intervention.

Britain signs treaties of commerce with Costa Rica and Guatemala.

1850   Britain and the United States sign the Clayton-Bulwer Treaty, which fails to settle their differences over each other's presence in the Mosquito protectorate and the Panama isthmus.

Britain signs treaties of commerce with the Dominican Republic and Peru.

The U.S. Senate passes the Fugitive Slave Act, requiring U.S. marshals to help slave owners recover fugitives and imposing fines on any person found guilty of harboring a runaway. The law increases sectional tension, leading to the Civil War.

1851   Congress decrees the abolition of slavery, effective in 1852.

Harriet Beecher Stowe publishes *Uncle Tom's Cabin,* an antislavery novel. It will become the nation's second best seller, after the Bible.

Sojourner Truth delivers her speech, "Ain't I a Woman?"

1853   A British-American claims commission awards $110,330 as compensation to the U.S. slave owners demanding the return of the *Creole* mutineers.

William Wells Brown's *Clotel: or, the President's Daughter,* the first African American novel, is published.

Final emancipation for Uruguayan slaves takes effect. Abolitionist principles are incorporated into the new national constitution.

1855   The southern U.S. filibuster, William Walker, establishes a brief dictatorship in Nicaragua, where he restores slavery and calls on the United States to annex Nicaragua as a slave state. Britain encourages the other four Central American governments to send troops to Nicaragua to oust Walker, who will face a Honduran firing squad in 1857.

1856   Britain and the United States experience a war scare over their respective differences in Central America.

In the face of the British guano monopoly, and claiming unfair British trading practices, the U.S. Congress passes the Guano Islands Act to claim ninety-four islands, rocks, and keys in the Pacific and Caribbean.

The first indentured servants from India arrive on Grenada.

1857   *Dred Scott v. Sandford* is decided by the U.S. Supreme Court. It defines the legal status of blacks in America and denies Congress the right to restrict slavery in the American territories. The decision defined the legal status of blacks, stating that blacks cannot become citizens of the U.S. and therefore may not sue in a federal court. It is disputed during the sectional crisis that leads to the Civil War.

1858   British railway engineer George Thompson begins the construction of Paraguay's central railroad.

1859   Admiral Thomas Cochrane's *Narrative of Services in the Liberation of Chili, Peru, and Brazil* is published.

1860   U.S. pressure succeeds in forcing Britain and Nicaragua to sign the Treaty of Managua, by which Britain transfers its sovereignty over the Miskito nation to Nicaragua, turning the protectorate into an "autonomous reservation."

Richard Burton's *The Lake Regions of Central Africa* is published; it is an example of travel literature written about Africa by its British explorers.

1861   *Incidents in the Life of a Slave Girl,* by Harriet Jacobs, is published under the pen name of Linda Brent.

1862   The Peruvian government transfers the guano export contract from the Gibbs monopoly to a group of Peruvian merchants, breaking the British control of the guano trade.

The British minister to Brazil, William Christie, orders a six-day blockade of Rio de Janeiro in retaliation for the arrest of British sailors. The British refusal to apologize or pay compensation leads the Brazilian government to suspend diplomatic relations. Britain seeks conciliation.

1863   Announced on September 22, 1862, the Emancipation Proclamation comes into effect, with a view to strengthening the Union cause abroad and preventing Britain's intervention on the side of the Confederacy.

The American Freedman's Inquiry Commission is established in March by U.S. secretary of war Edwin M. Stanton to determine the best course of action to improve the lives of freed African Americans.

1864   Following the ousting of the Blanco Party leadership and its replacement by the Colorado Party in Uruguay, assisted by Brazil, Paraguay goes to war with Brazil. The events will lead to the five-year War of the Triple Alliance.

1865   On June 19, Major General Gordon Granger, a Union officer, arrives in Galveston, Texas, with the announcement that the Civil War had concluded and all slaves were now free. His announcement inaugurated the celebration by African Americans of Juneteenth, which they still celebrate.

The five-year War of the Triple Alliance (Paraguayan War) breaks out between Paraguay and the combined forces of Brazil, Argentina, and Uruguay. The War of the Triple Alliance begins. It will last until 1870. It is considered the most devastating war in South American history. Roughly one hundred British military advisers, engineers, and surgeons will assist Paraguay, while tens of thousands from the allied countries will fight as the Triple Alliance. Sir Richard Burton's *Letters from the Battlefields of Paraguay* (1870) will raise European awareness of the desperate resistance of the besieged Paraguayans.

The Morant Bay Rebellion of Jamaica occurs. Approximately 500 black Jamaicans confront a militia of some 30 men guarding the Morant Bay Courthouse. The militia shoots seven blacks. The crowd responds by killing eighteen guards. Black Jamaicans write letters and petitions defending their actions and calling for the eradication of injustice; the British governor decrees the execution of nearly 500 innocent black Jamaicans.

1867   Diamonds are found in Cape Colony. Until this point, most diamonds have come from India and Brazil.

1868   Bolivian dictator Mariano Melgarejo ties the British ambassador to a donkey and parades him through a jeering crowd. Upon hearing of this, Queen Victoria literally crosses Bolivia off her map, declaring: "Bolivia no longer exists."

1870   A group of over forty black ministers and church leaders meets at Jackson, Tennessee, to form the Colored Methodist Episcopal Church in America (CMEC).

1871   The Leeward Island Federation is established, comprising Anguilla, Antigua and Barbuda, the British Virgin Islands, Montserrat, and St. Kitts and Nevis.

Edward Blyden, native of the Virgin Islands and resident of Liberia, moves to Freetown, Sierra Leone. From here he founds and edits *The Negro,* the first Pan-African journal in West Africa. He becomes convinced that Islam suits the African race better than Christianity. While resigning from the Presbyterian Church, in which he was a clergyman, he never formally adopts Islam. The one child of his who survives him, Isa Cleopatra, will give birth to Edward Wilmot Blyden III, whose Sierra Leone Independence Movement will help to win that nation's independence from Great Britain in 1961.

1873   The British-built Ferrocarril Mexicano railway is completed, linking Mexico City and Veracruz.

1876   King Leopold II of Belgium creates an international holding company, L'Association International Africaine, with the objectives of exploration and discovery of resources in the African continent and the mission to "civilize" African populations. The association quickly becomes an economically-driven monopoly advancing Leopold's interests.

The U.S. presidential election expedites the end of Reconstruction in those Southern states where it still prevails, bringing the return of white rule to those states in 1877. This paves the way for the disenfranchisement of Southern blacks that begins in the 1890s. It also leads to the spread throughout the South, especially from 1890 to 1910, of the Jim Crow segregation of African Americans and whites, which is judicially addressed in 1954 by *Brown v. Board of Education,* 1878

Henry Morton Stanley's *Through the Dark Continent* is published.

1879   The three-year War of the Pacific pits Chile against Peru and Bolivia. British merchants begin to cut their Peruvian ties and actively engage with Chile, following that nation's privatization of the guano industry.

The Cuban musical form of the *danzon* is publicly launched. It will quickly become the musical-cultural emblem of the country from 1879 to 1920.

1880   Cuba abolishes slavery, the last country in the hemisphere—except for Brazil—to do so.

1881   Muhammad Ahmad proclaims himself Al Mahdi al Muntazar and raises an army known as the Ansar to throw off the rule of the Ottoman Egyptians in present-day Sudan. The mahdi will become an eschatological figure who influences Islamist thought, including that of Osama bin Laden.

The Tuskegee Normal and Industrial Institute opens. Booker T. Washington is brought to the school; he stresses the need for practicality in education for African Americans.

1885   At the Berlin Conference, fourteen of the most powerful European nations divided and claimed the entire African continent for themselves. King Leopold II refers to Africa as a "magnificent . . . cake."

The Congo Free State is created, with King Leopold II as its autocratic ruler. His sadistic abuses of the African population are so extreme that when they are publicized, he is forced to turn the Congo over to the Belgian Parliament in 1908.

1887   Venezuela suspends diplomatic relations with Britain due to a dispute over the boundary between Venezuela and British Guiana.

1888   Britain unifies Trinidad and Tobago into a single colony.

Cecil John Rhodes forms De Beers Consolidated Mines, Ltd., which has since dominated the diamond business worldwide.

1890   The Baring Crisis, in which Argentina defaults on major British loans, is resolved through renegotiation rather than British military pressure, marking a shift in British-Argentine relations.

1891   Civil War erupts in Chile, where the activities of John T. North, the Nitrate King, have made the nitrate zone of Tarapacá into a British enclave.

1894   The Venezuelan government commissions former U.S. consul William Scruggs to produce a pamphlet, *British Aggression in Venezuela: The Monroe Doctrine on Trial,* drawing the United States into the boundary dispute between Venezuela and British Guiana.

1895   Following an aborted Miskito revolt during which Nicaraguan officials had arrested the British pro-consul, Britain demands reparations and prepares for war, sending steamships to Bluefields, and occupying Corinto. The United States declines to invoke the Monroe Doctrine.

U.S. secretary of state Richard Olney dispatches a note to the Foreign Office demanding that Britain agree to submit the Venezuela Boundary Dispute to arbitration. The implication is that the United States possesses an inherent right to intervene in diplomatic questions relating to the Western Hemisphere, a restatement of the Monroe Doctrine.

The British prime minister and foreign secretary, Lord Salisbury, protests to Washington that the United States has no right to interfere in the boundary dispute, representing a direct challenge to the validity of the Monroe Doctrine.

In a special message to Congress, President Grover Cleveland reaffirms the Monroe Doctrine and requests immediate funds for an international commission to investigate and decide on the dispute.

Booker T. Washington delivers his Atlanta Convocation Address. It will later become known as the "Atlanta Compromise" for supporting the segregationist practices imposed by whites.

1896   Prime Minister Lord Salisbury's cabinet overrules him and decides that Britain should submit to U.S. arbitration in the Venezuela Boundary Dispute.

The first organized resistance, by the Ndebele and Shona, emerges against European invasion in sub-Saharan Africa, taking place in present-day Zimbabwe. This became known as the first Chimurenga (struggle). The U.S. Supreme Court rules in *Plessy v. Ferguson* that "separate but equal" services for blacks and whites are constitutional, thus legally affirming racial segregation.

1897   Venezuela resumes diplomatic relations with Britain.

1898   The U.S. battleship *Maine* explodes mysteriously in the harbor of Havana, Cuba. British newspapers express the same degree of outrage as the American press, and the State Department receives condolences from British officials, including the Prince of Wales, the Duke of York, the First Lord of the Admiralty, and the Lord Mayor of London.

1899   The Anglo-Boer War begins, lasting until 1902. Britain gains the support of ardent Anglo-Saxonists such as Theodore Roosevelt and John Hay. U.S. anti-imperialists such as Mark Twain, Henry Adams, Carl Schurz, and Andrew Carnegie condemn the British and champion the Boers as underdogs.

Following U.S. president Grover Cleveland's call for an arbitrated settlement of the Venezuela Boundary Dispute, a Russian-British-American tribunal awards 94 percent of the disputed territory to British Guiana.

1900   The first West Indian cricket team tours England.

By 1900 the French have established rubber plantations on 9 million acres in present-day Zimbabwe.

Trinidadian Henry Sylvester Williams organizes the first Pan-African Conference in London, laying the foundations for the Pan-African Movement.

1901   As Venezuela protests suspected rebel insurgency from British Trinidad during its civil war, President Cipriano Castro orders a suspension in the payment of the interest on the foreign debt, most of which is owed to Britain.

1902   The British and German ministers in Caracas threaten military action if compensation is not forthcoming for Venezuela's illegal seizure of their ships and crews and for the claims of their nationals for redress of economic grievances.

British and German gunboats enter Venezuelan waters and seize all the Venezuelan naval vessels they encounter.

Britain, Germany, and Italy declare a formal blockade of the Venezuelan coast, with U.S. agreement.

British and German gunboats bombard the port of Puerto Cabello in retaliation against a perceived public insult to the British flag by Venezuelans on shore.

The will of Cecil John Rhodes establishes the Rhodes Scholarships to Oxford University for students from countries with present or former connections to the British Empire.

1903   British and German gunboats bombard Fort San Carlos in Venezuela.

Britain, Germany, and Italy lift the Venezuelan blockade in response to the announcement that Caracas will submit existing claims to the International Court of Arbitration at the Hague.

The Souls of Black Folk, by W. E. B. Du Bois, is published.

The Sokoto Caliphate falls to the British West African Frontier Force under Frederick Lugard.

1904   The Hague Court rules in favor of the blockading European powers and against Venezuela. In response, Latin American nations assert the Drago Doctrine, stating that foreign nations have no right to use military force to recover public debt.

1905   W. E. B. Du Bois founds, with Monroe Trotter, John Hope, and others, the Niagara Movement, with a platform calling for universal suffrage and equality in economic opportunity, education, and legal status for African Americans. The movement is the precursor to the National Association for the Advancement of Colored People (NAACP), formed in 1909.

1906   William Joseph Seymour starts the Pentecostal movement in Los Angeles, California. It will gain in popularity, eventually spreading to Africa.

1909   The National Association for the Advancement of Colored People (NAACP) is established, with the objectives of equality of rights, justice in the courts, opportunity for education and employment for black Americans, as well as the eradication of prejudice and the advancement of the political interests of black citizens. The U.S. government sponsors a revolt against Nicaragua's leader, José Santos Zelaya; he is forced into exile.

1910   The exclusive English department store, Harrod's, opens a branch in Buenos Aires, reflecting the impact of the British and Anglophile community.

In November, Lij Taffari Makonnen becomes emperor of Ethiopia and adopts the name Haile Selassie, meaning "Might of the Trinity."

1911   A Puerto Rican immigrant to the United States in 1891, Arthur Alfonso

Schomburg founds, with journalist John Edward Bruce, the Negro Society for Historical Research. Schomburg will amass a huge collection of rare materials documenting black experiences in the United States and England over the course of his life. This collection will become the Schomburg Center for Research in Black Culture in the Harlem branch of the New York Public Library.

1912   James Weldon Johnson's *Autobiography of an Ex-Colored Man* is published anonymously.

1913   Timothy Drew (Noble Drew Ali) launches an Islamic movement called the Moorish Science Temple. He will author his own "Holy Koran" in 1927.

1914   Following the outbreak of World War I, U.S. president Woodrow Wilson offers to mediate between Britain, Germany, and other belligerent powers.

The Anglo-Dutch Royal Dutch Shell Company makes huge discoveries of oil around Lake Maracaibo, placing Venezuela on the road to becoming the world's biggest oil exporter.

Lord Lugard of England, as governor-general of a region of Africa that combines the former empires of Oyo, Igbo, Bornu-Kanem, and Hausa-Fulani, names it Nigeria.

Jamaican Marcus Garvey founds the Universal Negro Improvement Association (UNIA) in Jamaica.

1915   The U.S. occupies Haiti. One of the results is the emergence of the Haitian black nationalist movement known as Noirisme, which seeks to study the country's African roots, with regard to language, religion, and folklore. Such study is best typified by Jean Price-Mars's *Ainsi parla l'Oncle*.

1916   Marcus Garvey arrives in Harlem, New York. He will establish a Harlem chapter of UNIA in 1917.

1917   After intercepting and decoding the Zimmerman Telegram, Britain transmits it to the United States in hopes of gaining an ally. The telegram from the German foreign minister promises to restore Texas, New Mexico, and Arizona to Mexico in return for a Mexican-German alliance against the United States.

The United States enters the war as an "associate" rather than as a declared ally.

Venezuela's first commercial oil well begins producing.

The East St. Louis riots, spawned from white racial hatred of African Americans, who had traveled north for work during World War I, claims the lives of thirty-nine African Americans and nine whites, while hundreds of African Americans are displaced from their homes by fire.

Following the East St. Louis riots, W. E. B. Du Bois, James Weldon Johnson, and others organize the Silent Protest Parade, which marches along Fifth Avenue from Harlem to lower Manhattan. It protests American racial hatred of African Americans as well as President Woodrow Wilson's hypocritical administration, concerned with democracy and equality abroad but not at home.

1918   The Armistice ending World War I is signed.

The Haitian, Charlemagne Massena Peralte, leads an unsuccessful attempt to oust U.S. troops from Haiti during the first U.S. occupation.

1919   The Paris Peace Conference assembles to draft treaties of peace between the warring nations of World War I.

The first Pan-African Congress is held in Paris. Another will follow in 1921.

The Treaty of Versailles is signed, dictating punitive terms to defeated Germany.

Oscar Micheaux produces *The Homesteaders,* becoming the first African American to produce a feature-length film.

Jessie Fauset assumes the position of literary editor of *The Crisis,* the NAACP's literary magazine. She will hold the position until 1927, and through it nurture a number of young talents (such as Langston Hughes) while publishing her own novels.

The Red Summer of race riots erupts. African Americans are targeted with brutality, intimidation, and murder in over 21 cities across the United States.

Prohibition begins, lasting until 1934. The Bahamas becomes a major transit point for smuggling alcohol into the United States.

Namibia becomes independent from Germany as a consequence of the Treaty of Versailles. South Africa administers Namibia under the League of Nations in an occupation that will last until 1990.

1921   Caribbean author René Maran's novel, *Batouala,* is published. It will win France's literary prize, the Goncourt.

1922   Egypt becomes independent of British colonial rule.

1923   The African American modernist literary work, *Cane,* by Jean Toomer, is published.

1924   Tunisian director Chemama Chikly makes *Ain el Ghezal* (The girl from Carthage), the first motion picture made by an African.

1925   *The New Negro,* edited by Alain Locke, an anthology celebrating African American poetry, fiction, and essays written mostly by African Americans, is published.

Noble Drew Ali opens the Moorish American Science Temple in Chicago.

C. Ernest Cadie leads the Denver African Expedition, a safari expedition traveling from Cape Town to the Mandated Territory of South West Africa, to study the Bushmen (the San people). The expedition planned to find the "missing link" and to "capture" some "wild" Bushmen in order to bring them to the United States, but eventually settled for attempting to make a film and taking many photographs. The latter were used in U.S. school textbooks, promulgating and perpetuating the stereotype of the "wild" Bushman.

1927   Following his pursuit by J. Edgar Hoover for mail fraud, Marcus Garvey is deported as an undesirable alien.

1928   British Guiana is declared a crown colony.

The West Indies cricket team plays its first ever Test match, at Lord's in London.

1929   In the Women's War of Nigeria, women palm oil producers protest against the impact of falling prices, increased taxation, and government marketing cartels. Over 50 women are killed when police fire on protesters. The British secure a monopoly over the palm oil trade by establishing the United Africa Company.

1930   The first Empire Games open in Hamilton, Ontario, Canada with over 400 competitors from Britain, Ireland, Canada, Australia, New Zealand, Bermuda, and British Guiana.

The first World Cup is hosted by Uruguay in Montevideo; the universalized rules of England's Football Association are applied.

Wallace Fard founds the Lost-Found Nation of Islam in Detroit, Michigan.

1931   South Africa enacts the Entertainment Law, forbidding the viewing of unapproved arts, including film and theater, and blocking freedom of expression in the creation of such works, particularly from a black perspective.

The League of Colored Peoples is founded in London by Dr. Harold Moody and modeled on the National Association for the Advancement of Colored People.

1933   The Roca-Runciman Treaty supersedes the Anglo-Argentine Treaty of 1904: the two governments negotiate special arrangements for mutual access to each other's markets.

Meeting in Paris, the Senegalese Léopold Sedar Senghor, Martinican Aimé Césaire, and Guyanese Léon Gontran-Damas found the literary-intellectual Négritude movement.

President Franklin Delano Roosevelt develops his Good Neighbor Policy toward the nations of Latin America, rejecting the Monroe Doctrine policy that the Theodore Roosevelt, Harding, Taft, Wilson, Coolidge, and Hoover administrations pursued.

1935   The BBC places a ban on the broadcasting of "hot music"—American jazz.

The Anglo-Uruguayan Trade and Payments Agreement secures the promise of "benevolent treatment" for British interests in Uruguay.

1936   Britain and Argentina renew the Roca-Runciman Treaty.

Italy occupies Ethiopia, 1936–1941.

1937   Wali Akram establishes the First Cleveland Mosque, the only orthodox mosque in America to be run entirely by indigenous Muslim converts. Around the same time, he develops the Moslem Ten-Year Plan, a proposal to address the economic and educational needs of African American Muslims in the midst of the Great Depression.

1938   Trinidadian C. L. R. James publishes *The Black Jacobins: Toussaint L'Ouverture and the San Domingo Revolution*, a historical study locating the Haitian Revolution in the tradition of the

Enlightenment revolutions of France and America.

1939   The Leeward Islands Federation is dissolved.

Black classical singer Marian Anderson performs at the Lincoln Memorial, having been denied the use of Constitution Hall by the Daughters of the American Revolution.

1940   Richard Wright publishes *Native Son.* It becomes a Book-of-the-Month Club selection and an immediate best seller.

1941   Eritrea becomes independent of Italy. It will be colonized by Britain.

1942   Britain and the United States establish the Anglo-American Caribbean Commission (AACC) with the goal of protecting postwar Western Hemisphere security, developing regional integration, and promoting agricultural and other research in the Caribbean. It is renamed the Caribbean Commission in 1946.

The Voice of America gives its first European broadcast via BBC transmitters.

The Allies launch Operation Torch to free French Northwest Africa from Axis occupation.

1943   The American Forces Network (AFN) begins broadcasting to American troops stationed in Europe, giving many Britons their first taste of American jazz and blues music. The BBC is hesitant about having its monopoly breached, but in the end submits to assurances that AFN will only act as an auxiliary to the BBC's own offerings.

The first program of *Caribbean Voices,* operated by the BBC from London, is broadcast on March 11. When broadcasting ceases in 1958, many of the hitherto unknown talents—including V. S. Naipaul, Una Marson, George Lamming, Sam Selvon, Edward Kamau Brathwaite, and others—had been recognized by publishers and critics in England and America.

The Congress of Racial Equality (CORE) stages the first successful "sit-in" demonstration against segregation in Chicago, IL.

1944   The International Monetary Fund and World Bank are created to aid multiple nations' economic and health crises.

1946   The United States and (reluctantly) Britain sign the Anglo-American Air Services (Bermuda) Agreement, forcing major British concessions and enabling the first significant U.S. incursions into European civil aviation routes.

The United Nations Education, Scientific, and Cultural Organization (UNESCO) is implemented on December 14.

1947   The Anglo-Uruguayan Payments Agreement transfers the ownership of British-financed railways, trams, and waterworks to the Uruguayan government.

Major league baseball in the United States becomes racially integrated.

1948   In Angola, coffee plantations expand from 297,000 acres to 1.2 million acres between 1948 and 1961.

South Africa adopts the segregationist and racist official policy of "apartheid." It will not be reversed until 1994.

The Organization of American States (OAS) is established in Bogota, Colombia, with the signing of its charter on April 30. Twenty-one Latin American and Caribbean nations, as well as the United States, are members. The organization will later expand to include Canada and nations of the English-speaking Carribean.

President Harry Truman approves the desegregation of the U.S. military and creates the Fair Employment Board.

1950   Poet Gwendolyn Brooks is the first African American to receive a Pulitzer Prize in any category.

Ralph Bunche receives Nobel Peace Prize. He is the first African American to win it.

1951   Libya becomes independent of Allied Administration.

1952   Malcolm Little joins the Nation of Islam and changes his surname to "X".

Gamal Abdul Nasser leads the overthrow of the Egyptian monarchy.

Eritrea becomes independent of Britain.

The novel *Invisible Man,* by Ralph Ellison, is published. It becomes one of the most influential and widely read novels of twentieth-century American literature.

1953   Queen Elizabeth II and Prince Philip visit Bermuda for a day—the first visit by a reigning British monarch.

Britain temporarily suspends the constitution of British Guiana after the popular election of Dr. Cheddi Jagan, leader of the People's Progress Party, prompts fears of a Marxist takeover in the country.

The Federation of Rhodesia and Nyasaland is formed. It includes the territories of present-day Zambia, Malawi, and Zimbabwe.

Fidel Castro, with a handful of revolutionaries, attempts to attack Cuban leader Fulgencio Batista's soldiers at the Moncada Army Garrison in Santiago de Cuba. Defeated, Castro is arrested, tried, and sentenced to fifteen years in prison; he is pardoned after serving just two years.

1954   The charter for the Kingdom of the Netherlands grants the Netherlands Antilles and Surinam the status of equal and autonomous partners within the kingdom, signaling the official end of colonial relations.

In *Brown v. Board of Education,* the Supreme Court rules segregated schools unconstitutional, overturning *Plessy v. Ferguson* (1896).

1955   Rosa Parks is arrested for refusing to give up her seat on a bus to a white man, prompting the Montgomery Bus Boycott, led by Dr. Martin Luther King Jr.

Emmett Till, a 14-year-old Chicago native, is lynched in Mississippi.

The Supreme Court orders the integration of schools "with all deliberate speed."

The Interstate Commerce Commission (ICC) orders the integration of buses, trains, and waiting rooms for interstate travel.

Marian Anderson becomes the first African American to sing at the Metropolitan Opera on January 7.

Trinidadian Claudia Jones, a member of the American Communist Party, is deported from America for "un-American activities" after serving jail time for her political activities. She is barred from entering Trinidad. Needing medical help, she seeks asylum in Britain; in 1958 she organizes the first black indoor carnival, held in 1959.

1956   The Southern Manifesto against school desegregation is signed by 101 congressmen.

Morocco, Tunisia, and Sudan become independent.

Nigeria's first commercial oil well, located in Oloibiri, in present-day Baylesa State, begins producing.

The Lonely Londoners, by Trinidadian-born Ssmuel Selvon, is published. It is the first Caribbean novel to employ dialect in both dialogue and narrative.

1957   Congress approves the Civil Rights Act of 1957.

Federal troops are sent to Alabama to enforce school desegregation.

Ghana becomes the first sub-Saharan African nation to gain independence from colonial rule.

The Southern Rhodesia African National Congress is formed. It is banned within two years.

François Duvalier, nicknamed "Papa Doc," is elected for a nonrenewable six-year term as president of Haiti; he will have himself reelected in a fraudulent election in 1961. He will rule Haiti uninterrupted until his death in 1971.

Martin Luther King Jr. becomes president of the Southern Christian Leadership Conference (SCLC).

1958   Guinea becomes independent.

Nigerian Chinua Achebe's first novel, *Things Fall Apart* (1959), is published.

Five years after the British Musicians' Union lifts its ban on U.S. musicians, English jazz player Ronnie Scott opens his legendary jazz club in London. It becomes a mecca for U.S. jazz musicians.

The Cuban Revolution, led by Fidel Castro, is successful in forcing out Fulgencio Batista.

Argentine-born Ernesto "Che" Guevara is made a Cuban citizen.

Radio Swan, financed by the U.S. Central Intelligence Agency, begins broadcasting to Cuba. Voice of America, a U.S. government-funded program, also begins broadcasting to Cuba. Considering its content to be propagandistic, Cuba will jam its signal.

Ofeu Negro (*Black Orpheus*) is produced by French director Marcel Camus. It wins the Academy Award for best foreign film.

Lorraine Hansberry's play, *A Raisin in the Sun,* is published.

1960   A sit-in is staged by four black students at a Woolworth's lunch counter in Greensboro, North Carolina.

The Student Nonviolent Coordinating Committee (SNCC) is founded in part to advance a more radical political response to segregation and Jim Crow racism than the Southern Christian Leadership Conference (SCLC). SNCC will lead freedom rides and protest American involvement in the Vietnam War. SNCC's members include Stokely Carmichael, Julian Bond, and Fannie Lou Hamer.

Congress passes the Civil Rights Act of 1960.

The People's National Movement announces that Trinidad and Tobago will seek independence outside of the West Indies Federation.

Between 1960 and 2000, crop yields in the developing world drastically increase, a result described by scientists as the Green Revolution.

Nigeria achieves independence from Britain. It becomes a republic in 1963.

The French government grants independence to French Cameroon. Ahmadou Adhijo, leader of the independence party Union Camerounaise, becomes Cameroon's first president.

The African nations Benin, Burkina Faso, Central African Republic, Chad, Democratic Republic of the Congo (formerly Zaire), Congo (Brazzaville), Côte d'Ivoire, Gabon, Madagascar, Mali, Mauritania, Niger, Senegal, Somalia, and Togo become independent.

1961   *I Speak of Freedom: A Statement of African Ideology,* by Kwame Nkrumah, the first president of independent Ghana, is published. The work is influential in shaping pan-African thought in the era of African decolonization.

Two works by LeRoi Jones (Amiri Baraka), *Preface to a Twenty Volume*

Suicide Note and the play *Dutchman,* are published.

With the help of the United Nations, British Cameroon organizes a referendum in which its northern half votes to join Nigeria and its southern half votes to join Cameroon.

Sierra Leone, South Africa, and Tanzania (then Tanganyika) become independent.

1962   An outbreak of rioting occurs after the U.S. Supreme Court orders the University of Mississippi to accept James H. Meredith as its first black student. Twelve thousand federal troops are employed to restore order and ensure his admission.

The West Indies Federation collapses, following the secession of Jamaica and Trinidad and Tobago, which declare their independence within the Commonwealth.

In the Bahamas, President John F. Kennedy and Prime Minister Harold Macmillan sign the Nassau Pact. To diffuse the crisis caused by President Kennedy's unilateral cancellation of the British-American Skybolt weapons system, the U.S. government agrees to make Polaris missiles available to the United Kingdom.

Britain passes the Commonwealth Immigrants Act, aimed at regulating the flow of non-European immigrants. Further acts will follow in 1968 and 1971.

In South Africa, Nelson Mandela is arrested for treason a second time and sentenced to five years in prison. In 1963, while in prison, Mandela is also charged with sabotage for plotting to overthrow the government through violence. In 1964, Mandela is convicted of sabotage and treason and is sentenced to life imprisonment on Robben Island.

Algeria, Burundi, Uganda, and Rwanda become independent.

1963   Martin Luther King Jr. writes "Letter from Birmingham Jail."

National support for civil rights swells after the police attack a Birmingham, Alabama, demonstration led by King.

A March on Washington demonstration for civil rights and jobs attracts more than 200,000. Martin Luther King Jr. delivers his "I Have a Dream" speech.

President John F. Kennedy is assassinated.

Kenya and Zanzibar become independent.

The Organization of African Unity is established.

Ousmane Sembène makes his first film, *Borom Sarret.* It changes the course of African film production, and Sembène will become the most prominent African filmmaker of the continent.

1964   Upon his return to the United States after visiting Mecca and performing the Islamic pilgrimage, Malcolm X breaks away from Elijah Muhammad and forms the Organization of Afro-American Unity, along with Muslim Mosque Incorporated, in New York City.

Three civil rights workers are murdered in Mississippi by white segregationists during the Mississippi Freedom Summer.

Martin Luther King Jr. receives the Nobel Peace Prize.

Congress passes the Civil Rights Act of 1964 and the Economic Opportunity Act.

Cassius Clay wins the world heavyweight boxing title, converts to Islam, and changes his name to Muhammad Ali.

The Museum of African Art is founded in Washington, D.C., by former U.S. Foreign Service officer Warren M. Robbins. It is renamed the National Museum of African Art in 1981.

Malawi and Zambia become independent.

The Bahamas are granted self-governing rule by the United Kingdom.

François Duvalier has himself elected president-for-life of Haiti. As its dictator, he will rule until his death in 1971. His son, Jean-Claude Duvalier, nicknamed "Bébé Doc," will rule as dictator of Haiti from 1971 until 1986, when he will be forced into exile.

1965   The era of major American military involvement in the Vietnam War begins, and continues to 1973.

Rhodesian prime minister Ian Smith unilaterally declares Rhodesia's independence from Britain. The United States joins Britain in imposing sanctions.

Prime Minister Harold Wilson and President Lyndon Johnson agree to cease oil shipments to Rhodesia. Ian Smith retaliates by blocking oil shipments to Zambia; the United States and Britain mount a joint airlift of millions of gallons of petroleum for the Zambian copper mines.

The Gambia becomes independent.

Alex Haley publishes *The Autobiography of Malcolm X: As Told to Alex Haley*.

On February 21, Malcolm X is assassinated in New York City.

Martin Luther King Jr. leads a march from Selma to Montgomery, Alabama.

The Watts riot in Los Angeles is the most serious single racial disturbance in United States history.

The Caribbean Artists Movement (CAM) is founded by Edward Kamau Brathwaite, John La Rose, and Andrew Salkey in London.

The Black Arts Movement is started by Amiri Baraka in Harlem.

The Wretched of the Earth, an anticolonial treatise by Martinique-born author Frantz Fanon, is published. He will follow this publication with *Black Skin, White Masks* in 1967.

1966   Barbados declares independence.

At a London constitutional conference, Bermuda—still a sovereign British dependency—adopts a new constitution with universal suffrage and a two-party parliamentary system. The constitution comes into effect in 1968.

British Guiana becomes the independent nation of Guyana.

Botswana and Lesotho become independent.

Yakubu Gowon becomes military dictator of Nigeria (1966–1975).

Jamaica Labrish, by Louise Bennett, is published.

Nigerian author Flora Nwapa's *Efuru,* the first novel written in English by a woman from black Africa, is published.

The Black Panther Party (BPP) is established, headquartered in Oakland, California.

The Black Power concept is adopted by CORE and SNCC.

The National Organization for Women (NOW) is founded.

Senator Edward W. Brooke, Republican of Massachusetts, becomes the first elected black senator since Reconstruction.

1967   Martin Luther King Jr. announces his opposition to the Vietnam War.

The worst race riot in U.S. history kills forty-three in Detroit; major riots occur in Newark and Chicago.

Thurgood Marshall becomes the first black U.S. Supreme Court justice.

The U.S. Supreme Court overturns laws against interracial marriage.

The West Indies Associated States (or the Federated States of the Antilles) is established, comprising Antigua, St. Kitts and Nevis (tethered to an unwilling Anguilla), Dominica, Grenada, St. Lucia, and St. Vincent and the Grenadines. All seek voluntary "associated status" within the British Commonwealth, but the Federation will progressively dissolve as the members opt for independence.

The black majority of the Bahamas defeats the mostly white government that has held power since self-rule began in 1964.

The Republic of Biafra comes into existence on May 30. A thirty-month civil war breaks out in July; it is the bloodiest war in modern Africa and the first black-on-black genocide of modern history.

U.S. guitarist Jimi Hendrix moves to London, where he reinvents the blues as a psychedelic music form.

Piri Thomas's autobiography, *Down These Mean Streets,* is published. It describes the conflict between national identification as Puerto Rican and racial identification as black.

The poet LeRoi Jones becomes a Kawaida minister, discards his slave name, and assumes the name Imamu Amiri Baraka (he later drops the title "Imamu").

1968 Martin Luther King Jr. is assassinated in Memphis.

Senator Robert F. Kennedy is assassinated in Los Angeles.

Equatorial Guinea, Mauritius, and Swaziland become independent.

1969 Moummar al-Qaddafi successfully overthrows the monarchy in Libya and is installed as Libya's leader on September 1. He has ruled the country since then.

While sleeping in their apartment, Fred Hampton and Mark Clark, Black Panther Party members, were assassinated by the Chicago police.

1970 The Nigerian-Biafran War ends officially on January 15, 1970. Over two million Biafrans had died by the time of its surrender, including one million Biafran children as a result of starvation and disease-induced kwashiorkor, a form of malnutrition.

1971 The U.S. Supreme Court approves busing as a method of desegregation.

François "Papa Doc" Duvalier dies in April. Power is passed to his son, Jean-Claude ("Baby Doc"). While he rules as president of Haiti, his corrupt financial schemes and lack of bookkeeping and financial accountability drive the country into widespread, deep-rooted poverty.

1972 Shirley Chisholm is the first black woman to run for U.S. president.

In spite of its British dependent status, Bermuda pegs its currency to the U.S. dollar.

The Jamaican band, Bob Marley and the Wailers, is signed to Island Records, a key moment in the internationalization of reggae music.

The first feature-length Jamaican film, *The Harder They Come,* is released, starring the reggae singer Jimmy Cliff and featuring his and other artists' music, bringing reggae to a worldwide audience.

News of the Tuskegee Syphilis Study breaks. The American public is outraged to discover that the African American male subjects had been denied therapeutic treatment, available since at least the 1940s.

1973 The Bahamas gains full independence from the United Kingdom on July 10.

The Caribbean Community and Common Market (CARICOM) is established by the Treaty of Chaguaramas on August 1, with the purpose of providing economic and social integration to Caribbean nations after the failure of the West Indies Federation. There are currently 15 full members.

Roberto Clemente becomes the first Hispanic baseball player to be inducted into the National Hall of Fame.

The Falashas (or Beta Isra'el, as they call themselves) of northwestern Ethiopia are recognized as Jews by the Sephardi chief rabbi; they will be recognized by the Ashkenazi chief rabbi in 1975.

1974   Grenada declares independence.

Ethiopian emperor Haile Selassie is overthrown in a military coup.

Jamaican-born Linton Kwesi Johnson publishes *Voices of the Living,* which marks the start of British reggae, or "dub," poetry.

1975   Upon his death, Elijah Muhammad's son, Wallace Deen Muhammad, is named as the new leader of the Nation of Islam. Wallace redirects the Nation toward orthodox Islam.

The Economic Community of West African States (ECOWAS) is formally created with the signing of the Treaty of Lagos on May 28. It includes 15 African states.

Angola, Cape Verde, the Comoros Islands, Mozambique, and São Tomé and Principe become independent.

Ntozake Shange's play, *for colored girls who have considered suicide/when the rainbow is enuf,* is published. It opens the following year and thrusts the author into immediate prominence; Shange's work becomes the second play by a black female author, after Lorraine Hansberry's *A Raisin in the Sun,* to reach Broadway.

1976   As the guerrilla war against white rule in Rhodesia continues under Robert Mugabe and Joshua Nkomo, British prime minister James Callaghan offers to oversee a constitutional conference to negotiate Rhodesia's independence.

President Nixon's secretary of state, Henry Kissinger, pledges American support for a settlement that would bring peace and majority rule.

Trinidad and Tobago declare themselves a republic and replace the queen with a president as head of state.

The Soweto Rebellion in South Africa begins. While protesting the government-enforced system of apartheid, blacks are shot in the back by government troops. Bishop Desmond Tutu will now support the global boycott of South Africa.

Western Sahara and the Seychelles Islands become independent. Through a 1975 deal organized by Spain, Morocco acquires two-thirds of Western Sahara and Mauritania one-third. The Saharan Arab Democratic Republic (SADR) declares itself in 1976 to represent the Saharan people; Mauritania renounces its territorial claims in 1978 and as a consequence Morocco moves to occupy the one-third of their former territory. As a consequence, SADR refugees flee to southern Algeria, where they are permitted to settle. The debate over territory, autonomy, and sovereignty continue in 2007 between Morocco, Algeria, and SADR.

Roots: Saga of an American Family, by Alex Haley, is published. It celebrates Haley's African heritage and his family's determination to survive the ravages of 200 years of slavery. It is an immediate best seller, with purchases of over 1 million copies in its first year. *Roots* earned Haley both the National Book Award and the Pulitzer Prize. The book prompted a television miniseries in 1977.

British Jamaican Linton Kwesi Johnson names himself "dub-lyricist" and helps to develop a still-lively tradition of black British spoken word poetry.

1977   A year after London renounces the Anglo-American Air Services (Bermuda)

Agreement of 1946, Britain and the United States sign the Bermuda II Agreement, which establishes a more equal framework for British-U.S. airline competition.

Louis Farrakhan forms a new Nation of Islam, revolting against the new leadership of the Nation under Wallace Dean Muhammad.

Novelist and activist Ngugi wa Thiong'o is imprisoned without trial for one year by Kenya's independent government under President Jomo Kenyatta. The imprisonment is the result of his involvement in directing his play, *I Will Marry When I Want,* about the neocolonial exploitation of the Kenyan working class.

Djibouti becomes independent.

1978   The U.S. Supreme Court disallows quotas for college admissions but gives limited approval to affirmative action programs.

Dominica declares independence. A royal commission recommends independence for Bermuda.

The Brazilian Movimento Negro Unificado is founded as the culmination of a rally protesting the death under torture of black worker Robson Silveira da Luz at police headquarters; the expulsion of four black athletes from the Tiete sport club; and the killing of black worker Nilton Lourenco by a policeman.

1979   St. Lucia declares independence.

Anwar Sadat and Menachem Begin win the Nobel Peace Prize for their diplomatic negotiations in the Israeli-Palestine conflict, which led to Egyptian recognition of Israel and Israeli withdrawal from the Sinai Peninsula.

Charged and convicted of the murder of a state trooper despite evidence to the contrary, Black Panther member Assata Shakur (JoAnne Chesimard) escapes from the Clinton Correctional Center and is granted political asylum in Cuba, where she still lives. In 1991 the FBI offered a $1 million bounty for her return to the United States.

Alice Walker edits *I Love Myself When I Am Laughing: A Zora Neale Hurston Reader.*

Nigerian author Buchi Emecheta's novel, *The Joys of Motherhood,* is published.

1980   UNESCO begins publishing a series of continental histories, beginning with *The General History of Africa.*

Zimbabwe claims independence, with Robert Mugabe as its first prime minister. Mugabe has remained the country's only ruler, as executive president, since 1987.

1981   Belize—formerly British Honduras—declares independence.

Antigua and Barbuda declares independence.

Emmanuel Dongala, novelist, poet, and playwright, forms the Théatre de l'éclair, now one of the best-known theater companies in Congo.

1982   A group of Argentine scrap-metal dealers land on the British island of South Georgia and hoist the Argentine flag. The Falklands War begins with Argentina's military seizure of the Falkland and South Georgia islands. Britain declares the 200-mile Falkland Island Maritime Exclusion Zone.

The British submarine *Conqueror* sinks the Argentine carrier *Belgrano* and over 300 of its crew. (In February 1985, Clive Ponting, an assistant secretary at the Ministry of Defence, will resign after leaking documents alleging that when it was attacked, the *Belgrano* was outside the Maritime Exclusion Zone and heading away from the British fleet.)

An Argentine Exocet missile sinks HMS *Sheffield,* while British marines and Special Forces begin a sustained ground assault on East Falkland Island. The Argentine air force attacks Royal Navy positions.

British forces move from their beachhead for the final assault on Port Stanley. The Falklands War ends with the surrender of Argentine forces at Port Stanley. The war has claimed approximately 650 Argentine and 250 British lives.

Sudanese John Garang leads a Dinka uprising against the Muslim-dominated, increasingly fundamentalist federal government of Sudan.

Alice Walker receives the Pulitzer Prize for her novel *The Color Purple.*

1983   The Federation of St. Kitts and Nevis becomes the last British Caribbean territory to declare independence, as well as the Western Hemisphere's smallest independent nation.

The United States and supporting Caribbean forces invade Grenada to overthrow the hard-line Marxist regime of Bernard Coard. The American failure to consult the British government causes friction between the Reagan and Thatcher administrations.

In September, Sudanese president Jafar Nimeiri announces the country will incorporate traditional Islamic punishments drawn from Shari'a (Islamic law). These laws will apply not only to Muslims, but to southern Sudanese and other non-Muslims as well.

1984   David Dabydeen's first volume of poetry, *Slave Song,* is awarded Britain's Commonwealth Poetry Prize.

August Wilson's *Ma Rainey's Black Bottom* opens on Broadway.

The Reverend Jesse Jackson is the first serious African American contender for the U.S. presidency, winning 17 percent of the popular vote in the Democratic primaries.

Vanessa Williams is crowned the first black Miss America.

1986   Martin Luther King Jr.'s birthday is officially celebrated as a national holiday.

At the World Cup in Mexico City, England's football (soccer) team faces Argentina in the final playoff, as they face each other in the World Cup tournament for the first time since the end of the Falklands War. Diego Maradona scores two goals to lead Argentina to victory, alleging that one had been scored by "the Hand of God."

Following Sudanese president Nimeiri's overthrow in 1985, elections are held. Tentative efforts are made to negotiate peace with the south.

As a mark of gratitude for U.S. assistance during the Falklands War, Prime Minister Thatcher allows British air bases to be used for American bombers attacking Libya.

Nigerian author Wole Soyinka wins the Nobel Prize for Literature, the first African to receive the award.

Annie John, Jamaica Kincaid's first novel, is published.

1987   Toni Morrison wins the Pulitzer Prize for *Beloved.*

August Wilson wins the Pulitzer Prize for his Broadway play, *Fences.*

Rita Dove wins the Pulitzer Prize for her poems, *Thomas and Beulah.*

1989   The National Patriotic Front of Liberia (NPFL), a guerilla force, splits into two factions with the execution of Liberia's dictator Samuel Doe, one led by Charles Taylor, the other by Prince Johnson. This rupture incites a bloody five-year civil war that ends with Taylor's election as president in 1997.

Arab-African relationships in Sudan, previously complementary, develop into serious conflict as an Arab nationalist group comes into power with the intent of eradicating groups who retain their distinct culture and language alongside the Arabic that they have accepted as a lingua franca. Alienation from the Arab-dominated Sudanese government leads various groups to sympathize with the Sudan People's Liberation Movement/Army (SPLM/A).

1990 Post–Falklands War diplomatic relations between Britain and Argentina are normalized.

South West Africa achieves independence from South Africa and renames itself Namibia.

After 27 years, Nelson Mandela is released from prison.

Producer, writer, and director Julie Dash receives the Sundance Film Festival's Best Cinematography award for *Daughters of the Dust*.

August Wilson wins the Pulitzer Prize for his play, *The Piano Lesson*.

Charles Johnson's *Middle Passage* wins the National Book Award.

1991 An uprising in Somalia leads to ousting of dictator Siad Barre. In the final period of his regime, all foreign aid was halted; after Barre is deposed, there is widespread hunger, and armed factions squabble over scarce food supplies.

Jean-Bertrand Aristide becomes president of Haiti, decisively winning with over 67 percent of the vote. He is overthrown in a September 29 coup by Raoul Cédras that Aristide and his supporters accuse President George H. W. Bush of supporting. Aristide flees to Venezuela.

The development of the first major museum display to examine the transatlantic slave trade and the slavery associated with it is begun in Liverpool. The exhibit, "Transatlantic Slavery: Against Human Dignity," opens in 1994. Nigerian Ben Okri receives the Booker Prize for his novel, *The Famished Road*.

Clarence Thomas, an African American, is confirmed as U.S. Supreme Court justice, despite Anita Hill's sexual harassment testimony.

1992 The United States intervenes in Somalia, calling it a "humanitarian effort" to protect aid workers distributing food.

Cameroon holds its first multiparty elections.

Riots spread through Los Angeles's South Central following the acquittal of the policemen accused of brutally beating Rodney King.

Carol Moseley Braun, Democrat of Illinois, becomes the first African American woman elected to the U. S. Senate.

A St. Lucian, Derek Walcott, receives the Nobel Prize for Literature.

1993 A bombing of the World Trade Center in Manhattan kills six and injures over 1,000; it precedes and is linked to the September 11, 2001 attacks on the WTC as an act of Islamic terrorism backed by Al Qaeda.

Toni Morrison receives the Nobel Prize for Literature.

Poet Yusef Komunyakaa wins Pulitzer Prize for *Neon Vernacular*.

Maya Angelou reads "On the Pulse of the Morning" at President Clinton's inauguration, becoming the first African American poet to participate in a U.S. presidential inauguration.

Sani Abacha becomes the military dictator of Nigeria, which he rules to 1997.

Eritrea becomes independent from Ethiopia and joins the United Nations.

A U.S. intervention in Somalia for peacekeeping leads to the deaths of 1,000 Somalians, including civilians and children, and 18 U.S. soldiers. The U.S hands over control of the intervention to the UN in May.

In Burundi, Tutsis—the ruling ethnic group of the nation despite its minority population—yield power after a Hutu wins the country's first democratic election. Killed in an attempted coup after serving only four months in office, his successor is killed in a suspicious plane crash in 1994. The Hutu leader of Rwanda is killed in the same plane crash.

1994   Nelson Mandela is inaugurated as president of South Africa. He will serve as president for three years before retiring.

Bishop Desmond Tutu is appointed head of South Africa's Truth and Reconciliation Commission.

A civil war erupts in Rwanda. At least half a million Tutsis and moderate Hutus are killed. Tutsi rebels win control, sending 1 million Hutus, fearful of revenge, into Zaire and Tanzania. The United Nations sets up refugee camps in Zaire.

Following three years of failed diplomatic and economic sanctions, U.S. forces land in Haiti on September 19. Aristide returns to office on October 15.

A U.S. occupation of Haiti begins, continuing into 2000.

Rita Dove is named U.S. poet laureate.

O. J. Simpson is accused of murdering his former wife and her friend. The ensuing trial grips the nation.

1995   In a Bermuda referendum, voters reject independence from Britain by a margin of three to one.

The Soufrière Hills Volcano erupts on Montserrat, destroying the southern half of the island. The majority of the population is evacuated, and Britain imposes a Maritime Exclusion Zone.

Nation of Islam minister Louis Farrakhan organizes the Million Man March on Capitol Hill in Washington, D.C.

Colin Powell is the first African American seriously considered as a presidential candidate of a major party.

1996   Rwandan Hutu militants, fearful of reprisals for the massacres of Tutsis who had taken up influential positions in the new government, force Hutu refugees to remain in exile in Zaire and Tanzania. In October–November, Zaire sinks into a crisis as civil war, sparked by Tutsi-Hutu fighting, cuts off more than half-a-million Hutu refugees from food and medical supplies. The emissary named by the UN to negotiate a cease-fire warns of a possible regional war between Hutus and Tutsis and another genocide like the one in Rwanda. There is also a threat of epidemic and mass starvation. Canada, the United States, and other nations begin forming a peacekeeping mission when the rebels in Zaire—mostly Tutsi—take over the refugee camps, sending the refugees streaming home.

Tanzania gives Hutu refugees less than a month to return to Rwanda; many flee in the other direction instead, to hide in the forests. Tanzanian troops head off the refugees and order them back; 300,000 return to Rwanda.

The British Royal Navy sends HMS *Brave* to the Turks and Caicos Islands to quell a civil uprising that in the end does not occur.

Jean-Bertrand Aristide leaves the presidential office of Haiti at the end of his first term.

1997   Charles Taylor is elected president of Liberia.

Ghanaian Kofi Annan is elected secretary-general of the United Nations. He will be appointed to a second, five-year term beginning in 2002.

South Africa attempts to obtain more affordable versions of the anti-viral AZT treatment for the HIV virus, which is available in most Western countries. The attempt is blocked by the world pharmaceutical industry, which spearheads a lawsuit based on intellectual property rights.

The United States imposes sanctions against Sudan that prohibit trade between the two countries.

1998   Former Chilean president Augusto Pinochet is arrested in London, following an extradition request by the Spanish High Court in order to try Pinochet for human rights violations. Senior English law lords hearing Pinochet's appeal fail to reach a decision.

Britain experiences a wave of celebrations marking the fiftieth anniversary of the arrival of the emigrant ship, *Empire Windrush,* from Jamaica, carrying the first sizable group of West Indians to arrive in Britain after World War II.

The secretary-general of the United Nations, Kofi Annan, publishes the report, *The Causes of Conflict and the Promotion of Durable Peace and Sustainable Development in Africa.*

The U.S. embassies in Kenya and Tanzania are bombed within minutes of each other. The death toll is 207 Kenyans, 11 Tanzanians, and 12 U.S. citizens; altogether, more than 4,000 are injured. Several of the injured will attempt without success to sue the United States for further compensation for their injuries. Four men linked to Al Qaeda will be convicted and sentenced to jail for life in May 2001 for their role in the bombings.

1999   The United States bombs factory buildings in Khartoum, Sudan, citing

intelligence of chemical weapons links. Following the bombings, the world political community questions the reliability of this intelligence.

Eritrean-Ethiopian border clashes turn into a full-scale war.

2000   Former president Pinochet is released from British custody and flies home to Chile, where he is subsequently declared mentally unfit to stand trial.

President Thabo Mbeki of South Africa's African National Congress government writes to world leaders, calling for "an African solution to an African problem," questioning scientific evidence linking the HIV virus with the AIDS disease and contrasting the disease's emergence through heterosexual contact in South Africa and its emergence in gay communities in the West. Mbeki's approach to the problem of HIV is strongly criticized by the world community.

Eritrea and Ethiopia sign a cease-fire that calls for a UN force to monitor compliance and oversee the withdrawal of Ethiopian troops from Eritrean land. The two nations sign a peace agreement in Algeria, establishing commissions to mark the border, exchange prisoners, return displaced people, and hear compensation claims.

2001   Libyan intelligence officer Abdelbaset Al-Megrahi is found guilty of the 1988 airplane explosion over Lockerbie, Scotland, following a trial before a Scottish court in the Netherlands. He is sentenced to life imprisonment.

Islamist militants fly hijacked airliners into the World Trade Center in New York City and the Pentagon in Washington, D.C. A fourth hijacked plane crashes in a Pennsylvania field. The terrorist atrocities result in the deaths of 2,973 victims by the official death toll.

Following the September 11 attacks on the World Trade Center and the

Pentagon, the United States declares war on terror on September 12.

The Taliban regime in Afghanistan refuses to extradite Osama bin Laden, whose Al Qaeda terrorist network is suspected of carrying out the September 11 attacks. The United States spearheads a wave of assaults on Al Qaeda and Taliban positions, while Britain's military response is channeled through the UN, NATO, and the European Union.

A portion of the Guantanamo Bay naval base in Cuba is used to imprison suspected Al Qaeda and Taliban terrorists, labeled "enemy combatants." More than 500 people of 35 different nationalities have been held there for six years, as of 2007. Many detainees allege they have been subjected to torture and other cruel, inhuman treatment.

Kofi Annan and the United Nations receive the Nobel Peace Prize.

Jean-Bertrand Aristide returns for a second presidential term in Haiti.

Trinidadian V. S. Naipaul receives the Nobel Prize for Literature.

Canonized on October 1, Saint Josephine Bakhita becomes the first African woman former slave to become a saint.

2002   In Afghanistan, the Taliban and Al Qaeda forces are largely routed. U.S. and British troops remain in support of the transitional government for humanitarian and logistical purposes and as combat operatives against remaining Taliban and Al Qaeda insurgents.

Chicago native José Padilla is arrested for plotting to explode a "dirty bomb." He will not be indicted until 2005; when arraigned, this accusation will not be among the charges.

The British government publishes a dossier asserting that the Iraqi dictator Saddam Hussein could launch chemical and biological weapons of mass destruction against British targets within forty-five minutes. U.S. secretary of state Colin Powell draws on this dossier to argue for the UN Security Council's resolution authorizing "serious consequences" if Iraq refuses to disclose the weapons.

2003   With the official justification being the elimination of Iraq's weapons of mass destruction, the United States and Britain launch Operation Iraqi Freedom—the Second Gulf War—in a bid to topple Saddam Hussein. Baghdad quickly falls to coalition forces, and Operation Iraqi Freedom is officially declared over after three weeks of fighting. The war has global repercussions as Arab nations from North Africa to Southeast Asia are assessed for their potential involvement with Islamist groups linked to Al Qaeda.

U.S. ambassador L. Paul Bremer is appointed administrator of the Coalition Provisional Authority (CPA), effectively the government of occupied Iraq.

BBC reporter Andrew Gilligan cites an unnamed senior British intelligence source in suggesting that the Blair government had exaggerated (or "sexed up") the Iraqi threat in order to make the case for war.

The Iraqi Governing Council is constituted with a broad-based membership from Iraq's major religious and ethnic sectors.

The UK's chief expert in Iraqi weapons, Dr. David Kelly, commits suicide following the British government's leaking of his name as Andrew Gilligan's source. The senior British law lord, Lord Hutton, commences an inquiry into the circumstances surrounding Dr. Kelly's death.

The CPA and the Iraqi Governing Council agree to full Iraqi governance and the dissolution of the CPA by June 30, 2004.

U.S. forces capture Saddam Hussein near his hometown of Tikrit. British, American, and other coalition forces continue to face attacks by pro-Saddam insurgents.

While alternately admitting and denying national responsibility for the Lockerbie bombing, Libya offers a multi-billion-dollar compensation package in return for the lifting of U.S. sanctions, which President George W. Bush announces early in 2004.

Charles Taylor is indicted by an international court for war crimes. He accepts political asylum from Nigeria.

The United States asks Jean-Bertrand Aristide to distance himself from Amiot Métayer. When Métayer is subsequently murdered, his supporters accuse Aristide of ordering him killed to improve his relations with the U.S.

The boundary commission in the Eritrea-Ethiopia dispute rules that the town of Badme is in Eritrea. Ethiopia calls the ruling unacceptable.

2004   Prompted by the investigative work for two documentaries about the 1955 murder of Emmett Till, the U.S. Department of Justice announces that the case is officially reopened.

Métayer's brother launches a rebellion that spreads to the city of Cape Haitien. From there the rebels march on the Haitian capital, Port-au-Prince. At the prodding of his former French and U.S. supporters, Aristide leaves Haiti on February 29 for initial exile in the Central African Republic. (Aristide later claims he was abducted by U.S. troops.)

Abdullahi Yusuf, reputedly an ally of Ethiopia, becomes Somalia's interim president.

International warrants for the arrest of Laurent Nkunda and Jules Mutebutsi are issued by the government of the Democratic Republic of the Congo in connection with the May–June 2004 crisis that resulted in killings, rapes of adults and children, and widespread looting.

2005   Hurricane Katrina, strengthening to a category five hurricane in the Gulf of Mexico, makes landfall along the Central Gulf Coast near Buras-Triumph, Louisiana, just east of New Orleans, as a category three storm and causes extensive devastation in life and commerce. It is estimated to cause $75 billion in damages and a death toll well over 1,000, with final figures not yet established. Areas affected include the Bahamas, South Florida, Louisiana (especially Greater New Orleans), Mississippi, Alabama, and the Florida Panhandle.

Out of a Comprehensive Peace Agreement signed by the government of Sudan and the Sudan People's Liberation Movement/Army (SPLM/A) comes the inauguration of the new government of Sudan on July 9. Omar al-Bashir is sworn in as president and John Garang, SPLM leader, as first vice-president. Garang dies in a helicopter crash. Salva Kiir is named first vice-president by the SPLM; he will hold the post of president of Southern Sudan and commander-in-chief of the SPLA.

Conflict and crisis in the Darfur region of Sudan is labeled an "unfolding genocide" by human rights groups. Colin Powell and Kofi Annan pay visits to the Western Sudan region. A UN panel recommends that the mass killings in the Darfur region be referred to the International Criminal Court (established in The Hague); tensions between allies grow, as the United States has not recognized the court in either principle or practice.

A dire food situation exists in Eritrea, the result of several droughts.

In October, Eritrea bans UN helicopter flights in its airspace.

The United Nations Security Council threatens Eritrea and Ethiopia with sanctions unless they return to the 2000 peace plan. Eritrea orders the expulsion of North American, European, and Russian peacekeepers from the UN mission monitoring its border with Ethiopia.

2006   Ellen Johnson-Sirleaf becomes Liberia's first female president. She is also the first female president of the modern African continent.

Charles Taylor, former president of Liberia and a war crimes fugitive in Sierra Leone, is captured in Nigeria on March 29. Taylor will be transferred to Liberian custody, and Liberia will transfer him for trial to the UN-backed Special Court for Sierra Leone.

Ethiopia admits that its forces are fighting in Somalia. The operation against Islamist militiamen is called "self-defensive." The statement reveals that Ethiopia is backing Somalia's interim government against Somalia's Union of Islamic Courts.

Ethiopian-backed Somali government troops capture the capital, Mogadishu,

hours after Islamist fighters flee the city.

Eritrea expels five UN staff as spies. A UN report says that Eritrea and six other countries have been providing supplies and arms to the Islamist administration in Somalia. Eritrea denies the report and issues its own report, which states that Ethiopia was arming the Islamist government.

In Burundi, the Forces nationals pour la liberation (FNL) and Force de la defense nationale (FDN) sign a comprehensive cease-fire agreement, following UNICEF's efforts to demobilize, reintegrate, and prevent the recruitment of child soldiers. The recruitment of children continues to be a grave concern for the UN.

A faction of the Sudan Liberation Army (SLA) forcibly recruits 4,700 refugees from camps located in eastern Chad, some of them children.

2007   A ceremony marks the beginning of Ethiopia's withdrawal from Somalia on January 23.

INTRODUCTORY ESSAYS

DEMOGRAPHY, DIASPORA, AND INTERNATIONAL RELATIONS

Amadu Jacky Kaba

People of black African and European descent are the two racial groups most dispersed across the globe. They can be found in statistically significant to substantial numbers almost everywhere on earth. Professor Ali A. Mazrui has pointed out that just as the sun never used to set on the British Empire in the first half of the twentieth century, in the twenty-first century the sun never sets on blacks or people of African descent, because they are spread out in statistically significant to substantial numbers in many countries and regions across the world. Outside of their ancestral continent, black Africans or people of African descent have their largest concentration in the Americas, or the Western Hemisphere.

The largest migrations to the Americas of people of black African descent have occurred in two stages in the past thousands of years: a relatively small degree of pre- and post-Columbus migration, and post–World War II or post–African independence migration. There may have been a relatively small, although potentially influential migration, of African people to the Americas prior to Columbus; however, these numbers are overshadowed by subsequent events.

The large-scale migration of Africans that this encyclopedia is concerned with took place in the post-Columbus period during the era of the slave trade, which began to grow rapidly the beginning of the 1600s. From this period to the end of the nineteenth century, estimates of fewer than 10 million to almost 100 million black Africans were brought to the Western Hemisphere as slaves, along with a small number who arrived as indentured servants. Generally, a scholarly range of 12 million to 14,650,000 is used. It is also important to recognize that there existed an internal movement of slaves in the Western Hemisphere, and from 1783 to 1810, roughly 170,300 slaves were brought to North America from the Caribbean and Africa combined

The third, post–World War II wave of African migration to the Western Hemisphere began in significant numbers in the 1960s, with the majority of the migrants going to North America. Indeed, it has been reported that more black immigrants have come to the United States from Africa since the 1960s than the total of Africans brought to North America during the entire slave trade. This assertion is based on the claim that of an estimated 12 million Africans brought as slaves to the Western Hemisphere, less than 5 percent (less than 600,000) of that total came to North America, meaning that the rise of the black population of the United States has been mostly through natural increase, that is, birth. In 1960, for example, there were 35,000 post–World War II African immigrants in the United States, and by the year 2002 that figure had increased to just over 1 million. This may mean that the number of children born in the United States to these post–World War II African immigrants may be greater than the total number of black Africans brought as slaves to North America. Overall, by the beginning of the twenty-first century, due to internal demographic increase and continuing migration from Africa, the proportion of people of black African descent has increased to the point where they comprise at least one out of every five people in the Americas.

DEMOGRAPHY, IMMIGRATION, AND THE INCREASE OF PEOPLE OF BLACK AFRICAN DESCENT IN THE WESTERN HEMISPHERE

The massive rise in numbers of people of black African descent in the Americas and the Caribbean has occurred mostly naturally, through birth, but a substantial portion of that increase has also occurred through post–World War II immigration, especially to the United States and Canada. Among the many racial and ethnic groups in the Western Hemisphere, people of black African descent have one of the highest rates of childbirth. This has resulted in a substantial increase in their populations all across the hemisphere. For example, in the United States, which has the second-largest black population in the Western Hemisphere (after Brazil), more black females have children than white females. In 2000, 44.8 percent of non-Hispanic white women age fifteen to forty-four in the United States were childless, while 39 percent of black women of the same age group were childless in that same year. In the Caribbean, which has a black majority population, as of 2005 the total fertility rate (children born per woman) was 2.16, slightly higher than the 2.1 children per woman that United Nations demographers indicate is required to replace or sustain a country's population. In Latin America (where at least 20 percent of the people are of black African descent), that figure for 2005 is 2.75 children on average born per woman.

AFRICA'S TOTAL AND REGIONAL POPULATIONS

Although Africa, especially sub-Saharan Africa, has the highest death rate among the regions and continents of the world, the continent as a whole continues to provide a substantial share of the estimated 80 million people added annually to the world's total population. For example, Africa's total population increased by an estimated 18 million, from 823 million to 841 million, between July 2001 and July 2002. This means that during this period, Africa contributed 22.6 percent of the 80 million people added to the total world population.

As of July 2005, Africa's total population was estimated at 887.2 million. Utilizing the classifications of the five regions of Africa (Eastern, Middle, Northern, Southern, and Western Africa [see Appendix]), out of this number, the regional populations were: 275.9 million (31.1 percent) for Eastern Africa; 254.74 million (28.7 percent) for Western Africa; 199 million (22.4 percent) for Northern Africa; 106.4 million (12 percent) for Middle Africa; and 51 million (5.7 percent) for Southern Africa. As of 2005, the average fertility rate (children born per woman) was: 4.24 for all of Africa; 2.91 for Northern Africa; 3.06 for Southern Africa; 4.93 for Eastern Africa; 5.19 for Middle Africa; and 5.10 for Western Africa. The ten most populous countries in Africa as of July 2005 were: Nigeria, 128.8 million; Egypt, 77.5 million; Ethiopia, 73 million; Democratic Republic of Congo, 60.1 million; South Africa, 44.3 million; Sudan, 40.2 million; Tanzania, 36.8 million; Kenya, 33.8 million; Morocco, 32.7 million; and Algeria, 32.5 million.

PEOPLE OF BLACK AFRICAN DESCENT IN LATIN AMERICA (EXCLUDING THE CARIBBEAN)

The twenty-two countries and territories that make up Latin America (excluding the Caribbean) are among the most racially diverse areas of the world. Various estimates exist as to the number or percentages of people of African descent in the region because of different methods of research; an accepted scholarly range is that there are between 90 and 150 million people of African descent in Latin America.

In Brazil, Panama, Cuba, and the Dominican Republic, people of black African descent comprise the majority.

Research by this author shows that out of the estimated total of 490 million people in Latin America in 2001, whites made up 182,690,461 (37.3 percent); Mestizos (a mixed race of whites and Indians), 152,751,357 (31 percent); Amerindians, 58,265,533 (11.9 percent); blacks, 16,071,290 (3.3 percent); mixed (blacks mixed with Indians, whites, or Mestizos), 73,844,229 (15.2 percent); and other racial groups, 7,217,685 (1.5 percent). If the definition of blacks in the United States (any person with a fraction of black African blood) were used in Latin America, the black population would be at least 90 million (18.5 percent of the total 490 million people in July 2001). As of July 2005, there were an estimated 518.6 million people in Latin American countries combined. If one were to use the 2001 percentage (18.5 percent) of people of black African descent in Latin America to get the actual number of their total as of 2005, it would amount to 96 million. But since people of black African descent tend to have more children than whites, one could claim that the actual number would be at least 100 million.

Using the definition of a black person in the United States, the countries in Latin America with statistically significant to substantial black populations as of July 2005 were Brazil, with 45 percent out of 186 million; Guyana, with 36 percent of 765,283; Colombia, with 21 percent of 43 million; and Uruguay, with 4 percent out of 3.4 million.

PEOPLE OF BLACK AFRICAN DESCENT IN THE CARIBBEAN

People of black African descent constitute the majority of the population of the twenty-four countries and territories that make up the Caribbean. As of the year 2001, the total population of the Caribbean was estimated at 36.9 million, with an estimated 65 percent of this total population being people of black African descent. As of July 2005, there were an estimated 38.7 million people in the Caribbean.

As of July 2005, the following Caribbean nations had these proportions of people of black African descent: 98 percent of the 2.7 million in Jamaica; 95 percent of the 8.1 million in Haiti; 85 percent of the 301,790 in the Bahamas; 62 percent of the 11.3 million in Cuba; and 58 percent of the one million in Trinidad and Tobago. Research by this author shows that as of 2003, there were at least 165 million (19 percent) people of black African descent out of the estimated 862 million people in the Western Hemisphere.

PEOPLE OF BLACK AFRICAN DESCENT IN NORTH AMERICA

Apart from Brazil, the United States has the largest black African population outside of Africa. As of July 1, 2004, there were 39.2 million blacks or African Americans in the United States. In Canada, according to the 2001 Canadian census, of the 29,639,030 people in that country, people of black African descent comprised 662,215 (2.2 percent).

RELATIONS BETWEEN PEOPLE OF AFRICAN DESCENT IN THE WESTERN HEMISPHERE AND AFRICA

There are three types of international relations between Africa and people of African descent in the Western Hemisphere. The first is between governments in Africa and those in the Western Hemisphere. The second type of relations between Africa and the Western Hemisphere is between individuals or groups or organizations comprising mostly people of African descent in the hemisphere and governments, groups, and individuals in Africa. The third type of international relations between Africa and the Western Hemisphere is through mainstream human rights organizations, foundations, and other activist organizations that lobby their governments in the Americas on behalf of poor countries, including African nations. It is worth noting that people of African descent are involved in all three types of relations with Africa. For example, for the first type of relations with Africa, the U.S. government in the beginning of the twenty-first century has developed a very positive partnership with most African nations that includes signing favorable trade agreements with most of them, which has increased substantially the number of immigration visas issued to Africans, and intervening in Liberia's bloody fourteen-year civil war. However, it is African Americans who have played an essential or important role in creating the environment for such positive relations between Africa and the government of the United States. Another important example of government-to-government relations between Africa and countries in the Western Hemisphere occurred between South Africa and

Haiti. During celebrations of Haiti's two hundredth year of independence, the government and people of South Africa gave the government and people of Haiti $10 million. In addition, to prevent a very bloody civil war between the then president, Jean-Bertrand Aristide, and an armed rebellion in Haiti, the South African government offered asylum to President Aristide, which he accepted.

The second type of relations between Africa and the Western Hemisphere is between individuals of African descent (including African immigrants) in the hemisphere and governments, civic organizations, and individuals in Africa. For example, in a summit in February 2003, the African Union (AU), a Pan African organization that includes Africa's independent nations, recognized the African Diaspora as the sixth region of the organization. The African American nonprofit relief organization, Africare, is reported to have donated over $400 million of assistance to Africa.

The African American female billionaire, Oprah Winfrey, has established a $10 million academic institution known as the Oprah Winfrey Leadership Academy for Girls in South Africa, and she has also spent $6 million on a program called Christmas Kindness in South Africa. The African American film actor Denzel Washington and his wife, Pauletta, are reported to have donated $1 million to the Nelson Mandela Children's Fund.

African immigrants in the United States are also increasing their assistance to Africa in various important ways. By 2005, African immigrants were sending an estimated $1 billion home annually as remittances. Also, an Ethiopian immigrant businessman in the United States, named Noah Samara, in 1999 launched a WorldSpace satellite radio orbiting above Earth, known as XM Radio, which broadcasts daily educational programs, including programming from CNN and the BBC, to remote areas in East Africa. Although the technology was American, Africa utilized it before the United States, which launched it two years later, in 2001.

The third type of relations between Africa and the Western Hemisphere is that between Africa and mainstream civic organizations and foundations in the Americas that provide all sorts of important assistance to African nations. One example of such organizations is the Bill and Melinda Gates Foundation, which has provided millions of dollars in grants to various nonprofit organizations in Africa to solve medical and other serious social problems there. These organizations work with both the government of the United States and black individuals in the hemisphere to find the best ways to provide meaningful assistance for various problems confronting Africa.

CONCLUSION

The large-scale migration of people of African descent to the Americas and the Caribbean began as the tragedy of the slave trade. However, the rise in population and the ongoing voluntary migration of people of black African descent in the Western Hemisphere shows that the history of African migration has not stayed one. Today, people of African descent, including African immigrants, in the Western Hemisphere are at the core of international relations between Africa and countries in the Americas.

APPENDIX: CLASSIFICATIONS OF REGIONS OF AFRICA

Eastern Africa

Burundi, Comoros, Djibouti, Eritrea, Ethiopia, Kenya, Madagascar, Malawi, Mauritius, Mozambique, Reunion, Rwanda, Seychelles, Somalia, Tanzania, Uganda, Zambia, Zimbabwe, and Mayotte (overseas department of France)

Middle Africa

Angola, Cameroon, Central African Republic, Chad, Republic of Congo, Democratic Republic of Congo, Equatorial Guinea, Gabon, and São Tomé and Principe

Northern Africa

Algeria, Egypt, Libya, Morocco, Sudan, Tunisia, and Western Sahara

Southern Africa

Botswana, Lesotho, Namibia, South Africa, and Swaziland

Western Africa

Benin, Burkina Faso, Cape Verde, Côte d'Ivoire, The Gambia, Ghana, Guinea, Guinea-Bissau, Liberia, Mali, Mauritania, Niger, Nigeria, Senegal, Sierra Leone, Togo, and Saint Helena (British overseas territory)

Source: Country/regional classifications by the United Nations Statistics Division, Department of Economic and Social Affairs. Retrieved on July 12, 2004. http://unstats.un.org/unsd/methods/m49/m49regin.htm.

References

Akukwe, Chinua, and Sidi Jammeh. "Africa-Diaspora Partnership: Issues and Challenges." *African Renaissance* 1, no. 2 (2004): 69–74.

Akukwe, Chinua, Sidi Jammeh, and Melvin Foote. "Africa and Its Diaspora: Institutionalising a Durable Partnership." *African Renaissance* 1, no. 2 (2004): 75–80.

American Community Survey Profile 2002. Washington, DC: U.S. Census Bureau, Government Printing Office, September 2, 2003.

Bachu, Amara, and Martin O'Connell. *Fertility of American Women: June 2000.* Washington, DC: U.S. Census Bureau, Government Printing Office, 2001.

Bernstein, Robert. *Hispanic Population Passes 40 Million, Census Bureau Reports.* Washington, DC: U.S. Census Bureau, Government Printing Office, June 9, 2005.

Canada Statistics. "Visible Minority Groups, 2001 Counts, for Canada, Provinces and Territories." 2001. http://www12.statcan.ca/english.

Central Intelligence Agency. *World Factbook.* Washington, DC: Central Intelligence Agency, 2001–2005.

Clark, Andrew F. "The Atlantic Slave Trade Revisited." *Journal of Third World Studies* 22, no. 1 (2005): 273–284.

Franklin, John H., and Alfred Moss Jr.. *From Slavery to Freedom: A History of African Americans.* 7th ed. New York: McGraw-Hill, 1994.

Kaba, Amadu Jacky. "Africa-U.S. Partnership in the 21st Century." *Chimera* 2, no. 1 (2004): 18–25.

Kaba, Amadu Jacky. "Africa's Migration Brain Drain: The Costs and Benefits to the Continent." *Chimera* 2, no. 3 (2004): 19–30.

Kraay, Hendrik. "Transatlantic Ties: Recent Works on the Slave Trade, Slavery, and Abolition." *Latin American Research Review* 39, no. 2 (2004): 178–195.

Mazrui, A. A. "The African Experience in Politics and Culture: From Monroe's Doctrine to Nkrumah's Consciencism." Lecture delivered under the sponsorship of the Center for Contemporary Culture of Barcelona, in Barcelona, Spain, January 13, 2003.

McMillin, James A. *The Final Victims: Foreign Slave Trade to North America, 1783–1810.* Columbia: University of South Carolina Press, 2004.

Profile of the Foreign-Born Population in the United States: 2000. Washington, DC: U.S. Census Bureau, Government Printing Office, 2001.

"Visible Minority Groups, 2001 Counts, for Canada, Provinces, and Territories." Statistics Canada. Retrieved on July 30, 2004. http://www12.statcan.ca/english.

Wright, Donald R. "Recent Literature on Slavery in Colonial North America." *Magazine of History* 17, no. 3 (2003): 5–9.

CULTURE AND RELIGION

Fabio Akcelrud Durão

In this essay, the abundance and variety of material on culture and religion in Africa and the Americas is meaningfully organized by framing culture according to three principles, namely (1) that if culture in general is in a process of continuous change, this assumes an extreme form in transatlantic exchange; (2) that culture is not completely autonomous, but always subject to some kind of material determination, the historical experience of slavery being only the clearest determining factor in Africa and the Americas; and (3) that cultural manifestations in general—but again, especially so in the region—contain, in themselves, something that transcends them, either through their form or through the effects they generate. Religious diversity, typical of Africa and the Americas, is explored by viewing religions in Africa and the Americas as changing in relation to their matrixes in Europe, Asia, or Africa; as part of an unending war for the minds of believers and for material resources; and as representing a unique realm for reconciliation in the transatlantic world taken as a whole. This essay shows that precisely through diversity and difference, opposition and conflict, Africa and the Americas are inescapably and inexorably interconnected.

CULTURE

Few terms have been so open-ended in the humanities and social sciences as that of "culture." Present everywhere, related to everything, it very easily loses all specificity and easily generates all sorts of contradictory statements. A great variety of points of view and increasing abundance of conflicting data become even more apparent when one focuses on the culture of Africa and the Americas as they constitute the Atlantic World. Three broad and basic principles may be useful to work out the mediation of this African American cultural profusion, without at the same time homogenizing the overwhelming wealth of differences that can be found in all cultures at any point in history and at any part of the globe. They could be termed the principles of constant mutability, inevitable determination, and immanent transcendence.

The first principle, the presence of constant mutability, concerns the nonoriginal nature of all culture, regardless of whether the concept be related to an isolated instance, as in a given local or national culture, or conceived as the result of regional or even continental interaction. No cultural formation has ever been pure or "authentic." That which is maintained, in a given ritual or celebration, must in the same movement both shape and accommodate those necessarily differing elements that always threaten to invade and spoil the reproduction of a given cultural practice. Thus, in spite of remarkable cases of constancy, it is safe to consider that transformation is more the norm than a deviance in the life of cultures, even (and sometimes especially) when members of a determinate group see themselves as perpetrators of a timeless and immutable tradition.

Indeed, cultural transformation becomes an undeniable fact when, instead of focusing on a particular group or community, one tries to frame the Atlantic World. For in the immense process of voluntary and forced migration into the Americas—the largest in history, involving, apart from settlers, from 12 to 20 million African captives, depending on the estimates—cultures simply *could not* remain the same. Members from enslaved families were torn apart from each other, and individuals from varied, oftentimes rival ethnic and tribal groups were strategically mixed together and thrown into a completely different and threatening milieu. Among slaves, contrasting habits had to be negotiated into new forms of conviviality and be accepted by all, thus encouraging a relative cultural unification that could not be found in the diversity of their native Africa. At the same time, the innumerable Native American social formations, spanning from nomadic smaller groups to highly complex social organizations, as in the case of the Aztecs, witnessed the invasion of their lands and the subjection of their work force to an unknown rhythm of production. The fates of indigenous groups varied a great deal. In some regions they were simply exterminated or reduced to a minimum; this happened in both the "white" South (Argentina, Chile, and Uruguay) and North America (United States and Canada), as well as in the Caribbean, where black slaves constituted the overwhelming part of the population. Elsewhere, Native Americans were dissolved in the constitution of racially mixed nations, as in the case of Brazil, or, finally, managed to survive to form the greatest substratum of the people, as in Bolivia or Peru.

And finally, it is important to remember that Africa itself was not left untouched by transatlantic exchanges. If already in the seventeenth and eighteenth centuries the slave trade brought about changes in social organization such as depopulation and increasing animosity among African peoples, in the nineteenth century Africa became a colonized continent too, a condition that for many critics persists until today. Africa thus began to share many of the problems experienced by Latin America—including political instability, increasing debt levels, and a gaping social fault line between rich and poor—even though Africa acted, and still does, as a supplier of labor force rather than its receptacle.

Any single cultural phenomenon in Africa and the Americas may be viewed as bearing the imprint of this mixed and intrinsically violent process of formation, a process that only became more complex with the arrival of successive waves of European and Asian immigration to the Americas in the nineteenth and twentieth centuries. When properly scrutinized, all cultural practices in the Transatlantic World—including also many of them that occurred in Europe—provide ample evidence of this history, from Cuban music to Afrofuturism, from pageants to classical music and drama. It is true that national differences created cultural particularities, and it is obvious that a North-South divide accounts for the inequalities in the volume of cultural artifacts produced in the richest country of the world, the United States, in comparison to an impoverished Latin America and an Africa plunged into misery. A clear view of this imbalance can be had, for instance, by simply comparing the number of films produced in each continent and their respective budgets. This poses a challenge, perhaps the greatest, to Afrocentrism: to call attention to the centrality of Africa without surrendering to cultural and historical reductionism. Be that as it may, it is important to keep in mind that even though it is tempting to imagine a place or time outside the mutual influence of Africa and the Americas, this temptation itself deserves to be scrutinized, quite frequently as a symptom of a world that for varying reasons has become unbearable.

In fact, imaginary misrepresentations are decisive not only within particular cultural contexts in Africa and the Americas, but also in the overall process of transatlantic exchange. For both Latin America and Africa, albeit in unequal degrees, the United States and Canada often appear as perfect stereotypes of wealth and abundance, places where need has no meaning, while the opposite also holds, when the countries of the North project on the rest of the Atlantic World, without much heed for differentiation, the reverse of all that is lacking to them: exuberant and exotic nature and peoples as a counterimage to urban standardization and humdrum everyday lives. But, again, this imbalance and dissymmetry should be viewed as an argument for, rather than a proof against, transatlantic interconnection. It corroborates the claim that cultural identity is itself relational, thus not self-established or autogenetically created, but on the contrary dependent on a *determinate* other to constitute itself.

The second important principle concerning culture in Africa and the Americas derives from the first principle of mutability or constant change. That culture is not an absolutely independent realm, being somehow related to material, concrete forms of daily life, and consequently contributing to the reproduction of society as a whole, is a claim generally accepted but which, once more, is all the more evident within the framework of the transatlantic world. It is often astonishing to realize that many of the cultural practices now viewed as in themselves autonomous, "naturally" associated to the identity of a given group or nation, emerged as strategies of survival in direct connection with their immediate environment. Brazilian *capoeira*, for instance, was first devised as a disguise for slaves to fight among themselves while appearing to dance. What today is a hybrid mixture of martial art and performance practiced worldwide had its roots in hardship, in the dehumanization of human beings. In many of the cultural manifestations discussed in the following entries, one can detect the coexistence of both a response or reaction to the surrounding environment and the presence of furtive utopic impulses: a desire for a better world, oftentimes expressed under the most adverse conditions, when even immediate subsistence cannot be taken for granted. The myth of the flying African, of slaves going back home in the same way as birds, is an obvious example of this, insofar as it provided an imaginary compensation and utopic outlet for life under slavery.

One should not think that partial social and economic determination play only a restrictive or shackling role in the lives of cultures in Africa and the Americas. For if cultures are not totally autonomous, neither are they completely reducible to specific ways of life or the reproduction of society. Without spontaneity and creativity, without the presence of something previously nonexistent, no culture can ever come into being. Interestingly enough, this additional "something" may often be found in a given artifact's capacity to promote the conciliation of opposites in its very form, thereby presenting, by means of its expression, something transcending itself. In samba, for instance, the body is divided into two parts, the legs and waist in continuous movement and the stomach and chest dexterously kept static. It would not be difficult to associate this contrast to the experience of Afro-Brazilians concerning the duality inherent to their post-abolition relationship to the law and civil society as a whole: formally endowed with the same rights as whites, in reality they were far from being on equal footing with them.

This spontaneous and creative moment attached to culture in Africa and the Americas does not have to be sought only in the formal aspects of cultural practices; it may also be found in the reaction or response they elicit. Take the singular passion for soccer in Latin America and Africa. Culture oftentimes loses its autonomy and spontaneity as it is absorbed by group or identity politics. This represented a danger for many of the movements of resistance, particularly against racial oppression, which in their desire to differentiate themselves from their (white) other adopted a prescriptive stance as to what members should do and how they should behave. By attempting to lead their group to what they thought would be the right way, activists could very easily see themselves in the position to dictate what the culture of their group should be like, especially if they wanted to purge it of extraneous elements. They thus ran the risk of acting against the very culture they fostered.

But an opposite threat to that of cultural surveillance and censorship must also be taken into account, namely, the belief in the absolute naturalness of culture. In a world where cultural manifestations are so prone to be turned into commodities, simply to renounce reflection becomes tantamount to abandoning culture to the demands of the market. This tension between creative impulse and rational assessment is constantly present in the everyday practice of participants in virtually all cultural groups in Africa and the Americas; a proper balance is tenuous and varies a great deal from case to case. When, for instance, does Carnival lose its status of a popular, in-the-street and color-blind party to become a commercial enterprise, mainly for tourists? When do participants degenerate into spectators (even of themselves)? When does the happiness expressed in Carnival reverse into an imperative to be happy because the show must go on? To be sure, selling what they do is often for marginalized groups, not only in Africa and Latin America, but also even in the United States and Canada, the only way to survive. But they always run the risk of converting the market into the final objective of such cultural manifestations, profit occupying the place of self-expression. The unavoidably creative aspect of culture is thus a highly ambiguous element, for if it may feed an industry of culture, it also continuously attests to the inextinguishable presence of collective life in Africa and the Americas.

RELIGION

In contrast to Europe, most of the former Soviet bloc, and a great deal of Asia (with perhaps the exception of India), where religion does not interfere directly in the public sphere, the region comprising Africa and the Americas is characterized by the deep-rooted and all-pervasive nature of its religious practices and beliefs. More than anything else, the strength of faith may be viewed as a common denominator placing the poorest and richest parts of the globe, Africa and the United States, on the same plane.

Religion's social comprehensiveness is paralleled by its diversity. The transatlantic world encompasses the greatest number and variety of religions in the world: from minority groups such as Jews, Buddhists, or Hindus through specifically local religions, to the main creeds of Catholicism, Protestantism, and Islam. Interestingly enough, this geographic multiplicity has its own temporal counterpart in the simultaneous presence of beliefs and practices belonging to different periods of history, from old shaman-led and magical cults, which originated in, and were congenial to, a pre-industrial world, to capitalism-tailored sects whose functioning is not unlike that of business enterprises. And, again, this raises the interesting question about the survival of pre-modern religious worldviews, which according to more narrow-minded sociological theories, should have vanished a long time ago. It is true that so-called traditional religions, mainly in Africa, have been in a process of gradual disappearance and, as will be discussed, have undergone continuous transformation; nevertheless, their unremitting effectiveness and influence in large stretches of Africa and, in very modified forms, of the Caribbean and black Latin America, is still something to be wondered at.

The specific religious nature of the Atlantic World also generates methodological problems. For a great deal of the African continent in the present (as well as for pre-Columbian Native Americans in the past), religion is so much enmeshed in everyday life, so much part of a holistic view linking the cosmos to one's basic daily routine, that studying it as a separate realm could only correspond to an artificial procedure, dictated as it should be by the rational need to classify and distinguish different social practices. In Cuban ritual music of African descent, for example, it would be unsatisfactory to sever the sacred origins from the more or less profane uses that it may be put to; religious ritual and secular spectacle here go hand in hand and cannot be dissociated.

Not even the boundaries dividing culture and religion can be unproblematically drawn in relation to Africa and the Americas. For many African and American believers, religion could not be placed *under* culture, even as a privileged part of it, but would have rather to be conceived *over* it, as the aim of all culture, the point where all cultural practices should converge. If dead religions may easily be situated within the culture that originated them, living creeds fiercely deny their particularities and refuse to relinquish claims to Truth and universality, especially against other faiths. For many Catholics, Muslims, and Protestants, their religions should not share the same theoretical framework with African traditional religions, the latter being properly "cultural," which would be but a codeword for "innocuous." This shows how religions in Africa and the Americas are as vital a theme as they are controversial and conflicting.

The three principles for framing culture described above are also fruitful in approaching the transformations, threats, and promises of religions in Africa and the Americas.

First of all, the principle of mutability also holds here, for when they were transplanted into the new continent, religious rituals had to pass through significant changes to varying degrees. To take an obvious example, when captives died in slave ships or when proper resources were not available in the Americas, which was almost always the case, African burial practices had to relinquish their original grandeur. But beyond particular rites themselves, it is important to observe that larger-scale religious transformations also took place, mainly in three different, if interconnected, ways. New beliefs emerged first by means of syncretism, the combination of apparently irreconcilable elements within the same religious outlook. Brazilian Umbanda and Candomblé, Caribbean Voodoo, Obeah, and Santeria blend Catholic saints with spirits—the *orixás* and *loas*—by whom ritual participants may actually be possessed. Another kind of change happened through the adaptation of already-existing creeds to the realities of the Americas, thus creating new hybrid entities. The Nation of Islam, for instance, claims the Muslim faith while its status as a true Islamic religion is refuted by many scholars and theologians. It could thus be interpreted as a working out of partial elements of Islam within a context of U.S. social and racial tension. The same could even be said of Pentecostalism, whose origins may also be traced back, through William Joseph Seymour, to the experience of slavery in the United States. Even though it is now accepted as a legitimate and respectable Protestant religion, Pentecostalism is best understood as a North American creation, and its immense success, which certainly derives from its intensity and caring for individual churchgoers, has its roots in a long tradition of black Protestantism that practiced a more communal and participative kind of worship. This could, again, be viewed as a clear reaction against and as compensation for the oppression brought about by slavery.

The third form of change involved established religions as they were transplanted to the Americas. For even Christianity and Islam themselves did not remain the same. As far as Catholicism is concerned, very early on Jesuit converters saw themselves confronted with the task of having to adapt their terminology to the Native American universe. How could one teach the doctrine of the Fall to Indians who simply could not understand the concept of guilt, let alone that of primordial sin? In what is today called Latin America, Catholic indoctrination had thus to be built taking pre-Columbian beliefs and religions as its basis and proceeding to work its way through and out from them. This process of adjustment has not yet stopped, and there is very little reason to believe that it will. Indeed, it is possible to regard, for example, liberation theology and its socially motivated and politically engaged re-reading of the teachings of Jesus as part and parcel of a long Latin American tradition of reappropriation of Catholicism.

Nor should it be imagined that changes happened only in the New World, for the African continent, too, has witnessed strong transformations in its religious configuration. Africa has long been associated with religious diversity, for the continent not only played a fundamental role in the history of Christianity, Islam, and Judaism; it was also the birthplace of a great number of native, tribal, animist religions. But what may have once been cohabitation and tolerance became confrontation very early on. Even before the Portuguese arrived in the sixteenth century, trade routes in North Africa were already bringing Islam to the continent, gradually supplanting traditional beliefs. With increasing

European presence since the seventeenth century, but most markedly from the nineteenth century on, Christianity too started to occupy an important position in the religious life of the continent. Waves of evangelization also included the reverse movement, when black preachers traveled from the Americas to Africa to profess Protestantism and Catholicism.

If religions were (and still are) an all-important aid for the survival of oppressed groups in Africa and the Americas, they were also (and still remain) a means of oppression and control. One way of seeing the history of religions in Africa and the Americas would be to relate it to an overall history of conflicts and animosity, which now would involve competition for the minds of believers. Tending to influence politics and to generate confrontation, religious intolerance is one of the greatest threats facing the Africa and the Americas of today. In the context of the transatlantic world, it is possible to identify at least fours fronts, both past and present, of an undying religious war.

The first one of them concerns the attack on pre-Columbian Native American beliefs, one of the first casualties in the colonizing process. These beliefs all but disappeared, even though faint traces of them may still be found scattered in popular superstitions. The second front is that of a good deal of the African continent, where religious tensions, involving mainly Christians and Muslims, but also traditional religions, persist. A full list of such confrontations would not be a short one, and it would have to include the 1994 genocide in Rwanda and the genocide in the Darfur region of the Sudan that began in 2003. The third front is that of the Americas themselves, where there seems to be an increasing push toward more unyielding kinds of faith. In the United States, religious war could first of all be verified, albeit not ostensibly, in several acts of conversion. It is hard not to see, for example, Muhammad Ali's or, more clearly, Malcolm X's turn to Islam as a political statement, the rejection of Christianity as the religion of the masters and of the status quo as much as the acceptance of Allah. But also from the point of view of dominant Christianity itself, connection to power, including governmental power, has not always been absent. It is not only the case that Protestantism and Catholicism—which of course have their own European history of war—to a greater or lesser extent had the status of "official" religions, but also that for many North Americans, implicitly present in the recent "war on terrorism" is a confrontation with Islam.

Finally, in Latin America, religious conflict has been renewed with the decline of Catholicism and Afro–Latin American religions as a consequence of the rise of so-called new evangelical, often Pentecostal, churches. In their worst forms, they may resemble commercial enterprises or self-help industries, sometimes with little connection to matters related to the Beyond such as immortality of the soul or the meaning of Creation. Catholic reaction came under the guise of the Charismatic Movement, which implemented several of the practices carried out by the new evangelical churches. It is not uncommon for the latter, in turn, to revert to rituals left behind by Catholicism, such as collective exorcism and an emphasis on the immediate presence of the devil and evil spirits in the world.

And yet, these conflicts demonstrate an openness to unique possibilities. For all the intensification of conflicts and the recrudescence of fanaticism and intolerance, religion in Africa and the Americas contains an unparalleled potential, to be found nowhere else in the world, in its capacity to mobilize collective energies that otherwise could never come into existence. If the widespread Latin American and African distrust of politics, the corrosion of personal and communitarian relationships, and the commercialization of most (if not all) spheres of life do not lead in Africa and the Americas to anomie, skepticism, or cynicism, this must be explained to a great extent by the role played by religions there. Reconciliation is an all-important term in this context, because for all the history of suffering and conflict—or perhaps precisely because of it—the fate of Africa and the Americas lies in their togetherness, their future very much depending on whether their forced conjunction may become a peaceful and equal integration. This would be the promise of religion, in fact of all religions, in Africa and the Americas.

> *See also:* African Methodist Episcopal Church; Afrofuturism; Atlantic World; Candomblé; Caribbean Artists Movement; Carnival, Latin American; Colored Methodist Episcopal Church; Cuban Music, African Influence in; Cuban Ritual Music, African Influence in; Drama, African American; Film (all entries); Nation of Islam; Négritude; Obeah; Ogun; Orisha; Pentacostalism; Religion (Africa); Transculturation; Voodoo

References
Arrighi, Giovanni. *The Long Twentieth Century.* New York: Verso, 1994.
Bailyn, Bernard. *Atlantic History: Concept and Contours.* Cambridge, MA: Harvard University Press, 2005.
Baucom, Ian. *Specters of the Atlantic: Finance Capital, Slavery, and the Philosophy of History.* Durham, NC: Duke University Press, 2005.
Bloch, Ernst. *The Principle of Hope.* 3 vols. Translated by N. Plaice et al. Cambridge, MA: MIT Press, 1995.
Bosi, Alfredo. *Dialética da Colonização.* São Paulo, Brazil: Companhia Das Letras, 1992.
Gilroy, Paul. *The Black Atlantic: Modernity and Double Consciousness.* Cambridge, MA: Harvard University Press, 1993.
Inikori, Joseph, and Stanley Engerman, eds. *The Atlantic Slave Trade: Effects on Economies, Societies, and Peoples in Africa, the Americas, and Europe.* Durham, NC: Duke University Press, 1992.
Jameson, Fredric. *The Political Unconscious: Narrative as a Socially Symbolic Act.* Ithaca, NY: Cornell University Press, 1981.
Mbiti, John S. *African Religions and Philosophy.* 2nd ed. Oxford: Heinemann, 1989.
Palmie, Stephan. *Slave Cultures and the Cultures of Slavery.* Knoxville: University of Tennessee Press, 1995.
Weber, Max. *The Protestant Ethic and the Spirit of Capitalism.* Translated by Talcott Parsons. Los Angeles: Roxbury Publishing, 1998.

ECONOMICS AND TRADE

Christopher Cumo

THE EMERGENCE OF AGRICULTURE AND THE PRE-COLUMBIAN AND AFRICAN CIVILIZATIONS

The earliest stone tools in Africa, dating to 2 million years ago, reveal that the ancestors of humans hunted or at least scavenged for food and imply a division of labor between males and females, with males hunting or scavenging game and females gathering plants. During the Old Stone Age, humans in Africa adorned their dead with beads made of seashells and ivory, implying trade in these items. Accompanying this activity was commerce in gold. In the first millennium BCE, humans in Africa began working iron without having, in contrast to the cultures of Europe and Asia, first smelted copper or made bronze, an alloy of copper and tin. Excepting Zambia, Africa is deficient in copper, providing little opportunity for the mining and use of this metal.

At the close of the Old Stone Age, humans settled the Americas, and around 6000 BCE, well before the Iron Age in Africa, began growing corn in Mexico and the Yucatan and potatoes in the Andes Mountains. Corn had spread north by the first century CE to the Great Lakes, though the potato would not reach this region until the seventeenth century as a product of the Columbian Exchange: the Spanish carried the potato to Europe in the sixteenth century, whence the tuber doubled back across the Atlantic to the Great Lakes a century later. In addition to corn and the potato, Native Americans grew several varieties of bean, squash, pumpkin, tomato, pepper, and tobacco. These crops, especially corn and the potato, made possible the empires of Mesoamerica and South America. The longevity of these empires evidences a regular food surplus, an achievement all the more remarkable given that pre-Columbian people had neither plow nor draught animal.

The existence of paved roads in these empires implies commerce. As did the inhabitants of Africa, pre-Columbian people traded gold. It, along with stylistic variations in pottery and elaborate burial, implies a division of wealth, with the affluent able to afford greater ornamentation than the poor. The peoples of the Arctic Circle fished and hunted seal. The nomads of Canada hunted moose and caribou. The Native Americans of the Pacific Northwest fished for salmon and traded seashells. The tribes of the Great Plains hunted buffalo, and the woodlands Indians east of the Mississippi River were farmers, hunters, and traders.

As in the pre-Columbian empires, agriculture undergirded the economy of ancient Africa. In contrast to the Americas, farming was not an indigenous development in Africa, at least not north of the Sahara Desert. Ancient Egyptians borrowed the crops and implements, notably the plow and sickle, from the Near East around 5000 BCE. Agriculture flourished on the strip of land inundated by the Nile River. Wheat and barley filled the granaries of the pharaohs and later of the Romans. Agriculture spread from Egypt west across North Africa. Whether farming spread south from Egypt or developed independently in sub-Saharan Africa remains open to question. Trade between Egypt and Nubia along the Nile and between Egypt and Ethiopia across the Red Sea leads one to suspect that agriculture migrated south along these routes. Yet the absence of the plow and sickle south of the Sahara confirms the lack of technological diffusion to Nubia and Ethiopia and implies an independent origin of agriculture in these areas. This view gains strength from the different suite of crops grown in sub-Saharan Africa: the yam and oil palm since 3000 BCE; sorghum since 2000 BCE; millet since 1000 BCE; and bananas since the first millennium CE. African farmers also grew rice, though its date of dispersal from Asia remains a matter of conjecture.

From an early date North Africa was part of the economy of the Mediterranean world. Alexandria, a city on the western edge of the Nile Delta, was a commercial hub that linked the western Mediterranean to the Near East and India. The merchants of Alexandria traded olive oil from Greece, wine from Italy and Gaul (what is today France), and wheat from Sicily and the Nile Valley. Rivaling these merchants were the Phoenicians in Carthage, which is today part of Tunisia. The Roman conquest of Carthage and Egypt united the Mediterranean in a single commercial zone. The presence of Roman coins throughout North Africa reveals the degree to which the Romans monetized the economy of this region. Conversely, their dearth in sub-Saharan Africa suggests the persistence of trade in kind. With the decline of the Roman Empire in the fifth century CE, North Africa reverted to trade in kind. The fragmentation of the economy in North Africa paralleled the economic decline that attended the collapse of the Mayan Empire in the ninth century CE. The cause of this collapse remains a matter of controversy, though it is probable that corn yields declined.

CONTACT ACROSS THE ATLANTIC: THE COLUMBIAN EXCHANGE AND THE SLAVE TRADE

Separate for millennia, the economies of Africa and the Americas converged after 1492. The Columbian Exchange brought corn to Africa and rice, via Madagascar, to the New World. Rice fueled the growth of the plantations in the Carolinas and Georgia and stoked the demand for labor. The dearth of money in pre-capitalistic America made it difficult to attract labor. The alternative was compulsion through indentured servitude and slavery. Indentured servitude, however, declined in the seventeenth century, leaving slaves to shoulder the plantation economy. Africans were more immune than Native Americans to European diseases and so were suitable as laborers. The European settlers of the Atlantic seaboard sought Africans not only for their labor but also for their knowledge of rice cultivation. Several scholars doubt that Europeans would have succeeded in growing the crop without African expertise. In addition to growing rice, Africans worked the sugar plantations of Brazil, the Caribbean, and Louisiana, the tobacco farms of Virginia and Maryland, and the cotton lands of the Lower South. Historians debate the magnitude of the slave trade. Estimates range from 4 million to 100 million slaves. Historian Philip Curtin has tallied 9.4 million, a number that may be as close to authoritative as one can hope to get. The trade enriched African and European middlemen but otherwise impoverished Africa, draining human capital from the continent.

The slave trade began to integrate Africa into the world economy, a process that accelerated during the period of European colonialism. The colonial economy benefited Europe more than Africa. European companies and governments took cash crops and natural resources from Africa, siphoning off the profits rather than reinvesting them in their colonies. The French extracted rubber from Zimbabwe, the British and Italians cocoa from Kenya and Ethiopia respectively, the Portuguese coffee from Angola, and the British oil from Nigeria. Under the tenets of laissez-faire, the governments of Europe paid scant attention to their companies with holdings in Africa, a policy that allowed business to exploit the colonies without fear of condemnation. In the nineteenth century, Belgian rubber companies kidnapped and killed recalcitrant workers in an effort to create a compliant labor force in what became the Democratic Republic of the Congo. In South Africa the discovery of diamonds in 1867 led the British to press men into working the mines for six months at a time. Wages were so low that wives had to send food to their husbands; otherwise the men would have gone hungry. When European governments intervened in the economy, they did so in favor of white settlers. The Land Act of 1913 gave nearly 90 percent of the land in South Africa to whites, an action that intertwined wealth with notions of racial superiority.

The Americas, like Africa, were European colonies: Latin America, excluding the Caribbean, was the possession of Spain and Portugal; the Caribbean of Great Britain, France, and the Netherlands; and North America of Britain, France, and Spain. South of the Ohio River the economy resembled that of Africa in its reliance on plantation agriculture and slavery. Cash crops for export predominated over the growing of food for sustenance. North of the Ohio River, however, free labor prevailed over slavery and small farms over plantations. The Columbian Exchange brought wheat to the Americas, where farmers cultivated it in New York and Pennsylvania. The Middle Colonies also abounded in corn for the feeding of livestock. Farmers grew potatoes and vegetables for the cities of the eastern seaboard. Boston, New York City, and Philadelphia were the commercial hubs of North America, linking Britain and the interior of the continent. British North America imported sugar, rum, and molasses from the Caribbean and manufactured goods from Britain and exported meat, grain, tobacco, indigo, and fish to these regions, tallying in exports one-sixth of colonial income. British mercantile policy prohibited the colonies from manufacturing textiles and other goods but protected American shipping from foreign competition. Shipbuilding employed from 5 to 10 percent of the colonial work-force, making it the second largest employer after farming, which totaled 90 percent of workers.

In the sixteenth century the Portuguese, Spanish, British, and French fished for cod and the Basques hunted whale along the coast of Newfoundland. While drying fish ashore, the French traded knives, axes, trinkets, and fur with Native Americans. By the end of the sixteenth century, French traders had reached the mouth of the Saguenay River. To advance the fur trade the French formed alliances with tribes of Native Americans. By the mid-seventeenth century, France—under the tenets of mercantilism—sought fur, tim-ber, fish, and grain from Canada. The French crown envisioned trade among Canada, the French Caribbean, and France. By the mid-1670s fur traders had reached the eastern rim of Lake Superior. Farmers fed the French and British garrisons in Canada and shipped grain to New England.

NEW NATIONS AND THE SHAPING OF THE WESTERN HEMISPHERE

The colonies of British North America were the first European possessions to gain inde-pendence, though autonomy did not lead the United States to repudiate trade with Britain. From 1784 to 1789 trade between the United States and Britain totaled 95 per-cent of the pre-Revolution mark and by the mid-1790s exceeded it by 30 percent. Com-merce in the interior of the continent lagged behind transatlantic trade. The Mississippi River was a conduit north and south, but the Ohio River spanned only a fraction of the breadth of North America. Business needed a route from the Atlantic seaboard to the Mississippi River and ultimately to the Pacific Ocean. Between roughly 1790 and 1820 private companies built toll roads, but these were less efficient than water transit. Four horses could transport 4.5 tons only 18 miles in a day by road but 100 tons 24 miles in the same time by water. Inventor Robert Fulton accentuated this advantage in 1807, launching the first steamboat on the Hudson River. To benefit from water transit, New York opened in 1825 the Erie Canal, linking the Hudson River and Lake Erie. So lucrative was trade on the canal that New York had recouped the cost of digging it by 1832. Three additional canals built between 1832 and 1856 linked Lake Erie and the Ohio River, allowing merchants to ship products from New York City to New Orleans by water. Even greater in stimulating trade were the railroads. In 1831 the United States had 13 miles of track; in 1836 more than 1,000 miles; in 1840, 2,818 miles; and in 1849, 9,021 miles. The completion of the first transcontinental railroad in 1869 made it possible to ship goods across the country. The railroad pulled trade and people west, a process Congress spurred in 1862 by passing the Homestead Act. The act stimulated farming on the Great Plains by selling public land to farmers for a small fee. Beyond the corn belt of the Midwest were the cattle ranches of the Southwest and the wheat farms of the Great Plains. Beyond these were the citrus and vegetable growers of California and the Rio Grande.

As did the British and French in North America, Spain and Portugal applied the tenets of mercantilism in their colonies, seeking a favorable balance of trade to gain gold and silver. Accordingly, Spain and Portugal mined these metals throughout Latin America. Mexico's yield of gold doubled between roughly 1820 and 1840. Silver production in Peru doubled in the 1830s. Prospectors discovered new veins of silver in Chile and the yield of copper rose from 3.3 million pounds (1.5 million kilograms) in 1820 to 27.1 million pounds (12.3 million kilograms) in 1850. In 1913 Mexican mines produced roughly one-third of the world's silver. That year tin and silver were the leading exports in Bolivia, silver and copper in Mexico, and gold in Colombia. Chile and Peru exported silver and Brazil gold. Cash crops remained a staple of Latin America. Argentina exported corn, wheat, and meat; Brazil coffee and rubber; the Dominican Republic cocoa and sugar; Ecuador, Haiti, and Venezuela cocoa and coffee; Guatemala coffee and bananas; Panama bananas and coconut; Puerto Rico sugar and coffee; Uruguay wool and meat; Columbia, El Salvador, and Nicaragua coffee; and Paraguay tobacco. In 1913 Argentina totaled $510 million in exports, Brazil $315.7 million, Cuba $164.6 million, Mexico $148 million, and Chile $142.8 million. As in Africa, the concentration of agriculture on cash crops left Latin America short of food for local consumption. Imports made up the difference. By 1913 Latin America imported the largest fraction of its goods from the United States.

At the turn of the nineteenth century, the Canadian economy centered on shipbuilding and cod fishing along the Atlantic coast and the fur trade north of the Great Lakes. After 1820 Great Britain increased its import of wheat from Canada and the United States to feed its urban population. Spurred by the European market and the clearing of forest, agriculture spread west with settlement, the St. Lawrence canal system, and the railroad. Improvements in technology, farming methods, and varieties of wheat boosted Canadian wheat exports from 2 million bushels in 1896 to more than 150 million bushels in 1921. As had the United States, Canada drew farmers west with cheap land. After 1896 prospectors flocked to the Klondike and Yukon to seek gold. The demand for manufactured goods in the West and a high tariff stimulated the growth of industry in central Canada. Sensitive to opportunity, U.S. investors poured more than $600 million into Canadian mines and factories between 1900 and 1913. As in the United States, workers in Canada sought to bargain collectively with employers. By 1914, 166,000 workers had unionized, 140,000 of them in the Knights of Labor, the Industrial Workers of the World, and other international unions.

THE INDUSTRIAL REVOLUTION AND NEW CAPITALISM

By the nineteenth century the United States was in the throes of the Industrial Revolution. Starting with the first textile mills around 1790, factories swept the United States after 1800. The value of manufactured goods tallied $483 million in 1840, $1 billion in 1850, and $2 billion in 1860, a figure nearly equal to the value of the food and fiber produced by U.S. farms. By 1894 U.S. factories were outproducing Britain, France, and Germany combined. In 1901 U.S. Steel held more than $1 billion in capital. A new managerial elite arose to command American industry. Its leaders bent women and children to the grind of the factory for subsistence wages. Labor fought back in a series of bloody strikes between 1877 and 1894. The last of them sank in a swamp of travails: in 1893 some 500 banks and 16,000 businesses went bankrupt, plunging the United States into a four-year depression. Henry Ford recast the relationship between labor and the market for wages and prices in a context in which poverty deprived the poor of the ability to buy consumer goods. In 1913 Ford raised wages at Ford Motor Company to five dollars a day and priced cars within the means of consumers. The production of cheap standardized goods at the heart of Fordism defined the U.S. economy into the era of personal computers.

Fordism arose at a critical moment. Industry flourished amid protectionism. The open shop prevailed over trade unions, allowing business to dictate wages. Yet agriculture did not share in the prosperity that industry enjoyed. Nations retaliated against the Payne-Aldrich Tariff Act of 1908 by raising their own tariffs, shutting out American exports. Dependent on exports, American farmers suffered. Farm prices fell between 1919 and 1921, plunging U.S. agriculture into a depression. This depression undermined purchasing power, a cornerstone of Fordism, and the spread of economic woes to banking and business ushered in the Great Depression. Between October 1929 and May 1933 unemployment rose from 500,000 to 15 million, nearly one-third of workers. Between these years, Gross Domestic Product (GDP) fell nearly 30 percent. Manufacturing plummeted 54 percent, construction 78 percent, and investment 98 percent. Drought on the Great Plains exacerbated the ills of agriculture, turning soil into dust in the mid-1930s. Dust storms in 1935 destroyed wheat farms in Kansas and Nebraska, spurring landless laborers to seek work in California. The efforts of the New Deal to return people to work achieved partial success but only the production of armaments in World War II lifted the U.S. economy from the Great Depression.

THE TWENTIETH CENTURY AND ONWARD: WAR, PROSPERITY, AND POVERTY

Wartime prosperity did not end with the return of peace in 1945. The cold war goaded Congress into perpetuating wartime expenditures on the military. The postwar increase in the birthrate fueled the consumption of goods and services. Contractors applied the lessons of Fordism in building cheap, standardized houses in the suburbs. In homage to the automobile, Congress in 1956 began the construction of an interstate highway system, a public works project that rivaled the New Deal in creating jobs.

The postwar growth of the economy ended in the 1970s. The southern corn leaf blight, a fungal disease, destroyed 15 percent of the U.S. corn crop in 1970. Some farmers along the Ohio and Mississippi rivers lost their entire crop. In 1973 the Organization of Petroleum Exporting Countries suspended the shipment of oil to the United States to protest American support of Israel in the Yom Kippur War. Oil prices leapt 350 percent that year. High petroleum prices spiked inflation and eroded purchasing power. Republican legislators responded in the 1980s by cutting taxes on the rich and reducing federal expenditures. Business fled the United States in search of low wages. Nike, for example, closed its factory in Oregon, moving to South Korea and then to Indonesia. Bereft of jobs in manufacturing and mining, the Northeast and Great Lakes became pockets of poverty. Attending this decline was the rise of California's Silicon Valley in the production of semiconductors and personal computers. Telecommunications and biotechnology may revolutionize the twenty-first-century economy, as did the automobile the twentieth century.

The first facilities to resemble factories in Latin America were the sugar mills of Brazil and the Caribbean and the meat-processing houses along the Río de la Plata. About 1830, home production of clothing gave way in Mexico to textile mills, which spread thereafter throughout Latin America. The construction of railroads after 1870 improved the transport of goods, and the spread of power plants after 1880 supplied business with electricity. In 1913 factory production totaled $619 million in Argentina, comprising 16.6 percent of its GDP, and $184 million in Chile, comprising 14.5 percent of its GDP. By World War I three-quarters of manufacturing in Latin America was concentrated on the processing of food and the manufacture of textiles. Not all countries shared in this growth. As late as 1925, factory production totaled only $58 million, or 6.7 percent of GDP, in Colombia. World War I increased the demand for oil from Mexico and Venezuela, copper from Peru, tin from Bolivia, and nitrates from Chile. Great Britain imported meat and sugar from Latin America, but the export of coffee and bananas from the region fell amid wartime restrictions on shipping. The Allies barred German goods and investment from Latin America. The dearth of German investment and the postwar indebtedness of Britain brought the United States to the fore. U.S. investment in Latin America, totaling $1.6 billion in 1914, rose to $5.4 billion in 1929. The United States bought 29.7 percent of Latin American exports at the beginning of World War I and 45.4 percent in 1918. Latin America received one-quarter of its imports from the United States in 1913 and 41.8 percent in 1918.

Latin America's dependence on U.S. markets and capital imperiled the region when the U.S. economy contracted in the late 1920s. Between 1928 and 1932 the value of Latin American exports fell 64 percent. During these years the volume of exports plummeted 69 percent in Chile. Between 1929 and 1932 Argentinean exports declined from $1.5 billion to $561 million. The recovery of exports brought Latin America out of the Great Depression. After 1932 the volume of exports increased in Bolivia, Ecuador, the Dominican Republic, and Haiti. Between 1932 and 1939 the value of Cuban exports doubled. Excluding Mexico and Argentina, the value of Latin American exports rose 53 percent during these years. As had been the case during World War I, World War II stimulated demand for Latin American exports.

War's end left the region in a precarious position. The cold war drew U.S. capital to Europe. Latin America made do with small loans. Unable to attract capital, Latin American industry did not expand to meet domestic and international demand. To fill the gap between demand and supply, Latin America imported goods by expanding the money supply, but this expansion caused inflation. Between 1955 and 1960 prices rose 38 percent per year in Argentina, 28 percent per year in Brazil, 25 percent per year in Uruguay, and 24 percent per year in Chile. Between 1965 and 1970 the annual rate of inflation averaged 48 percent in Brazil, 44 percent in Uruguay, 29 percent in Chile, and 20 percent in Argentina. As in the past, Latin America turned to exports to buoy the economy. After

World War II cotton cultivation and cattle ranching swept the Pacific littoral. The rise of Communism in Cuba led the United States to turn to the rest of Latin America for sugar. By the late 1970s Guatemala totaled 80 percent of world exports of cardamom. But exports bumped up against ecological constraints. By the 1970s Peru had depleted its fisheries and intensive agriculture had eroded soils in Haiti. The expansion of pasture at the expense of forest diminished rainfall and increased global temperatures. These woes reached a crisis in the 1980s. In 1982 Mexico suspended repayment of its debt, followed over the next two years by nearly every other country in Latin America. The region responded by cutting imports and government spending and increasing exports. Between 1985 and 2000 exports from Latin America more than tripled. During these years exports from Mexico and the Dominican Republic leapt more than seven times and from Chile more than four times. Between 1993 and 2000 inflation in Latin America fell from 876.6 percent to 8.7 percent. Despite these trends, 35 percent of Latin Americans in 2000 lived below the poverty line. The poor comprised three-quarters of the population in Honduras, 65 percent in Nicaragua, 58 percent in Ecuador, 49 percent in Colombia, and 42 percent in Bolivia.

The expansion of the early twentieth century gave way to the Great Depression in Canada. Dependent on exports, Canadian farmers and merchants saw their income fall with the price of wheat, fish, and lumber. Between 1929 and 1932 the volume of wheat exports plummeted 75 percent. As it had in the United States, drought bedeviled the Canadian prairie in 1934 and 1937, diminishing wheat yields in these years to one-third of their 1928 level. The contraction of agriculture depressed trade along railroads and the demand for manufactured goods. GDP fell 40 percent between 1929 and 1932. In May 1933 unemployment peaked at 32 percent and hovered above 10 percent until 1939, when the production of armaments for World War II returned people to work. As in the United States, the demand for labor drew women in Canada into factories. In an effort to manage wartime production, the Canadian government limited the right of workers to strike and rationed sugar, tea, coffee, butter, meat, and gasoline. The return of prosperity and the end of rationing boosted the sale of automobiles, televisions, and appliances after 1945. As did Americans, Canadians flocked to suburbs and shopping malls. The postwar growth of consumerism drew people from countryside to city, swelling the ranks of labor. By 1950 one-third of Canadian workers, 1 million men and women, had joined unions. In emulation of the American Federation of Labor and the Congress of Industrial Organization in the United States, the Trade and Labour Congress and the Canadian Congress of Labor merged in 1956. The Trans-Canadian Highway linked city and suburb. Construction had begun in 1949, the highway opened in 1962, and the final miles were laid in 1970. Reliant on the automobile, Canadians suffered a quadrupling of oil prices in 1973 and 1974. This increase drove up prices 9 percent in 1973, double the rate of inflation in 1972. To combat inflation, Canada increased interest rates to 20 percent in 1981 to contract the money supply. Unemployment peaked at 13 percent in December 1982, the highest since the Great Depression. To restore prosperity Canada has since the 1980s reoriented trade toward the United States, its largest importer, and away from the European Union.

As did the United States, Latin America, and Canada, Africa succumbed to the Great Depression. Between 1929 and 1932 the value of African exports nearly halved. As it had in the United States and Canada, drought exacerbated the depression, reducing crop yields in West Africa in 1931. By the late 1930s, however, Africa, like the United States, Canada, and Latin America, had rebounded. As in Latin America, exports catalyzed this recovery. In 1938 African mines produced 97 percent of the world's diamonds, 95 percent of cobalt, 46 percent of gold, and 40 percent of chrome. World War II stimulated the demand for food and raw materials from Africa, particularly after Japan in 1942 sealed off French Indochina from the Allies. Yet price controls forced African merchants to increase exports without a concomitant rise in profits. The end of price controls in 1948 allowed merchants to realize profits denied them during the war. As had World War II, the Korean War stoked the demand for exports from Africa. Between 1950 and 1957, GDP more than doubled in Zimbabwe and Kenya and increased 84.5 percent in South Africa, 78.7 percent in the Belgian Congo, and 70.2 percent in Uganda. Between 1960 and 1975, however, the growth in the GDP of Africa was less than 5 percent per year and just 2 percent in 1975. The cost of imports into Africa rose from $5 billion in 1965 to $22 billion in 1973. Between 1960 and 1975 agriculture declined from 41.3 percent of GDP to 30.3 percent, mining rose from 4.4 percent to 7.3 percent, manufacturing and the generation of electricity from 10 percent to 12 percent, and construction from 5 percent to 8 percent. As in Latin America, exports have grown in value in several African countries. Between 1976 and 1991 exports in Nigeria increased from 23 percent of GDP to 36 percent, in the Congo from 26 percent to 39 percent, in Mauritania from 31 percent to 42 percent, and in Mauritius from 38 percent to 44 percent. In 1995 Angola sent 64.5 percent of its exports to the United States and Canada, the Congo 36.5 percent, Gabon 31.8 percent, and Benin 22.2 percent. That year exports from Angola totaled $3.9 billion, from Côte d'Ivoire $3 billion, from the Democratic Republic of the Congo $2.5 billion, and from Gabon $2.4 billion. As is true of Latin America, inequality plagues the economy of Africa. Venture capitalists are funding the growth of technology firms in Nigeria, a country in which oil pumps $120 million a day into the economy. Yet Nigeria's income per person was less than $500 in 2003. Niger, Chad, Mozambique, Eritrea, Malawi, Sierra Leone, Liberia, and Guinea Bissau totaled less than $250 in income per person and Ethiopia and Burundi just $90 per person in 2003.

See also: Colonialism; Economic Community of West African States; Globalization; International Monetary Fund; Mercantilism; Slavery (Economics); World Bank; World Trade Organization

References

Atack, Jeremy, and Peter Passell. *A New Economic View of American History: From Colonial Times to 1940.* New York: W. W. Norton, 1994.

Bulmer-Thomas, Victor. *The Economic History of Latin America since Independence.* Cambridge: Cambridge University Press, 2003.

Cardenas, Enrique, Jose Antonio Ocampo, and Rosemary Thorp, eds. *An Economic History of Twentieth-Century Latin America.* Hampshire, UK: Palgrave, 2000.

Horn, Michiel. *The Great Depression of the 1930s in Canada.* Ottawa, ON: Canadian Historical Association, 1984.

Kayizzi-Mugerwa, Steve, ed. *The African Economy: Policy, Institutions, and the Future.* London: Routledge, 1999.

McCalla, Douglas. *Planting the Province: The Economic History of Upper Canada, 1784–1870.* Toronto: University of Toronto Press, 1996.

Mshomba, Richard E. *Africa in the Global Economy.* Boulder, CO: Lynne Rienner, 2000.

Ouellet, Fernand. *Economic and Social History of Quebec, 1760–1850.* Toronto: Macmillan, 1980.

Rich, Patricia Gray, ed. *Latin America: Its Future in the Global Economy.* Hampshire, UK: Palgrave, 2002.

ARTS, LITERATURE, AND SPORT

Sarah Boslaugh

African culture has enriched Western culture in many ways, and African influence is particularly evident in countries where persons of African descent are in the majority (e.g., Jamaica) or constitute a sizable minority (e.g., the United States): in those countries persons of African descent combined elements of African and Western culture to create a vibrant African American (or Afro-Cuban, Afro-Brazilian, etc.) culture. Cultural sharing works in both directions, however, and Western culture has been an important influence on many aspects of modern African culture. This essay will discuss the mutual influences of African and Western culture in dance, music, literature, film, the visual arts, and sport.

DANCE

Dance is an important aspect of many African cultural groups. Not surprisingly, Africans brought their dance traditions with them to the Americas and developed new forms of expression there, combining their traditions with those they encountered in the Americas. A similar process took place when Africans migrated from villages to cities within Africa. One result of this cultural mixture was the creation of national or pan-African dance companies, the first of which was les Ballets Africains.

Many popular dance forms common in the Americas can be directly traced to their African roots, including the mambo, samba, rumba, cumbia, and the Brazilian dance–martial art form known as *capoeira*. Tap dancing, a performance type of dance created in nineteenth-century America, combines African rhythms with Irish and Scottish dance steps. Many of the greatest tap dancers in history have been African Americans, including Bill "Bojangles" Robinson, Fayard and Harold Nicholas, Gregory Hines, and Savion Glover. African Americans working in modern dance have also developed a distinctive style that combines African and Western traditions. Leaders in this regard include Katherine Dunham, who founded the first African American modern dance company, and Alvin Ailey, who studied with Dunham and later founded the Alvin Ailey Dance Theater.

MUSIC

African influence on Western culture may be most obvious in music. It is difficult to imagine what American popular music, or for that matter world popular music, would sound like without the contributions of African Americans. For example, they created jazz, an art form that is recognized and enjoyed all over the world. Jazz is continually evolving and many different types of jazz are currently performed around the globe, from early styles such as Dixieland through swing and bebop to more modern forms such as free jazz and fusion. In fact, jazz has in a sense returned to its roots by crossing the Atlantic in the opposite direction. Thanks in large part to radio broadcasts and recordings as well as performances by touring American and European artists, jazz became popular in African cities and distinctive local jazz styles have developed in many different African countries. Among the greatest composers and performers in the history of jazz are Joseph "King" Louis Armstrong (considered by many to be the greatest jazz musician of all time), William "Count" Basie, Edward Kennedy "Duke" Ellington, Ella Fitzgerald, Billie Holiday (Eleanora Fagan), Miles Davis, and Charlie Parker.

Many other types of popular music were strongly influenced by African traditions, as well. Reggae, which combines elements of many types of music, including jazz, blues, ska, and calypso, was created by Afro-Jamaicans in the 1960s. Soul music, a style of popular music that combines elements of traditional African American gospel music and popular rhythm and blues with the popular song form, was developed in the late 1950s and 1960s in the United States. Hip-hop or rap music, which was developed in the 1970s by African Americans and Latinos in the borough of The Bronx in New York City, has since become popular all over the world. Some trace the spoken or "rapping" technique, an important part of hip-hop performance, back to the griot or itinerant singer-poets of West Africa, as well as to the insertion of spoken sections within songs by African American artists such as James Brown and Isaac Hayes. Even the Caucasian-dominated musical genres of bluegrass, old-time, and country music owe their distinctive sounds partly to African influence. The banjo, a central instrument in all three styles of music, is descended from an African instrument first brought to the United States by enslaved Africans.

Many popular Latin American types of music also show the influence of African customs. For instance, samba was developed in Rio de Janeiro in the early twentieth century, primarily by Afro-Brazilians from Bahia. Characteristics of samba were later combined with jazz elements and this gave rise to bossa nova, a type of music popular worldwide in the 1960s and featured in the Academy Award–winning movie *Orpheu Negro* (1959; *Black Orpheus*). Two world-famous styles of popular music came from the Afro-Trinidadian community: calypso and steel pan. Cuban popular music forms such as the son, the rumba, and the danzon draw on African traditions, as do the more modern hybrids: the mambo and the cha-cha-cha. There has been a revival of interest in Cuban popular music recently due to the success of the 1999 film *The Buena Vista Social Club*. Some of the greatest performers of Cuban popular music have been Afro-Cubans, including Machito (Frank Grillo), Ibrahim Ferrer, and Celia Cruz.

LITERATURE

The influence of European culture on contemporary African writers is most obvious in their use of European languages such as English and French and in their use of Western forms such as the novel. The works of the Nigerian Wole Soyinka, winner of the Nobel Prize for Literature in 1986, are an outstanding example of how artistic results may be achieved through the combination of traditional African and modern Western culture. Other English-speaking Africans who have achieved recognition in contemporary literature include Chinua Achebe (Nigeria), Ben Okri (Nigeria), Anthony Appiah (Ghana), and Bessie Head (South Africa-Botswana). Outstanding African writers in French include the philosopher Frantz Fanon (Martinique-Algeria) and the statesman and poet Leopold Senghor (Senegal).

African Americans played only a small role in American literature until after the Civil War, primarily because most had neither the education nor the freedom to enable them to write. One exception was Phillis Wheatley, the first African American to receive recognition as an author. Another was Frederick Douglass. Interestingly, both Wheatley and Douglass had to defend their works against charges of inauthenticity, that is, the claim that they had been written by someone else, since some of their contemporaries believed African Americans were incapable of writing fine literature. After the Civil War, the debates about the place and future of African Americans were often carried out in the writings of Booker T. Washington (e.g., *Up from Slavery,* 1901) and W. E. B. Du Bois (e.g., *The Souls of Black Folk,* 1903).

The first time African American writers as a group became central to American literature was during what is now called the Harlem Renaissance of the 1920s and 1930s. Another name for the Harlem Renaissance was the New Negro Movement, after the term the "New Negro," coined in 1925 by Alain LeRoy Locke. These terms conveyed the belief that African Americans could now cast off their heritage of servitude and define for themselves what it meant to be African American. Both labels are apt, as the Harlem Renaissance saw a veritable explosion of creative activity from African Americans in many fields, including art, literature, and philosophy.

One reason the Harlem Renaissance was possible was the fact that many African Americans migrated from the rural South to northern cities, including New York City, during World War I, the 1920s, and the 1930s. The increased numbers of African Americans living in small geographic areas naturally fueled a sense of community. Furthermore, in northern cities these internal migrants experienced freedoms and opportunities that had not been available to them in the South. These two factors encouraged African Americans to seek to redefine themselves socially and politically.

African American writers are now firmly established as a vital part of the American literary canon. Ralph Ellison's fame rests primarily on his novel *Invisible Man* (1953), which won the National Book Award for fiction. In it, he uses the metaphor of invisibility to express his disconnection from the largely Caucasian world around him. Although he wrote many books, Richard Wright is best known for his novel *Native Son* (1940) and the autobiographical volume, *Black Boy* (1945). Gwendolyn Brooks was the first African American to win a Pulitzer Prize (in 1950, for poetry) and also published novels and essays as well as encouraging the younger generation of African American poets. Lorraine Hansberry's play, *A Raisin in the Sun,* which takes its title from a Langston Hughes poem, won the New York Drama Critics' Circle Award as the best play of 1959. Alex Haley's novel, *Roots: Saga of an American Family* (1976), won both a Pulitzer Prize and a National Book Award and was adapted into a television mini-series that was the highest-rated program of its time. Maya Angelou, perhaps best-known for reading a poem at the 1993 inauguration ceremony of President Bill Clinton, wrote the best-selling autobiographical *I Know Why the Caged Bird Sings* (1970) as well as numerous volumes of poetry. Other contemporary African American writers include the poets Audre Lorde and Nikki Giovanni; the poet and playwright Amira Baraka (Leroi Jones); the novelists Toni Morrison, Alice Walker, and John Edgar Wideman; and the playwright Ntozake Shange. African Americans have also achieved success in genre fiction, including Samuel R. Delany in science fiction and Walter Mosley in detective novels.

The most distinguished African American playwright is probably August Wilson (Frederick August Kittell), whose greatest works form a series of ten plays chronicling African American life in the twentieth century. Wilson won Pulitzer Prizes in 1987 for *Fences* and in 1990 for *The Piano Lesson.* George C. Wolfe, a noted Broadway director, achieved great success with his play *The Colored Museum* (1986). The best-known contemporary Afro-Caribbean writer is probably the poet Derek Walcott, born in St. Lucia and resident in Trinidad; he won the Nobel Prize for Literature in 1992. The poet Kamau Brathwaite (Barbados) was in the forefront of those emphasizing the importance of African influence in Caribbean culture; he has published over twenty-five books of poetry as well as historical and critical works. Other important contemporary Afro-Caribbean writers include the poets Wilson Harris (Guyana) and Linton Kwesi Johnson (Jamaica) and the novelists Merle Hodge (Trinidad), Michelle Cliff (Jamaica), and Jamaica Kincaid (Antigua).

FILM

Opportunities for persons of African descent in film have been limited until the last decades of the twentieth century due to a combination of deliberate exclusion and lack of access to education and funding. The greatest number of opportunities were available for performers, both as actors and actresses (although in a limited range of roles) and as singers and dancers. One exception was the "race movies" made in the United States in the first half of the twentieth century, primarily for African American audiences. These films not only featured African American actors and actresses in leading roles, but were often written and produced by African Americans. Three of the most influential directors and producers in this genre are Omar Micheaux and George and Noble Johnson. The first African American to direct a Hollywood film was Gordon Parks, with *The Learning Tree* in 1969; other African American directors of this generation include Melvin van Peebles and Ossie Davis. Today a number of African Americans are working as film directors, both in Hollywood and independently; they include Spike Lee, John Singleton, and Julie Dash. Notable African Canadian directors include Clement Virgo and Stephen Williams.

Several outstanding directors of African descent have come from the French-speaking Caribbean. Rassoul Labuchin's *Anita* (1980), the first film made in the Haitian Creole language, tells the story of a young girl working as a domestic servant in Port-au-Prince. Martinique-born Euzhan Palcy achieved international renown with her first feature film, *Rue Cases Nègres* (Sugar Cane Alley) in 1983 and has also directed *A Dry White Season* (1989) and *Aimé Césaire: A Voice for History* (1994). Christian Lara, born in Guadeloupe and working primarily in France, has directed a number of French-language films concerning Caribbean subjects, the best-known of which is *Sucre Amer* (1998). Raoul Peck's feature, *L'Homme sur les quais* (1993), set in Haiti in the 1960s, was the first Haitian film released in U.S. theaters.

In Colombia, José Agustín Ferreyra was an exception to the usual rule that film direction was a role reserved for Caucasians. Ferreyra, who was often referred to by the nickname "El Negro" because of his African heritage, directed many films in the first half of the twentieth century. Many Brazilian films have focused on the life of Afro-Brazilians, including the Academy Award–winning *Ofeu Negro* (1959), by the French director Marcel Camus; *Rio Zona Norte* (1957), by Nelson Pereira dos Santos; and *Cidade de Deus* (2002), by Fernando Meirelles and Kátia Lund. However, as in the United States, few Afro-Brazilians had the opportunity to direct films until the late twentieth century. The current generation of Afro-Brazilian directors includes Waldyr Onofre, Antonio Pitanga, and Silvana Afram. Since the Cuban Revolution in 1959, focus in Cuban film has shifted from the primarily Caucasian landowning class to the history and current reality of ordinary Cuban citizens. A number of films have looked at the role of race in Cuban society, past and present, including *La Última cena* (1976), by Tomás Gutiérrez Alea, and *Cecilia* (1981), by Humberto Solás.

VISUAL ARTS

Relatively few African American artists worked in the mainstream of the visual arts until the twentieth century. An early exception was Henry Osawa Tanner, the son of an African Methodist Episcopal minister who spent much of his adult life in Paris. Although most of his paintings are of religious subjects, he is best-known for his sensitive portraits of African Americans, including *The Banjo Lesson* (1893). The Harlem Renaissance also included a number of visual artists, such as Lois Mailou Jones, William H. Johnson, Jacob Lawrence, Romare Bearden, and Palmer Hayden. The works of Bearden and Lawrence in particular have become part of the canon of twentieth-century American art. The photographers James Van Der Zee and Gordon Parks (who was also a novelist and filmmaker) also achieved success in the mainstream art world. Younger African Americans who were or are successful in the visual arts include Jean-Michael Basquiat, Carrie Mae Weems, Faith Ringgold, and Martin Puryear.

WESTERN SPORTS

Western sports were introduced to Africa primarily by Europeans. Sometimes sports were taught directly as part of a colonizing or missionary endeavor and at other times Africans simply observed and imitated European games. For instance, soccer became popular in South Africa after Africans observed the game as played by British soldiers serving in the Boer War. Few Africans were successful in sports at the world-class level until the 1960s;

exceptions included the boxers Louis Faal of Senegal, Dick Tiger and Hogan Bassey of Nigeria, and Roy Ankrah of Ghana. Participation in international sports became an expression of national identity for many newly independent African countries in the 1960s, and many countries participate in international sporting events such as the Olympics and the Football (Soccer) World Cup. This national and pan-African pride is also celebrated at the Pan-African or All-African Games, first held in 1965.

Given the opportunity to train and compete at the world-class level, African athletes have excelled at many sports. Runners from East Africa, particularly Kenya and Ethiopia, currently dominate middle- and long-distance races all over the world. Among the first to achieve success at the world level were Abebe Bikila, who won the Olympic marathon in 1960 and 1964, and Kipchoge (Kip) Keino, who won the 1,500 meters at the 1968 Olympics and the steeplechase at the 1972 Olympics. Africans also star in football (called soccer in the United States): many play on European teams, and the national teams of Nigeria and Cameroon in particular have distinguished themselves in World Cup competition. In basketball, the Nigerian Hakeem Olaujuwon was the first African to play at a world-class level, starring first for the University of Houston and then for the Houston Rockets of the National Basketball Association (NBA). A number of African players have since played in the NBA, including Manute Bol of Sudan, Michael Olowokandi of Nigeria, and Dikembe Mutombo of Congo. In addition, many Africans also play professional basketball in Europe, and the African continent has been represented at the world championships and Olympic Games by several teams, including Angola, Senegal, and Nigeria.

African Americans have suffered discrimination in sports throughout most of American history. Legal segregation in public accommodations, including schools and recreational facilities, meant that the African American community had to develop its own support networks and institutions. For instance, the first two great African American tennis players, Althea Gibson and Arthur Ashe, both received critical assistance early in their careers from Dr. Walter Johnson, a Virginia physician and tennis player. Gibson also developed her game at Florida A & M College, a traditionally black school, and in competitions of the American Tennis Association, founded in 1916 to promote tennis among African Americans. In 1950 Althea Gibson became the first African American woman to compete in the U.S. national tennis championships, and she was the first to win a Grand Slam title, winning singles titles at the French Open (1956), Wimbledon (1957, 1958), and the U.S. Open (1957, 1958). In 1963 Arthur Ashe was the first African American to play on the U.S. Davis Cup team, and he was the first African American man to win singles titles at the U.S. Open (1968) and Wimbledon (1975).

The most remarkable example of segregated sports in the United States may be the simultaneous existence of the all-black Negro Baseball Leagues and the all-white American and National Leagues (also called the "Major Leagues"). The Negro Leagues achieved their greatest success from the 1920s through the 1940s, when their all-star teams regularly beat white all-star teams. Outstanding players from this era include Josh Gibson of the Homestead Grays, Satchel Paige of the Kansas City Monarchs, and Cool Papa Bell of the Pittsburgh Crawfords. Some Negro League teams continued to exist after Major League baseball began to integrate in 1946, after Jackie Robinson was signed by the Brooklyn Dodgers of the National League. However, the best African American players chose to play in the Major Leagues when possible, and the Negro Leagues ceased to exist after 1960. In the integrated era (since 1946), many of the best players in Major League baseball have been African American, including Willie Mays, Reggie Jackson, Bob Gibson, and Roberto Clemente. Many professional boxing champions over the years have been of African descent, including Jack Johnson, Joe Louis, Sugar Ray Robinson, and Muhammad Ali in the United States and Sergio Eligio Sardinas Montalvo of Cuba, better known as "Kid Chocolate." Cuban boxers have only competed as amateurs since 1962, but they dominate Olympic competition; among their greatest champions are the Afro-Cubans Teofilo Stevenson and Felix Savon. Football (soccer) is the most popular sport in many parts of the world, and many of the best players from the Western Hemisphere have been of African descent. These include arguably the greatest player of all time, Edson Arantes Do Nascimento of Brazil, better known as Pelé. Current outstanding players of African descent include Ronaldo (Ronaldo Luiz Nazario da Lima) of Brazil and Freddie Adu (born in Ghana, currently residing in the United States), who at the age of fourteen became the highest-paid soccer player in the United States.

The relationship of Africa and the Americas in the arts and athletics has been mutually beneficial in many ways. Western culture would look very different today were it not for the contributions of Africans living in the Americas. For instance, it is difficult to imagine what contemporary popular music would sound like if all African influences were removed from it, or what modern art and dance would look like without the influence of African folkloric traditions. African culture has also been enriched by Western influence; jazz, for instance, a type of music created in the Americas by persons of African descent, has re-crossed the Atlantic and become a vital part of modern African cultural life. This cultural exchange continues today in the vibrant artistic creations of persons of African descent living on both sides of the Atlantic.

See also: Brathwaite, Kamau; Brazilian Culture; Brooks, Gwendolyn; Calypso; Clemente Walker, Roberto; Cliff, Michelle; Cuban Music, African Influence in; Du Bois, William Edward Burghardt; Ellison, Ralph Waldo; Fanon, Frantz; Fauset, Jessie; Film (Caribbean); Film (Latin America); Film (North America); Film (South America); Garvey, Marcus; Guinea Dance; Haley, Alex; Hansberry, Lorraine; Head, Bessie; Hip-Hop; Hurston, Zora Neale; Johnson, Linton Kwesi; Kincaid, Jamaica; Locke, Alain LeRoy; Lorde, Audre; Marley, Robert Nesta; Mays, Willie Howard; Morrison, Toni; Music (African); Negro Leagues; Nigeria, Drama in; Reggae; Robinson, Jack Roosevelt; Shange, Ntozake; Soyinka, Wole; Toomer, Jean; Walcott, Derek; Washington, Booker T.; Wideman, John Edgar; Wright, Richard

References

Alexander, George. *Why We Make Movies: Black Filmmakers Talk about the Magic of Cinema.* New York: Broadway Books, 2003.

Ashe, Arthur. *A Hard Road to Glory: A History of the African American Athlete.* New York: Amistad, 1993.

Conyers, James L., Jr., ed. *African American Jazz and Rap: Social and Philosophical Expressions of Black Expressive Behavior.* Jefferson, NC: McFarland, 2001.

Ervin, Hazel Arnett. *The Handbook of African American Literature.* Gainesville: University Press of Florida, 2004.

Gioia, Ted. *The History of Jazz.* Oxford: Oxford University Press, 1998.

Lewis, Samella S. *African American Art and Artists.* Berkeley: University of California Press, 2003.

Long, Richard A. *The Black Tradition in American Dance.* London: Prion, 1995.

Reid, Mark. *Black Lenses, Black Voices: African American Film Now.* Lanham, MD: Rowman and Littlefield, 2005.

Ross, Charles K., ed. *Race and Sport: The Struggle for Equality on and off the Field.* Jackson: University Press of Mississippi, 2004.

Smithe, Jonathan P., ed. *African Literature: Overview and Bibliography.* Hauppague, NY: Nova Science Publishers, 2002.

Watson, Steven. *The Harlem Renaissance: Hub of African American Culture, 1920–1930.* New York: Pantheon Books, 1995.

Welsh-Asante, Kariamu. *African Dance: An Artistic, Historical, and Philosophical Inquiry.* Trenton, NJ: Africa World Press, 1996.

Africa and the Americas

A

ABOLITIONISM

Abolitionism refers to the political and social means by which different groups in slaveholding nations, including enslaved and formerly enslaved peoples themselves, tried to end chattel slavery. An expanded definition of abolitionism would include both formal political processes and the efforts by slaves to free themselves through revolt, escape, and the creation of communities outside the control of slaveholders, such as the Maroon societies of the Caribbean and Latin America. The demise of slavery in Europe, the United States, and Latin America was the direct result of multifaceted abolitionist efforts.

The first white group to publicly prohibit slavery in its ranks in colonial America was the Society of Friends, also known as the Quakers, beginning in 1755. Refusing to subscribe to the artificial hierarchy of the races, the Quakers viewed everyone as equal in God's eyes. American Quakers began their mission by first discontinuing the practice of slave trading and ousting from their religious community those who would not desist from the practice. Abolitionist sentiment grew not only because of religious belief, but also because through the course of colonial American history, slaves sought to revolt and escape,

as in the New York City revolt of 1712. While the direct result of this particular uprising was a new set of laws to restrain more tightly the movements of black people, such events also became opportunities for American Quakers to advocate more openly for the general and gradual manumission of the colonial slave population.

The issue of abolitionism did not come to the forefront more broadly in colonial America until the dawn of the American Revolution of 1775. Both free and enslaved blacks found themselves in a complicated position when the British offered emancipation for slaves who joined Loyalist forces. A significant number fought on the British side during the Revolution, seeking refuge in Nova Scotia, Canada, and elsewhere after the British defeat. In the United States, abolitionism was somewhat successful during the last quarter of the eighteenth century, especially in the northern states. Some Americans saw the absurdity of fighting for freedom while continuing to deny others the same freedom for which the war was being fought. As a result, there was a gradual abolition of slavery in the North. The southern United States did not follow suit; since large numbers of slaves resided in the southern states, slaveholders feared reprisals. Following the news of Toussaint

Louverture's successful slave revolt in 1791, which led to the establishment of the Republic of Haiti, southern whites actually tightened their states' slave laws. Southern states also remained economically dependent on plantation slavery. Consequently, southern states became determined to hold on to that institution.

The first European nation to abolish the slave trade, prohibiting the traffic of new slaves from Africa to the Americas but not emancipating slaves or their descendants, was Britain. Working in conjunction with their American counterparts, the British Quakers began the first European abolitionist activities by presenting a petition against slavery to the British Parliament in 1783. In 1787 the London Committee to Abolish Slavery was established through the collaborative efforts of the Quakers and evangelical Christians. The British Quakers, through the Committee to Abolish Slavery, then assisted in the creation of other abolitionist organizations that included parishioners of Baptist and Methodist congregations along with members of marginalized groups such as women and industrial workers. Britain passed the Abolition of the Slave Trade Act in 1807. The Emancipation Act would be passed in 1833, freeing slaves over the course of five years; the measure included a period called "apprenticeship" and provided compensation for slave owners. All slaves in the British Empire were free by 1838, including slaves in the colonies of Jamaica, Barbados, Sierra Leone, Cape Town, and the Bahamas.

British abolition and emancipation would be a model for abolition in other European nations. Between 1847 and 1848 the Swedish and Danish governments worked to bring about emancipation to their perspective colonies of the West Indies. In 1848, following political turmoil at home and a slave revolt on Martinique, France emancipated slaves within the French Empire, including the colonies in Guadeloupe, Martinique, French Guiana, and Senegal. In 1863 the Dutch emancipated the remaining slaves in their Caribbean colonies. In 1873 Puerto Rico was in the midst of abolishing slavery. By 1886, with Puerto Rican slavery nearing its end, Cuba followed the Puerto Rican paradigm and moved toward abolition.

However, as slavery was abolished in Europe's Western Hemisphere possessions, the United States steeped itself even more in the practice, and consequently the divide between northern and southern states hardened. Revolts and religious reforms reignited Northern calls for the abolition of Southern slavery while the success of southern cotton plantations further convinced southerners of the necessity of slavery. For Northerners, continued violence was a reason for abolition, while Southerners saw it as a reason to tighten their control over slaves.

The American Anti-Slavery Society was a key northern abolitionist organization. This group included William Lloyd Garrison, the editor of the weekly publication *The Liberator* (1831), and Harriet Beecher Stowe, who wrote a serially published novel, *Uncle Tom's Cabin* (1852). In addition to well-intentioned whites, voices of freed and escaped slaves such as Frederick Douglass and Sojourner Truth made strong abolitionist arguments. These black voices described the horrors of slavery in the first person and reached audiences in a different way than either the rhetoric of Garrison or the extremely successful fiction of Stowe.

Stowe's novel further fueled concern about slavery and abolition at a pivotal time. America was expanding and the expansion of slavery within the growing country was a major issue. Some Northerners saw slavery as a sin that needed to be eradicated from all parts of the country, so the idea of slave expansion was completely unacceptable. Opposing this viewpoint were those who saw a failure to spread slavery as meaning a loss of ground to Northern abolitionists. The Missouri Compromise of 1820 had kept the United States balanced between free and slave states by prohibiting slavery above the 36th parallel. However, with the passing of the Kansas-Nebraska Act of 1854, in which both states were allowed to vote on whether or not to allow slavery, the Missouri Compromise was dissolved. The changing balance of power between pro- and antislavery forces would thus play a major role in the American Civil War that began in 1861.

In 1863 President Abraham Lincoln issued the Emancipation Proclamation, freeing all slaves in Confederate-controlled areas. In December 1865, after the defeat of the Confederacy earlier that year, the Thirteenth Amendment was ratified, freeing all slaves.

During the nineteenth century, slavery existed in parts of Latin America, especially former Spanish colonies. The issue of abolition did not gain the attention of the world as it did in other places with greater numbers of slaves, such as the United States. Because of the smaller number of slaves and the marginal financial opportunities they offered their owners, abolishing slavery in places like Mexico and Venezuela was not difficult. From the 1820s through the 1860s, Latin American countries all but abolished slavery as a whole. Peru emancipated its 45,000 slaves in 1821, Mexico emancipated its 3,000 slaves in 1822, and Chile emancipated its 4,000 slaves in 1823. The Central American Federation, composed of Costa Rica, El Salvador, Guatemala, Honduras, and Nicaragua, emancipated its collective lot of 3,000 slaves in 1824, Bolivia emancipated its 1,500 slaves in 1846, Colombia emancipated its 20,000 in 1851, Ecuador emancipated its last 2,500 slaves in 1852, Argentina passed a law making all members of its society equal in 1853, and Uruguay emancipated its slave population in the same year.

In contrast to the United States, where slavery was a major part of the economy, slave labor in Latin America was largely used by a small elite. While such a class was rich, it was generally not so large as to monopolize the moral debate concerning slavery. In some specific cases, the general well-being of the country required or profited from the abolition of slavery, as was the case with Uruguay. In an attempt to secure their own liberty from Brazil, Uruguay's rebel government officials freed the slave population so that the slaves could join their army. The economic and political reality in Latin America was reinforced by the fact that slaves there were more likely to escape, maintain their freedom through Maroon communities, and actively revolt.

Brazil was the last stronghold of state-sanctioned slavery in the West. It ended there in 1888 with slaves refusing to continue to work under existing harsh conditions of involuntary servitude and government soldiers refusing to force compliance. Ironically, the abolition of Western slavery ended in a way similar to how slave abolition began—with slaves trying to annihilate the systematic hell that unjustly bound them. Brazilian abolition took so long to occur in large part because the great numbers of slaves had been made part of the fabric of the country for over three centuries, from the time of Portuguese colonization through independence. Slaves occupied a very important role in the society and were essential to the economy. Like the United States, which had ended slavery twenty-three years earlier, Brazil profited greatly from slavery. Unlike from the United States, however, Brazilian society was not so morally divided about the issue of slavery that it was prepared to enter into a civil war. As the black population grew, including a large number of free persons, political thinking changed. Additionally, the political leadership began to consider the slavery issue in terms of its effects on Brazil's national labor market, its ability to continue functioning within the international market, and the safety of citizens. The culmination of all of these factors led to Brazil's final abolition of slavery.

Abolition in Africa took place in the context of the changing structure of African slavery as a consequence of the European slave trade and European colonialism in the late nineteenth century. Slaveholding was extensive in Africa. There were about 2 million slaves, according to some estimates, in northern Nigeria when the British began to establish colonial rule there at the end of the nineteenth century. However, an important distinction often needs to be made between chattel slavery in the Americas, in which enslaved people were considered simply a particularly valuable commodity, and African systems of slavery. Although chattel slavery existed, many African systems of slavery, prior to the growth of transatlantic slavery, resembled ancient Greek or Roman slavery in

that the enslaved person was not eternally relegated to the lowest rung of a caste system from which no upward mobility was possible. However, the growth of transatlantic slavery led to the dramatic destruction of much of Africa's human capital through increased warfare, kidnappings, and enslavement. Kidnappings of Africans for the trade became so rampant that, just as there were concentrated abolitionist efforts to end slavery in the West, there were concerted efforts to end slave trading in Africa.

As the demand for slaves grew, so did African resistance. Groups fought off slavers when they could and found other means of resistance as well. For example, a number of tribes in central Africa used the region's complex terrain defensively, changing their hunting and cultivation practices so as to better hide their presence.

From about 1830 until the early twentieth century, European countries tried to bring an end to slavery in Africa. The abolition of slavery there was closely tied to colonialism. The governments of colonial powers, which had themselves outlawed slavery at home and within their own empires, sought to abolish the institution in Africa. While part of the interest that these governments had in abolishing slavery in Africa was humanitarian, there were also other, less benign motives. These included using abolitionism as a justification for colonial domination to the public at home and developing a labor force abroad. In French colonies in the early nineteenth century, slaves were emancipated only after serving fourteen years as indentured laborers under the control of French colonial administrations. In British colonies, emancipation was also gradual. In the case of northern Nigeria for example, laws were put into place that sought to slowly minimize slavery. For example, in 1901 the children of slaves were legally born free.

Unlike in Europe or the Americas, the abolition of slavery in the colonies tended to have a patchwork quality. The pace and extent of abolition and emancipation in colonial areas depended greatly on the extent to which the colonial administration depended on the goodwill of local rulers who might hold slaves, on the balance of economic advantages and disadvantages, and on the desire to maintain a stable labor pool. As in the United States, abolition and emancipation under colonial rule often meant not a transition to economic freedom but a shift to sharecropping or other forms of labor with minimal social mobility.

Overall, while abolitionism did not completely remove slavery from the face of the planet—especially as slavery existed in parts of Africa into the early 1900s—it did help to end the human travesty in large part of the Western Hemisphere. And even though forms of labor exploitation existed throughout the nineteenth and twentieth centuries, the attitude of tolerance and general acceptance toward such practices changed significantly in large part because of abolitionism. Members of the abolitionist movements took the position that human rights superceded the right of individuals to make profits at the expense of their fellow humans. That position has since become a norm for many people within the Western Hemisphere.

Ordner Taylor

See also: Abolitionism, British; American Revolution; Civil War, American; Colonialism; Douglass, Frederick; Emancipation Proclamation; Human Rights; Nova Scotia, African American Diaspora in; Quakers; Slave Narratives; Slave Revolts/Maronnage; Stowe, Harriet Beecher; Truth, Sojourner; Tubman, Harriet; World Anti-Slavery Conventions (1840, 1843)

References
Baronov, David. *The Abolition of Slavery in Brazil.* Westport, CT: Greenwood Press, 2000.
Broadhead, John Romeyn. *Documents Relative to the Colonial History of the State of New Cork; Procured in Holland, England, and France.* Vol. 5. Edited by E. B. O'Callaghan. New York: AMS Press, 1969.
Davidson, Basil. *The African Slave Trade.* Boston: Back Bay Books, 1980.
Harrold, Stanley. *The Abolitionist of the South, 1831–1861.* Lexington: University of Kentucky Press, 1995.
Klein, Martin A. *Slavery and Colonial Rule in French West Africa.* Cambridge: Cambridge University Press, 1998.
Manning, Patrick. *Slavery and African Life: Occidental, Oriental, and African Slave Trades.* Cambridge: Cambridge University Press, 1990.
Rassner, Ronald M. "Palmares and the Freed Slave in Afro-Brazilian Literature." In *Voices from Under: Black Narrative in Latin American and the Caribbean,* edited by William Luis. Westport, CT: Greenwood Press, 1984.
Rout, Leslie B. *The African Experience in Spanish America, 1502 to the Present Day.* Cambridge: Cambridge University Press, 1976.

ABOLITIONISM, BRITISH

The role of the United Kingdom in the abolition of both the slave trade and slavery during the nineteenth century was extensive. From the late eighteenth century, Britain progressively turned against slave trading and then against the very practice of slavery itself. A change in opinion by the British people transformed Britain from being the biggest Atlantic slave trader into actively pursuing a multifaceted antislavery policing operation within the Atlantic

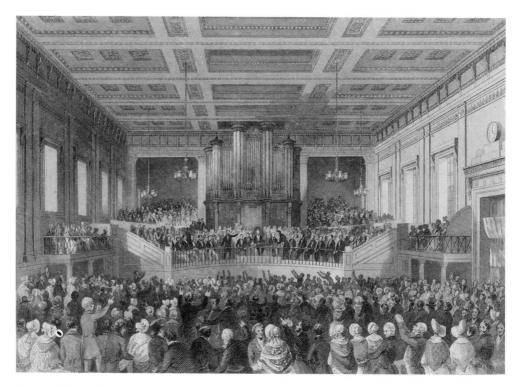

Exeter Hall in London, England, filled with a large crowd for the Anti-Slavery Society meeting in 1841. (Library of Congress)

Basin. This involved a plethora of instruments, including international anti-slave trading treaties, diplomatic pressure, leading by example, and military intervention. By the late nineteenth century, both the slave trade and the practice of slavery had not only been suppressed in the Atlantic but also banned in all advanced countries.

By 1807 the British had already exported approximately 3,120,000 people into bondage. Merchants from the wealthy ports of Liverpool and Bristol operated an extensive chain of slave installations along Africa's Atlantic coast, where goods were taken and exchanged for slaves, which were then shipped across the notorious Middle Passage to the Americas. The trade was extremely lucrative; for some traders, profits could reach in excess of 100 percent. One of the principal uses for slaves was in the labor-intensive sugar trade—in the Caribbean and in Louisiana in southern North America—that enabled Britain to dominate the sugar trade. By 1805 the nation was accounting for approximately 55 percent of world sugar production, a figure that was still rising. The economic incentives for the continuance of slavery were enormous, but these were further reinforced by various social incentives. As slave trading could generate rapid wealth, it was also a path to respectability in the class-ridden society of the late eighteenth century.

However, hostility toward slavery had been growing in Britain within certain humanitarian and religious circles since the mid-eighteenth century. These groups believed the trade corrupted all aspects of social and economic life within the British

Empire and beyond. By the 1770s the antislavery movement had gained momentum and was further reinforced by the decision of Lord Mansfield in the Somerset case of 1772, which decreed that any slave who set foot within the United Kingdom was immediately a free citizen. Real progress commenced, however, when two leading antislavery campaigners, Zachary Macaulay and William Wilberforce, started to mobilize grassroots movements to end the trade in slaves. Along with other abolitionists, such as Granville Sharpe, they came to be known as the Clapham Sect and operated with evangelical fervor. Pressured by their work, the Houses of Parliament passed An Act for the Abolition of the Slave Trade in 1807. From this moment, slave trading was illegal throughout the British Empire. Nevertheless, the abolitionists were still not content. By 1814, 806 antislavery petitions, signed by 750,000 people, were sent to Parliament. This next thrust formed part of the antislavery movement, and the Anti-Slavery Society was founded in 1823 to campaign for the outlawing of slavery itself. In 1833, ten years later, this was finally achieved with the passing of the Slavery Abolition Act, although a period of apprenticeship was introduced for slaves between 1834 and 1838.

Neither the slave trade nor slavery would be eliminated by two mere acts passed by the British government. Those engaged in the trade would need to be actively pursued. As Adam Hochschild has pointed out, "the Atlantic slave trade depended on the fact that most of the societies of Africa—chiefdoms, kingdoms large and small, even groups of nomads—had their own systems of slavery" (p. 16). Further, many European nations and Middle Eastern merchants were engaged in the trade. It was truly systemic, and most of those societies showed few signs of abolishing either the slave trade or the practice of slavery. The abolitionists believed that slavery had to be proactively stopped and wanted to use all the available instruments of the British state to achieve their goal. As Lord Castlereagh, the then foreign secretary, wrote of the abolitionist movement in 1814: "The whole nation is bent upon this project. I believe that there is hardly a village which has not met and petitioned upon it. Both houses of parliament are pledged to press it and ministers must make it the basis of their policy" (Johnson, p. 328).

The British had been in pursuit of slave traders since the 1807 Act. In order to stamp out the trade, the Royal Navy's power was used in an attempt to sweep the African and American seas of slave ships. This resulted in the dispatch of the British West Africa Squadron, a pioneer of gunboat diplomacy, to arrest recalcitrant traders engaging in the slave trade from ports within British territory. This was how the operation started, but the British found it increasingly difficult. At first they used their dominance—especially after the defeat of France in 1815—to entice and pressure other European nations into signing treaties that enabled the mutual searching of suspected slave ships in international waters. Such treaties were not very successful, however, as many nations turned a blind eye to the trade in practice. Some even attempted to cash in on the trade that Britain sought to end. British sugar production had fallen by 25 percent in the 35 years since 1807 and would account for only 15 percent of the world total by 1850 (a drop of 40 percent since 1807), whereas sugar production increased in rival (slave-based) economies by 210 percent. There was now an economic as well as a moral stimulus for the enforcement of the ban. Britain could not allow its economic competitors to benefit from a trade it had itself abandoned. The British, therefore, became considerably more aggressive.

The Houses of Parliament authorized the unilateral searching of intransigent nations' ships, with or without their consent. It was decreed that slave traders were to be treated like pirates, meaning that they could face the death penalty. The slave traders were also to be rooted out at the source. Slave installations in Africa were bombarded and burned and local chiefs were forced into signing treaties that demanded that they prevent, or arrest, traders operating within their kingdoms. In 1850 the prime minister, Lord Palmerston, went further still and sent Her Majesty's gunboats into an undeclared war against Brazil, which eventually forced the Brazilian government into banning the trade altogether. Lord Palmerston then turned his attention toward the similar trade operating between Africa and the Middle East.

In all, the British intercepted 1,635 slave ships, liberated over 150,000 slaves at sea, and had reduced the trade by approximately 80 percent by the middle of the nineteenth century. The suppressing of the slave trade has been estimated as costing the British almost 2 percent of their economic output over sixty years; furthermore, at the height of the operation, about one-third of the Royal Navy's military assets were involved. With the Union's victory in the American Civil War and unrelenting British pressure elsewhere, the slave trade between Africa and the Americas would eventually cease as a sizable organized practice, which would lead to considerable economic restructuring on either side of the Atlantic. Further, the Royal Navy's mapping and exploration of the African coast during the antislavery operations helped to pave the way for the opening of Africa to European penetration during the New Imperialism in the latter nineteenth century.

James Rogers

See also: Abolitionism; Apprenticeship (British Empire); Britain: People of African Origin and Descent; British Empire; Slavery (History); Wilberforce, William; World Anti-Slavery Conventions (1840, 1843)

References

Eltis, David. *Economic Growth and the Ending of the Transatlantic Slave Trade.* New York: Oxford University Press, 1989.

Hochschild, Adam. *Bury the Chains: The British Struggle to Abolish Slavery.* London: Macmillan, 2005.

Hyam, Ronald. *Britain's Imperial Century, 1815–1914.* Basingstoke, UK: Macmillan, 1993.

Johnson, Paul. *The Birth of the Modern: World Society 1815–1830.* London: Phoenix Giant, 1991.

Kaufmann, Chaim, and Robert Pape. "Explaining Costly International Moral Action: Britain's Sixty-year Campaign against the Atlantic Slave Trade." *International Organization* 53, no. 4 (1999): 631–668.

Morris, Jan. *Heaven's Command: An Imperial Progress.* London: Faber and Faber, 1998.

ACHEBE, CHINUA (1930–)

Chinua Achebe is the most widely read, translated, and taught modern African writer. Chinua Achebe's first novel, *Things Fall Apart,* published in 1958, has become a classic. The tragedy of Okonkwo, who abhors the corruptive influence of Western civilization in his Umuofia community and dies fighting against the alien, is a historical fictionalization of African society during the European colonial invasion of the nineteenth century.

Achebe was born on November 16, 1930, at Ikenga, Ogidi, in Igboland, southeastern Nigeria. He hails from a family of Christian converts, and his father, Isaac Okafor Achebe, was an evangelist. *Things Fall Apart* is an epochal allegory on the passing of traditional glory and the beginning of modern disenchantment. The heroic and suicidal father, Okonkwo, belongs to an old order and his children, represented in the experiences of the despised and apostate first son, Nwoye, and the beloved and demoniac first daughter, Ezinma, belong to the new dispensation.

Achebe studied at Government College, Umuahia, and he was a pioneer student at the premier London University College, Ibadan, Nigeria, where he matriculated in medicine and graduated in classics. He taught at the University of Nigeria, Nsukka, and at several American universities, including Bard College in Annandale-on-Hudson, New York, where he still teaches. His studies in European imperial literature were the immediate catalyst for Achebe's vocation as a writer. Achebe feels that the British colonial district officer and writer, Joyce Cary, portrays his African characters in the novel, *Mister Johnson,* as stupid and naïve. Achebe's widely anthologized essay, "An Image of Africa," is canonical in the postcolonial and race discourse of Joseph Conrad's novel, *Heart of Darkness* (1902). Achebe argues that Conrad misrepresents his African characters as nameless types, "dumb brutes," and "prehistoric" savages. The continuing animalization of the African image in the writing of such an Anglophile as J. M. Coetzee demonstrates the corrosive influence of Conrad and Cary

and tends to justify the caustic criticism of Achebe.

As Achebe says in his essay, "The Novelist as Teacher" (1965), it is against the demeaning background of colonialist literature that he takes up the novel genre to present a vision of African history and humanity that challenges and defies European depictions of precolonial history as simply a long stretch of simple savagery. This defiant persona of the colonized African, the Shakespearean "Caliban," or the psychotic subject as a speaking subject "talking back" to the master, is a signifying self-identification and liberation from a debasing objectification.

The foregoing is Achebe's creative discovery as the father of African literature. It has also been the springboard of his influence over succeeding generations of African writers from the mid-twentieth century to the twenty-first century. Beginning from his novels *Things Fall Apart, No Longer at Ease* (1960), *Arrow of God* (1964), *A Man of the People* (1966), and *Anthills of the Savannah* (1987), through his Biafran War poetry and his collected essays to his short fiction and children's writing, Chinua Achebe remains the most widely read, translated, studied, sought after, and honored African writer worldwide because of the global accessibility of his discourse on the preservation of universal human integrity.

Obi Iwuanyanwu

See also: Literature, African; Nigeria

References

Achebe, Chinua. "The Novelist as Teacher." In *Morning Yet on Creation Day.* Garden City, NY: Anchor Books, 1975.

Achebe, Chinua. "An Image of Africa: Racism in Conrad's *Heart of Darkness.*" In *Hopes and Impediments: Selected Essays.* New York: Anchor Books, 1989.

Achebe, Chinua. *Things Fall Apart*. New York: Anchor Books, 1994.

Booker, M. Keith, ed. *The Chinua Achebe Encyclopedia*. Westport, CT: Greenwood Press, 2003.

Iwuanyanwu, Obi. "Achebe's Poetic Drive." *Sentinel Poetry Quarterly* 5 (September 2005): 23–48.

AFRICA, NORTH

The physical boundaries of the region recognized as North Africa have varied tremendously throughout history. Some consider North Africa to comprise only the former French colonies of Tunisia, Algeria, and Morocco, also known as Le Maghreb. However, the Arab Maghreb Union (AMU), founded in 1989, includes Mauritania, Morocco, Algeria, Tunisia, and Libya, although disputes over the former Spanish territory of Western Sahara have sometimes stood in the way of AMU unity. At present, North Africa is generally understood to be all the northern part of the African continent: the area situated between the Sahara Desert and the Mediterranean Sea, and extending from the Atlantic Ocean in the west to the Red Sea in the east.

Because of its historical relation to the Greek and Roman empires, North Africa is generally seen by scholars to be more closely related to Europe than to sub-Saharan Africa. This perception, however, has been sustained by climatic, racial, and religious arguments that are ultimately artificial. The two regions have in fact a long history of contacts as well as deep-rooted religious, cultural, and political ties. The oldest link between North and sub-Saharan Africa, however, is economic, and it dates back to the ninth century BCE, when trans-Saharan trade networks began flourishing as a result of the markets created on the Mediterranean coast by the Carthaginian Empire.

From an Arab perspective, North Africa is known as al-Maghrib (The West), since it was the site of the massive westward expansion of the Islamic Empire. This expansion started in the seventh century, when General Uqbah ibn Nafi's Arab army invaded the region, and culminated in the annexation of southern Spain by General Tariq ibn Ziyad in 711. Arab expansion in North Africa set a precedent for later European endeavors in the Americas, emblematized in Columbus's voyage in 1492. This was the same year that the city of Granada fell to the Christian Reconquista, which marked the end of the Islamic states in Spain.

Today, North Africa is almost entirely Sunni Muslim, with the exception of a few minorities such as Coptic Christians in Egypt and Sephardic Jews in Morocco and Tunisia. Morocco in particular maintained close ties with its former Jewish citizens living in Israel. In the 1970s, King Hassan II of Morocco (1929–1999) paved the way for peace negotiations in the Middle East and the signing of the Camp David Accords between Israel and Egypt in September 1978. The indigenous inhabitants of North Africa, the Imazighen or Amazigh, better known by their Arabic name as Berbers, have almost uniformly converted to Islam. Although their language subsists in its various dialects, they often equally claim an Arabic identity and are sometimes called Arabized Berbers by anthropologists.

In spite of the similar economic and political circumstances of Latin America and North Africa, both legacies of European colonialism, North Africa's American contacts have been mostly limited to ties with the United States. This is especially true for Morocco, Algeria, and Tunisia, which constitute the westernmost edge of the Arab world and are therefore geographically closer. Thus, North Africa eventually became a crucial figure in American conceptions of "the Arabs."

Morocco is the North African country with the longest history of political links to the United States. In fact, the Sultanate of Morocco in 1777 was one of the first states to seek diplomatic relations with the newly independent United States. Contacts between the two countries grew significantly after World War II, and especially after the 1942 military landing of mostly American Allied troops near the cities of Casablanca, Oran, and Algiers. In January 1943, U.S. president Franklin D. Roosevelt met with the sultan of Morocco, Mohammed V (1909–1961), during the Casablanca Conference and encouraged him to seek independence from French colonial rule.

After World War II, Morocco occupied a major place in the American imagination and became a focus of literature, art, and media. The writings of the American author Paul Bowles (1910–1999), who settled in the city of Tangiers in the late 1940s, drew the American public's attention to the country. Later on, Morocco became a favorite destination for American tourists—especially hippies in the late 1960s—and grew increasingly important in relation to the American movie industry. Indeed, Morocco moved from providing the setting of movies made in Hollywood, such as *Casablanca* (1942), to being the shooting location for numerous films such as Orson Welles's *Othello* (1949). In later Hollywood productions, Morocco's landscapes stood in place of a wide gamut of geographical locations, ranging from the Arabian Peninsula (*Lawrence of Arabia,* 1962) to Somalia (*Black Hawk Down,* 2001).

During the cold war, Morocco generally sided with the United States, while neighboring states usually adopted neutral positions. Tunisia, for instance, observed a policy of neutrality because it depended on foreign aid for its development and maintained good relations with both the United States and the Soviet Union in order to reduce its reliance on either one.

Throughout the 1980s and 1990s, cultural links between the United States and Morocco were reinforced in the field of education. The Moroccan American Commission for Educational and Cultural Exchange, established in 1982, administers a wide range of research grants and facilitates academic and cultural exchanges between American and Moroccan scholars. In 1995 the first private English language university in North Africa was inaugurated in the town of Ifrane, with contributions from Saudi Arabia and the United States.

Most of North Africa's foreign trade links are with Europe. However, attempts to expand commerce and economic exchanges with the United States have moved transatlantic connections forward. Tunisia's economic relations with the United States have advanced in spite of disagreements over the Gulf War in the early 1990s, and trade accords between the two countries have been negotiated since Morocco's signing of a free trade agreement with the United States in 2004. After Mauritania's independence from France in 1960, the SOMIMA mining company began exploiting copper deposits in the Akjoujt region, partly thanks to U.S. investments, but the mine was closed in 1978. In 2001 Mauritania took further steps toward developing its mineral resources by allowing a North American mining company to prospect for precious metals in the Akchar region.

With the growing interest in Islam and the Arab world that has emerged since the 1970s, and especially since the September 11, 2001 attacks on the World Trade Center and the Pentagon, the Arab side of North African identity has been paramount, and today, more often than not, the region is considered part of the Middle East rather than Africa. For instance, al-Zammouri—enslaved by Spaniards in 1511, named after his native Berber town of Azemmour on the Atlantic coast of Morocco, and brought to what is now Florida in 1528—is now celebrated as the earliest Arab immigrant to the New World in a permanent exhibit in the Arab-American National Museum in Dearborn, Michigan. That the full complexities of a Berber-Arab identity could thus be elided is a testament to the American interest in North Africa mainly as a portal into the Arab world.

Consequently, although Sudan is usually considered to be in East Africa, it has sometimes been included in North Africa because the northern part of the country is largely dominated by Arabic speaking Muslims who identify themselves as Arabs. Tensions between northern and southern Sudan have resulted in armed confrontations throughout the 1980s and 1990s and erupted in a violent conflict in the Darfur region when an Arab militia was created in response to attacks on government installations. Hostilities reached such proportions that in 2005 the situation in Darfur was described as genocide against the "non-Arab" population, and it remains a major problem in Sudan. Various countries, including the United States, have supported a plan to send UN peacekeepers to Darfur and have put pressure on the Sudanese government to bring an end to the fighting.

Ziad Bentahar

See also: Algeria; Libya; Mauritania; Morocco; Sudan (Darfur Region); Tunisia

References

Edwards, Brian. *Morocco Bound: Disorienting America's Maghreb, from Casablanca to the Marrakech Express.* Durham, NC: Duke University Press, 2005.

Gelb, Norman. *Desperate Venture: The Story of Operation Torch, the Allied Invasion of North Africa.* New York: William Morrow, 1989.

Morse, Kitty. "Esteban of Azemmour and his New World Adventures." *Saudi Aramco World* 35, no. 2 (March–April): 2–9.

Prunier, Gérard. *Darfur: Ambiguous Genocide.* Ithaca, NY: Cornell University Press, 2005.

Taha, Abdulwahid Dhanun. *The Muslim Conquest and Settlement of North Africa and Spain.* London: Routledge, 1989.

AFRICA, PRECOLONIAL

The term "precolonial Africa" can refer to any period of African history prior to the conquest and occupation of the continent by Europe. It is often used also to refer specifically to the century prior to direct European colonization of Africa, from approximately 1780 to 1884, the year when the Berlin Conference laid down the guiding principles for European powers to carve up Africa among themselves. It is hard to generalize about Africa's development during this period, as the continent exhibited a wide variety of regional variation in terms of political, economic, social, and cultural change generated both by external and internal forces, such as Western military technology, economic pressures of the shift from slaving to "legitimate trade" and the impact of the Industrial Revolution, European exploration, and missionary activity associated with Christianity. All of these activities would free Europe from the fringes of the continent, establishing "informal empires" that would subsequently be transformed into formal ones at the end of the century. In addition to a changing relationship with Europe and North America, precolonial Africa also experienced internal forces that rocked the continent, including the rise of jihadist movements in West Africa, the emergence of new commercial empires in East Africa, tentative steps toward modernization in North Africa, and the explosion of new military powers in South Africa.

In North Africa, the precolonial century saw the decline of the Ottoman Empire's control and the increase of European powers' influence, indirectly via the gun trade and directly via intervention and occupation. North Africa had begun to be incorporated into the Ottoman Empire in 1517 but had not experienced many benefits of such an association. Repeated bouts of plague and drought resulted in drastic demographic decline, economic stagnation, and political instability. By the nineteenth century, there was little loyalty toward the Ottomans and local leaders began to exert their independence from Istanbul. In Egypt the Mamluk Beys outmaneuvered the Ottoman sultan, and in 1760 Ali Bey set Egypt on a new path of autonomy. When the French invaded in 1798 to undermine British influence in the region, Egyptian nationalism flared and new military and administrative opportunities opened up to young, ambitious men. In 1805 Muhammad Ali turned on his Ottoman counterparts, seized control of Egypt, declared himself "pasha," and began the expansion of Egypt's control in the region. More importantly, Ali began the

modernization of Egypt. His activities soon threatened British interests in Asia. As such, the British undermined his efforts and stalled his progress. Ali's success in Egypt was also linked to expansionist policies on slaving that negatively impacted the peoples of Nilotic Sudan. His influence, at its peak, reached into modern-day Ethiopia and northern Uganda, to the corner of Zaire, and into Darfur. The stateless peoples of the Upper Nile, predominantly the Dinka, experienced the brunt of the trade and remember it as a time of insecurity and devastation, a time when "the earth was spoilt." It is also the time when the foundations for the Sudanese conflicts of the late twentieth and early twenty-first century were laid between the Arab and African populations of the Sudan.

Under Muhammad Ali's successors, Egypt opened itself to foreign investors and began to incur growing debts to European bankers. Modernization was clearly desirable, but it was expensive, and by the 1870s Egypt was unable to repay or meet interest payments on its loans. As a result, Britain and France took control of Egyptian finances, setting up an "informal empire" in which Egypt might claim formal sovereignty but had to act under the direction of European powers even though technically it was still an autonomous province of the Ottoman Empire. Informal empire gave way to formal when, in 1880, Britain took control of the Egyptian government and by extension gained the Sudanic territories. But in 1881 a local rebellion flared in Sudan under the leadership of Muhammad 'Ahmad ibn 'Abdallah, who declared himself as Mahdi. The Mahdi seized Khartoum and established control throughout northern Sudan. This independent caliphate was allowed to exist until 1898, when the British committed themselves to full colonization of the region.

While North Africa renegotiated its relationship with old and new empires and made tentative steps toward modernization, a religious revival movement whose roots came from the north swept across West Africa and established a series of new and powerful Islamic empires. Over many years and miles, Islam was introduced slowly into West Africa via the trans-Saharan trade routes. Muslim merchants traveled the routes bringing the faith with them, versions of Islam that were often not orthodox Sunni. Over time Islamic religious brotherhoods became important in the routes' entrepôts, and the Qadiriyya emerged as the most influential. West African rulers often adopted Islam for its secular economic and political benefits, and while some became devout Muslims, many did not, and even fewer attempted to enforce Islamic law or practice on their populations. As a result, Islam became more of a class religion, and while elements crept into traditional African religious practices, the majority of West Africans neither converted to nor practiced devout Islam. Muslim clerics were frustrated with the state of affairs but could do little. From the seventeenth century on, however, some clerics began to confront the situation aggressively through the use of jihad, not only against non-Muslims but also—and primarily—against rulers who were not devout or who tolerated non-Islamic practices within their kingdoms.

The main participants in the Islamic reform movements were the Fulbe from Futa Toro in the north of the savannah near the Senegal River. Due to their location, the Fulbe had been among the earliest

groups in West Africa to convert to Islam, and they were also among the first to wage jihad with the result of establishing small imamates in the seventeenth century. In 1725 Alfa Ibrahim Bin Nuhu established Futa Jalon; in 1769 Suleiman Bal established Futa Toro, and subsequently a third imamate was established between Futa Jalon and Futa Toro. These early Islamic states were but the forerunners of an even more extensive jihadist movement of the precolonial era: the most influential, the Sokoto Caliphate, founded by Usman dan Fodio in 1804, had by the 1830s incorporated all of Hausaland in what is today northern Nigeria and northern Cameroon. Usman dan Fodio, a Fulbe scholar of the Qadiriyya brotherhood, capitalized on the rivalry between the Hausa states and internal discontent among the populations to conquer non-Fulbe states. The Hausa rulers could not match the organization of dan Fodio's followers, let alone their zealous motivation. Fulbe clerics became the new ruling class in Hausaland, and Usman dan Fodio's success inspired other Islamic reformers in the region, including Sheikh Ahmadu Lobbo of Masina, who had been part of Usman dan Fodio's movement in Hausaland.

Within the area where Fulbe herdsman made up the majority of the population, Ahmadu Lobbo in 1818 led a movement for clerical control over the Fulbe, a kind of internal jihad. His troops conquered Jenne, Timbuktu, and Macina, and he established a second new caliphate at Hamdullahi. Unlike that of Usman dan Fodio, his caliphate experienced tensions with the old ruling classes of the conquered cities and came into conflict with another caliphate, that of Sheikh Umar Tal. Unlike Usman dan Fodio and Ahmadu Lobbo, Umar Tal was a member of a new Islamic brotherhood founded in North Africa called Tijanyya. After making the pilgrimage to Mecca, he took the title, al-Hajj Umar and founded a base in Futa Jalon where he recruited followers and imported guns from coastal European contacts. Al-Hajj Umar conquered the non-Islamic Bambara states as well as Islamic states including Hamdullahi in 1862, and he established the largest Islamic empire in West Africa, the Caliphate of Futa Jalon.

The legacy of these three Islamic states in the region is important even today. Once established, they brought order, reformed administration, and an expansion of trade to the region. The new reformers overthrew old systems of rule and created a new ruling class. The jihadists strengthened the faith of believers and caused extensive conversions of non-Muslims to Islam. However, non-Muslims also felt the brunt of the negative impacts of the empires, including forced conversions, loss of status, and increased slaving via the trans-Saharan trade routes. As power shifted from old empires to new ones, Islamic reformers were not the only ones to seek out new opportunities. In the upper Niger region, Samori Ture organized a powerful army that held off the French for fifty years. A controversial character, Ture has been remembered as an empire builder, a brilliant military strategist, a nationalist, and an anticolonialist as well as an opportunist and a tyrant. While he was establishing a new empire, the once-powerful Oyo Empire finally disintegrated as Fulani jihadists from the north penetrated its territory and internal administrative crisis rocked its foundations. As a result, groups once under Oyo's control began jockeying for supremacy. A series of wars broke out between the principal

Yoruba states of Ijaye, Ibadan, Egba, and Ijebu as they all sought supremacy in the face of Oyo's decline. These conflicts disrupted trade between 1840 and 1893 to such an extent that the British intervened on the side of Ibadan. As a result of Oyo's decline and the conflicts between Yoruba states, the kingdom of Dahomey began making incursions into Yorubaland. Initially, the incursions were motivated by Dahomey's extensive slaving practices, which had depopulated their traditional slave-raiding grounds, but when the British abolished the slave trade, the incursions were motivated by a desperate desire for productive land to grow the new crops the Europeans desired. Dahomey's economy would never recover from the shift from slaving to legitimate trade, and ultimately the kingdom fell to the Egba.

Despite the decline of many traditional African kingdoms, West Africa was not dominated solely by new Islamic powers. In what is today Ghana, the Asante emerged as a powerful empire among the Akan principalities, with a strong, centralized state and diversified economy. In addition to gold wealth, the Asante established a well-equipped army and soon came into conflict with their coastal neighbors, the Fante. Although the suppression of the slave trade temporarily impacted the Asante economically, they quickly retooled their economic activities and continued their expansionist drive in the region. Conflict with the coastal kingdoms and their rising strength also brought the Asante into conflict with the British. Although both groups were interested in the benefits of trade, they spent the majority of the precolonial century engaged in a long series of wars, ending with British annexation of the Asante Empire in 1901.

In West Africa, religious purification and political decay allowed for the development of new empires. In East Africa, political boundaries were also modified, but primarily due to shifting commercial activities in the region. Coastal trading networks were increasingly controlled by Oman, causing new currents of trade to push into the interior as far as Lake Victoria. Demands for ivory and slaves created a system of trading networks that involved the Nyamwezi of central Tanzania and the Swahili and Afro-Arabs from the coastal ports. The British, as well as the sultans of Oman, benefited from Oman's centralization of power on the Arabian coast. As a result of the growing interior trade, the sultan of Oman moved his capital from Arabia to Zanzibar to dominate better the coastal ports from Mombasa to Kilwa. The island of Zanzibar was transformed into a commercially based kingdom, aided by the British. Its major economic activities were centered around newly established, lucrative clove plantations on the island and continued trade in ivory and slaves from the mainland. These products ensured a steady supply of guns from the British, which was then used to protect Zanzibar's control of trade routes and to foment conflict on the mainland to ensure a steady supply of slaves when necessary.

Zanzibar's commercial enterprises flourished and dominated East Africa until the 1860s, when the British Royal Navy finally neared its goal of effectively interdicting the slave trade and Britian's pressures against slavery in Africa continued. Sultan Bargash faced a difficult position in 1873 as the trading posts were dependent on slaving, but the British threatened to end their support if he did not agree to end the trade. He accepted an antislavery treaty to ensure continued British protection of the clove plantations and further British military support that increased his control over the coastal region, despite the discontent of the mainland slavers. What the Zanzibar example illustrates is the continuing incorporation of Africa into a global economic network that was increasingly dominated and dictated by Europeans. It also indicates the benefits of cooperating with Europeans to gain access to military technology. The trade relations between African and European states were dominated by the gun trade, and those African rulers who were able to access that technology could easily dominate their neighbors and enemies. As a result, new interior states sprang up as guns made their way into the continent.

Military weaponry may have been used by Africans to protect trade and commercial interests in East Africa, but in South Africa, Africans used it for conquest and expansion in conjunction with new African military tactics, resulting in one of the most profound migrations of people the continent had ever witnessed.

Indeed, most scholars examine precolonial South Africa through the lens of two great migration experiences: the Mfecane and the Great Trek. Both were seminal events in the history of the region. The Mfecane is a Nguni word used to describe the profound disruptions caused by the rise of the Zulu under the leadership of Shaka. By the mid-eighteenth century, population pressures and traditional cattle-raiding practices were creating land tensions among population groups. Three leaders emerged at this time: Sobhuza of the Ngwane, Zwide of the Ndwandwe, and Dingiswayo of Mthethwa. These men developed a new method of military organization that integrated local age/grade sets into army regiments, armed them with European weapons, and used them as infantry against their enemies. They all clashed with each other but were not able to dominate the region due to the emergence of a young Zulu named Shaka. Shaka created a highly trained infantry unit and introduced a short stabbing spear as well as the famous "cow's horns" fighting formation. In 1818 Shaka emerged as the undisputed master of the region. He established his empire via military conquest, expanded his forces, and traded guns with the English. Shaka's swift rise to power disrupted the region through forced migrations of people who, as they moved, came into conflict with other groups over resources. The success of the Zulu gave rise to smaller new states that adopted Zulu military tactics for their own gain and security.

While much of South Africa was wracked by the Mfecane, Africans were not the only ones having to migrate to protect their way of life in the precolonial period. Between 1835 and 1841 between 6,000 and 10,000 Afrikaner men, women, and children trekked northward from the Cape Colony to the Natal and Transvaal. The "voortrekkers" were the descendants of Dutch settlers who had come to the Cape Colony after Holland took over Portuguese interests on the Cape of Good Hope and established a way station in 1652. The Dutch initially were not interested in colonizing the area and actually attempted to prevent contact with the native populations of Khosian and Bantu speakers. But the way station was quickly transformed into a full-scale settlement, and Dutch settlers soon arrived, bringing with them strong agricultural traditions and strict Calvinist Christianity. Known as Boers, the settlers

also quickly established a society with rigid racial prejudices. As the colony went from Dutch to British rule, it was inevitable that the attitudes of the Boers would come into conflict with those of the British, especially after Britain abolished slavery. In response to British authority, the Boers set out on their Great Trek north to establish new colonies far from British rule. The Mfecane had depopulated northward territory and the Boers relocated their families. But clashes with the British could not be avoided, especially after discoveries of gold and diamonds. In addition, tensions between the Boers and African populations increased, and the British could not ignore the Boers' independent existence as Britain annexed an increasing amount of territory in South Africa. The rest of the precolonial era in South Africa focused predominantly around the expansion of British control of both the African and European population in the region through the Zulu Wars and the Anglo-Boer Wars of 1880–1881 and 1899–1902, respectively, as well as the activities of Cecil Rhodes and the conquest of central South Africa.

The South African precolonial experience illustrates a number of changes in the relationship between Africa and Europe, many of which can be seen throughout the continent during this era. It is clear that the abolition of the slave trade and movement to legitimate trade created tensions and caused economic difficulties for many African kingdoms. From the north to the south and the east to the west, this transition was not easy for many African states. Many had participated in the trade and now had to find a replacement commodity, and a great number were confused over the new policy against slaving. Africans showed great resourcefulness and adaptability, so that by 1880 the mainstays of Africa's external trade economy were ivory, gum, cloves, beeswax, honey, wild coffee, peanuts, cotton, rubber, and palm oil. Europe's Industrial Revolution had created almost an inexhaustible demand for fats and oils. Slave trading posts were converted to outlets for the new trade, and additional commercial enclaves were established. Many of the new products were plantation based and, due to transportation costs and logistics, were concentrated on the coasts. As the slave trade contracted to localized regional markets, new economic opportunities emerged for some Africans able to engage in cash crop agriculture. The early terms of trade benefited Africans as the demand for their products was high and the prices for European imports low. But this would not continue, and by the end of the precolonial era, the benefits had shifted drastically in favor of European interests.

The search for new resources in the continent also spurred European exploration. Steamships navigated Africa's rivers and medical advances against malaria and yellow fever brought down the last barriers to European penetration of interior Africa. But pursuit of economic gain was not the only motivating factor in Europe's domination of precolonial Africa. Scientific advance and inquiry were also prime motivators in the movement inland. In 1788 the African Association of England formed to send explorers to collect scientific information about Africa, and in 1821 the Geographic Society of France followed suit. Through the expeditions of men such as Mungo Park, Dr. David Livingstone, Heinrich Barth, Sir Richard Francis Burton, John Hanning Speke, and Antoine d'Abbadie, Europe "discovered" Africa. This so-called discovery was spurred and directed by a complex and often problematic mixture of inquiry, acquisition, and transformation represented by exploration, economic development, and missionary activity.

Part of the changing dynamic between Africa and Europe during the precolonial age was the introduction of Christianity. In 1800 Christianity was confined to only the coastal regions of Africa, but by 1880 there were a great number of missionary societies active deeper and deeper within Africa. Nineteenth-century Europe underwent a kind of Christian revivalism represented by new humanitarian concern and missionary zeal. This resulted in a great deal of Christian influence on the designs for informal empire that the European powers had in Africa. As a result of missionary activities, African societies were divided into further factions: a small Christian, European-educated African elite and a larger group of traditional and illiterate Africans. There is clear evidence of African openness to new technologies and interest in modernization. The developments in precolonial Africa indicate African peoples' ability to adapt to profound economic, political, and social changes. There was also no indication that Africans thought of themselves as inferior to Europeans, as evidenced in the diplomatic correspondence from African rulers to European heads of state or in the Ethiopian victory over the Italians. But what a majority of African rulers did not realize was that they were living in a precolonial age. The Europe that clung to the coasts of the continent had undergone a massive transformation via the Industrial Revolution and was no longer content to pursue free trade and informal empire. With that economic transformation emerged a new technology gap between Africans and Europeans in the form of new weaponry. While African rulers had armed themselves with European weaponry of the previous age, European powers now had breech-loading rifles. And so within two decades, all of Africa except Liberia and Ethiopia fell to European occupation. By the onset of the twentieth century, the incredibly diverse and complex variety of independent African states and peoples were lumped into forty artificially created colonies. The speed and suddenness of the transition between the precolonial and colonial age in Africa was shocking to Africans, and the subsequent impact destroyed the tentative steps Africa was taking toward independent modernization during the precolonial era, leaving a legacy that the continent is still struggling to overcome.

Heather Theissen-Reily

References

Afigbo, Adiele, et al. *The Making of Modern Africa.* Vol. 1, *The Nineteenth Century.* London: Longman, 1993.

Ajayi, A. *UNESCO General History of Africa.* Vol. 6, *The Nineteenth Century until the 1880s.* Berkeley: University of California Press, 1998.

Bennet, Norman. *Arab versus European: Diplomacy and War in Nineteenth Century East Central Africa.* New York: Holmes and Meier, 1986.

Crais, Clifton. *White Supremacy and Black Resistance in Pre-industrial South Africa.* Cambridge: Cambridge University Press, 1992.

Hamilton, Carolyn. *Terrific Majesty: The Powers of Shaka Zulu and the Limits of Historical Invention.* Boston: Harvard University Press, 1998.

Hilliard, C. B., ed. *Intellectual Traditions of Pre-Colonial Africa.* Boston: McGraw-Hill, 1998.

Martin, Bradford G, *Muslim Brotherhoods in Nineteenth Century Africa.* Cambridge: Cambridge University Press, 2003.

McCaskie, T. C. *State and Society in Pre-colonial Asante.* Cambridge: Cambridge University Press, 2003.

Smith, Robert. *Warfare and Diplomacy in Pre-colonial West Africa.* Madison: University of Wisconsin Press, 1989.

Thornton, John. *Africa and Africans in the Making of the Atlantic World.* Cambridge: Cambridge University Press, 1998.

AFRICA, WEST

West Africa has been an historical focal point for the African continent's economic and political development. The region has been pivotal to the transatlantic slave trade, European colonial expansion, and U.S. interests in Africa during and after the cold war. Across its history, West Africa experienced long periods of migration and as a result contains a plethora of cultural, ethnic, linguistic, and religious groups. Rich in mineral resources, West Africa has long drawn in outside interests, first via the early Muslim-controlled trans-Saharan trade routes and then via Europe's coastal trading stations for the transatlantic slave trade. Early economic development in the region resulted in the development of entrepôts (ports of trade) in lucrative and expansive trade routes that created, in turn, powerful precolonial African states; Islamic empires; European colonies; and, finally, independent nation states. The migration of peoples and the expansion of trade routes also encouraged the expansion of Islam and Christianity into the area, adding to an already complex mix of animist African religions. Today, the region contains the modern states of Benin, Burkina Faso, Cape Verde, Côte d'Ivoire, Gambia, Ghana, Guinea, Guinea-Bissau, Liberia, Mali, Mauritania, Niger, Nigeria, Senegal, Sierra Leone, and Togo. The boundaries of these nations are the legacy of the colonial era and, consequently, tend to cut across ethnic, cultural, and religious lines. Indeed, all of West Africa's modern states, except Liberia, were created by European colonialism.

Geographically, West Africa refers to the area that stretches from the Nile Valley and Sudan westward to the Atlantic Ocean. It is bordered to the north by the Sahara Desert and extends southward through the savannah belt and the forest regions to the coast. Consequently, West Africa is an area of vast economic variance with climatic zones whose characteristics go from the extremes of desert to tropical rain forest. Four main vegetation belts stretch across the region: the Sahara in the north; the Sahel, a semi-arid region south of the Sahara; the savannah; and the southern coastal region. The savannah belt has long been the site of agricultural activities, including the production of groundnuts, sorghum, and millet. Agricultural activities in areas of cleared forest include the production of cocoa, yams, coffee, and cassava. In the Sahel the population engages in herding and related activities. West Africa also contains some of the continent's greatest rivers: the Gambia, Niger, Senegal, and Volta. These rivers and their tributaries provide vital trade routes both internally and to and from the Atlantic Ocean.

Prior to European expansion, West Africa saw constant transregional migration as populations traveled through the Sahara and Sahel and into the forest regions. The earliest settlers in the region appeared around 12,000 BCE. Subsequently, substantial migrations of agriculturalists and pastoralists would take place until around 2000 BCE. With the onset of the Iron Age in 400 BCE, the region witnessed the establishment of more settled and sophisticated civilizations, and evidence shows

extensive sedentary farming and herding practices by the fifth century CE. The region's largest ethnic groups, the Yoruba, Ibo, Nupe, Fon, and Asante, developed powerful kingdoms through trade and by harnessing the resources of the savannah and the forest. From 500 CE to 1600 CE the states of Ghana, Mali, and Songhay dominated the region, benefiting from the lucrative camel caravans that crossed the Sahara Desert.

The region and its emerging kingdoms were first integrated into a larger economy via a series of lucrative trans-Saharan trade routes that extended down from the North African coast. Between 200 and 700 BCE, a network of caravan routes using camels connected West Africa to the larger Arab world. This trade system transformed the region economically, culturally, and politically. Demand for gold led to an increase in mining in what are now Ghana, Senegal, and Nigeria. This gold had global importance; prior to the discovery of the Americas, Europeans received the majority of their gold supplies from West Africa via these trade routes, and West African gold motivated Europeans to make direct contact with the African kingdoms, bypassing the Muslim Afro-Berber traders who controlled the Saharan routes. Additionally, Africans traded ivory, gum, kola nuts, and slaves for Mediterranean and Eastern goods such as silk, cotton, beads, mirrors, dates, and salt. From 500 to 1600 CE, Ghana, Mali, and Songhay emerged as dominant kingdoms with large urban centers on the economic basis of these caravan routes.

Alongside the trade in gold, West Africa also had an extensive and growing slave trade. The slave trade along trans-Saharan routes dates to approximately the ninth century and served primarily the

Mediterranean. Arab peoples justified enslaving Africans on religious grounds and used them for military service, administration, domestic service, and concubinage.

Extensive trade facilitated the urbanization of the region; cities such as Jenne, Gao, Timbuktu, and Kumbi all became both trading centers and centers of culture and learning. This development was linked to the introduction of Islam into the region. By the tenth century, Muslim Berbers controlled the trade routes and the routes became conduits for not only goods and economic activities but also for the expansion of Islam. The mid-eleventh century incursions of the Almoravids into the region also facilitated the expansion of Islam as Muslim scholars traveled the routes. The cities of Gao and Timbuktu become important centers of trade and Islamic study.

By the eleventh century many rulers in the southern Sahara and the Sahel had accepted Islam. Conversion brought legal, political, administrative, cultural, and economic benefits to elites, and Islam spread to the ruling classes and mercantile elite. African elites did not force the conversion of their populations and Islam did not disrupt indigenous African shamanist and animist beliefs. Still, as Islam spread into the region, it united some ethnic groups and laid the foundations for the development of Islamic states such as Kanem and the small Hausa states at the southern ends of the caravan routes such as Kano and Katsina.

By the fourteenth and fifteenth centuries, the focus of trade was shifting from the Sahara to the Atlantic as Europeans arrived on the coast of West Africa, seeking direct contact with the Africans who controlled the sources of gold and other goods. The Portuguese were the first to arrive due to the invention of the caraval, a ship that

could sail into the wind and whose hull construction could overcome the strong oceanic currents. Hugging the African coastline, the Portuguese arrived on the Guinea coast in 1445 and established Elmina, a fortress on the coast, in 1482. While the Portuguese expeditions were sent by Prince Henry the Navigator, whose interest in Africa included scientific, political, and religious concerns, economic motives became paramount.

The Portuguese brought the first African slaves to Lisbon in 1441. While Prince Henry the Navigator hoped to convert them to Christianity and return them to Africa as missionaries, the result was the start of the transatlantic slave trade. The trade expanded substantially when the Spanish conquest and occupation of the Caribbean and the Americas led to a precipitous decline of the indigenous population as a consequence of disesase and abuse. Acute labor shortages threatened the expansion of the plantation system in the Spanish colonies. By 1521 both the Portuguese and Spanish were taking Africans captives directly from the western and central coasts of Africa, as well as relying on African middlemen for slaves. As the European colonial presence in the Americas grew, so did the demand for labor, especially after the introduction of sugar cane. Soon, Spain and England were both importing slaves into their American colonies from Africa. The Dutch, French, Swedish, Danes, and Germans were also active along the West African coast. Competition between European powers was fierce. Areas of the coast quickly were named by Europeans based on the products they found there: the Grain Coast, Ivory Coast, Gold Coast, and Slave Coast. It was the Slave Coast that would experience the most intensive

European involvement in West Africa between the sixteenth and nineteenth centuries as a result of the transatlantic slave trade.

Added to the older trans-Saharan trade in slaves, the transatlantic slave trade expanded the scale of African slavery. The two slave-trading systems were conducted simultaneously for almost four centuries. While the transatlantic slave trade was far more extensive, both systems removed millions of people from the continent and resulted in a large global economic network. The sheer size and geographical reach of the transatlantic slave trade led to profits that dwarfed those of the trans-Saharan trade.

The transatlantic slave trade would become the centerpiece of European–West African relations for centuries. The Dutch, using their strong naval power, wrested control of the Gold Coast of West Africa from the Portuguese. Under the Dutch, the slave trade grew rapidly. After 1650 the Dutch, French, and English also developed plantations in the Caribbean and North America. After 1700 the British took control of the slave trade from the Dutch and the slave trade reached its peak in exports, replacing gold as the main export out of West Africa and blending the Gold Coast into the Slave Coast. By the eighteenth century, the enslavement of Africans for the transatlantic trade was also carried out by African coastal kings and the elders of West and Central African societies. Very few Europeans marched inland to capture slaves. However, when African rulers seemed recalcitrant to expand their slaving activities outside of traditional practices, Europeans were quick to foster conflict among African societies to increase the number of slaves taken as prisoners of war.

They did so by trading guns for slaves and creating alliances with one group against another.

The impact of the slave trade on West African governments, economies, and societies was varied. Wealth and power in West Africa moved away from the Sudan and Sahel toward the coast, causing the once lucrative and expansive trans-Saharan routes to decline drastically after 1700. Some groups were able to expand as a result of participating in the trade and acquiring European firearms, which gave them a technological advantage over their neighbors. By 1730, 180,000 guns had been sent to West Africa. New coastal populations of urban entrepreneurs, artisans, and traders, often the mixed-race offspring of European traders and African women—for example, the Wolof Signares of Goree and Saint-Louis—spurred the economic reorientation of West Africa from the north to the south. But many societies suffered greatly from the increase in warfare. Some African rulers, such as King Agaja of Dahomey in 1724 and those of Futa Toro in 1789, tried to stop the trade but were unable to gain widespread support. Groups without central governments became easy prey for the trade, and African industry stalled as the most productive adults were seized and manufactured goods poured in from Europe, undermining local African industries. African societies were devastated culturally, economically, and politically by the prolonged crisis of losing their most productive members. By the time of the British abolition of the slave trade in 1807, much damage had already been done across the centuries. European and American activities in West Africa were not limited to trade but also included promoting Christianity. While guns tended to interest African rulers more than the Bible, Christian missionaries set out to establish a presence in West Africa and experienced varied levels of success, especially after the 1827 establishment of Fourah Bay College in the British repatriation colony of Sierra Leone. Sierra Leone was founded by Granville Sharp in 1787 as a settlement for London's black poor, black American Loyalists fleeing the American Revolution, and rebel Jamaican former slaves, known as Maroons, as well as those Africans recovered from slaving ships at sea. The colony had a difficult beginning and experienced conflicts with the local Temne and Mende peoples. Nonetheless, it ultimately became a base for the British missionary activities.

Following the Sierra Leone example, Captain Paul Cuffe, a successful African American and Quaker shipowner in the United States, attempted to gain American support for a repatriation colony in Africa. On December 21, 1816, prominent Americans, including James Monroe, Andrew Jackson, Henry Clay, and Daniel Webster, became members in the newly formed American Colonization Society (ACS). In 1819 the ACS received $100,000 from Congress, and two years later it established a settlement on the west coast of Africa. As in Sierra Leone, the early settlers faced disease and hostile natives while also lacking sovereignty, as the colony was managed by the ACS. Despite these hurdles, between 1824 and 1864, 19,000 African American repatriates settled in Liberia, in addition to 5,000 recaptured Africans from slave ships.

Although the British and the French had become the dominant European powers in West Africa by the nineteenth century, European hegemony in West Africa was challenged by an Islamic revivalist movement that swept across the Sahel. In the nineteenth century, Islamic religious brotherhoods were no longer willing to coexist with traditional African practices, and a series of Fulani-led jihads swept across Western Sudan seeking to purify the faith in the region. These jihadist movements led to the establishment of powerful Islamic states in the Sahel, including Uthman dan Fodio's Fulani Empire in the first decade of the nineteenth century, which defeated the Hausa states, followed in 1818 by Seku Amadu's Massina Empire, which defeated the Bamber, and, in the 1860s, by El Hadj Umar Tall's Tokolar Empire, which came to control most of Mali. These empires controlled the Sahel region until the late nineteenth century, when European powers extended their control from the coast inland. The British and French quickly consolidated their control over West Africa under the principles of the Berlin West Africa Conference of 1884–1885. Britain established indirect rule over the Gambia, Sierra Leone, Ghana, and Nigeria, and France established direct rule over Senegal, Guinea, Mali, Burkina Faso, Côte d'Ivoire, and Niger (French West Africa). Germany claimed Togoland but quickly lost it after World War I, and the territory was turned over to Britain and France by the terms of the Treaty of Versailles. The only area in West Africa not claimed and colonized by Europeans at this time was the nation of Liberia, because of its ties to the United States.

The Great Depression of the 1930s, frustrations with colonial rule and racism, and the presence of an increasing number of educated Africans returning from abroad resulted in the rise of militant demands against the colonial system. While early nationalist movements pressed for a more representative system, younger Africans called for the full dismantling of colonial rule. During and after World War II, Britain and France responded to reformist demands. In 1946 France liberalized its colonial governments and Britain introduced new colonial constitutions that allowed the election of more Africans to colonial governments. But these mild reforms were not sufficient. Between 1944 and 1948 the first mass-based political parties began to emerge in West Africa, the first in the continent. The National Council of Nigeria, the Convention People's Party in Gold Coast, and the Rassemblement Democratique Africaine in French West Africa all committed themselves to winning full independence. The most influential of all emerged in Ghana under Kwame N'krumah, who became the major influence in independence movements within West Africa.

In 1957 Ghana became the first sub-Saharan colony to achieve independence; subsequently, Britain dismantled its colonial control in the region. France followed suit and, by 1960, all major French colonies in sub-Saharan Africa were on their way to independence. N'krumah and the independence movements of West Africa were influential in promoting Pan-Africanism and connecting West African intellectual and political leaders into a global network of black intellectuals that included Aime Cesaire, W. E. B. Du Bois and Marcus Garvey, all of whom advocated a common destiny for all black African peoples around the world and an emphasis on African cultural community and spirituality against European and U.S. materialism.

By 1974 all West African colonies had gained their independence. Independence led to a mix of one-party rule and democracies. Much of the region's post-independence era has been characterized by great potential but also great failings. Independent West Africa has suffered from high levels of political corruption and instability. Early movements toward democracy fell to the imposition of oppressive one-party states, military dictatorships, and autocratic rulers. The cold war divided the region between U.S. and Soviet spheres of influence, resulting in the empowerment of West African militaries and their generals while economic development languished.

During and after the cold war, conflicts over economic resources, complicated by ethnic tensions, have fueled brutal civil wars. Petroleum and regional competition caused the bloody Biafran secessionist movement and civil war between 1967 and 1970. Conflicts also broke out in Sierra Leone, Liberia, and Côte d'Ivoire, with resources such as diamonds fueling the conflicts. Ghana and Burkina Faso experienced military coups and the region's conflicts have created immense refugee and humanitarian crises.

Political and economic development has been complicated by increasing environmental challenges and crises. The region experienced devastating droughts in 1968–1974, 1977–1978, and 1983–1985 and the desert edge of the area is expanding. The resulting aridity and soil desiccation leads to the further removal of forests as farmers attempt to survive. Lake Chad, which lost 90 percent of its area between 1960 and 1983, illustrates the severity of the problem of desertification; whole countries such as Niger and Mali risk turning into deserts.

As a result of the political, economic, and environmental problems facing the region, there have been serious attempts at interstate cooperation. However, competition over economic resources, including diamonds and oil, continues to fuel conflicts, and the legacy of colonialism continues to keep trade and economic development oriented to the southern coast and overseas rather than among West African countries themselves. In an effort to address such concerns, a concentrated effort was made in 1975, when the Treaty of Lagos established the Economic Organization of West African States (ECOWAS). This organization included all West African nations and has sought to promote trade, cooperation, and self-reliance among its members. In the last decades of the twentieth century, it also became a vehicle for resolving regional conflicts collectively. Responding to the threat to regional security posed by civil war in Liberia in the 1990s, which included conflict with neighboring Sierra Leone, ECOWAS intervened militarily with ECOMOG, the ECOWAS Monitoring Group, a multinational armed force. ECOMOG has intervened in the internal conflicts of Liberia, Sierra Leone, and Guinea-Bissau with some limited success in ending the region's brutal conflicts. However, ECOMOG troops are generally ill-equipped and poorly trained and have been implicated in human rights abuses. Still, the attempt to find regional solutions may aid West Africa's stability.

As the twenty-first century opens, positive signs of political change are visible. Sierra Leone and Liberia have ended their conflicts and their governments are focused on rebuilding and reconciliation; former Liberian president Charles Taylor, whose soldiers committed shocking and systematic atrocities, was arrested as a war criminal and faces charges in the International Criminal Court. Throughout the region there are other examples of a peaceful transition to genuine multiparty constitutional systems of government, as in Senegal.

West Africa's global cultural influence is considerable. The region has produced some of the continent's most influential writers, such as Nigerian authors Chinua Achebe and Wole Soyinka, and Buchi Emecheta and Ama Ata Aidoo of Ghana. Musicians from the region have popularized their traditional musical forms of expression, such as Palm Wine music from Sierra Leone; M'balax, most associated with Youssou N'Dour; Makossa by Manu Dibango; and Juju by Iko Darro and King Sunny Ade. Other West African musicians have fused traditional music with black American forms to create new forms of expression; the best known, Afrobeat, was popularized by Fela Anikulapo-Kuti of Nigeria. While West Africa was first integrated into the Atlantic World via a brutal traffic in humanity, today the region's connections across the Atlantic come primarily through immigration of choice. With the Hart-Cellar Immigration Act of 1865 in the United States, African immigration boomed and the U.S. census of 2000 indicated that over one-third of all immigrants from Africa to the United States come from West Africa. The region's wealth of natural resources also ensures continued integration in the Atlantic World and the international global economy.

Heather Theissen-Reily

References

Achebe, Chinua. *Things Fall Apart.* New York: Anchor, 1994.

Boahen, Adu. *Topics in West African History.* New York: Longman, 1986.

Collins, Robert. *Western African History.* New York: Marcus Wiener Publishing, 1990.

Crowder, Michael. *West Africa*. New York: Longman, 1977.

Davidson, Basil. *West Africa before the Colonial Era: A History to 1850*. New York: Longman, 1998.

Gomez, Michael, and Martin Klein. *Reversing Sail: A History of the Africa Diaspora*. Cambridge: Cambridge University Press, 2004.

Soyinka, Wole. *You Must Set Forth at Dawn*. New York: Random House, 2006.

Webster, J. B., and Adu Boahen. *West Africa since 1800*. New York: Longman, 1980.

AFRICAN INSTITUTION, THE

The African Institution was an early-nineteenth-century British abolitionist group that was formed after Britain's abolition of the slave trade in 1807. Out of the environment following abolition came a new antislavery group, the African Institution. Virtually all of the top abolitionists of the day were involved, including Granville Sharp, William Wilberforce, and Thomas Clarkson. The group planned to promote Africa's well-being—by, among other things, spreading practical information throughout the continent—and circulate useful information about Africa throughout Britain. Later, the group also pushed for emancipation and lobbied for more direct action in order to stop Africa's slave trade. The group also supported British pressure for other European countries to end their trading and maintained close correspondence with North American abolitionists.

Limited financial resources hampered the effectiveness of the African Institution in pursuing these programs, but the group did manage to keep African and antislavery issues at the heart of Britain's foreign policy. This was relatively easy, given the close personal connections that top group members enjoyed with many prominent British politicians. These connections, however, did not guarantee the African Institution complete success in pursuing its goals.

The efforts of the group in developing Africa are most clearly seen in Sierra Leone, a colony that seemed an ideal testing ground for projects. The close attention that the organization gave Sierra Leone ensured that the colony stayed on the minds of relevant segments of the British government. The group recommended that slaves freed from captured slave ships be settled in Sierra Leone. While how much credit the group deserves for Sierra Leone's increasing success and stability is debatable, it certainly did all it could toward building up the colony. The organization also advocated on Paul Cuffe's behalf as he attempted to bring American free blacks to the colony, though Cuffe, an American free black Quaker, only managed to bring several dozen colonists to Sierra Leone before his death in 1817. The involvement with Cuffe and Sierra Leone demonstrated clearly the group's transatlantic focus.

The group's activities would change and expand with the times. Members supported the creation of slave registries in all of the West Indian possessions; the registries were expected to improve slave conditions and also inhibit illegal slave importation. The group also collected information on the East African and Indian Ocean slave trades and corresponded with Henri Christophe, Haiti's first and only black king.

Foreign slave trading also became a more and more important issue for the African Institution. The group kept British diplomats well supplied with antislavery literature at the congresses of Vienna, Aix-la-Chapelle, and Verona, while also working to keep the British delegations on track in terms of raising slave-trade issues with other nations' delegations. Other European powers did, in fact, either modify or abandon their slave trades during the first quarter of the nineteenth century, a partial success for which the African Institution can take some credit.

The African Institution was an organization whose primary goals were only partially fulfilled, however. Though the group's agenda did become part of national planning and international concern because of its connections with the British government, these contacts did not ensure the pursuit of all of its plans. Nonetheless, the African Institution was the primary national British antislavery organization between 1807 and 1823, when it was largely replaced by the new Antislavery Society. The African Institution came to an effective end in 1827.

Wayne Ackerson

See also: Abolitionism, British; Britain: People of African Origin and Descent; Sierra Leone; Wilberforce, William

References
Ackerson, Wayne. *The African Institution (1807–1827) and the Antislavery Movement in Great Britain*. Lewiston, NY: Mellen Press, 2005.
Davis, David Brion. *The Problem of Slavery in the Age of Revolution, 1770–1823*. New York: Oxford University Press, 1999.

AFRICAN METHODIST EPISCOPAL CHURCH

The African Methodist Episcopal (AME) Church is a Christian evangelical church founded to embrace a congregation with an African heritage and to spread Christian gospel to African Americans and people of African descent around the globe. It established missions to Liberia and Sierra Leone. The AME Church followed the Christian tradition of evangelizing and spreading the gospel. The AME Church was formed as a protest against the treatment of African Americans by the white members of the St. George Methodist Episcopal Church in Philadelphia. In November 1787, Bishop Richard Allen led a group of African Americans out of the predominately white church after they were pulled off of their knees while praying during the church service. Although African Americans were always expected to stand when seating was limited, there were even fewer places available than usual during that November worship service, since the church was constructing a larger gallery. Therefore, the seats previously designated for blacks were needed for white members. Being pulled off their knees during prayer catalyzed the formation of the independent African Methodist Episcopal Church. Officially established in 1816, the "African" in the title connected the new denomination with an African heritage.

Although it separated from the Methodist Episcopal Church, the AME Church and its leaders maintained the strong Methodist commitment to John Wesley's philosophy, including evangelizing the world. However, the AME Church felt a special commitment to spreading the Christian gospel to African Americans and people of African descent around the globe. Early in its history, the AME Church sent missionaries such as David Smith and William Paul Quinn to perform missionary work in the West and South. In Canada, the AME Church worked among escaped slaves, founding the British Methodist Episcopal Church in 1856. Missions to the

Portrait of Richard Allen with other African Methodist Episcopal bishops. Founded in 1787 by Richard Allen and Absalom Jones, the African Methodist Episcopal Church is the oldest black religious denomination in the United States. The church was formed as newly imposed segregated practices forced blacks to sit in the balcony, away from the white congregation. (Library of Congress)

South after the Civil War are credited with transforming the AME Church from a small northern community to a national church and the largest black Methodist denomination.

The year 1816 also marked the formation of the American Colonization Society (ACS), founded by Robert Finley, a white Presbyterian from New Jersey. Finley, who opposed the harsh treatment of slaves, argued for a government-funded colony on the west coast of Africa for the freed blacks of America. Finley felt that blacks, once out of slavery, could prosper, and he hoped the creation of such a colony would lead to the abolition of slavery. He also hoped the colony would bring the gospel to Africa and remove an unacculturated group from America.

There were varying views of the ACS within the AME Church. In 1820 Bishop Daniel Coker of the AME Church established the first ACS colony in Liberia. However, Richard Allen and many of his supporters distrusted the ACS and began seeing Africa as a reminder of a perceived black inferiority and a lack of readiness to become full American citizens. Although the AME Church retained the title "African," the word was removed from thousands of black schools, churches, and benevolent societies across America. While the 1830s saw a marked decline in emigration and association with Africa in the AME Church, the church remained committed to evangelical work at home and abroad.

Foreign missions began early in the church's history. In 1820 an AME missionary, Daniel Coker, began evangelizing Africans in Liberia and Sierra Leone. In the 1830s the AME Church sent Scipio Beanes and Richard Robinson to establish AME churches in Port au Prince, Haiti. Led by Bishop Henry McNeal Turner in the 1880s and 1890s, the church renewed its interest in international missionary work. In 1896 the AME Church accepted the Ethiopian Independent Church of South Africa into the denomination. The South African church would become the largest of the AME Church's foreign branches.

The first permanent AME mission in Africa began in Liberia in 1878, led by Samuel Flegler. Flegler, as well as his successors—Clement Irons, S. J. Campbell, and, in the 1890s, William H. Heard—all made fleeting efforts to evangelize Africans. In 1915 the total AME membership in Liberia was 436. The AME Church had slightly better success in Sierra Leone. From its inception, the Freetown congregation successfully attracted emigrants from Canada who had fled to Sierra Leone during the American Revolution. In 1885 the Freetown membership was in sharp decline, however, so the leadership requested an official affiliation with the AME Church to boost its sagging numbers. The AME Church sent J. R. Frederick to establish the congregation. Along with Edward Blyden, Frederick instituted a Dress Reform Society that encouraged the acceptance of traditional African clothing and language, which was a departure from previous missionary philosophies in the church, which had emphasized the importance of embracing Western dress and culture. In 1888 another AME missionary, Sarah Gorham, opened a small mission 75 miles inland at Magbele. By 1891 the Sierra Leone Church had over 500 members. Lack of funding remained a recurring issue. Gorham's mission closed in 1894 and in 1897, Frederick's congregation withdrew its affiliation with the AME Church.

Women played a large role in the AME Church's missionary efforts. From the inception of the Women's Mite Missionary Society in 1874, led by Mary A. Campbell, its first president, the organization raised money for local societies and missionary work in Haiti, Santo Domingo, and West Africa. Sara J. Duncan served as the general superintendent of the AME Church's Woman's Home and Foreign Missionary Society. However, women faced obstacles to their full participation in the missionary process and some, such as Amanda Smith, found the limitations placed upon female missionaries in the AME Church too restrictive. In April 1865, Smith joined the Mother Bethel AME Church in Philadelphia. In November 1870, at the Fleet Street AME Church in Brooklyn, New York, Smith felt the Holy Spirit was calling her to preach. Smith gained renown speaking before white and black audiences at "holiness" revivals. Because the AME Church would not sponsor female missionaries traveling abroad unless their husbands accompanied them, some women in the AME Church worked with white denominations that had fewer prohibitions against female missionaries. In 1878, in conjunction with the white Methodist Episcopal Church, Smith engaged in missionary efforts across the globe and eventually traveled to London, India, and Africa. In 1890 she returned to the United States and became involved with the Woman's Christian Temperance Union in Chicago. Although many of the fledgling communities founded by male and female missionaries in the church struggled for their existence throughout the nineteenth century, the commitment of the AME Church to foreign missions rarely wavered.

Julius Bailey

See also: Christianity (African American); Liberia; Sierra Leone

References

Angell, Stephen W. *Bishop Henry McNeal Turner and African-American Religion in the South.* Knoxville: University of Tennessee Press, 1992.

Campbell, James T. *Songs of Zion: The African Methodist Episcopal Church in the United States and South Africa.* Chapel Hill: University of North Carolina Press, 1998.

Dodson, Jualynne E. *Engendering Church: Women, Power, and the AME Church.* Lanham, MD: Rowman & Littlefield, 2002.

AFRICAN SQUADRONS

African Squadrons were naval patrols mainly organized by the British whose main duty was to intercept slaver ships. Although the English had been the major slave traders in the eighteenth century, the British Parliament passed a bill in 1807 by virtue of which the slave trade was considered illegal. This bill had been finally adopted thanks to Thomas Clarkson's and William Wilberforce's efforts and the support of the British prime minister, Lord Grenville. In the United States the issue of slavery had already been present at the framing of the Constitution in 1787, but the only measure concerning slavery taken at the time was a section of the document barring Congress from abolishing the African slave trade for a twenty-year period. At the end of those twenty years, Congress passed the Slave Importation Act (1807)

that on the one hand censored the international exportation of slaves but on the other did not affect the U.S. internal or coastal slave trade. The centrality of cotton production in the southern states and the huge demand for Cuban sugar and coffee were partly responsible for the measures adopted by the U.S. Congress in 1807.

The British organized squadrons—for example, the British West Africa Squadron—to implement the law and to ensure that there were not any British ships trading in slaves along the African coast. Soon these squadrons demanded the right to board and inspect ships of neutral and enemy lands such as the United States and France. The United States did not want the British to investigate their ships. The Royal Navy practice of impressment, by which it seized U.S. vessels indiscriminately, caused tensions between the two nations. Ships of other slaver nations, such as Portugal and Spain, began throwing the human cargo overboard when chased by the Royal Navy in order to avoid capture, both to lighten the weight of their ships, as well as to disguise their purpose.

In 1819 the American Congress passed the Slave Trade Act, by which President James Monroe allowed warships to play an active role in detecting and suppressing the trade in human beings. The Slave Trade Act also created Liberia as a West African country in which newly freed slaves could resettle. Monroe required U.S. ships to detect and take into custody any ship with the American flag that was involved in the slave trade. The first five U.S. navy vessels sent to Africa to fulfill their squadron duty were the *Cyane, Hornet, John Adams, Alligator,* and *Shark.*

The conditions under which the squadrons had to work were terrible in terms of temperature and sanitary conditions. Surgeons in the ships could only treat the symptoms of many mosquito-induced fevers and illnesses. The two-year period assigned to an African Squadron was a painful test for any member of the crew. The American African Squadron was far less successful than the British squadrons. During the nineteenth century about 7,750 slaving voyages were attempted, but only 21 percent of the ships were captured by the African Squadrons. In the first seventy years of the nineteenth century, approximately 200,000 Africans were shipped, of which 10 percent were rescued by these naval patrols.

Laura Gimeno-Pahissa

See also: Abolitionism, British; Slavery (History)

References

Blackburn, Robin. *The Making of New World Slavery.* New York: Verso, 1997.

Eltis, David. *The Rise of African Slavery in the Americas.* Cambridge: Cambridge University Press, 2000.

Kolchin, Peter. *American Slavery.* New York: Penguin, 1993.

Lovejoy, Paul. *Transformations in Slavery.* Cambridge: Cambridge University Press, 1983.

Thomas, Hugh. *The Slave Trade.* New York: Simon & Schuster, 1997.

AFRICAN UNION

On May 25, 1963, thirty African heads of state assembled in Addis Ababa, Ethiopia, and signed a charter for the Organization of African Unity (OAU) before a 500-person delegation of ministers, nationalist party leaders, a United Nations (UN) representative, and the Chilean ambassador from the Organization of American States (OAS). The OAU established four organs in a descending order of hierarchy: the Heads of State and Government; the Council of Ministers; the General Secretariat; and the Commission of Mediation, Conciliation, and Arbitration. In 2002 the OAU was reconfigured as the African Union.

The Pan-African philosophy of the OAU was rooted in a transnational movement of black leaders from the Americas, Europe, and Africa that emerged at the beginning of the twentieth century. W. E. B. Du Bois, known as the Father of Pan-Africanism, attended the founding Pan-African Congress of 1900 and later presided over the historic Fifth Pan-African Congress of 1945 convened in London, where future OAU leaders Kwame N'krumah and Jomo Kenyatta were present. Du Bois bequeathed the leadership of the Pan-African Congress to N'krumah, who then spearheaded the formation of the West African National Secretariat in 1946, the Union of African Socialist Republics in 1946, and the Committee of Independent African States in 1958. These unions, along with the UN declaration of the Year of Africa in 1960 and a series of closed and open deliberations amongst the Monrovia and Casablanca blocs, were instrumental in forming the OAU.

Domestic and international affairs in the United States also affected the political evolution of the OAU. The OAU's denunciation of brutality against civil rights protesters in the Jim Crow South caused great alarm in the U.S. State Department and compromised the OAU's official policy of neutrality during the cold war. But some OAU member states facilitated U.S. cold war initiatives by condemning Soviet aggression in Africa, accepting U.S. aid for development, and lauding the efforts of the

United Nations secretary-general Kofi Annan addresses the African Union Summit in Banjul, Gambia on July 1, 2006. (UN Photo by Mark Garten)

federal government in thwarting the violent backlash of racist segregationists. Malcolm X returned from a 1964 meeting of the OAU inspired by its call to African unity yet questioning the merit of independent states that accepted U.S. foreign aid.

Upon its founding, the OAU immediately confronted the tensions wrought by language barriers, the geographical divides inherited from the colonial era, and the official policy of noninterference in the internal affairs of member states. Starting in the mid-1970s, the OAU attempted to mitigate the economic devastation of famine and debt repayment through initiatives like the Lagos Plan, and its first troop dispatch went to Chad to settle a military conflict in 1981. In the early 1990s the OAU began deliberations on the HIV/AIDS pandemic occurring throughout sub-Saharan Africa. In 2002 the African Union replaced the

OAU to form a counterweight to the European Union and economic globalization. It had the mission of creating one African currency, one defense system, and an AU head of state. The January 2006 summit of the fifty-three member states of the AU met in Khartoum, Sudan, to discuss the recent dispatch of AU troops to Sudan, HIV/AIDS, and the conflicts in northern Uganda, the Congo, and Algeria.

Margaret M. Stevens

See also: Economic Community of West African States; N'krumah, Kwame; Pan-African Congress; Pan-Africanism.

References

Brown, Michael B. *Africa's Choices: After Thirty Years of the World Bank.* Boulder, CO: Westview Press, 1996.

Boutros-Ghali, Boutros. "The Addis Ababa Charter: A Commentary." *International Conciliation,* no. 546 (January 1964): 25–32.

Murray, Rachel. *Human Rights in Africa: From the OAU to the African Union.* Cambridge: Cambridge University Press, 2004.

N'krumah, Kwame. *Africa Must Unite.* New York: Praeger, 1963.

Salim, Salim Ahmed. *The OAU at 30: Reflections on the Past and Prospects for the Future.* Addis Ababa, Ethiopia: OAU Information Service, 1993.

Wallerstein, Immanuel. *Africa, the Politics of Unity: An Analysis of a Contemporary Social Movement.* New York: Random House, 1967.

AFROCENTRISM

Afrocentrism is an African American ideological and educational movement supporting and promulgating pride in peoples of African descent by locating the origins of black civilization in Egypt. A major facet of Black Nationalist historiography, Afrocentrism asserts the significant contributions of black peoples to human history and culture. A challenge to Western cultural paternalism, Afrocentrism posits not only that black culture provides a credible alternative to European culture, but also that European culture is in some ways itself derivative of black culture. Proponents of Afrocentrism would accept and even embrace that idea that it provides a radical historical, cultural, and political perspective, but they would reject the charge of critics that it depends too much on pseudo-historical claims and speculation.

Afrocentrism has its basis in the widely accepted theory that humankind developed on the fringes of the forests and plains of East Africa and from there spread to all corners of the world. The centerpiece of Afrocentrism is the claim that the Pharaonic civilization of the Nile Valley was in many of its essential aspects an African, rather than a Mediterranean or a Middle Eastern, civilization. Since the Pharaonic civilization had great influence throughout the Mediterranean world, the subsequent ascendancy of Greek civilization—and through it, Roman and Western civilization—can therefore be seen as also owing a significant debt to cultural sources in black Africa. Critics have argued that Afrocentrists have grossly overstated the general influence of the Nubian kingdoms on Pharaonic civilization and the impact of their relatively brief hegemony over the lower Nile Valley near the end of the Pharaonic epoch.

Afrocentrism began in the United States as an educational movement intended to address deficiencies in the education of African American students. Central to addressing other deficiencies was the perception that the denigration of black culture left African American students with a diminished sense of self-esteem and that the obvious way to raise the self-confidence of African American students was, therefore, to celebrate the past achievements and the future possibilities of black culture.

Critics have argued that Afrocentrism serves only to further isolate African Americans from the mainstream, Eurocentric culture. But proponents have countered that the teaching of an Afrocentric curriculum would also serve to broaden the perspectives of students with European ancestries and would enhance their ability, as well as that of African Americans, to function meaningfully within an increasingly multicultural world.

The most prominent proponent of Afrocentrism has been Molefi Kete Asante, whose *The Afrocentric Idea* (1987) remains the seminal text in the movement's history. He has subsequently authored the influential collection of essays, *Malcolm X as Cultural Hero and Other Afrocentric Essays* (1993). Another notable Afrocentrist has been the historian Yosef ben-Jochannan, whose books have included *Black Man of the Nile* (1970) and *Africa: Mother of "Western Civilization"* (1971).

Martin Kich

See also: Black Athena; Literature, African American; Négritude; Race, History of

References

Asante, Molefi K. *Kemet, Afrocentricity, and Knowledge.* Trenton, NJ: Africa World Press, 1990.

Asante, Molefi Kete, and Ama Mazama, eds. *Egypt vs. Greece and the American Academy: The Debate over the Birth of Civilization.* Chicago: African American Images, 2002.

Conyers, James L., ed. *Afrocentric Traditions.* New Brunswick, NJ: Transaction, 2005.

Dompere, K. K. *Africentricity and African Nationalism: Philosophy and Ideology for Africa's Complete Emancipation.* Langley Park, MD: I.A.A.S., 1992.

Gilroy, Paul. *The Black Atlantic: Modernity and Double Consciousness.* Cambridge, MA: Harvard University Press, 1993.

Gray, Cecil Conteen. *Afrocentric Thought and Praxis: An Intellectual History.* Trenton, NJ: Africa World Press, 2001.

Henderson, Errol Anthony. *Afrocentrism and World Politics: Towards a New Paradigm.* Westport, CT: Praeger, 1995.

Keto, C. Tsehloane. *The Africa-Centered Perspective of History: An Introduction.* Laurel Springs, NJ: K. A. Publishers, 1991.

Keto, C. Tsehloane. *Vision and Time: Historical Perspective of an Africa-Centered Paradigm.* Lanham, MD: University Press of America, 2001.

Mazama, Ama. *The Afrocentric Paradigm.* Trenton, NJ: Africa World Press, 2003.

Ziegler, Dhyana, ed. *Molefi Kete Asante and Afrocentricity: In Praise and in Criticism.* Nashville, TN: James C. Winston, 1995.

AFROFUTURISM

Afrofuturism is an African American literary and artistic movement addressing the transatlantic issues of displacement, home, and belonging. In speculative fiction, some of the major recurring themes have included alien intrusion and subjugation, forced displacement, and the quest to return to the native land and to regain a lost sense of cultural location. All of these themes would have a very natural appeal to African American writers and readers, and yet until the last few decades of the twentieth century, there was little African American visibility in the genres of science fiction and science fantasy.

At the literary forefront of the Afrofuturist movement has been the Jamaican-Canadian novelist Nalo Hopkinson. She is best known for her novels *Brown Girl in the Ring* (1998) and *Midnight Robber* (2000), in which she focuses on Afro-Caribbean women dealing with the dislocation that they experience in other settings. Beyond their inventive narratives and compelling themes, the novels are notable for their use of Afro-Caribbean dialect.

Hopkinson's African American forerunners in the genre have included, most prominently, the American novelists Samuel R. Delany and Octavia Butler, both of whom have won major awards. Delany has earned a reputation as a novelist interested in intellectual movements and cultural theories. In almost all of his novels, he has treated the intersections of language, myth, and artistic expression. His most acclaimed novels have included *Babel–17* (1966) and *The Einstein Intersection* (1967). Butler is best known for her five-volume Patternists series (1976–1984), which focuses on a group of telepaths who are obsessed with creating a race of superhumans. More recently, she has written the Xenogenesis trilogy (1987–1989), which treats a postapocalyptic world in which aliens conduct genetic experiments with human beings. Afrofuturism is not just a literary movement. It has drawn adherents from across the whole spectrum of the arts. Some of the more prominent of these artists have included George Clinton, Kodwo Eshun, McLean Greaves, Lee "Scratch" Perry, Keith Piper, Sun Ra, and Fatimah Tuggar.

Martin Kich

See also: Literature, African American

References
"Afrofuturism." *Social Text* 71, no. 2 (Summer 2002).
Nelson, Alondra, ed. *Afrofuturism*. Durham, NC: Duke University Press, 2002.
Rollins, Lisa M. "Models of Black Resistance: Negritude, New Negroism, and Afrofuturism." MA thesis, Claremont Graduate University, 2000.

AGRICULTURE

Historically, agriculture arose independently in Africa and the Americas, but is followed, from the fifteenth century to the present, by extensive exchanges of crops and farming practices. Evidence from paleobotany points to the Americas rather than Africa as the earlier region of plant domestication, a surprise given that humans colonized the Americas only around 10,000 BCE, making them the last of the habitable continents to be settled. Despite this late date of settlement, the transition to agriculture was rapid. The oldest corncobs establish that humans first grew corn as early as 6000 BCE in southern Mexico and the Yucatan. At the same time, the people of the Andes Mountains began to grow the potato. These two crops made possible the empires of Mesoamerica and South America. The longevity of these empires evidences a regular food surplus, an achievement all the more remarkable given that pre-Columbian people had neither plow nor draught animal. The collapse of the Mayan civilization may signal a decrease in corn yield in the ninth century CE, a decline one hypothesis attributes to the spread of an insect-borne corn virus. This hypothesis implies a genetically uniform corn crop, though it need not imply monoculture. Pre-Columbian agriculture was diverse enough to include several varieties of bean, squash, pumpkin, tomato, pepper, and tobacco in addition to corn and potato.

The 4,000 years between the settlement of the Americas and the rise of agriculture contrast with the more than 100,000 years that separate these events in Africa. Anatomically, modern humans originated in Africa 130,000 years ago, and they must have gathered plants for food from the outset. Despite the long association between people and plants, humans in Africa did not make the transition to agriculture on their own. Rather, the inhabitants of the Nile River Valley borrowed crops and implements, notably the plow and sickle, from the Near East around 5000 BCE. The Nile Valley is well suited to the requirements of agriculture; the annual innundation of the Nile deposits enough silt to free farmers from the need to fertilize their soil. Barley and wheat had the same importance in Egypt as corn and potato had in the Americas. The small farmer, averse to risk, must have prized barley for its drought tolerance, an attribute the first-century CE Roman writer Columella noted in his *On Agriculture*. Along with barley, farmers grew emmer and einkorn wheat for porridge, bread, and beer. By the Roman period, Egypt was the granary of the Mediterranean Basin. In addition to barley and wheat, Egyptian farmers grew peas, lentils, chickpeas, and several types of vegetable. Egypt was the model for agriculture throughout North Africa. Farmers in sub-Saharan Africa cultivated a different group of crops. The cultivation of both the yam and oil palm dates to 3000 BCE, sorghum to 2000 BCE, millet to 1000 BCE, and bananas to the first millennium CE.

Having been separate for millennia, the agricultural systems of Africa and the Americas moved toward one another after 1492, though convergence has been incomplete. The voyages of Christopher Columbus awakened Europeans to the possibility of transferring crops in both directions across the Atlantic Ocean. Europeans dictated the terms of this exchange, and they concentrated on the cultigens of Eurasia and the Americas rather than on those of Africa. Even had they adopted an "Africa first" strategy, they would have bumped up against biological and ecological constraints. Soils are thin in many regions of Africa and vulnerable to erosion. The clearance of forests exacerbates the problem of erosion. Soils in equatorial Africa tend to be acidic, requiring the application of calcium carbonate before they can be farmed. The tropical climate of equatorial Africa has hindered the transplanting of crops from temperate regions, in part because the diseases of tropical Africa have been a barrier to the introduction of crops. The potato is adapted to cool weather and spread rapidly to northern Europe after 1500 but not to tropical Africa, where fungal diseases afflict the crop. Tobacco, indigenous to Virginia, grows poorly in the thin soils of Africa, in part because it rapidly depletes the soil of nutrients. Corn, on the other hand, is native to the warm climate of Mesoamerica and, more than any other crop, has transformed

African agriculture. Europeans introduced corn into Africa around 1500, planting it wherever they established colonies. So successful has corn been that it dethroned sorghum and millet as the leading crop in several regions of Africa. Between 1976 and 1980 corn tallied 37 percent by weight of all crops harvested in eastern and southern Africa, whereas sorghum and millet combined for only 14 percent. The percentages are similar in sub-Saharan Africa. Only in West Africa has corn not displaced sorghum and millet.

From the perspective of biology and ecology, the transfer of crops from Africa to the Americas should have been straightforward. Sorghum, for example, is well suited for cultivation throughout the midwestern United States. As late as 1970 farmers in western Ohio grew it on a few thousand acres, but by 1980 soybeans, a crop that swept the Midwest after World War II, had replaced sorghum. As with soybeans, corn has excluded African crops from the Americas. Corn was the primary cultigen when Europeans began to settle the Americas in the sixteenth century. Rather than reconfigure agriculture, Europeans deepened their dependence on corn, forging the Midwest into a monolith of corn and hogs. The result is a stable system of production that farmers could change only at prohibitive cost. More than any other African crop, rice transformed American agriculture. Native to East Asia, rice came to colonial America from Ghana in 1672. During the 1680s Europeans planted a hardy variety of rice from Madagascar along the Carolina coast, whose marshland and climate are ideal for rice cultivation. The farmers of Carolina exported 1.5 million pounds of rice in 1710, 18 million in 1730, and 76 million in 1770.

Rice was a plantation crop. If the interchange of crops between Africa and the Americas was incomplete, the rise of the plantation nonetheless marked a stark convergence of the agricultural systems of these regions in the form of African labor and the crops of Africa, the Americas, and Eurasia. Sugar fueled the growth of the first plantations. In 1493 Columbus brought sugar, a crop native to northern India, to the Caribbean. The Portuguese, who had established sugar plantations as early as 1441 in the Old World, carved out in 1538 the New World's first sugar plantation in Brazil. The British followed suit in Barbados, Jamaica, and the Leeward Islands in the seventeenth century, as did the French in Louisiana after 1700. Production grew in Jamaica from 500 tons in 1669 to 7,100 tons in 1691 and in the Leeward Islands from 1,505 tons in 1678 to 8,015 tons in 1699. Britain's sugar islands more than tripled production between 1663 and 1698. North of the sugar plantations of Brazil, the Caribbean, and Louisiana and the rice plantations of Carolina were the tobacco lands of Virginia and Maryland. In 1612 John Rolfe transplanted a variety of tobacco from Trinidad to Virginia. In 1627 Virginia exported 500,000 pounds of tobacco, in 1635 it exported 1 million pounds, and in 1660, 15 million. Cotton was the last crop to sink roots in the plantations of America. The cotton lands stretched from Georgia to Texas. Two types of cotton vied for the market. Long staple cotton grew along the Carolina and Georgia coast but yields declined inland, where short staple cultivars prevailed. The cotton gin eased the separation of seeds from the fiber, thereby removing the bottleneck in production. The southern United States produced 3,000 bales of cotton in 1790,

178,000 in 1810, 732,000 in 1830, and 4.5 million in 1860. By 1850 this region produced two-thirds of the world's cotton. Plantations, whether they grew sugar, rice, tobacco, or cotton, devoured African slaves. Between 1526 and 1810, 10 million slaves crossed the Atlantic. During these years the plantations of Brazil absorbed 3.6 million slaves, the Caribbean 3.3 million, Spanish Florida 1.5 million, and British North America and the United States 400,000. Among the Caribbean Islands, the Leeward Islands imported 2,000 slaves between 1640 and 1650, 10,100 between 1651 and 1675, and 32,000 between 1676 and 1700. Intent on controlling slaves through drudgery, the British planters in the Caribbean forced slaves to toil without benefit of the plow. Plantation agriculture substituted labor for technology, the reverse of the trend toward mechanization on farms that employed free labor.

Technology occupied a prominent place in the agriculture of the United States from its early days. Among his accomplishments, Thomas Jefferson designed a plow, and from the eighteenth century the agricultural societies offered prizes for the development of farm implements. The horse-drawn reaper of 1833 and the steel plow of 1837 launched a series of innovations that have culminated in the modern planter and combine. Science was the other side of the coin. Proponents of agricultural innovation championed the application of science to farming. George Washington advocated federal support for agricultural science, and in 1862 Congress created the U.S. Department of Agriculture and gave states land to establish agricultural and mechanical colleges. The agricultural experiment stations were the research arm of these colleges, and in the early twentieth century, they began breeding high-yielding crops. Hybrid corn swept the midwestern United States in the 1930s and 1940s and Mexico, South America, and Africa after 1950. High-yielding varieties of potato in the United States and the South American highlands and wheat in North Africa supplanted traditional cultivars after 1940. Fertilizers, herbicides, insecticides, and irrigation doubled yields. These new cultivars were genetically uniform. Although they were resistant to a range of pathogens, the evolution of new strains of pathogen left farmers vulnerable to losses. The spread of corn viruses through the valleys of the Mississippi and Ohio rivers in 1945 and between 1962 and 1964, the Southern Corn Leaf Blight throughout the United States in 1970 and 1971, and the Late Blight of Potato in Ecuador and Peru since 1997 have diminished yields between 15 and 90 percent.

The formative years during which science and technology came to shape agriculture coincided with the period of European colonialism in Africa. As had been the case in the Caribbean and British North America, plantations monopolized wealth. Large farmers grew cash crops for export at the expense of food for local consumption. By 1900 the French had established rubber plantations on 9 million acres in Zimbabwe. In Angola coffee production increased from 4,000 tons in 1920 to 118,000 tons in 1961. Coffee plantations expanded from 297,000 acres to 1.2 million acres between 1948 and 1961. By 1974 Angola was the world's third-leading coffee grower. Colonial Nigeria exported cocoa, palm oil, and groundnuts. The Shire Highlands of Malawi produced cotton, coffee, and tobacco. Planters required peasants to work their estates as many as six months a year in lieu of rent, a policy that

undermined subsistence farming. Uganda, Tanzania, Sudan, Mali, Burkina Faso, Senegal, and Nigeria produced cotton; Senegal groundnuts; Zaire palm oil; and Ghana, Cameroon, Kenya, and Ethiopia cocoa. In Gambia planters converted land from rice, a staple of the peasant, to groundnuts for export. In Guinea rubber and groundnuts displaced rice.

Postcolonial Africa has tried with varying success to feed its burgeoning population by growing food for domestic consumption rather than cash crops for export. In 1968 Nigeria launched a program to increase land under irrigation from 32,000 acres to 677,000 acres in ten years. Much of the $2.7 million Nigeria earmarked for the program lined the pockets of contractors rather than benefiting farmers, while the country's population grew faster than food supply. In 1970 Nigeria imported just 1.6 percent of its food, but by 1979 that figure had jumped to 21 percent. Between 1977 and 1981 grain imports rose from 1.4 million tons to 1.3 billion. Other countries fared better. Starting in 1932 farmers in Senegal supplanted groundnuts with millet, manioc, and taro for domestic consumption. In Kenya beans and bananas have diversified an agriculture that once concentrated on coffee and cocoa. Between 1966 and 1970 sub-Saharan Africa exported on average 1.3 million tons of grain per year. In 1981 Zimbabwe exported 1 million tons of its record 215 million tons of corn.

At issue is whether farmers in Latin America and Africa can replicate the model of intensive agriculture. The proponents of this model assert that only the growing of high-yielding crops can avert famine in Africa and other populous regions. Opponents point to the ecological and human costs of intensive agriculture. Monoculture robs the land of its native foliage, hastens erosion, and depletes nutrients. The use of agrochemicals pollutes groundwater and endangers wildlife. Mechanization displaces labor, pushing the rural poor into overcrowded cities. Intensive agriculture squeezes the small farmer between low commodity prices and the high cost of agrochemicals. Small farmers launched the Neolithic Revolution in the villages of Peru and Egypt. Whether they can survive in an era of highly capitalized agriculture and global markets is an open question.

Christopher Cumo

See also: Agriculture, Sustainable; Development, International; Green Revolution; Rice in the African Diaspora

References

Cohen, Ronald, ed. *Satisfying Africa's Food Needs: Food Production and Commercialization in African Agriculture.* Boulder, CO: Lynne Rienner Publishers, 1988.

Dunn, Richard S. *Sugar and Slaves: The Rise of the Planter Class in the English West Indies, 1623–1713.* Chapel Hill: University of North Carolina Press, 1972.

Harrison, Paul. *The Greening of Africa: Breaking through in the Battle for Land and Food.* New York: Penguin Books, 1987.

Littlefield, Daniel C. *Rice and Slaves: Ethnicity and the Slave Trade in Colonial South Carolina.* Baton Rouge: Louisiana State University Press, 1981.

McCann, James. "Maize and Grace: History, Corn, and Africa's New Landscape, 1500–1999." http://www.ruafrica. rutgers.edu/events/media/ maize_and_grace_jamesmccann[1].pdf.

AGRICULTURE, SUSTAINABLE

In 1987 the UN's Brundtland Commission defined "sustainable development" as meeting people's needs today without compromising the ability of generations in the future to meet their own needs; in turn, sustainable agriculture generally refers to an agriculture that is economically viable, socially equitable, and environmentally sound, not only at the present, but also for the future. This paradigm, initially rooted in the environmental and organic food movements of the United States and Europe, has become increasingly visible in the arena of agricultural development, with particular implications for Africa and the Americas. In developing countries, sustainable agriculture stands as an alternative to extractive colonial and postcolonial plantations of export crops planted in monoculture, and it has been largely embraced as an alternative to the Green Revolution's "silver bullet" package of hybrid varieties and agrochemical inputs, which has largely failed to deliver its promised results to smallholder farmers. Indeed, small farmers who adopted the new Green Revolution technologies found that yields of new hybrid crop varieties often fared more poorly on their marginal land than their own traditional varieties. Similarly, mechanization and monocropping as prescribed by extensionists contributed to increased rates of soil degradation on hillside farms, as well as to increases in pest and disease infestation and concomitant pesticide use.

Unlike the input-intensive approach of the Green Revolution, sustainable agriculture is knowledge-intensive, founded on agroecological principles. Sustainable agriculture's agroecological approach is not a one-size-fits-all technical solution—there is no panacea recipe of broad-spectrum pesticides, precise fertilizer dosages, or silver bullet genetically modified seed purporting to solve world hunger. Rather, agroecology uses knowledge of ecological processes to work within the framework of a particular existing natural system in order to enhance beneficial biological relationships. Instead of a package of inputs, sustainable agriculture relies on a set of guiding principles that can be adapted in unique fashions to a particular agroecosystem.

First, dependence on external inputs such as fertilizer and pesticides should be minimized in conjunction with the improvement of on-farm nutrient cycling. This includes the cycling of crop residues back into the soil, as well as integration of livestock into the farming system and extensive applications of organic matter such as manure, compost, or mulch. By "closing the system," nutrient losses and the unnecessary importation of off-farm inputs can be reduced. Where conventional chemical agriculture focuses on "feeding the plant" with measured doses of synthetic mineral fertilizer, sustainable agriculture emphasizes instead "feeding the soil" with organic matter in order to compensate for topsoil lost to erosion from tillage, wind, and rain and to revitalize soil microbial populations. Soil microbes metabolize organic matter, releasing nutrients in the mineral form available for uptake by plants. In addition to serving as a nutrient-rich feedstock for microbes, soil organic matter absorbs moisture, vital in the sandy, arid soils of the Sahel and parts of the Americas. Additionally, it acts as glue holding together soil particles, slowing erosion.

The second principle of sustainable agriculture is the enhancement of functional biodiversity. This is accomplished in a number of ways. By maintaining habitats for beneficial insects that parasitize pest species, a farmer can reduce dependence on pesticides. Application of organic matter fosters soil microbial diversity, helping to stem soil-borne pests and pathogens as well as improving nutrient cycling. Increased spatial and temporal crop diversity helps to buffer the farming system from environmental or market shock. Unlike in a monoculture system, when a falling price or crop failure spells economic disaster or food insecurity for a farmer, a diverse cropping system spreads out environmental or market risks across several crops. If a crop's price falls or if the crop fails due to pest or disease pressure, a farmer relies on his other crops. Similarly, polycultures also serve as barriers to the rapid spread of host-specific pests and diseases. A pest specific to a particular crop can quickly destroy a monoculture, whereas in a polyculture or intercropped system, the pest's trajectory is broken by the presence of other plant species.

Third, the enhancement of beneficial interactions or "mutualisms" between agroecosystem components is fundamental. For example, the inclusion of nitrogen-fixing leguminous plant species into a cropping system improves soil fertility, just as the presence of beneficial insect populations can reduce pest pressure and thereby improve crop performance. Finally, the integration of existing farmer knowledge (of soils, insects, crops, and so on) as the basis of enhanced management techniques promotes sustainability of practice. Unlike conventional industrial agricultural production, sustainable agriculture is site-specific and rooted in a farmer's knowledge of his fields and farm. Sustainable agriculture is imbedded largely at the field and farm levels and is adapted to the heterogeneity of specific local agroecosystems and farming practices. Indeed, many sustainable agriculture approaches are built on foundations of local knowledge. For example, Haitian farmers have developed a range of techniques to address the constraints they face, such as erosion, pests, and volatile markets. Rock walls and residue embankments slow erosion. They rely on polycultures of maize, sorghum, taro, yams, malanga, pigeon pea, and cowpea, and numerous multipurpose trees to enhance soil fertility and control pests. Similarly, in many parts of Africa, farmers have developed strategies to rehabilitate degraded soil by stopping erosion with rock bunds that trap nutrient-rich sediment. Velvetbean, a nitrogen-fixing cover crop, is widely used in coastal West Africa and East Africa as fertilizer, erosion control, and animal fodder. Throughout the world, development projects employing sustainable farming techniques have boasted significant crop yield increases.

Sustainable agriculture, however, addresses more than simply ecological sustainability and productivity. In addition to being environmentally sound, it must also both be economically viable for the long term and socially equitable. For example, while industrial-scale U.S. conventional and organic agriculture are economically viable, they are both still monoculture systems that rely heavily on off-farm inputs (either synthetic or organic) and exploit cheap Latin American migrant labor. A more sustainable system would remain profitable, provide workers with decent working conditions and a living wage, and be more biologically diverse with fewer off-farm inputs.

While total sustainability may seem an impossible goal, an asymptote that can never quite be reached, the paradigm of sustainable agriculture serves as a framework to help improve the long-term stewardship of the land for current and future generations. Helping to buffer farmers from the risk of crop failure due to global-warming-induced climatic variability, sustainable agriculture is of particular interest to farmers in the drought- and hurricane-prone zones of Africa and the Americas. Additionally, sustainable farming practices can help protect developing country farmers from the economic variability associated with increasingly globalized markets, guaranteeing a modicum of income and food security.

Nathan C. McClintock

See also: Agriculture; Biotechnology; Globalization; Green Revolution

References

Altieri, Miguel. *Agroecology: The Science of Sustainable Agriculture.* 2nd ed. Boulder, CO: Westview Press, 1995.

Nicholls, C. I., and M. A. Altieri. "Conventional Agricultural Development Models and the Persistence of the Pesticide Treadmill in Latin America." *International Journal of Sustainable Development and World Ecology* 4 (1997): 93–111.

Pretty, Jules N. *Regenerating Agriculture: Politics and Practice for Sustainability and Self-Reliance.* Washington, DC: Joseph Henry Press, 1995.

Reij, Chris, and Ann Waters-Bayer. *Farmer Innovation in Africa—A Source of Inspiration for Agricultural Development.* London: Earthscan Publications, 2001.

AIDOO, AMA ATA (1942–)

Ama Ata Aidoo is a prominent Ghanaian woman novelist and dramatist, writing in English and addressing women's issues in Africa and in Europe. Relentlessly confronting patriarchal attitudes in culture and society, Aidoo has probed into the intricate relationship between the neocolonial mentality and African women's condition in her composite literary production and through her political activism.

Born in the Central Region of Ghana, she studied at Cape Coast and at the University of Ghana, where she produced *The Dilemma of a Ghost* (1965), thereby entering the male-dominated African literary scene. The play centers on Ato's return to Ghana with his African American wife, Eulalie, and dramatizes the latter's conflict with her in-laws, highlighting burning issues like the cultural gap between Africans from different continents, the duty of motherhood, and African involvement in the slave trade. The theme of slavery recurs in her next play, *Anowa* (1970). In the late nineteenth century, the eponymous protagonist defies societal pressure and marries the man she loves, but his trading in humans will lead her to another rebellion, this time against her husband, and to a tragic conclusion.

Stylistically, both plays recover traditional literary genres, such as the folktale. Her fiction is similarly molded. *No Sweetness Here* (1970) is composed of eleven stories where storytelling, plurality of voices, and direct speech recreate in Ghanaian English the communal atmosphere of oral literature. Worth mentioning is "For Whom Things Did Not Change," where the old servant, Zirigu, cannot distinguish his former colonial master from his present Ghanaian ones. In her first novel, *Our Sister Killjoy* (1977), narrated alternately through prose and poetry, the Ghanaian protagonist Sissie travels to Germany and London on a scholarship, experiences the contradictions of European society, stigmatizes the neocolonial alienation of Africans who choose to live there, and finally returns home.

Between the late 1960s and the 1980s, she taught and lectured in Ghanaian, Tanzanian, Kenyan, and U.S. universities, besides actively engaging in politics as director of institutions such as the Ghana Broadcasting Corporation and the Arts Council in Ghana. Beginning in 1982 she served as Ghana's secretary for education for eighteen months. She later moved to Zimbabwe, where she published her poetry in *Someone Talking to Sometime* (1985), a collection of colloquial pieces dominated by a pensive mood, with a section on her experiences in New Orleans. The early 1990s saw another collection of poems on African and gender matters, *An Angry Letter in January* (1992) and the novel *Changes* (1991), winner of the Commonwealth Writers Prize, which follows the vicissitudes of the divorced working woman Esi and her controversial choice to marry for love a man who already has one wife. Using polygamy as a possible alternative for an educated woman in today's Accra, and alternating (as in *Killjoy*) prose with poetry and scriptlike dialogues as a way to revitalize the continuum of traditional verbal discourses, *Changes* confirmed Aidoo's penchant for experimentation and her restlessness with imposed forms and ideas. *The Girl Who Can and Other Stories* (1997) followed in its wake, reaffirming her belief in the emancipation of African women as a necessary step toward national advancement—also a guiding principle in her essays and in her involvement with women's associations and NGOs. She has also published two books for children, *The Eagle and the Chickens and Other Stories* (1989) and *Birds and Other Poems* (1989).

Pietro Deandrea

See also: Feminism and Women's Equality
   Movements, African; Ghana; Literature
   African

References
Aidoo, Ama Ata. *The Dilemma of a Ghost.*
   Harlow, UK: Longman, 1965.
Aidoo, Ama Ata. *Changes—A Love Story.* New
   York: CUNY, Feminist Press, 1991.

Azodo, Ada Uzoamaka, and Gay Wilentz, eds. *Emerging Perspectives on Ama Ata Aidoo.* Trenton, NJ: Africa World Press, 1999.

Odamtten, Vincent O. *The Art of Ama Ata Aidoo: Polylectics and Reading against Neocolonialism.* Gainesville: University of Florida Press, 1994.

AKAN

Akan is a Ghanaian linguistic and cultural group whose folk culture, especially proverbs and textile art, define them as a people. The Akan are one of the best-known cultural groups in Africa. Four million strong, they are the largest cultural grouping of Ghana, representing approximately half of the country's population. The Akan Abusua (family), or clans, include the Ahanta, Akuapem, Akwamu, Akyem (Abuakwa, Bosome, Kotoku), Asante, Bono, Fante, Kwahu, Nzema, Sefwi, and Wassa.

The Asante and Fante are the two largest of these subgroups. While the political, social, religious, and customary practices of the Akan are very similar, each clan shares a common cultural heritage and language, which—added to their historical tradition of group identity and political autonomy—contributed to the formation of individual nation-states during the pre-colonial period.

Linguistically, the collective term "Akan" refers to a group of languages belonging to the Kwa subfamily of the Niger-Kordofanian language family spoken in both Ghana (south of the Volta River) and Côte d'Ivoire. What distinguishes one group from another are their linguistic variants (dialects), which include Akuapem, Asante, and Fante; the former two are referred to as Twi. Akan is the first language of approximately 44 percent of Ghana's population, with Asante Twi being the most widely spoken of the variants. Making use of figurative speech, the Akan are probably best known for their proverbial wisdom. Proverbs, popular maxims used to express practical truths gained through experience and observation, are expressed by the Akan not only in words but also through music, particularly traditional drumming, and dance, as well as through textile art, specifically adinkra and kente cloths. Proverbs constitute an important characteristic of the Akan languages and are used to imbue communication with life.

It is through proverbs that we gain a better understanding of the Akan outlook on existence, both physical and spiritual. What distinguishes the Akan from many of the other cultural groupings in Ghana is that they are a matrilineal people, tracing their lineage and inheritance through the mother's bloodline. Most importantly, although Christianity and Islam attempted to colonize their spirituality, they have not departed from their ancestral and spiritual culture, which defines them as Akan.

Religion, understood in a broad sense, is the foundation upon which Akan society and culture is built. Cosmologically, the Akan universe is essentially spiritual. In addition to their belief in a Supreme Being (Nyame), Mother Earth (Asase Yaa), and a host of intermediaries (Abosom), the Akan believe in the omnipresence of the ancestors (Nsamanfo), made evident by daily acts such as the pouring of libation and the throwing on the ground of the first morsel of food, as well as by periodic ancestral ceremonies. Akan culture is ancestral in that the Akan believe that the Nsamanfo, although they no longer occupy physical space on earth, maintain important roles in each person's life. The most important of their roles is that of direct messenger to Nyame, as opposed to the Abosom, who are messengers from Nyame. It is believed that the Nsamanfo are spiritual beings with the power to bring good fortune to the living, specifically members of their lineage, or if dissatisfied, to show their displeasure by causing ill fortune, sickness, and so on. They may manifest themselves in human form, in dreams, or through trance, and their spiritual presence may be invoked to assist the living. Prayers, offerings, and sacrifices are most often offered to them to seek their blessings and to avoid any misfortune. Spirituality, therefore, permeates all aspects of Akan society, and most activities are informed by its ancestral cosmology and culture.

Yaba Amgborale Blay

See also: Ancestor Worship; Ghana; Religion (Africa)

References
Buah, F. K. *A History of Ghana.* London: Macmillan Education, 1980.
Opoku, K. A. *West African Traditional Religion.* London: FEP International Private, 1978.

AKRAM, WALI (1904–1994)

Wali Akram was the founder of the First Cleveland Mosque and author of the Moslem Ten-Year Plan. Akram was born Walter R. Gregg in Bryan, Burleson County, Texas. He studied electrical engineering at Prairie View State Normal and Industrial College before working a series of odd jobs. He moved to St. Louis, Missouri, during the early 1920s where he met Sheik Ahmad Din, a local leader of the nonconformist Ahmadiyya Movement in Islam. Akram converted to Islam, took on his Muslim name, and a year later married his wife, Kareema. After studying Islam for several years, he became a missionary in the Midwest and eventually settled in Cleveland, Ohio. There he helped to establish an Ahmadiyya mosque, but within a few years the African American congregation became distrustful of the motives and activities of the movement's Indian missionaries. Akram and most of the congregation rejected their Ahmadiyya connections and beliefs and turned toward orthodox practices of Islam.

In 1937 the First Cleveland Mosque was established, becoming the only orthodox mosque in America to be run entirely by indigenous Muslim converts. At about the same time, Akram developed the Moslem Ten-Year Plan, a proposal to address the economic and educational needs of African American Muslims in the midst of the Great Depression. Akram later toured the nation in an effort to unite all American Muslims and in 1943 was elected president of the United Islamic Society of America. In 1957 he became one of the first African Americans to officially make the pilgrimage to Mecca and was thereafter known as Al-Hajj Wali Akram. He spent the remainder of his career advocating the Ten-Year Plan and leading his mosque as imam until he retired in the early 1980s.

Brent Singleton

See also: Islam, African American

References
Dannin, Robert. *Black Pilgrimage to Islam.* Oxford: Oxford University Press, 2002.
Lo, Mbaye. *Muslims in America: Race, Politics, and Community Building.* Beltsville, MD: Amana Publications, 2004.

ALGERIA

Algeria's territory, the second largest of any African nation, consists mostly of a desertic region in the south that is separated from the coastal plains of the Mediterranean shore by the Atlas Mountains. A significant amount of Algeria's foreign exchange consists of the export of petroleum and natural gas products to the United States. Algeria was under the domination of a weakening Turkish Ottoman Empire when France invaded it in 1830 in response to a diplomatic dispute dating back three years earlier. France's main purpose at the time was to impose a naval blockade to solve the problem of Turkish-sanctioned piracy in the Mediterranean. As early as 1847, the French incorporated the territory of Algeria into France proper. Consequently, France was more attached to Algeria than to its other colonies, which made the war of decolonization that led to Algeria's independence in 1962 particularly violent. To obtain independence, the Algerian National Liberation Front (FLN) employed diplomatic activity abroad—particularly in Egypt and at the United Nations—as well as guerilla warfare and urban terrorism that the French army countered with the use of torture.

Algeria's struggle for independence set an example for other decolonizing African nations in the 1960s. From the African American perspective, Algeria was a model of resistance against racism. The writings on the Algerian Revolution by the West Indian psychiatrist Frantz Fanon were an inspiration for the foundation of the Black Panther Party by Huey Newton and Bobby Seale in 1966.

Malcolm X had a close relationship with Ahmed Ben Bella, the first president of independent Algeria. Additionally, Malcolm's meeting with Taher Kaid, the Algerian ambassador to Ghana, in May 1964 had a particularly great influence on him. Furthermore, Malcolm and the Cuban revolutionary Che Guevara were expected to strengthen the links between North Africa and the Americas by appearing as keynote speakers at an international conference in Algeria in February 1966. However, the venture was undone by Malcolm's assassination and by Ben Bella's imprisonment after a coup led by Colonel Houari Boumedienne on June 19, 1965.

Later on, in January 1981, Algeria played a major role in mediating the release of U.S. hostages held in Iran. However, Islamism became an increasingly important part of Algerian politics. After the army canceled the January 1992 second round of elections for the National People's Assembly following the victory of the Islamic Salvation Front (FIS) in the first round in December 1991, violence by Islamist groups escalated into a yet-unresolved civil war.

After September 11, 2001, the U.S. government studied terrorist and counter-terrorist tactics in French Algeria. In 2003 Gillo Pontecorvo's film, *The Battle of Algiers* (1966), which documents three years of the Algerian war for independence, was screened at the Pentagon as a case study to better understand the problems faced by the United States in Iraq.

Ziad Bentahar

See also: Colonialism; Decolonization, African; French Empire; Malcolm X; Terrorism

References

Ageron, Charles-Robert. *Modern Algeria: A History from 1830 to the Present.* Trenton, NJ: Africa World Press, 1991.

Isham, Christopher, Richard Clarke, and Michael Sheehan. "The Battle of Algiers: A Case Study." Disc 3. *The Battle of Algiers,* DVD. Directed by Gillo Pontecorvo. The Criterion Collection, 2004.

'ALI PASHA, MUHAMMAD (1769–1849)

Muhammad 'Ali Pasha (Mehmet Ali) was the viceroy of Ottoman Egypt, conqueror of Sudan, and founder of Egypt's Muhammad

'Ali dynasty, its last dynasty. He was also an important reformer in Egypt. Born in Kavala, a fishing village on the Macedonia coast, he was probably of Albanian ethnic origin. After Muhammad 'Ali's father, Ibrahim Agha, died, he was reared by the governor of Kavala. He married one of the daughters of the governor. She eventually became the mother of five of his ninety-five children. While in Kavala he became involved in the Greek tobacco trade. His experiences with tobacco may have contributed to his commercial interests later in life.

In 1798 Muhammad 'Ali went with an Ottoman expedition to drive the French out of Egypt. As a young officer he fought in battles against the French and British. The French withdrawal from Egypt in 1801 created a power vacuum. Muhammad 'Ali gained control of Egypt and in 1805 was appointed as the Ottoman sultan's *wali* (viceroy) in Egypt, with the rank of pasha ("ruler").

The French invasion initiated great changes in the traditional social structure of Egypt, changes that Muhammad 'Ali found useful to perpetuate. Between 1805 and 1812 he abolished the Mamluk Beys and their obsolete military class. Muhammad 'Ali Pasha's reforms ushered in the modern Egyptian army. He worked to reorganize Egypt after the *nizam jaded* (new order) instituted by Sultan Selim III (1789–1807). He promoted new industry and improved the agricultural system, the irrigation system, and the administrative system in order to strengthen his position within Egypt. In 1818 Muhammad 'Ali destroyed the Wahabbi movement in Arabia. In 1821 he conquered Sudan. He also fought against the Greeks in their war of independence, but his fleet was destroyed at the

Battle of Navarino on October 20, 1827. 'Ali Pasha fought two wars against Sultan Mahmud II (1831–1833 and 1838–1841). He defeated an Ottoman army at the Battle of Nezib (June 24, 1839). However, Britain and other Europeans stopped his expansion and prevented him from making Egypt independent.

In 1841 Muhammad 'Ali's family became an Egyptian dynasty, lasting until King Farouk was dethroned and exiled in July 1952. Muhammad 'Ali died on August 2, 1849 at Alexandria.

Andrew J. Waskey

See also: Africa, Precolonial; Egypt

References

Dodwell, Henry. *The Founder of Modern Egypt: A Study of Muhammad 'Ali.* Cambridge: Cambridge University Press, 1931.
Fahmy, Khaled. *All the Pasha's Men: Mehmed Ali, His Army, and the Making of Modern Egypt.* Cambridge: Cambridge University Press, 1997.

ALI, MUHAMMAD (1942–)

Muhammad Ali was the three-time world heavyweight boxing champion who now travels the world promoting peace and humanitarian causes. Born Cassius Marcellus Clay in Louisville, Kentucky, he won the heavyweight title in 1964, defeating Sonny Liston is what was at the time thought to be one of the greatest upsets in the history of the sport. Immediately following this victory, he revealed publicly that he was a disciple of Elijah Muhammad's Nation of Islam, a Black Nationalist religious organization that promoted racial separatism and stood in contrast to the leading integrationist figures of the Civil Rights Movement like Martin Luther King Jr. Shortly afterwards, he changed his name from

Muhammad Ali (right) and Howard Cosell (left) on "Speaking of Everything with Howard Cosell" on WABC radio in 1965. (Library of Congress)

Cassius Clay to Muhammad Ali, a symbolic rejection of his ties to the slaveholders after which his family had been named.

Three months after he won the championship, Ali left the United States to embark on a month-long tour of Africa, visiting Ghana, where he met with President Kwame N'krumah, Nigeria, and Egypt, where he spoke with President Gamel Abdul Nasser. The trip furthered Ali's belief that he was a world champion whose duty was to represent people all over the globe, not just in the United States.

Ali's most formidable articulation of himself as a worldwide figure occurred during 1966 and 1967, when he resisted being drafted into military service during to the Vietnam War. Ali believed that American intervention in Vietnam was driven by the same forces that had denied blacks first-class citizenship in the United States. He believed that the war was a racist one, a cog in the apparatus that white people around the world had used to conquer and disfranchise nonwhites. His draft resistance and outspoken defiance of the United States government came with a heavy price, as Ali was convicted of draft evasion, sentenced to five years in prison, stripped of his championship, and exiled from boxing for three-and-a-half years. During this period, although he remained out of prison while appealing his case, Ali was unable to box or to leave the country. Nevertheless, he became a hero to millions around the globe who understood that his sacrifice paralleled their own freedom struggles against oppression. His conviction was overturned by the Supreme Court in 1971, paving the way for the resumption of his boxing career.

For the next several years, Ali pursued the championship, eventually earning a match against titleholder George Foreman. The fight was the first world heavyweight championship match held in Africa, and it took place in Kinshasa, Zaire. It was held there because President Mobutu Sese Seko paid $10 million for the right to host the bout, believing that it would bring his country the kind of publicity that would add up to increased tourism and industry for his poverty-stricken nation. The bout also had great symbolic value because it marked the return of the Black Nationalist Ali to Africa, thus materializing his assertions that blacks around the globe were unified in struggle. Although Foreman was heavily favored to retain the crown, Ali scored a stunning knockout in the eighth round, cementing his status not only as an all-time great fighter but as a hero to poor people worldwide.

Michael Ezra

See also: Civil Rights Movement

References

Ali, Muhammad, with Richard Durham. *The Greatest: My Own Story*. New York: Random House, 1975.

Hauser, Thomas. *Muhammad Ali: His Life and Times*. New York: Touchstone, 1991.

Remnick, David. *King of the World: Muhammad Ali and the Rise of an American Hero*. New York: Random House, 1998.

ALI, NOBLE DREW (1886–1929)

Noble Drew Ali was the founder of the Moorish Science Temple Islamic movement and the author of *The Holy Koran of the Moorish Science Temple of America* (1927). Originally named Timothy Drew, he was born in North Carolina in 1886. Ali was self-taught, receiving no formal education. Little is known about his early life except that he worked as a railway expressman in New Jersey. As an adult he visited the Middle East and became a Muslim.

On his return to New Jersey in 1913, he launched an Islamic movement called the Moorish Science Temple. It attracted many blacks, as Ali taught his members that if they were of Asiatic or Moroccan origin, that they were superior to the white man and that they must have their own identity. To further this, he issued identification cards and wrote instructional pamphlets for his followers. In addition, in 1927 he authored his own *Holy Koran*, which contained forty-eight chapters wherein he illustrated his philosophy. He considered himself a new prophet to black Americans.

Ali encouraged his followers to establish businesses to achieve economic independence, to take care of their health, to be industrious, and to invest in the education of their children. He believed that a begging people would never attain success or enjoy a prosperous life. Ali did not advocate the separation of blacks from whites or the emigration of blacks to Africa, as was preached by his predecessor, Marcus Garvey. For Ali, America was the homeland for blacks because they were Americans. He warned his followers against violence. Because of his approach, the American government did not perceive Ali and his movement to be a threat to the government.

The Moorish Science Temple nonetheless expanded and new temples in Philadelphia, New Jersey, Chicago, and Detroit were built. Even though Ali claimed his was an Islamic movement, most perceived it as a nationalist movement with little connection to Islam. Differing from mainstream Muslims, the members of the Moorish Science Temple did not observe the five daily and Friday prayers, nor did they fast in the month of Ramadan. In addition, Ali's followers called him the Prophet rather than the Prophet of Islam, Muhammad bin Abdullah of Mecca. They also believed that Noble Drew Ali's Koran was the Book of Guidance, rather than the Arabic Qur'an. In fact, much of Ali's teachings were actually in contradiction to mainstream Islamic guidelines. Ali was a suspect in the assassination of his rival, Shaikh Claude Green; he himself died a violent death in July 1929 as a result of a beating he received from Green's followers. With Ali's death, prominent members of the Moorish Science Temple fought for leadership positions, killed one another, and ultimately brought on the collapse of the movement. Today, only a few claim to be members of the Moorish Temple, mostly in New York.

Yushau Sodiq

See also: Garvey, Marcus; Islam, African American

References

McCloud, Aminah B. *African American Islam.* New York: Routledge, 1995.

Rashad, Adib. *Islam, Black Nationalism, and Slavery: A Detailed History.* Beltville, MD: Writers Inc., 1995.

Turner, Richard Brent. *Islam in the African American Experience.* Indianapolis: Indiana University Press, 1997.

AMERICA, CENTRAL

Extensive links between Africa and Central America have existed since the first Spanish colonies, and large numbers of people with African ancestry live in the Central American countries of Guatemala, Belize, Honduras, El Salvador, Nicaragua, Costa Rica, and Panama. Most live on the Caribbean coastline of these countries. El Salvador, without an eastern coastline, has the smallest number of people of African descent.

The early Spanish voyages brought slaves to the Caribbean and, soon after, to Central America. There were African slaves on the first Spanish expedition to Guatemala, led by Pedro de Alvarado, in 1524. Alvarado, the governor of Guatemala from 1527 until 1531, was one of the most bloodthirsty of the conquistadors and fought fierce battles resulting in the Spanish conquest of all modern-day Guatemala and much of modern-day El Salvador. Most of the early slaves were used in construction work and in the search for gold. While dying after his horse fell on him during an expedition against the Indians in 1541, he left orders for all his slaves to be freed.

The first documented reference to African slaves being brought for sale in Central America was the arrival of a Spanish ship from Santo Domingo that arrived at San Pedro (Honduras) on January 5, 1543. There is also a report of a ship bringing slaves to Central America two years earlier. Most of these early slaves seem to have been first taken to the West Indies to work on plantations, where they were assigned to do the hard manual labor required. As the Spanish population increased in Central America, some of the slaves were transferred to the region. One reason was the death, mainly from disease, of many Indians, whom the Spanish had initially relied on as manual laborers.

In 1548 all Indian slaves were officially freed (although many became bonded laborers), at which time it was estimated that each Spanish household in San Salvador had about twelve slaves. By 1550 a sufficient number of slaves resided in San Salvador to make some worry that there were too many, and there were also increasing numbers of black freedpersons in the region. Many of the latter worked as day laborers on farms under dreadful conditions, while others worked in domestic service, often alongside slaves. Both they and slaves were involved in the cultivation of indigo and sugar, mining for silver, dock and road construction, and shipbuilding. In isolated parts of the countryside, especially on *estancias* where cattle were bred, the differences in condition between slaves and freedpersons were sometimes minor, with freedpersons working as bonded laborers. In 1570 an account of the Kingdom of Guatemala noted that there were 10,000 blacks and mulattos (descendants of blacks and Europeans) living in it, with African slaves costing 200 pesos, as against an Indian male slave, who would cost only 15 pesos. There are some descriptions of the Africans in Central America during the seventeenth century. Slaves in San Salvador were selling from between 150 and 500 pesos for males and 250 to 500 pesos for females. In some areas slaves dominated the population. In 1610 there were 3,500 African slaves in Panama City alone, with the city having a population of 1,007 whites, 146 mulattos, and 148 free blacks. By contrast, the small town of Cartago, in the central part of Costa Rica, remained largely white, with only 41 blacks out of a total population of 578. Overall, in the Kingdom of Guatemala there were an estimated 20,000 blacks and 10,000 mulattos in the 1650s. By this time the population was being divided, racially, into sixteen

categories. Apart from Europeans, blacks, mulattos, and Indians, the term *mestizo* was being used to define those who were mainly of European or Indian descent, but possibly with some African antecedents; *zambos* and *coyotes* referred to descendants of Indians and Africans. During this period, the number of new slaves being brought to the region from Africa declined considerably and many urban slaves were transferred to work on sugar plantations and *estancias*. The Spanish sought to reduce their reliance on slaves, with many blacks being freed or leaving their owners. The arrival of the English, however, in what was later to become British Honduras (and then Belize), resulted in many Jamaican slaves being brought to the Central American mainland. Some Dutch plantations in Costa Rica also used slaves.

By the eighteenth century most of the slaves in Central America were owned by religious orders, particularly the Dominicans and Jesuits, who operated some of the wealthiest sugar plantations and indigo mills. An account of one sugar plantation and mill near Amatitlán, owned by the Dominicans, noted that there were 900 slaves employed there, and a much smaller number of free blacks who had been exempted from military service and the *corvée* (compulsory labor for public works projects such as road construction). In 1770, three years after the king of Spain had ordered the suppression of the Jesuit order, many slaves that had been owned by the order remained in San Salvador. A 1781 census of the Salvadorean estates noted some 600 blacks working there.

During the second part of the Seven Years' War (1756–1763), the Spanish saw an opportunity to eject the British from their bases along the eastern, Caribbean coast region of Nicaragua, but they failed to do so. The British left of their own accord in 1782 but continued to use slaves in British Honduras until slavery was abolished in the British Empire in 1833. In 1775 slave owners petitioned the colonial authorities to exact harsher penalties on people who harbored escaped slaves, but to no avail. However, measures were adopted to reduce nighttime gatherings of slaves. During this period—the last decades of the eighteenth century—the Spanish were facing many problems regarding the administration of slaves. As slaves could invoke royal *amparo* (protection) for particular grievances, the treatment of them improved considerably. In fact, there are records to show that royal funds were spent in connection with the feeding, doctoring, christening, marriage, and burial of slaves in Central America owned by the king. During the 1790s the Código negro español provided for religious instruction to slaves and also stipulated that slaves working in domestic service should be given an allowance of two pesos a year. It was even possible for a slave of one owner to marry a slave who had a different owner, and once married, the code said, "they should not live apart." However, despite the legal code, only royal and ecclesiastical slaves were ever guaranteed this condition.

Around this time the *garifuna*—blacks of African descent who traced their origins to slave plantations on the Caribbean island of St. Vincent—appeared in Central America. Most of them were moved, en masse, in 1797–1798, by the planters on St. Vincent in response to a sustained pattern of resistance and rebellion. Many were landed at Roatán in the Bay Islands of Honduras and others were moved to British Honduras, where slavery continued

for many years. These new migrants in Honduras were often known as the Caribs, although writers of the period refer to them as Trujillanos (because many blacks lived in the port of Trujillo) and Vincentinos, as well as Morenos. Most made their living from the sea, by fishing, with the vast majority of them residing within less than a mile of the Honduran coast. Some still worked on indigo plantations, but many were involved in the cutting of mahogany. The black populations in the interior had largely assimilated with the Indian population, so few retained a black identity there.

Slave populations continued to decline through the nineteenth century. From 1810 onward there was unrest among many of the elite families of Spanish Central America as nationalist sentiment rose. By 1810, indigo had also replaced cacao as the major export crop, leading to a decline in the demand for slaves. Cacao had needed a labor force all year around, as had sugar. For indigo, however, a large pool of labor was needed for only two months of the year. Therefore, gradually over time, many indigo plantations came to prefer hiring seasonal labor rather than "looking after" slaves for the whole year. Furthermore, indigo did not require much machinery.

On September 15, 1821, the first step toward independence in Central America occurred when Mexico ceded from Spain. In that year a census was held throughout Central America and in one village, Pueblo de los Esclavos (town of slaves), close to the Honduras-Guatemala border, no individual slave owner was mentioned, although 395 men and 376 women, ranging in age from five months to 100 years old, were living in a village that appears to have been established by the colonial authorities. This peculiar demography suggests the complex situation of slavery and freed slaves in Central America.

On June 29, 1823, the Central American Federation—consisting of modern-day Costa Rica, El Salvador, Guatemala, Honduras, and Nicaragua (Panama was a part of Colombia until it gained independence in 1903)—detached itself from Mexico. One of the early actions of the new Central American Federation was to abolish African slavery. This became Article 13 of the Federation's 1824 Constitution, with slaves being declared free on April 17, 1824. Abolition was confirmed by the federation's National Constituent Assembly. Each of the Federation's constituent states ratified the law, led by Costa Rica on May 24, 1824. Part of the reason for abolition was that by this time there were relatively few slaves in Central America, with many farmers more reliant on Indian labor. Sources indicate that there were only 50–200 slaves in Costa Rica and 800 in Guatemala.

During the 1830s many more Africans migrated to Honduras from Grand Cayman, further augmenting the African population of the Bay Islands of Honduras, which became a largely English-speaking Protestant enclave in the country. Some British administrators felt that, as a result, the Bay Islands should become British and, in fact, it was not until 1860 that Britain recognized Honduran sovereignty over them.

Although the Liberals, who dominated the Central American Federation, had freed the slaves, many Africans were concerned about the Liberals' goal of reducing the power of the Roman Catholic Church. As a result, Africans briefly closed the ports of Omoa and Trujillo in a campaign of civil unrest.

Although the former Spanish colonies of Central America had outlawed slavery, it existed in British Honduras, which was under Spanish rule, where slaves were still an important factor in the economy of the settlements. In 1814 the restored Spanish king, Ferdinand VII, had agreed to allow British settlements in British Honduras. Two years later, some Britons tried to carve out territory along the Mosquito Coast of Nicaragua. This latter operation was abandoned. However, many more slaves were brought to British Honduras to make the plantations more viable; in particular, a large number were brought from Barbados. However, this led to trouble in British Honduras, as slaves began protesting against their condition. Gradually, although the number of blacks grew, that of slaves fell. As the total population rose from 2,824 in 1816 to 4,107 in 1826, that of slaves declined from 2,742 to 2,468 during the same period. Part of this resulted from the escape of some slaves from British Honduras to neighboring Guatemala, where slavery had been abolished. The British demanded the return of the slaves. This led to massive internal debate in Guatemala, with Guatemalan politicians being eager to avoid offending Britain but unwilling to hand back the slaves.

During the 1850s American adventurer William Walker led a small band of Americans into Central America. His aim was to provoke U.S. military intervention that, Walker hoped, would result in U.S. annexation of the region. Walker hoped for support from the English-speaking people in Honduras but those of African descent were worried that Walker was a supporter of slavery. Walker made himself president of Nicaragua on July 12, 1856, and some 2,500 American adventurers and mercenaries, along with a number of southern plantation owners, arrived soon afterward. In the year in which he was president of the country, Walker declared English to be the official language of Nicaragua and also legalized slavery. Walker had initially been against slavery but now seems to have felt that its reintroduction would help gain some support for his cause from slave states in the United States. The use of the English language and the legalization of slavery were both very unpopular with Liberals in the country, who had originally offered him some support. They also feared that the United States might annex Nicaragua, a move which Walker might well have hoped for. The Liberals turned against him, and when Walker tried to invade neighboring countries, his forces were driven back. He himself was forced to flee. In 1860 he returned but was captured and handed over to the president of Honduras, who had him executed.

As with the much earlier creation of Liberia in 1847, there were also plans to establish black colonies in Central America. The main reason given to U.S. president Abraham Lincoln—during whose presidency this idea was resurrected—for such colonies was that they could check the British and the Mexicans who might otherwise consider taking over the region for themselves. At that time the French were heavily involved in Mexico with Emperor Maximilian, and Elisha O. Crosby, U.S. minister to Guatemala, claimed that the idea of a colony of "free blacks" would achieve "two good things"—remove large numbers of blacks from the United States and block a possible Mexican expansion. The humanitarian aspect of such a colony does not seem to have been a major consideration. U.S. Postmaster General Montgomery Blair suggested in June 1861

that many black colonists might be moved to some parts of Mexico, but Guatemala seems to have been the favored location.

The Central American countries were rather cautious about these plans, varying from polite interest to opposition. Victoriano Castellanos, the acting president of Honduras, thought it might be a good way of working unused land, especially on the Caribbean coastline. In early 1862 President José María Montealegre of Costa Rica asked his legislative assembly, on hearing of the idea, to investigate whether lands could be set aside for the project. His foreign minister was less convinced and wanted further discussions. By contrast, Nicaragua was hostile, especially when John P. Heiss, a Southern U.S. businessman who had settled in the country, wrote a letter, published in the government-sponsored newspaper, which suggested that these freed slaves might control the local economy with the help and extraterritorial protection of the United States. He never raised any racial objections, however, and it is possible that after Walker's failed bid to take over the country six years earlier and his unpopular plans to reintroduce slavery, Heiss knew that complaints along these lines might fall on deaf ears. Very soon Nicaragua managed to persuade El Salvador and Costa Rica to join them in rejecting the scheme. On October 7, 1862, U.S. Secretary of State William Seward asked Abraham Lincoln to suspend all plans for moving blacks to Central America, and Lincoln agreed.

By the 1860s people of African descent in Central America were living mostly along the Caribbean coastline. They were needed to work on banana plantations, and American and British firms welcomed the fact those who were from the British West

Indies were English-speaking and also mainly Protestant. Initially, many came from Jamaica, which had been undergoing an economic depression since the 1860s, and later many came from the Windward Islands; St. Kitts (in the Leeward Islands); and many other places, including British Guiana and British Honduras. To keep wages low, the companies tended to bring in more immigrants than were actually needed. As the men were brought over on contracts, the British colonial government did not feel any obligation to intervene. However, protests by locals led the Honduras government to start placing restrictions on immigration in 1903. Seven years later, in June 1910, police connected with the Vaccaro brothers' fruit company were involved in the shooting deaths of three black West Indian employees, creating an international incident. The British government complained and eventually, through the arbitration of King Alfonso XIII of Spain, the matter was adjudicated in favor of the British. Tensions remained, and in 1929 the government of Honduras finally banned immigration from the West Indies. Many of the families remained in Honduras and Costa Rica—indeed, one of the highest concentrations of African Costa Ricans is in the city of Limón, on the Caribbean coast, where they work for the United Fruit Company.

Many West Indians of African ancestry moved to Panama to help with the construction of the Panama Canal. Most faced considerable discrimination and worked in terrible conditions during the canal's construction. There were also many black residents and employees of the Canal Zone who, although technically Panamanian citizens, came from the West Indies, were English-speaking, and Protestant. When the United States ended its control of the canal, many chose to leave Panama, but a large number remained.

Although many of the people of African descent in the former Spanish colonies in Central America had long since lost their connections with Africa, many of the British administrators in British Honduras had served in Africa. Robert W. Harley, the lieutenant governor from 1882 until 1884, had been administrator in the Gold Coast, in modern-day Ghana. Of the governors, Cornelius Moloney had been administrator in Gambia and governor of Lagos (Nigeria) before becoming governor of British Honduras in 1891–1897; Ernest Sweet-Escott had been administrator of the Seychelles before being transferred to British Honduras in 1904; his successor, Eric John Eagles Swayne, had been governor of British Somaliland. Harold Baxter Kittermaster, who was governor from 1932 to 1934, had been governor of British Somaliland, later becoming governor of Nyasaland; his successor, Alan Cuthbert Maxwell Burns, who was governor from 1934 to 1940, went on to be governor of the Gold Coast and then of Nigeria. John Hawkesworth, the first post–World War II governor of British Honduras, had been chief commissioner of Ashanti; his successor, Patrick M. Renison, went on to be the penultimate governor of Kenya; and John W. Paul, governor from 1966 until 1972, had been governor of Gambia.

Since the 1970s there has been massive interest, not only locally, but also worldwide, in African musical styles from Central America. Some musicologists have found similarities between the music in Belize and the rhythms from southeast Nigeria from where, it is believed, many of the slaves may have originally come—especially River

State, Efiks, and Calabris. Blended with Western instruments, the music is now known as *brukdown*. There is also *paranda,* a style that tends to be even more African. A leading figure in Belize's music scene, Andy Palacio, offers an English-Garifuna style popular in the United States, Cuba, Britain, and West Africa.

Although there are other *garifuna* musicians and singers in Central America, especially in Honduras, none have achieved much fame beyond their locality. Much of their music, known locally as the *congo,* features upright drums and a female call-and-response chorus. A few writers have pointed out similarities with some black Cuban and Haitian music. The other type of African music common in Central America is based on the calypso of the West Indies. Dance in Honduras is also heavily influenced by the rhythm of African music.

The place of Africans in Central America has received heightened scholarly interest beginning in the latter half of the twentieth century. Prominent are Wilbur Zelinsky's study, "The Historical Geography of the Negro Population of Latin America" (1949), and more recently, William V. Davidson's "The Garifuina of Pearl Lagoon" (1980), a study of an historically African American town in Nicaragua. Such studies demonstrate the complex historical and cultural mixtures that characterize the African experience in Central America.

Justin Corfield

References

Davidson, William W. "The Garifuina of Pearl Lagoon: Ethnohistory of an Afro-American Enclave in Nicaragua." *Ethnohistory* 27, no. 1 (1980): 31–47.

DiLorenzo, Kris. "The Blacks of Central America." *Crisis* 93, no. 6 (1986): 28–31, 34, 60–62.

Echeverri-Gent, Elisavinda. "Forgotten Workers: British West Indians and the Early Days of the Banana Industry in Costa Rica and Honduras." *Journal of Latin American Studies* 24, no. 2 (May 1992): 275–308.

Fiehrer, Thomas. "Slaves and Freedmen in Colonial Central America: Rediscovering a Forgotten Black Past." *Journal of Negro History* 64, no. 1 (1979): 39–58.

Gabbert, Wolfgang. "Cultural Cleavages in Central America: The Case of the Afro-Americans and the National State in Costa Rica." *Asien, Afrika, Latinamerika* (Switzerland) 27, no. 2 (1999): 159–178.

Leiva Vivas, Rafael. *Trafico de esclavos negros a Honduras.* Tegucigalpa, Honduras: Editorial Guaymuras, 1982.

Mellafe, Rolando. *Negro Slavery in Latin America.* Berkeley: University of California Press, 1975.

Rout, Leslie B., Jr. *The African Experience in Spanish America: 1502 to the Present Day.* Cambridge: Cambridge University Press, 1976.

Schoonover, Thomas. "Misconstrued Mission: Expansionism and Black Colonization in Mexico and Central America during the Civil War." *Pacific Historical Review* 49, no. 4 (1980): 607–620.

Stone, Michael Cutler. "The Afro-Caribbean Presence in Central America." *Belizean Studies* 18, nos. 2–3 (1990): 6–42.

Westerman, George W. "Historical Notes on West Indians on the Isthmus of Panama." *Phylon* 22 (Winter 1961): 340–350.

Zelinsky, Wilbur. "The Historical Geography of the Negro Population of Latin America." *Journal of Negro History* 34 (April 1949): 153–221.

AMERICAN COLONIZATION SOCIETY

As early as the colonial period, repatriation was considered a favorable solution to the perceived problems posed by a growing free black population in what would become the United States. Southern whites feared that large groups of freed African Americans living in their midst would encourage slave insurrection and lead to

African village in Liberia established by the American Colonization Society, ca. 1822. (Library of Congress)

miscegenation. In the North, many resented the competition that freed blacks created in the urban labor market. Meanwhile, the American Revolution forced many to apply rights theory to the plight of the African American, and the abolitionist movement was well underway by the dawn of the nineteenth century. A number of diverse interests, then, were present in Washington, D.C., in December 1816, when the American Colonization Society (ACS) was founded.

The ACS's ultimate goal was to establish a colony along the West African coast, and it called upon the federal government to allocate resources to facilitate settlement of African Americans. To appease slaveholding legislators and philanthropists, the ACS emphasized that it was not opposed to slavery and asserted that free blacks, not slaves, posed the greatest threat to society.

However, a number of ACS supporters believed that by repatriating African Americans, whites could begin to undo some of the wrongs committed during the Atlantic slave trade. Nevertheless, land was ceded along the Atlantic coast for the repatriation of free blacks only, to be named Liberia after the Latin word for "freedom." The first ACS-sponsored voyage to Liberia left in 1820.

The American Colonization Society administered the colony of Liberia until its independence in 1847. While the Americo-Liberians had initiated efforts to patrol the Atlantic coastline, where slave trading continued despite a U.S. ban, southern U.S. legislators accused them of undermining their slave-based economy. As the debate over states' rights raged in the United States, the federally funded ACS found itself on the defensive. It reiterated that the organization sought only to remove African Americans from the country, not to bring about an end to slavery. This line brought them into conflict with American and British abolitionists. William Lloyd Garrison led the charge against the ACS, accusing it of pandering to politicians and of racism and hypocrisy for characterizing African Americans as "nuisances" while expecting them to "civilize" native African Liberians. Garrison's criticism contributed to a marked decrease in migration to Liberia during the 1840s, as well as to the withdrawal of funding by the ACS's American and British benefactors. A weakened ACS, combined with increased Americo-Liberian calls for self-determination, hastened Liberian independence.

Carmen Lenore Wright

See also: Abolitionism; Delany, Martin Robinson; Liberia

References

Beyan, Amos J. *The American Colonization Society and the Creation of the Liberian State: A Historical Perspective, 1822–1900.* Lanham, MD: University Press of America, 1991.

Smith, James. *Sojourners in Search of Freedom: The Settlement of Liberia by Black Americans.* Lanham, MD: University Press of America, 1987.

AMERICAN FREEDMEN'S INQUIRY COMMISSION

The American Freedmen's Inquiry Commission is a bureau that was established to determine the social conditions resulting from the emancipation of American slaves in 1863. In response to Abraham Lincoln's 1863 Emancipation Proclamation freeing African Americans in Confederate-held territory from the bondage of slavery, the U.S. secretary of war, Edwin M. Stanton, established the American Freedmen's Inquiry Commission in March 1863. Stanton appointed three commissioners with the task of collecting testimony to determine the best course of action to protect and improve the lives of freed African Americans. The commission was composed of Samuel Gridley Howe, James McKaye, and Indiana U.S. representative Robert Dale Owen, all social reformers and abolitionists. The commission collected testimony from army personnel, slaveholders, government officials, abolitionists, and former slaves throughout the United States and Canada. From the testimonies of these individuals and visits made to different parts of the United States and Canada, the commission was able to determine the social conditions resulting from emancipation.

The commission drafted three preliminary reports before submitting its final version to the secretary of war on May 15, 1864. The commission believed that emancipation would not be complete until full civil and political rights were established for all freed African Americans. To ensure civil and political rights, the commission suggested the establishment of a temporary government agency to assist former slaves in their transition to freedom. The Bureau of Refugees, Freedmen, and Abandoned Lands, known as the Freedmen's Bureau, distributed food, clothing, provided medical assistance, leased abandoned and confiscated land, and helped establish educational opportunities for African Americans.

Michael LaMagna

See also: Civil War, American; Emancipation Proclamation

References

Blassingame, John W. *Slave Testimony: Two Centuries of Letters, Speeches, Interviews, and Autobiographies.* Baton Rouge: Louisiana State University Press, 1977.

Frankel, Oz. "The Predicament of Racial
Knowledge: Government Studies of the
Freedmen during the U.S. Civil War."
Social Research 70, no. 1 (2003): 45–81.

Sproat, John G. "Blueprint for Radical
Reconstruction." *Journal of Southern
History* 23, no. 1 (1957): 25–44.

AMERICAN MISSIONARY ASSOCIATION

The American Missionary Association
(AMA) was founded after the *Amistad*
affair by prominent abolitionists to work
for the end of slavery. In addition to its
antislavery work, it also founded ten black
colleges to provide higher education to
African Americans during and after the
Civil War. Founded in 1846 through the
consolidation of various abolitionist
societies, the American Missionary Association was a nondenominational organization with the goal of ending slavery.
Although the association claimed not to
be affiliated with a particular religion, the
strong connection between the AMA and
the Congregational Church was apparent.
The origin of the AMA can be traced to
the *Amistad* affair of 1839, an incident
wherein Africans aboard the slave ship *La
Amistad* mutinied against their Spanish
captors off the coast of Cuba. Established
to defend the Africans, members of the
Amistad Committee, including Lewis
Tappan and Simeon Jocelyn, later joined
together to form the AMA. The commitment of the AMA to social justice and the
abolition of slavery can be seen in the
assistance its members provided to freed
slaves.

The legacy of the AMA is the educational opportunities it provided African
Americans during and after the Civil War.
It opened over 500 schools at all educational levels throughout the South. Eventually, the AMA transferred control of its
elementary and secondary schools to the
local public school systems and focused on
higher education for African Americans.
This resulted in the establishment of the
predominately black colleges of Atlanta
University, Berea College, Dillard University, Fisk University, Hampton University,
LeMoyne-Owen College, Talladega College,
and Tougaloo College. The commitment of
the AMA to promoting equality was not
limited to African Americans; they also
worked on behalf of Native Americans, immigrant groups, and others.

Michael La Magna

See also: Abolitionism; *Amistad* Case, The

References

DeBoer, Clara Merritt. *Be Jubilant My Feet:
African American Abolitionists in the
American Missionary Association,
1839–1861.* New York: Garland
Publishing, 1994.

Richardson, Joe Martin. *Christian
Reconstruction: The American Missionary
Association and Southern Blacks,
1861–1890.* Athens: University of Georgia
Press, 1986.

AMERICAN REVOLUTION

"I do hereby further declare all indentured
Servants, Negroes, and others . . . free, that
are able and willing to bear Arms"
(Lanning, 2000, p. 201). With this Proclamation of 1775, John Murray, earl of
Dunmore and royal governor of Virginia,
officially invited all men of African descent
to join the British in their efforts to suppress Patriot insurgencies. Blacks fought in
substantial numbers for both the Royal and
Continental armies during the American
Revolution (1775–1783), most often giving their allegiance to whichever side they
felt would best ensure their freedom.
Dunmore's decision to free Virginia's slaves

By his Excellency the Right Honourable JOHN Earl of DUNMORE, his Majesty's Lieutenant and Governour-General of the Colony and Dominion of Virginia, and Vice-Admiral of the same:

A PROCLAMATION.

AS I have ever entertained Hopes that an Accommodation might have taken Place between *Great Britain* and this Colony, without being compelled, by my Duty, to this most disagreeable, but now absolutely necessary Step, rendered so by a Body of armed Men, unlawfully assembled, firing on his Majesty's Tenders, and the Formation of an Army, and that Army now on their March to attack his Majesty's Troops, and destroy the well-disposed Subjects of this Colony: To defeat such treasonable Purposes, and that all such Traitors, and their Abetters, may be brought to Justice, and that the Peace and good Order of this Colony may be again restored, which the ordinary Course of the civil Law is unable to effect, I have thought fit to issue this my Proclamation, hereby declaring, that until the aforesaid good Purposes can be obtained, I do, in Virtue of the Power and Authority to me given, by his Majesty, determine to execute martial Law, and cause the same to be executed throughout this Colony; and to the End that Peace and good Order may the sooner be restored, I do require every Person capable of bearing Arms, to resort to his Majesty's S T A N-DARD, or be looked upon as Traitors to his Majesty's Crown and Government, and thereby become liable to the Penalty the Law inflicts upon such Offences, such as Forfeiture of Life, Confiscation of Lands, &c. &c. And I do hereby farther declare all indented Servants, Negroes, or others (appertaining to Rebels) free, that are able and willing to bear Arms, they joining his Majesty's Troops, as soon as may be, for the more speedily reducing this Colony to a proper Sense of their Duty, to his Majesty's Crown and Dignity. I do farther order, and require, all his Majesty's liege Subjects to retain their Quitrents, or any other Taxes due, or that may become due, in their own Custody, till such Time as Peace may be again restored to this at present most unhappy Country, or demanded of them for their former salutary Purposes, by Officers properly authorised to receive the same.

GIVEN under my Hand, on Board the Ship William, *off* Norfolk, *the* 7th *Day of* November, *in the* 16th *Year of his Majesty's Reign.*

D U N M O R E.

G O D SAVE THE K I N G.

Lord Dunmore's Proclamation of November 1775, giving freedom to all Virginia slaves who are willing to take up arms for the British cause. (Library of Congress)

was counter to Continental commander-in-chief George Washington's initial impulse to keep African Americans from participating in the war. Within weeks of Dunmore's address, several hundred blacks had volunteered to fight in Dunmore's Ethiopian Regiment, and by the end of the war, more than 2,000 slaves enlisted in this unit.

When the thirteen American colonies broke away from Great Britain in 1775, nearly 20 percent of the residents of the United States were of African descent, the vast majority of them enslaved. Despite General Washington's ambivalence about the enlistment of African American soldiers, blacks fought valiantly for the Patriot side from the onset of the conflict. Crispus

Attucks, a young sailor and former slave, was killed during the Boston Massacre (1770) when British troops fired on a riot. African Americans participated alongside Continental forces in the early battles at Lexington, Concord, and Bunker Hill in 1775. By 1777, General Washington had altered his position on the enlistment of blacks. Faced with a shortage of troops, Washington was forced to incorporate African Americans into his war effort, and by the end of the Revolution, more than 5,000 blacks had served in the Continental army and navy. Agrippa Hull, Price Hall, Cornelius Lenox Remond, and Cuff Whitmore were among the many African Americans who served with distinction for the American cause.

Nevertheless, more blacks died fighting for Britain, many being slaves recruited away from their American owners by the British army. While the lure of freedom was strong, escape was extremely dangerous for slaves. In 1740 South Carolina passed a law that permitted whites to kill any slave caught outside of his owner's premises—even if the slave did not resist arrest. In 1755 Georgia enacted a similar code, whereby rewards were given for the bodies of dead male slaves. For those slaves who did make it safely to the British lines, there was no guarantee of protection. According to Boston King, a former slave who later recorded his experiences, Loyalist commanders were often known to leave ill African Americans to die or heal on their own. Yet African Americans proved invaluable to the British, especially as guerrilla fighters who could carry out attacks on the communities of their former owners. Colonel Tye was the most renowned of these combatants. Originally a slave in Monmouth County, New Jersey, Tye escaped and joined

Dunmore's Ethiopian Regiment in 1775. With his special knowledge of local terrain and facilities, Tye led raids on Patriot homes, where food and fuel were stolen in surprise attacks. Although the British never officially commissioned blacks, Tye eventually joined a group called the Black Brigade, which was instrumental in the efforts to protect New York City in the latter years of the war.

Both the Continental and Royal navies also sought the services of black men. As many as 25 percent of the African Americans who participated in the Revolution worked on ships; escaped slaves often went to sea in order to reduce the chances of being captured by their former owners. Though African American sailors were most often assigned to common labor (they were much cheaper to hire than whites), their efforts as pilots benefited both navies. The vast majority of black sailors worked in the vicinity of Maryland and Virginia, and in some instances, white Patriots were allowed to avoid enlistment if they substituted one of their slaves to serve in their place.

In 1782 Britain and the United States came to terms on a treaty that allowed for American independence. As part of the agreement, British forces were required to return any property—including slaves—that was taken from Patriots during the war. Sir Guy Carleton, acting commander of the British forces, would not grant this request, as his government had promised freedom to anyone who fought for the British cause. In order to create an official record of those who had participated in the war, British brigadier general Samuel Birch began to document the names of black Loyalists in "The Book of Negroes." At the end of the war, approximately 4,000 black men, women, and children left the United States for the United Kingdom, Jamaica, and Nova Scotia. (Many of those who relocated to Nova Scotia were uncomfortable in North America and eventually fled to Sierra Leone.) Other black Loyalists were unsuccessful in their attempts to leave the United States, and like many blacks who fought for the Patriot side, they eventually migrated to Florida or American Indian territories. Although over 100,000 slaves escaped during the war, a great number of these men and women were returned to slavery after the conflict. And while Vermont had banned slavery as early as 1777 and was soon followed by other northern states, slave owners in the American South continued to import slaves to replace those who escaped during the Revolution. Despite the fact that the Declaration of Independence (1776) espoused democracy and personal liberty, approximately 20 percent of the American population would be denied the rights of citizenship for almost another century.

Clark Barwick

See also: Attucks, Crispus; Nova Scotia, Black Refugees in

References

Horton, James Oliver, and Lois E. Horton. *In Hope of Liberty: Culture, Community, and Protest among Northern Free Blacks, 1700–1860.* New York: Oxford University Press, 1997.

Knoblock, Glenn A. *"Strong and Brave Fellows": New Hampshire's Black Soldiers and Sailors of the American Revolution, 1775–1784.* Jefferson, NC: McFarland, 2003.

Lanning, Michael Lee. *Defenders of Liberty: African Americans in the Revolutionary War.* New York: Citadel Press, 2000.

Quarles, Benjamin. *The Negro in the American Revolution.* New York: Norton, 1973.

AMISTAD CASE, THE

The *Amistad* case was a nineteenth-century trial that defined issues of property and rights in the United States in relation to the transatlantic slave trade. A Spanish schooner named *Amistad* left Havana for Port Principe, Cuba, on June 28, 1839. The ship carried a captain, cook, crew, two "owners" of African captives, the captain's slave, and fifty-three African captives, including forty-nine men, three girls, and a boy. The captives had been recently kidnapped from West Africa and brought to Havana aboard the slaver, *Tecora*. Four days out of the harbor during the voyage from Havana to Port Principe, the African captives, in the middle of a stormy night, revolted and took over the ship. One African, Sengbe Pieh, whom the Spanish men named Joseph Cinque before he entered the *Amistad* ship, led the rebellion. The captain and cook were killed, and two of the crew were either killed or escaped in a small boat. Two of the captives were killed as well. The Africans spared the two "owners," Jose Ruiz and Pedro Montes, since, having little or no contact with the modern sea vessel, they needed assistance in operating the ship. Threatening the two white men, Cinque forced them to steer the ship back to Africa under careful watch, ensuring that they were moving eastward. However, the whites, discussing in their own language strategies to rebel, began to move the ship north and west during the night, when the sun was down and the stars, a navigational tool unknown to the blacks, were out. For almost two months, the rebels and their former "owners" sailed and drifted within the vast waters of the Atlantic, pushing and pulling the ship east during the day and northwest during the night.

On August 26, 1839, Cinque and a few other Africans, seeking food and water, anchored the ship off the shore of Montauk Point on Long Island, New York, and went ashore with a few gold doubloons that they had found on the ship. Shortly after, Lieutenants Richard W. Mead and Thomas R. Gedney, patrolling the coastal waters aboard the U.S. Navy's *Washington,* spotted the tattered ship. They found a large number of blacks and two whites aboard it, along with gold doubloons and other valuables. As this situation seemed unusual to the military men, they disarmed the blacks, arrested them, and towed the ship and its contents to New London, Connecticut. After an initial hearing regarding what had happened on the ship, Judge Andrew T. Judson announced that a September hearing would decide if the blacks should stand trial for murder. All the blacks, with no one to post bond, were transported to the nearby New Haven jail.

During the first hearing in mid-September 1839, Judge Smith Thompson of the District Court of Connecticut in Hartford ruled that the case was to be tried in Connecticut, but since the incident occurred on the high seas and did not involve U.S. citizens, the courts had no jurisdiction regarding the murders. However, the issue of whether or not the slaves were property would be decided in another trial. After the initial trial, abolitionists supporting the slaves hired Josiah W. Gibbs, professor of linguistics at Yale College, to assist in breaking the language barrier that was obstructing the Africans' voices. Gibbs, after learning some of the Mende language from Cinque, found James Covey, a Mende native, freed captive from a slaver, and sailor for a British patrol ship. Covey agreed to serve as a translator for the *Amistad* Africans.

The second trial, which began on November 19, 1839, in Hartford, was postponed after two days, until January 7, 1840. The defense lawyers presented witnesses to support their claim that the *Amistad* captives were not from Cuba but from Africa, and since the international slave trade had been abolished the act of transporting the Africans was illegal. Professor Gibbs testified that the captives did not speak Spanish, but only Mende. Judge Andrew T. Judson announced on January 13, 1840, that the *Amistad* captives were born free and thus should be delivered to President Martin Van Buren for transport back to Africa. The defense team appealed the case to the U.S. Supreme Court, and a third trial took place. Tappan gained assistance from former president John Quincy Adams, who argued brilliantly on behalf of the captives. Justice Joseph Story, on March 9, 1841, announced that the *Amistad* blacks were kidnapped Africans and that they could either stay in America as free blacks or return to Africa. The group, which became known as the *Amistad* Africans via newspapers and magazines, decided to return to Africa and arrived in Sierra Leone in mid-January 1842.

John Kille

See also: Abolitionism; Slave Revolts/Maronnage; Slavery (History)

References

Cable, Mary. *Black Odyssey: The Case of the Slave Ship Amistad.* New York: Penguin, 1971.

Chase-Riboud, Barbara. *Echo of Lions.* New York: Morrow, 1989.

Jones, Howard. *Mutiny on the Amistad: The Saga of a Slave Revolt and Its Impact on American Abolition, Law, and Diplomacy.* New York: Oxford University Press, 1986.

Owens, William A. *Slave Mutiny: The Story of the Revolt on the Schooner Amistad.* New York: John Day, 1953.

ANANSE

A spider-trickster and hero of the folktales from the Akan ethnic group (in modern Ghana) who was transported with the slave trade to many areas of the Americas, Ananse (also spelled "Anancy," "Anansi," "Annancy," "Nancy," and "Nansi") has remained a protagonist of Afro-Caribbean lore. He is also still employed in various ways by contemporary Ghanaian, Caribbean, and black British writers.

Like other human and animal tricksters from all over the world, the Akan spider (also existing under different names in several West African groups' tales) profanes all ethical and religious beliefs by being selfish, mean, hypocritical, vulgar, and sexually exuberant—his only goal being the satisfaction of his own biological needs. At the same time, though, Ananse helps focus attention on the nature and limits of the taboos he breaks, thus creatively regenerating them. When he is sentenced to death by the sky-god Nyame for one of his mischievous tricks, Ananse tells his son Ntikuma to dig a tunnel underground, dive into it, and make an appeal for his father's life: believing that he is hearing the voice of the earth goddess Asaase Yaa, Nyame frees Ananse. In this case the spider-trickster ridicules the supreme deity, but at the same time he brings to the fore the validity of the balance between earth and sky, Asaase and Nyame, female and male element—a fundamental principle in Akan society. Ananse here assumes a role as link between the physical and the supernatural dimensions, but sometimes he becomes a creator or, better, a catalyst of creation, thanks to the etiological endings of his tales. Further functions carried out by his tales include enabling children to develop autonomy and peer relations, acting as a safety valve for social attrition, and entertaining.

Ananse's import for contemporary Ghanaian authors became particularly evident during the independence period, when the national policy of recovering native cultures led many playwrights (such as Efua Sutherland, Joe De Graft, Martin Owusu, and Yaw Asare) to abandon Western naturalistic models and to include the storytelling format—and therefore Ananse—in their plays. The disillusionment of the following historical phase was conveyed by the Ghanaian novelist Ayi Kwei Armah in his *Fragments* (1969), where Ananse becomes symbolic of the greed for material wealth that is corrupting the ideals of independence. Ananse's multifaceted nature, then, allows various, if not opposed, forms of borrowing by writers at the turn of the twenty-first century.

The Middle Passage transported Ananse to many Caribbean areas: his presence is registered in the slaves' lore from Barbados, Belize, Costa Rica, Curaçao, Haiti, Jamaica, Suriname, Trinidad, and the Virgin Islands, among other places; in the United States, he survived as the African American female trickster Ann Nancy (or Aunt Nancy) from South Carolina and Georgia. In the new, ruthless context of Caribbean plantations, Ananse sheds his godlike qualities and acquires more earthly features. His subtle cunning, the art of the weak, is used not only to ensure sheer survival, but also to deceive and overthrow the powerful. In one of the most common tales, he boasts that Tiger is no more than his riding horse. When Tiger confronts him, he pretends to be sick and asks Tiger to carry him on his back so that he can meet the people and deny what he has said; Tiger accepts, and is thus humiliated when the spider rides him like a horse. In the entertaining storytelling sessions among slaves, Ananse's outwitting of bigger animals could be seen as a vicarious rebellion against slave owners and overseers.

Yet the rawness of slavery keeps the tales firmly anchored to an extreme realism: sometimes Ananse is defeated; he also outwits weaker creatures (presumably standing for fellow slaves); and his cruelty could occasionally be identified with the overseer's. Once again, his attributes include extreme opposites, and the spider-trickster may represent, for a slave audience, its hero, object of hatred, and scapegoat all at the same time. Generally speaking, Ananse shows how cunning and indirection are necessary tactics for surviving in a racist and dangerous environment. From the start of the twentieth century, Walter Jekyll, Martha Warren Beckwith, and Philip Sherlock successfully popularized "Anancy tales" in print. Laura Tanna's *Jamaican Folktales and Oral Histories* (1984), a result of tale-collecting fieldwork from 1974 to the early 1980s, proves that the tradition is still alive, albeit dormant.

In a pattern similar to what happened in Ghana, the emergence of Ananse in Caribbean written literature after a long period of colonial neglect coincided with the recognition of the literary dignity of folk forms. This recognition was pioneered by the popularization of tales and poems in dialect by Louise Bennett through books, drama, radio, and television. Contemporary works that have found inspiration in Ananse's role as a sly underdog include V. S. Reid's historical novel, *New Day* (1949), where shrewd Anansean strategy is suggested as the way Jamaican self-government in 1944 was attained, and Trevor Rhone's play *Smile Orange* (1971), where the hotel waiter Ringo astutely exploits tourists to improve his status. Ananse's bossy connotations are best rendered through the ambiguous politician Arthur in *Couvade* (1974), a play by Michael Gilkes.

Contemporary Caribbean authors have also creatively developed Ananse's folkloric features into new forms. Some depart from the misogyny that often characterizes Ananse lore to infuse the spider's adventures with a gender-oriented significance, as in Velma Pollard's poem "Anansa" (1988). Wilson Harris transforms Ananse's metamorphic powers—traditionally, he can change from spider to man and modify his own shape—into a linguistic technique, namely a prose that erodes any fixed polarization, thus merging different characters, reality and dream, in the oneiric ambience of the Guyanese forest. A similar "Anansean technique" can be found in the novels by the Ghanaian Kojo Laing, while Edward Kamau Brathwaite identifies such a transformative potential with the attitude of disruptive creativity that poetry should always have toward its language. Andrew Salkey published three volumes of stories in which the spider-trickster is confronted with contemporary issues such as nuclear weapons or the Vietnam War, whereas Roy Heath turns him into the bizarre simpleton protagonist of his two novels, *Kwaku* (1982) and *The Ministry of Hope* (1997). Finally, black British authors such as John Agard, Maggie Harris, and Beryl Gilroy employ Ananse as an image capable of reactivating a link with their Afro-Caribbean roots.

Pietro Deandrea

See also: Akan; Bennett, Louise; Caribbean Literature; Folklore, African; Gilroy, Beryl Agatha

References

Agard, John. *Weblines*. Newcastle, UK: Bloodaxe, 2000.

Pelton, Robert D. *The Trickster in West Africa—A Study in Mythic Irony and Sacred Delight*. Berkeley: University of California Press, 1980.

Salkey, Andrew. *Anancy's Score*. London: Bogle-L'Ouverture, 1973.

Sutherland, Efua Theodora. *The Marriage of Anansewa*. Harlow, UK: Longman, 1975.

Tanna, Laura. *Jamaican Folktales and Oral Histories*. Kingston: Institute of Jamaica Publications, 1984.

Tiffin, Helen. "The Metaphor of Anancy in Caribbean Literature." In *Myth and Metaphor,* edited by Robert Sellick. Adelaide, Australia: Centre for Research in the New Literatures in English, 1982.

ANCESTOR WORSHIP

Ancestor worship is the anthropological term for veneration of ancestors in African religions. In his anthropological work, *Principles of Sociology* (1885), Herbert Spencer coined the term "ancestor worship" to understand the relationship between members of a community that celebrated their departed members through sacrifice and offering. Although many African cultures honor their ancestors through libations and the giving of food, some scholars have questioned the appropriateness of applying the term wholesale to African religions. Nonetheless, the veneration of the dead is a central practice of most African communities. The offerings of food and drink symbolize the continuation of the relationship between surviving and departed members of the community, the latter being still viewed as a central component of the family, sometimes having a larger role and impact in the community than the living. The rituals spiritually bond the ancestors to their surviving family members and are symbolized through the exchange of gifts and favors. The ancestors often continue the role they played in the community while alive, such as a maternal or paternal role. Not only do the living desire to honor their departed, but the ancestors also desire to be remembered and venerated in the community. As keepers of the customs and laws, ancestors play an important role in the present. As such, most African traditions prioritize continued communication with the dead. Because of the presumed continuity in family relationships, the term "worship" becomes even more problematic. Because of the fluidity of many African religions, it is difficult to isolate the veneration of ancestors from the larger cultural context and components of the African cosmology.

In contrast to many Western traditions, death in many African cultures is a gradual process, and the boundaries between the natural and supernatural realms are blurred. After physical death, the departed individual remains a part of the community through the memories of friends and relatives. If the dead person appears in the community, she or he must be recognized by name. In many cultures, the current members must have had a direct experience of the individual while she or he was alive and be able to recall the individual's name, personal traits, values, words, and important life moments. In general, the departed appears only to the eldest members of their family and very rarely to the young. In some cultures, the appearance of a particular insect or animal such as a caterpillar or hyena may also indicate the arrival of an ancestor. Ancestors also visit living members through dreams and divination. If neglected, the departed can bring tragedy upon the community to draw

attention to the neglected elements of the relationship, forcing the living to respond and correct the situation through prayer and offering. In most cultures, the rituals are performed as preventative measures rather than in response to calamity. Similarly, the ancestors do not seek to harm their descendants, but to guard life and warn them of potential trouble. Ultimately, misfortune serves to restore harmony in the community. Religious specialists in the community are often the ones who analyze and diagnose the cause of the misfortune. Good family health, prosperity, survival to adulthood, and a good birthrate would all be seen as signs of harmonious relationships with the ancestors. As long as the dead are recognized by a member of the community, they may appear for as long as four or five generations.

Because the eldest member of the community most often knew the departed for the longest period of time, she or he often performs or supervises the ritual ceremonies to honor the dead. Often a symbolic meal is served as an act of remembrance. The sacrifices offered to the departed are particularly important, because living members who have forgotten their ancestors face illness or misfortune from their mistreated dead family members. However, in most societies a central virtue of ancestors is patience, and therefore calamity comes only after all other reminders are exhausted. The role of sacrifice is not to exile the ancestors or limit their power, but to restore the relationship and receive blessings from their descendants. Ancestors can also intervene in the community unprovoked and can be scolded by the living for their unwarranted behavior and intrusion in the community. After the last individual who knew the dead person dies, the departed becomes completely dead and moves outside of immediate familial ties. Rather than vanishing out of existence, the departed become part of the spirit world. While they may still appear to living members or speak through a medium, in most African societies ancestors become part of the intermediary spirits between a God (High God), sometimes referred to as the Great Ancestor, and human beings.

Until that point, ancestors play a large role in daily life. Presenting proper sacrifice and offering, carrying out the instructions of ancestors given either while they were alive or during an after-death experience, becomes essential to maintaining harmony in the family and community. Because of the ancestors' continued influence in the community, children were believed, in many African societies, to bare the physical and personality traits of departed members. It follows that children are named after ancestors and are expected to go into the profession or sphere of life in which the departed excelled. In this way, the spirit of the ancestor continues to influence the present and future of the community.

Because of this view of death, marriage becomes essential to ensuring that persons, through the memories of their children, will remain a part of the community. Barrenness is seen as a curse, since it limits the continuation and rebirth of ancestors in the children of the community. Burial rites are very important, because if they are absent or incorrectly performed, the transition of the dead to the spirit realm can be delayed and the dead may wander the world as ghosts. In many societies, the burial rites are a long process that includes the preparation of the body, which is often expensive, a wake, several periods of mourning, and elaborate decorations for the grave,

often including the personal items of the deceased person or objects or activities that they enjoyed. While the offerings and ceremonies range from simple to more formal rituals and sacrifices, the veneration of the ancestors is a prevalent trait in most African societies.

Julius Bailey

See also: Akan; Burial, African Practices in the Americas; Religion (Africa)

References

Magesa, Laurenti. *African Religion: The Moral Traditions of Abundant Life.* Maryknoll, NY: Orbis Books, 1998.

Mbiti, John S. *The Prayers of African Religion.* Maryknoll, NY: Orbis Books, 1975.

Mbiti, John S. *African Religions and Philosophy.* Portsmouth, NH: Heinemann, 1999.

ANGOLA

Located on the southwest coast of Africa, the Republic of Angola has a population of approximately 10,978,000, with 40 percent of the country covered by forests and woodlands. The Portuguese arrived in the region in 1482 and gradually took over first the coastal areas and then the hinterland. In 1589 a Portuguese governor was appointed, and Angola remained a Portuguese colony until November 11, 1975, when it gained its independence. Owing to its connections with Portugal, Angola had many ties with Brazil in terms of trade, shipping, and cultural exchanges. Some of the early Portuguese seafarers sailed from Angola to Brazil, with Angola being a source of slaves for South America. One of the men who sold Angolan slaves to French military establishments in the Caribbean was Pierre Escourre from Bordeaux. Later, Angola was also a source of cuttings and seedlings for agricultural crops that were developed in Brazil. When Angola was a Portuguese colony, a number of Brazilians came to work in there, and in 1974, when the bulk of the white population of Angola was airlifted out of the country, quite a number settled in Brazil.

U.S. missionaries have long been interested in Angola, especially after U.S. journalist Henry Morton Stanley passed through a part of Angola in 1877 after locating David Livingstone. William Taylor (1821–1902), from Rockbridge County, Virginia, was elected a missionary bishop of the Methodist Episcopal Church in 1884, and for the next twelve years he supervised missionaries going to, among other places, Angola. One of these, Héli Chatelain (1859–1908), was born in Switzerland but moved to New Jersey where he studied theology. Becoming a U.S. citizen, in 1889–1890 he was in Angola as a guide and translator for the American Eclipse Mission and was U.S. consul in Louanda (now Luanda) in 1891–1892. Returning to the United States, he was the author of several linguistic works and *Folk-Tales of Angola,* published in Boston in 1894. He then returned to Angola, residing there from 1897 until just before his death. At the same time, Merlin W. Ennis (1874–1964) was working in Angola, having translated the Bible into Umbundu and writing *Umbundu: Folk Tales from Angola* (1902). He founded the Elende Station in Angola in 1906, remaining there until 1944, when he retired to Lexington, Massachusetts. Another U.S. citizen in Angola was Reed Paige Clark (1878–1958). An economic adviser to the Liberian government, he was consul in Louanda from 1919 until 1924.

Ralph Edward Dodge (b. 1907), from Terril, Iowa, was to play a small but very important part in Angola's history. After training as a missionary, he went to Angola under the auspices of the Board of Missions of the Methodist Episcopal Church in Angola from 1936 until 1941, and again from 1945 until 1950. During his second term there he met a young man who was working with the Luanda Public Health Service and helped him apply for a scholarship to study medicine at the University of Lisbon. The man, Agostinho Neto (1922–1979), went to Portugal, but his studies were suspended for two years owing to his political activities, so the American Methodist Church provided him with a scholarship to finish his degree. Returning to Angola, Neto was jailed, released, and jailed again. He then escaped to Morocco, from where he led the nationalist struggle, becoming a dedicated Marxist. On November 11, 1975, Neto was proclaimed Angola's first president, leading the Communist government through four years of civil war until he died in 1979.

The Americas were heavily involved in the civil war. On the one hand, the U.S. government backed the União Nacional para a Independência Total de Angola (National Union for the Total Independence of Angola or UNITA) rebel movement of Jonas Savimbi, which opposed the Neto government. While Neto's government did recruit some U.S. mercenaries, of much greater military importance was the large number of Cuban soldiers who served in Angola in support of the Neto government. At the conflict's height, 2,500 Cubans were serving in Angola. As a result of this connection, many Angolans studied in Cuba, with quite a few settling in Havana.

In spite of the war in Angola, trade between the United States and Angola rose between 1982 and 1984 from $856 million to $1.1 billion. At the same time, the U.S. government was sending millions of dollars to UNITA. In addition, the United States was a venue for the sale of many diamonds sold by the movement to finance its army. When Cuban soldiers finally left Angola in 1989, elections were held, with international peacekeepers provided by many countries, including Argentina. After these elections, opposition to the Marxist government from the United States declined, although Savimbi contested the results and the war started again, although on a much smaller scale than before and ending with Savimbi's death in 2002. On May 19, 1993 the United States recognized the Angolan government. Ambassadors were exchanged, with Edmund T. DeJarnette serving as the first U.S. ambassador to the country in 1994–1995, succeeded by Donald K. Steinberg and then Joseph Gerard Sullivan. In 1980, 3,853 people born in Angola were residing in the United States. In 1990 the figure was 2,252. No figures are available for 2000.

Justin Corfield

See also: African Methodist Episcopal Church; Cuba; Peacekeeping and Military Interventions; Portuguese Empire

References

Blashford-Snell, John. *In the Steps of Stanley.* London: Hutchinson, 1975.
Piper, Mark. "Cuban Military Mails in Angola." *American Philatelist* 115, no. 2 (February 2001): 150–157.
Stockwell, John. *In Search of Enemies: How the C.I.A. Lost Angola.* London: Andre Deutsch, 1978.
Wilcken, Patrick. *Empire Adrift: The Portuguese Court in Rio de Janeiro.* London: Bloomsbury, 2004.

ANIKULAPO-KUTI, FELA (1938–1997)

One of Africa's most popular musicians and most famous dissidents, Nigerian Fela Anikulapo-Kuti, was larger than life and rebellious to the core. His influence in the popular culture of the United States and Europe has increased in recent years due to fascination with his heroic persona. Best known by his first name, Fela reflects the circularity of influence within the African Diaspora: a musician from Lagos absorbed American funk and the Black Power Movement and synthesized these elements into afrobeat, which in turn influenced Western musicians. The cross-cultural essence of afrobeat appeals to contemporary audiences accustomed to music that mixes different styles.

Fela's family was solidly Christian and middle class. While Fela attended the Trinity College of Music in London from 1958 to 1963, he was exposed to classical music and American jazz. He formed his first band, Koola Lobitos, and they performed a popular West African dance music, highlife.

After a return to Nigeria, Fela toured the United States in 1969. There, the band was renamed Nigeria 70 and he was introduced to the Black Power Movement. Inspired by Malcolm X, Fela—upon returning to Lagos later that year—changed his name from the Anglicized "Ransome" to "Anikulapo," which in Yoruba means "one who wears death in his pouch." The band's name was changed to the Pan-African Afrika 70, and the music evolved into a new style, afrobeat. The driving sound of afrobeat incorporated highlife, rock, and the funk of James Brown and featured multiple electric guitars and African instruments. Lyrics, in the lingua franca of pidgin, ridiculed Africans emulating their colonial masters as well as the Nigerian military and government.

The American counterculture of the late 1960s manifested itself in Fela's lifestyle. He openly smoked marijuana and conducted interviews dressed only in bikini briefs. Fela's outspokenness led to jail time in 1974. In 1977 he declared his commune, the Kalakuta Republic, autonomous, and the military responded violently. Upping the ante the following year, Fela entered politics with his Movement of the People Party. An emphasis on politics over music caused band members, including drummer Tony Allen, to quit, and the music suffered.

In 1981 the band was renamed Egypt 80, reflecting Fela's spiritual conversion, which was informed by Egyptologist and Afrocentrist thought. At Fela's nightclub, the Shrine, performances were preceded by elaborate Yoruba ceremonies. For most of the remainder of Fela's career, political dissent continued overshadowed his music. Fela died of AIDS in 1997.

Fela's influence was felt by David Byrne, Brian Eno, Jimmy Cliff, Miles Davis, Branford Marsalis, James Brown, and Bootsy Collins. Many rap and hip-hop artists have sampled Fela, and DJs mix Fela with dance music to create afro-house. Ginger Baker, Lester Bowie, and Roy Ayers collaborated with Fela. Fela's son Femi carries on his father's political and musical heritage and is a leading AIDS activist. Recent tributes include the CD *Red, Hot + Riot: The Music and Spirit of Fela Kuti* (2002) and "Black President: The Art and Legacy of Fela Anikulapo-Kuti," an exhibition organized by the New Museum of Contemporary Art in New York City during 2003.

Monica Berger

See also: Black Power Movement; Hip-Hop; Jazz and the Blues; Jazz, African; Music (African)

References

Darnton, John. "Nigeria's Dissident Superstar." *New York Times Magazine,* July 24, 1977, 10–12, 22–28.

Olaniyan, Tejumola. *Arrest the Music!: Fela and His Rebel Art and Politics.* Bloomington: Indiana University Press, 2004.

Olorunyomi, Sola. *Afrobeat!: Fela and the Imagined Continent.* Trenton, NJ: Africa World Press, 2003.

Schoonmaker, Trevor, ed. *Fela: From West Africa to West Broadway.* New York: Palgrave Macmillan, 2003.

Veal, Michael E. *Fela: The Life and Times of an African Musical Icon.* Philadelphia, PA: Temple University Press, 2000.

ANNAN, KOFI (1938–)

Kofi Annan, a Ghanaian citizen, was secretary-general of the United Nations from 1997 to 2007. Annan is best-known as the seventh UN secretary-general and the first elected by UN staff. His first term as secretary-general ran from January 1997 until January 2002; subsequently, he was appointed by acclamation to a second five-year term of office beginning in January 2002. Annan was born in Kumasi, Ghana, on April 8, 1938. Annan's first position with the UN was with the World Health Organization's budget office in 1962. Before his tenure as secretary-general, Annan served in numerous important UN posts. As secretary-general, he placed considerable emphasis on maintaining an international commitment to Africa, as is evident in his influential 1998 report, *The Causes of Conflict and the Promotion of Durable Peace and Sustainable Development in Africa.* In April 2001, calling it his personal mission, he issued a five-point "Call to Action" addressing the HIV/AIDS epidemic and proposed the establishment of a Global AIDS and Health Fund.

Annan acted with diplomacy in volatile political situations involving Iraq's compliance with Security Council resolutions (1998), civilian rule in Nigeria (1998), a stalemate between Libya and the

Security Council (1998), violence in East Timor (1999), Israel's withdrawal from Lebanon (2000) and further efforts to resolve Israeli-Palestinian conflict, and combating terrorism (2001–2007). He called for a Global Compact to share the benefits of globalization fairly. In 2001 he and the UN received the Nobel Peace Prize, on which occasion he was credited with bringing new life to the UN.

Alana Trumpy

See also: Ghana; Health, Public; Human Rights; Terrorism; United Nations

References

Meisler, Stanley. *A Man of Peace in a World of War.* New York: Wiley, 2006.

Koestler-Grack, Rachel A. *Kofi Annan.* New York: Chelsea House Publications, 2007.

ANTHROPOLOGY

At the turn of the twentieth century, anthropologists like Felix von Luschan (1854–1924); Franz Boas (1858–1942); and Boas's U.S. followers Alfred L. Kroeber (1876–1960), Robert Lowie (1883–1957), Edward Sapir (1884–1939), Ruth Benedict (1887–1948), and Margaret Mead (1901–1978), contributed to a new understanding of cultural systems by introducing new concepts of comparative approaches. These anthropologists initiated a paradigmatic shift in the social sciences from the biological to the cultural sphere. Their research changed notions of American democracy and its promise of equality in political, social, economic, and cultural history. Anthropologists' early commitment to overcoming traditional stereotypes regarding the supposed inferiority and primitiveness of African cultures provided some of the ideological groundwork for political organizations such as the National Association for the Advancement of Colored

People (NAACP), with its thirty-two founding members, among them W. E. B. Du Bois (1868–1963), William E. Walling, Mary White Ovington, and Henry Moskowitz, and the Association for the Study of African American Life and History, led by trailblazers such as Robert E. Park, Jessey E. Moorland, and Carter G. Woodson.

Anthropologists like Boas, Benedict. and Alexander Goldenweiser (1880–1940) reevaluated aesthetic products of African peoples. In the wake of the new developments within pragmatic philosophy that were initiated by John Dewey, Boas and his followers promoted the revolutionary concept of cultural pluralism. The leading African American intellectual of the early twentieth century, W. E. B. Du Bois, recognized in Boas a seminal figure in the challenge of overcoming the color line. "Franz Boas came to Atlanta University where I was teaching history in 1906 and said to a graduating class: You need not be ashamed of your African past; and then he recounted the history of black kingdoms south of the Sahara for a thousand years. I was too astonished to speak. All of this I had never heard and I came then and afterwards to realize how the silence and neglect of science can let truth utterly disappear or even be unconsciously distorted" (Du Bois, 1939, p. vii).

Boas was a pioneer in modern anthropology and is commonly referred to as the "father of American anthropology." The Boas school created an important link between African American culture, modernism, and multiculturalism. In addition to addressing specialized audiences through scholarly journals and books, Boas, Sapir, and Benedict reached not only a broad white audience but also the black community by contributing articles to *The Crisis, Opportunity, The Nation, The Liberator,* and *The New Republic.* These activities fostered crosscurrents of thinking on the nexus of race, culture, and democracy, thereby injecting African American arts with vigorous productive energy. For example, Sapir became a member of the writers' workshop of Jean Toomer (1894–1967) in Chicago, and Boas's student, Zora Neale Hurston (1891–1960), employed scientific fieldwork in Eatonville, Florida, as a basis for a new vernacular prose style in novels such as *Jonah's Gourd Vine* (1934), *Their Eyes Were Watching God* (1937), and *Moses, Man of the Mountain* (1939).

In the 1920s the increasing self-awareness and cultural self-reliance of African Americans found its most prominent expression in the artistic movement called the Harlem Renaissance. The Harlem Renaissance writings fostered transatlantic literary interest in African American vernacular language and culture, particularly in European capitals such as Berlin, London, and Paris. Of equal importance was the exuberant reception of jazz music, African American dance, and the visual arts.

Some of the groundbreaking beginnings of the new school of American anthropology can be traced back to Germany. Under the guidance of Adolph Bastion (1826–1905) and Rudolph Virchow (1821–1902), Felix von Luschan became a central figure at the Museum für Völkerkunde (Museum of Ethnology) in Berlin. Committed to the principle of collecting and analyzing cultural artifacts comparatively and inductively, the so-called "salvage anthropology," Luschan elevated African art to a signifier of complex cultural systems comparable to those of European cultures. Thereby, he departed from

established anthropological strategies that drew their inspiration from the philosophical racial discourses of thinkers such as David Hume (1711–1776) and Immanuel Kant (1724–1804). Kant's belief that Africans were mentally child-like and intellectually inferior to Europeans was discredited by Luschan's fieldwork on sub-Saharan art and its analysis, comparison, and, ultimately, display in Berlin museums His collection of Benin art and publications led to a reevaluation of African art that challenged long-standing categories of "superior" and inferior" peoples based on concepts of race.

In 1915 Luschan lectured in the United States, where he confronted the question of the "color line," informed Booker T. Washington (1856–1915) about his findings, conducted research on the heredity of African American immigrants, and popularized a nonracialist vision of the human species. With references to sensationalist and racist European displays of Africans in zoos, Luschan criticized racial activists such as Jörg Lanz von Liebenfels (1874–1954) and Hermann Klaatsch (1863–1916) and his followers in a lecture at the University of Illinois in 1915. "[They] connect the tall Negroes with the gorilla, and the African Pygmies with the chimpanzee, the Chinese with the orang[utan] and the Japanese with the Gibbon" (Smith, 2002, p. 32). American scientists like William Benjamin Smith (1850–1934) and Robert W. Shufeldt (1850–1934) had, according to Luschan, hardly anything to say on the race question from a scientific standpoint. Luschan held that too much of racial discourse was socially constructed. Despite his endorsement of racial tolerance, Luschan remained an ambiguous personality who slowly moved into the Darwinian camp, supporting colonialism, eugenics, and German nationalism, a tendency that found its most ardent expression in Eugen Fischer (1874–1967) and Hans Gunther (1891–1968). They propelled the disciplines of anthropobiology and human genetics. In Germany, these scientific aberrations played into the hands of National Socialist claims of "Aryan" supremacy and the genocide plan of the "final solution."

At the Berlin museum, Franz Boas conducted research on the language and culture of various tribes of Africa and Alaska, which led to his substantial criticism of "scientific" racism as propelled by physical anthropology. When Boas emigrated to the United States in 1886, he was confronted with outspoken racism against immigrants and African Americans. Following Luschan, Boas was able to free anthropology from its pseudo-scientific justification of racist attitudes regarding physical inferiority and of proto-fascist, elitist, concepts in Europe. He used methods of anthropometry (physical anthropology and their techniques of measuring head sizes and shapes) to counter the assumption of racial formalism regarding the stability of human "types." Boas warned that by confining considerations on the question of race in the United States to the intermixture of European types, it would be clear "that the consent that is felt by many in regard to the continuance of racial purity of our nation, is to a great extent imaginary" (Boas, 1974, p. 322).

In his immensely popular and provocative book, *Anthropology and Modern Life* (1928), Boas held that environment, culture, and language affect mental functioning rather than physical characteristics. With his research on black Egyptianism and Ethiopianism, he continued to advocate

the complexity and greatness of West African civilizations. With books such as *The Mind of Primitive Man* (1911) or *Race, Language, and Culture* (1940), Boas not only provided scientific proof to counterbalance notions of African primitivism. He also initiated far-reaching projects to foster a strong sense of self-awareness among Africans and African Americans, thereby enhancing racial pride. Boas encouraged gifted African American students to pursue anthropological research and continue an academic career despite the tremendous obstacles of racial prejudice within academia. Among those who felt stimulated by his call to "scientific arms" were Zora Neale Hurston, Arthur Huff Fauset (half-brother of the Harlem Renaissance writer Jessie Fauset), and James F. King. Boas proved that the social and natural environment played a crucial role regarding the performance of specific tasks. These findings refuted the belief that only northern Europeans brought the proper biological and racial features to the American context, making them alone fit for assimilation to the "American way of life." The unsettling conclusions of Boas's research caused great public uproar and resistance among conservative elites.

Alain Locke drew on Boas in his essay, "The Eleventh Hour of Nordicism" (1935), where he explained in respect of the race question, "that this situation is finally changing after nearly two decades dominated by such attitudes is due to the influence of just a few strong dissenting influences—the most important of which has come from the militant but unquestionably scientific school of anthropologists captained by Professor Boas. They have dared, in season and out, to challenge false doctrine and conventional myths, and were the first to bring the citadel of Nordicism into range of scientific encirclement and bombardment. An essay in itself could be written on the slow but effective pressure that now has ringed the Nordic doctrines and their advocates round with an ever-tightening scientific blockade" (Locke, 1983, p. 232). The Boasian school held that cultural contacts are a source of creative growth for individuals and societies. Instead of insisting on a traditional concept of Western civilization following a singular evolutionary plan, cultural pluralism in the sense of Boas and his students recognized that all cultures are mixed and constantly undergo transformations. These ideas opened new perspectives on American contributions to modernity and its cultural hybridity.

Frank Mehring

See also: Art, African; Du Bois, William Edward Burghardt; Ethnicity; Exploration and Explorers, Africa; Folklore, African; Harlem Renaissance; Hurston, Zora Neale; Race, History of; Transculturation

References

Boas, Franz. *The Mind of Primitive Man.* New York: Macmillan, 1911.

Boas, Franz. *Anthropology and Modern Life.* New York: Norton, 1928.

Boas, Franz. *Race, Language, and Culture.* New York: Macmillan, 1940.

Boas, Franz. *Race and Democratic Society.* New York: J. J. Augustin, 1945.

Boas, Franz. "Race Problems in America." In *A Franz Boas Reader,* edited by George W. Stocking Jr. New York: Basic Books, 1974.

Du Bois, W. E. B. *Black Folk Then and Now.* 1939. Millwood, NY: Kraus-Thomson Organization, 1975.

Hurston, Zora Neale. *Mules and Men.* Philadelphia: J. B. Lippincott, 1935.

Kroeber, Alfred Louis. *Anthropology.* New York: Harcourt, Brace, 1933.

Locke, Alain, "The Eleventh Hour of Nordicism: Retrospective Review of the Literature of the Negro for 1934." In *The Critical Temper of Alain Locke,* edited by Jeffrey C. Stewart. New York: Garland, 1983.

Luschan, Felix von. *Die Altertümer von Benin.* Berlin and Leipzig, Germany: Vereinigung Wissenschaftlicher Verleger Walter de Gruyter, 1919.

Mead, Margaret. *Anthropologists and What They Do.* New York: F. Watts, 1965.

Smith, John David. "W. E. B. Du Bois, Felix von Luschan, and Racial Reform at the *Fin de Siècle.*" *Amerikastudien/American Studies.* 47, no.1 (2002): 23–38.

ANTIGUA AND BARBUDA

Antigua, Barbuda, and the uninhabited Redonda constitute an island nation in the Lesser Antilles of the eastern Caribbean Sea. The vast majority of Antigua and Barbuda's population are the descendants of the thousands of African slaves who were brought to the islands to work on sugar plantations. The colony of Antigua and Barbados was administratively part of the Leeward Islands from 1871 until 1967, when it entered into free association with Britain. It achieved full independence in 1981. The official language of the nation of Antigua and Barbuda is English. It is composed of six parishes and is a constitutional monarchy, with Queen Elizabeth II as its titular head. The largest of the islands, with 108 square miles (280 square kilometers), Antigua has an intricate coastline, with reefs and shoals. Barbuda is a flat coral island of 62 square miles (161 square kilometers). A game reserve has been created in Barbuda owing to its woods and great variety of wildlife. The island has also become a sanctuary for the frigate bird.

The original inhabitants of the islands were pre-agricultural Amerindians who populated the islands around 3000 BCE. After them, groups of Saladoid people, and subsequently Arawaks and Caribs, settled on the islands. Columbus disembarked on Antigua during his second voyage in 1493 and renamed the island after the Church of Santa Maria la Antigua in Seville, Spain. The Spanish and French established minor settlements, and in 1632 Antigua was colonized by the first English settlers.

The soil of both Antigua and Barbuda was highly fertile. As it happened with the rest of the English colonies in the Antilles, the growing of tobacco and other experimental crops was soon discarded in favor of sugar, by far the most profitable business. In order to grow sugar, the land was divided into vast plantations, and the first Irish Catholic indentured servants were imported to work on them. Because of the climate and tropical diseases, these "white slaves" were in a few years replaced by Africans.

Although slave rebellions were as frequent as in the rest of the English territories, the density of the forests in the interior provided the slaves with another way of breaking away from their cruelest servitude: self-governing maroon communities of escaped slaves flourished, at least as long as the plantation owners did not deforest the woods. Other means of slave resistance ranged from neglecting one's labor to sabotage to suicide. African slaves also contested their owners' tyranny by adapting African customs and cultural traditions to their Caribbean space. The successes of slave rebellions and the diversity of the cultural origins of African slaves led to a rich and complex variety of local traditions.

Slaves in Antigua and Barbuda were officially emancipated in 1834, although former slaves often remained economically dependent on working for former plantation owners. Harsh labor conditions persisted well into the twentieth century. In 1939 the Antigua Trades and Labour Union was created to regulate and ameliorate the harsh labor conditions. However, agriculture is still important, though the sector nearly collapsed in 1972 when the sugar industry closed down. Since the 1970s its economy has being growing steadily. Although the main industry of the nation has become tourism, manufacturing is steadily growing, the main industries being those involved in the processing of agricultural products.

Virginia Fernández Canedo

See also: British Empire; Pre-Columbian America; Slave Revolts/Maronnage

References

Klein, S. Herbert. *La esclavitud Africana en América Latina y el Caribe.* Translated by Graciela Sánchez Albornoz. Madrid: Alianza Editorial, 1986.

Montiel Martínez, Luz María. *Negros en América.* Madrid: Editorial Mapfre, 1992.

APPIAH, KWAME ANTHONY (1954–)

Kwame Anthony Appiah is a philosopher, historian, novelist, and literary critic of the late twentieth and early twenty-first centuries. Born of a Ghanaian father and an English mother, Appiah has used his writings to bridge the philosophical divide between Africa and America by deconstructing traditional racial identities in his writing. He is one of the most important philosophers of Africa, race, identity, and ethics of his lifetime.

Appiah was born on May 8, 1954, in London to a Ghanaian father, Joe Appiah, a politician and lawyer in Ghana, and a British mother, Peggy Cripps, an author and historian. Appiah grew up in Kumasi, Ghana. He later earned his BA (1975),

MA (1980), and PhD (1982) in philosophy from Cambridge University. After graduating from Cambridge, Appiah took a variety of teaching positions in the United Kingdom, Ghana, South Africa, and United States, including a professorship at Princeton University in Princeton, New Jersey.

While Appiah is an important linguistic philosopher, his works on race and ethnicity have earned him his greatest acclaim and criticism. Many of Appiah's books and articles discuss the epistemology of being African, the history of Africa, and the metaphysics and ethics of identity, especially African identity. The inspiration for his philosophical tracts on race and identity stem from his own varied identity as an Anglo-Ghanaian gay man. His books discussing Africa or race, which stem from his Ghanaian experiences and heritage, include *The Ethics of Identity* (2005), *Africana: The Encyclopedia of African and African American Experience* (2003), *Bu Me Bé: The Proverbs of the Akan* (2002), *Color Conscious: The Political Morality of Race* (1996), and *In My Father's House: Africa in the Philosophy of Culture* (1992).

In My Father's House and *Africana* are Appiah's two most famous works on African and African American identity, culture, and history. The book *In My Father's House* deconstructs Pan-African identities that are based upon color or race, which he believes are not correct biological categories for determining an identity. The book also shows how Africa can learn from the West and still keep local, regional, and continental cultural identities based upon shared experience, not race- or color-based essentialism. As a professor of Afro-American Studies and philosophy at Harvard University (1991–2002), Appiah teamed up with

Harvard scholar Henry Louis Gates Jr. to create *Africana*. The idea originated with the famous African American scholar W. E. B. Du Bois in the early twentieth century; Du Bois thought that African American history and European American scholars grossly misportrayed African and African American culture. Scholarly experts wrote the over-3,000 encyclopedia entries in *Africana*.

Brett Bennett

See also: Akan; Du Bois, William Edward Burghardt; Enlightenment Philosophy; Ethnicity; Gates Jr., Henry Louis; Ghana; Race, History of; West, Cornel

References

Appiah, Kwame Anthony. *In My Father's House: Africa in the Philosophy of Culture.* New York: Oxford University Press, 1992.

Appiah, Kwame Anthony. *The Ethics of Identity.* Princeton, NJ: Princeton University Press, 2005.

Appiah, Kwame Anthony, and Peggy Appiah. *Bu Me Bé: The Proverbs of the Akan.* Accra, Ghana: The Center for Intellectual Renewal, 2002.

Appiah, Kwame Anthony, and Amy Gutman. *Color Conscious: The Political Morality of Race.* Princeton, NJ: Princeton University Press, 1996.

APPRENTICESHIP (BRITISH EMPIRE)

Apprenticeship is the term for the transitional four-year period (1834–1838) between slavery and its full abolition that occurred in most of Britain's slave-based colonies. A compromise between pro- and antislavery forces, apprenticeship allowed slave owners continued access to the unpaid labor of their former slaves, adding compensation in the form of labor for their loss of human property to the £20 million in monetary compensation they received. Initially proposed as a twelve-year period during which formerly enslaved people would become the "apprentices" of their former owners, the system envisaged by the British Abolition Act of 1833 was to last for six years. In the end, apprenticeship produced such opposition on the part of both former slaves, who objected to the delay in the attainment of "full freedom," and former slave owners, who opposed the increased imperial intervention that accompanied it, that it was abolished in 1838.

The British Abolition Act set out the broad outlines of apprenticeship, while local details were worked out in colonial legislation (for those "old" colonies with their own elected legislatures, such as Jamaica and Barbados) and in Orders in Council (for the more recently acquired crown colonies, such as Trinidad, which had no elected chamber). The British act legislated that children under the age of six became completely free. Other former slaves became "apprentices" and were designated either "praedial" (agricultural) or "nonpraedial" workers. Praedial apprentices owed their masters or mistresses forty-five hours of unpaid work per week, four and a half hours of which were to be allocated to work on provision grounds, parcels of land on which slaves could cultivate their own food. Nonpraedial apprentices—mostly domestic workers—could be required to work unlimited hours and were to be freed after four years, in 1838, while praedials would be freed after six, in 1840. Former slaveholders could no longer legally inflict direct punishment, corporal or other, on their apprentices. Apprentices had the right to purchase their freedom by undergoing a complex process of valuation. The system was overseen by a new group of state officials, the stipendiary or special magistrates, who adjudicated in cases of offences

committed under the terms of the abolition act. (Criminal acts, such as theft, were supposed to be tried in the common law courts, although in practice, many stipendiary magistrates heard such cases as well.) Stipendiary magistrates, presented in the law and in some of the historiography as neutral third parties, consistently ruled more frequently in favor of apprenticeholders than apprentices. While many magistrates were openly racist and pro-planter, the imbalance in outcome of cases derived at least as much from the content of apprenticeship law, which aimed to enforce a system of unfree labor, as it did from the personal bias of individual magistrates.

Apprenticeship was one of a number of gradual abolition plans proposed in British governmental circles in the early 1830s. Like the other schemes proposed, the apprenticeship system assumed that neither slave owners nor slaves were equipped for life in a society organized around free labor and that both needed a period of training and state supervision before adopting their new roles, envisaged to be those of employer and employee. The choice of the term "apprenticeship" invoked an imagined state of tutelage for former slaves who were not, however, apprenticed in the sense of learning a skill or a trade, but rather to the state of being free—that is, contract-making—people. For instance, the designers of the system hoped that apprentices and apprenticeholders would make contracts for labor beyond the mandated forty-five hours per week, although in practice this took place relatively rarely.

The design of apprenticeship incorporated efforts to reconstruct the gender relations and identities of enslaved people. Monogamous Christian marriage was encouraged, while women and men were marked out as different kinds of people through the prohibition of flogging for women while it remained a punishment that could be inflicted, at the order of a stipendiary magistrate, on men. Colonial governors and stipendiary magistrates exhorted apprenticed men to take on the role of head of household and provider for their nuclear families.

The colonial legislatures of Antigua, Bermuda, and the Virgin Islands decided to forego an apprenticeship period. In those colonies, slavery was fully abolished on August 1, 1834, superseded in many cases by legislation governing vagrancy and contracts that imposed severe controls on formerly enslaved people. Elsewhere in the Caribbean, apprenticeship came into force on August 1, 1834, while in the Cape Colony (South Africa) it began on December 1, 1834. In several places, including St. Kitts and some Jamaican parishes, apprentices' initial reaction to their new status took the form of strikes and protests demanding an end to compulsory unpaid labor. These were suppressed by British military force. Such conflicts were symptomatic of a wider range of daily struggles that belied the many initial reports of the system's success. Some of these conflicts arose over issues created by the apprenticeship system, for example, the work and subsistence of free children or the organization of the hours of the compulsory working week. Others revolved around concerns that had led to conflict during slavery, such as religious freedom, the extent of deference expected by planters of unfree workers, the work requirements placed on breast-feeding women and mothers of many children, and the provision by masters and mistresses of clothing, dietary protein, and health care. These were long-standing conflicts, but they were played out during apprenticeship at heightened intensity because of apprentices' raised expectations and apprenticeholders' efforts to extract as much short-term profit as possible from their apprentices in the knowledge that the system would be short-lived.

British abolitionists soon realized that apprenticeship had not ended the oppression of former slaves. Making use of information supplied largely by missionaries, they publicized the problems of the system and pressured the Colonial Office to increase the regulation of apprenticeship. By 1837 they were campaigning strongly in favor of the system's immediate abolition. Ultimately, the colonial legislatures, under heavy pressure from the Colonial Office, decided to abolish apprenticeship completely from August 1, 1838. These decisions were taken for a variety of reasons, including planters' desire to escape "interference" by the Colonial Office and stipendiary magistrates; pressure from British abolitionists; and fear of mass strikes and uprisings on the part of praedial apprentices when the nonpraedials achieved freedom.

The British system of apprenticeship became a model in some respects for other emancipations in the Atlantic World. These included the *patronato* system of Cuba and Puerto Rico, the apprenticeship system in Suriname, and the Freedmen's Bureau regulation of freedpeople's lives and labor in the U.S. South.

Diana Paton

See also: Abolitionism, British; American Freedmen's Inquiry Commission; British Empire; Slavery (History)

References

Eudell, Demetrius. *The Political Languages of Emancipation in the British Caribbean and the U.S. South.* Chapel Hill: University of North Carolina Press, 2002.

Holt, Thomas. *The Problem of Freedom: Race, Labor, and Politics in Jamaica and Britain, 1832–1938.* Baltimore, MD: Johns Hopkins University Press, 1992.

Paton, Diana. *No Bond But the Law: Punishment, Race, and Gender in Jamaican State Formation, 1780–1870.* Durham, NC: Duke University Press, 2004.

Scully, Pamela. *Liberating the Family? Gender and British Slave Emancipation in the Rural Western Cape, South Africa, 1823–1853.* Oxford: James Currey, 1997.

Williams, James. *A Narrative of Events, since the First of August 1834, by James Williams, an Apprenticed Labourer in Jamaica.* Edited by Diana Paton. Durham, NC: Duke University Press, 2001.

ARCHITECTURE

Cultural contact between Europe, the Americas, and Africa has influenced the architectural structures of each. Architecture refers to the art and science of designing buildings and structures. While the definition of what architecture is varies from one place to other, that is, from one culture to another and from historical period to period, "good" architecture nonetheless is widely acknowledged to contain three core elements: beauty, utility, and solidity. With regards to the architecture of Africa and the Americas, a number of distinct models may be seen.

Architecture in the Americas goes back for literally thousands of years, but it underwent fundamental change following the colonizing of both the North and South American continents by Europeans from the sixteenth century onward. However, prior to the arrival of European influence, Native Americans lived in highly developed societies with distinct customs; rules; beliefs; and, significantly, built forms. Often designed with regional differences due to, for example, the influence of local climate,

availability of building materials, and the distinct ways of life of particular Native American groups, edifices ranged from earth mounds in West Virginia (United States) and the elaborate, and large-sized, pole-framed dwellings of the Iroquois Indians in New York State (United States) to the snow and ice houses of the Inuit and Yupik in the Canadian Arctic and Alaska (United States) and the temples of the Aztecs (Mexico). In places such as Central America, large-scale stone pyramids, thoroughfares, and cities were erected—for example, Tenochtitlan and Teotihuacán in Mexico—that highlight the importance of architecture to the cultural expression and rituals of native peoples such as the Aztecs, Mayans, and Toltecs. In South America, too, peoples like the Incas created elaborate structures and urban settlements as their empires grew; an example is Machu Picchu in Peru, which was erected on a mountain peak. Yet with the arrival of Europeans in the 1500s, many native design cultures vanished, like that of the Meso-American peoples mentioned previously, and indigenous design forms in some instances even adopted westernized forms, for example, gables at the front of the longhouses erected by Atlantic Indians in the United States.

Until the late 1800s and early 1900s, European traditions hugely influenced the design of American buildings. In Brazil, architecture was dependent on Portugal for inspiration until the 1800s, and in Mexico, Spanish design was hugely influential until the 1900s. With the rise of industrialization, the lessening influence of the colonial motherland and the rise of independent nations, and the search for national design styles, architecture in the Americas took on new forms. In so doing, it utilized new materials, such as steel, and new technologies, such as the mechanical elevator. North American cities, as a result, adopted new vertical scales, led by Chicago and New York from the 1890s, with their many-floored skyscrapers that are today synonymous with U.S. cities. Representing the large egos, mercantile status, and substantial riches of private corporations, these buildings had a practical advantage in places such as Manhattan, in New York City, by providing a structural means to circumnavigate the problem of a scarcity of central urban land. Many skyscrapers today, especially those in New York, are world famous even if extreme. High-rise building in the Americas has somewhat slowed due to the impact of the September 11 terrorist attacks of 2001 on New York's World Trade Center. However, tall building design, very much part of the move toward modernist designing, is well and truly rooted in the Americas. Frank Lloyd Wright's design and open-plan influence, consolidated by the likes of Mies Van der Rohe and Philip Johnson, ensured that North American cities have tall buildings erected to geometric shapes with metal and glass facades and horizontal bands across the tops. Modernism has also taken hold in South America as well, in part because of the influence of Le Corbusier, who visited Brazil in the 1920s and 1930s and who consequently helped style the original forms of architects such as Oscar Niemeyer and Lucio Costa.

In Africa, traditional design forms, as in the Americas, have a significant richness, with the northern area of sub-Saharan Africa having been influenced in past centuries by Arabic culture while the southern area of the continent was affected by the Bantu peoples and their cultures. Similarly to Native American architecture, Native African designing was influenced by available materials, or lack thereof, as in the case of the holy city of Lalibela, in Ethiopia, which was erected from natural rock. Hence the widespread use of uncomplicated, unfussy materials like adobe for bricks; wood or woven leaves and branches for roofs, which are applied to roundhouses in Togo and Benin; painted facades of mud edifices in Nigeria; thatched roofs in the Congo; and wooden-ribbed housing in Cameroon, elements of which also were adopted in other places such as North and South America following the onset of slave exportation by European nations. Travel and conquests by Africans such as the Moors brought Muslim architecture to Europe, particularly Spain. Significantly, too, African architecture in Egypt during the reign of the pharaohs—with its decorative columns and horizontal and vertical lines that help create balanced, ordered edifices of large scale—influenced the rationally minded ancient Greeks, who in turn inspired the Romans and subsequently most of Western Europe as part of the cultural awakening of the Renaissance. In short, Africa indelibly influenced the palette of European architectural evolution, while soon after Europe, in turn, fundamentally shaped Africa.

Modern Africa has been profoundly affected by the processes of slavery and colonization by European nations such as France, Germany, Portugal, and Britain from the 1500s. European vernacular design was brought to Africa for the purpose of erecting public buildings and residential buildings for the elites of African colonial society, that is, the non-native population. With regards to housing, a notable designer was Arts and Crafts–inspired Herbert

Bet Giyorgis (St. George's), one of a number of rock-hewn churches built under Lalibela, a Christian king of Ethiopia during the twelfth and thirteenth centuries. (iStockPhoto.com)

Baker in South Africa, a British designer who amalgamated local stone, thatch, and timber with an adaptation of the vernacular (Cape gable). Similarly, local elites combined elements of Western design vocabularies with local traditions, and in so doing created a hybrid architectural culture. With regard to public architecture, classical designing was often employed and hybrid forms were not permitted as colonizing authorities steadfastly maintained control over the styles to be used in order to continue to highlight status hierarchies and support existing colonial contexts. However, the British, for instance, slowly shifted away from importing design styles to adopting components from local styles.

Even so, the history of African architecture is closely related to the politics of colonial rule. From the mid-1900s, the changing cultural condition in Africa created by the move from colonialism to independence brought a major architectural shift as Africa for the first time experienced a move toward modernism. At the end of the colonial period in the 1950s, modern architecture was employed as a means to display the intended colonial welfare state, yet after independence new governments and elites utilized modernism as a means to convey strength, optimism, and hopefulness about Africa's future.

Ian Morley

See also: Africa, Precolonial; Architecture, Plantation; Art, African; Pre-Columbian America

References

Elleh, Nnamdi. *African Architecture: Evolution and Transformation.* New York: McGraw-Hill, 1996.
Prussin, Labelle. *African Nomadic Architecture.* Seattle: Washington University Press, 1995.
Segre, Roberto, ed. *Latin America in its Architecture.* New York: Holmes & Meier, 1981.

ARCHITECTURE, PLANTATION

The knowledge of African slaves and the conflicts inherent in transatlantic slavery would play a central role in the architecture and design of plantations. Plantations in the New World were important economic units, and their architecture and design reflected the knowledge and skills brought by African slaves to the Americas, the economic interests of plantation owners, and the inherent conflicts between masters and slaves. Africans would, in effect, influence architectural design in the Americas through their presence on the plantation.

The Caribbean, Brazil, and the United States offer important examples of plantation architecture and design.

Slaves were greatly utilized in the Caribbean and, because of the limited amount of arable land, the homes of these slaves were located on the plantation where the soil could not be tilled. These homes were one-to-two-room huts that were square or rectangular in shape and were arranged in neat rows. The huts were constructed of available materials, which varied from island to island. These slave dwellings were built by the planters and also, sometimes, by the slaves. The floors were tamped earth and sometimes held a raised platform for a bed. The walls were constructed out of wattle, a weaving of branches, vines, or split bamboo over a plaster of clay. Roofs were made of palms. All these techniques of construction and similar types of materials were in wide use in West Africa. In Brazil, a certain type of architecture called the *fazenda,* or plantation house, was developed from the 1500s to the 1800s. The arrival and use of slaves, which assured the survival of the colonial economy in Brazil, demanded a separation of master and slaves. Most of these plantation houses were built in the Portuguese baroque or neoclassical style; the change from baroque to neoclassical was inspired by European architect Grandjean de Montigny. Montigny designed various buildings and spread a distinctive type of architecture in Rio de Janeiro, Brazil. A key feature of these plantations was separate quarters for the slaves. These dwellings were usually laid out in a square-shaped configuration to form an open courtyard directly behind the plantation house. On some of the larger plantations, the owner had outbuildings that were used for housing the abundance of slaves surrounding the great house. The *fazenda* of Freguesia is on one of the oldest sugar plantations in Bahia, Brazil. It was built in the eighteenth century and was heavily influenced by the Portuguese baroque style. African slaves played a role in building the project. The chapel is the crowning element of this plantation and is heavily adorned with baroque-style architecture.

Between 1837 and 1840 Brazil produced over 90 percent of all coffee exports in the world. As in the case of sugar, plantations and slaves were prevalent. Also, due to the great demand for the tanks that held the coffee and the sluiceways that transported it, slaves were commonly utilized in their production. The slave quarters on the coffee plantations were laid out in the same square configuration and courtyard as on the sugar plantations. One of the more prominent coffee plantation homes in Brazil was the *fazenda* called Retiro, located in Rio de Janeiro. It is a stunning example of a square-shaped plantation with a large, open courtyard. The house was owned by the Werneck family and was landscaped by Roberto Burle Marx. It is one of the few plantation homes that has been designated a national monument. Once again, the slaves and owners worked together to create a beautiful, two-story, baroque-style plantation. The African slaves stayed in the outbuildings and in the courtyard apartments as well. This architectural feature perpetuated the separation of slave and owner.

In the United States, slavery influenced the layout and general function of plantation design much as in Brazil. New spatial layouts were devised to maintain the slaves' functionality while concealing their role in the hierarchical realm of the plantation. African influence on architecture in the

United States can be best exemplified by looking at Mount Vernon, Monticello, and the plantation of Thomas Spalding.

George Washington's Mount Vernon home in Virginia was built between 1730 and 1787, and it displays the architectural elements required for the patriarchal plantation system. The first feature to be noticed is the placement of the mansion on the site. The "big house" is placed on higher ground than the main entrance path, enhancing the structure's monumental feel. This impression is increased by the large amount of land in front of the house and the large trees surrounding it. It is further enforced by the curve of the service lane toward the slave quarters, which were placed so as to be completely invisible from the main house. This separation is rendered even more complete by making the back walls of the slave quarters completely solid, thus, forming a wall-like barrier to the garden area of the main house. Even though this arrangement was created for the benefit of the plantation owner, it served a purpose for the slaves as well. The separation between master and slave gave the slaves a sense of privacy while in their common sleeping and living areas. In this sense, privacy contributed to the function of the structures. Privacy was probably one of the only ways in which the slaves were able to define and control their own environment at Mount Vernon.

Yet even though the presence of slaves had a noticeable impact on the architecture conceived at Mount Vernon, the design scheme at Thomas Jefferson's Monticello was even more attuned to the hierarchical gap between master and slave. First, slaves had a more direct impact on the architecture of Monticello because they participated in its actual creation. For the lack of available white craftsmen, the slaves of Monticello served in their stead. The slaves who worked on Monticello served as cabinetmakers, carpenters, masons, bricklayers, and smiths. Their high skill level proves that slaves were capable of creating their own architectural designs and putting them into production, although they generally lacked the freedom to display such abilities.

Whatever freedom the slaves had in creating and building Monticello was crushed by its design, for the slaves were completely separated from the realms of the plantation owner. A number of the design features at Monticello allowed for the slaves to be readily available for service while remaining hidden. They included a rotating door that had semicircular shelves on one side and tiny stairways unobtrusively located in the cross-passageways from different wings. Such ingenious architectural features as these allowed the slaves to perform all of their necessary tasks and move throughout the house without imposing themselves upon the refined environment of their master. Along with the interior features, the general layout of the plantation highlighted the presence of the master and the expendability of the slave. At Monticello, the main house was at a consistently higher ground level than any slave walkway or housing compound. Therefore, Jefferson was able to incorporate a passageway from the main house to the slave quarters that was completely invisible from any vantage point of the mansion. Also, Jefferson devised the surrounding landscape and structures of Monticello so that one could not see from the parlor the slaves as they performed the daily functions of the plantation. It is believed that Thomas Jefferson's incorporation of such designs was influenced by a study of the slave castle at Elmina on the West African coast. There, hidden access routes were utilized to connect the upper realms of the white man to the lower recesses, where the slaves were kept for exploitation. However, no matter the initial influence for his design schemes, Jefferson's home is a significant landmark in the development of plantation design.

Yet apart from plantation design, one must also observe the treatment of slaves in city settings. In contrast to the designs and spatial layouts utilized in the plantation settings, city homes had to incorporate the same separation between master and slave without the option of simply placing the slave dwellings some distance away. The proximity of slaves to each other increased their opportunities to communicate and organize uprisings. Therefore, keeping all these factors in mind, many designs placed the main house near the street, with minimal housing for the slaves at the very back of the site. These structures were usually surrounded by very high walls and open only to the main house. This development, along with the omission of alleys, made it impossible for the slaves to focus their attention on anyone besides their master. Building these structures was difficult because it took time, materials, and land away from the wealthy white population; thus, the idea of slaves "living out" became popular at this time. This meant that slaves lived in warehouses, utility sheds, and stables. In these places, African people began to demonstrate their ability to understand and develop architecture of their own. Many slaves in these settings rearranged and created new spaces to suit their various needs. Gradually, as moving slaves away from their masters became more frequent,

African people began to build sheds and shanties on the outskirts of towns.

In the nineteenth century, slaves were used to build plantations in the U.S. South. In Georgia, skilled slaves made a distinctive contribution to the culture of coastal locations. An example is the site of Thomas Spalding, a slave owner on the island of Sapelo. There, Spalding used his slaves to build his mansion as well as his sugar mill, cotton gin, and other machinery. Spalding not only depended upon his slaves to build his plantation, but also used them in running it. An example of such a slave is Sandy Maybank, who belonged to Charles C. Jones and who directed the construction of Jones's rice mill and supervised all milling operations. The buildings on Jones's site were constructed of materials the slaves found in their environment. These materials consisted of a mixture of crushed sea shells, water, lime, and mud, a combination called Tubby. The layout of Spalding's and Jones's plantations is also important. To accommodate the slaves, many plantations had all the necessary facilities for their care and maintenance. In most cases, these plantations were arranged to be like modern small cities. For example, Spalding's plantation on Sapelo Island had a hospital, a building for the care of slave infants, and slave quarters that were designed facing a main street with yard space at the back for gardening. Although most of the plantation was destroyed during the U.S. Civil War, some of the slave quarters remained, illustrating the durability of the building construction.

The influence that Africans had on plantation architecture differed with each project. Sometimes the slaves were skilled craftsmen, as at Monticello, and sometimes they were merely laborers. During the slavery era, a separation of master and slave was required, and the separation can be seen directly in the way architecture was produced during the eighteenth and nineteenth centuries in the United States. The infusion of Africans into American society brought new ways of constructing and new ways of designing in the United States.

Mohammad Gharipour

See also: Architecture; Plantations and Plantation Systems; Slavery (History)

References
Crain, Edward E. *Historic Architecture in the Caribbean Islands.* Gainesville: University Press of Florida, 1994.
Hughes, David. *Afrocentric Architecture: A Design Primer.* Columbus, OH: Greyden Press, 1994.
Johnson, Charles, and Patricia Smith. *Africans in America: America's Journey through Slavery.* New York: Harcourt Brace, 1998.
Vlach, John Michael. *Back of the Big House: The Architecture of Plantation Slavery.* Chapel Hill: University of North Carolina Press, 1993.

Jean-Bertrand Aristide, a former Catholic priest, became the first democratically elected president of Haiti in late 1990. (UPI)

ARISTIDE, JEAN-BERTRAND (1953–)

Jean-Bertrand Aristide, a charismatic priest of Haiti's poor, served three times as his country's president, in 1991, 1994–1996, and 2001–2004. Aristide was born on July 15, 1953, to a family of peasants of moderate means outside Port-Salut in southwestern Haiti. When he was still an infant, and after the death of his father, the Aristide family moved to the capital, Port-au-Prince. Educated by Salesian priests, Aristide studied in Israel, Greece, and Canada. He was ordained a priest on July 3, 1982. In 1985 he was assigned to the St. Jean Bosco parish in one of Port-au-Prince's slums.

Aristide quickly acquired a reputation for courage, as he delivered fiery sermons targeting dictator Jean-Claude Duvalier (Baby Doc) and his henchmen, the Tontons Macoutes. This earned him the hatred of Duvalier and his successors, who ruled Haiti during the period of instability that followed Duvalier's departure (1986–1991) and made him the target of up to seven assassination attempts. On September 11, 1988, as Aristide was preaching mass at St. Jean Bosco, armed gunmen assaulted the church, killing thirteen before setting the building on fire. (Aristide miraculously escaped.) Another devoted, though less violent, enemy was Haiti's Catholic hierarchy, which resented Aristide's revolutionary message and his sympathy for the theology of liberation, a liberal reading of the Gospel popular in Latin America during the 1970s and 1980s. The Salesians expelled Aristide from the order in December 1988. (Aristide renounced the priesthood in October 1994.)

Aristide's message was highly popular with Haiti's poor. He dared to stand up against the Macoutes who tyrannized the country's inhabitants. His anti-American rhetoric was in tune with most Haitians' political convictions. In a country plagued by widespread poverty and deep inequalities, he professed interest in, though not outright adoption of, Communism. A dark-skinned Haitian, he capitalized on the dark-skinned majority's resentment against the mulatto minority that dominated Haiti's economic life. Aristide astutely delivered most of his speeches in creole, the French-African dialect used by poor Haitians, rather than the academic French that the Haitian elite traditionally favored. When presidential elections monitored by the international community were held on December 16, 1990, Aristide won a decisive first-round victory with 67.48 percent of the vote.

Political controversy plagued Aristide's first presidency (February 7, 1991–September 30, 1991; October 15, 1994–February 7, 1996). His decision to raise the minimum wage angered the country's economic elite and foreign donors; the army grew restless after Aristide fired most of its senior officers shortly after gaining office. But criticisms focused mostly on Aristide's human rights shortcomings. On April 4, 1991, former president Ertha Pascal-Trouillot was sent to the national penitentiary, then put under house arrest. She was released only after intense international pressure. In a famous September 27, 1991, speech, Aristide made a nominal apology

for the practice called Père Lebrun, or necklacing, a torture popular among his supporters that consisted in throwing a tire filled with burning gasoline around a suspected Macoute's head. Raoul Cédras, whom Aristide had appointed as interim commander-in-chief, overthrew Aristide in a September 29 coup that Aristide and his supporters accused U.S. president George H. W. Bush of supporting. Aristide flew to Venezuela and exile.

In 1993 Aristide settled in Washington, D.C., and asked U.S. president Bill Clinton to help restore him to power. Following three years of failed diplomatic and economic sanctions, U.S. forces landed in Haiti on September 19, 1994. Aristide returned on October 15. He left office at the end of his first term in February 1996, then returned for a five-year term in February 2001. Aristide's second presidency was marked by economic and political turmoil. Opposition parties, accusing Aristide's supporters of electoral fraud, boycotted the 2000 presidential elections, then denounced Aristide's presidency as illegitimate. They also accused Aristide of sponsoring political assassinations, either through the Haitian National Police or through paramilitary groups known as *chimères* (chimeras). Due to political instability, foreign donors canceled most of the funds pledged following the U.S. intervention of 1994.

In the fall of 2003 the United States asked Aristide to distance himself from Amiot Métayer, who led a group of *chimères* called the *armée cannibale* (cannibal army) in the city of Gonaïves. When Métayer was subsequently murdered, his supporters accused Aristide of ordering Métayer killed to improve his relations with the United States. In February 2004

Métayer's brother Butter allied himself with Louis-Jodel Chamblain, the leader of a paramilitary group who had terrorized Haiti in 1991–1994, and former police chief Guy Philippe. They launched a rebellion that soon spread to the city of Cap Haïtien, then marched on the capital, Port-au-Prince. At the prodding of his former French and U.S. supporters, Aristide left Haiti on February 29, 2004, for an initial exile in the Central African Republic. (Aristide later claimed he had been abducted by U.S. troops.) Following Aristide's departure, four major power centers emerged in Haiti: remnants of Aristide's *chimères*; Philippe's troops; French and American peacekeepers; and Gérard Latortue, chosen by a committee representing Haiti's various political parties to become interim prime minister.

Jean-Bertrand Aristide married Haitian-American lawyer Mildred Trouillot in February 1996. They have two daughters.

Philippe R. Girard

See also: Duvalier, Jean-Claude; Haiti; Human Rights

References

Aristide, Jean-Bertrand. *La vérité en vérité.* Port-au-Prince, Haiti: Le Natal, 1989.

Aristide, Jean-Bertrand. *In the Parish of the Poor.* New York: Orbis Books, 1993.

Aristide, Jean-Bertrand, and Christophe Wargny. *Jean-Bertrand Aristide: An Autobiography.* New York: Orbis Books, 1993.

Danner, Mark. "Haiti on the Verge." *New York Review of Books* (November 4, 1993): 25–30.

Danner, Mark. "The Prophet." *New York Review of Books* (November 18, 1993): 27–36.

Danner, Mark. "The Fall of the Prophet." *New York Review of Books* (December 2, 1993): 44–53.

Girard, Philippe. *Clinton in Haiti: The 1994 U.S. Intervention in Haiti.* New York: Palgrave MacMillan, 2004.

Wilentz, Amy. *The Rainy Season: Haiti since Duvalier.* New York: Simon & Schuster, 1989.

ARMS TRAFFICKING

Arms trafficking refers to the buying and selling of weapons to military and paramilitary groups internationally, both through state-sanctioned and extralegal transactions. In Latin America and Africa, arms trafficking has been part of regional conflicts and conflicts between external powers that are conducted through third and fourth parties in proxy warfare. For Latin America, most arms trafficking during the cold war served American and Soviet proxy conflicts. During the same period, African arms trafficking served regional conflicts to overturn or maintain disputed governing bodies.

Modern arms trafficking in Latin America was heavily tied to U.S. regional and international interests during World War II and the cold war. During World War II, Latin American nations declared their allegiance to the Allies and received great financial assistance from the United States. Relying on U.S. monetary support and military power, Latin American governments subsequently leveraged their position during the cold war by using the specter of impending Communism to claim that any internal conflicts would favor Soviet-style policies. In response, the United States often provided aid in the form of weapons, military training, and equipment to quash violently such uprisings. In a mirror image, Latin American revolutionary groups received similar arms support from Cuba, Eastern Europe, and the Soviet Union.

While direct overseas weapons deliveries or sales and formal military assistance dominated the twentieth century, more recently a secondary international arms system was introduced to Latin America by private arms deals with guerilla forces, typically funded by narcotics sales. Coca cultivation, processing, and distribution groups hire guerilla forces for protection. Profits from narcotics trafficking, in turn, are used by the revolutionary groups to purchase weapons. In some cases the arms sales are private legal purchases, but usually private sellers and dealers illegally transport these weapons to Latin America. In other cases, arms sales have been made by purchasing surplus weapons from postconflict U.S.-Soviet proxy war regions. The private and internal trafficking of weapons dominates today's Latin American market.

In contrast, Africa's arms traffic after World War II was made possible by military aid from multiple parties, such as China, Iran, the United States, the Eastern Bloc, and the Soviet Union. Decolonization in the 1960s created a power vacuum. In this context, money and weapons were provided to bolster groups supporting capitalism, socialism, Communism, or rule governed by the Islamic faith. Intense conflicts arose in Sudan, Gambia, Mozambique, Angola, South Africa, and other areas. The vast majority of weapons used in these regional conflicts were manufactured elsewhere and partly shipped as official aid packages. The majority of the military hardware in such shipments did not consist of large weapons systems such as aircraft, tanks, or naval vessels, but rather assault weapons, mines, field-expedient artillery, and mortars. Africa lacked the necessary infrastructure to utilize and maintain mechanized infantry.

Vast numbers of assault weapons were sent to Africa with complex consequences. A domestic cottage industry emerged to retrofit civilian weapons to accept military ammunitions. South Africa established small arms productions facilities. When the cold war ended, massive aid shipments from the U.S. and Eastern Bloc nations declined; by that time, however, there were so many weapons on the black market that it was nearly three times more expensive to purchase small arms officially than to acquire them extralegally.

As monetary aid from the United States and the Eastern Bloc dried up, Latin America's and Africa's black markets became the driving forces behind further arms transfers. Latin American conflicts and arms hoarding are typically restricted to either official military forces or guerilla elements. However, in Africa, enough weapons had been shipped by the end of the cold war so that small arms could be more easily obtained. Furthermore, Africa lacks the infrastructure necessary to control the threat of arms. Additionally, in contrast to Latin America, many African governments rely on weapons as a means to maintain their own power.

Disarmament and arms control remain difficult in both Latin America and Africa. Weapons in one region often circulate to neighboring countries after a conflict. This was the case with Mozambique and South Africa; Rwanda and the Democratic Republic of the Congo; and, on a larger scale, Peru and Colombia. Even if disputed areas are settled by formal disarmament methods, a lack of secure handling and corruption amongst personnel charged with the transfer and destruction of such arms results in the weapons being sold back or exchanged for other goods. Arms are often shipped along channels similar to those used for contraband items such as rhino horn, fur, ivory, and narcotics.

Josiah Baker

See also: Cold War; Decolonization, African; Military Forces; World War II

References

Adekanye, 'Bayo. "Arms and Reconstruction in Post-Conflict Societies." *Journal of Peace Research* 34.3 (August 1997): 359–366.

Brayton, Abbott A. "The Politics of Arms Limitations in Africa." *African Studies Review* 26, no. 1 (March 1983): 73–89.

Vines, Alex. "Angola and Mozambique. The Aftermath of Conflict." *Conflict Studies* 280 (May–June 1995): 1–27.

Willet, Susan. "South Africa: Arms Trade Dilemma." *International Security Digest* 541.1 (November 1994): 47–74.

ART, AFRICAN

African art includes expressive art forms such as painting, sculpture, photography, textiles, pottery, beadwork, metal, and wood from the Stone Age to the present, shaped by travel and trade within the African continent and between Africa and the Americas. From its ancient civilizations to contemporary culture, Africa has been a continent of extraordinary artistic creativity. A vast diversity of art traditions and forms are produced and practiced by people living in a wide variety of landscapes: deserts, mountains, rain forests, and savannahs, large cities and small rural villages. Local traditional faiths have a long oral tradition providing explanations for the creation of the world, and the visual arts serve along with religion to teach and provide instructions in moral values, social conduct, and philosophical beliefs.

Evidence of the origins of artistic expression in Africa emerges from the early prehistoric period to ancient Nubian and Egyptian dynasties. Along with the art form, whether cave painting, pyramid, sculpture, mask, textile, or beaded necklace, there is a distinct connection between the use of these objects, religion, and other social systems.

Stone Age

The impulse to create art has prehistoric beginnings found in the ancient rock paintings north of the Sahara Desert in the Tassili n'Ajjer region of Algeria (ca. 8000–6000 BCE). These early Stone Age pictures are composed of symbols and images cut into rock or painted with naturally occurring pigments such as ocher (yellow clay), kaolin (white chalk), and charcoal (black ash). They portray animals and horned figures, goddesses and hunters, and scenes of everyday life, all rendered in remarkably detailed naturalism.

Ancient Art

In the north, ancient civilizations along the great Nile River in Egypt included the Kush kingdom in Nubia (ca. 800 BCE) and the Egyptian dynasties with their artistic splendor. Both Nubia (located in both Egypt and Sudan) and Ethiopia became important sites for early Christianity. The divine ruling kings commissioned the finest paintings and sculpture to serve as a system of sacred communication between the human and spiritual worlds.

In sub-Saharan Africa (countries located south of the Sahara Desert), ancient pottery heads were excavated in the town of Nok in northern Nigeria and dated to ca. 800 BCE–200 CE. The heads were at one time part of full human figures. Clothing and ornaments depicted on the surviving figures portray body adornments and dress nearly identical to those found several centuries later, ca. 900–1400, in figures from the Yoruba city of Ife. Ife is considered the sacred site of creation for the Yoruba people living in southwestern Nigeria. Ife flourished as a great center for the arts, where the finest bronze workers were commissioned by the Oni (owner) of Ife. The

Cave paintings of people with cattle, ca. 4000 BC–2000 BC, at Tassili-n-Ajjer, in the Sahara Desert of Algeria. (Corbis)

artists were notable for their highly skilled technique of *cire-purdue* (lost-wax) casting, as well as an elegant realism, attention to the finest detail, and idealized renderings of important royal ancestors.

Beginning in the fifteenth century, the legendary kingdom of Benin began to extend its power and authority over a wide area of Nigeria. The skill of the Ife craftsmen was so highly valued and celebrated that the Oba (king) of Benin had them move into his royal family compound. The Oba commissioned a dazzling array of objects highlighting himself and queen mother, their spiritual wealth and affiliations signifying wisdom, high rank, dignity, and achievement. The works incorporated images of court officials, chiefs, political allies, and conquered men. The Oba's warrior exploits and divine power were recorded and commemorated on large carved ivory tusks, inserted in cast bronze heads and displayed on royal ancestral shrines. Thousands of objects were created and installed in the Benin palace over several centuries immortalizing the king and reflecting the historical importance of the royal ruling lineage.

Nineteenth and Twentieth Centuries: Art and Transformation

Carved wood masks, both sacred and secular, are one of Africa's best-known and expressive art forms. The purposes, functions, and contexts in which they are used are

Statue for the soul of a local Nubian prince, ca. first–third century AD found in the excavations of Karanoq, ancient Nubia. (Giraudon/Art Resource, NY)

which may be painted or anointed with sacrificial material, but also distinct clothing often adorned with cowry shells, bells, mirrors, coins, plant fiber, animal hair, teeth, and other symbolic attachments. The dancer may also wear special arm and leg ornaments along with rattles or whisks held in the hand. In other words, the emphasis is on the complete ensemble and how it moves with motion and gesture and activates communication during a ceremonial performance. Geometric patterns and colors further identify the mask's association with natural forces and phenomena such as rivers, mountains, trees, winds, heaven, and earth. Once transformed, the masked character may even channel a spirit language such as low guttural sounds or high-pitched whistles. The dancer's intent is to conceal his earthly identity in order to transform and embody the invisible spirit that is

diverse and complex. Masks are carved to represent a range of distinct ancestors, animals, or natural forces that have particular significance to the individual family lineage or community. Masquerades are performed during rites of passage from adolescence to adulthood. They entertain while also communicating important social values and behavior, they mark the beginning and end of the agricultural seasons, and they emerge at funerals to provide the deceased a safe journey into the spiritual world.

Their appearances before audiences on these special occasions often include music, drumming, singing, and stunningly vigorous dance before a gathered audience. This is accomplished by donning a full costume comprised of not only the carved mask,

Bronze casting of Ife king, ca. thirteenth-century Nigeria. (Werner Forman/Art Resource, NY)

called to visit the human community during important ceremonial performances.

Masks display an astonishing variety of form. Each style can be identified as distinct and representative of a particular ethnic group and area. The Yoruba of southwest Nigeria, for instance, are considered one of the largest and most prolific art-producing peoples in West Africa. Yoruba carvers use one of the more naturalistic approaches when rendering the faces of ancestors and other special characters. For example, Gelede masqueraders perform at annual ceremonies honoring the ancestral mothers and the powerful community of deceased female elders. The masks provide a symbolic function by reinforcing and protecting the memory of the departed mothers.

Animals from the surrounding landscapes play an important role in masked

Initiation mask representing antelope, Democratic Republic of Congo, ca. twentieth century. (Manu Sassoonian/Art Resource, NY)

societies. The appearance of the Chi-Wara antelope headdresses of the Bamana peoples of Mali signals the beginning and end of the planting and harvest season. The antelope represents the mythical ancestor who helped to guide this agricultural community to plant bountiful harvests. Danced in male and female pairs, the masqueraders wear the carved headdresses attached by a basketry cap on the top of their heads. Their bodies are covered with full raffia costumes, signifying the uncultivated forest area. The dancers carry two long sticks, and in a bent posture they mimic the graceful movements of the antelope.

The Dogon of Mali incorporate masked dancers into collective dry-season funerary rituals, which take place over six days, during which individual and group performances are carried out by a special group of initiated men. The complex

Ceremonial mask from Angola representing a female ancestor, ca. twentieth century. The scars indicate tears associated with the ritual separation of sons from their mothers. (Manu Sassoonian/Art Resource, NY)

Dongon tribesmen in traditional masks, Mali. (Corbis)

ceremony, called *dama,* is an elaborate presentation that can include more than seventy masked characters. One of the most frequently seen is the *kanaga* mask, which is highly abstract in form. The *kanaga* mask is carved in a rectangular form worn over the face, with twin slats at the top. The dancers move in whirling, dynamic motions.

The Mende of Sierra Leone are exceptional for their women masqueraders, members of the all-female Sande society that is unique among masking societies in Africa. The women dance in their own helmet masks, worn over the head to the shoulder, called Sowei. The Sande society is responsible for the training, initiation, and socialization of young girls into adulthood. The male counterpart is the Poro society, whose members also use masks during rites of passage and often represent the town authority in both judicial and social matters.

Art and the Spiritual World

Figure carvings are among the most central and essential of objects commissioned for use in context with important sacred and secular rituals. These powerful symbolic images function as sites of worship and devotion to a particular deity or invisible force in the spiritual realm. They support the individual or community with a private place to come to petition for protection, prosperity, and personal welfare.

To influence the spirit to engage with the human world, some figures are carved in a highly abstract style by inventing an earthly form for a spiritual force. Still others function as a site for a specialist priest to activate the shrine figure by pouring a libation or blood sacrifice from an

Carving of female figure with offertory bowl. Luba, Congo. Nineteenth century. (Yale University Art Gallery/Art Resource, NY)

animal, usually a goat or chicken, which is then cooked and eaten as part of a community feast. In addition, iron nails or blades can be inserted into the carved figure to swear an oath of atonement, healing, and reconciliation. These rituals are seen as a process that helps to set the earth and heaven in a world of balance and harmony.

Carvings are commissioned to commemorate important warrior kings, leaders, or chiefs. These can function as memorials to both the deceased and the living and as a visual biography of the history of important town lineages. Women and children are also an important theme in figure sculpture. This image of maternity symbolizes the importance of the role of women in giving birth and increasing the community.

Among the carved wood sculpture of the Luba in the Democratic Republic of the Congo can be found the female figure. Representing the spiritually powerful wife of the diviner holding a bowl, it signifies the important role of women to contain life and offer sacred substances at encounters with the divine king.

Art and Royalty

The Ashanti of Ghana are historically associated with vast natural resources of pure gold that was both mined and traded by them. A spectacular array of cast gold was made as emblems of the authority of the king, treasures entrusted to him by the Akan state and passed on to his successors. The paramount chiefs are known to wear

Ashanti soul washer's gold badge. Ghana. (The Newark Museum/Art Resource, NY)

gold rings on every finger, multiple bracelets, an abundance of *kente* cloth often woven to include threads of gold, and layers of gold amulets and charms. As part of the king's arrival on ceremonial occasions, he is followed by a retinue of attendants who carry umbrellas, fans, weapons, and shields to symbolize both worldly and spiritual protection.

Stools are the principal and most fundamental symbols of the Akan state. Both secular and sacred, functional and symbolic, the soul of the leader is transferred to his "seat" at death. The Golden Stool of the Ashanti is considered their most sacred and spiritually powerful object. Seen only on rare ceremonial occasions in public, it sits on its own throne, one higher than the king himself.

Contemporary African Art

Africa today continues to be the home of creative artists working and producing in a multitude of mediums: painting, sculpture, photography, textiles, pottery, beadwork, metal, and wood. Travel, imported materials, and new technologies have allowed contemporary artists to generate new forms and reach beyond the borders of their towns and cities to embrace Europe, the Americas, and Asia, reflecting the continued vibrancy of African cultural expression.

Deborah Stokes

See also: Africa, Precolonial; Cush Kingdom; Kente Cloth; Nigerian Traditional Dances; Religion (Africa)

References

Bascom, William. *African Art in Cultural Perspective: An Introduction.* New York: Norton, 1973.

Beier, Ulli. *Contemporary Art in Africa.* New York: Praeger, 1968.

Boone, Sylvia A. *Radiance from the Waters: Ideals of Feminine Beauty in Mende Art.* New Haven, CT: Yale University Press, 1986.

Cole, Herbert M., ed. *I Am Not Myself: The Art of African Masquerade.* Monograph Series, no. 26. Los Angeles: Fowler Museum of Cultural History, Regents of the University of California, 1985.

Drewel, Henry J., and John Pemberton. *Yoruba: Nine Centuries of African Art and Thought.* New York: Center for African Art and Harry Abrams, 1989.

Phillips, Tom, ed. *Africa: Art of a Continent.* London: Prestel, 1996.

Visona, Monica Blackmun, Robin Poyner et al., *A History of Art in Africa.* New York: Harry Abrams, 2001.

Willett, Frank. *African Art.* New York: Thames & Hudson, 1993.

ATLANTIC WORLD

The "Atlantic World" is a critical and theoretical concept for cultural study through transatlantic, circum-atlantic, and point-specific analysis of peoples, goods, intellectual production, and health issues. The Atlantic World as a unit of study and analysis is a relatively new concept. It most literally refers to a geographic region, but it also encompasses the identification of a shifting set of identities as exerted by this region's various components. It is usual to begin with Columbus's voyages from 1492 and the intersection of Europe, the African Atlantic, and the Americas that they heralded. David Armitage has identified three frameworks of analysis for the Atlantic World: "circum-Atlantic history," which emphasizes a holistic approach to the Atlantic region; "trans-Atlantic history," which centers on a comparative approach; and "cis-Atlantic history," which identifies a particular point or region within a wider Atlantic context. The concept of an Atlantic World seeks to outline the manner in which the inhabitants of this world were enmeshed: by the goods extracted and produced in one area and consumed elsewhere; by flowing intellectual and cultural currents; by kinship networks; and by diseases emanating from afar.

We can broadly periodize our study of this region into three eras. The sixteenth and seventeenth centuries saw the creation of an Atlantic World as a European oceanic frontier analogous to the Mediterranean. Initial movements emanated primarily from the Iberian Peninsula, and the cultural and political ties that bound them to the Americas gradually became more formal. The next three centuries saw the development of more "modern" colonial relationships, the beginning of whose end has been traced by some to the slave revolts and black revolutionary activity against French forces in Haiti, or St. Domingue, in the late eighteenth century. The abolition of slavery in the Western Hemisphere by 1888 provides another possible end point for this era. This may be problematic for our understanding of an Atlantic World, however, given that it was not until the middle of the twentieth century that slavery was abolished in much of Atlantic Africa.

In the twentieth century, rather than the Americas being Atlanticized by European and African expansion, the opposite effect could be detected: as the United States rose to world predominance, the European state system lost its traditional structures and influences could be exerted from West to East. Indeed, this phenomenon even characterized what Paul Gilroy labels as a particularly "black Atlantic" culture. Thus, in the twentieth century, the African American intellectual, W. E. B. Du Bois, could articulate a "double consciousness" that referred to a dual mindset in which Africa and the Americas equally and mutually influenced a developing "Atlantic" mentality.

Thus, inherent in a scholarly identification of an Atlantic World linking Africa and the Americas is a challenge to notions of national exceptionalism on either side of the Atlantic Basin. Set within this world during both its colonial and national eras, the United States had more similarities with than differences from other colonies and new nations in the Americas and the eastern Atlantic. Networks, therefore, came about that consisted of people of African descent in the United States and in Canada and British and American abolitionists. Such networks allowed these groups to organize migrations from West to East rather than East to West. They were responsible for the British colony of Sierra Leone and the American settlement of Liberia, for example.

Indeed, we may view the American Revolution from within a wider Atlantic World that encompassed Africa, the

Americas, and Europe. In this light, it did not lead to any explicit changes in the structure of the British state. Rather, in an Atlantic context, it produced a more abstract change in notions of British nationhood. We may view this difference through a comparison with the Caribbean Atlantic world during the same period. The revolution in the mainland American colonies did not create an allied sense of Jamaican-ness, for example. Rather, with the loss of white Americans from the British Empire, white inhabitants of the Caribbean identified themselves more closely with this same Empire, making race, rather than liberty, a key factor in its makeup. In the context of an Atlantic World, then, the American Revolution created a new distinction between nations defined by a conception of liberty and empires whose identities were formed in racial terms. Indeed, such a cis-Atlantic approach may even provide a new interpretative framework for the westward expansion of slavery as well as the dispossession of Native Americans in the United States during the nineteenth century. The notion of an Atlantic World may thus complicate any "exceptionalist" approaches to the study of U.S. history.

It is important to note that many of the European settlers in the Atlantic World maintained a self-conscious collective identity that emphasized a shared endeavor, albeit one that was often in competition with those with whom it was shared. Whether we analyze this world in its Anglo-American, Ibero-American, or Franco-American contexts, many of those involved would have identified themselves as being from particular localities, or even economic guilds, as opposed to larger nation states. This may, for example, explain often complicated Anglo-French and Huguenot-Dutch alliances, which allowed access to the Caribbean under Hispanic control in the first and second periods of Atlantic expansion. Early Caribbean sugar producers were advised by Dutch experts who had honed their skills in Portuguese settlements on the Brazilian Atlantic, which connected them to the Amazon. Moreover, it was the Portuguese experience (ironically medieval in nature) in utilizing enslaved peoples in Atlantic Africa that could be translated into more modern colonial terms in the Western Atlantic and transferred to other European powers.

Recent scholarship, however, points to medieval, and even biblical, precedents for the formation of this Atlantic World. Quasi-religious legends such as the land of Ophir, the islands of the seven cities, or the mythical figure of Prester John provided medieval means to conceptualize the region's expansion in the early modern, and even modern, era. One may also highlight the medieval encounters between Europeans and the indigenous inhabitants of the Canary Islands, Madeira, the Azores, and the African Atlantic littoral. The *guanches* of Tenerife, for example, were not regarded in the fourteenth and fifteenth centuries as either white European or black African. They therefore provided a kind of conceptual halfway house between Europe and the Americas, given that European perceptions of indigenous Caribbean societies in the early modern period reflected the same ambiguities.

Indeed, early-fifteenth-century Portuguese and Italian encounters with the African Atlantic coast were in many ways medieval and feudalistic in origin. European naval power could not be fruitfully deployed in coastal battles along the African Atlantic littoral, which had a specialized and difficult maritime culture that consisted of uncharted seas and narrow coastal inlets. This meant that any African counterforces did not need to engage outside of coastal waters. African vessels were often designed for coastal trade, given their earlier experiences of connecting trading boats with Saharan caravans, which would meet the vessels at tributaries or inlets. In this way, a natural African naval advantage often obliged Europeans (and European interlopers) to trade on African terms. This might include the payment of customs, duties, and gifts. Interestingly, experience like this in Atlantic African contexts would be incorporated into Western Atlantic encounters in the following centuries. For example, the Venetian traveler Alvise Ca Da Mosto, who acted on behalf of the Portuguese, often deferred to African rulers and customs, while other Portuguese representatives dealt with African Atlantic polities in feudal—rather than colonial—terms.

Ironically, the institution of slavery, which dominates our understanding of a developing transatlantic world, in many ways developed because of medieval, rather than colonial, similarities between existing networks of African and Arab slavery and Iberian forms of feudal labor. Only with the growth of capitalistic structures would the Middle Passage rupture these medieval continuities and characterize the Atlantic World in more colonial terms, buttressed by commodities produced through an often ruthless system of plantation slavery in areas such as Brazil, the Caribbean, and North America.

We should thus be aware of the disparity between African and European migration in this Atlantic World. For example, between 1600 and 1800, over one million Europeans migrated to British America, including mainland and Caribbean colonies, compared to well over two million Africans during the same period, the vast majority of whom went to the Caribbean. In the entire Atlantic World, including areas such as the parts of Brazil administered by the Dutch and Portuguese, over 7.5 million African captives moved across the Atlantic to the Americas in the period before 1800. Indeed, the idea of an Atlantic World in fact helps us to understand the manner in which slavery, and the production of sugar, developed according to a pattern of linked environmental and socioeconomic change. Portuguese feudal links with Atlantic Africa allowed local forms of forced labor to be transferred into a more formal structure in the Atlantic islands of Madeira, São Tomé, and the Azores. Here, patterns and experiences provided a model that other groups would use in the Caribbean and the Americas, giving rise in the Atlantic World to what some scholars label the "plantation complex." In Madeira, a model was created in which large tracts of land were cleared, enslaved people were imported, and complicated sugar mills built. On the other side of the Atlantic, Hispaniola's sugar production depended on technology developed in these arenas, as well as inflows of capital and debt served by merchants whose livelihoods were made in the Eastern Atlantic.

We should not, however, allow our analysis of the growth of trans-Atlantic slave systems to paint a picture of an Atlantic World that was divided between coerced labor, in its "new" frontiers, and labor induced by currency, in its "old" ones. In hubs such as Amsterdam and London, for example, guilds, indentured servants, and sharecroppers often found themselves inserted in a monetarized economy.

Moreover, Old World Atlantic cities such as Bordeaux, whose industry came in the seventeenth century to be dominated by New World connections, demonstrated that the periphery of the region could often influence, and change, what historians would label as the "center."

The Atlantic World could also produce new, syncretic identities. Forms of European Christianity could either be forced upon unwilling populations in the Americas or could combine with indigenous beliefs to create new systems. Similarly, Creole culture might develop in the region, where enslaved, or previously enslaved, Africans could mold Christian concepts with older African customs and beliefs within a new context that could itself continually alter these identities according to changing circumstances. Indeed, it is with this idea in mind that we are brought back to the revolutionary black Atlantic identity in Haiti, influenced as it was by local Creole and European identities and events. The combination of the two at the end of the eighteenth century uniquely demonstrates the specifically "Atlantic" world that scholars deploy as the most appropriate analytical tool in such circumstances. Sharing a stage with the French Revolution and the Napoleonic Wars, Haiti's fifteen-year struggle for racial emancipation and national independence challenged notions about racial hierarchy that were gaining legitimacy in an Atlantic World dominated by Europeans and the slave trade. It also demonstrates, however, that the concept of an Atlantic World is more than a mere tool of analysis. Rather, these new intersections of Creole and European identities formed from within the Atlantic context, were often self-consciously perceived in contemporary terms.

Societies in the Atlantic World were not necessarily located along the Atlantic Ocean itself: Africans could live far away from the Atlantic African coast but nonetheless find themselves ensnared in the slave trade through Saharan Arab slave networks that connected to newer Atlantic European ones. Many Amerindians far away from the Atlantic coast encountered pathogens, flora, and fauna that transformed their lives before they even met a European arriving from an Atlantic hub. It is through the analysis of such interconnections that we see the validity, and usefulness, of the notion of an Atlantic World.

Gideon Mailer

See also: Colonialism; Columbian Exchange; Creole/Criollo; Diaspora; Mexico (Afro-Mexican Identity); Pre-Columbian America; Slavery (History)

References

Armitage, David, and Michael Braddick, eds. *The British Atlantic World, 1500–1800.* New York: Palgrave Macmillan, 2002.

Bailyn, Bernard. "The Idea of Atlantic History." *Itinerario* 20 (1996): 19–44.

Canny, Nicholas, and Anthony Pagden, eds. *Colonial Identity in the Atlantic World, 1500–1800.* Princeton, NJ: Princeton University Press, 1987.

Curtin, Philip. *The Rise and Fall of the Plantation Complex: Essays in Atlantic History.* 2nd ed. Cambridge: Cambridge University Press, 1998.

Elliott, John H. *The Old World and the New, 1492–1650.* Cambridge: Cambridge University Press, 1970.

Gilroy, Paul. *The Black Atlantic: Modernity and Double-Consciousness.* Cambridge, MA: Harvard University Press, 1993.

Klooster, Wim. "The Rise and Transformation of the Atlantic World." In *The Atlantic World: Essays on Slavery, Migration, and Imagination,* edited by Wim Klooster and A. Padula. Upper Saddle River, NJ: Prentice Hall, 2004.

Schwartz, S., ed. *Implicit Understandings: Observing, Reporting, and Reflecting on the Encounters between Europeans and Other*

Peoples in the Early Modern Era. Cambridge: Cambridge University Press, 1994.

Thornton, John. *Africa and Africans in the Making of the Atlantic World, 1400–1800.* 2nd ed. Cambridge: Cambridge University Press, 1998.

ATTUCKS, CRISPUS (1723–1770)

Crispus Attucks was an African American hero of the American Revolution. In what has become known as the Boston Massacre, he was shot down in the street on March 5, 1770, while leading a protest against the presence of British troops. Attucks's father was a slave brought to Boston from Africa, his mother a Natick Indian. He was enslaved in Framingham, Massachusetts, until age twenty-seven, when he ran off to sea. Except that he was employed as a sailor and sometime rope maker in Boston, little is known about the twenty-year span between Attucks's escape from slavery and the time of his involvement in the Boston Massacre. As a runaway slave and a sailor, Attucks must have been attuned to the various abuses of power under which the British held their subjects throughout the Atlantic World, not the least of which was the press gang—an institution many equated with slavery. Thus, it is not surprising that his sympathies were with the colonists, who were largely against the British occupation. From the moment of his death until this day, Attucks has been lionized as an American hero; indeed, Boston colonists continued to memorialize his death until the signing of the Declaration of Independence, and Boston abolitionists established Crispus Attucks day in 1858. For many, he remains a symbol of the way in which African Americans throughout American history have laid

Crispus Attucks, an African American killed in the Boston Massacre, became a symbol of the American struggle for independence. (Library of Congress)

down their lives for key American values, even as they have struggled to reap the full reward of those values.

Matthew D. Brown

See also: American Revolution

References

McLeese, Don. *Crispus Attucks: Heroes of the American Revolution.* Vero Beach, FL: Rourke Publishing, 2005.

Hiller, Zobel. *The Boston Massacre.* New York: W.W. Norton, 1970.

AVELLANEDA, GERTRUDIS GÓMEZ DE (1814–1873)

The first published book of Gertrudis Gómez de Avellaneda, *Sab* (1841), is considered by critics such as Catherine Davis to be the only feminist-abolitionist novel published by a woman in nineteenth-century Spain or its slaveholding colony, Cuba. Poet, novelist, and playwright, often

Portrait of Gertrudis Gómez de Avellaneda. Published in 1841, her most controversial novel, Sab, *has been compared to* Uncle Tom's Cabin *as a literary protest against slavery. (Library of Congress)*

called la Avellaneda or Tula, she was born in Camaguey, Cuba, in 1814, and died in Madrid, Spain, in 1873. Throughout her lifetime, the Cuba of her birth remained a slaveholding colony of Spain. Nonetheless, the sociopolitical realities of nineteenth-century Cuba eventually led to a Cuba that sought independence beginning in 1868. Cubans abolished slavery in 1886, and gained independence from Spain in 1898. La Avellaneda's life and writings announced, if not foreshadowed, the circular trajectory of this dialectic: subjugation-emancipation-subjugation, slavery-postslavery-slavery.

Because of her mastery of rhyme and meter as well as her output, impressive both in quantity and quality, la Avellaneda is considered to be first and foremost a poet. Although she claims to have started writing poetry at the age of nine, her first extant poem was written in 1836 aboard a frigate taking her from Cuba to Europe. Many of her poems carry the theme of nostalgia for the country of her birth. It was not until 1859 that she would return to Cuba, where she remained until 1864 before returning to Spain.

It is important to note that *Sab* was published eleven years before *Uncle Tom's Cabin.* Set in the Cuban countryside, the novel traces the demise of slaveholding Cuban society. It is the story of a mulatto slave's unrequited love for Carlota, his master's daughter, who is engaged to Enrique Otway, a greedy Englishman with fair, rosy skin, blue eyes, and golden hair. Sab, the tormented slave who gives the novel its name, feels that his soul is free, although his body is enslaved and base, and at the same time is convinced that no woman could possibly love him or want to join her fate to that of a poor mulatto. His feelings predate pride in Cuban blackness because he is very much ashamed of what he calls his accursed race and is literally dying to be white. The novel calls for the immediate abolition of slavery and the manumission of all slaves. Upon publication, it was banned in Cuba, and la Avellaneda omitted it from her complete works.

There is much debate over the question of la Avellaneda's patriotic affinities. According to the critic Hugh Harter, no dichotomy existed, and the accusation that she had turned her back to Cuba deeply hurt her since, much like the characters in her plays and novels, she exemplified Cuba, or the union in the New World of the Spanish, the African, and the Indian. The idiosyncratic circumstances of her birth allowed her to be both the colonizer and the colonized. Just like her protagonist, Carlota, la Avellaneda was the colonizer for all the obvious reasons, for she was the privileged daughter of the slaveholding gentry;

she was also the colonized, because she herself was a *criolla,* a Cuban, a woman, and a child of Cuba, of a subordinated people.

Beatriz Rivera-Barnes

See also: Caribbean Literature; Cuba; Literature, Latin American; Spanish Empire

References

Cotarelo y Mori, Emilio. *La Avellaneda y sus obras: Ensayo biográfico y crítico.* Madrid: Archivos, 1930.

Gómez de Avellaneda, Gertrudis. *Sab.* Manchester, UK: Manchester University Press, 2001.

Harter, Hugh A. *Gertrudis Gómez de Avellaneda.* Boston: Twayne, 1981.

Kirkpatrick, Susan. *Románticas: Women Writers and Subjectivity.* Liverpool, UK: Liverpool University Press, 1989.

Luis, William. *Literary Bondage.* Austin: University of Texas Press, 1990.

AVIATION

Following the Wright brothers' first flight in 1903, many people in the Americas and in Africa became interested in aviation, but few considered the possibility of travel across the Atlantic until the first transatlantic flights in 1919. The first nonstop flight across the North Atlantic, by British aviators John Alcock and Arthur Brown in July 1919, aroused much interest in flying. Seeing the possibilities in Africa, South African pilots Pierre van Ryneveld and Quentin Brand in 1920 were the first to fly from Cairo to Cape Town.

In 1922 Portuguese naval pilot Sacadura Cabral and his commanding officer, Vice Admiral Gago Coutinho, the navigator, decided to take up the challenge. They flew from Lisbon to Rio de Janeiro. Although they stopped on the Cape Verde Islands and crash-landed on St. Paul's Rock, off the coast of Brazil, technically they were the first pilots to fly from Africa to any part of the Americas. Altogether, their flight used three Fairey IIID floatplanes. After their crash on St. Paul's Rock, a local plane that was loaned to them seemed incapable of reaching mainland Brazil, so they cabled Portugal for another plane. It arrived but had been damaged while at sea, and a third plane had to be used. They eventually made it to Pernambuco and then to Rio de Janeiro. In spite of their problems, they were regarded as the first to fly the South Atlantic and won a $50,000 prize. One of the original planes is on display at the Maritime Museum in Lisbon, and a replica of the plane is on display on the embankment to the River Tagus at Belém parish, Lisbon.

With many other records being broken, in 1926 Ramón Franco, younger brother of Francisco Franco, later dictator of Spain, piloted a flight from Spain to Argentina. His plane also stopped in the Canary Islands and the Cape Verde Islands, making him the first Spaniard to fly from Africa to the Americas. He touched down in Fernando de Noronha, Brazil, and then flew on to Pernambuco, Rio de Janeiro, Montevideo, and Buenos Aires, spending a total of fifty-nine hours in the air. Ramón Franco was killed in 1938 during the Spanish Civil War en route to bombing Valencia.

In May 1927 Charles Lindbergh completed the first solo, nonstop transatlantic flight; on October 14–15 of the same year, Frenchmen Dieudonne Costes and Joseph le Brix flew a Breguet 19 from Saint Louis, Senegal, to Port Natal, Brazil, the first nonstop aerial crossing from the mainland of Africa to the Americas. Another French pilot, Jean Mermoz, flew from Dakar for Brazil on May 12, 1930, to inaugurate the first airmail service across the South

Atlantic, but he crashed into the sea and had to be rescued.

The next major move in the field of aviation was the transport of passengers. In 1930 the German airship Graf Zeppelin crossed the South Atlantic, going over the Azores. On March 20, 1932, zeppelins began their first regular transatlantic flights, from Germany to Brazil, some passing over Africa.

After these records, aviators tried their hand at achieving other "firsts." On January 6, 1931, when the Italian general Italo Balbo led twelve Savoia-Marchetti S55s from Portuguese Guinea to Brazil, they became the first formation to cross the South Atlantic. Mermoz and his crew flew from Senegal to Brazil, nonstop, in 17 hours, 27 minutes, on January 16, 1933, the fastest journey from the African mainland to the Americas at that time. Mermoz joined up with the famous French pilot Antoine de Saint-Exúpery to fly in Argentina—Mermoz was lost after his plane disappeared, believed crashed, while flying from Dakar to Natal (Brazil). Saint-Exúpery had flown extensively in French West Africa before moving to South America. Soon after Mermoz flew, Jim Mollison flew from London to Senegal and then to Brazil, becoming the first person to have flown across both the North Atlantic and the South Atlantic solo.

On November 11–13, 1935, New Zealander Jean Batten flew from Senegal to Brazil in a Percivall Gull, being the first woman to fly solo across the South Atlantic. She was late arriving in Rio de Janeiro, and the Brazilian air force set off to look for her. They eventually found her plane bogged on a beach 175 miles away; she was in a nearby fishing village. After patching up the plane, she flew to Rio and was awarded the Brazilian Order of the Southern Cross, the first British woman not in the royal family to receive the award. She subsequently flew to Montevideo and then to Buenos Aires.

On August 15, 1937, Lufthansa started seaplane flights from the Azores to New York, refueling from seaplane tenders stationed along the route. The military importance of the Azores as a refueling stop was recognized by the British, who occupied it during World War II, along with the Americans. In May 1947 it was used as a base for the planes involved in the first aerial refueling of British flights from London to Bermuda.

After World War II civil aviation grew rapidly. On January 1, 1946, an Avro Lancastrian from British South American Airways was the first commercial flight to leave London's new Heathrow Airport. Nowadays, passenger flights flying from African cities are, of course, regular services connecting Africa and the Americas.

Justin Corfield

See also: Cape Verde; Military Forces; World War I; World War II

References

Lascano, Diego M. *Saltando el charco: Imágenes y crónicas del cruce aéro del Río de la Plata entre 1907 y 1940.* Montevideo, Uruguay: Librel Editores, 1999.

Longyard, William H. *Who's Who in Aviation History: 500 Biographies.* Novato, CA: Presidio Press, 1994.

Mackersey, Ian. *Jean Batten: The Garbo of the Skies.* London: Macdonald, 1990.

Rivero, Clara. "Antoine de Saint-Exúpery en la Argentina." *Todo es Historia* (Buenos Aires), no. 395 (June 2000): 82–93.

B

BAHAMAS

The Bahamas has cultural retentions from Africa that can be traced through its political history from colonization and slavery to independence. An archipelago of over 700 islands and 2,400 cays, the Bahamas is an independent nation in the Caribbean. The islands of the Bahamas are located in the Atlantic Ocean, just east of Florida in the United States and north of Cuba and Hispaniola. The Bahamas extends over 760 miles and is regarded as having the clearest and most beautiful water in the world. The 700 islands that make up the Bahamas include 30 inhabited islands, and the total estimated land area is 5,358 square miles, with the highest land elevation being 206 feet on Mount Alvernia in Cat Island. Overall, the terrain of the Bahamas is flat with some rounded hills, and its climate—controlled by the Gulf Stream—is subtropical to tropical. The islands of the Bahamas stand with numerous coral reefs on two shallow submarine banks, and all the islands, rocks, and cays are made up of limestone. The capital of the Bahamas is Nassau, which is on the island of New Providence, where about 70 percent of the population resides. The remaining major islands are called the Family Islands, and they include Grand Bahama, Abaco, Andros, Bimini, Berry Islands, Eleuthera, Cat Island, Exuma, San Salvador, Long Island, Acklins, Crooked Island, Rum Cay, Mayaguana, Ragged Island, and Inagua.

People and Culture

The population of the Bahamas, according to the 2000 census, totaled 306,611, and people from the Bahamas are known as Bahamians. Some 85 percent of the Bahamian population is of African descent, 12 percent is of European descent, and 3 percent is Asian and Hispanic. The official language is English, spoken by almost all inhabitants, and many people also speak Bahamian patois or dialect. The Bahamas is a religious country; it has more churches per capita than any other nation in the world. Christianity is the main religion, and Baptists form the largest denomination, followed by the Anglican and Roman Catholic churches. Some people, especially in the southern and eastern islands, practice Obeah, which is an African religious and spiritual practice similar to Voodoo and Santeria.

The rich cultural heritage found in the Bahamas can be traced to its African legacies. Obeah, bush medicine, Bahamian patios, the Junkanoo festival, and Bahamian dances, folktales, and music all have origins in Africa. Bush medicine is the use of medicinal plants to cure common ailments. The Bahamian dialect or patios came from the country's European and African heritage, with a vocabulary and sentence structure similar to other creolized languages across the African Diaspora. The Bahamian festival Junkanoo was created during slavery to celebrate the days free from work during the Christmas season, and its African roots lie in the use of goatskin drums. Junkanoo is celebrated twice per year, on Boxing Day and New Year's Day, and the festival has thrived since the 1800s. The music of Junkanoo is very distinct, using goatskin drums, cowbells, and horns. Other forms of Bahamian music include goombay and rake-and-scrap. Fire dances, ring plays, and jumping dances are Bahamian dances with African roots. Additionally, Bahamian folktales and oral stories reveal the country's African heritage with characters and stories that can be traced directly to West Africa and shared across the African Diaspora.

History

The original inhabitants of the Bahamas were Lucayan Tainos, a subgroup of the Arawaks. Archaeologists have asserted that many Amerindians in the Caribbean islands shared similar languages and culture, and they are often referred to as Tainos, which means good or noble. When Columbus landed in 1492 on the island of San Salvador in the eastern Bahamas, he believed he was in the East, specifically India, and therefore mistakenly called the native people Indians. After observing the shallow sea around the islands, he spoke the words *baja mar*, meaning shallow water or sea, and this effectively gave the area the name Bahamas. The Lucayan Tainos were known to be very peaceful, and they lived off the land and ocean through farming and fishing. They built sturdy thatch huts, used stone tools, and made pottery. Moreover, they had well-defined social, political, and religious systems; however, Europeans treated them as primitive and even childlike. When Columbus arrived in the Bahamas, there were an estimated 50,000 Lucayan Tainos inhabiting the islands. He enslaved them and shipped them off to Hispaniola and Cuba to work in mines. Slavery, disease, and other hardships wiped out entire tribes within twenty-five years of European contact.

Spain lost interest in the Bahamas after colonizing other islands such as Hispaniola and Cuba. As a result, most of the Bahamian islands remained uninhabited for over one hundred years until England laid claim to the archipelago. The first major settlement was established in 1648 on Eleuthera by dissident English Puritans, known as the Eleutheran adventurers, who arrived in the Bahamas seeking religious freedom. The adventurers gave the island its name, and despite experiencing food and supply shortages, the group established settlements across Eleuthera and Abaco. During the late 1600s and the early 1700s, the Bahamas became a major stronghold for pirates and privateers. It was an ideal place for piracy because of its numerous islands and harbors, which made exceptional hiding places. Some famous pirates associated with the Bahamas include Blackbeard, Calico Jack, Anne Bonny, Mary Read, and Sir Henry Morgan, among others. They used Nassau as one of their major ports.

After the Bahamas became an official British colony in 1717, the United Kingdom ruled through governorships. The first governor-general of the Bahamas was Woodes Rogers, a former privateer. He successfully expelled the pirates and restored commerce. From the mid-to-late 1700s, however, the Bahamas was still considered to be a failing colony by many of the governors after Rogers. The population of the Bahamas during that time was only a few thousand people, almost half of them slaves. During the American Revolution, the British government issued land grants to American colonists who were still loyal to England. They sought refuge in the Bahamas and brought their slaves with them. They were known as the Loyalists and settled in Eleuthera, Abaco, and New Providence. The sparse population of the Bahamas tripled in a few years because of these new residents and their slaves. The new planters started to grow cotton, but the soil was unsuitable for that crop, and the plantations soon failed. But the Loyalists and other ruling classes in the Bahamas tried to maintain the plantation system because it was the foundation of their wealth and status.

After Britain outlawed the slave trade in 1807, the planters and merchants in the colonies fought vehemently against emancipation. As a result, slavery was not outlawed in the British colonies until 1834, and in the Bahamas, the Emancipation Act was not fully enforced until August 1, 1838. Furthermore, it did not mean complete freedom for the slaves. Rather, they became indentured labor for many years with little or no pay; in addition, former slave owners received monetary compensation from Britain for the freed slaves. While land was supposed to be allocated to the former slaves, for the most part they never actually received what they were promised. But in some cases, specifically in New Providence, former slaves did receive plots of land. Aside from some land allocation,

for over a century black Bahamians were treated with very little respect by the white ruling classes. The political climate of the Bahamas has been strongly affected by the inequality of whites and blacks. After emancipation, the education provided for blacks in the Bahamas during the mid-to-late 1800s was substandard, which served to maintain white dominance for many decades. The poor condition of education for blacks continued through the 1950s, while the majority of whites were educated abroad or at expensive private institutions. The lack of education and the poverty among blacks created considerable resentment toward the white ruling classes. Most black Bahamians could not vote because of a law limiting the franchise to propertyholders, which ensured the continuance of white rule. This law was repealed in 1886, nominally expanding the franchise to the larger black population, but that did little to change economic and political dominance by whites. The ruling white Bahamians believed they were superior to black Bahamians, and this produced inequality and segregation. Laws against discrimination were passed in 1956; however, tensions and prejudice remained.

The Bahamas was granted self-governing authority by Britain in 1964, and the mostly white government remained in power until defeated by the black majority party in 1967. The Bahamas gained full independence from Britain on July 10, 1973, and the country has for the most part flourished since becoming an independent nation.

The economic changes in the Bahamas from the end of slavery to the dependence on tourism at the turn of the twenty-first century have been tumultuous. During the U.S. Civil War, the economy prospered as a consequence of Confederate blockade running because Britain used Nassau as the port of exchange between British vessels carrying manufactured goods and Confederate boats carrying Southern cotton. (The Union blocked British ships from entering Southern ports between 1861 and 1865.) The next boom in the economy started in 1919 as a result of Prohibition in the United States, with the Bahamas becoming a major transit for smuggling alcohol into the United States. However, the end of Prohibition in 1934, along with the later collapse of the sponging industry, devastated the economy. It revived during World War II, when the Bahamas served as an Allied air and sea way station in the Atlantic, a function that created many jobs. The tourist and banking industries began growing in the Bahamas during the 1950s, but major expansion began during the years of radical economic, political, and social changes from 1963 to 1973. The Bahamas has become a stable, developing country that is heavily dependent upon tourism and offshore banking.

Angelique V. Nixon

See also: American Revolution; British Empire; Civil War, American; Columbus, Christopher; Creole/Criollo; Folklore, African; Obeah; Slavery (History)

References

Craton, Michael. *A History of the Bahamas.* 3rd ed. Waterloo, ON: San Salvador Press, 1986.

Craton, Michael, and Gail Saunders. *Islanders in the Stream: A History of the Bahamian People.* Vol. 2. Athens: University of Georgia Press, 1998.

Eneas, Cleveland W. *Bain Town.* Nassau, Bahamas: Timpaul Publishing, 1976.

Glinton, Patricia. *An Evening in Guanima: A Treasury of Folktales from The Bahamas.* Nassau, Bahamas: Guanima Press, 1994.

Glinton-Meicholas, Patricia. *More Talkin' Bahamian.* Nassau, Bahamas: Guanima Press, 1995.

Rouse, Irving. *The Tainos: Rise and Decline of the People Who Greeted Columbus.* New Haven, CT: Yale University Press, 1992.

Williams, Eric. *From Columbus to Castro: The History of the Caribbean.* New York: Vintage Books, 1970.

BAKHITA, JOSEPHINE, SAINT (1869–1947)

Canonized on October 1, 2001, Josephine Bakhita is the first African woman former slave to become a saint. Born in Africa but brought to Italy, Bakhita not only converted to the Catholic religion but also entered the convent. Bakhita is one of the few African nuns who lived in Europe. Following a practice common to nineteenth-century abolitionism in the United States, Bakhita dictated her own life story, following the suggestion of her prioress. Her biography has caught the attention of a varied audience, and she has been the inspiration for a musical show and a documentary film.

Bakhita was born in Olgossa in the region of Darfur in Sudan around 1869. She grew up in a large wealthy family. Her father was a respected kinsman to the tribal chief. Bakhita's family first experienced slavery when the eldest daughter was kidnapped by slave merchants who had previously ransacked the village. Bakhita, then only six years old, was witness to the brutal capture. Bakhita herself was captured by two Arabs at the age of eight or nine while she was in the fields searching for herbs in the company of a friend. Once she was captured, the little girl, separated from her friend and in shock, could not even remember her own name and was called Bakhita by her captors, which means "the lucky one" in Arabic. In the company of the slave traders and other slaves who were captured later, a bare-footed Bakhita walked through small villages, towns, and deserts for months. She was sold five times and tried to escape once, but she was caught.

Bakhita recalls the time she spent at a Turkish general's house as having been the most dreadful of all. Although not a day passed without some kind of physical punishment being inflicted on Bakhita, her most terrible experience took place when she was tattooed. This was a customary practice that raised the slave's market value and the prestige of the masters who owned them. As a result of this commonly practiced marking of the slaves, 192 incisions were inflicted on Bakhita's breasts, arms, and stomach. For more than three months Bakhita remained motionless and suffered in excruciatingly painful agony. This nightmare continued until the Italian consul in Khartoum, Callisto Legnani, visited the Turkish general and became interested in Bakhita's future. In 1883, having been a slave for almost fifteen years, Bakhita was purchased by Legnani with the intention of freeing her later. The consul's family took good care of her during the two years they remained in Sudan. In 1885, when the consul was recalled to Italy, Bakhita asked to travel with him, and the Legnani family accepted. Once in Italy, Bakhita eventually chose to stay at the Canosian sisters' Catechumenate, where she could be instructed in the Catholic religion. Bakhita, entrusted to the Canosian sisters, was baptized on January 9, 1890. She was around twenty-one years of age. When baptized, she received three Christian names: Josephine, Margaret, and Fortunata. Bakhita remained in the Cathecumenate for four years before deciding to enter the convent.

On December 7, 1893 Bakhita joined the novitiate at the Institute of the Cathecumenate in Venice, starting her religious career. She took her vows on December 8, 1893, and became a Canosian sister. However, due to her lack of formal education, she was relegated to the household chores. She worked in the sacristy and as a doorkeeper. From Venice she was first posted to Schio, near Venice, in 1902. At the request of her mother superior, Bakhita wrote down her story in 1910, while she was still in Schio. Apparently, Bakhita received hundreds of visitors, and it was this circumstance, together with the prospect of collecting money and gaining vocations for the missions in Africa, that led Bakhita's superior to request her now to dictate her life to Italian writer Ida Zanolini. The biography was published in 1930 under the title *Storia Meravigliosa* (Wonderful story). It not only sold well but also attracted hundreds of visitors to the Canossian convent. In view of Bakhita's growing popularity, she was sent to the Canossian novitiate in Vinercate, to be more conveniently located for travel all over Italy. On her superior's advice, Bakhita was sent to various convents to give talks on her life in Africa, her experience in slavery, her conversion, and her decision to embrace the Christian religion. In her broken Italian, which is preserved in the original text, Bakhita gave voice to her heartbreaking story.

Bakhita, affectionately called "madre moretta" (little black sister), suffered from chronic arthritis and asthmatic bronchitis, which became progressively aggravated until she died at Schio, Italy, on February 8, 1947, following an attack of pleurisy. She was buried in an aristocratic family vault. The canonization process started when Pope John Paul II proclaimed her Blessed Bakhita at St. Peter's Square on May 17, 1992. Years later, the same Pope John Paul II proclaimed her a saint on October 1, 2001.

Maria Frias

See also: Catholicism; Chikaba; Religion
(Africa); Sudan (Darfur Region)

Reference
Ukken, Clare. *Bakhita: From Slavery to
Sanctity.* Nairobi, Kenya: St. Paul, 1993.

BARAKA, AMIRI (1934–)

Amiri Baraka is an African American poet,
essayist, and dramatist who spurred the Black
Arts Movement (1960–1975). The rage
expressed by black dramatists in the 1960s
may have peaked with the arrival of Amiri
Baraka (formerly LeRoi Jones) on the
theatrical scene. Baraka was born Everett
LeRoy Jones in Newark, New Jersey, on
October 7, 1934. The depression of the
1930s, World War II, and the assassinations
of Malcolm X, Martin Luther King Jr., and
John F. Kennedy in the 1960s provoked his
disenchantment with world and American
politics and with America's racial policies. In
1957, following his undesirable discharge
from the Air Force, for which he had no re-
grets, Baraka moved to New York City.

*Amiri Baraka, poet and leading force in the Black Arts
Movement. (Library of Congress)*

On settling in Greenwich Village,
Baraka devoted time to writing poetry and
experimenting with drama. The Beat community in New York City afforded him the
atmosphere to develop an art that has been
defined as "populist modernism." Populist
modernism integrated "populist" black experiences with those aspects of modernist
Western literature and literary theory that
were considered excellent and, therefore,
appropriate. His involvement with the Beat
movement, from 1957 to 1962, was the
first phase of Baraka's rebellion against the
bourgeois separation of life and art, since it
was at this time that he began to suscribe to
the notion of art as an extension of the
artist. To reinforce this ideal, he advocated
bohemianism, an antibourgeois stance that

attacked bourgeois life and aesthetic styles.
By the mid-1960s Baraka was becoming in-
creasingly involved with Pan-Africanism,
protest rallies, and the African American
Civil Rights Movement. At the same time,
Baraka was drawn to to the ideas of the
Nation of Islam, and the radicalism of
Malcolm X, particularly by his contention
that racial confrontation was inevitable.

As part of his pursuit of revolutionary
and nationalistic ideals, Baraka in 1967
became a Kawaida minister, discarded his
"slave" name—LeRoi Jones—and assumed
the name Imamu Amiri (sometimes spelled
"Ameer") Baraka. Imamu, a Muslim title
and Swahili word, signifies "spiritual
leader," while Amiri, an Arabic (Berber)
name, means "prince." Baraka, also an
Arabic name, means "blessed," "sanctity,"

or "holiness." In 1974 Baraka dropped the title "Imamu" after he became a Marxist-Leninist.

Baraka's anger and pronationalist stance are traceable to his political views and activities, in the course of which he had a number of clashes with the police and white racists. In 1967, for example, he was thrown in jail for a misdemeanor that was never proven. Affected by this background, the explosion of racial anxiety and violence in the 1960s, and the emergence of black artistic, religious, and political movements within and beyond America, Baraka's drama championed aggressive solutions to America's black crisis. In all, therefore, his emergence as an activist was part of an ongoing artistic and political evolution that spanned the period from the 1950s through the 1970s.

The impact of Baraka's transatlantic background on his drama was partly manifested in his emergence as a major spokesman for the 1960s Black Arts Movement, which centered on experimentation with African sociodramatic and religious traditions. In his reliance on African ritual forms, which he restructured within a black American context, Baraka borrowed from a belief system that forged a close and sacred tie between the people and their social and natural environment. It is a relationship culled from the ancient inseparability of religious practice and secular events, as expressed in folklore, ceremonies, or festivals. Although these ritual paradigms underwent transformation when they resurfaced in the New World, Baraka sought to reclaim in the United States the basic role they had in African society.

African ancestral models also surfaced in Baraka's support for and commitment to the Black Theatre Movement, an offshoot of the Black Arts Movement. Both movements shared the quest for a viable, antiracist, independent black theatre and influenced the founding of Baraka's Black Arts Repertory Theatre in 1965 and his Spirit House Movers and Players troupe in 1968. Activities of the Repertory Theatre and Spirit House centered on the ideals of Baraka's Black Revolutionary Theatre manifesto, which defied the ambivalence he associated with integrationist drama and which further demonstrated his interest in African socio-artistic values. Presented in 1965, the manifesto heralded the revolutionary drama of the 1960s, which was essentially anti-liberal, anti-academic, and anti-European. The Revolutionary Theatre put white America on trial in a manner that brought about its symbolic but hostile confrontation with the black world. As the chief exponent of the Revolutionary Theatre, Baraka played a leading role in defining a more practical task for black drama, one that advanced themes of black survival while teaching the people the relevance of struggle. In advocating rebellion in art and ideas, the Revolutionary Theatre sought to radicalize or destroy European sociodramatic ethics by refusing to endorse the reformist character that Baraka identified in pre-1960s black dramas.

To fulfill the goals of the Revolutionary Theatre, Baraka borrowed from customary African rituals and sacrifice. His confidence in ritual evolved around his nationalistic "return" to ancestral precepts. In preserving this sacred worldview, his Revolutionary Theatre adopted a rite-of-passage structure that thrived on violence and sacrificial rebirth. In part, therefore, Baraka presented black drama as an extension of the oral traditions of Africa and as a genre rooted in specific African sensibilities.

As his revolutionary drama progressed, Baraka's status as black nationalist also developed. He increasingly incorporated black-based music, dance, language, and lifestyles as integral parts of his form, and in this way, he retained a deliberate black and African-rooted rhetoric. His tapping from a broad range of performance elements was based on a desire to involve his audience emotionally, intellectually, verbally, and physically so that his audiences were much like the traditional African spectator-participants who become a fundamental part of performance through their choric presence. Up until its demise, the Revolutionary Theatre was reinvigorated by the reciprocal energy that it distributed among its audience.

Beyond the incorporation of several related genres, Baraka's ritual drama was a bloody rite, one of exclusion and vengeance, purging black society of white profanity. Whites were symbolically judged and exterminated along with their black accomplices, a pattern aimed at ingraining the Revolutionary Theatre's message in the consciousness of its primary audience of blacks. Bloody sacrifice became Baraka's formula for black rebirth and American regeneration, which is why his revolutionary plays were structured on recurring archetypal, thematic, and stylistic traits.

The functional basis of Baraka's drama was thus situated in a spiritual dimension aroused and sustained through ritual. The communality generated by ritual supported his ideology and retained certain liturgical qualities that derived from his African background. As in African ritual systems, the Revolutionary Theatre did not distinguish the sacred from the secular, ritual from theatre, or theatre from life. It encompassed the total experience and aspirations of the black community.

In essence, violence was a principal ritual instrument in Baraka's revolutionary dramas. Beyond a strong and sadistic desire to kill whites, his plays demonstrated the possibility of change through force and determination. In this regard, Baraka found Antonin Artaud's Theatre of Cruelty theory germane to the intensity of his Revolutionary Theatre and borrowed from its brutal and exorcist suggestions, especially in his *Four Black Revolutionary Plays* (1969).

Some of Baraka's plays initially deviate from a ritualistic pattern, but they end with ritual murders, thereby preserving the efficacy of ritual sacrifice. The following are among his most salient plays falling within this category: *The Toilet* (1963), *Dutchman* (1964), *Experimental Death Unit #1* (1965), *Home on the Range* (1968), *Junkies are Full of (Shhh . . .)* (1968), and *The Death of Malcolm X* (1969). Other Baraka plays explore race relations in dramatic contexts that are rituals in themselves. As rituals, Baraka's plays manifest more obvious African influences, a trend crowned by his decision to tap from African ritualistic and mythical sources in *Slave Ship* (1967). Other plays that adhere to this structure are *The Slave: A Fable in a Prologue and Two Acts* (1964) and *Great Goodness of Life: A Coon Show* (1967). Then again, there are those other Baraka plays that are consciously situated within fantasy worlds. When he explores his ideologies in such fantasy worlds, Baraka becomes a mythmaker who devises sacred space for ritual display. Within this realm he escapes the restriction to "real" characters and settings, exploring other innovative possibilities. Baraka plays that belong to this fantasy category include *The Baptism* (1966), *Black*

Mass (1965), and *Madheart: A Morality Play* (1967). In general, Baraka's style, aims, and themes set a violent, autonomous, and defiant tone for black drama of the 1960s and spurred African American playwrights on to more daring and richer experimentation.

Phillip Effiong

See also: Black Power Movement; Drama, African American; Pan-Africanism

References

Baraka, Amiri. *The Autobiography of LeRoi Jones/Amiri Baraka.* New York: Freundlich Books, 1984.

Baraka, Amiri. Four Black Revolutionary Plays, All Praise to the Black Man. Indianapolis, IN: Bobbs Merrill 1969.

Harris, William J., ed. *The LeRoi Jones/Amiri Baraka Reader.* New York: Thunder's Mouth Press, 1991.

Hudson, Theodore R. *From LeRoi Jones to Amiri Baraka: The Literary Works.* Durham, NC: Duke University Press, 1973.

Sollors, Werner. *Amiri Baraka/LeRoi Jones: The Quest for a "Populist Modernism."* New York: Columbia University Press, 1978.

Stewart, James T. "The Development of the Black Revolutionary Artist." In *Black Fire: An Anthology of Afro-American Writing,* edited by LeRoi Jones and Larry Neal. New York: William Morrow, 1968.

BARBADOS

The most easterly of the Caribbean islands, Barbados has been an independent state within the British Commonwealth since 1966. The nation's head of state is the British monarch. Its official language is English, but Bajan—the national dialect—is the most spoken. The capital of Barbados is Bridgetown. The low, flat island is 166 square miles (430 square kilometers) and forested with mahogany, palm, casuarinas, and other tropical species. More than 90 percent of the population is of African heritage.

Barbados's first inhabitants came from the South American coasts in the fourth century CE. Arawaks and Caribs populated it around the eighth century. In 1536 a Portuguese sailor, Pedro Campos, named the island Los Barbados because the long roots of the fig trees reminded him of beards (*barbas* in Portuguese). The Spanish arrived in 1518, though they did not settle there until 1536. By 1550 there remained no Indians on the island.

When Captain Henry Powell landed a party of English settlers on the island in 1627, it was virtually deserted. They experimented with such crops as tobacco, cotton, indigo, and ginger. These first crops turned out to be unprofitable: Barbadian tobacco could not compete with the excellent tobacco from Virginia, and landowners had to pay higher taxes to export it to England. From the middle of the seventeenth century, Barbados would become the center of a growing sugar industry. An epidemic disease that killed most of the population resulted in a concentration of land into the hands of a small number of landlords, who turned the land into a few vast plantations. A number of rich families who had fled from England due to the Civil War took refuge in Barbados and invested their wealth in the nascent sugar business. Barbados soon became the most populated and productive of the English colonies in the Caribbean.

The industry of sugar brought about the birth of a plantation society, dependent on the work of thousands of slaves who were imported from Africa as the labor supply from Europe began to decrease around 1660. In 1643 there were 6,000 black people on Barbados; in 1835, when slavery was finally abolished, almost 90,000 black slaves were emancipated.

African beliefs and cultural heritage often survived in Barbados. The Barbadian slave code regarded slaves as bestial and as recalcitrant pagans unworthy of missionary efforts. The fact that slaves were regarded as not human enough to convert to Christianity favored the survival of African beliefs on the island. Notably, the earliest calls for a repatriation of the descendants of slaves who wished to return to their ancestral lands were made by black Barbadians. These utopian impulses later inspired Marcus Garvey's more radical Back-to-Africa movement.

After emancipation in 1834, sugar cultivation remained a major part of the Barbadian economy. Although the traditional sugar industry collapsed in the late 1960s, the production and export of sugar is still an important sector of Barbados's economy. At the start of the twenty-first century, tourism provides almost a half of the gross national product.

Virginia Fernández Canedo

See also: British Empire; Garvey, Marcus

References

Klein, S. Herbert. *La esclavitud Africana en América Latina y el Caribe.* Translated by Graciela Sánchez Albornoz. Madrid: Alianza Editorial, 1986.

McFarlane, Anthony. *El Reino Unido y América: La Época Colonial.* Translated by Jacinto Antolín. Madrid: Editorial Mapfre, 1992.

Montiel Martínez, Luz María. *Negros en América.* Madrid: Editorial Mapfre, 1992.

BARNET, MIGUEL (1940–)

Miguel Barnet is an expert on Afro-Cuban culture, as well as a novelist, an anthropologist, and a poet. He was born in Havana, Cuba, in 1940 and opted to remain in Cuba, faithful to Fidel Castro's regime.

Beyond his literary and scholarly work, Barnet has served many roles in the expansion of Cuba's presence in the global community. Barnet was one of the founders of the Cuban Academy of Sciences as well as the Fernando Ortiz Foundation. He is also a member of Cuba's Chamber of Deputies and the Cuban representative to UNESCO.

To date Barnet has published seven books of poetry, numerous ethnographic studies, and five ethnographic novels. He has helped give rise to a new genre through his renowned *Biography of a Runaway Slave* (1966), one of the origins of what has become known as "testimonial" fiction in Latin American letters A remarkable testimony that uses established ethnographic field practices, *Biography* is the product of a very special encounter. In 1963 Barnet followed up on an article about a nursing home that had several residents who were over 100 years old. It was in that nursing home that he first met the 103-year-old Esteban Montejo and began to interview him. Montejo's life was unique in many ways. He was born a slave on a sugar plantation in 1860 and, in his own words, "lived through it all." He could not understand how the African gods allowed slavery. In fact, Montejo blamed it on the color red. In Montejo's eyes, when the Portuguese arrived in Africa, they lured Africans to their boats with red kerchiefs, and since black men have always liked red, they were caught, put in chains, and taken away to be sold as slaves. Alongside such myth-making, Montejo's memories are unique, not least of all because he was able to remember differences between Congos, Mandingos, Gangas, Carabalís, Musungo Congos, and Lucumís. It would have been impossible to find a former slave in the United States able to do the same. Such memories suggest that Latin American slaves enjoyed greater cultural autonomy than their North American counterparts and explains why many African traditions are still very much alive in the Latin American world, particularly in the Caribbean and in Brazil. After running away from a sugar plantation, Montejo spent several years in the woods, hiding until slavery was abolished. He then fought in the Cuban war of independence from Spain and witnessed the takeover of Cuba by the United States—through trickery, in his opinion. Until Castro's revolution, Montejo worked as a day laborer. Barnet immortalized Montejo and, through him, the intricacies of Cuba's complex history of slavery and abolition.

Beatriz Rivera-Barnes

See also: Cuba; Literature, African American

References

Barnet, Miguel. *Biography of a Runaway Slave.* Translated by Nick Hill. Willimantic, CT: Curbstone Press, 1994.

Luis, William. *Literary Bondage: Slavery in Cuban Narrative.* Austin: University of Texas Press, 1990.

Ortiz, Fernando. *Cuban Counterpoint: Tobacco and Sugar.* Durham, NC: Duke University Press, 1995.

BAROTSELAND

Barotseland, the land of Lozi kings and their constituents, is an historical kingdom with borders that once included western Zambia, eastern Angola, and Namibia's Caprivi Strip. Today, its heartland remains intact in Zambia's Western Province. It is an area famous in the literatures of anthropology and African history due to the scholarship of Max Gluckman and Gwyn Prins, and its unique history of colonial-era contact—from the nineteenth-century travels of David Livingstone to a visit by Britain's queen mother, Elizabeth, in 1957. It is perhaps best-known for its spectacular pageant, Kuomboka, which occurs when the waters of the Zambezi River flood the surrounding plain. During Kuomboka, the Lozi king (Litunga) rides a black-and-white striped barge that is equipped with 100 paddlers, two drum orchestras, and a giant elephant superstructure and leads a flotilla of thousands across lily-studded waters to dry land.

The area now known as Barotseland did not acquire this name or recognition as a unified kingdom until the reign of King Lewanika at the close of the nineteenth century. The region's history spans five broadly defined periods: predynastic, the arrival of the Luyana dynasty, the Kololo interregnum, the colonial era, and integration into the nation-state of Zambia. Archaeological evidence and oral histories suggest that a Lunda princess (known alternately as Mbuyu, Mwambwa, and Mbuywamwambwa) from the Katanga region of the Democratic Republic of Congo led her followers to the upper Zambezi plain sometime between the fifteenth and seventeenth centuries. Shortly thereafter she abdicated power in favor of her son, Mboo. All Lozi kings trace their descent back to Mboo and retain their authority through visits to the graves of the royal founders. Until the 1830s this dynasty was known as Luyana. During the mid-nineteenth century, the Luyana kings lost power, and the region was occupied by Sotho-speaking Kololo leaders from the south. Lubosi Lewanika had reestablished Luyana political control by 1885, but after nearly fifty years of intermarriage and exchange with Kololo, fundamental linguistic and cultural transformations had occurred.

"Lozi" and "Barotseland" both refer to the fusion of Kololo and Luyana language and culture along the upper Zambezi River.

King Lewanika established a golden era for Barotseland. He was a skilled politician who created a kingdom from the twenty-five constituent populations living in the Zambezi plain, inviting representatives from each community to his court. During his reign (1878–1884, 1885–1916), he negotiated with the British to establish Barotseland as a protectorate—not a colony. He became an international presence when he was among a select number of African kings to attend the coronation of England's Edward VII in 1902. His talents extended beyond the political arena. He was a renowned artist who carved wood and ivory, wove baskets, and trained apprentice artists at his court. By 1905 he had established a Native Curios Shoppe at Victoria Falls and was selling Lozi art works to European and American traders, missionaries, and colonial officers. In addition, he worked with missionaries to establish the first schools in the region.

All six kings to reign in the past century have been descendants of Lewanika. His son, Sir Mwanawina, signed the Barotseland Agreement of 1964 that joined the Barotseland Protectorate to Northern Rhodesia to form the modern nation of Zambia. The current king, Lubosi Imwiko II, is Lewanika's grandson. In addition to serving as king, he is a successful entrepreneur who is working to improve environmental conservation policies for the region.

Karen Milbourne

References

Caplan, Gerald L. *The Elites of Barotseland, 1878–1969: A Political History of Zambia's Western Province.* Berkeley: University of California Press, 1970.

Gluckman, Max. *Economy of the Central Barotse Plain.* Manchester, UK: Manchester University Press for the Rhodes-Livingstone Institute, 1941.

Gluckman, Max. *Essays on Lozi Land and Royal Property.* Livingstone, Northern Rhodesia: Rhodes-Livingstone Institute, 1943.

Mainga, Mutumba. *Bulozi under the Luyana Kings: Political Evolution and State Formation in Pre-colonial Zambia.* London: Longman, 1973.

Milbourne, Karen E. "Diplomacy in Motion: Art, Pageantry, and the Politics of Creativity in Barotseland." PhD dissertation, University of Iowa, 2003.

Prins, Gwyn. *The Hidden Hippopotamus: A Reappraisal in African History, the Early Colonial Experience in Western Zambia.* Berkeley: University of California Press, 1980.

BAUZÁ, MARIO (1911–1993)

A gifted musician, excellent composer, and superb arranger, Mario Bauzá was one of the founders and leading figures of Afro-Cuban or Afro-Latin jazz. He began clarinet lessons at the age of five and became a member of the Havana Philharmonic at twelve as a bass clarinetist. He accompanied Antonio María Romeu's orchestra on his first trip to the United States in 1926.

Fascinated with jazz, Bauzá made the switch to saxophone after hearing the legendary Coleman Hawkins. Bauzá was equally impressed by black-owned clubs, restaurants, record companies, and radio stations in the United States, which he viewed as an alternative to the discrimination he had faced in his native land. In the 1940s and 1950s, however, Bauzá criticized some of the New York Latin-based bands that refused to hire African-Latin musicians. Bauzá settled in New York in 1930. The opportunity to play with Antonio Machín's group motivated him to learn the trumpet, lore has it, in less than two weeks. He was Chick Webb's trumpeter from

1933 to 1938, and became the musical director of Webb's band in 1934. Bauzá played with Cab Calloway's band from 1939 to 1941 and in the latter year he joined Machito's Afro-Cubans, where he remained until 1975.

His 1943 composition "Tanga" is considered one of the first, if not the first, Afro-Cuban jazz composition. Bauzá's classical training and experience in big-band swing orchestras helped remake the Machito band. His "Cubop City" (1948) and "Mambo Inn" (1950), co-authored with pianist René Hernández, became hits, the latter a staple of the Count Basie Band. Bauzá's knack for bringing together great artists (Ella Fitzgerald and Chick Webb; Dizzy Gillespie and Cab Calloway) was legendary. Bauzá facilitated the collaboration between Gillespie and Chano Pozo, which engendered a new phase in Latin jazz history. Bauzá, despite his huge contributions, did not receive the recognition he deserved until late in life with The City of New York Mayor's Award of Honor for Arts and Culture in 1984 and an eightieth birthday concert in his honor. In the early 1990s he recorded three albums, starting with *Tanga* (1992) and followed by *The Time Is Now* (1993). In 1993 Bauzá, already diagnosed with cancer, went back to the studio for one last session that resulted in *944 Columbus* (his address), released posthumously in 1994. To the very end, Bauzá displayed his impeccable musicianship, professionalism, wit, and creativity.

Alan West-Durán

See also: Cuban Music, African Influence in; Jazz and the Blues; O'Farrill, Arturo "Chico"

References

Acosta, Leonardo. *Raíces del Jazz latino, un Siglo de Jazz en Cuba*. Baranquilla, Colombia: Editorial la Iguana Ciega, 2001.

Chediak, Nat. *Diccionario de Jazz Latino*. Madrid: Fundación Autor, 1998.

Roberts, John Storm. *Latin Jazz, the First of the Fusions, 1880s* to *Today*. New York: Schirmer Books, Macmillan, 1999.

Yarnow, Scott. *Afro-Cuban Jazz*. San Francisco: Miller Freeman, 2000.

BBC CARIBBEAN SERVICE AND *CARIBBEAN VOICES*

The British Broadcasting Corporation (BBC), a London-based broadcasting service, launched the program *Caribbean Voices* to promote the creative and critical work of Caribbean artists. The BBC operated a Caribbean Service (1938–1958) from London that broadcast music, interviews, poetry, plays, short stories, critical debates, and personal messages (during World War II) to the people of the Caribbean. Programs evolved from the pioneering work of a Jamaican freelance scriptwriter, Una Marson, who joined the BBC as an established poet, playwright, and journalist. In Kingston in the 1930s, Marson had run a literary Readers and Writers club and published *The Moth and the Star* (1937).

In London during 1938, Marson devised programs for the BBC, including music from St. Vincentian pianist William Wilson and Cyril Blake's Band, whose performances were broadcast from BBC studios. She went on to produce *Calling the West Indies* during World War II, which she conceived as a means for West Indian service people to keep in touch with families back home. In 1941 Marson was appointed a full-time program assistant on the Empire Service and promoted to West Indies producer in 1942. She also contributed her own work to the poetry magazine *Voice,* edited by Eric Blair (George Orwell), who was at the time working in the BBC's Indian section. On one of the programs she was featured alongside a distinguished set of writers including M. J. Tambimutto, William Empson, and T. S. Eliot. *Voice* was a successful venture that inspired Marson to produce her own Caribbean version of the literary magazine. Entitled *Caribbean Voices,* the first program was broadcast on March 11, 1943. Subsequent programs broadcast the published work of Neville Guiseppe of Trinidad; John Wickham, Barbadian editor of *Bim*; and Jamaican poets Constance Hollar and Ruth Horner. In the early years of the program, Marson struggled to find published contributors who were from the Caribbean and living in Britain. The situation changed when, in 1946, Henry Swanzy took over the production and began to seek out unpublished work, drawing on material from Caribbean and British-based writers. From 1954 to 1956, V. S. Naipaul edited the program, followed by Edgar Mittelholzer. By the time broadcasting ceased in 1958, many of the hitherto unknown talents had been recognized by publishers and critics in England and America.

The importance of the program is reflected in the contributors who were featured as readers or short-term editors, namely, George Lamming, Sam Selvon, Edgar Mittleholzer, Andrew Salkey, John Figueroa, Vidia Naipaul, Shake Keane, Frank Collymore, Claude McKay, and Edward Kamau Brathwaite. Trinidadian Michael Anthony was encouraged by Naipaul to write and to develop a new Caribbean aesthetic that English literary magazines found unfamiliar. *Caribbean Voices* provided a creative catalyst and was a precursor to the Caribbean Artists Movement (CAM). One of *Caribbean Voices*'s contributors was Edward Kamau Brathwaite, a founder member of CAM. Brathwaite understood the importance of creating opportunities for writers, artists, and cultural activists to meet, cajole each other, and criticize each other's work. The BBC Caribbean Service also provided income for Samuel Selvon and George Lamming, who survived, if only minimally, solely on their earnings from writing. The BBC fraternity increased opportunities for contact with the London literary intelligentsia and with publishers. These activities were increasingly male-oriented. However, a number of women writers contributed to *Caribbean Voices*. In addition to Hollar and Horner, later contributors included Louise Bennett, Gloria Escoffery, Barbara Ferland, Vivette Hendriks, Mary Lockett, Stella Mead, Daisy Myrie, and Dorothy Phillips. Gloria Escoffery and Pauline Enriques both broadcast from London, but the majority of women contributors sent in work through Caribbean-based agents like Cedric Lindo.

The program's broadcast tapes were erased, but written scripts survive in the BBC's archives. John Figueroa trawled through fifteen years of scripts to edit a two-volume collection of poetry from the programs: *Caribbean Voices: Dreams and Visions* (1966) and *Caribbean Voices: The Blue Horizons* (1970). For a colonized region with no sense of a literature of its own, *Caribbean Voices* filled a void and established a lineage for writers and critics. The program trafficked in creative output in a quite unique way. Writing produced in the Caribbean and sent to London for broadcast made the reverse passage into the radio-listening homes of a geographically vast and diversely populated Caribbean region.

Sandra Courtman

See also: Jamaica, Women's Role in; Marson, Una; McKay, Claude; Reggae

References
Caribbean Service: BBC Written Archives. Caversham Park, Reading, UK.
Figueroa, John. *Caribbean Voices.* Vol. 1, *Dreams and Visions.* London: Evan Brothers, 1966.
Figueroa, John. *Caribbean Voices.* Vol. 2, *The Blue Horizons.* London: Evan Brothers, 1970.
Jarrett-Macauley, Delia. *The Life of Una Marson, 1905–65.* Manchester, UK: Manchester University Press, 1998.
Walmsley, A. *The Caribbean Artists Movement, 1966–1972.* London: New Beacon Books, 1992.

BENIN, REPUBLIC OF

The Republic of Benin, with an estimated population of 7,863,000 and an area of 43,483 square miles, dates back to the pre-colonial kingdom of Abomey and has had complex trade relations with Europeans since the fifteenth century and with the Americas in the modern era. Benin was formerly known as Dahomey and was also a former French colony that gained full independence from France in 1960.

Dahomey was an active player in the transatlantic economic order and owed her rise and splendor to the profits of the slave trade that supplied cheap labor for mines and plantations in the Americas from 1450 to 1870. The coastal town of Ouidah was one of the most important centers of the slave trade in the nineteenth century. There can be seen the remains of the ancient port from which slaves were boarded and shipped to the New World. This loss and dislocation of population were detrimental to the economy of precolonial Benin, more so than for most other areas of Africa because of the particular intensity and consistency of slave exports. The exports, on the other hand, provided revenues, which were used for the purchase of imports, including new goods and new technology. Ouidah is the birthplace of Voodoo, later in vogue in the Americas, namely in Brazil, the Caribbean, and the West Indies. In Porto Novo, the reconstructed rooms of the Da Silva museum at the former house of the Da Silva family demonstrate the privileged position of the descendants of the Brazilian slaves who returned to Benin after the abolition of the transatlantic slave trade.

After its difficult beginning as an independent country, when it was plagued by governmental instability, economic troubles, ethnic rivalries, and social unrest that led to military intervention, Benin embraced democracy in 1989 with a characteristic fervor that catapulted it onto the African stage as a model of political and economic reforms. These democratic successes have earned the country U.S. interest and support because they fall in line with American foreign policies. Indeed, starting in the 1990s, the United States elevated African democratization to a central priority of its foreign policy toward the continent.

Benin has strengthened its ties with the United States, Canada, Brazil, and the main international lending institutions. The current administrative cabinet is sprinkled with technocrats who have studied or worked in North America. Benin is a prominent destination for many American governmental and nongovernmental agencies.

The United States Agency for International Development (USAID) oversees the implementation of U.S. assistance programs in the Benin Republic, and the agency has established an integrated focus for its central objectives, which include sustainable economic development, improved health and nutrition, recognition and protection of basic human rights, accountability, and strengthened environmental protection as well as democracy in Benin.

One of the main current projects of USAID's operations in Benin is to reform the education system. USAID is helping the Benin government to replace the old French system (described as authoritarian and based on rote learning) with a system allowing for student initiative and active learning. USAID also sponsors the training of Benin government officials in Western accounting and financial management practices. The agency has also assisted at the telecenter of the Songhai Center located in Porto Novo, a project aimed at fostering a mode of development based on a thoroughly scientific approach to agriculture and small-scale industry, combined with self-sufficiency, honesty, integrity, and a highly developed sense of community.

In various parts of the country, and especially in the rural areas, U.S. Peace Corps volunteers are active in social development projects. Africare-Benin, a U.S.-funded organization, focuses on the basic development areas of food, water, and health, as well as the promotion of democratic governance, poverty reduction, the development of information and communications technology, and women's education. The U.S.-based Catholic Relief Services (CRS) has an office in Benin, and its outreach projects have been significant. The National University of Benin (UNB) has established interuniversity cooperation with U.S. institutions such as Wayne State University, the State University of New York at Oswego, Bowling Green State University, Wake Forest University, and Agnes Scott College.

Music is a sphere of significant American influence. As far back as the nineteenth century, freed Brazilian slaves and their descendants introduced samba music; they adapted it to the sound of big-band jazz and added African percussion instruments. Renowned singer Angélique Kidjo does an excellent mixture of Afro-punk, reggae, samba, salsa, jazz, rumba, zouk, and makossa. Gangbé Brass Band explores the rich Voodoo culture and ancient songs of Benin, which are combined with jazz melodies to produce a powerful contemporary sound. Starting at the end of the 1990s, hip-hop bands, including Benin's most popular rappers, Sakpata Boys and H2O, created a modern dazzling rap based on the multitude of Beninois traditional rhythms and instruments. Ardiess started out in 1997 as a purely modern rap group that based its music on U.S. rap but has since added some local melodies. A confirmation of the extent of the influence of U.S. hip-hop on the African musical scene was the Pan African Hip-Hop Festival held in Cotonou, Benin, in 1999.

Emmanuel A. Odjo

See also: Reggae; U.S. Agency for International Development; Voodoo

References

Harbeson, John W. "Externally Assisted Democratization." In *Africa in World Politics: The African State System in Flux*, edited by John W. Harbeson and Daniel Rothchild. 3rd ed. Boulder, CO: Westview, 2000.

Manning, Patrick. *Slavery, Colonialism, and Economic Growth in Dahomey, 1640–1960*. Cambridge: Cambridge University Press, 1982.

Webster, James Bertin, and Adu A. Boahen. *History of West Africa—The Revolutionary Years, 1815 to Independence*. New York: Praeger, 1970.

BENNETT, LOUISE (1919–)

Louise Bennett is a Jamaican-born author of poetry and radio segments and a fixture of Jamaican theater. She employs Jamaican creole and focuses on the Jamaican woman in her art. Known as Louise Bennett-Coverly or "Miss Lou" to her fans from Jamaica and Canada, Bennett fascinates audiences with her wit and performances.

Bennett is one of the first Jamaican authors to focus on the Jamaican woman in her literature. She was a fixture of Jamaican radio and theater from the 1960s into the 1980s. Her better-known published works are *Jamaica Labrish* (1966) and *Selected Poems* (1982), as well as *Aunty Roachy Say* (1993), which is a collection of "Miss Lou's Views," her witty radio segments dating back to the 1960s. Aunty Roachy speaks in Jamaican creole, with a pervasive use of Jamaican proverbs to gain her audience's attention and achieve an immediate effect. The arguments ingrained in common Jamaican proverbs are universally understandable; for instance, "yuh sleep wid dog, yuh ketch im flea."

For some Jamaicans, Bennett's overt usage of Jamaican creole and Jamaican proverbs throughout her repertoire was problematic; it suggested a "lowness" or coarseness in opposition to the more "appropriate" use of Standard English, even if her poetry and radio segments were quite thought provoking and well crafted. But Bennett persisted and eventually won over the majority, who came to appreciate Bennett's attention to the daily trappings of life in Jamaica, whether her poetic discussions revolve around the Jamaican language, social climbing, manners, traffic conditions, gun court, rent control, or international concerns such as Jamaica's relationship with England. This last point comes through well in her poem "Colonization in Reverse" (1966), where she humorously describes the wave of Jamaicans moving to England.

Bennett has received numerous honors befitting her cultural contributions to Jamaican culture. In 1961 Queen Elizabeth II bestowed on Bennett the honor of Member of the Order of the British Empire. In 1974 she received the prestigious Order of Jamaica.

David W. Hart

See also: Creole/Criollo

References
Bennett, Louise. "Colonization in Reverse." In *Selected Poems,* edited by Mervyn Morris. Kingston, Jamaica: Sangsters, 1982.
Bennett, Louise. *Aunty Roachy Say.* Kingston, Jamaica: Sangsters, 1993.
Cooper, Carolyn. "Noh Lickle Twang: An Introduction to the Poetry of Louise Bennett." *World Literature Written in English* 17 (1978): 317–327.
Cooper, Carolyn. *Noises in the Blood: Orality, Gender, and the "Vulgar" Body of Jamaican Popular Culture.* Durham, NC: Duke University Press, 1993.
Doumerc, Eric. "Louise Bennett and the Mento Tradition." *Ariel* 31, no. 4 (October 2000): 23–32.
Morris, Mervyn. *Is English We Speaking.* Kingston, Jamaica: Ian Randle Publications, 1999.

BERLIN WEST AFRICA CONFERENCE

The European struggle over control of the Congo played a crucial role in the Berlin West Africa Conference of 1884–1885 and the subsequent partition of tropical Africa. While the colonization of Africa had previously been marked by a series of bilateral rivalries and agreements, especially between the French and British, a number of European powers held interests in the

Congo River and its surrounding territory. Organized by Chancellor Otto von Bismarck of Germany, the Conference was part of a longer series of colonial negotiations and anxieties surrounding free trade and navigation. The result was an important new development for African colonization. Rather than bilateral, the international conference set a precedent for multilateral European negotiations over shared and competing colonial interests. Delegates from Austria–Hungary, Belgium, Denmark, France, Great Britain, Italy, the Netherlands, Portugal, Russia, Spain, Sweden, and the Ottoman Empire met to discuss the fate of the African continent.

The Conference set out to provide an international framework for regulating European relations in Central Africa. For the sake of free trade, European diplomats attempted to establish international access to the Congo and Niger rivers, while at the same time negotiating territorial claims. Often, the territorial compromises led to boundaries that divided native populations. Rather than prevent potential conflict, these agreements soon had European powers scrambling to establish spheres of influence in tropical Africa simply for their currency in international negotiations.

Though its final resolutions were mostly vague and limited, the Conference became a powerful symbol in the European imagination. The Conference was, for example, widely publicized in European newspapers as the final carving up of the African continent. Though a large map of Africa hung over the meeting and though the Conference had been called as a result of the fierce race to colonize and influence sub-Saharan Africa, the Conference was chiefly interested in a code of conduct for such rapid expansion. Though local economic competition and political conflict were clearly important, the primary concern centered on European diplomacy. The drafted resolutions focused on principles for navigation channels, international law, and humanitarian responsibilities (the slave trade was formally abolished). Rather than a formal partitioning of tropical Africa, Conference delegates were far more interested in the African coast, which had already been divided up and, as a result, posed trade and navigation problems for interior control.

The Conference's first principle, referred to as the hinterland doctrine, stated that a power which claims a portion of coastal territory also reserves the right to its adjacent inland area. Countries were discouraged from attempting to establish territory directly inland of another power's coastal control. Nevertheless, the dimensions of this principle were vague in practice. France, for example, unsuccessfully argued that British Nigeria was a hinterland of Algeria. Equally unclear, the Conference proposed a second principle of effective possession, by which treaties would be legally and internationally valid. Anxious to avoid challenges to their own territorial possessions, most European diplomats agreed to respect previous treaties as a matter of principle.

The most important principle, transformative for African colonization, was that of "effective occupation." Effective occupation applied, however, only to newly acquired territories, coastal territories, and formal colonies. Rather than organize the colonization of the African interior, this principle not only contributed to the fierce pace of colonization, but it put an additional premium on the subjugation—violent, if necessary—of native peoples.

The forceful control of a population—effective occupation—became a prerequisite for an unchallenged territorial claim.

Brandon Jernigan

See also: Abolitionism, British; British Empire

References

Chamberlain, M. E. *Scramble for Africa.* 2nd ed. New York: Longman, 1999.

Forster, Stig, Wolfgang J. Mommsen, and Ronald Robinson, eds. *Bismarck, Europe, and Africa: The Berlin Africa Conference 1884–1885 and the Onset of Partition.* New York: Oxford University Press, 1988.

Wesseling, H. L. *Divide and Rule: The Partition of Africa, 1880–1914.* Translated by Arnold J. Pomerans. Westport, CT: Praeger, 1991.

BERMUDA

Covering an area of 22.7 square miles (58.8 square kilometres), Bermuda lies 650 miles (1,050 kilometers) east of the U.S. coast. An archipelago of 7 islands and 170 islets and rocks, the largest island is referred to as Main Island. Owing to its strategic location, both the United States and Canada had military bases on Bermuda until the last decade of the twentieth century. This old colony of the British Empire has become one of the United Kingdom's self-governing overseas territories. Under Bermuda's constitution, which was approved in 1968, the English monarch, represented by the governor, is the head of state. A referendum on independence took place in 1995, but it was soundly defeated. Hamilton became the administrative capital in 1815 (until then, St. George had been the capital city of the colony). About three-fifths of Bermudians are of African descent—thousands of slaves were brought to Bermuda before Britain outlawed the slave trade in 1807. The territory has a market economy based on tourism—more than 500,000 tourists visit the island every year—and international finance—thanks to its low income taxes, Bermuda is one of the most important financial centers in the world.

Throughout the sixteenth century, Bermuda was a stopping point for Spanish and Portuguese sailors seeking water and food on their way to the New World. In 1609 the Sea Venture, the flagship of an expedition sent to relieve the colony of Jamestown led by the Virginia Company's admiral Sir George Somers, wrecked off the coast of Bermuda. The survivors became the first English community in the previously uninhabited island, which soon was formally claimed for the English crown. Indian and African slaves began to be transported to Bermuda by 1617, and soon the slave population outnumbered the white settlers.

Due to the limited area of the island and the poor quality of its tobacco, Bermuda never succeeded as an agricultural colony. Before long, however, Bermuda's farmers noticed the value of the Bermuda cedar; the island was soon reforested with this species of juniper native to the area. Such an excellent wood allowed the islanders to establish a fairly thriving shipbuilding industry. The Bermuda sloop, light and extremely easy to direct, became a success not only in the Caribbean, but also in the West Indies and Europe. Hundreds of slaves were taken from Bermuda's farms to be trained as shipwrights. Fishing, whaling, and other naval-related economic activities were central to Bermuda. Its predominantly maritime economy led to the employment of many slaves as sailors; they enjoyed a higher degree of autonomy than most colonial plantation slaves.

The Turks Islands, in close proximity, were deforested and devoted to the extraction of salt, which became a pillar of the island's economy. Mary Prince, a Bermudian woman born in slavery in 1788, was re-sold as a punishment for her insolence and was sent by her new owner to work in the salt ponds. In her narrative, *The History of Mary Prince, A West Indian Slave,* published in London in 1831, Prince exposes the harsh conditions of Turks Islands slavery.

From the second half of the twentieth century, racial issues have been central to the political history of the islands. The first Bermudian political party, the Progressive Labour Party, was created in 1963 to represent the nonwhite population. The multiracial United Bermuda Party was placed in power soon after the nation became self-governing and was returned to office in subsequent elections. These apparently pro-equality governments did not put an end to social tensions, and in 1977 rioting broke out. Since then, efforts have been made to put an end to racial discrimination.

Virginia Fernández Canedo

See also: British Empire; Prince, Mary; Sailors

References

Klein, S. Herbert. *La esclavitud Africana en América Latina y el Caribe.* Translated by Graciela Sánchez Albornoz. Madrid: Alianza Editorial, 1986.

Montiel Martínez, Luz María. *Negros en América.* Madrid: Editorial Mafre, 1992.

BEYALA, CALIXTHE (1961–)

A prolific francophone Cameroonian novelist and advocate of immigrants' and women's rights, Calixthe Beyala has spent most of her life as a voluntary exile in France and elsewhere, having left Africa as a teenager. Her work explores the intersection of race and gender within the context of exile and cultural hybridity. Crossing geographical borders, it is from the standpoint of exile that her work endeavors to fight racism and misogyny in the francophone world and beyond. Several of her novels concentrate on the themes of African diaspora and immigrant identity and have been well received by audiences in the Americas, notably in Quebec and the francophone Caribbean; she is a frequent participant in literary salons in North America and Europe, giving a voice to the voiceless that resonates throughout the francophone world in her novels, political writings, and interviews.

Her novels, letters, and political essays portray the lives of women and children in postcolonial West Africa and the lives of those living abroad in Europe. She treats themes such as poverty, prostitution, work and exploitation, childhood, and immigration, common threads in francophone literature today on both sides of the Atlantic. She employs erotic imagery and metaphors in her discussion of female sexuality, bodily difference, and identity. Exile from Africa is presented with nostalgia, though the African scenes she paints present a world of violence, of objectification, of physical abuse and rape, of prostitution, of multiple pregnancies and abortion, of polygamous families, of female genital mutilation practices, of famine. She explores the ambiguity of immigrant identity and integration among African immigrants living abroad— for instance, in the Belleville neighborhood of Paris. She portrays strong female figures in exile who maintain their traditional culture through cooking and storytelling. Her major works that have been translated into English are are *C'est le soleil qu m'a brûlée* (1987; *The Sun Hath Looked Upon*

Me, 1996), *Tu t'appeleras Tanga* (1988; *Your Name Shall be Tanga*, 1996), and *Le petit prince de Belleville* (1992; *Loukoum: The Little Prince of Belleville*, 1995).

Sarah Gordon

See also: Africa, West; Cameroon; Diaspora; Literature, African American

References

Beyala, Calixthe. *The Sun Hath Looked Upon Me.* Translated by Marjolijn de Jager. New York: Heinemann, 1996.Beyala, Calixthe. *Your Name Shall be Tanga.* Translated by Marjolijn de Jager. New York: Heinemann, 1996.

Darlington, Sonja. "Calixthe Beyala's Manifesto and Fictional Theory." *Research in African Literatures* 34, no. 2 (2003): 41–52.

Hitchcott, Nicki. "Comment cuisiner son mari à l'africaine: Calixthe Beyala's Recipes for Migrant Identity." *French Cultural Studies* 14 (2003): 211–220.

BIAFRA

Biafra is the eastern region of Nigeria that briefly became a sovereign republic (1967–1970). The Republic of Biafra came into existence on May 30, 1967, by the proclamation of General Chukwuemeka Ojukwu, then military governor of Nigeria's South Eastern Region, following an edict of the Eastern Region Constituent Assembly. The new independent country was comprised of the Igbo, Efik, Ibibio, Ijaw, Kalabari, Ogoja, and Ogoni ethnic groups. The name was adopted from the ancient West African kingdom of Biafra, on the inlet of the Atlantic coastline that early Portuguese explorers called the Bight of Biafra.

Two immediate causes led to the breakaway of the Eastern Region of Nigeria into a sovereign republic. First was the northern Nigerian military officers' countercoup of July 29, 1966, in which about 200 Igbo officers and men of the Nigerian army were killed, including the country's first military head of state, General J. T. U. Aguiyi-Ironsi. Second was the May, July, and September 1966 Nigerian genocide against Igbo settlers in other parts of Nigeria, but mainly in the north. All these created a pervasive sense of insecurity for the lives and properties of Igbo and other eastern ethnicities in the old Nigerian nation. The growing animosity between Nigeria's political leaders heightened the cultural and religious tensions between the south and the north.

Nigeria's first military coup d'état, on January 15, 1966, upset the delicate political balance between the country's three dominant ethnic groups: the Igbo, Yoruba, and Hausa-Fulani. Northern leaders interpreted the coup as a ploy by the Christian Igbo to usurp political power from the Arab and Muslim Hausa-Fulani. The consequences were the coup of July 29, the bloodiest in modern Africa and the first black-on-black genocide of modern history, in which an estimated 50,000 Igbo settlers in northern Nigeria were butchered in a state-programmed wave of ethnic cleansing. Over 1 million survivors of the ensuing nationwide pogrom fled back to the Igbo traditional homeland in the east to help found Biafra as a protection against the brutality of Nigeria.

Yakubu Gowon, a northerner who became Nigeria's second military head of state, refused to recognize the sovereignty of Biafra. He declared a state of emergency, subdivided the existing four regions of Nigeria into twelve states, and ordered a military invasion of the Eastern Region. The thirty-month civil war that broke out in July 1967 displayed Biafra's ingenuity through the technological inventiveness of its research and production unit (RAP), the efficiency of its military forces, and the perseverance of its people. As a test of its successful diplomacy, Biafra gained varying recognitions from France, Gabon, Haiti, Ivory Coast, Israel, Portugal, South Africa, and Tanzania.

The Nigerian government, however, hid under the Biafran oil and armament proliferation interests of its British and Soviet Union sponsors to unleash further acts of genocide against Biafran civilians. Nigeria's Egyptian pilots bombed the Igbo Awgu market, and the Nigerian army wiped out an entire population of old men and male children in the Igbo town of Asaba. In spite of the interventions of the Vatican, the World Council of Churches, the International Red Cross, the United States, and others, Nigeria imposed an economic blockade against Biafra. Under the program of "starvation as a legitimate weapon of war," the Nigerian government ordered the afternoon downing of a Swedish Red Cross plane on June 5, 1969.

About 1 million Biafran children died of starvation and *kwashiorkor,* a debilitating disease brought upon by malnutrition. Over 2 million Biafrans had died by the time of its surrender on January 12, 1970. The Nigerian-Biafran War officially ended on January 15, 1970, but the continuing agitation of the Movement for the Actualization of the Sovereign State of Biafra (MASSOB) attests to the rampant marginalization of the former Eastern Region and the failure of the Nigerian government postwar projects of reconstruction, rehabilitation, and reconciliation.

Obi Iwuanyanwu

See also: Hausa; Igbo; Nigeria; Yoruba

References

Forsyth, Frederick. *The Biafra Story: The Making of an African Legend.* Baltimore, MD: Penguin Books, 1969.

Ojukwu, Chukwuemeka Odumegwu. *Biafra.* New York: Harper & Row, 1969.

Sherman, John. *War Stories: A Memoir of Nigeria and Biafra.* Indianapolis, IN: Mesa Verde Press, 2002.

Soyinka, Wole. *The Open Sore of a Continent: A Personal Narrative of the Nigerian Crisis.* New York: Oxford University Press, 1996.

Uzokwe, Alfred Obiora. *Surviving in Biafra: The Story of the Nigerian Civil War.* New York: Writers Advantage, 2003.

BIOTECHNOLOGY

Biotechnology or, more specifically, plant biotechnology, is a broad term referring to a variety of techniques used to isolate the DNA of plants and control their genetic makeup. Three techniques are widely used in plant breeding and propagation worldwide, and have specific applications for food and fiber crops in Africa and the Americas. The first is tissue culture (or cloning), which uses cell tissue of a parent plant to regenerate a new plant. This technique is used to clone disease-free propagules from African and American staple food crops such as sweet potatoes, yams, cassavas, bananas, and potatoes. Tissue culture is central to many plant-breeding programs and is used to reproduce rapidly improved crop varieties. The second biotechnology is called marker-assisted selection. This technique allows scientists to isolate and mark specific genes that express particular traits. It is used by breeders to select for beneficial traits, providing the essential foundation for the third, and most controversial, biotechnology: genetic engineering, the creation of genetically modified organisms (GMOs). Genetic engineering involves the manipulation of the genetic makeup of a plant via the transfer of DNA between different varieties, species, and genera, as well as between plants and animals, in order to introduce a new trait to a plant.

Most commonly, genetically modified (GM) crops are designed to resist attack by a particular insect pest or plant pathogen. One of the most common GMOs is *Bt* corn and cotton. *Bt (Bacillus thurengiensis)* is a naturally occurring bacterium that is toxic to the larval stage of many pests and has been used as a timed, topical application by organic farmers for decades. In *Bt* corn and cotton, however, the gene expressing toxicity in *Bacillus* has been isolated and inserted into the corn and cotton DNA. The corn and cotton tissue of the GMO then expresses the *Bt* trait of toxicity and is toxic to larvae throughout the crop's life. Other GM crops express herbicide resistance, so that an application of herbicide will kill surrounding weeds but will not damage the crop itself. Scientists are also developing rice that contains beta-carotene in order to stem vitamin A deficiency in developing countries.

Advocates of biotechnology have promoted GMOs as the key to the next Green Revolution—the original one being the post–World War II advances in crop and fertilizer technology that massively boosted production between the 1950s and 1980s—capable of feeding a rapidly growing world population. In Africa and Latin America, the Consultative Group on International Agricultural Research (CGIAR), an international consortium of crop- and region-specific research centers, has been actively promoting research and development of GMOs for use in developing countries. Over the last decade, GMOs have come to dominate several commodity crops in the United States, such as corn, soybeans, and cotton. Worldwide GMOs are grown on nearly 50 million hectares, a number that is increasing rapidly. Advocates argue that pest and herbicide resistance reduces the need for other, potentially harmful, agrochemicals.

While the biotech industry has heralded such pest and herbicide resistance and increased yields, consumers worldwide have raised concerns over potential risks, including long-term effects on public health and the environment, as well as on the economic systems of developing countries. These potential risks, coupled with the higher cost of GM seed, have led many farmers in the developing world to be skeptical of the technology's potential and to resist its introduction into local farming systems by agribusiness and development agencies. While GMOs may lead to increased production in the short term, environmental and socioeconomic realities may ultimately constrain biotech's potential to feed populations in the less-industrialized world.

Critics argue that because GMOs are a relatively new technology, the long-term ramifications of their presence in the food system have not yet been evaluated. Concerns include the possibility that widespread use of antibiotic marker genes (that identify the plant as a GMO) may induce resistance to therapeutic or prophylactic antibiotics in humans and livestock. Additionally, the biotechnology industry has not yet elucidated the potential for GMOs to create allergens, food toxins, or immune system reactions.

Industry and international organizations have maintained that GMOs are safe for consumption; yet many farmers, consumers, and scientists alike fear the potential for genetic contamination via pollination or through the "horizontal gene flow" of GM DNA taken up by soil bacteria. Concerns that herbicide-resistant genes could transfer into weed species, or that the recombination of GM transgenes into virus or bacteria could produce new pathogens, have not been fully investigated. In addition to affecting pest species, the *Bt* pesticide gene inserted in cotton and corn also affects beneficial insects that many smallholder farmers rely on for maintenance of an acceptable threshold of pest pressure. The toxin has been found to remain in soil for several months, potentially destabilizing soil ecology and threatening soil fertility by destroying microorganisms that transform organic matter into mineral nutrients available to crops. Researchers have already observed increased pest resistance to *Bt* in GM crop systems. Similarly, herbicide-resistant GMOs may ultimately lead to an increase in broad-range herbicide, ultimately resulting in increased resistance by weed species.

Perhaps most importantly, however, critics argue that biotechnology as a solution to solving world hunger problems is a narrow-sighted and naïve approach. They argue that by focusing their efforts and resources on finding a "silver bullet" panacea that simply increases food production, biotech advocates distract from identifying the fundamental root causes of poverty in the developing world. Poor distribution and low purchasing power are the primary obstacles to food security. Additionally, under neoliberal economic restructuring, involving the expansion of "comparative advantage" export agriculture, many traditionally agrarian developing countries are moving from food self-sufficiency to food import dependency.

The debate over biotechnology has significant implications in Africa and the Americas and has been central to debates over trade, aid, and development in these regions. In 2001 both the Mexican National Biodiversity Commission and a controversial peer-reviewed article reported the contamination of two local varieties of Mexican maize by GM DNA, despite a ban on GMO importation. In Brazil, the world's largest soybean producer, herbicide-resistant (Roundup Ready) soybeans and *Bt* cotton are growing more popular among industrial-scale farmers, despite legislation banning GMO sales. In Africa, several governments are establishing committees to assess biotechnology risks and to draft legislation concerning GMO foods. The GMO controversy came to the forefront of public awareness when, in September 2002, the government of Zambia rejected U.S. food aid during a famine on the grounds that it contained GM corn. Other countries followed suit, claiming that GMOs in their food system might contaminate potential crop exports to GMO-free markets in Europe. Others fear that North American and European biotechnology firms will isolate indigenous genetic resources and patent them (biopiracy) for use in newly developed GM crops, which will then be sold back to developing world farmers, trapping them in a neocolonial relationship of technological dependency.

Nathan C. McClintock

See also: Agriculture; Agriculture, Sustainable; Green Revolution

References

Altieri, Miguel A., and Peter Rossett. "Ten Reasons Why Biotechnology Will Not Ensure Food Security, Protect the Environment, and Reduce Poverty in the Developing World." *AgBioForum* 2, nos. 3–4 (1999): 155–162.

DeVries, J., and G. Toenniessen. *Securing the Harvest: Biotechnology, Breeding, and Seed Systems for African Crops.* New York: CABI Publishing, 2001.

Omamo, Steven, and Klaus von Grebmer, eds. *Biotechnology, Agriculture, and Food Security in Southern Africa.* Washington, DC: IFPRI, 2005.

Patel, Raj, with Alexa Delwiche. "The Profits of Famine: Southern Africa's Long Decade of Hunger." *Backgrounder* 8, no. 4 (2002): 1–8.

BIRCHTOWN (BIRCH TOWN)

Birchtown is the Nova Scotian community of free blacks, founded in 1783, that was once the largest free black settlement on the North American continent. Three of the six settlements founded by the freed blacks who accompanied the Loyalists to Nova Scotia in 1783 as refugees from the War of Independence were called Birch Town. They were all named in honor of Brigadier Samuel Birch, a former British commandant of New York City, who had issued many of the black refugees passports. The largest of the Birchtowns, and the only one that survives, lay near Shelburne, on the southwestern coast of Nova Scotia. At its peak in the mid-1780s, Birchtown was the largest free black settlement on the North American continent.

Birchtown was founded by Loyalist Stephen Blucke, leader of the black community in New York. Appointed to take charge of the evacuation of the fugitive slaves, Blucke personally led some 1,500 freed blacks to Port Roseway (Shelburne), Nova Scotia, where he arrived in August 1783. On the instructions of Governor John Parr, the freed blacks were set down at the head of the northwest arm of Shelburne Harbour (now Birchtown Bay), five miles west of the "Loyalist city" of Shelburne.

There, after a first year in which government supplied rations, they struggled to survive by fishing and hiring themselves out as woodcutters and land clearers. The land was rocky and swampy and subsistence agriculture was inadequate to feed the people. The community was in decline by the late 1780s, and by 1791 the residents were receptive to the West African emigration and resettlement scheme proposed by the Sierra Leone Company. Thanks to Blucke's opposition to this early Back-to-Africa movement, however, many of Birchtown's people did not join the emigration. This in turn made possible the survival down to the twenty-first century of Birchtown as a sustainable black community. In 1993 it was designated a site of national historic significance.

Barry Cahill

See also: Blucke *or* Bleucke *or* Bluck, Stephen; Nova Scotia, Black Refugees in

References

Niven, Laird, comp. *Birchtown Archaeological Survey (1993): The Black Loyalist Settlement of Shelburne County, Nova Scotia, Canada.* Lockeport, NS: Roseway Publishing, 1994.

Niven, Laird, and Stephen A. Davis. "Birchtown: The History and Material Culture of an Expatriate African American Community." In *Moving On: Black Loyalists in the Afro-Atlantic World,* edited by John W. Pulis. New York: Garland Publishing, 1999.

Robertson, Marion. *King's Bounty: A History of Early Shelburne, Nova Scotia.* Halifax, NS: Nova Scotia Museum, 1983.

BLACK ARTS MOVEMENT

The Black Arts Movement (BAM), also called the Black Aesthetics Movement, was a literary and artistic development among African Americans from the mid-1960s through the mid-1970s. Ideologically grounded in the Civil Rights Movement, the Black Muslims, and the Black Power Movement, it was a "sixties" revolution pursuing radical social change through art. Whereas the Harlem Renaissance of the 1920s and early 1930s asserted the maturity of African American art and protested racial inequality on American soil, the Black Arts Movement sought the elevation of the status of blacks through social engagement. Writers and artists associated with the BAM embraced black cultural nationalism, adopting Black English vernacular (especially the kind of English used by Malcolm X) and a defiant tone in both speech and writing. While the Harlem Renaissance was centered in New York City, the BAM was a nationwide cultural development arising not only in the Northeast but also in such areas as Chicago, St. Louis, Los Angeles, and the Deep South. Publishing firms, theater troupes, and music associations meeting the specific needs of blacks were also established during this period. Both the Harlem Renaissance and the Black Arts Movement, however, turned to the history, culture, and spirituality of precolonial Africa for inspiration.

Important events leading to BAM included the passage of the Civil Rights Act of 1964 and the Voting Rights Act of 1965 and the assassination of Malcolm X in February 1965. Considering the Civil Rights Movement based on the philosophy of nonviolent resistance to be a failure, black militants asserted that racial equality in America could be achieved only through black separatism and social engagement. The death of Malcolm X inspired the playwright Amiri Baraka (LeRoi Jones)— regarded as the father of the Black Arts Movement—to collaborate with like-minded black artists to found the Black Arts Theatre/School (BART/S) in Harlem,

New York, in March 1965. In 1968 he and Larry Neal edited an important compendium, *Black Fire: An Anthology of Afro-American Writing* (1968), in which Neal described BAM as an ideological arm of the Black Power Movement. Other Black Arts ideologues included Houston A. Baker Jr., author of *Long Black Song* (1972); Addison Gayle Jr., editor of *The Black Aesthetic* (1971) and *Way of a New World* (1975); and Hoyt Fuller, editor of the periodical *Negro Digest* (renamed *Black World* in 1970) and author of *Return to Africa* (1971), a collection of essays written upon returning from a trip to Africa.

Among the most notable writers associated with the Black Arts Movement were Toni Morrison, Ishmael Reed, Ntozake Shange, Alice Walker, Amiri Baraka, Gwendolyn Brooks, Hoyt Fuller, Nikki Giovanni, Maulana Ron Karenga, Sonia Sanchez, Haki R. Madhubuti (formerly Don L. Lee), Eldridge Cleaver, and Angela Davis. A relatively short-lived movement, BAM was a landmark development in African American cultural history in its emphasis on social engagement, Black English, racial separatism, and Pan-Africanism. It has inspired not only younger black writers and artists but also writers of Native American and Hispanic American heritage. The black speech style popularized by the movement survives in rap music.

John J. Han

See also: Literature, African; Baraka, Amiri; Black Power Movement; Brooks, Gwendolyn; Civil Rights Movement; English, African American Vernacular; Harlem Renaissance; Morrison, Toni; Sanchez, Sonia; Shange, Ntozake

References
Clark, Cheryl. *"After Mecca": Women Poets and the Black Arts Movement.* New Brunswick, NJ: Rutgers University Press, 2005.

Lawrence, David. *"Negotiating Cooly": The Intersection of Race, Gender, and Sexual Identity in Black Arts Poetry.* PhD dissertation, University of Missouri-Columbia, 2003.

Sell, Mike. *Avant-Garde Performance and the Limits of Criticism: Approaching the Living Theatre, Happenings/Fluxus, and the Black Arts Movement.* Ann Arbor: University of Michigan Press, 2005.

Smethurst, James Edward. *The Black Arts Movement: Literary Nationalism in the 1960s and 1970s.* Chapel Hill: University of North Carolina Press, 2005.

BLACK ATHENA

Martin Bernal's *Black Athena: The Afroasiatic Roots of Classical Civilization* (1987) argues that Africa, particularly Egypt, had a substantial role in shaping classical Greek culture and the texts that are often considered sources of European and Western culture. This role, Bernal argues, has been ignored by scholars in the nineteenth and twentieth centuries who sought to promote a vision of Western civilization in which Africa had little or no influence. In the United States, the raging debate that followed the publication of *Black Athena* has exposed contemporary America's continuing sensitivity to questions of race and inheritance. Indeed, while Bernal's work sought merely to enter into the academic debate concerning the debt that European (and therefore American) civilization owed to the influence of African cultures, the implication of its revisionist history has found favor among antiracist and civil rights organizations in America. Therefore, the significance of *Black Athena* revolves around the veracity of its central thesis. As Bernal has written, if his work truly demonstrates that African civilizations played a highly significant role in the constitution of the ancient Greek culture that informed all European societies, then racist discourse can no longer return to the ideas that blacks are inherently uncivilized or that blacks must become like the white European if they are to enjoy "civilization." As such, *Black Athena,* as revisionist history, encourages the empowerment of America's black community, and insists that African and African American self-perception change—that it step outside of the kind of discursive limitations that saw Leopold Senghor's negritude movement willingly embrace the notion that Africa stood as the emotional correlate to the ancient Greek intellect.

Bernal's *Black Athena* is a wide-ranging piece of scholarship that employs a host of interpretive systems—including linguistic, historical, archaeological, and mythological—to argue for a revision of the influence of Africa on the intellectual and cultural development of Europe. The core ideas of the book are the result of two intertwined assertions. The first is Bernal's claim that the way in which we currently understand the origins of ancient Greece is significantly different from that of earlier generations. Bernal argues that in earlier centuries, ancient Greek culture had always been understood as the product of the insertion of Egyptian and Phoenician (read African) civilizations. However, this "Ancient model," as Bernal calls it, was seemingly replaced by our current understanding of ancient Greece as the product of a series of invasions from the north by Indo-European speakers—the "Aryan model." It is from this claim that Bernal makes his second assertion that one can trace the fall of the Ancient model to certain external forces operating around the second half of the eighteenth century. Bernal highlighted factors such as a Christian reactionism that favored the study of Greek culture over Egyptian civilization, since it could not tolerate any suggestion that some Egyptian religious traditions were older than the Hebrew Bible; the rise in the concept of "progress," which ensured that the very antiquity of Egyptian civilization became unpalatable to a Europe that exhibited blind interest in only those societies that were considered to be dynamic and developing; and a Romantic Hellenism that was stimulated by the Greek War of Independence in the early nineteenth century, which Bernal claims was interpreted as a struggle between Europe on one hand and the continents of Africa and Asia on the other.

Bernal asserts that the growth of an institutionalized racism, premised on "scientific" claims of objective proof of the inherent superiority of Caucasian races, accounts for much of the historical rewriting that occurred at the turn of the nineteenth century. As such, even though the attention of Bernal's work seems to be split between two fundamentally different projects— *Black Athena* as a revisionist history of the last three millennia of the Mediterranean area, and *Black Athena* as a work of historiography, which is to say, an examination of the way in which these ancient Mediterranean cultures have been written about from the fifth century BCE to the present day—it retains the singular focus of unveiling the processes that systematically underestimated, deflated, and marginalized the importance of African cultures to world history.

While the *Black Athena* debate is perhaps best-known as an Internet phenomenon, nevertheless, initial interest in its arguments and methodology actually began with academia's response to what was perceived as an antagonistic piece of scholarship. After

all, Bernal's work seemed to imply that all Western historical and archaeological scholarship was in some manner racist and, to a certain extent, anti-Semitic.

Early academic responses to Bernal's work included a special issue of the journal *Arethusa* (1989), which contained papers given at the 120th meeting of the American Philological Association; a special issue of the *American Journal of Archaeology* (1990); and a dedicated issue of the *Journal of Women's History* (1993), which contained a symposium on Bernal's work. While many academic responses to *Black Athena* began by acknowledging the important role that it played in reigniting interest in the genealogical relationships between ancient civilizations, the overwhelming majority of these responses highlighted serious flaws in Bernal's theses, methodologies, and evidence. No collection of responses has questioned the scholarship behind Bernal's work more than Mary Lefkowitz and Guy Rogers's collection, *Black Athena Revisited* (1996).

In this collection, noted linguists Jay Jasanoff and Alan Nussbaum express fundamental misgivings about Bernal's linguistic evidence for claiming that Europe inherited a massive lexicon from Egyptian and Semitic languages. Jasanoff and Nussbaum conclude that Bernal made no effort to go beyond the realm of appearances, while choosing to ignore and misrepresent known facts about the history of individual word forms. Similarly, Edith Hall argues that Bernal's use of Greek mythological narratives in support of his composition of the "Ancient model" is deeply flawed because of his selective and reductive use of source materials. Indeed, the claim that Bernal's more complex assertions about modern scholarship fail to stand up to any kind of rigorous examination because of his selective use of sources is one that is repeated in the criticism of writers such as Robert Palter, Robert Norton, and Richard Jenkyns.

While Bernal has largely accepted criticism of his rather monolithic consideration of certain academic disciplines, it is certain that such criticism has done little to temper the force that *Black Athena* exerts beyond the walls of academia. Clearly, his work has proven to be an important and necessary catalyst for America's continuing dialogue on race and the manner in which the relationship between white and black is conducted. Moreover, it has revitalized the question of how history should be taught in institutions of education, and along with it re-politicized all aspects of the African American genealogy.

Grant Hamilton

See also: Afrocentrism; Négritude; Race, History of

References

Bernal, Martin. *Black Athena: The Afroasiatic Roots of Classical Civilization.* Vol.1, *The Fabrication of Ancient Greece 1785–1985.* New Brunswick, NJ: Rutgers University Press, 1987.

Bernal, Martin. *Black Athena: The Afroasiatic Roots of Classical Civilization.* Vol. 2, *The Archaeological and Documentary Evidence.* New Brunswick, NJ: Rutgers University Press, 1991.

Lefkowitz, Mary, and Guy Rogers, eds. *Black Athena Revisited.* Chapel Hill: University of North Carolina Press, 1996.

BLACK CLASSICAL SINGERS

Black classical singers negotiate issues of race and audience in music on the American stage and internationally. From the mid-nineteenth century, black Americans have excelled as classical singers. They have, however, had two major obstacles to overcome. First, prejudice excluded them from opera houses, and many whites regarded their concerts more as freak shows than artistic events. Second, since the time when African Americans have been allowed to the sing at the nation's major opera houses, they have frequently been characterized as possessing a distinctively dusky or "Negro" sound that particularly suits them for certain roles. (A blindfold test comparing, say, Leontyne Price and Leonie Rysanek would disprove that easily.) Black sopranos, for example, were pressured into performing the dramatic role of Verdi's Ethiopian princess, Aida, even though their voices were far too light for the part. By the year 2000, blacks were overcoming these stereotypes and functioning as regular members of the operatic and concert community.

The leading black singers of the nineteenth century, sopranos Elizabeth Taylor-Greenfield (1820s–1876), Marie Selika (ca. 1849–1937), and Sissieretta Jones (1869–1933) were compared favorably with white divas Jenny Lind and Adelina Patti, sang for presidents of the United States and British royalty, and yet were never offered an operatic role. Jones could have been recorded (the phonograph became usable roughly in 1900) but never was. Tenor Roland Hayes (1887–1968), who attended Oberlin College in Ohio and was a sensational concert singer in Europe and America, deeply inspired Marian Anderson and pioneered in mixing Negro spirituals and hymns with classical music on his programs. His one surviving record of spirituals (he destroyed some early recordings) from his old age is immensely important for the history of singing. The aged Patti compared his voice and technique in its prime to the great tenors who had first sung the operas of Verdi and Donizetti in the mid-nineteenth century, and the elegance of Hayes's phrasing and dynamics offer a glimpse into a lost world of singing that only a handful of artists have recalled.

Two black singers of different temperaments dominated the American concert stage in the first half of the twentieth century. Marian Anderson (1897–1993) of Philadelphia and Paul Robeson (1898–1976) of Princeton, New Jersey—born some fifty miles and a year apart and possessing, respectively, two of the most beautiful contralto and bass voices ever heard—both concertized extensively in Europe to win recognition in America. Both integrated classical and folk songs with Negro spirituals in their programs, calling attention to their equal beauty, and both became involved in the Civil Rights Movement. Robeson, an outspoken socialist and supporter of the Soviet Union, lost his passport, his fortune, and ultimately his health and his mind for his unwillingness to compromise his principles during the early days of the cold war. Anderson, a placid and religious woman, became a symbol of the struggle for civil rights when she sang at the Lincoln Memorial in 1939, having been denied use of Constitution Hall by the Daughters of the American Revolution. Late in her career, on January 7, 1955, she also became the first black person to sing at the Metropolitan Opera in New York.

Although several blacks sang at the Metropolitan after Anderson's debut, the African American opera singer came of age when Leontyne Price (1927–) received a forty-five-minute ovation following her debut in 1962 as Leonore in Verdi's *Il Trovatore.* Born in Mississippi, she first excelled in the performance of contemporary

Opera singer Leontyne Price dressed in costume for Anthony and Cleopatra *at the Metropolitan Opera House in New York City in 1966. (Library of Congress)*

songs, most notably, Samuel Barber's *Hermit Songs.* She was also a notable lead in *Porgy and Bess,* Jewish composer George Gershwin's opera about Charleston, South Carolina, blacks, where she sang opposite her husband, the superb bass William Warfield. Price's limitless top register and tonal beauty were unmatched in the contemporary field of great sopranos who sang at the Met. Peerless in Verdi and Puccini, she disappointed her many supporters by venturing into Wagner and Strauss only on record and learning few new roles. Although she retired from the Met in 1987, she has continued to give concerts into her seventies. Replacing Marian Anderson as a national icon, it was appropriate that she sang her signature tune, "God Bless America," in the memorial concert in her adopted New York City immediately following the September 11 terrorist attack.

Several superb singers followed in Price's footsteps from the 1960s to 1980s.

Soprano Martina Arroyo took many of the same parts with a richer lower and middle register although less spectacular top. Mezzo-soprano Grace Bumbry—at age twenty-four the first black to sing at Wagner's Bayreuth Festival, appearing as a voluptuous Venus in *Tannhauser*—later sang soprano roles, as did her sometime rival, Shirley Verrett. Both mezzos offered immensely dramatic interpretations and a fire that Price and Arroyo lacked: Bumbry excelled as an erotic Salome, Verrett as Lady Macbeth, and both as Eboli and Amneris in Verdi's *Don Carlo* and *Aida*. Coloratura Reri Grist and lyric tenor George Shirley never received equal publicity but were among the best singers of the day.

In the last two decades of the twentieth century, the two most famous black classical singers were sopranos Jessye Norman and Kathleen Battle. Although possessing beautiful voices—Battle a delightful light one, Norman a rich dramatic soprano that she has used in unusual repertory such as Janacek, Rameau, and French song—they became known as much for their personalities as their vocal gifts. Norman has been criticized for construction of a pretentious, larger-than-life persona; the Metropolitan Opera fired Battle for her extreme displays of temperament. On the other hand, lyric–coloratura soprano Barbara Hendricks and contralto Denyce Graves are noted for their generosity—Hendricks for her work with the poor and refugees for the United Nations, and Graves—who possesses one of the deepest and most moving contraltos ever heard—for her work with students and charities in the United States. Other African American singers—tenor Vinson Cole, basses Willard White and Simon Estes, sopranos Mavis Martin and Roberta Alexander, and mezzos Hilda Harris and Florence Quivar—are among the finest working in the early twenty-first century. Lacking the publicity machines of the "Three Tenors" and no longer astonishing audiences by their very presence on stage, black singers are becoming part of the mainstream of American vocal music.

William Pencak

References

Davis, Peter G. *The American Opera Singer.* New York: Doubleday, 1997.

Pleasants, Henry. *The Great Singers.* 2nd ed. New York: Simon & Schuster, 1986.

Story, Rosalyn M. *And So I Sing: African-American Divas of Concert and Song.* New York: Warner Books, 1990.

BLACK PANTHER PARTY

The Black Panther Party was a radical black intellectual and political organization. It promoted Black Nationalism and resistance as an alternative to the integrationist Civil Rights Movement.

In the late 1960s, the Black Panther Party (BPP) gained national attention as one of the most revolutionary formations in American history. Emerging in the crucible of the Black Power Movement, the BPP rejected the Civil Rights Movement's strategy of nonviolent civil disobedience and advocated armed struggle against America's white supremacist–capitalist state. Viewing urban black communities as colonies occupied by a system of hostile white police, the BPP fearlessly contested the power of the state to brutalize black citizens. Established in October 1966 and headquartered in Oakland, California, the BPP both influenced and was influenced by local and global affairs. Stimulated by Malcolm X's black nationalism, Mao Zedong's axiom of "picking up the gun," and Frantz Fanon's and Che Guevera's theories of revolutionary violence, Huey P. Newton and Bobby Seale, students at Oakland's Merritt College, founded the BPP in 1966 based upon a radical critique of racial oppression and class domination. The Black Panther Party's newspaper, *The Black Panther*, served as the organization's major source of communication throughout urban America.

Huey Newton, the organization's theoretician, wrote the party's platform and program, delineating "What We Want" and "What We Believe." The program's elements included power and self-determination for the black community, decent housing, critical education, full employment for black people, self-defense, the termination of police brutality and murder of black people, and the freedom of all black prisoners. One of the Black Panther Party's initial activities was an armed patrol of the Oakland police to ensure that police did not brutalize and murder black residents and, also, to inform urban residents of their legal rights. This effort was key to the Panthers' ability to recruit members during the organization's early stages of development. One of the most important functions of the party was to provide a number of community survival programs, which included free breakfast for children, free health clinics, and liberation youth schools. As a vanguard formation, the Black Panther Party regarded its survival programs as contributing to the revolutionary transformation of black consciousness and of America's repressive state apparatus.

As a dimension of the Black Power Movement's politics of indictment against America's systemic anti-black racism, the Black Panther Party contributed to the ongoing evolution of radical black political thought. Beginning as a Black Nationalist formation, the party quickly repudiated that ideology by embracing revolutionary nationalism, which sought to combine anti-racist and anti-capitalist perspectives. More and more, Huey Newton advanced the position that black Americans were colonized in much the same way as were the people in Africa, Asia, and Latin America, whose nations western Europeans had subjugated since the nineteenth century. It was this sense of solidarity with colonized and oppressed peoples around the world that encouraged Newton to advance the position of revolutionary internationalism in 1970. Newton argued that the United States no longer was a nation but an empire that dominated the world. Accordingly, the bourgeoisie that Marxist-Leninist adherents sought to defeat was international in character. Overthrowing this international enemy demanded an international strategy; it required the unity of struggle among the workers of the world, according to Newton.

In the face of changing world dynamics, most especially the war in Vietnam, the Panthers' efforts to refine the concept of internationalism resulted in a transition to revolutionary intercommunalism, a belief that stressed a collective striving for anti-colonialism and the self-determination of peoples, who were otherwise dispersed throughout the colonial world. This new ideology was put forward at the turbulent September 1970 Revolutionary People's Convention in Philadelphia. The idea of intercommunalism grew out of the Panthers' fundamental ideological position on internationalism. In the face of U.S. world capitalism and imperialism, the BPP called for the world's oppressed peoples to unite and fight under the banner of revolutionary intercommunalism.

It was in the context of these rapidly shifting political ideas, together with increasing repression from the U.S. government, that members of the Black Panther Party traveled throughout Europe, Asia, Latin America, and Africa to establish relations with international activists and leaders of socialist nations. In 1968, at the invitation of Japanese radicals, BPP leaders Kathleen Cleaver and Earl Anthony gave a series of speeches that criticized the war in Vietnam and the use of nuclear weapons. In the same year, the BPP minister of information, Eldridge Cleaver, fled to Cuba in order to escape charges related to an April 6, 1968, Panther-police shootout in Oakland, California. Three years later the party sent a representative to the annual celebration of the Cuban Revolution.

Significantly, the North African nation of Algeria—a nation that sheltered many exiled Panthers—officially acknowledged the connection between African and African American liberation struggles by inviting black artists and political activists to the First Pan-African Cultural Festival began in July 1968. In addition to an invited ensemble of radical activists, writers, scholars, poets, actors, playwrights, and jazz musicians, Panther leader Eldridge Cleaver reemerged in Algiers, Algeria. BPP members met numerous international revolutionaries, including representatives from liberation movements in Palestine, Vietnam, and South Africa.

Thereafter, Black Panther Party members were to receive numerous invitations from international revolutionaries and progressive governments. As a result of close ties between the Panthers and the North Korean Embassy in Algiers, North Korean diplomats invited Cleaver to attend the International Conference on Revolutionary

Poster of Black Panther Eldridge Cleaver. Active throughout the 1960s and 1970s, the Black Panthers promoted civil rights and self defense. (Library of Congress)

Journalists in the Democratic People's Republic of Korea in 1969. This initial visit led to another invitation by North Korean officials the following year. A contingent, calling itself the American People's Anti-Imperialist Delegation and representing a cross section of progressive organizations and forces—the Black Panther Party, the Red Guard, the women's liberation movement, the radical media, and representatives of the antiwar movement—met Cleaver in North Korea and toured the country. Unexpectedly, the Vietnamese ambassador in Pyongyang invited the American delegation of progressive activists to North Vietnam, where they were honored on August 18, 1970, during a celebration of International Day of Solidarity with Black People of the United States.

Eldridge Cleaver initiated additional BPP exchanges with African revolutionaries. As a result of a 1971 invitation from the Congolese Socialist Youth Union, he led a delegation of Panthers from Algeria to the People's Republic of the Congo in order to attend the International Conference of Solidarity with the People under Portuguese Domination. In the Congo, members of the Panther contingent, which included Kathleen Cleaver, established relations with African freedom fighters from Guinea-Bissau, Mozambique, and Angola. Also participating were socialist youth delegations from North Africa, Asia, Eastern Europe, and the Soviet Union—all of which articulated their support for the struggle against Portuguese colonialism.

It also was in the early 1970s that the Black Panther Party established international links with the People's Republic of China. In September 1971, following his release from prison, Huey Newton led a delegation of Panthers, including Central Committee member Elaine Brown, to China. This visit set the stage for a larger BPP contingent in 1972—a visit to China that allowed Panther delegation members to observe the practice of Marxism-Leninism in relationship to the everyday life experience of Chinese people.

As the 1970s progressed, the Black Panther Party experienced mounting internal contradictions as well as increased repression by the U.S. government. Severe tensions emerged between California and New York Panther members, which resulted in a public split between Huey Newton and Eldridge Cleaver. The public display of party division affected the party's international contingent, contributing to an increasingly precarious situation in Algiers for Panther expatriate Cleaver, his family, and other BPP members. Moreover, murders of New York and California Panthers ultimately led Huey Newton to purge numerous party members.

In addition to internal problems, the Panthers faced increasing repression from the U.S. government in the form of the FBI's Counter Intelligence Program (COINTELPRO), which was set in motion in the late 1960s. This state terror campaign decimated Panther leadership and rank-and-file membership. With the assistance and support of the FBI and local police informants, urban policemen raided Panther offices and homes in cities across America and deliberately shot and killed numerous Panthers. Killed while asleep in their apartment on December 4, 1969, Fred Hampton and Mark Clark were two of the most prominent Panther members assassinated by the Chicago police. As internal contradictions mounted and state repression intensified, the Black Panther Party, as a revolutionary formation, declined between 1974 and 1977.

Floyd W. Hayes III

See also: Black Power Movement; Civil Rights Movement; Malcolm X; Pan-Africanism

References

Cleaver, Kathleen. "Back to Africa: The Evolution of the International Section of the Black Panther Party (1969–1972)." In *The Black Panther Party Reconsidered,* edited by Charles E. Jones. Baltimore: Black Classic Press, 1998.

Clemons, Michael L., and Charles E. Jones. "Global Solidarity: The Black Panther Party in the International Arena." In *Liberation, Imagination, and the Black Panther Party: A New Look at the Panthers and Their Legacy,* edited by Kathleen Cleaver and George Katsiaficas. New York: Routledge, 2001.

Foner, Philip S., ed. *The Black Panthers Speak.* New York: J. B. Lippincott,1970.

Hilliard, David, and Lewis Cole. *This Side of Glory: The Autobiography of David Hilliard*

and the Story of the Black Panther Party.
Boston: Little, Brown, 1993.

Jeffries, Judson L. *Huey P. Newton: The Radical Theorist.* Jackson: University Press of Mississippi, 2002.

Seale, Bobby. *Seize the Time: The Story of the Black Panther Party and Huey P. Newton.* New York: Random House, 1970.

BLACK POWER MOVEMENT

The Black Power Movement was a political movement linked with the Black Panther Party, the Black Arts Movement, and Afrocentrism that fostered political and educational support for a positive valuation of black racial identity and the right to self-defense.

The Black Power Movement had its beginnings in the ideology of the Civil Rights Movement. Both movements were interested in bringing about equality for the African American community. In fact, the roots of the Black Power Movement can be linked directly to the philosophy of Martin Luther King Jr. and other leaders of the Civil Rights Movement. The Black Power Movement, however, moved away from the peaceful protests of the Civil Rights Movement and became a movement that called for more active and confrontational resistance to segregation, Jim Crow policies, and legalized discrimination in the United States. The term "Black Power" was first used by Adam Clayton Powell in a speech at Howard University, but it was made popular in 1966 by Stokely Carmichael, the national chairperson of the Student Nonviolent Coordinating Committee (SNCC), in Greenwood, Mississippi. The idea of the Black Power Movement was expressed in many ways during the 1960s and 1970s; most noticeable were the raised fists of black athletes at the 1968 Olympic Games in Mexico and the change in hair and clothing styles during the 1960s and 1970s. A critical change that the Black Power Movement brought about was the use of the word "black" instead of "Negro" to identify African Americans.Malcolm X, born Malcolm Little, prominent leader of the Nation of Islam and later the head of the Muslim Mosque Inc., also provided a foundation for the Black Power Movement. Malcolm X's insistence on self-defense, and on the maintenance of black cultural values, traditions, and history were a point of reference for the younger generation of African Americans in the 1960s. While these individuals supported the goals of the Civil Rights Movement, they were concerned that the nonviolent approach of King and his followers put them in a position where they had to wait for their rights. The leaders of the Black Power Movement asserted the need for equal rights today, not tomorrow, and they were willing to pursue that goal, in the words of Malcolm X, "by any means necessary." While this assertion by Malcolm X has been interpreted to represent a call to violence, it was in fact a call to action and a call to community. It reflected a desire to effect change in all aspects of the African American experience in America. This desire was perhaps best exhibited in the actions of the Black Panther Party. Huey Newton, Eldridge Cleaver, and Bobby Seale, the cofounders of the organization, established a ten-point program that included an insistence that African Americans had the right to self-defense. While much attention has been given to this assertion, the Black Panther Party was also instrumental in providing much needed support in African American communities, including but not limited to soup kitchens and breakfast programs for schoolchildren. In addition, the party was instrumental in making a tangible connection between the struggles of minority communities and other working-class communities.

A critical aspect of the Black Power Movement was a call for African Americans to define the world in their own terms. The response to this call took on numerous forms. In the artistic realm of the black community, the Black Power Movement was paralleled by the Black Arts Movement, which included the works of such artists as Amiri Baraka (born Everett LeRoi Jones), Sonia Sanchez, and Nikki Giovanni. These artists used their creativity to form a new, more radical image of the African American as one who was unwilling to remain stagnant in the face of racism and oppression. This image also advanced, as an ideal, the individual as a person who is culturally, nationally, and internationally aware. This international awareness was particularly critical, as it included an acknowledgement of the transnational link between Africa and individuals in the African Diaspora. The role of Africa in the culture, traditions, and ideology of African Americans was exhibited in the art, literature, and styles developed during the 1960s and 1970s. Particularly noticeable was the return to natural, more Afrocentric, styles of dress and hair styling.

Other important leaders of the Black Power Movement included Maulana Karenga, the founder of Kwanza, and Angela Davis, an activist and teacher. Created in 1966 and based on a range of African religions, Kwanza emphasizes seven principles of familyhood: *umoja,* unity; *kujichagulia,* self-determination; *ujima,* collective work and responsibility; *nia,* purpose; *kuumba,* creativity; and *imani,* faith.

These principles helped to emphasize the philosophical outlook of the movement and its desire to initiate change in the black experience in America. Kwanza was instrumental in reestablishing a tangible connection between African Americans and their African past; the principles provided a transnational perspective for the African American community, affirming the continued strength and value of the African past within African American culture. Angela Davis was instrumental in voicing the needs of women at a time when much emphasis was on racial uplift. Davis discussed racial injustice while promoting women's rights.

The Black Power Movement, coupled with the Black Arts Movement, was vital in reaffirming a sense of race pride, a sense of community that was both national and transnational. Like the Black Power Movement, the Black Arts Movement asserted a sense of pride in African Americans' African heritage and a desire to return to an "authentic" African American identity, one that emphasized the African in African American. The ideologies and philosophies of the Black Power Movement continue to impact both the cultural and political perspective of the African American community. The Black Power Movement was also influential in the development of international movements, such as African internationalism and Pan-Africanism.

J. A. Brown-Rose

See also: Afrocentrism; Baraka, Amiri; Black Arts Movement; Black Panther Party; Civil Rights Movement; Malcolm X; Sanchez, Sonia; Student Nonviolent Coordinating Committee

References
Breitman, George. *Malcolm X Speaks: Selected Speeches and Statements.* New York: Grove Weidenfeld, 1990.

Collier-Thomas, Betty, and V. P. Franklin. *Sisters in the Struggle: African American Women in the Civil Rights and Black Power Movement.* New York: New York University Press, 2001.

Tyson, Timothy B. *Radio Free Dixie: Robert F. Williams and the Roots of Black Power.* Chapel Hill: University of North Carolina Press, 2001.

Van De Burg, William. *New Day in Babylon: The Black Power Movement and American Culture, 1965–1975.* Chicago: University of Chicago Press, 1992.

Van De Burg, William, ed. *Modern Black Nationalism: From Marcus Garvey to Louis Farrakhan.* New York: New York University Press, 1997.

BLACK STAR LINE

The Black Star Line (BSL) was established in 1919 by Marcus Garvey, in line with his vision to promote racial uplift through black-owned enterprise. The goal of the steamship line was to promote trade in the Atlantic while providing transportation for blacks who wanted to return to Africa as part of Garvey's efforts to recolonize and rejuvenate Liberia. The three-ship fleet was funded through the sale of stock to initially eager blacks in North, Central, and South America and the Caribbean.

Hopes were high at the outset of the BSL's endeavors, as the corporation provided a rare example of black economic independence in the New World. Challenges, however, soon followed. Stiff competition in the industry and racism made shipping contracts difficult to procure. Also, the poor condition of the vessels, high maintenance costs, and bad decision making on the part of the ships' crews often meant that voyages were delayed or not completed. Merchandise was often spoiled, consumed, or lost as a result, and many of the BSL's clients soon became creditors.

These factors, combined with financial mismanagement by officials of Garvey's Universal Negro Improvement Association (UNIA), resulted in criticism of Garvey in both the black and white press and difficulty in obtaining credit.

Despite these obstacles, the BSL continued to enjoy support from a large segment of the black population. Garvey toured constantly, encouraging blacks to purchase stock in a flagship to be named the *Phillis Wheatley.* When financial problems and questionable business dealings made it clear that such a ship was not forthcoming, further criticism ensued. Garvey's difficulties culminated in an FBI investigation and charges of mail fraud. The legal challenges that followed resulted in the failure of the Black Star Line and Garvey's conviction and deportation.

Carmen Lenore Wright

See also: Garvey, Marcus; Titanic; Universal Negro Improvement Association, The

References

Cronon, Edmund. *Black Moses: The Story of Marcus Garvey and the Universal Negro Improvement Association.* Madison: University of Wisconsin Press, 1955.

Lewis, Rupert, and Patrick Bryan, eds. *Garvey: His Work and Impact.* Mona, Jamaica: University of the West Indies, 1988.

BLUCKE OR BLEUCKE OR BLUCK, STEPHEN (1752–1795?)

Stephen Blucke was a black American Loyalist and founder of the Nova Scotian settlement, Birchtown.

Leader of the African American community in New York City during the seven-year British occupation (1776–1783), Blucke led the postwar migration to Nova Scotia of the largest body of black refugees—fugitive slaves declared free by British military proclamations. Though referred to as "Colonel" because he was placed in overall charge of some twenty-one companies of fugitive slave evacuees, Blucke was a civilian, not a soldier; the only colonelcy he ever held was command of the black militia in Shelburne, Nova Scotia. The embarkation list of refugee slaves evacuating New York (the "Book of Negroes") treats Stephen Blucke as if he were black. In fact he was mulatto, born free in Barbados, probably of a planter father and black mother. He was well-educated and highly literate. It is not known when or why he first came to New York, but he was clearly there throughout the British occupation. Sir Guy Carleton, who became British commander-in-chief in 1782, appointed Blucke to lead the evacuation of some 1,500 freed blacks to Port Roseway (Shelburne), Nova Scotia, where they arrived in August 1783. Blucke named the separate black settlement, established five miles away, Birchtown, in honor of a former commandant of the city of New York who had issued many of the fugitive slave passports. For several years Birchtown was North America's Negropolis, the largest freed black settlement on the continent.

Blucke ruled the black community as if he were a magistrate, but he did not live among the refugees or even near them. Nor were he and they treated equally. His 200-acre farm lot—five times the size of the other black land grants—was at Churchover, on the southwestern shore of Shelburne Harbour. His "spacious house," where, tradition says, he entertained Prince William Henry in October 1788, lay on the road from Shelburne to Birchtown; it was still standing eighty years later. In September 1784 Blucke's status as paramount leader of

the black refugees was recognized by Governor Parr, who commissioned him lieutenant colonel of the black militia in the district of Shelburne. Blucke was both the black community's headman and its go-between with the white community. While most of the black people were, or became, Baptists or Methodists, Blucke—as befitted an honorary member of the white establishment—was an Episcopalian, renting a pew in Shelburne's Christ Church (Church of England). He also served as schoolmaster at Birchtown under the auspices of the Society for the Propagation of the Gospel in Foreign Parts.

Blucke, who had never been a slave, did not actively oppose the resettlement scheme to Sierra Leone, but he was out of sympathy with what he considered an African adventure that would divest the refugees of hard-won land in return for a distant promised one. Blucke's disenchantment with the scheme, which was supported by all the other black leaders and most of the freed black community in Nova Scotia and New Brunswick, ensured the survival—down to the present day—of Birchtown, a dispersed rural community that is now one of Canada's national historic sites. All the other black refugee communities in Nova Scotia were depopulated or simply disappeared as a result of the exodus to Sierra Leone in 1791–1792. The loss of about half the local black population—a plentiful supply of cheap labor—was an economic factor contributing to the rapid decline of Shelburne township in the 1790s. More were leaving Shelburne than were staying, and Blucke was among the former. He disappears from the records in April 1796 and probably left soon after. His reasons for doing so are unknown, but may relate to his having entered into a bigamous marriage with his wife's ward, Isabella Gibbons, who bore him children.

Barry Cahill

See also: Birchtown; Nova Scotia, Black Refugees in

References

Cahill, Barry. "Stephen Blucke: The Perils of Being a 'White Negro' in Loyalist Nova Scotia." *Nova Scotia Historical Review* 11, no. 1 (June 1991): 129–134.

Hodges, Graham Russell, ed. *The Black Loyalist Directory: African Americans in Exile after the American Revolution.* New York: Garland, 1996.

Ranlet, Philip. *The New York Loyalists.* 2nd ed. Lanham, MD: University Press of America, 2002.

Walker, James W. St. G. *The Black Loyalists: The Search for a Promised Land in Nova Scotia and Sierra Leone, 1783–1870.* 1976. Reprint, Toronto: University of Toronto Press, 1992.

Edward Wilmot Blyden, Liberian educator and statesman. (Library of Congress)

BLYDEN, EDWARD WILMOT (1832–1912)

A Pan-African intellectual, statesman, and educator, Edward Wilmot Blyden was born in St. Thomas in the Virgin Islands of free parents. Blyden was the first West Indian to make an important contribution to the emergence of Pan-Africanism. He also laid the foundations for West African nationalism and the negritude movement.

At an early age Blyden decided to become a clergyman. In May 1850 he went to the United States, where he tried to enroll at Rutgers Theological College. His rejection on the basis of his skin color was one of the main reasons why he migrated to Liberia in December 1850. He continued his formal education at Alexander High School in the capital, Monrovia. In 1858 he was ordained a Presbyterian minister and became the principal of Alexander High School. In 1861 and 1862 he served as Liberia's commissioner to Britain and the United States. From 1862 till 1871 he was professor of classics at Liberia College, a post which he combined for some time with that of secretary of state of Liberia.

In 1871 Blyden moved to Freetown, Sierra Leone, where he founded and edited *The Negro,* the first Pan-African journal in West Africa, and on two occasions he led government expeditions into the interior. Between 1871 and 1884 he was based again in Liberia, where he alternated between important academic and governmental positions. After 1885 Blyden divided his time between Sierra Leone, Liberia, and Lagos, Nigeria. He contributed to their development in his capacity as educator and statesman and as the founder of several journals and newspapers that promoted West African nationalism.

He died in Freetown in 1912. Only one of his eight children, Isa Cleopatra, survived him. She was the mother of Edward Wilmot Blyden III, whose Sierra Leone Independence Movement organization helped to win Sierra Leone's independence from Great Britain in 1961. In spite of his many important functions, Blyden found time to express his views on race and Africa in lectures, reviews, articles, pamphlets, and books. His most influential writings are *A Voice from Bleeding Africa* (1856), *Liberia's Offering* (1862), *Christianity, Islam, and the Negro Race* (1887), *West Africa before Europe* (1905), and *African Life and Customs* (1908). Blyden adhered to the idea that humankind was divided into different races that were distinct but equal—none was inherently superior or inferior. He tried to prove in his lectures and writings, to both black and white, that the African was equal to other races. He mentioned the contributions that Africa had made to humanity before the arrival of the Europeans and also highlighted individual black achievement. In addition, he encouraged Africans at home and in the diaspora to study African history and culture and take pride in their skin color. His practice of giving the word "negro" a positive interpretation and of capitalizing it was one of several means he used to instill a new racial consciousness in Africans. It is this practice, more than any other, that has earned him the label of forerunner of the negritude movement.

Blyden's racial ideas affected his views on religion. His expeditions into the interior of Africa, where he observed Islam's influence, and his discussions with scholarly African Muslims gradually convinced him that Islam suited the African "race" better than Christianity, as it emphasized brotherhood and lacked racial prejudice.

Blyden resigned from the Presbyterian Church in 1886 but never formally adopted Islam. For the remainder of his life, he tried to promote Islam among Africans and facilitate an understanding between Islam and Christianity in Africa. Between 1901 and 1906, for example, he was director of Muslim education in Sierra Leone and taught English and other "western" subjects to Muslim youth with the aim of bridging the gap between the Muslim and Christian communities in the British protectorate.

Throughout his life, Blyden worked toward the establishment of a modern West African state that would protect and promote the interests of peoples of African descent and serve as a symbol of African power. He saw Liberia as the stepping-stone of this project. Its development would encourage the settlement of other nation-states that in time would form, with Liberia, a West African state. To enhance Liberia's development, he influenced the Liberian government to encourage selective repatriation from the Americas. He was convinced that Africans in the Americas were the key to integrating Africa into the modern world due to the role that they had played, mostly against their will, in the economic development of the Americas. He also tried to achieve his political goal by actively championing the merging of Liberia and Sierra Leone into one nation.

Blyden's work contains many inconsistencies. He espoused racial equality while at the same time advocating the separation of the races and expressing a fear of racial mixture. Drawing upon examples from the United States, Blyden argued that there was antipathy among the races and that only by keeping them apart could the African race fully develop and demonstrate its talents. He backed his claim that people of mixed race were inferior to those of pure parentage largely by offering evidence from Liberia. He presented Liberia's mulattos as a retarding influence on its progress. They were, in his opinion, physically weaker and more corrupt than full-blooded Africans. Equally inconsistent and ambivalent are his remarks on European colonialism. On the one hand, he regarded European colonial rule as a negative influence that dismantled traditional beliefs and customs, while on the other, he welcomed it as a vehicle of progress for Africa. These contradictory ideas, however, have not prevented generations of Pan-Africanists and West African nationalists—from Casely Hayford and Marcus Garvey to George Padmore and Kwame N'krumah—from acclaiming Blyden as a great teacher.

Henrice Altink

See also: Garvey, Marcus; Islam, African American; Liberia; Négritude; N'Krumah, Kwame; Pan-Africanism

References

Hanciles, J. J. "Edward W. Blyden and the West African University: Race, Mission, and Education." *Zimbabwe Journal of Educational Research* 10, no. 3 (1998): 235–249.

Lynch, Hollis R. *Edward Wilmot Blyden: Pan-Negro Patriot, 1832–1912.* Oxford: Oxford University Press, 1967.

Lynch, Hollis R., ed. *Black Spokesman: Selected Published Writings of Edward Wilmot Blyden.* London: Frank Cass, 1971.

Turner, R. B. "Edward Wilmot Blyden and Pan-Africanism: The Ideological Roots of Islam and Black Nationalism in the United States." *Muslim World* 87, no. 2 (1997): 169–182.

BOATBUILDING

The boats designed and constructed by Africans on both sides of the Atlantic were vital in the transportation of goods and workers. Drawings and descriptions of huge hollowed trees that held as many as eighty people appear frequently in travelers' and traders' accounts. These canoes, called *pirogues* or *pettiaguers* by French traders, were engineered for a wide range of tasks in varying water conditions—slow, plant-clogged rivers, rushing rapids, and the turbulent Atlantic surf along the coasts. African societies controlled their own interior waters throughout the Atlantic slave trade with these vessels, sometimes meeting the European ships at the mouths of rivers with warriors to prevent further incursion. Europeans found that African sailors' skill and experience, along with their watercraft, which were suitable for local waters, could navigate the treacherous surf and bring terrified captives from barracoons to the Europeans' tall-masted sailing ships.

The African boatbuilding method of hollowing a single large tree was combined with the watercraft techniques of Native Americans in South America, the Caribbean, and in North America. By the late nineteenth century a multilog *pettiauger,* invented by an enslaved African man known to history only as "Aaron," had proven its usefulness, especially for dredging oysters. There were 7,000 such watercraft on the Chesapeake Bay by 1900.

Related industries of naval stores and lumbering were developed with African American labor in the South, beginning with colonial times. In the decade before the U.S. Civil War, the pine forests of North Carolina, South Carolina, and Georgia, worked almost entirely by slave labor, provided most of the naval stores for the country. In the first half of the nineteenth century, the turpentine and lumber industries moved to the Gulf Coast of Louisiana and Texas in the general westward migration of southern slaveholders and planters.

Jean Libby

See also: Sailors; Technology Transfers

References

Bolster, W. Jeffrey. *Black Jacks: African American Seamen in the Age of Sail.* Cambridge, MA: Harvard University Press, 1997.

Ramold, Steven J. *Slaves, Sailors, Citizens: African Americans in the Union Navy.* DeKalb: Northern Illinois University Press, 2002.

BOLIVIA

Bolivia is a multicultural and multiethnic republic located in the heart of South America. The country's racial diversity, as in many African and Latin American countries, has served as both a resource and a challenge. Over half (55 to 60 percent) of its population of nine million is Native American (20 to 25 percent Aymara, 35 to 40 percent Quechua, and a small percentage of primarily Guaraní lowland Indians). However, these statistics are relative and fluid and are culturally defined. For example, in the 2001 census, 62 percent of Bolivians claimed an indigenous identity, signficantly more than in previous censuses. A second, racially mixed group of Mestizos (called *cholo* in Bolivia) are descendants from unions between Spanish colonizers and indigenous peoples and are some 30 to 40 percent of the population. White Bolivians comprise some 5 to 15 percent of the population, and a fractional percentage are Afro-Bolivians (blacks, mulattos, and black Indian, or *zambo*), the descendants of African slaves imported into Bolivia and forced to work the silver mines of Cerro Rico in the colonial city of Potosí and the coca leaf plantations of the northern inter-Andean valleys. There are also citizens of North African, Middle Eastern, Asian, and European extraction, such as Dutch and German Mennonites and Jewish refugees.

Bolivia has been landlocked since the loss of its seacoast in 1883 and is encircled by the five South American countries of Peru, Chile, Argentina, Paraguay, and Brazil. The country's landmass, which totals 621,371 miles (1,098,581 square kilometers), or about the combined size of Texas and California, incorporates a wide range of topography and climate. These range from the snow-capped Andean Mountains, to the chilly, windswept plateau known as the Altiplano in the west, to the fertile valleys and the lush subtropical and tropical savannahs and rainforests in the east. Administratively, the country is divided into nine departments, three in the Andean region (La Paz, Oruro, Potosí), three in the valleys (Cochabamba, Chuquisaca, and Tarija), and the three largest in the subtropical and tropical zones (Santa Cruz, Beni, and Pando).

Colonialism established in Bolivia, as in most African and Latin American countries, both a racist and an authoritarian political tradition. In the decades from independence in 1825 to the formation of civilian political parties in the 1880s, white and Mestizo military dictators (*caudillos*) dominated civic life. The rule of a white, civilian oligarchy during the first half of the twentieth century ended with the Bolivian National Revolution of 1952, which instituted land reform and universal suffrage, nationalized the mines, provided extensive educational and social welfare benefits, and for the first time recognized the Indians (at least in law) as full citizens of the republic. After an accommodation with the United States—the undisputed hegemonic power in Latin America—economic aid flowed into the needy country. However, in 1964 a military coup—the first among many—interrupted the reform process and influenced Ernesto "Che" Guevara, fresh from his guerrilla campaigns in Africa, to try to replicate the Cuban Revolution in Bolivia in 1967 and spark a continent-wide revolution.

In 1982, after eighteen years of authoritarian and military rule, Bolivia held free and fair elections. Despite continued poverty and a massive debt crisis (the bane of many developing countries), Bolivians continued to struggle for rights and democratic government. In December 2005 the long process of democratization culminated in the election of the country's first president of indigenous descent. President Evo Morales Aima received an unprecedented mandate of 54 percent of the popular vote—the largest since the revolution.

In Bolivia, as with many countries of Africa, regionalism, localism, and ethnic diversity have been powerful impetuses for divisiveness and underdevelopment. Bolivia has been described as a land divided into the extractive export economy (silver, tin, and other minerals) of the Andean region and the semifeudal agricultural economy of the lowlands. And as with many third world countries, a rugged geography has hindered development and national integration. Bolivia is popularly viewed as an Andean and Indian country because until the late twentieth century nearly two-thirds of the population lived in the Andes and inter-Andean valleys. Also, the largely white and Mestizo (a mixture of white Spanish and Aymara and Quechua Indians) ruling class of the highland departments dominated national politics during most of Bolivia's colonial and modern history.

However, two-thirds of the country's land mass lies in the subtropical and tropical lowlands in the east. Moreover, since the 1960s the massive population influx into and socioeconomic development of the eastern departments, especially resource-rich Santa Cruz, has shifted the balance of political and economic power eastward. Today, with the mineral and economic base of the highlands in steep decline, the wealthy and entrepreneurial Cambas (the ethno-regional term for eastern lowlanders) are more reluctant to transfer wealth to the central government's coffers in La Paz (the administrative capital) and to support the poorer Kollas (the ethno-regional term for indigenous citizens of the highlands). Despite significant economic development and regional decentralization in the 1990s, this highland versus lowland bifurcation has intensified. Cruceños (citizens of Santa Cruz) demand more regional autonomy and political and economic decentralization and threaten to secede if denied.

As in African countries such as Nigeria, Rwanda, and Sudan, uneven political and economic development has exacerbated regional-ethnic tensions. Economically, the decline of Bolivia's tin mining sector after 1985 forced thousands of unemployed and desperate highland miners to migrate to the lowlands. Many became growers of coca leaf, a legal crop until a U.S.-inspired Bolivian law criminalized production in nontraditional growing regions.

Unfortunately, economic necessity and profit enticed some Bolivians into the production of cocaine paste. As the Andean drug war became increasingly militarized and violent and human rights abuses increased, Bolivia's coca farmers, who continued to grow the primary ingredient for the drug trade, organized into a powerful growers' federation. Since the late 1970s the predominantly localized struggle has grown into a national social movement (similar to new, grassroots social movements across Africa and Latin America) and political party, the Movement toward Socialism (Movimiento al Socialismo, MAS), which brought Evo Morales, leader of the growers' union, to the presidency. The coca leaf, which has been grown in Bolivia since ancient times by the indigenous peoples and used in native medicine and religious and cultural ceremonies, became the symbol of nationalism, ethnic pride, and opposition to U.S. imperialism.

It has been in Bolivian Yungas (the tropical inter-Andean valleys north of La Paz) where coca has been grown traditionally and remains legal. There, thousands of Afro-Bolivians (perhaps 25,000) settled and farmed coca and other crops. The status of Afro-Bolivians, descendants of the approximately 100,000 slaves brought to the country from the Congo and Angola during colonial times, remains precarious economically and culturally, and the government did not include them in the 2001 census. Afro-Bolivians, unlike Afro-Latin Americans in many other countries, are a very small percentage of the population. The struggle to retain a distinct racial and cultural identity and the process of intermarriage or creolization created a black Aymara-speaking subculture in the Yungas. In dress and customs the black heritage has largely blended with those of the Aymara Indians and become an integral part of national folkloric dance and music. Examples are the Morenada dance of black slaves from the Altiplano and the Caporal dance of the Spanish overlords to the Saya music of the Yungas, which combines Andean instruments with African percussion and rhythms.

Many Afro-Bolivians welcomed the election of an Indian president and his promise to end white colonialism and discrimination and extend ethnic and racial inclusion. Still, rather than increase the rights of peoples in relation to the state—especially for groups historically disempowered and discriminated against—some feared that greater autonomy for diverse ethnic communities might revive a negative tribalism, which has hampered nation building in Latin America and Africa in the past.

Bolivia, the poorest country in South America, with two-thirds of its population at or below the poverty line, has been victimized (as have many African and Latin America countries) by the neoliberal economic, restructuring, and privatizing policies of the International Monetary Fund (IMF) and the World Bank. Within the country, grassroots social movements have aggressively opposed the dark side of globalization. In 2000, the citizens of Cochabamba hit the streets and for the next several years waged the Water War against the Bechtel Corporation's privatization of the city's water system. Lives were lost in the struggle. Not unlike the the case in South Africa, privatization had doubled and tripled rates for the city's poor majority. A similar water privatization scheme was attempted and failed in El Alto, in the Altiplano heights above La Paz. Finally, the Gas War, which erupted in 2003, was a popular uprising against the privatization of oil and gas resources. It culminated in the fall of two governments and the May Day nationalization decree of 2006, which increased state control and revenues from this last major resource.

The Gas War has been so explosive politically in large part because it represented the country's last resource war. Its colonial and national history was marred by the relentless exploitation of the country's mineral resources (much as with diamonds in South Africa and the Congo and petroleum in Nigeria and Angola) to the benefit of foreign colonizers and investors and local dictators and oligarchs. The people remained impoverished. Moreover, nationalism compounded the popular outrage because the government in 2002 sought to send newly discovered natural gas resources to U.S. markets via Chilean ports. Bolivia has had a traditionally conflictive relationship with Chile, which defeated Bolivia in a resource war over control of rich desert nitrates. In the War of the Pacific from 1879 to 1883, Bolivia lost its coastal territory and became landlocked.

Like the fourteen landlocked African countries, Bolivia believes it has been geographically and developmentally handicapped by the absence of a seacoast in terms of sovereign access, resources, and trade. Indeed, the thirty-one landlocked developing states—almost half in Africa—are some of the poorest countries with the weakest growth rates, and like Bolivia (and Paraguay in Latin America) are often marginalized in the global economy. Bolivia has joined with the developing world and Africa's landlocked states to form an alliance at the Third United Nations (UN) Conference on the Law of the Sea (UNCLOS III) to gain concessions from neighboring coastal states. Bolivia's landlocked status has contributed to national frustration and inspired extensive diplomatic campaigns to regain sovereign access to the sea, such as the 2004 agreement with Peru to exchange natural gas for access to the sea.

Waltraud Q. Morales

See also: Globalization; International Monetary Fund; World Bank

References

Gill, Lesley. *Teetering on the Rim: Global Restructuring, Daily Life, and the Armed Retreat of the Bolivian State.* New York: Columbia University Press, 2000.

Hudson, Rex A., and Dennis M. Hanratty, eds. *Bolivia: A Country Study.* 3rd ed. Washington, DC: Government Printing Office, 1991.

Klein, Herbert S. *Bolivia: The Evolution of a Multi-Ethnic Society.* 2nd ed. New York: Oxford University Press, 1992.

Kohl, Benjamin, and Linda C. Farthing. *Impasse in Bolivia: Neoliberal Hegemony and Popular Resistance.* New York: Zed Books, 2006.

Morales, Waltraud Queiser. *Bolivia: Land of Struggle.* Boulder, CO: Westview Press, 1992.

BRAND, DIONNE (1953–)

Dionne Brand is a Trinidadian-born, Canadian-based writer and political activist. She was born in Guayguayare, a small village in the very south of Trinidad. At the age of seventeen she left the Caribbean to study in Toronto, Canada, where she has been based since. Throughout her career, Brand has combined creative and political writing with action. Art and politics, for her, are inextricably linked forms of expression in coming to terms with issues of colonial and neocolonial exploitation, racism, sexism, and the riddles of diasporic identity. Brand has belonged to the Communist Party and, while acknowledging Marxism's failures, still remains dedicated to ideas of just distributions of wealth and labor; she has engaged in numerous community activities, for instance, in the Black Education Project or as counselor for the black West Indian community at the Immigrant Women's Center in Toronto;

also, she worked for the Agency of Rural Transformation in Grenada until U.S. troops invaded in 1983. Her innumerable encounters in these and many other capacities with individual histories of displacement and victimization, yet also with female courage and love, have manifestly influenced her creative writing as well as her nonfictional work.

Examples of her political writing are *Rivers Have Sources, Trees Have Roots* (1986, with Krisantha Sri Bhaggiydatta), *Black Women at Work* (1987), *Bread out of Stone* (1994), and *A Map to the Door of No Return* (2001), covering a broad range of topics from feminism and lesbianism via issues of race and representation to larger historical perspectives on the African Diaspora. Moreover, in *Older Stronger Wiser* (1989), *Sisters in Struggle* (1991), and *Long Time Comin'* (1993), she also expressed herself in documentary film.

In her creative writing, Dionne Brand has for a long time concentrated her efforts on poetry. She made her debut in 1978 with *'Fore Day Morning* and a book of poetry for children, *Earth Magic*. The volumes that followed were increasingly political in scope, for instance, *Primitive Offensive* (1982); *Chronicles of a Hostile Sun* (1984), a poetic reaction to her involvement in the Grenadian revolution of 1983; *No Language is Neutral* (1990); the governor-general's award-winning *Land to Light On* (1997); and *Thirsty* (2002). In all her poetry, however, political thrust goes hand in hand with emotional depth and a careful sense for language and its rhythms, ranging from Trinidadian creole to Toronto slang.

Brand's fictional prose fundamentally benefits from her lyricism. An earlier volume of short stories, *Sans Souci* (1988), was followed by two novels, *In Another Place,*

Not Here (1997) and *At the Full and Change of the Moon* (1999); they intimately explore the political, cultural, and historical upheavals in the Caribbean and their diasporic extensions in the North American and European metropolises. Dionne Brand's acute feeling for the intricacies of inter-human relations and the complexities of displaced identity, her combination of political and artistic vision, have established her as one of the most exiting Canadian and Caribbean writers today.

Lars Eckstein

See also: Caribbean Literature; Feminism and Women's Equality Movements, Transatlantic

References

Brand, Dionne. *Bread out of Stone: Recollections on Sex, Recognitions, Race, Dreaming, and Politics.* Toronto: Coach House, 1994.

Joseph, Clara A. B. "Nation Because of Differences." *Research in African Literatures* 32, no. 3 (2001): 57–70.

Walcott, Rinaldo. *Black Like Who? Writing Black Canada.* Toronto: Insomniac, 1997.

BRATHWAITE, KAMAU (1930–)

Kamau Brathwaite is an award-winning Caribbean poet, cultural critic, and historian. He was born in Bridgetown, Barbados, on May 11, 1930 and was christened Lawson Edward Brathwaite. After secondary school in Barbados, he won a coveted scholarship to study history at Cambridge University in England from 1950 to 1953. He then traveled to Ghana, West Africa, where he worked as an education officer from 1955 to 1962. Afterwards, he traveled back to the United Kingdom and completed his PhD in history at the University of Sussex in 1968. Brathwaite's journeys through Europe and Africa led him back to the Caribbean, and he taught at the

University of West Indies in Kingston, Jamaica, for nearly thirty years. In his seventies, Brathwaite divides his time between teaching as a professor of comparative literature at New York University and his home in Barbados.

Brathwaite is a prominent figure in the field of Caribbean literature, and his expansive work has been vital to Caribbean Studies. Brathwaite's experiences and travels in Africa greatly influenced his academic and creative work. He is best-known for exploring and revealing the African presence in the Caribbean through culture, history, and literature. During his impressive career, Brathwaite has continuously worked to forge a Caribbean voice through his message of cultural and regional pride that calls for unity among Caribbean people and countries. He has done this not only through his work as a historian, poet, and cultural critic, but also through his active work in forming the Caribbean Artists Movement and returning to the Caribbean to work and teach. During his time in Jamaica, Brathwaite became a central figure in developing the formal study of Caribbean literature and culture.

Brathwaite's historical works include the foundational text, *The Development of Creole Society in Jamaica, 1770–1820*, which reveals the central role that African slaves had in forming the social and cultural particulars that make up the unique culture of present-day Jamaica. In addition, Brathwaite has written many critical essays and lectures that have been essential in the creation of a critical aesthetic and context for Caribbean literature. A number of his important essays are in the valuable collection *Roots: Essays in Caribbean Literature* (1993), which captures the depth of his critical work from the 1950s to the 1980s.

Moreover, Brathwaite has insisted on the significance of creole languages across the Caribbean, and this clearly shows in his poetry.

Brathwaite has published over twenty-five books of poetry, and his unique style reveals the interconnections of the African Diaspora, links between the Caribbean and Africa, and the similarities among different islands in the region. His major poetic works include *Ancestors* (2001), *The Arrivants: A New World Trilogy* (1973), *Barabajan Poems, 1492–1992* (1994), *Black + Blues* (1976), *Dream Stories* (1994), *Middle Passages* (1992), *Shar* (1990), *Soweto* (1979), *Third World Poems* (1983), and *The Zea Mexican Diary* (1994), among others. Brathwaite has won numerous awards and honors for his outstanding work, including the Neustadt International Award for Literature; the Casa de Las Americas Prize for poetry and literary criticism; and fellowships from the Guggenheim, Fulbright, and Ford Foundations.

Angelique V. Nixon

See also: Caribbean Artists Movement; Caribbean Literature.

References

Brathwaite, Doris Monica. *A Descriptive and Chronological Bibliography (1950–1982) of the Work of Edward Kamau Brathwaite.* London: New Beacon Books, 1988.

Brathwaite, Kamau. *The Development of Creole Society in Jamaica, 1770–1820.* Oxford: Clarendon Press, 1971.

Brathwaite, Kamau. *The Arrivants: A New World Trilogy.* London: Oxford University Press, 1973.

Brathwaite, Kamau. *Black + Blues.* Havana, Cuba: Casa de Las Americas, 1976.

Brathwaite, Kamau. *Soweto.* Mona, Jamaica: Savacou, 1979.

Brathwaite, Kamau. *Third World Poems.* London: Longman, 1983.

Brathwaite, Kamau. *Shar.* Mona, Jamaica: Savacou, 1990.

Brathwaite, Kamau. *Middle Passages.* Newcastle, UK: Bloodaxe Books, 1992.

Brathwaite, Kamau. *Roots: Essays in Caribbean Literature.* Ann Arbor: University of Michigan Press, 1993.

Brathwaite, Kamau. *Barabajan Poems, 1492–1992.* Kingston, Jamaica: Savacou North, 1994.

Brathwaite, Kamau. *Dream Stories.* London: Longman, 1994.

Brathwaite, Kamau. *The Zea Mexican Diary.* Madison: University of Wisconsin Press, 1994.

Brathwaite, Kamau. *Ancestors.* New York: New Directions Books, 2001.

Brown, Stewart, ed. *The Art of Kamau Brathwaite.* Bridgen, UK: Cromwell Press, 1995.

Reis, Timothy, ed. *For the Geography of Soul: Emerging Perspectives on Kamau Brathwaite.* Trenton, NJ: Africa World Press, 2001.

Rohlehr, Gordon. *Pathfinder, Black Awakening in The Arrivants of Edward Kamau Brathwaite.* Tunapuna, Trinidad: G. Rohlehr, 1981.

Williams, Emily Allen. *The Critical Response to Kamau Brathwaite.* Westport, CT: Praeger Publishers, 2004.

BRAZIL

Brazil's geology, population, social differentiation, history of enslavement of Africans, and contemporary politics have all helped to shape its history. With a population of 180 million and 3,286,470 square miles (8,511, 965 square kilometers)of territory, the Federative Republic of Brazil is the fifth largest country in the world and the sixth most populated. Comprising twenty-six states and a Federal District, it is divided into five regions and occupies a central position in Latin America as a whole, being not only the biggest country of the region in size and population, but also the most industrialized and economically advanced. Geographically and geologically, Brazil is a privileged land. Even though regional differences in climate, relief, and vegetation

are sharp, as could be expected given the country's size, natural catastrophes such as hurricanes, earthquakes, or blizzards are unknown to Brazilians. Temperatures seldom fall below the freezing point, and when they do, it is normally in the mountains in the South. Snow is rare; when it comes, it becomes a tourist attraction. Increasing heat, on the other hand, is a phenomenon Brazilians have been forced to cope with. Due not only to global warming but also to the devastation of natural forests and fast, unplanned urbanization, it is not uncommon for many cities like Rio de Janeiro to experience temperatures surpassing 100 degrees Fahrenheit (38 degrees Centigrade) for several successive days (or even weeks). As elsewhere, climatic changes have brought an intensification of calamities related to the weather, mainly floods or droughts, which now may happen simultaneously in different parts of the country. Brazil remains extremely rich in natural resources, including minerals (coal, iron, limestone, aluminum, copper, and amianthus), abundant fertile soil and water supplies—about 9 percent of the globe's reservoir, especially in the Amazon River, the greatest of the world's rivers in water capacity, bringing around 4.2 million cubic feet of water per second into the Atlantic. The country's most precious possession is the Amazon rain forest, which spreads over an area of 2.1 million square miles (5.5 million square kilometers), roughly 60 percent of the forest's total extension, and contains one of the world's richest sources of biodiversity. Deforestation, however, is rampant, reaching an average of over 8,880 square miles (23,000 square kilometers) per year since 2001, according to government data provided by the Brazilian Institute for Geography and Statistics.

Brazil's population has become increasingly urban. In the 1940s just 31 percent of Brazilians lived in cities; as of 2007 more than 80 percent do. São Paulo and Rio de Janeiro are among the biggest metropolises in the world, with total populations of respectively of 10.215 and 15.318 million. The growth of cities took place in an unorganized way, mainly through internal migration from the Northeast, where conditions of living were the worst in the country, to a quickly industrializing Southeast, where jobs could be found. Migration flows to Southeast states have decreased since the 1980s, being redirected toward areas of more recent settlement such as the states of Mato Grosso, Rondônia, Tocantis, and Roraima. Yet the effects of uncontrolled resettlement can be felt in the presence of slums, called *favelas,* at the outskirts of every big city in the country. These have come to occupy an increasingly important place in Brazilian culture and society. Concentrating the poor and the Afro-Brazilian population, they can be very violent places where the state authority is at times virtually absent and which thus have their own rules and codes of behavior. The *favelas* were (and are still) sites of intense cultural production, being the birthplace of much of which is now typical of Brazil, such as samba.

Regional unevenness is paralleled by extreme social differentiation. Brazil has one of the worst distributions of wealth in the world. According to government estimates, in 2000 the richest 10 percent of the population held 47.6 percent of the country's wealth, whereas the poorest 60 percent owned only 18 percent of it. Although parameters to determine poverty vary a great deal, geographers agree that the number of poor Brazilians is around 42 million. The situation is even worse in the distribution of land, where the top 1 percent of owners have 46 percent of the fertile soil in their hands. And yet, conviviality in Brazil is much more unproblematic than these numbers might suggest. In fact, one of the greatest achievements of Brazilian culture was to unify such economically, ethnically, and regionally unequal populations. Diverse cultural expressions such as soccer, popular music, and dietary habits (rice and beans are eaten every day throughout the country) represent important elements of junction, together with the predominant Catholic religion. The media, particularly the powerful Globo Network and its soap operas, have also been central to the homogenization of the Brazilian imagination, even though patterns of Brazilian cordiality have long since been a typical trait of the land before the arrival of modern media.

Brazilian history is complex in that it shares several features with the rest of Latin America while differing in other important aspects. In common with other Latin American countries, Brazil has its colonial past, characterized as it was more by exploitation than by exploration. In contrast to New England, for example, where pioneers intended to colonize and develop the land, most Portuguese settlers saw Brazil (named after a tree, the Brazil wood, from which comes a red dye) as a place one could profit from. The scars of exploitative colonization are still felt today, and for many historians, Brazil's numerous problems may be derived from its colonial social structure. The colonial period was characterized by two fundamental demographic transformations: the extermination of Native Brazilians and the forced migration of black slaves. The former were reduced from a population of around 5 million before the arrival of the Portuguese in 1500 to less than 350,000 at the end of the twentieth century, and while the number of slaves brought to Brazil is still a matter of dispute, estimates varying from 3 to 13.5 million, it is agreed that until 1888, the year of abolition, the average survival time of slaves on plantations did not exceed five years.

Political independence from Portugal came in September 7, 1822, in what would prove to be a typically Brazilian way of conducting politics. Instead of fighting for liberation as other Latin American countries did, Brazil was "declared" independent by Dom Pedro I, son of Dom João VI, king of Portugal. This happened as the result of a political process in which the Brazilian elites managed to convince the prince that it was safer to keep the government in the hands of a Portuguese-Brazilian royal family in an independent land than to risk losing control of the country in a revolution led by local leaders. The Brazilian Empire did not last long, however, being abolished through a military coup that established the republic on November 15, 1889. Again, change came from above, through an alliance of the military with a national agricultural bourgeoisie dissatisfied with imperial centralization and taxation, with popular involvement in the emperor's overthrow being minimal. Again, resistance to political change was less traumatic than it could have been, for even though monarchists in the South fiercely opposed the republic, civil war and territorial fragmentation were avoided.

Democracy has always been fragile in Brazil. Strictly speaking, it did not exist in the so-called República Velha (Old Republic, 1889–1930), where participation was restricted (women, for instance were not allowed to vote) and elections manipulated.

The Revolution of 1930, led by Getúlio Vargas, put an end to this and inaugurated the populist period in Brazilian history, which would last until 1964. These were years of great change, when an agrarian, coffee-exporting Brazil started giving way to an industrial and urban country, most clearly exemplified by the construction of the new capital, Brasilia—a whole city built up in a couple of years from scratch, a perfect instance of speedy modernization. During the Vargas years (1930–1945; 1950–1954), positive institutional developments in labor legislation—such as the minimum wage, paid vacations, and pensions—and in education took place side by side with strict social control, periodic curtailment of press freedom, and occasional political persecution.

Populist attempts to reconcile the interests of the working classes with those of property owners proved untenable, for when President João Goulart started to bend toward the former, a military coup ensued in 1964, leading to a dictatorship that would last until 1989. Strongly affected by the cold war, this period—like the Vargas years—witnessed the combination of political repression and economic development, but now on a greater scale. Communists were persecuted and hundreds died and were tortured (although on a smaller scale than elsewhere at this time, as in Chile and Argentina). On the other hand, in the 1970s Brazil exhibited the world's greatest rates of economic growth. Democracy was fully restored only in 1989, inaugurated by the first direct election for president since 1962. Since then Brazil has been passing through the freest period in its political history and may indeed be viewed as one of the most democratic countries in the world, although political democracy still awaits the coming of economic and social democracy.

Fabio Akcelrud Durao

See also: Brazilian Culture; Colonialism

References

Fausto, Boris. *A Concise History of Brazil.* Translated by Arthur Brakel. Cambridge: Cambridge University Press, 1999.

Hollanda, Sérgio Buarque. *Raízes do Brasil.* 26th ed. São Paulo, Brazil: Companhia das Letras, 2003.

Instituto Brasileiro de Geografia e Estatística. http://www.ibge.gov.br.

Kinzo, Maria D'Alva G., and James Dunkerley, eds. *Brazil since 1985: Politics, Economy, and Society.* Washington, DC: Brookings Institution Press, 2003.

Page, Joseph A. *The Brazilians.* Reading, PA: Addison Wesley, 1995.

Roett, Riordan. *Brazil: Politics in a Patrimonial Society.* 5th ed. Westport, CT: Praeger, 1999.

BRAZILIAN CARNIVAL

Brazilian Carnival is officially celebrated on the Sunday, Monday, and Tuesday before Ash Wednesday, although it normally begins on Friday. The etymology of Carnival is dual. It may derive from the Latin *carrus navalis,* which designated the carriage in the form of a ship that held the image of the god who presided over a celebration in the ancient world. Or, it might be the corruption of the Italian *carnevale,* from the Latin *carne vale* (farewell to meat), which refers to the custom of eating all the meat available before Lent.

Although Carnival is a celebration that defines the country's cultural identity, its origin is European. The *entrudo* (entrance), the first form of carnival celebration, was brought by the Portuguese in the seventeenth century and was very popular until the early twentieth century. It was very aggressive, consisting mainly in throwing at random water, flour, and "scented fruit" (oranges and lemons made of wax and stuffed with homemade perfume) at other people. There were two kinds of *entrudos,* the familiar, or homely one, and the popular, or street *entrudo.*

Against the barbarous *entrudo,* the Brazilian upper class had, by the 1850s, envisaged a new way of celebrating Carnival: the masked and costumed ball, an idea imported from Paris. The Great Societies, groups of revelers that would parade every year through the streets of Rio de Janeiro, were another novelty imported from Europe with great success.

The masked balls and the parades of the Great Societies constituted the Grand Carnival; however, the popular Small Carnival was also developing, with its parades: the *cordões* (laces), *ranchos* (ranches) and *blocos* (blocks). *Ranchos* and *cordões* derived from the slaves' religious processions; the tunes were played with African instruments of percussion. The *ranchos* had their own music style: the *marcha-rancho* (the ranch march), played by wind instruments and percurssion. The *blocos* had a smaller number of participants and were not as organized. With the appearance of the samba schools in the 1920s, the *cordões* and *ranchos* gradually disappeared. But the *blocos* are still very much alive. Instead of sambas, the *blocos* revelers sing carnival marches.

The first mention of the samba dates from 1893. The samba mixes traditional African rhythms, the *batuques,* with popular urban rhythms like the *maxixe.* In the 1920s, small carnival groups formed by young samba composers—such as Cartola, Carlos Cachaça, and Ismael Silva e Heitor dos Prazeres, adapting elements of *ranchos, cordões,* and *blocos*—would soon become

Performers from the Beija-flor samba school dance in Rio de Janeiro's premier Carnival parade February 8, 2005. (Corbis)

the first samba schools. The first official competition took place in 1932.

Nowadays the samba schools parade is a huge spectacle in which thousands of revelers participate, wearing rich and colorful costumes arranged among the thirty or more sections of the samba schools. They all sing an original samba specially composed for the occasion based on a theme, the *enredo,* envisaged by the *carnavalesco,* the creative designer. The *enredos* are generally about Brazil's history, the more critical ones satirizing current moral or political issues. The rhythmic section is the *bateria* (battery).

Rio de Janeiro Carnival has become a model for the rest of the country. In the late 1950s, however, a new form of carnival appeared in Salvador, Bahia, with *trios elétricos. Trios elétricos* are trucks that support huge loudspeakers and platforms on which the singers and musicians perform. The *trios elétricos* play Axé and other music styles with a strong influence of African and Caribbean rhythms. Typical also of Bahia carnival are the *blocos afro* blocks, such as the *Filhos de Gandhi* that also parade during Carnival. Recife and Olinda, two cities in the northeast state of Pernambuco, also have important Carnival celebrations, where the *blocos* of *frevo,* a typical musical style, predominate.

Roberto Ferreira da Rocha

See also: Brazil; Brazilian Culture; Carnival, Latin American; Portuguese Empire

References

Ferreira, Fernando. *O livro de ouro do carnaval brasileiro.* Rio de Janeiro, Brazil: Ediouro, 2004.

Queiroz, Maria Isaura Pereira de. *Carnaval brasileiro: O vivido e o mito.* São Paulo, Brazil: Brasiliense, 1992.

BRAZILIAN CULTURE

Brazilian culture reflects a wide range of culturally and racially hybrid identities. Some scholars have argued the primary influences have been the Portuguese, Africans, and Indians, organically interacting so as to form what is now called Brazilian culture.

Recent students of the sociology of culture, however have rejected this view suggesting a greater degree of complexity. Such a view, it is argued, disregards successive flows of immigrants who arrived later in Brazil, including the Japanese, Germans, Italians, and Arabs. Second, and more fundamental, is the observation that the Portuguese, Africans, and Native Brazilians played (and still do) essentially different roles in the formation of the country and its culture. It is true that Indians left their mark, mainly in the names of places and dietary habits, and that miscegenation in Brazil, its mixing of races, has been intense. Native Brazilians, however, very early on saw their numbers drastically reduced through disease and killing, so that their present role in society is negligible. African slaves constituted the basic workforce in colonial and imperial Brazil, and black and Mestizos still do. Finally, people of European descent formed the ruling classes and continue to do so. "White" culture has always been turned to the outside, to Europe and later the United States (not always without envy), while "black" culture was shaped through an internal process of self-definition, as the millions of slaves who were forced into Brazil had to adapt themselves to an oppressive environment. There is not a single sphere of Brazilian culture that was not affected by African influence, while at the same time there is no African element of culture brought to Brazil that

has been left untransformed. Brazil's cultural singularity as a Portuguese-speaking country with a black-based, mixed population is the key factor in explaining why cultural exchange and mutual influence with other South American countries has been much less intense than one might at first expect.

In order to fully grasp such a complex and rich realm as Brazilian culture, it is methodologically useful to approach it alongside a fundamental axis embedded within an ambiguity in the concept of "culture" itself, which may be considered either as (1) the whole set of practices and experiences of a given group or (2) as the body of privileged symbolic artifacts deemed the worthiest of a country. Brazilian culture would then be constituted in the tension between the specificity of the "spontaneous" mode of being of Brazilians and the heritage of formal or erudite culture. Indeed, it is a thesis generally accepted that the most important Brazilian cultural manifestations emerged as a result, in one way or another, of a mixture of the two, with each influencing the other. Brazilian popular culture has always referred to "high" culture, either consciously or unconsciously, for legitimization and inspiration. Consider the two most important Brazilian cultural manifestations, music (especially, but not only, samba) and soccer. Samba associations are called samba *schools* (*escolas de samba*), and the most important dancers, the flag-bearer (*porta-bandeira*) and her protector (*mestre-sala*), were modeled after aristocratic figures and dressed accordingly. Soccer, interestingly, was imported from England—as the Portuguese vocabulary attests (*futebol, gol, penalty,* and so on)—and was at the beginning an elite pastime.

However, mixtures of popular and dominant culture very often did not take place freely, but rather as strategies of survival and means of resistance, as in the case of much of Afro-Brazilian culture. Instances of this may be found everywhere. Capoeira, half dance, half fight, was devised by slaves as a way of fooling their masters, who would never allow their property to be damaged. Umbanda and Candomblé, religions based on spirits, the *orixás,* that possess believers, may be regarded as a fusion of African deities with other figures, including Catholic saints; they emerged as a compromise allowing slaves to give vent to their religiosity while apparently following the official creed. Even such an apparently neutral practice as eating still bears the marks of oppression: *feijoada,* Brazil's national dish, a rich meat stew in black beans, was originally slave food, the putting together of leftovers (ears, tails, and feet of cows and pigs) in a nutritious, energy-giving base of beans.

But mixtures also occurred when erudite culture allowed itself to be swayed by the energies of the (most of the time uncultivated) people. In fact, it is possible to support the claim that every single major Brazilian artist incorporated popular elements in her or his work. This is valid for Brazilian music as a whole: Bossa Nova worked out the mixture of jazz and samba; Chico Buarque combined sophisticated lyrics with rhythms from the jerry-built shack neighborhoods, the *favelas;* Caetano Veloso and the Tropicália movement merged avant-gardist self-consciousness and rebellion to a festive Brazilian ethos. It is true even for strictly so-called high culture, which also borrowed from popular customs and practices. A short list of examples would include architect Oscar Niemeyer, who besides being the planner of Brasilia is also well known for the Sambódromo in Rio; such great names of Brazilian literature as Joaquim Machado de Assis, Guimarães Rosa, Clarisse Lispector, Carlos Drummond de Andrade, and João Cabral de Mello Neto; painters Cândido Portinari and Tarsila do Amaral; the music of Heitor Villa-Lobos and Camargo Guarnieri; the dramaturgy of Augusto Boal; and Paulo Freire's pedagogy—to name just some of the most prominent persons in the arts.

And yet it remains an open question whether culture's potential for mutual influence and modification is unlimited. In a country marked by great social inequalities, the unifying role of culture is constantly being challenged. If traditionally one of the most remarkable traits of Brazilian culture has been its capacity of mixing everything, thus avoiding ghettoization, there are clear signs now that this function of culture is under great strain. Symptoms of this include the walling-up of apartment complexes; the fencing-off of public squares; and the creation of fortresses for the rich, paralleled by the sealing-off of the *favelas,* now dominated by drug dealers, from intercourse with the world outside. Even Brazil's tolerant and accommodating Catholicism has been lately challenged by uncompromising and unyieldingly belligerent new evangelical Protestant churches. Whether Brazilian culture will prove strong enough to incorporate these fragmenting tendencies into its melting pot remains to be seen.

Fabio Akcelrud Durao

See also: Brazil; Colonialism

References

Azevedo, Fernando de. *Brazilian Culture: An Introduction to the Study of Culture in*

Brazil. Translated by William Rex Crawford. New York: Macmillan, 1950.

Freyre, Gilberto. *The Masters and the Slaves: A Study in the Development of Brazilian Civilization.* Translated by S. Putnam. Berkeley: University of California Press, 1986.

Schwarz, Roberto. *Misplaced Ideas: Essays on Brazilian Culture.* New York: Verso, 1992.

Wasserman, Renata R. Mautner. *Exotic Nations: Literature and Cultural Identity in the United States and Brazil, 1830–1930.* Ithaca, NY: Cornell University Press, 1994.

BRINDIS DE SALAS, VIRGINIA (CA.1920–CA.1958)

Virginia Brindis de Salas was a black female poet who explored African and Latin American identity in Uruguay. Brindis de Salas, who published during the 1940s, is the pioneer of black women writers in Spanish America. She is highly regarded as the preeminent female black poet of Uruguay and is to this day considered one of the most radical and controversial of all Afro-Uruguayan writers. After Pilar Barrios, who is referred to as the poet laureate of Afro-Uruguayan literature, she is the second black Uruguayan writer whose work appeared in book form. She published two volumes of poetry, *Pregón de Marimorena* (The call of Mary Morena) in 1946 and *Cien cárceles de amor* (One hundred prisons of love) in 1949.

Pregón de Marimorena, a collection of ballads, tangos, songs, and *pregones,* is the more innovative of the two volumes. Brindis de Salas takes the *pregón,* a vendor's street cry, and molds it into poetic form in order to draw attention to the life of a poor black woman, Marimorena (Brown Mary). From sunup to sundown, Marimorena walks the streets of Montevideo with her heavy load, selling the daily newspaper.

Reminiscent of the toil and sweat of slaves, the melodic and melancholic cry of Marimorena evokes her pain as she struggles to earn enough for a day's meal for her family. As the central protagonist of the collection, Marimorena reflects the triple burden of being black, female, and poor in Uruguay in the 1940s. At the same time, the poet sharply criticizes Uruguay's social marginalization of its black population and focuses on the actions of the powerful against the powerless. In turn, the story of Marimorena brings to light the social, economic, and racial stratifications of the country.

Still seeing the contradictions between black reality and white reality, Brindis de Salas wrote *Cien cárceles de amor.* A continuation of the themes in *Pregón de Marimorena,* the collection reflects the ambivalent attitude of Uruguay toward its Afro-Uruguayan citizens. The poet challenges the Uruguayan community to reexamine itself as it embraces the music and dance of Afro-Uruguay while at the same time maintaining the second-class status of Afro-Uruguayan citizens. Therefore, many of the poems address the social and economic imprisonment imposed on Afro-Uruguay by the dominant culture. The poems in this volume continue to testify to the daily obstacles, the racism, the social inequities, and the oppression experienced by the black Uruguayan community and illustrate what it means to be black in Uruguay.

Overall, Brindis de Salas transformed the silent voices of her community into speech. Both volumes represent an early attempt to erase the invisibility of black Uruguayan citizens and the struggle to make their voices heard. To that end, the themes of racism, discrimination, and poverty dominate both volumes and reveal insight into the Uruguay of the past and the sociopolitical issues facing black Uruguayans today.

In *Cien cárceles de amor,* the editor notes that a third volume of poetry, *Cantos de lejanía* (Songs from faraway), is forthcoming; however, that collection was never published. Leading black periodicals such as *Nuestra Raza* (1917–1948), which were the storehouses of the legacy of Afro-Uruguayan intellectualism, folded. In the study of those periodicals and other historical documents, little is revealed about the life and later literary productivity of Brindis de Salas; perhaps in the years to come, the mystery of her life will unfold.

Caroll Mills Young

See also: Cabral, Cristina Rodriguez; Uruguay

References

Brindis de Salas, Virginia. *Pregón de Marimorena.* Montevideo, Uruguay: Sociedad Cultural Editora Indoamericana, 1946.

Brindis de Salas, Virginia. *Cien cárceles de amor.* Montevideo, Uruguay: NP, 1949.

Young, Caroll M. "The Historical Development of Afro-Uruguay's Intellectual Movement: A Coalition in Black and White." *PALARA,* no. 6 (Fall 2002): 84–93.

Young, Caroll M. "The Unmasking of Virginia Brindis de Salas: Minority Discourse of Afro-Uruguay." In *Daughters of the Diaspora,* edited by Miriam DeCosta Willis. Kingston, Jamaica; Miami, FL: Randle Press, 2003.

Young, Caroll M. "From Voicelessness to Voice: Womanist Writing of the Afro-Uruguayan Press." *Afro-Hispanic Review* 23, no. 2 (Fall 2004): 33–39.

BRITAIN: PEOPLE OF AFRICAN ORIGIN AND DESCENT

Britain's multiracial society of the early twenty-first century has been several centuries in the making. There is evidence of Africans in Britain as part of the Roman armies of occupation and as rare visitors in medieval times. More Africans came to the British Isles during the age of reconnaissance, when English ships began trading down the African coast. By the end of the sixteenth century, the number of Africans in London excited sufficient hostility that a royal injunction stated that they be expelled from the realm. During the seventeenth and eighteenth centuries, the expansion of direct trade with Africa and the development of transatlantic commerce, particularly the African slave trade, resulted in an increase in the number of Africans coming to the British Isles. Some Africans came as seamen, travelers, or occasionally as persons attached to embassies, but the majority of black people entered the country from the American colonies. They were brought into Britain as slaves or servants, their status often being blurred.

By the mid-eighteenth century there may have been 10,000 black people living in Britain, probably more men than women. Most were in London and the major trading ports of Bristol and Liverpool, but several thousands were scattered throughout the country. They were engaged in a variety of jobs, often as servants, with some aristocratic families employing blacks in livery, while small black boys were "pets" to certain elite women. But blacks were also laborers, artisans, prostitutes, soldiers, and seamen. The evidence for this comes primarily from registers of baptism, marriage, and death; poor law accounts; jail records; and newspapers. Most black people were illiterate. However, by the end of the century there were a few educated and professional black men and women. These included former slaves who wrote accounts of their experiences, such as Ukawsaw

Gronniosaw; Olaudah Equiano, who claimed in his autobiography, published in 1798, to have been born in West Africa; Ignatius Sancho, who was a friend of the novelist Lawrence Sterne and the actor David Garrick; Joseph Emedy, an accomplished violinist and composer; and John Naimbanna, son of a West African ruler, who was sent to Britain to be educated.

Most black people in eighteenth-century Britain came to the country in some way due to the African slave trade. Thus, their position was often a servile one and their color and race a badge of discrimination. However, despite a certain amount of scholarly literature exploring racial attitudes in that century, the picture of popular attitudes to race is still unclear. Black people were not sufficiently numerous to constitute a threat to the host communities; many records, for example of prisoners, often do not mention color or race; working-class black and white people lived close to each other, and intermarriage seems to have been common. There is also evidence that some slaves brought to Britain fled but then negotiated with their masters to return in exchange for a wage, adequate clothing, and gentle treatment. It would seem that in certain instances, African slaves and servants were demanding and gaining rights similar to those sought by white apprentices and servants.

The position of black slaves in Britain was ambiguous. James Somerset, a slave brought to England from Boston, Massachusetts, fled his master but was recaptured. Granville Sharpe and fellow antislavery activists secured a writ of habeas corpus and brought Somerset to court from the ship where he had been imprisoned. Chief Justice Mansfield's important judgment in June 1772 stated that no master could forcibly remove a slave from Britain. Contrary to many sources, the judgment did not end black slavery in Britain. A few years later, the black population of Britain increased with the arrival of several hundred black loyalists, many being former slaves who had served with the British forces during the American Revolution. Many were poor and swelled the number of those seeking relief, particularly in London parishes. A resolution to this domestic problem, and a cause supported by Equiano, was the settlement of poor blacks in the new colony of Freetown in West Africa in 1787.

More research needs to be done to quantify and analyze the composition of the black population of Britain in the first half of the nineteenth century. Did it decline in size due to intermarriage of black men and white women? How many people from Africa and the Americas entered Britain at this time? Baptismal registers indicate that there was a small indigenous black population, including men such as Thomas Birch Freeman, son of a black father and a white mother, born in Hampshire and subsequently the premier Wesleyan missionary in West Africa, and William Cuffay, born in Chatham and in 1849 transported to Tasmania for his Chartist activities. Intermarriage may have reduced the more visible black presence in Britain, but as the country's maritime trade increased and London in particular became a commercial crossroads of an expanding empire, so the number of black people coming to Britain probably grew. Many were undoubtedly itinerant, as was part of the black population of the seafaring parishes of east London, Liverpool, and Bristol. However, there were also black settlers, along with children and students coming from Africa and the Caribbean colonies for education.

The size of Britain's black population in the mid-nineteenth century is unknown, but it may have been in the vicinity of 10,000 people. Part of that population seems to have been fairly mobile. In the major ports, most notably London, Liverpool, and Bristol, black seamen formed part of a growing cosmopolitan population. New black communities also developed in Bute Town, Cardiff, in the late nineteenth century, and in South Shields, on the northeast coast, by the early years of the twentieth century. The black population was composed not only of laborers and artisans, but from the 1830s onward of black preachers and speakers, both men and women, who toured British towns, often to denounce American slavery and racism. For example, the African American Methodist, Zilpha Elaw, preached widely in Britain in the 1840s, as in later decades did better-known figures, such as William and Ellen Craft, Frederick Douglass, and Ida B. Wells. In addition, a steady stream of black entertainers came to Britain, where they appeared on public platforms throughout the country. Ira Aldridge, the African American actor, is perhaps the best-known, but there were also Zulu dancing troupes, Zulu choirs, and the famous Fisk Jubilee Singers. Some of these overlap with black people who were skilled tradespeople and professionals, a frequently ignored section of Britain's black population in the late nineteenth and early twentieth centuries. A steady stream of men, and some women, from the African and Caribbean colonies entered Britain to study in schools, universities, and hospitals. Some remained, or maintained a base in Britain, to practice as doctors, lawyers, dentists, journalists, and clergymen. Samuel Coleridge-Taylor, the distinguished black composer, was the son of a West African doctor who worked in Britain.

Although the black population of Britain in 1911 has been estimated at 10,000, the actual figure is not known, as the census did not ask questions about race or color. As in earlier generations, the concentration of black communities was in the major port cities, although black people were to be found in almost every town and county. Racial discrimination had increased in the second half of the nineteenth century. It was fueled by "scientific" theories of race developed at mid-century; by popular responses to the Indian Rebellion (1857–1858) and the Morant Bay Rebellion in Jamaica (1865); by a growing public arrogance associated with the conquest and possession of overseas empire, fanned by popular mass literature; and by the belief, associated with eugenics, that miscegenation led to racial degeneration. Black people visiting and living in Britain encountered overt and covert forms of racial discrimination when they sought accommodations, employment, insurance, and interracial marriage. Black Britons were not permitted to become officers in the armed forces, and black nurses who had been offered places in hospitals were rejected when their color became known to matrons. In 1919 serious racial violence aimed at black people occurred in several cities, mainly Liverpool.

Racial discrimination increased during World War I as black people tried to enlist while others came to Britain for war work. Trade unions were much more likely than professional associations to reject applicants on grounds of color. The Pan-African Conference, held in London in

1900, was one attempt to promote the interests and welfare of black people and to criticize imperialism. Other small political groups followed, organized by black professionals and students: the African Progress Union, the West African Students' Union, the League of Coloured Peoples, the International Africa Service Bureau, and the Pan-African Federation. There were also black-owned newspapers and magazines: the *African Times and Orient Review, African Telegraph, WASU, The Keys,* and *The Black Man.* From the 1920s through the 1940s, these small and often financially weak political groups with their often irregular publications campaigned against the "color bar," opposed racism and colonialism, and demanded legislation to guarantee equal civil rights for black people.

The work of lobbying against racism increased during World War II as black workers and soldiers from the empire and black GIs from the United States entered Britain. Racial tensions increased, often heightened by the imported Jim Crow rules of the U.S. military and the prejudices of its white personnel. When the Fifth Pan-African Congress met in Manchester in August 1945, the British race relations were still uneasy and there was no strong, active political group to represent the interests of black people. This was particularly unfortunate as black immigration, mainly from the Caribbean, increased in response to Britain's postwar labor shortage. This new and significant movement of immigration was marked by the arrival of the *Empire Windrush,* carrying nearly 500 Jamaican immigrants, in June 1948. In the next decade over 150,000 black immigrants, most from the Caribbean, entered Britain in search of work. They were joined by many thousands of people from the Indian subcontinent. Britain was becoming a multiracial society, although new immigrants tended to be concentrated in the older, inner areas of the large cities.

Entry to Britain was unrestricted for Commonwealth citizens. Black immigrants brought skill and enterprise, new cultures with popular music and dance, different foods, and charismatic Christian worship in new black churches. Continuing immigration inevitably led to some communal tension, which increased when economic recession brought fiercer competition for scarce housing and jobs. A number of politicians exploited racial tensions and helped give voice to growing demands that black immigration into Britain be controlled. In August and September 1958, serious race riots broke out in the Nottingham and Notting Hill areas of London. This discouraged the government from pushing ahead with legislation to curb immigration, as ministers did not wish to be seen as being swayed by mob violence. However, the Commonwealth Immigrants Act, passed in 1962, attempted to regulate the flow of non-European immigrants. Further legislation followed in 1968 and 1971, tightening the rules of entry. This legislation encouraged black immigrants to stay in Britain and also to bring their dependents into the country before the measures took effect. Thus, ironically, the Act of 1962 helped increase Britain's black population and ensure that the country would be a multiracial society.

Legislation of the 1960s and 1970s curtailed voluntary immigration of workers from the Caribbean and South Asia. It did not, however, end black immigration to Britain. In the last thirty years of the twentieth century, a steady flow of black immigrants, mainly from Africa, continued.

Refugees from famine, war, and economic hardship were admitted into the country, many coming from Ethiopia, Eritrea, Somalia, and the Congo, countries that had not been part of the former empire. The immigrants included many professionally trained people who have greatly benefited the British economy. One result is that there is a growing black middle class in Britain. Black men and women have become school principals, chief constables, doctors, business executives, members of Parliament, cabinet ministers, trade union leaders, bishops, lawyers, and award-winning novelists. However, this should not mask the fact that problems remain: racism lurks in important institutions, particularly among the police; communal tensions are provoked by racist political groups; and many young black men are alienated from a society that appears to have failed them.

David Killingray

See also: Diaspora; Morant Bay Rebellion; Notting Hill Carnival in London

References

Fryer, Peter. *Staying Power: The History of Black People in Britain.* London: Pluto Press, 1984.

Gerzina, Gretchen Holbrook. *Black England: Life before Emancipation.* London: John Murray, 1995.

Gerzina, Gretchen Holbrook. *Black Victorians/ Black Victoriana.* New Brunswick, NJ: Rutgers University Press, 2003.

Green, Jeffrey. *Black Edwardians: Black People in Britain, 1901–1914.* London: Frank Cass, 1998.

Gundara, Jagdish S, and Ian Duffield, ed. *Essays on the History of Blacks in Britain.* Aldershot, UK: Avebury, 1992.

Ramdin, Ron. *Reimaging Britain: 500 Years of Black and Asian History.* London: Pluto Press, 1999.

Shyllon, Folarin. *Black Slaves in Britain.* Oxford: Oxford University Press, 1974.

Shyllon, Folarin. *Black People in Britain, 1555–1833.* Oxford: Oxford University Press, 1977.

Walvin, James. *Black and White: The Negro in English Society, 1555–1945.* London: Allen Lane, 1971.

BRITISH EMPIRE

The British Empire fundamentally shaped political structures, national boundaries, and civil conflicts across the continents of Africa and the Americas. Once a minor Roman colony, Britain formed an empire that, at its most expansive, encompassed more than one-fifth of the globe; the diverse population of its imperial subjects exceeded 400 million.

The Expansion of Britain's Overseas Empire

Under Tudor rule (1485–1603), Britain began to explore and settle outside of Europe and the British Isles as a result of its improved seafaring capabilities. The merchant marine system not only strengthened English shipbuilding and seafaring but also established important mercantile institutions, such as the Massachusetts Bay Company and the British East India Company. The well-financed Royal Navy became centrally organized and rose as Europe's foremost naval force after defeating the Spanish Armada in 1588.

With superior seafaring capabilities, British interest in exploration grew. In 1578, while circumnavigating the globe, Sir Francis Drake landed in northern California and claimed it for the English crown, naming it Nova Albion. Drake's claim was not, however, followed by settlement. In 1583 Sir Humphrey Gilbert formally declared Newfoundland an English colony and, five years later, Sir Walter Raleigh organized the first colony in Virginia at Roanoke Island. These early attempts at settlement, however, lacked full metropolitan support. Both the settlements in Newfoundland and Roanoke were shortly abandoned as a result of food shortages, difficult marine navigation, and conflict with indigenous American peoples.

Despite initial setbacks, the Virginia Company, chartered in 1606, became the first successful enterprise. Its settlement at Jamestown in the colony of Virginia became the first permanent overseas settlement and it received sustained metropolitan support due to the commercial success of tobacco. By the mid-eighteenth century, the population of the mainland American colonies exceeded 1.25 million, not including nearly 350,000 African slaves or former slaves.

The economic relationship between Britain and its American colonies was governed by a series of Trade and Navigation Acts. These acts, which helped to support chartered monopoly companies by restricting trade to British ships, required that all goods imported by the colonies be channeled through England. All exported goods to foreign markets were also tightly regulated, and colonies typically specialized in a single export, such as tobacco in Virginia and sugar in the West Indies. With a shortage of labor in the colonies, African slaves became increasingly important to the export of raw goods, especially labor-intensive crops like sugar. Additional acts, such as the Wool, Iron, and Hat Acts, protected imperial markets for domestic industries by restricting the colonial manufacture of certain domestic goods. This economic system came to be known as mercantilism. Colonies were both suppliers of raw goods and exclusive markets for British manufactured products.

The Americas soon became a crucial site of Anglo-French conflict, which escalated into the Seven Years' War (1756–1763). Although Britain emerged victorious, its relationship with the mainland American colonies was inevitably altered. During the conflict, colonists shirked metropolitan regulations—often, for example, smuggling molasses from the French West Indies. While Britain attempted to reassert its imperial power, colonists continued to maintain and extend their new sense of self-governance. In fact, with the rival French removed from North America, mainland British colonists were less dependent on their home government for protection. Moreover, during the war Britain's national debt had doubled. Rather than bolstering the economy, its new monopoly in the Americas forced Britain to maintain a significant military presence in Quebec, where 100,000 French colonists and more than 250,000 Native Americans were now under British imperial rule. In 1763 Native American resistance erupted in a massive rebellion, known as Pontiac's conspiracy, which spread through the upper Ohio Valley. As a result of heavy debt and increased military presence, new duties were placed on a wide range of products imported by the colonies, such as foreign molasses, newspapers, and tea.

After defeating France, Britain acquired the majority of North American colonial territory. Its new mainland acquisitions extended north to Quebec, west to the Mississippi, and south to Florida. In the Caribbean, British territory included Jamaica, the Bahama Islands, the Leeward Islands, and the newly acquired Windward Islands. This height of expansiveness marked the peak of the early British Empire, which would be fundamentally altered as a result of the rebellion of most of the mainland American colonies in 1776.

The loss of thirteen mainland American colonies, however, did not prove disastrous for the British Empire. In fact, no longer responsible for defending the colonies, Britain soon found trade profitable in the absence of direct political control. The empire's reliance on mercantilism gave way to laissez-faire capitalism. With advanced industry at home and the foremost naval fleet, Britain strategically expanded its economic and political influence through an informal empire based on liberal free trade. As a result of resistance to further colonization in the Americas by former colonies such as Argentina and the United States, Britain's new policy of informal empire became particularly effective. By helping to enforce this resistance with its Royal Navy, Britain effectively prevented other European powers from establishing formal rule or economic advantage.

During this period, Britain also outlawed the slave trade (1807) and pressured other nations to do the same. Nevertheless, slavery was not officially abolished in British colonies until 1834, with a subsequent six-year term of apprenticeship.

Despite its new reliance on trade, Britain continued to acquire territories. New colonies were founded in the Pacific. Following the abolition of slavery, Britain formally established the colony of Sierra Leone in West Africa as a settlement for freed slaves. Moreover, the defeat of Napoleonic France in 1815 left Britain the strongest colonial power, with newly acquired French colonies, including Trinidad, Malta, Gibraltar, and the Cape of Good Hope.

British New Imperialism and the Colonization of Africa

Although the British Empire came to rely on economic influence, it pursued an even more aggressive competition for overseas territories between the 1870s and the outbreak of World War I in 1914. Historians refer to this period as British New Imperialism. The emergence of European doctrines of racial superiority, which often denied the capability of nonwhite peoples for self-governance, also contributed to this renewed interest in direct imperial control.

Largely unoccupied by European powers until the late nineteenth century, Africa became the primary target of this "new" imperialism. As of 1875, significant European holdings in Africa were limited to French Algeria and Britain's Cape Colony. By 1914, however, only the kingdom of Ethiopia and Liberia, a settlement of former American slaves, remained outside formal European control. Fearing a threat to its economic dominance, Britain contended for its share of African territories. In 1875 the British government bought Egyptian khedive Isma'īl's shares in the Suez Canal to secure control of the waterway, an important trade route between Britain and India. Egypt was heavily indebted to European powers as a result of building the Suez Canal, which had been financed by a combination of French and Egyptian interests, and dual financial pressure by France and Britain shifted to outright British occupation in 1882.

When France, Belgium, and Portugal held disputing claims on the lower Congo River, European powers met to formalize the orderly partition of Africa in 1884–1885 at the Berlin West Africa Conference. Britain's military occupation of Egypt also led to an interest in controlling the Nile

Valley. As a result, in 1896–1898 British and Egyptian troops conquered neighboring Sudan, a former colony of Egypt. Britain's decision to divide the Sudan into two separately controlled colonies exemplified the British strategy of "divide and rule." By manipulating and intensifying already-existing conflict between ethnic, religious, and racial communities, British strategy attempted to prevent subjugated populations from uniting against them.

In the 1840s a British colony, Natal, was established on the southern borders of the Zulu kingdom. By the 1870s Britain had become interested in uniting the various British colonies, Boer republics, and independent African groups for the sake of sustained economic development. The economically stable Zulu kingdom, however, posed a threat to this policy. As a result, the British high commissioner in South Africa, Sir Henry Bartle Frere, provoked a war against the Zulu king, Cetshwayo, believing the Zulu army to be desperately outmatched by British imperial forces. On the contrary, when the war began in 1879, the British experienced their greatest defeat in colonial history. The success against the British, however, exhausted the Zulu army, and British reinforcements soon flooded into southern Africa. After a series of campaigns, British troops eventually advanced to the Zulu capital, Ulundi, burning it to the ground. Rather than annex the kingdom of Zululand, the British divided it into thirteen smaller realms—a divisive strategy that resulted in a decade of civil war among the Zulu.

Though Britain consolidated its South African colonies following the Anglo-Zulu war, its imperial control also faced a persistent threat from the Boers, a British term for the Dutch farmers in southern Africa

who fiercely resisted subordination to Britain. The Boers rebelled against British rule in 1880 and declared the Transvaal independent. In the ensuing conflict, known as the First Boer War, or Transvaal War, a series of defeats forced the British to sign a truce recognizing the self-governance of a Boer republic of the Transvaal.

Later, mounting conflict over the Boers' overtly racist treatment of black Africans and British interest in the Transvaal, a chief supplier of gold, led to the South African War of 1899–1902, also known as the Second Boer War. After defeating the Boers, Britain united its Cape Colony and Natal Colony with the former Boer republics of the Orange Free State and Transvaal. In 1910 these former colonies and republics became the Union of South Africa, a self-governing dominion.

Despite its policy of free trade, Britain emerged in 1914 as holding the most extensive overseas empire. It included not only the subcontinent of India, but also a substantial share of African territory that far exceeded the holdings of other European powers.

From Empire to Commonwealth

Following World War I the British Empire acquired former German and Ottoman territories in what would become its final major expansion. As the British Empire incorporated new territories, the heavy costs of war, economic decline, and growing nationalist movements undermined Britain's capacity to maintain its sprawling empire. Although it brutally repressed nationalist resistance in Ireland, India, and the Middle East, Britain also expanded the autonomy of white-settler Dominions such as Canada and South Africa. In fact, although

Dominions had no voice in declaring war, each enjoyed international recognition when, as separate signatories of the Treaty of Versailles (1919), they entered the League of Nations.

Conferences of British and colonial prime ministers had occurred periodically since 1887. In an important set of Imperial Conferences in the late 1920s, multiple Canadian challenges to imperial authority led the way to full Dominion independence. The Balfour Declaration in 1926 and the Statute of Westminster in 1931 formally established the full independence of Dominions. Each became autonomous, free from British interference, independent in international relations, and officially equal in status to Britain. Its imperial power permanently weakened, the British Empire was transformed into a Commonwealth, a voluntary association between Britain and its former colonies.

In the 1930s widespread Caribbean unrest, including the 1938 labor rebellion in Jamaica, led the British government to appoint the West India Royal Commission to recommend constitutional reform. After World War II, Britain attempted to repeat the dominion model in decolonizing the Caribbean. However, following the failed attempt to establish a West Indian Federation (1958–1962), former colonies separated into independent nations after Jamaica and Trinidad and Tobago refused to accept the proposed distribution of powers. In 1959 Britain conceded full Jamaican independence, and self-governance was gradually extended to other former Caribbean colonies. Though several colonies, such as Guyana and Trinidad and Tobago, maintained their formal allegiance to the British monarch, they soon revised their status to become republics.

Britain also attempted to establish a dominion model in decolonizing Africa, but it, too, was unsuccessful. Britain maintained its influence in Egypt through treaty and partial occupation for more than thirty years after Egypt's formal independence (1922). In 1956, however, Egypt severed all constitutional links to Britain. Ghana, the first former colony declared a dominion in 1957, soon demanded recognition as a republic. Other African nations followed a similar pattern throughout the 1960s: Nigeria, Tanganyika, Uganda, Kenya, and Malawi. In fact, only Gambia, Sierra Leone, and Mauritius retained their dominion status for more than three years.

Brandon Jernigan

See also: Abolitionism, British; Berlin West Africa Conference; Jamaica; Kenya; Malawi; Nigeria; Trinidad and Tobago; Uganda

References

Hargreaves, John D. *Decolonization in Africa.* 2nd ed. New York: Longman, 1996.

Hart, Richard. *From Occupation to Independence: A Short History of the Peoples of the English-Speaking Caribbean Region.* Sterling, VA: Pluto Press, 1998.

Hornsby, Stephen J. *British Atlantic, American Frontier: Spaces of Power in Early Modern British America.* Lebanon, NH: University Press of New England, 2005.

Johnson, Robert. *British Imperialism.* New York: Palgrave, 2003.

Louis, William Roger, ed. *The Oxford History of the British Empire.* 5 vols. New York: Oxford University Press, 1998–1999.

Miers, Suzanne, and Martin Klein, eds. *Slavery and Colonial Rule in Africa.* Portland, OR: Frank Cass, 1999.

Morgan, Philip D., and Sean Hawkins, eds. *Black Experience and the Empire.* New York: Oxford University Press, 2004.

Moyles, R. G., and Doug Owram. *Imperial Dreams and Colonial Realities: British Views of Canada, 1880–1914.* Toronto: University of Toronto Press, 1988.

Smith, Simon C. *British Imperialism, 1750–1970.* New York: Cambridge University Press, 1998.

Sued-Badillo, Jalil, Pieter C. Emmer, Bridget
    Brereton, and B. W. Higman, eds. *General
    History of the Caribbean.* 6 vols. London:
    Macmillan, 1997–1999.
Wesseling, H. L. *Divide and Rule: The Partition
    of Africa, 1880–1914.* Translated by Arnold
    J. Pomerans. Westport, CT: Praeger, 1996.

BROOKS, GWENDOLYN (1917–2000)

Born on June 7, 1917, Gwendolyn Brooks, a black poet, won the Pulitzer Prize for poetry in 1950—the first African American to win a Pulitzer in any category. She went on to receive countless awards and honors during her lifetime. One of her many posthumous honors was the renaming of the Illinois State Library as the Gwendolyn Brooks State Library on June 6, 2003. A published poet at the age of thirteen, Gwendolyn Brooks would publish numerous works including two autobiographies, a single novel, and volumes of poetry such as *A Street in Bronzeville* (1945), *Annie Allen* (1949), *The Bean Eaters* (1960), *In the Mecca* (1968), *Riot* (1969), *Family Pictures* (1971), *The Tiger Who Wore White Gloves* (1974), *Beckonings* (1975), *Primer for Blacks* (1980), *To Disembark* (1981), *Gottschalk and the Grande Tarantelle* (1988), *Children Coming Home* (1991), and her final volume of poetry, published posthumously, *In Montgomery* (2003).

Gwendolyn Brooks's mother, Keziah Wims Brooks, influenced Brooks's life and works. Gwendolyn Brooks revealed this influence through autobiography, novel, and poetry. She made operative her mother's refrain, "Brighten your corner where you are," when she spoke to the universal, through the particular, from her corner on the South Side of Chicago. Brooks proclaimed in her first autobiography, *Report*

Poet Gwendolyn Brooks holding a copy of her book, A Street in Bronzeville, *published in 1945. Brooks was the first African American woman to win a Pulitzer Prize. (Library of Congress)*

From Part One (1972) and in other works, that she speaks to all black people as she pointedly articulates in her call. Even prior to this clarion call, the centrality of the black subject and the assumption of a black audience prevailed. Africanisms permeate the works of Gwendolyn Brooks, whether she crafted these works prior to the Fisk University Black Writers' Conference in 1967 or subsequent to the conference.

In the late 1960s there was a redirection of Brooks's voice to her people. This redirection manifested itself in major decisions that marked lifetime and life-altering changes, such as the move from white-owned Harper and Row to black-owned Broadside Press. Redirection of her voice resounded further when Brooks confessed a disregard for the white audience response and critical reception of her works. Brooks's inscription of meaningful, pronounced Africanisms in the black experience is not coincidental but conscious. For instance, the poem "To Those of My Sisters Who Kept Their Naturals" (1980) continues the concern and dialogue about black hair, for it is really about image and competing definitions of beauty. Brooks celebrates the the natural hair that stands the test of time.

In Gwendolyn Brooks's only novel, *Maud Martha* (1953), the author crafts a coming-of-age story about an intelligent young black woman who develops a keen awareness of life in Chicago as she moves from childhood to adulthood while reflecting on sibling, marital, and familial relationships at each level of her development. Brooks consistently makes of vital importance all facets of black life, depicts black people as subjects, and captures the events of the past, the concerns of the present, and the promise of the future as she harnesses the interconnectedness of life and the unity of all worlds—the living, dead, and unborn.

Jacqueline Bryant

See also: Haley, Alex; Literature, African American

References

Bennett, Lerone, Jr. "The Soul of Gwendolyn Brooks." In *Say That the River Turns: The Impact of Gwendolyn Brooks,* edited by Haki R. Madhubuti. Chicago: Third World Press, 1987.

Bryant, Jacqueline, ed. *Gwendolyn Brooks' Maud Martha: A Critical Collection.* Chicago: Third World Press, 2002.

Joyce, Joyce Ann. *Warriors, Conjurers, and Priests: Defining African-centered Literary Criticism.* Chicago: Third World Press, 1994.

Madhubuti, Haki R., ed. *Say That the River Turns: The Impact of Gwendolyn Brooks.* Chicago: Third World Press, 1987.

Wright, Stephen Caldwell. *On Gwendolyn Brooks: Reliant Contemplation.* Ann Arbor: University of Michigan Press, 1996.

BROUWER, LEO (1939–)

Born Juan Leovigildo Brouwer Mesquida in Havana, Cuba, Leo Brouwer is a Cuban composer, conductor, and pedagogue whose work reflects an African musical heritage. The breadth of his repertoire includes solo performances, chamber music, symphonies, concertos, and film scores; he is also highly regarded as a composer for the classical guitar. Brouwer is one of the first truly international composers in post-revolutionary Cuba.

Music was a part of Brouwer's heritage and a constant in his life. His artist mother taught him melodies from an early age. After his parents' divorce, Brouwer was raised by his maternal grandmother, through whom he came into contact with his great uncle, Ernesto Lecuona (a famous Cuban composer, arranger, and band leader), who noticed Brouwer's aptitude for music. At the age of twelve he was introduced to the guitar through his father and immediately showed prodigious talent. Brouwer went on to study with Cuba's great composer and virtuoso guitarist, Isaac Nicola, and made his professional debut at age sixteen for the Musical Youth Organization of Cuba. His career as virtuoso guitarist ended when a car accident in the early 1970s damaged his hand; from then onward he concentrated on composing. Although Brouwer briefly studied in the United States—he attended the Julliard School of Music and the Hartt College of Music—it was in Cuba where his interest in composition developed, both on his own and with various teachers, from the time he was introduced to the guitar. He was mainly a composition autodidact. His oeuvre is generally divided into three periods. The first (1955–1964) was seen as "nationalistic," the second (1964–1974) as avant-garde, and the third (1974–2002) as hyper-romantic. Brouwer entered a fourth stage of melismatic minimalism after returning to Cuba in 2002–2003 after many years of work in Europe. One continuous thread throughout his entire work is the abiding influence of African Yoruba rhythmic cells. Brouwer's ability to combine the classical tradition with the popular is a stylistic feature of the Afro-Cuban tradition. This inheritance, originating in the slave trade, fused African rhythms with European musical forms into a unique sound that is distinctly Cuban. Brouwer, however, has transformed it with his study of the avant-garde and its aleatoric compositional techniques.

Brouwer was one of the founding members and the eventual director of the Instituto Cubano del Arte e Industria Cinematográficos. In the 1960s this collective reinscribed the *trovador* tradition into the Nueva Trova, which formed part of a Latin American protest song movement reaching out to the United States and Europe. It was a conscious effort to minimize the demarcation line between performer and audience so prevalent in classical music.

Brouwer is renowned for his conducting and has led some of the world's greatest orchestras. He founded Orquesta de Córdoba in Spain in 1992 and remained its artistic director until 2001. He also wrote the scores for films such as *La Ultima Cena* (1976) and *Like Water for Chocolate* (1993).

His pieces are played internationally in "classical" recitals, exams, and conservatories.

They contain the transcultural heritage of Cuba, classical music infused with the idioms taken from Cuba's history, a unique blend of African and European influences.

Rhayn Jooste

References

Brouwer, Leo. *La Musica, Lo Cubano y La Innovacion* Havana, Cuba: Letras Cubanos, 1989.

Brouwer, Leo. *Gajes del Oficio*. Havana, Cuba: Letras Cubanos, 2004.

Hernández, Isabelle. *Leo Brouwer*. Havana: Editora Musical de Cuba, 2000.

Moore, Robin. "Music in Socialist Cuba." In *The New Grove Dictionary of Music and Musicians,* edited by Stanley Sadie. Vol. 6. London: Macmillan, 2001.

Sublette, Ned. *Cuba and Its Music, from the First Drums to the Mambo*. Chicago: Chicago Review Press, 2004.

BROWN, WILLIAM (1783–1816?)

William Brown was a black female sailor of the early nineteenth century. Suzanne Stark's groundbreaking study, *Female Tars: Women Aboard Ship in the Age of Sail* (1996), points to the extraordinary fact that several remarkable women passed as male sailors in the British Royal Navy in the eighteenth and early nineteenth centuries. Perhaps the most striking example cited by Stark is a black woman, born in Edinburgh, Scotland, who went under the assumed name William Brown—her given name is unknown. Little is known about William Brown, save what is written in the records of the Royal Navy. They indicate that she was "a smart, well-formed figure, about five feet four inches in height, possessed of considerable strength and great activity" (Stark, p. 87). The *Annual Register* confirms that William sailed aboard English warships from 1804 to 1816, rising to the distinguished post of captain of the foretop. The best sailors were made "captains" of various parts of the ship; the best captain was the captain of the foretop, the topmost section of the forwardmost mast on the ship. Her duties required great physical strength and courage, as she was required to ascend the mast high above the deck to handle sails, even in the worst weather. Her position also required the strongest of leadership skills, as she was required to inspire and organize a team of men as they handled the sails. Overturning every conceivable racial and gender assumption of her day, William had so earned the respect and admiration of her fellow sailors that, after she was found to be a woman, she was eventually allowed to rejoin her old crew. In June 1816 William joined a new ship, the *Bombay*, and at that point she disappeared from public record.

Matthew D. Brown

See also: Britain: People of African Origin and Descent; Sailors

Reference
Stark, Suzanne J. *Female Tars: Women Aboard Ship in the Age of Sail.* Annapolis, MD: Naval Institute Press, 1996.

BRUSSELS ACT

The Brussels General Act of July 2, 1890, made official the terms settled upon during the Brussels Convention, which was attended by representatives of the European colonial powers. The convention's goals were twofold. First, the imperial powers wished to ban the slave trade. While slavery and slave trafficking had been banned entirely in the New World by 1888, Arab traders continued to maintain a vigorous trade along the Indian Ocean's coastline.

Second, the act prohibited the sale of firearms to Africans. This act came only five years after the Berlin Conference, during which the British, French, Germans, Belgians, Dutch, Spanish, Portuguese, and several others established the boundaries of their territorial possessions in Africa. After that the imperialist powers found themselves in armed conflict with Africans who struggled to maintain their autonomy. White settlers in South Africa were among the many groups who had sought to prevent arms from falling into Africans' hands, as the latter had been acquiring weapons from traders in return for slaves and concessions. Eventually, the British and Boer authorities came to recognize that this served to perpetuate the slave trade and pose an increased military challenge.

With the Brussels Act, previous regulatory efforts were strengthened and Europeans were provided with an advantage in their efforts to enforce colonial rule and quell opposition from both Africans and Arab traders. Arms sales were restricted in the area known as the "slave trade zone," the sale of high-precision weapons was limited to a few individuals, and government armies remained able to purchase arms. These stipulations reinforced the technological superiority that the Europeans held over native African armies and kept the most advanced weapons in the hands of European powers. Although the act was not always fully enforced, the concerted efforts made to disarm Africans became an important factor in the consolidation of European rule, especially in the southern part of the continent.

Carmen Lenore Wright

See also: Berlin West Africa Conference; Colonialism; Slavery (History)

References

Boahen, A. Adu. *General History of Africa.*
Vol. 7, *Africa under Colonial Domination
1880–1935.* Abridged ed. Berkeley:
University of California Press/UNESCO,
1990.

Meirs, Sue. "Notes on the Arms Trade and
Government Policy in Southern Africa
between 1870 and 1890." *Journal of
African History* 4 (1971), 571–577.

BUNCHE, RALPH (1904–1971)

Ralph Bunche was the first African American diplomat to advise a U.S. presidential administration. Although he is best-known for brokering an Arab-Israeli truce in 1949, his work on Africa was critical to shaping U.S. foreign policy and United Nations (UN) policies toward African decolonization. At the 1945 conference held in San Francisco, during which the foundations for the UN were laid, Bunche helped draft those sections of the UN charter concerned with the future of regions still under colonial rule. His expertise on Africa led him, as the U.S. undersecretary to the UN, to be appointed to head the Trusteeship Division, the committee responsible for aiding regions transitioning to self-governance and independence.

Bunche began his career as a scholar studying anthropology and colonialism throughout sub-Saharan Africa. In 1936 he published a brief work, *A World View of the Race,* arguing that race and racialized ways of thinking were becoming a dominant means of organizing social relations and relations of inequality on a global basis. Already active in civil rights work, Bunche's public service shifted direction with the onset of World War II. During the war Bunche served as the head of the Africa

United Nations diplomat Ralph Bunche speaks with Dr. Kwame N'krumah, prime minister of Ghana, at a reception given for N'krumah by the Harlem Lawyers' Association at the Harlem Armory in 1958. (Library of Congress)

division of the Office of Strategic Services of the United States, the nation's first centralized agency dedicated to strategic intelligence gathering. His service led him further into diplomatic and public life. For his work at the UN, Bunche was awarded the Nobel Peace Prize in 1950. He was the first person of African descent to receive that award.

Bunche subsequently continued his international work. In 1954 he was appointed undersecretary-general of the UN. In 1956, after the Suez Canal crisis, Bunche returned to the problem of peace in the Middle East as the director of peacekeeping operations. These would occupy him for the next decade, including supervising operations in Congo (later Zaire) in 1960.

As a public figure, Bunche argued for the importance of self-governance for people still under colonial rule, believing that self-governance was a critical feature of future international stability and peace. He further insisted that self-governance was a basic human right. These were arguments that carried weight in the context of the search for international stability after World War II.

At the same time, he was a controversial figure, precisely because of his accomplishments and visibility. During the cold war he was often presented by the U.S. government to the larger world as a sign of national racial progress, despite the government's continued support of segregation and black disenfranchisement. Bunche himself fought strenuously against racism and for civil rights in the United States.

Drawing upon his global perspective, Bunche's intellectual contributions to the American Civil Rights Movement were considerable. At times, he viewed civil rights organizations in the United States as insufficiently attentive to the poverty that came as a consequence of racial inequality. Bunche argued strongly for viewing the black struggle in the United States as part of the larger global struggle of colonial peoples for democracy, self-determination, and human rights.

Richard Juang

See also: Civil Rights Movement; Decolonization, African; Peacekeeping and Military Interventions; United Nations

References

Holloway, John Scott. *Confronting the Veil: Abram Harris Jr., E. Franklin Frazier, and Ralph Bunche, 1919–1941.* Chapel Hill: University of North Carolina Press, 2001.

Urquhart, Brian. *Ralph Bunche: An American Odyssey.* New York: W. W. Norton, 1988.

BURIAL GROUND (NEW YORK CITY), AFRICAN

In 1991, during construction of a new federal building in lower Manhattan in New York City, the remains of a large African American burial ground were uncovered. Eventually, the remains of 419 bodies were removed from what is now the largest extant African American colonial burial ground in the United States. This rediscovery of a burial ground in the heart of the modern city highlighted the well-documented but hitherto largely ignored history of slavery and free black presence in the northern United States. African Americans had been buried at the site from at least the early eighteenth century, and they included conspirators from the 1712 New York slave revolt. It is thought that around 20,000 African Americans were buried there during the colonial period and into the early nineteenth century. The burial ground was kept outside the city limits of the time and was restricted to African Americans.

New York mayor David Dinkins and U.S. representative Augustus Savage of Illinois halted construction work during 1991 and 1992 so that proper archaeological excavation could take place, and researchers at Howard University were invited to undertake the painstaking work of removing and examining the human remains. This examination gave rise to new evidence about African origins and the transition from Africa to America. The site offers evidence for the continuation of African customs and beliefs.

New Yorkers were determined that the site itself would become a permanent memorial to those Africans who helped to build the city but are ignored in almost all histories. Thus, various artworks and

Pallbearers in Baltimore, Maryland, carry a hand-carved mahogany coffin containing human remains from an African burial ground discovered in downtown Manhattan in 1991. This coffin and three others are on a ceremonial procession back to New York for reburial. The remains of more than 400 free blacks and slaves that had been studied at Howard University since being uncovered during construction of a federal building, are scheduled to be reburied near New York's City Hall. (AP/Wide World Photos)

memorials were commissioned to stand in the building on the site and in an Interpretative Center alongside it. These include the work *Africa Rising* (1998), by Barbara Chase-Riboud, in the lobby of the federal building, and a work commissioned in 2005, titled *Ancestral Libation Chamber,* by Rodney Leon. Commemorating African contributions to the United States, Leon's work will include a memorial wall, pillars to mark the burial ground's entrance, and a map of the cemetery itself.

In October 2003 the remains of the bodies were re-interred in hand-carved

coffins from Ghana in a service replete with African ceremonial. Guest of honor Maya Angelou spoke to the thousands present to pay tribute to their African ancestors. In February 2006, after vigorous lobbying, the African Burial Ground was officially designated a national monument.

Alan Rice

See also: Burial, African Practices in the Americas; Museums and Transatlantic Slavery

Reference
La Roche, Cheryl J., and Michael L. Blakey. "Seizing Intellectual Power: The Dialogue at the New York Burial Ground." *Historical Archaeology* 31, no. 3 (1997): 84–106.

BURIAL, AFRICAN PRACTICES IN THE AMERICAS

African burial practices in the Americas include traditions and practices honoring the dead through retained and adapted cultural forms between Africa and the Americas. The retentions and transformations of African burial practices in the Americas provide the greatest amount of evidence about how the African past has influenced ethnic identity formations of African people in the New World. The most salient characteristic of this influence involves the so-called ancestors, that is, the "living dead." Africanist anthropologists, ethnographers, and historians agree that traditional African cosmology concerning death incorporated a continuum between the natural and spiritual worlds. African ontology, a holistic understanding of existence based on Africans' belief in this continuum of experiences, provided practical reinforcement. As a result, the continuum between life and death in African societies was most immediate and relevant in their funeral rituals.

Africans' relationships with the deceased symbolized the significance of the continuum. Dead people had power either to interfere maliciously or to intervene benevolently in earthly matters. Therefore, comforting the living during their bereavement was somewhat secondary to honoring the departed, because satisfied souls would find no reason to be malevolent toward survivors. Consequently, proper respect to the deceased shaped some behaviors of the living. Acceptable burials meant large attendance, food offerings, performance of appropriate dirges, interring personal objects belonging to the deceased, and elaborate funeral processionals. These funerary behaviors secured this connection between the living and the dead, exhibiting African practicality within spirituality. In fact, homage to their deceased represented the most common manifestation of how the sacred and secular coexisted within African burial practices. Misunderstood by early European observers from the fifteenth century as ancestor worship, the reverence assigned to deceased family or clan members had to do with an adulation of the deceased via an acceptance of their newly acquired power as otherworldly beings.

Involuntary migration across the Atlantic World and chattel slavery in the Americas did not destroy the continuation of African cosmological orientations manifested in burial practices, especially the centrality of respect for the departed through funerary displays. The "first burials" among Africa's dispersed people were aboard slave ships. Suicide, slave revolts, despondency, and disease made death at sea common occurrences for human cargo. The "watery grave" of the Atlantic Ocean, or Middle Passage, was also a metaphorical conduit away from horrific peril. Water, in some

African societies, signifies the divide between life and death. For example, as soon as funerary rites had been concluded, a departed soul began its journey across the river that marked the boundaries of life and death. The Ga and Lodagaa peoples of Ghana and the Bakongo from Angola, in particular, represented death as the voyage of a soul who had crossed a river, believing the end of human life was a voyage through the waters of death that separated the unseen world of the living from the world of the departed. Therefore, dying at sea could have been seen as a pilgrimage or departure to another existence as well as an escape from a horrific experience; hence, while those who survived the Middle Passage had crossed over into bondage, those who died had joined their ancestors, going back to a spiritual, African existence.

Slave cemeteries eventually replaced the aquatic tombs that the initial, dispersed Africans had created. Whether enslaved Africans died on islands such as Barbados, Antigua, or the Bahamas or on plantations in Virginia, South Carolina, Georgia, Alabama, Mississippi, or Louisiana, enslaved people retained their humanity and customs by culturally responding to human death. Traveler accounts, memoirs, and interviews with freedpersons all confirm that across both the antebellum South and the islands of the Americas, enslaved people insisted on observing their customary funerary rites. In fact, few slaveholders made the mistake of denying their human property the options of paying proper attention to their dead. Furthermore, urban archaeological finds in major U.S. cities such as New York and Dallas, as well as studies in folk beliefs about death, have all confirmed taboos concerning proper burial among West Indians and southern blacks, particularly in the cultures of the Sea Islands. For example, Africans from the continent and American-born Africans believed that grave dirt was also a common element in magic, healing, and witchcraft. The dirt from a grave was believed to be so powerful that taboos and superstitions regarding its usage abounded, dictating the very steps of those in the funeral processions as well as the movements of grave diggers and other mourners.

Evidence of similarities between Africans on the continent and their descendants dispersed across the Atlantic can still be seen when modern visitors frequent slave cemeteries. Specifically, enslaved people, like their African predecessors, also customarily interred personal items with the deceased. People believed that the deceased could become a restless spirit who resented the possibility of other people coveting their possessions and, therefore, returned to the world of the living to access and use his or her own belongings. As a result, some dispersed Africans adhered to a cultural practice of burying personal items as an obligation in the best interest of the family. Similarly, utilitarian grave decorations from St. Louis, Missouri, New Orleans, Louisiana, and Jacksonville, Florida, and throughout the Caribbean prove that Africans across the Atlantic World placed at grave sites functional paraphernalia like bottles, tea and flower pots, broken dishes, tools, cigar boxes, lamps, weapons, and even gold. Such items reflect Africans' traditional practicality regarding the continuum between life and death.

In addition to the influence of the departed on interment and grave decorations, mourning rituals and funeral displays of Africans in the Atlantic Diaspora also reference the African past. The actual funeral services for an enslaved person, however,

did not have to follow immediately after their death or burial. Time off work had to be provided by slaveholders to attend slave funerals because forced labor dictated the events of dispersed Africans' lives. Consequently, enslaved people commonly held night funerals during the antebellum period. These gatherings were traditionally attended by large numbers of people regardless of relation or local residence, and two burial practices legitimized the slave community's last rites: the presence of a slave preacher who would offer a flattering eulogy and the participation of lamenting slave women. African women in certain Akan societies and enslaved women of the antebellum South both demonstrated intense emotive displays. The funeral dirges of the Akan women in Ghana serve as sufficient comparisons to the mourning exhibitions of grieving enslaved women. In Africa, such a showing of grief would be an appropriate and expected behavior; also, these expressions of bereavement also could be cited as a refutation against possible accusations of witchcraft or wrongdoing in the death, especially the death of a husband. Across the Atlantic, such female funeral displays confirmed the worth of the deceased and conferred upon the community the permission to acknowledge the significance of its personal loss regardless of the slaves' supposedly powerless positions. A dead slave had neither productive nor reproductive benefit for slaveholders.

Before slavery was abolished throughout the New World, these burial practices had already assisted in the formation of a distinct diaspora, the African Atlantic. The growing number of burial societies and mutual aid associations on behalf of bereaved families during the postslavery period prove that funeral rites were considered essential characteristics of freedom. In the United States and Brazil, especially, African American and Afro-Brazilian communities institutionalized traditional burial practices after emancipation by organizing different types of benevolent groups. Even the poorest community member could join a benevolent society, especially those mutual aid organizations sponsored by local churches. Benevolent societies had memberships that included undertakers. The "society undertaker" provided professional death care for those individuals, families, and groups who joined burial associations. African American morticians, or society undertakers, were paid in cash from the dues and membership fees of society members, making death-care providers the wealthiest and most socially mobile members of the African American community. Benevolent societies, consequently, represented an embryonic equivalent of modern-day insurance companies. In fact, African-influenced burial practices should be cited as the root of the African American insurance and funeral industries.

LaTrese Evette Adkins

References

Creel, Margaret Washington. *"A Peculiar People:" Slave Religion and Community-Culture among the Gullah.* New York: New York University Press, 1988.

Godboldte, Catherine I. "Ancient African Traditional Funeral Ceremonies and the Funeral Ceremony of the Historic African American Church." PhD dissertation, Temple University, 1995.

Mbiti, John S. *African Religions and Philosophy.* 2nd ed. Oxford: Heinemann, 1989.

Raboteau, Albert J. *Slave Religion: The "Invisible Institution" in the Antebellum South.* New York: Oxford University Press, 1978.

Wright, Robert Hughes, and Wilber B. Hughes III. *Lay Down Body: Living History in African American Cemeteries.* Detroit, MI: Visible Ink Press, 1996.

BURKINA FASO

Previously known as Upper Volta, Burkina Faso is a West African nation with a population of over 13 million, as of 2007, drawn from more than fifty ethnic groups and largely living in urban areas. It is just south of the Sahara Desert, with only 13 percent of the land being arable. Formerly a part of French West Africa, the province of Upper Volta was created in 1919. From 1932 until 1947 it was abolished, forming the southeastern section of French Sudan. It gained its independence as the Republic of Upper Volta on August 4, 1960, and was renamed the People's Republic of Burkina, or Burkina Faso, on August 4, 1984. Although largely dominated by France, U.S. missionaries were active in the area in the early twentieth century. The White Fathers of Africa sent missionaries to Upper Volta from 1900; the Foreign Missions Department of the Assemblies of God from 1921; the Christian and Missionary Alliance from 1923; the Sudan Interior Mission from 1930; the Worldwide Evangelization Crusade from 1939; and the Africa Inter-Mennonite Mission (formerly the Congo Inland Mission) from 1978.

Being a landlocked country, with little in the way of natural resources—in fact, it is one of the poorest countries in the world—most of the connections between Burkina Faso and the Americas have been in terms of relations with the United States, with U.S. scholars studying aspects of the country. The nation's isolation has created much interest in the country among U.S. ethnographers. Some other American countries, such as Canada and Jamaica, have shown interest in Burkina Faso, mostly its music. Canadian artist Pauline Julien, from Quebec, spent five months in Burkina Faso in 1993, and musicians from Burkina Faso have toured several countries in North and South America and the Caribbean.

When Upper Volta became independent in 1960, the United States sent its first ambassador, Ralph Borden Reams. He was posted to Ouagadougou, the capital, from 1960 until 1961. The next ambassador, Thomas Stuart Estes, was there from 1961 until 1966 and later was co-author of *The Department of State* (New York, 1976). Elliott Skinner, born in Port of Spain, Trinidad, was the third ambassador. He became a U.S. citizen in 1943, and as an anthropologist he did research in West Africa during the 1950s. He earned his doctorate in 1955 and then became a visiting professor at the Department of Anthropology at Columbia University. Advancing to associate professor in 1963, Skinner was only the second African American to attain a tenured position in any Ivy League university. His book, *The Mossi of Upper Volta: The Political Development of a Sudanese People,* was published by Stanford University in 1964, and two years later Skinner was nominated by President Lyndon Johnson as ambassador to Upper Volta, a position he held until 1969. President Sangoulé Lamizana made him grand commander of the Upper Volta National Order. After his term, Skinner returned to academia as professor of anthropology at Columbia University. He wrote *African Urban Life: The Transformation of Ouagadougou* (1974) and *The Mossi of Upper Volta: Chiefs, Politicians, and Soldiers* (1989).

Another U.S. scholar who did research on Upper Volta in the 1950s was Peter B. Hammond of California, who conducted research in Upper Volta in 1954 until 1956, subsequently becoming assistant professor of anthropology at the University of Pittsburgh and then at Indiana University. In 1983 Captain Thomas Sankara came to power in Burkina Faso. His four years in power witnessed government austerity drives, a massive increase in health care, and the ejection of members of the U.S. Peace Corps. The U.S. ambassador from 1987 to 1990, David H. Shinn, was the author of the *Historical Dictionary of Ethiopia* (2004). In 1990 an international observer team went to Ouagadougou in response to the nation's political problems; the Canadian contingent was led by Yvon C. Tarte.

Several U.S. institutions hold substantial collections of artifacts from Upper Volta, especially the Detroit Institute of Arts. In addition, much research into Burkina Faso has been undertaken by Canadian and U.S. academics, especially in the realms of health and agriculture. The outputs include Richard Maclure's work on rural programs at Stanford University and Joanny Zongo's work on the Sorghum Shoot Fly in Burkina Faso at McGill University. Other North Americans connected with Burkina Faso include Charles F. Ames from Harvard University, who worked with Foster Parents Plan International in Ouagadougou; Joseph Bonenfant from Quebec, Canada, who taught at the University of Ouagadougou from 1977 to 1979; and Canadian doctor Chunilal Roy, who was the Canadian honorary consul in Burkina Faso. Burkina Faso is probably best-known through the music group Farafina, which has toured much of the Americas.

Justin Corfield

See also: French Empire

Reference

Skinner, Elliott. *African Urban Life: The Transformation of Ouagadougou.* Princeton, NJ: Princeton University Press, 1974.

BURUNDI

This small landlocked country in central Africa has a population of 6,231,000 (2004), three-quarters of whom live in urban areas. Most of the country is high plateau grassland, and the area that became Burundi was originally a part of German East Africa. After World War I the territory called Ruanda-Urundi (including modern-day Rwanda and Burundi) was annexed by Belgium, which ruled it under a League of Nations mandate and later as a United Nations Trusteeship. It gained its independence as the Kingdom of Burundi on July 1, 1962, becoming the Republic of Burundi on November 28, 1966.

When the British invaded German East Africa in 1914, they were aided by French, Belgian, and Portuguese contingents. However, most of the fighting was carried out by the British and colonial soldiers. These included several men connected with Argentina, including Claude Henry Forster and Richard Hewitt Talbot. The former contracted fever, dying in France, and the latter, who was awarded the Military Cross, returned to Buenos Aires at the end of the war and died in October 1919, only a few days after disembarking. Other Britons from Argentina who served there included W. L. Jordon and Jack Browne, who were, respectively, captain and sergeant in the East African Expeditionary Force, and B. V. Douglas, who worked in the British Transport Service.

There has been very little contact between Burundi and the Americas, except for the United States. From there some missionaries, under the auspices of the Free Methodist Church of North America, came to Burundi to work in 1935. Alan P. Merriam, an ethnomusicologist from Northwestern University and later the

University of Indiana, studied Burundi's music during the late 1950s. At this time the United States also became an importer of Burundi coffee, and later it imported Burundian postage stamps. It has also provided financial aid and training. One of the main researchers in Burundi under the Belgians was Melchior Mukuri, who completed a doctoral thesis on Burundi at Université Laval in Canada. When Burundi held elections in 1961, just prior to gaining its independence, one of the UN observers was the Canadian lawyer Martial Asselin, who was lieutenant governor of Quebec in 1990–1996.

The United States recognized Burundi upon its independence. Donald Albert Dumont was U.S. minister in 1962–1963 and then ambassador until 1966. He was replaced by George W. Renchard, who was ambassador until 1969. Thomas P. Melady succeeded Renchard as U.S. ambassador. Melady would later write *Burundi: The Tragic Years* (1974). With his wife, he later co-authored *Idi Amin: Hitler in Africa* (1977).

Throughout the 1960s there was substantial conflict and civil war between Hutus and Tutsis, Burundi's two major ethnic groups. In 1966, King Ntare V would be deposed, the culmination of years of strife in which thousands died. Between 1966 and 1972, Burundi was a republic with a degree of stability. However, in 1972, the year Melady left Burundi, the country was rocked by a massive Hutu revolt. The resulting repression was followed by the death of about 100,000 Hutu, causing U.S. senators Edward Kennedy and John Tunney to call for an international team to act regarding the "situation" in Burundi. When trouble broke out again in 1995, after genocidal events in neighboring

Rwanda, U.S. president Bill Clinton urged Burundi to "say no to violence and extremism." Later the same year, former U.S. president Jimmy Carter served as a mediator between Hutu and Tutsi factions in Burundi and Rwanda. Since then the situation in the country has been much more settled and tourists are returning to Burundi and neighboring Rwanda to see the mountain gorillas. Since the last years of the twentieth century, Burundi has established significant trade relations with the People's Republic of China, causing the United States some concern.

Justin Corfield

See also: British Empire; Central African Republic; French Empire

Reference

Eggers, Ellen K. *Historical Dictionary of Burundi.* Lanham, MD: Scarecrow Press, 1997.

CABRAL, AMILCAR (1924–1973)

A Marxist revolutionary and national liberationist, Amilcar Cabral was born in Bafata, Portuguese Guinea, and raised in Cape Verde. His father, Juvenal Cabral, an elementary school teacher, was a noted political activist who dedicated himself to improving the living conditions of farmers and civil servants in the region.

Growing up under Portuguese colonialism during the era of Portugal's fascist dictator António de Oliveira Salazar, Cabral experienced firsthand the exploitation and oppression, including mass starvation, suffered by the poor and working classes of Cape Verde. Cabral began his political activity during high school, taking on the assumed name Labrac.

In 1945 Cabral journeyed to Lisbon to attend the Agronomy Institute on a scholarship. During this period he actively engaged in democratic struggles and participated in antifascist student organizations. Cabral also formed student organizations devoted to African liberation from the colonial powers.

Cabral returned to Guinea and Cape Verde in the early 1950s and took up employment as an agronomist. His work took him to villages throughout the country, and based on his observation of extreme poverty and exploitation and his involvement with the diverse communities he visited, Cabral began to formulate an analysis of local social conditions and appropriate strategies for liberation from the colonial regime.

Cabral played a central part in the formation of the Partido Africano de Indepencia de Guine e Capo Verde (PAIGC; African Party for the Independence of Guinea and Cape Verde) in 1956. The PAIGC would become the primary force of national liberation struggles against the Portuguese. In 1963 the PAIGC launched an all-out campaign of armed struggle against the colonial regime. Within two years it had liberated large areas of land from the Portuguese and brought the areas under the leadership of the PAIGC.

In 1972 Cabral initiated a National People's Assembly, based on a popular vote for representatives of the liberated territories, in preparation for national independence. In January 1973, only months before the national liberation struggle claimed victory, Cabral was assassinated by a former colleague operating with the assistance of Portuguese agents who had infiltrated the PAIGC.

Cabral's writings on armed struggle and his theories on the value of national culture as an essential element in resistance to foreign domination have influenced revolutionaries worldwide. His work was taken up by armed struggle movements in the United States, notably the Black Liberation Army, as well as by socialist movements in Grenada and Guyana.

Jeff Shantz

References

Chabal, Patrick. *Amilcar Cabral: Revolutionary Leadership and People's War.* Cambridge: Cambridge University Press, 1983.

Chailand, Gerard. *Armed Struggle in Africa: With the Guerrillas in "Portuguese" Guinea.* New York: Monthly Review Press, 1969.

Davidson, Basil. *No Fist is Big Enough to Hide the Sky: The Liberation of Guine and Cape Verde: Aspects of an African Revolution.* London: Zed Books, 1981.

McCullough, Jock. *In the Twilight of Revolution: The Political Theory of Amilcar Cabral.* London and Boston: Routledge & Kegan Paul, 1983.

CABRAL, CRISTINA RODRÍGUEZ (1959–)

Cristina Rodríguez Cabral is a black female Uruguayan author. The granddaughter of Elemo Cabral, one of the lead editors of *Nuestra Raza* (Our race), the longest-running black periodical in Uruguay's history, Cristina Cabral comes from a family rooted in the civil rights movement and the black literary tradition of her country. Hailed as one of the most talented writers since those contributing to *Nuestra Raza* (1917–1948), she is the first published black woman writer after Virginia Brindis de Salas to continue the legacy of Uruguay's black literary tradition.

In the fifteen years that span her career, Cabral's work includes nine books of poetry, three essays, and one travel journal. As of 2007, she is completing the manuscript,

"Otro exilio" (Another exile), a volume of poetry. Although Cristina Cabral completed most of her work, which consists mostly of love poems and poems of introspection, in Uruguay, her ideas shifted when she moved to Brazil in 1988 and the United States in 1997. Influenced by the religious practices of Afro-Brazilians and the Afrocentric culture and philosophy she found in the United States, her poetry became more radical. Over the course of her travels, the subject matter of her poetry shifted to the racism, oppression, social injustice, and racial and gender disparities Afro-Uruguayans face. The complex experiences she faced in the United States dictated the voice of her newer poetry. Cabral questions and compares the similarities and differences between her two worlds, Uruguay and the United States. Her collection, *Memoria y Resistencia* (1998; Memory and Resistance), written in the United States, illustrates her struggle to define herself as an outspoken black woman warrior between two contradictory worlds.

Historically, Cristina Rodríguez Cabral has broken ground in the educational arena, wherein she is among a handful of black Uruguayan college graduates. After moving to the United States, she completed a master's degree in teaching English as a second language at Indiana University of Pennsylvania in 1999. Since then, Cabral has lived in Columbia, Missouri, where she is completing a docoral program at the University of Missouri. She is completing her doctoral thesis on the novels of Manuel Zapata Olivella, known as the "Dean of Afro-Hispanic literature." She will be the first Uruguayan black woman to hold a doctorate degree.

Caroll Mills Young

See also: Afrocentrism; Brindis de Salas, Virginia; Uruguay

References

Britos Serrat, Alberto. *Antología de los poetas negros uruguayos.* Montevideo, Uruguay: Ediciones Mundo Afro, 1990.

Lewis, Marvin A. *Afro-Uruguayan Literature: Post-Colonial Perspectivas.* Lewisburg, PA: Bucknell University Press, 2003.

Young, Caroll Mills. "Crossing Borders/Crossing Boundaries: Cristina Cabral's Memoria y Resistencia." In *Daughters of the Diaspora: Afra Hispanic Writers,* edited by Miriam DeCosta-Willis. Kingston, Jamaica: Ian Randle Press, 2003.

CALABAR

Calabar is a city of present-day Nigeria that was a transatlantic slave port. A city in the far southeast of Nigeria, it is situated on the Cross River, eight miles north of the Atlantic Ocean. Calabar was a transatlantic slave port throughout the seventeenth and eighteenth centuries and later a palm oil trading port. Mangrove swamps link the creeks to the southwest, while to the east the city is bounded by the Qua River. The climate is equatorial with heavy rainfall between May and October and a dry season between November and April. The city is surrounded by bush and forested areas, where small cultivators produce palm oil, cassava, yams, and bananas. The city is a conurbation of several "towns" (*obio*) and has a population of around 500,000.

Creek Town (Obio Oku) is the oldest settlement in Calabar, founded by migrants from the hinterland in approximately the fourteenth century. The Efik, Qua, and Efut people all established fishing communities, followed by further settlements down river at Old Town (Obutong), Duke Town (Atakpa), and Henshaw Town (Nsidung). These settlements later became known collectively as Old Calabar to distinguish the city from New Kalabar, a port to the west of Bonny on the Niger River. The Old Calabar "towns" were involved in the transatlantic slave trade by the eighteenth century, and between 1720 and 1830 one million slaves left from Calabar, most on British vessels.

Each town (*obio*) was headed by a king (*obong*) who controlled a trading monopoly over the supply of slaves captured in the interior. In the "'trust trade" system, European traders advanced goods to Efik middlemen, who supplied slaves from inland. European traders were forbidden to settle ashore or own land in the city, so they traded from ships moored in the Calabar River. Detailed accounts of the Calabar slave trade exist in the form of the letters, bookkeeping records, and diaries of European and Efik traders, including the description by the French trader Barbot of a visit in 1689 and the diary of the Efik trader Antera Duke, written between 1785 and 1788.

During the nineteenth century the slave trade declined. Calabar became a center for the export of palm oil to industrial Britain, where it was used to process detergents. Under the political control of Great Duke Ephraim from Duke Town, palm oil production increased between 1814 and 1834. The rulers of the Efik towns founded plantations for the cultivation of palm oil around the city in Okoyong and Akpabuyo. Plantation work was done by people who had been acquired by Efik traders as slaves before the transatlantic slave trade ended. Great Duke Ephraim forged close links with European traders such as the British trader Sir John Tobin, later the mayor of Liverpool.

The trust trade system had increased the power of the kings as mediators and European traders were required to pay each

Efik king "comey" duty to trade in his territory. By the 1840s several powerful Efik rulers had emerged, including King Eyo Honesty II in Creek Town and King Eyamba V in Duke Town, and by the 1860s, some former slaves within Efik towns were also prominent palm oil traders. The Ekpe secret society became a powerful source of authority used to resolve trade disputes, with Efik rulers, former slaves, and European traders all being members.

In 1841 King Eyo Honesty II and King Eyamba sent a letter to Queen Victoria, via a Liverpool-based palm oil trader, asking about new agricultural techniques, new European weaponry, and the Bible. A response came from the United Secession Church (USC), a Scottish Presbyterian denomination active in the campaign to abolish slavery. The USC considered that a West African mission could assist in the replacement of the slave trade with legitimate trade and sent seven missionaries to Calabar from its Jamaica mission in 1846.

The missionaries were the first Europeans permitted to settle ashore in Calabar, and they were allocated land by Eyamba V in Duke Town and by King Eyo Honesty II in Creek Town. The first conversion did not come until in 1853, when Esien Esien Ukpabio became the first of many teachers from Calabar to start mission schools throughout the Cross River region in the nineteenth and twentieth centuries. Efik rulers were reluctant to convert; King Eyo Honesty II translated for the mission but never became a Christian, arguing that his patronage of the mission was his contribution to the church and that he did not consider conversion necessary.

From 1861, when the British consul established a headquarters in Calabar, the city became a center of colonial administration. Trade treaties were signed between the consul and Efik traders, drawing the Calabar region into the 1885 Oil Rivers Protectorate. In 1899 the charter of the Royal Niger Company was withdrawn, and the administration and regulation of trade was passed to the colonial government. In 1900 Calabar became the seat of colonial government for the new Protectorate of Southern Nigeria. Calabar also became a center of protest against colonial taxation by women market traders in 1925, and then again in 1929, when the Women's War spread through large parts of Calabar Province. In the run up to independence in 1960, Calabar was part of the Eastern Region when the three-region federal state was established in 1947. Calabar was also part of the region that declared independence as Biafra in 1967, the city being recaptured by federal forces in the autumn of 1967.

Calabar remained a busy port up until the decline of the palm oil export trade in the 1960s. With the expansion of road and rail networks throughout eastern Nigeria and the development of the oil industry, Port Harcourt replaced Calabar as the main southeastern port. Today Calabar is the state capital of Cross River State. The city's economy rests upon its role as an administrative center and as a regional marketplace for the predominantly agricultural economy of Cross River State. Calabar is an important historic center for Presbyterianism in Nigeria, and it is also home to several international religious organizations, including the Brotherhood of the Cross and Star and many new Pentecostal ministries.

Philippa Hall

See also: Efik; Nigeria; Palm Oil; Slavery (History)

References

Eyo, Ekpo, ed. *The Story of Old Calabar*. Lagos, Nigeria: National Commission for Museums and Monuments, 1986.

Hackett, Rosalind. *Religion in Calabar: The Religious Life and History of a Nigerian Town*. New York: Monton de Gruyter, 1989.

Hackett, Rosalind. "Charismatic/Pentecostal Appropriation of Media Technologies in Nigeria and Ghana." *Journal of Religion in Africa* 28, no. 3 (1998): 258–277.

Marshall-Fratani, Ruth. "Mediating the Local and the Global in Nigerian Pentecostalism." *Journal of Religion in Africa* 38, no. 3 (1998): 278–313.

Mbon, Friday. "The Quest for Identity in African Religious Movements." In *New Religious Movements and Society,* edited by G. Ludwar Ene. Bayreuth, Germany: African Studies Series, 1991.

CALYPSO

The calypso is a popular and sometimes satirical song in rhymed verse dealing with topical social and political subjects, most associated with Trinidad. It was traditionally performed extempore and is usually played in 2/4 or 4/4 time. It is often, though not necessarily, associated with the steel pan on which it is played, especially around Carnival time.

Calypsonians use the song as a vent for political and social grievances, employing satire to this effect. The calypso shapes and reflects social opinion and is therefore often considered the voice of the people. Because it expresses, defines, and mobilizes political consciousness, calypso may have an overt or subtle influence on politics and so has an important role in society. In its function as social complaint, the calypso resembles the American blues and the contemporary Jamaican blues. In fact, calypso was born out of an act of self-preservation in the face of the dehumanizing conditions of slavery in the tradition of the African American folksong. It may, however, also be used as an invitation to revelry.

There have been many suggestions by researchers as to the origin of the words "calypso" and "kaiso" (another name given to the song). Some suggest that it might have come from the Carib word for a joyous song, "carieto," that might have developed into "cariso"; from the French patois derivation "carrousseaux" or "caillisseaux" from "carrousse," French for carousal; from "caliso," a Spanish word used for a St. Lucian song; or from "careso," a song in the Virgin Islands. The most popular view, however, is that it may be a derivative of the West African Hausa word, "kaito," a cry of approval. Researchers, including the renowned calypsonian, Attila the Hun, agree that this word may have developed into "kaiso" and then further evolved into "calypso."

Another calypsonian, The Roaring Lion, proposes that the calypso is a derivative of the French *ballade* of the thirteenth century and was infused with various rhythms in the West Indies to arrive at its form today. Although this view is not widely accepted, Frederick Gordon Rohlehr, an eminent scholar in the field of calypso, also compares the art form in its "vague cosmopolitanism and richly incongruous parentage" with the history of Trinidad, in which the island passed from one European nation to another. He agrees that different groups in Trinidad claim to have influenced the music form and that its origins are therefore unclear. He argues, for example, that different Creole rhythms, including the Castillian in its Creole Trinidadian form and the Habañera, may also be responsible for the form of calypso.

Calypso has, however, been linked to the kalinda, to which stick-fighters chanted and fought. The chantwell, or lead singers, of the stick-fighting groups functioned as social commentator and haranguer and so may be considered very early calypsonians. The chantwells, however, were thought to possess supernatural powers, and so their pronouncements of the injury the opponent would receive were taken seriously. The songs, usually sung extempore, therefore became statements of prowess, strength, manhood, and identity. The stick-fights represented a ritualized violence and were an expression of the sexual energy of a frustrated people. It was in this context that the calypso developed. The chantwells' songs became a sort of calypso war as each tried to outdo the other, and it is from this tradition that the "picong" (from the French "piquant," meaning stinging or biting) and the "grand charge" (empty and melodramatic boasting and threatening) associated with calypso developed. Because of its connection with stick-fighting, calypso was originally associated with a particular section of the lower classes called the "jamette group." "Jamette" was the French patois word for "diametre," French for "diameter," and referred to the group that fell below the diameter of social decency. The calypso was therefore a music developed by outcasts challenging their position and asserting their identity. However, after emancipation, the development of the calypso became closely aligned to the development of Carnival that had previously been a festival for the white Creole upper classes during slavery but had now changed to a celebration observed largely by underprivileged blacks.

Calypso is an oral art form and often employs the dialect of the people. It is therefore performance-centered, with the audience playing an important part. Showmanship is therefore an important part of the calypsonians' performance and is reflected in their characteristic gaudy dress in the latest fashions or in costumes depicting the theme of their song. The calypsonians also often choose sobriquets to reflect their invincibility, frequently choosing names of famous warriors or other names suggesting invincibility and combat such as Duke of Wellington, Lord Executor, Atilla the Hun, and the Roaring Lion. Others use the titles "Lord" or "Mighty," as in Mighty Spoiler, Lord Kitchener, and Mighty Sparrow, to suggest grandeur.

The calypso has traditionally been considered a male-dominated arena, although some research has shown that women have sung calypsos since the nineteenth century, and there has been mention of at least two female chantwells. Two other known calypsonians singing around the time of World War II were Lady Iere and Lady Thelma. After that, there were very few female calypsonians until the 1960s, when Calypso Rose began singing and was later joined by other female artistes.

The emergence of tents that organize and manage the performances have been a significant development in the calypso arena. In the early days after emancipation, the masqueraders and the calypsonians would gather in a barrack yard tent to practice and to showcase their talents in the weeks before Carnival. These humble yard tents, however, have since developed into the sophisticated and well-organized tents of today. The tents are also linked to the various calypso competitions that developed out of this tradition. The two most important competitions are the Calypso Monarch, held on Dimanche Gras night, or Big Sunday, that precedes the revelry on Carnival Monday morning, and the Road March. While the Calypso Monarch is a formal competition, the Road March is decided on the basis of popularity, that is, the most played song by the Carnival bands on Carnival Monday and Tuesday. It tends to be more of a party song suited to "jumping up" on Carnival Day.

Gisele Ramphaul

References

Best, Curwen. *Barbadian Popular Music and the Politics of Caribbean Culture.* Rochester, VT: Schenkman Books, 1999.

Elder, J. D. *The Calypso and Its Morphology.* Port of Spain, Trinidad, and Tobago: National Cultural Council, 1973.

The Roaring Lion (Rafael de Leon). *Calypso from France to Trinidad: 800 Years of History.* San Juan, Trinidad: General Printers of San Juan, 1987.

Rohlehr, Gordon. *Calypso and Society in Pre-Independence Trinidad.* Port-of-Spain, Trinidad and Tobago: Gordon Rohlehr, 1990.

Warner, Keith Q. *The Trinidad Calypso: A Study of the Calypso as Oral Literature.* London: Heinemann, 1982.

CAMEROON

Cameroon is an African nation with an important regional, ethnic, cultural, linguistic, colonial, and independence history relating to Africa and the Americas. Although technically a Central African country, Cameroon is a bridge zone between Central and West Africa because it possesses physical and cultural features of both regions. In fact, Cameroon is so richly varied in its physical and cultural features that it is commonly referred to as "Mini Africa" or the "Crossroads of Africa." The capital of Cameroon is Yaoundé; the largest city is Douala.

Slightly bigger than the American state of California, Cameroon boasts five distinct geographical regions: the Coastal Lowlands, the Southern Plateau, the Central or Adamawa Plateau, the Western Highlands, and the Northern Lowlands. These five geographical regions encompass three climate zones: the tropical zone in the south, the savannah zone in the center, and the semi-arid zone in the north. Each of these three climate zones sustains a different agriculture. The primary crops of each region include: bananas, cocoa, coffee, palm oil, tobacco, and timber in the tropical zone; cotton, rice, and maize in the savannah zone; and cotton, maize, and millet in the semi-arid zone. Cameroon is also home to Mount Cameroon (13,428 feet), which is an active lava volcano and West Africa's tallest mountain.

The history of the region that is now Cameroon extends far beyond any written record. Indeed, archaeological evidence indicates that the region has been inhabited by humans for 30,000 years. Archaeological evidence also suggests that a large civilization thrived near the shores of Lake Chad in northern Cameroon around 500 BCE. By the thirteenth and fourteenth centuries, numerous farming societies occupied the region. These societies were connected through an extensive trade network in which cowry shells and *bikie* (small metal rods) were used as forms of currency.

The region's first European encounter occurred in 1472 with the arrival of Portuguese explorers. Upon discovering a wealth of shrimp in the region's estuaries, these Portuguese explorers named the area Rio dos Camaros, or River of Shrimp, a name that later gave rise to the contemporary name, Cameroon. By the sixteenth century the Portuguese, Dutch, French,

British, and Spanish were involved in a large-scale slave trade, whereby inhabitants of Cameroon were systematically captured, transported across the Atlantic Ocean in the hulls of ships, and sold in the New World as slaves. With the abolition of the slave trade in the early 1800s, the British and Germans diverted their attention to the development of trade in commodities such as ivory and rubber.

Although Cameroon's earliest interactions with European powers began in the late fifteenth century, it was not until 1884, when the Duala kings signed a treaty with Germany, that the colonial era in Cameroon officially began. Despite Cameroonian resistance, Germany remained the colonial power until World War I (1914–1918), when it was defeated by the Allied Powers (including, among others, Britain, France, Italy, and the United States).

In 1919 the League of Nations produced a mandate that divided Cameroon between Great Britain and France. France received the larger eastern half. In addition to supervising the continued exploitation of Cameroon's resources, colonial administrators in French and British Cameroon built infrastructure (roads and bridges) and implemented land regulations, tax and inheritance laws, crop marketing systems, marriage reform, and Westernized educational systems.

The end of World War II saw the birth of several Cameroonian political parties and a demand for national independence. On January 1, 1960, the French government granted independence to French Cameroon, with Ahmadou Adhidjo, the founder and leader of the Union Camerounaise (UC), as its first president. In 1961, with the help of the United Nations,

British Cameroon organized a referendum in which the northern half voted to join Nigeria and the southern half voted to join Cameroon. Soon afterward, Cameroon became a federal republic with ten provinces, two prime ministers, and one president. In 1972 the creation of a national constitution replaced the federal republic with a united republic. Ten years later Adhidjo, citing health problems, resigned from his post and handed the presidency to his prime minister, Paul Biya. Biya created his own political party, the Rassemblement démocratique du people camerounais (RDPC; Democratic rally of the Cameroon people), and offered single party rule as a solution to the country's divisive regional and ethnic differences. In 1991 Biya was pressured to authorize a constitutional amendment that established a multiparty system and, in 1992, the nation held its first multiparty elections. In 2007, after three presidential elections (all of which have been criticized for being rigged), Paul Biya continues to hold the Cameroonian presidency.

Cameroon's primary exports include petroleum, agricultural products (cocoa, coffee, and tobacco), and timber. With its rich oil resources and prime agricultural conditions, Cameroon was one of sub-Saharan Africa's most prosperous countries from the 1960s to the early 1980s. However, the fall of cash-crop prices in the early 1980s triggered an economic crisis from which Cameroon has yet to fully recover. In the late 1980s Cameroon turned to the International Monetary Fund (IMF) and the World Bank for help. In response, the IMF and the World Bank implemented a Structural Adjustment Program (SAP). Although designed to stimulate long-term development, the immediate measures called for by the SAP—currency devaluation, increases in food prices and interest rates, decreases in wages and hiring rates, trade liberalization, removal of input subsidies, and decreases in budget deficits—created further economic hardships for Cameroonians.

With a population of 16 million, Cameroon boasts as many as 250 ethnic groups, each with its own language, spiritual practices, and sociopolitical structures. The majority ethnic groups of each region included the Tikar, Bamoun, and Bamileke in the west; the Fulbe, Massa, and Muktale in the north; the Douala, Bakweri, and Isubu in the south; and the Makakozine in the east. While Cameroon's official languages are French and English, most Cameroonians, regardless of ethnicity, speak two or three indigenous languages. In 2005 the distribution of religion among Cameroonians was as follows: 40 percent indigenous religions, 40 percent Christianity, and 20 percent Islam. Although the state wields great political influence in Cameroon, traditional political structures, such as the chiefdom, still play an important role. For example, among the chiefdoms of the Bamileke, the chief, or *fon,* mediates local disputes and oversees the general well-being of the chiefdom. The *fon's* state-related responsibilities include the signing of birth, marriage, and death certificates and the supervision of tax collection.

Given its great linguistic and cultural diversity, it is not surprising that Cameroon is rich in music and dance. Two of the most popular music styles are the Makossa and the Bi-Kutsi. Both music styles are accompanied by a specific dance of the same name. The Makossa was made popular by Cameroonian musicians Petit Pays and Manu Dibango, and the Bi-Kutsi was made popular by Cameroonian musicians Les Têtes Brulées and Roger Bekono.

Cameroon's contribution to the literary world is significant. Among Cameroon's most famous writers are Mongo Beti and Calixthe Beyala. Mongo Beti (1932–2001) was a novelist and essayist who spent forty-two years of exile in Rouen, France. A tireless advocate for human rights and environmental protection, Beti's works include *Ville Cruelle* (1954), *Remember Ruben* (1974), and *L'histoire du fou* (1994). Calixthe Beyala (1964–) wrote her first novel, *C'est le soleil qui m'a brulée* (It is the Sun Which Has Burnt Me) (1987) at the age of twenty-three. Since then, she has published fourteen novels, all of which examine the experience of women in West Africa and France. Beyala resides in Paris with her husband and two children.

As the world becomes increasingly interconnected, people of all nationalities are making new homes in countries other than those of their birth. Cameroonians are no exception. Indeed, Cameroonians of all ages and occupations live everywhere from Paris, France, to Toronto, Canada, to Washington, D.C.

With 17,000 Cameroonian residents, France has the largest Cameroonian population outside of Cameroon. Cameroon's influence in France is notable. A walk through the Chateau Rouge quarter in Paris' eighteenth *arrondissement* (district) reveals numerous Cameroonian restaurants, boutiques, and markets. The Cameroonian community in France is distinguished by the fact that, among all other African communities in France, it has the greatest number of students seeking higher education.

Abigail Dumes

See also: Agriculture; Coffee; Colonialism; Decolonization, African; Diaspora; Exploration and Explorers, Africa; Fulani; International Monetary Fund; Religion (Africa); Slavery (History); World Bank

References

Barley, Nigel. *The Innocent Anthropologist: Notes from a Mud Hut.* London: British Museum Publications, 1983.

Bocquené, Henri. *Memoirs of a Mbororo: The Life of Ndudi Umaru, Fulani Nomad of Cameroon.* New York: Berghahn Books, 2002.

Delancey, Mark W. *Cameroon: Dependence and Independence.* Boulder, CO: Westview Press, 1989.

Fowler, Ian, and David Zeitlyn, eds. *African Crossroads: Intersections between History and Anthropology in Cameroon.* Providence, RI: Berghahn Books, 1996.

Konigs, Piet, and Francis B. Nyamnjoh. *Negotiating an Anglophone Identity: A Study of the Politics of Recognition and Representation.* Boston: Brill Books, 2003.

CANADA (AFRICADIAN CULTURE)

When George Elliott Clarke's two-volume anthology, *Fire on the Water: An Anthology of Black Nova Scotian Writing,* was published in 1991, he suggested the existence of a unique, ethnoregionally defined Atlantic Canadian diasporic culture of African descent: Africadian culture. The anthology traced this claim to 1785 and, by covering two centuries, suggested a continuity of textualization. It claimed this continuity as ethnic coherence under a heading that, as Clarke admitted, was his own coinage: "Africadian." The term is witty as well as ironic. A compound neologism, "Africadian" combines the African background with the Mi'kmaq Indians' word for "land," which the early French colonizers took over to name the colony L'Acadie in the sixteenth century. Both constitutive parts denote territory rather than race, pointing to the fact that Africadian culture has a distinct land base. The survivors and refugees of the War of Independence (1776–1783) and the War of 1812 (ending in 1815) who cast their lot with the British rather than stay in the United States settled in free communities, where they were joined by escapees on the Underground Railroad.

In view of the rather small body of texts collected in the anthology dating to before 1900, the claim to an ethnoregional cultural identity is not easily supported diachronically as long as only literature is concerned. Many of the extant texts are sermons, autobiographical sketches, and minutes of Baptist meetings. However, together with texts from oral traditions (orature) they establish the basis, which Clarke has described as "sermon, song, and story," on which the existence of Africadian culture since its early days, and Africadian literature as a predominantly post–World War II phenomenon, was founded and continues to prosper. While the constituent parts are similar to the tradition found in African American communities in the United States, it needs to be noted that their diasporic situation, and the abolition of slavery in British North America before it was abolished in the United States, provided a considerable difference in cultural context—for example, anthropologist Arthur H. Fauset noted during a research trip in Nova Scotia that many Africadians had never heard of the Brer Rabbit tales popularized in the United States by white writers like Joel Chandler Harris. The adherence to and practice of Baptist beliefs, and the blending of the inherited cultures of the Africas and Americas with British North American, German, Acadian French, and Mi'kmaq Indian elements, resulted in a unique cultural formation.

The event that contributed substantially to the construction of a historical and political identity out of the roughly two-dozen settlements throughout the province was ironically one of destruction: one of the largest African settlements in the province was Africville, a densely populated but impoverished settlement at the north end of the Narrows, where the channel between Halifax and Dartmouth opens into the Bedford Basin. Dating back to the early 1800s and badly damaged in the terrible Halifax explosion of 1917, Africville had suffered a long history of neglect. This changed in the late 1950s, when Halifax city officials decided on improving the living conditions of Africville's inhabitants. They condemned and subsequently razed Africville. The inhabitants were moved to new housing projects with better sanitation and living conditions.

Ironically, the cultural identity of the obliterated settlement soon started to manifest itself anew in creative formats. The destruction of Africville, including the Campbell Road Church, bulldozed under the cover of night to prevent protests, resulted in a retroactive wave of identification with Africville as an imagined cultural and spiritual center. Young Africadians who had been children at the time of the resettlement, or who like George Elliott Clarke did not even have personal firsthand experience of living in Africville, were the first generation that received an education and training in the liberal arts, which enabled them to voice an artistic expression of their cultural identity that became heard not only within but also and increasingly outside their community. The marginalization of Nova Scotia within Canada, and the double marginalization of Africadians in the Maritimes, ensured a growing audience and interpretive community after the 1980s, in keeping with the increasing

self-confidence of Canadian writing on the whole.

Since the publication of *Fire on the Water*, Clarke's lobbying and the superior quality of many of the Africadian literary and other artistic creations have directed considerable reader response as well as a certain amount of critical attention to this unique ethnoregional formation. Early-twentieth-century figures like the opera singer Portia White and the African United Baptist Association moderator Dr. Pearleen Oliver have attained the status of cultural icons for the community, and new authors, playwrights, and artists are inscribing themselves into the Maritime Canadian cultural fabric, aided by the fact that a number of writers collected already in volume 2 of *Fire on the Water* are really multitalents, like actors Walter Borden and Frederick Ward, filmmaker Sylvia Hamilton, and singers Delvina Bernard and Raymond L. Parker. The members of the female quartet *Four the Moment* are highly successful singers of a unique blend of modern artistic song, spirituals, blues, and Nova Scotian folk tunes. Among the themes central to contemporary Africadian literature, Africville is gradually being superseded by a more global outlook for cultural orientation. However, the central function of Africville as a sociohistorical point of integration should not be underestimated. Interestingly enough, most Africadian authors writing on Africville took an ambivalent stance. In George Elliott Clarke's poem, "Campbell Road Church" (1983), Africville is introduced as a "beautiful Canaan of stained glass and faith," but the lurking nostalgia is immediately subverted in the next lines: "made shacktown of shattered glass and shame, / rats rustling like a mayor's robe." Rats also play an instrumental role in George Boyd's terrifying teleplay *Consecrated Ground* (1999). David Woods's poem "Africville: A Requiem" recounts the impossibilities of adjustment after the relocation, notably for older people. The closest one gets to straight nostalgia is the recreated walk through the settlement in Charles R. Saunders's 1989 story, "A Visit to Africville, Summer 1959."

Africa and the relation to Africa as a focal moment of identity creation features more prominently in the poems of Maxine Tynes than in the work of other Africadian poets and writers. A Dartmouth, Nova Scotia, teacher, she has to date published four volumes of poetry, all of superior quality. Feminist and African themes dominate her volume, *Borrowed Beauty* (1987); in *The Door of My Heart* (1993), Tynes explores the poetic power of her polio disability in hauntingly beautiful images, drawn from experience in good humor and self-irony.

Irony and a subtle sense of humor are also a trademark of George Elliott Clarke's poetry and prose. To this mélange he adds a fascinating mixture of a traditional tone, showing awareness of both oral forms and African American literary models, and a "high" tone, informed by Clarke's extremely wide learnedness and appreciation of world literature from the classics through the Italian and French Renaissance to the British and American modernists. Before *Fire on the Water* he had already published a highly acclaimed volume of poetry, *Saltwater Spirituals and Deeper Blues* (1983), which already showed distinct traces of this form. The next volume, *Whylah Falls* (1990),was simply a masterpiece. It has since been turned into a CBC radio drama and provided the basis for a stage play in 1997. The opera libretto *Beatrice Chancy* (1999) playfully reenacts the classical theme of *The Cenci* (a verse drama by Shelley and given several operatic treatments), while *Québécité: A Jazz Libretto in Three Cantos* (2003) ventures into operatic jazz. *Blue* (2001) introduced a much sadder tone and pessimistic viewpoint in his poetry, and in the novel *George and Rue* (2005), Clarke followed the story of two of his cousins who were tried for murder in rural New Brunswick in 1950.

In 2001 Clarke won the prestigious Governor General's Award for poetry (for *The Execution Poems* [2000]). Other Africadian writers like Maxine Tynes, Faith Nolan, and Sylvia Hamilton have also received stipends, prizes, and public acclaim. With their success, and with the resulting self-confidence, Africadia has come to serve, twenty years after its "invention" by George Elliott Clarke, as a common denominator for the cultural self-expression of Maritime people of African descent: a clandestine group within the Canadian multicultural patchwork with an ethnoregional identity that is both unique and productive.

Wolfgang Hochbruck

See also: Birchtown; Nova Scotia, African American Diaspora in; Nova Scotia, Black Refugees in

References

Clarke, George Elliott, ed. *Fire on the Water: An Anthology of Black Nova Scotian Writing.* 2 vols. Lawrencetown Beach, NS: Pottersfield Press, 1991.

Dalhousie Review 77, no. 2 (1997). Special Issue: Africadian Literature.

Davidson, Arnold E. "Whylah Falls: The Africadian Poetry of George Elliott Clarke." In *Down East: Critical Essays on Contemporary Maritime Canadian Literature,* edited by Wolfgang Hochbruck and James O. Taylor. Trier, Germany: Wissenschaftlicher Verlag Trier. 1996.

CANDOMBLÉ

Candomblé is a Brazilian syncretic religion of West African origins. The emergence of the religious practices of Candomblé in the New World coincided with the relocation of Yoruba, Ewe, and Bantu peoples, who were taken from their African homelands, enslaved, and transported to Brazil by ship. (This began as early as the sixteenth century and continued into the late nineteenth century, when slavery was abolished in Brazil.) Candomblé became a particularly African form of cultural and spiritual resistance to slavery and served as an affirmation and unification of its members' distinct cultural identities. Under slavery, practitioners of Candomblé succeeded in identifying the Catholic iconography of the saints with their own gods and therefore could remain faithful to their own religious principles while appearing to be true Catholic converts.

Followers of present-day Candomblé believe in a pantheon of gods or spirits, often called *orixás,* in accordance with Yoruba tradition. Ultimately, Candomblé acknowledges a strong relationship between human beings and nature, and the *orixás* function as mediators who intervene in everyday life in order to improve human experience, both physically and spiritually.

Their religious rites and ceremonies take place in *terreiros* and are officiated by spiritual guides, both male (*pai de santo* or *babalorixá*) and female (*mãe de santo* or *ialorixá*), literally father or mother of the saints. Most notably, it is women, rather than men, who have traditionally held the more significant leadership roles in Candomblé. Professed believers, known as *filhos* and *filhas de santo,* or sons and daughters of the saints, are often initiated into a lifelong relationship with certain *orixás,* to whom they pay tribute through ceremonial dances throughout the calendar year. During Candomblé ceremonies, it is believed that *orixás* manifest themselves by possessing or mounting the bodies of the *filhos* and *filhas de santo,* and these manifestations are later interpreted by the *pai de santo* or *mãe de santo.* Some of the most celebrated *orixás* are Iemanjá (goddess of the sea), Xangô (god of lightning and thunder), Ogun (god of war), and Iansã (goddess of the souls of the dead). Each *orixá* has his or her own particular cries, sacred offerings, holy objects, preferred colors and special attire.

Nicole L. Sparling

See also: Brazilian Culture; Orisha; Religion (Africa); Voodoo; Yoruba

References

Curto, José C., and Renée Soulodre-La France, eds. *Africa and the Americas: Interconnections during the Slave Trade.* Trenton, NJ: Africa World Press, 2005.

Greenfield, Sidney M., and André Droogers. *Reinventing Religions: Syncretism and Transformation in Africa and the Americas.* Lanham, MD: Rowman & Littlefield, 2001.

Pierson, Donald. *O Candomblé da Baía.* Curitiba, Brazil: Editora Guaíra Limitada, 1942.

CAPE COAST CASTLE

Cape Coast Castle was the center of the gold and transatlantic slave trade in the sixteenth through eighteenth centuries. As European trade along the Gold Coast intensified in the seventeenth century, Cape Coast Castle emerged as one of the most important trade enclaves of the region. After changing hands several times, the castle became the administrative center of England's African trade and in the nineteenth century played a role in the creation of England's Gold Coast colony.

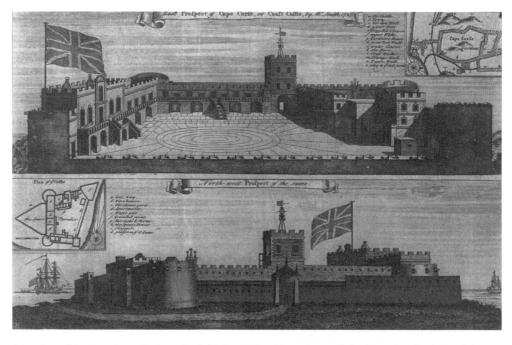

Two views of the Cape Coast Castle on the Gold Coast, West Africa. Originally built in 1653 for the Swedish Africa Company for trade in timber and gold, the Castle was later used in the transatlantic slave trade. (Library of Congress)

When the Portuguese first arrived on the Gold Coast during the late fifteenth and early sixteenth centuries, they called the area Cabo Corso, meaning "short cape." The English later changed it to Cape Coast. Cabo Corso was a short distance from the first Portuguese trade enclave on the Gold Coast, Elmina, established to serve as a base to acquire gold. In 1655 at Cabo Corso, the Swedes built their fort, Carolusburg, which changed hands numerous times before the English finally gained control of it in 1664. The English captured Cape Coast Castle to establish a coastal presence not only for gold but for the growing slave trade. After its creation, the Royal African Company decided to make the castle its coastal administrative center and quickly began work to rebuild, expand, and strengthen the original Swedish structure. as with all of the other

European trade enclaves being created along the Gold Coast, the English did not possess enough power to take the land from the local peoples and were therefore, until the imperialism of the late nineteenth century, tenants. This meant that the English made regular ground rent payments for the land upon which the castle stood, along with numerous customs payments. As the English gained control of and started to re-build the castle, they concurrently began to develop a relationship with the local Fetu peoples. Cape Coast Castle stood upon a rock jutting out into the water, and it was this rock that housed the local Fetu god Tabarah and his wife, Neyeir. After the Fante brought the Fetu into the Fante confederation, the English relied upon the Fetu to maintain their economic relationship with the Fante. When the Company of Merchants Trading to Africa replaced the

Royal African Company in 1750, it found the castle to be in a decrepit state and engaged in a long and expensive period of rebuilding and expanding it. They had, by the end of the slave trade, turned it into one of the best built and strongest structures on the coast. After a series of riots at Cape Coast at the turn into the nineteenth century, Cape Coast Castle served as a new administrative center for the development of England's Gold Coast colony.

Ty M. Reese

See also: Company of Merchants Trading to Africa; Fetu of Cape Coast; Royal African Company; Slavery (History)

References

Daaku, Kwame Yeboa. *Trade and Politics on the Gold Coast, 1600–1720: A Study of the African Reaction to European Trade.* Oxford: Clarendon Press, 1970.

Davies, K.G. *The Royal African Company.* New York: Atheneum, 1970.

Lawrence, A. W. *Trade Castles and Forts of West Africa.* Stanford, CA: Stanford University Press, 1964.

CAPE VERDE

A group of fifteen small islands, the Republic of Cape Verde is a former Portuguese colony with a population of approximately 482,000. Colonized in 1495, it was one of the first Portuguese colonies in Africa. As with many African island nations, its historical role as a transit point for transoceanic trade was considerable. Indeed, most of the land is not arable and the nation suffers regularly from droughts; consequently, the economic fortunes of the islands are closely tied to maritime trade.

Close to the West African coast, Cape Verde has had strong historical ties both westward to the Americas and eastward to the African continent. By the sixteenth century the islands were among the major transit points for the transatlantic slave trade conducted by European nations. The African coast east of Cape Verde soon became known as the Slave Coast. Cape Verde prospered as a place where ships could be easily resupplied as they crossed the Atlantic. By the early eighteenth century, American ships involved in the slave trade and in whaling were also arriving in Cape Verde. Even after the end of the slave trade, Cape Verde would keep its role as a port for transatlantic shipping.

Additionally, after the end of slavery, many Cape Verdeans emigrated to Portugal, the United States, and South America. In the United States, many settled in the New England port cities of New Bedford, Massachusetts, and Providence, Rhode Island. More generally, the nineteenth and twentieth centuries have seen what could be called a Cape Verdean diaspora as people sought better economic opportunities abroad. Now more Cape Verdeans and their descendants live abroad than live on the islands themselves. Money returned from individuals and families abroad make up a considerable amount of the nation's income. The New England communities of Cape Verdeans still thrive today. Indeed, the significant Cape Verdean presence in New England has led Cape Verde to maintain a consulate in Boston, Massachusetts, as well as an embassy in Washington, D.C.

With its longstanding colonial history, it is not surprising that Cape Verde, despite its small size, would also give birth to a leading anticolonial figure, Amilcar Cabral, and be a significant participant in anticolonial struggle in the years after World War II. Born in Cape Verde, Cabral was a founder of the African Party for the Independence of Guinea and Cape Verde

(PAIGC) (Partido Africano de Indepencia de Guinea e Capo Verde). By 1960 the PAIGC would be active in the war for liberation against the Portuguese in Guinea-Bissau. This war occurred in the context both of Guinea-Bissau's fight for independence and the cold war conflict between the United States and Soviet Union; PAIGC forces were supplied by Soviet-allied nations.

Cape Verde's post–cold war history has been peaceful. Since 1992, Cape Verde has been a multiparty democracy. Its stability has enhanced its relations with the United States, and in 2006, North Atlantic Treaty Organization (NATO) military forces conducted their first training operations in Africa on Cape Verde's island of São Vincente.

Richard Juang

See also: Africa, West; Cabral, Amilcar; Immigration, United States; Portuguese Empire

References

Halter, Marilyn. *Between Race and Ethnicity: Cape Verdean American Immigrants, 1860–1965.* Urbana: University of Illinois Press, 1993.

Lobban, Richard A. *Cape Verde: Crioulo Colony to Independent Nation.* Boulder, CO: Westview Press, 1998.

CARIBBEAN ARTISTS MOVEMENT

The Caribbean Artists Movement (CAM) (1966–1972) was a British-centered arts movement of the 1960s and 1970s, seeking a new aesthetic that reflected the rich cultural heritage of the West Indies. CAM grew out of the cultural dynamic of West Indians exiled in London during the 1960s and the early 1970s. The organization found inspiration in the Harlem Renaissance movement of the 1920s in the United States in that it brought together visual artists, performers, and critics seeking a new aesthetic for Caribbean arts that would reflect the rich cultural heritage of the West Indies. Its founders contended that the musical elements in calypso and ska corresponded to a jazz aesthetic in the Caribbean novel. CAM existed officially for only six years, from 1966 to 1972, but it advanced Caribbean and black British writing, art, criticism, and publishing in a dynamic and far-reaching way. CAM provided a public space, through open meetings and conferences, to debate the role of the arts in the context of an emerging "postcolonial" identity. Jamaican cultural critic Stuart Hall explained to a CAM meeting in 1968 that "The task of any intellectual and any writer in relation to the next generation of West Indians in Britain is to help them see, speak, understand and name the process that they are going through" (Jaggi, 2000, p. 8).

CAM's activities were extended through its members' travels back and forth between Britain and the Caribbean. CAM's journal *Savacou,* edited by Edward Kamau Brathwaite, provided a necessary platform for creative writing and cultural criticism, dedicating whole issues to new experimentation in form, such as the issue titled "New Poets from Jamaica—An Anthology" in 1979–1980.

The founding members of the organization were Edward Kamau Brathwaite, John La Rose, and Andrew Salkey in 1966. Many well-known figures were associated with the movement, including C. L. R. James, Stuart Hall, Wilson Harris, Ronald Moody, Aubrey Williams, Kenneth Ramchand, Gordon Rohlehr, Louis James, Ivan Van Sertima, James Berry, Donald Hinds, Linton Kwesi Johnson, Christopher Laird, and Errol Lloyd. By the time CAM members came together in London, the Caribbean arts were established through a substantial quantity of fiction, poetry, plays, and art exhibitions in Britain. In spite of a growing market, the production of new material was not matched by the critical attention that it deserved.

Anne Walmsley was an original member, and she was able to use her insider knowledge and contacts later to research and publish the history of the movement in *The Caribbean Artists Movement* (1992). There she addressed the movement's absence from cultural histories of the period in Britain and in the Caribbean. She explained the conditions that prompted CAM's formation and charts the development of the movement through its subsequent public readings, critical debates, exhibitions, conferences, and publications. A number of women artists, writers, and performers (for example, Althea McNish, Merle Hodge, and Marina Maxwell) as well as wives and partners of CAM activists contributed to the organization's success, although the list of key members as they appear in the blurb of Walmsley's book would suggest that CAM was an exclusively male club. CAM also circulated and publicly debated the scholarship of Lucille Mathurin-Mair and Elsa Goveia.

CAM's undoubted achievement lies in its nurturing of talented new Caribbean writers, artists, critics, and historians and in circulating, through its journal *Savacou,* debates on work that would otherwise have been produced in a critical void. CAM inspired the next generation of black British artists, including Linton Kwesi Johnson and Fred D'Aguiar. It ensured that Caribbean literature, history, and culture would be taught on the Caribbean Examination Council's (CXC) school curricula. The movement also strongly influenced the formation of the specialist publishing houses New Beacon Books and Bogle-L'Ouverture. The organization found it difficult to maintain London as its activity base with a membership scattered throughout the Caribbean, Britain, Europe, and North America. In 1972 official activities declined, although unofficial networks continued to be effective, operating through members like Andrew Salkey, who maintained an address book of the most significant Caribbean artists throughout the world.

Sandra Courtman

See also: Brathwaite, Kamau; Caribbean Literature; D'Aguiar, Fred; James, Cyril Lionel Robert; Johnson, Linton Kwesi

References

Francis, Donette. "Cosmopolitan Patriots: West Indian Intellectuals between Home and Metropole." PhD dissertation, New York University, 2001.

Jaggi, Maya Jaggi. "Stuart Hall: Prophet at the Margins." *Guardian,* July 8, 2000.

Patterson, Nerys. "Letter: The English Cradle of Caribbean Artists." *The Independent,* November 16, 1993.

Walmsley, Anne. *The Caribbean Artists Movement 1966–1972.* London: New Beacon Books, 1992.

Walmsley, Anne. "A Sense of Community: Kamau Brathwaite and the Caribbean Artists Movement." In *The Art of Kamau Brathwaite,* edited by Stewart Brown. Bridgend, UK: Seren, 1995.

CARIBBEAN COMMUNITY AND COMMON MARKET

Established in 1973, the Caribbean Community and Common Market (CARICOM) is an international trade group representing Caribbean nations that promotes economic development and social welfare. CARICOM was established by the Treaty of Chaguaramas, which came into effect on August 1, 1973. CARICOM was the culmination of fifteen years of lobbying for regional integration, coming in wake of the failure of the West Indies Federation (1958–1962) and the establishment of the Caribbean Free Trade Association (CARIFTA) in 1965.

CARICOM has fifteen full members: Antigua and Barbuda, the Bahamas, Barbados, Belize, Dominica, Grenada, Guyana, Haiti, Jamaica, Montserrat, St. Kitts and Nevis, St. Lucia, Suriname, St. Vincent and the Grenadines, and Trinidad, and Tobago. Associate members include the British Virgin Islands, the Turks and Caicos Islands, Anguilla, the Cayman Islands, and Bermuda.

CARICOM aims at helping members achieve economic and social integration. Some of its objectives include improving standards of living and work by developments in health, education, transportation, and telecommunications. It also seeks to expand trade and boost international competitiveness by leveling the global playing field for member states.

CARICOM has created several institutions designed to carry out these objectives. These include the Conference of Heads of Government and the Community of Council Ministers. The Conference is the main arm of CARICOM and the final authority for important matters. Its decisions are generally taken unanimously. The Council is the second-highest organization of CARICOM and is responsible for formulating policies concerning cooperation in areas such as education, health, labor, and foreign policies.

The Conference and the Council are assisted by the Council for Trade and Economic Development, the Council for Foreign and Community Relations, the Council for Human and Social Development, and the Council for Finance and Planning. Other major bodies of CARICOM are the Legal Affairs Committee, the Budget Committee, and the Committee of Central Bank Governors. Institutions under the auspices of CARICOM include the Caribbean Disaster Emergency Response Agency, Caribbean Meteorological Institute, Caribbean Environment Health Institute, Caribbean Agriculture Research and Development Institute, and Assembly of Caribbean Community Parliamentarians. Associate institutes of CARICOM include the Caribbean Development Bank, University of Guyana, University of the West Indies, Caribbean Law Institute, and Secretariat of the Organization of Eastern Caribbean States.

Though CARICOM has advocated a regional vision, the export economies of its members still depend heavily on nonmember countries. Nevertheless, CARICOM has made major strides toward attaining its objectives. The development of the Caribbean Single Market and Economy (CSME), for example, was designed to represent a single economic space where people, goods, services, and capital move freely and so enable members to lobby collectively on the international stage. The Treaty of Chaguaramas was revised in 2001 to facilitate this; the revision included the establishment of the Caribbean Court of Justice (CCJ) to settle disputes relating to the CSME and serve as an appellate court for member states that have severed ties with the Privy Council in the United Kingdom.

Though the Caribbean is multicultural and multiethnic, the majority of its people are of African descent, and thus African cultural retentions are found in all aspects of Caribbean society. In recognition of its cultural and historical ties with Africa, CARICOM has sought cooperation with African nations. Members of CARICOM were very vocal in their opposition to apartheid in South Africa and the latter's occupation of Namibia. After apartheid fell and Nelson Mandela became president of South Africa, CARICOM agreed on a regional mission to provide technical assistance and explore trade and investment relations with South Africa. Other efforts toward cooperation with South Africa have included launching the African Caribbean Business Development Bureau in 1998 to strengthen business ties between the two regions and various meetings between members of CARICOM and of the South African government, notably, Nelson Mandela and his successor, Thabo Mbeki.

Not only has CARICOM been forging links with South Africa, but also with other African nations. Members of CARICOM work with Africa as the African, Caribbean, and Pacific (ACP) Group of States to lobby the European Union (EU) in matters often relating to trade. Such relations are governed by the ACP-EU Conventions, that is, the four Lomé conventions and their successor, the ACP-EU Partnership Agreement, commonly referred to as the Contonou Agreement, signed in 2000. The ACP can be formally traced to the Georgetown Agreement, ratified in Guyana in 1975. The ACP states enjoy preferential treatment in the EU market for export products including sugar, rice, bananas, and groundnuts and receive aid in certain key areas of the environment, society, and economy.

Other notable achievements of CARICOM include the establishment in 1994 of the Association of Caribbean States and the Caribbean Forum of African, Caribbean, and Pacific States, which provide major linkages. At the global level, CARICOM strengthened its negotiating base, and in 1997, the Regional Negotiating Machinery was established to coordinate its external negotiations.

Nicole Plummer

See also: Barbados; Cuba; Jamaica; Mandela, Nelson; South Africa, History and Politics; West Indies Federation

References
Caribbean Community. *Basic Facts on CARICOM.* Georgetown, Guyana: Caribbean Community Secretariat, 1983.
Caribbean Community (CARICOM) Secretariat. http://www.caricom.org.
CARICOM Secretariat. *CARICOM: Our Caribbean Community: An Introduction.* Kingston, Jamaica: Ian Randle Publishers, 2004.
Pollard, Duke E., ed. *The CARICOM System: Basic Instruments.* Kingston, Jamaica: Caribbean Law Publishing, 2003.

CARIBBEAN LITERATURE

Caribbean literature includes Anglophone, Francophone, Hispanophone, and Dutch-language literature of the Caribbean, addresses cultural and historical influences, and fosters arts movements. The literature of the Caribbean reflects the complexities of the geography and history of the region. In its strictest sense, the Caribbean comprises those islands located in the Caribbean Sea. The languages spoken on each island reflect the history of colonization and enslavement, and former colonial languages often exist side by side with local creoles. The bulk of published literature has been in English, French, Spanish, and Dutch, although concerted efforts toward the development of literary creoles has fueled some artistic movements, and several significant works exist in Haitian creole and Papamientu (a Dutch creole). Before the end of the fifteenth century, the Caribbean islands were inhabited by Native Americans, primarily Arawak, Taino, and Carib. The rapid influx of European invaders in the early sixteenth century led to their extermination. In order to replace the labor force and exploit the islands for sugar, coffee, and other cultivation, the Europeans captured African men, women, and children who were brought to the Caribbean as slaves. Slavery was practiced into the nineteenth century, and in this period there was very little literary output.

The earliest literature was for the most part written by Europeans and their descendants and included historical logs. Mid- to late-nineteenth-century authors included the influential essays of the Cuban, José Martí, who championed a vision of a united Americas free of interference from United States and European expansionism into Latin America. By the mid- to late- nineteenth century Caribbean literature took the form of letters, the occasional journal; and, in the French-speaking islands, a form of exoticist sentimental writing called *doudouisme*. In the twentieth century, Caribbean literature has flowered prodigiously and has expanded and developed its definition by addressing the question of which languages and cultures of the Caribbean can articulate the themes and forms of its literature. One of its central concerns is the relationship between orality (primarily storytelling, which is an important part of folk heritage, as well as such musical forms as calypso) and writing. Other themes that pervade the literature are coming to terms with history and memory (particularly in light of the legacies of colonization and slavery), urbanization, relations between local and global politics, and the desire to record the spoken language of localized communities, be they Arawak, Haitian Creole, or Papamientu.

Anglophone

Among the generation of Caribbeans writing in English who came to prominence between the 1930s and the 1950s, the first to make a statement about the group's collective characteristics was George Lamming, a poet and broadcast journalist, in his book *The Pleasures of Exile* (1960). He noted the influence of a Trinidadian audience in encouraging already-established writers like Edgar Mittelholzer, Ernest Carr, Lafcadio Hearne, and Samuel Selvon (all of whom wrote primarily fiction). He also pointed to the common experience of this generation of writers, who had all chosen to leave the Caribbean for significant periods of time, most of them to reside in Britain. The historian and author C. L. R. James (best-known for his influential study of the Haitian Revolution, *The Black Jacobins* (1938) and his writings on cricket as a cultural phenomenon in the West Indies) and V. S. Naipaul (who would go on to become a Nobel Prize winner) were among these. Another important figure in early Anglophone Caribbean writing was Jean Rhys, whose novel *Wide Sargasso Sea* (1966) offered a different, West Indian perspective of the events in Charlotte Bronte's *Jane Eyre.*

Among the best-known poets are Derek Walcott, Edward Kamau Brathwaite, Wilson Harris, and Linton Kwesi Johnson. Walcott, of St. Lucia, who has also been a prolific playwright and prose writer, was awarded the Nobel Prize for Literature in 1993 following the appearance of his epic poem *Omeros* in 1990. Brathwaite, born in 1930 in Barbados, spent time in Ghana in 1955–1962. He advocated the use of "nation-language," which he described as an authentic linguistic expression of Caribbean cultures.

Later generations of writers include several key female figures who have led the way in thinking about gender equality in the context of the Caribbean. Paule Marshall and Michelle Cliff have explored psychological dimensions of women's experience, while Merle Hodge and Erna Brodber have been more concerned with cultural and linguistic questions. The region is also rich in theatrical traditions, especially on the island of Jamaica. One innovative group is the Sistren Theater Collective, which features collective writing by a theater group comprised of working-class women.

Travel writing also continues to be an important genre. Here, Caryl Phillips is recognized as a leading figure.

Francophone

The poet Saint-John Perse is sometimes regarded as the father of modern French Caribbean poetry. Born on the island of Guadeloupe to French colonial parents, he spent his youth in the Caribbean before emigrating to France and then traveled for much of his life. His adoption of ancient Greek forms influenced later poets who saw parallels between the Greek and Caribbean archipelagoes; however, his ancestry and emigration from the Caribbean make him a controversial father figure. Other key writers in the early development of Francophone literature include Suzanne Lacascade, whose novel, *Claire solange: Âme africaine,* appeared in 1920, and René Maran, who became the first black person to win France's literary prize, the Goncourt, for his

1921 novel, *Batouala.* Both novels explored (if obliquely) the relationship between Caribbean and African identities, a theme that became more prominent in the next generation of writers.

In the 1930s the Martiniquan, Aimé Césaire, and the French Guyanese, Léon Damas, joined with a fellow student at the Lycée Louis-le-Grand, the Senegalese Leopold Sedar Senghor, to establish a journal, *L'Étudiant noir* (The black student), which became the foundation for a movement known as Négritude. Négritude was a literary movement that sought to reclaim black cultures and reveal their inherent and historical creative potential. Négritude would develop differently in its African and Caribbean contexts. Aimé Césaire, René Ménil, Suzanne Césaire, and several others formed the *Revue tropique,* which appeared between 1941 and 1945. Aimé Césaire's best-known work, *Notebook of a Return to the Native Country* (1939) first drew the attention of the surrealist poet, André Breton, in 1941, and led to an association between the surrealist movement and some Négritude writers.

Another key early figure was the Haitian novelist, Jacques Roumain, who not only helped introduce Communism to Haiti but also, with his novel *Masters of the Dew* (completed in 1944; published in 1947), inaugurated a tradition of socialist realist fiction that portrayed the experiences of peasants. Later Haitian novelists of note include Marie Chauvet, René Depestre, and Edwidge Danticat, who writes in English and is part of the Caribbean diaspora in the United States.

The continued political status of Guadeloupe and Martinique as overseas departments of France has made for a complex understanding of identity on those islands. The first writer to try to theorize the implications of this ambiguous status is Edouard Glissant, whose essays in *Caribbean Discourse* (1981) complement a prolific career as a poet, novelist, playwright, and teacher. His notion of *antillanite* sought to characterize the essential identity of the French Caribbean. Other writers, such as Maryse Condé and Simone Schwartz-Bart, have taken a more ethnographic approach, valorizing the particular linguistic traits of the region, and have developed the art of storytelling as well. A more recent literary movement, the *creolistes,* led by Raphael Confiant, Patrick Chamoiseau, and Jean Bernabé, have made this approach even more pointed by seeking to change the use of the French language to reflect creole modes of thought.

Hispanophone

As mentioned above, the earliest key figure in modern Cuban letters was José Martí. Another important figure is Roberto Fernandez Retamar, whose essay on the Shakespearean character, Caliban, as a potential emblematic figure for the Americas has been highly influential. Among the poets, Nicolás Guillén, who advocated the *negrismo* movement in tandem with the Harlem Renaissance and the French Négritude movement, also did much to shape Caribbean poetic approaches to sound and to articulate a relationship with Africa. In addition to significant ethnomusicological work in Cuba, Guillén's contemporary, Alejo Carpentier, wrote several novels, among them, *Lost Footsteps* (1953) and *Concierto Barroco* (1974). Cuba continues to sustain a robust literary life with such authors as Nancy Morejón, Severo Sarduy, and Pedro Juan Guttiérez.

Puerto Rican literature also reflects the complexities of the island's history, and particularly the impact of urbanization on successive generations. The seminal dramatic work is René Marqués's *La Carreta* (1953) which tells the story of a peasant family faced with land dispossession. Poetry has flourished both on the island and among diasporic communities, particularly in the enclaves of New York-based descendants of Puerto Ricans, and has fostered the rise of performance poetry through the Nuyorican Poets Café. Well-known Boriqueño poets include Rosario Ferré, Edwin Torres, and Julia de Burgos. There are also important novelists, including Mayra Santos Febre and Luis Rafael Sánchez.

Dominican writers include the young fiction writer, Rita Indiana Hernandez. Two diasporic Dominican authors writing in English are Junot Díaz and Julia Alvarez.

Dutch

Caribbean literature in Dutch has garnered increasing critical attention in recent years. The first Dutch Caribbean novel was *My Black Sister,* by Cola Debrot (1935), while Frank Martinus Arion is the first author to have his works translated into English.

Tsitsi Jaji

See also: Brathwaite, Kamau; Caribbean Artists
   Movement; Cliff, Michelle; Condé, Maryse;
   Creole/Criollo; James, Cyril Lionel Robert;
   Johnson, Linton Kwesi; Marshall, Paule;
   Martí, José; Négritude; Walcott, Derek

References

Benitez-Rojo, Antonio. *The Repeating Island:
   The Caribbean and the Postmodern
   Perspective.* Translated by J. Maraniss.
   Durham, NC: Duke University Press,
   1996.

Gikandi, Simon. *Writing in Limbo: Modernism
   and Caribbean Literature.* Ithaca, NY:
   Cornell University Press, 1992.

Glissant, Edouard. *Le discours antillais.* Paris: Gallimard, 1981.

Lamming, George. *The Pleasures of Exile.* London; New York: Allison and Busby, 1960.

Richardson, Michael, ed. *Refusal of the Shadow: Surrealism and the Caribbean.* Translated by Krzystztof Fijalkowski and Michael Richardson. New York: Verso, 1996.

Van Neck-Yoder, Hilda. "Introduction: Special Issue on Caribbean Literature from Suriname, the Netherlands Antilles, Aruba, and the Netherlands." *Callaloo* 21, no. 3 (Summer 1998): 441–446.

CARNIVAL, LATIN AMERICAN

Carnival has been celebrated throughout Latin America since colonial times. The best-known places for Carnival celebration are Bolivia, the Caribbean, Cuba, and Colombia. Some of these different types of Carnival syncretize different cultural traditions: European, African, and Amerindian.

One of the most traditional Carnival sites in Latin America is the city of Oruro, in central Bolivia. It has its origin in the Andine invocations to Pachamama, the Mother Earth, to the Tío Supay, the Devil, and to the Virgen de la Candelária, or Virgen del Socavon, the saint patroness of the local miners. The Oruro Carnival is celebrated on the Saturday before Ash Wednesday, when more than forty groups wearing lavishly colorful traditional costumes and masks perform for the audience different styles of dances and music over a five-kilometer-long (3.1-mile-long) course. The best-known of these dances is La Diablada, which represents the fight between good and evil as personified by the Archangel Gabriel and the Devil, respectively. The dance of the Caporales has its origin in Afro-Bolivian traditions and makes fun of the black overseer of slaves of the Yunas. The dance called El Tinku represents the encounter between fighters. The Morenada is a music and dance style from the fringes of the Bolivian Andes that possesses both African and native elements. The black and white mask of the Morenada dancer represents the ethnic hybridity of the Bolivian people. Tobas is the dance style of an ethnic group from the mouth of the River Pilcomayo, and it represents its warring attitude in the defense of ancestral traditions. The whole celebration takes around eighteen hours.

Carnival in Colombia has existed since the eighteenth century. Although of European origin, it has incorporated African and Amerindian elements. Carnival was censored by the Colombian authorities in the main cities of the country—Bogotá, Cartagena, and Popayan—until the turn into the twentieth-first century. It has been celebrated in Barranquilla, in northern Colombia, and Pasto, in the south. The Carnival of Barranquilla, by far the most traditional of Colombia, takes place in the four days before Lent. Traditional dance styles are performed during the Barranquilla Carnival, such as Cumbia and Garabato, and on Saturday the Orchestra Festival presents Caribbean and Latin bands.

In Trinidad, the Carnival season lasts for a month before Ash Wednesday. The official music style of the celebration is the calypso, and there are competitions of steel-pan orchestras and huge parades, with revelers wearing elaborate costumes. African culture has a huge influence in Cuban Carnival due to the intense slave traffic in the nineteenth century. Because the African Diaspora in Cuba is somewhat recent, the different ethnic groups were able to maintain their cultural traditions in the mutual aid and social clubs of free and slave blacks known as *cabildos*. Later the *cabildos* became responsible for organizing the religious celebrations that are the origin of Cuban Carnival. Cuban Carnival does not always coincide with the period that precedes Lent. However, in Havana, where it used to be celebrated in June or July, it is now marked in February.

Roberto Ferreira da Rocha

See also: Brazilian Carnival; Calypso; Cuban Music, African Influence in

References

Candela, Mariano. *Carnaval de Barranquilla: Patrimonio oral e intangible de la humanidad.* Bogota, Colombia: Amalfi Editores, 2004

Ortiz, Fernando. *Contrapunteo cubano del tabaco y el azucar.* Madrid: Cátedra, 2002.

Noted inventor George Washington Carver at the Tuskegee Institute, Alabama in 1942. (Library of Congress)

CARVER, GEORGE WASHINGTON (1864–1943)

George Washington Carver was an African American inventor, researcher, agronomist, and educator. He was born in southwest Missouri (near present-day Diamond) in 1864 to a slave named Mary and was raised by Moses and Susan Carver. As a child, he won recognition from family and community as a "plant doctor." In his teens, Carver attended school and worked in various parts of Missouri, Kansas, Minnesota, and Iowa. In September 1890 Carver began studying art at Simpson College in Indianola, Iowa, and in 1891 he moved to the Iowa State College of Agriculture and Mechanic Arts in Ames, where he earned a BS in 1894 and an MS in 1896, both in agriculture. In the fall of 1896, Carver moved to Alabama to teach and conduct research at the Tuskegee Institute, where he would spend the rest of his professional life. His diverse experimental interests involved finding uses for plant materials, from industrial applications such as paint to domestic applications like creating an affordable and balanced diet. This led him to study vegetables, including the cow pea, the sweet potato, and the peanut, with which he is most identified. Between his classes at Tuskegee and his many public lectures across the country, Carver taught and inspired generations of students and came to embody black scientific achievement and uplift. Until his death in 1943, Carver spent his career studying nature with the goal of harnessing it for the good of humankind, starting with the "man furthest down."

Alex Feerst

See also: Agriculture; Tuskegee Institute

References

Kremer, Gary R. *George Washington Carver in His Own Words.* Columbia: University of Missouri Press, 1987.

McMurry, Linda O. *George Washington Carver: Scientist and Symbol.* New York: Oxford University Press, 1981.

CASAS, BARTOLOMÉ DE LAS (1484–1566)

Bartolomé De Las Casas, bishop of Chiapas, is regarded as the most influential figure of the movement for the protection and freedom of the Indians in the early years of the Spanish colonization of America. He is also remembered for his role in the development of the by then nascent export of African slaves to the colonies. Born in Seville, Spain, in 1484, Bartolomé De Las Casas was the only male son of a lower-class baker. Following his father's example—Pedro De Las Casas had joined Columbus's crew on his second voyage to the Indies—Bartolomé enlisted in Governor Nicolás de Ovando's expedition in 1502. Excited by the possibility of riches and social promotion, the young De Las Casas, during his first years in the colonies, behaved in the manner of any other Spanish colonist. He worked in the gold mines of Haina and Cibao in Santo Domingo and even participated as a soldier in de Ovando's campaigns against the natives in Haiti and Santo Domingo, although he did not mention it later in his writings. In 1505 De Las Casas obtained his first *encomienda* (the *encomienda* was the equivalent in the Indies to an old Spanish feudal institution of patronage, a form of personal domination of the natives) in Santo Domingo, and in 1514 he was rewarded with another one in Cuba by Diego Velázquez, on whose expedition De Las Casas had taken part as a missionary.

Months later, in May 1514, he was to renounce his *encomienda* and liberate the Indians under his jurisdiction, influenced by the Dominicans' sermons against both that institution and the conquest itself. The ire of the Spanish colonists was raised by De Las Casas's announcement of the illicitness of the institution and of the atrocious nature of the Spaniards' deeds. The priest traveled to Spain in 1515, where he stayed for five years and where he would return several times during his life, trying to persuade the crown and the ecclesiastical hierarchy of the need to put an end to the *encomiendas* in America and thus save the decimated Indians from exploitation and genocide. His influence upon Charles V was so great that he almost persuaded the monarch to return the kingdoms of Peru to what De Las Casas consideredtheir legitimate lords, the Incas.

In order to save the native population of the New World, De Las Casas proposed that, instead of using Indians, colonists could employ the labor of African slaves. Ancient philosophical and theological traditions supported this idea, based on the fallacy that slavery was the natural condition of black Africans. It is now widely known that De Las Casas inadvertently provided an ethical excuse for the massive development of this dreadful trade in the American colonies.

The influence of the Dominican on later Spanish pro-slavery currents of thought was such that three centuries later, his arguments were used to oppose the abolition of slave trade by the delegates who were drawing up Spanish Constitution of 1812. A document was received by the delegates from antiabolitionist colonists in Havana which said that they were not to blame for the exploitation of African slaves, which, they claimed, would never have happened except for De Las Casa's proposal to save the Indians by importing African labor.

De Las Casas felt utter remorse years after proposing his "providential" plan, his main act of repentance being the recording of the tragic situation of thousands of enslaved African men and women in his writings. That was all he could do, however, since by the 1530s, the traffic of black Africans to the American colonies was an essential part of the colonial enterprise.

Critics have tended to emphasize over the centuries what they have regarded the paternalistic–indigenist posture of De Las Casas. During the twentieth century, however, some have highlighted the Dominican's interest in the cultural heritage of the American peoples subjugated by the Spaniards, which in his opinion was comparable to those of the Greeks and Romans, and what has come to be called his *teoría de la restauración,* according to which it was necessary to restore the defeated Indian lords to their previous status.

De Las Casas left a significant legacy. Both the adoption of the New Laws in 1542, designed to protect the Indians, and his *A Short Account on the Destruction of the Indies* (1552), the work that inspired the Spanish Black Legend and influenced Montaigne's theories of indigenous New World culture and its relation to Old World culture. These stand out as the major contributions of De Las Casas's fairly intricate, and always contradictory, work.

Virginia Fernández Canedo

See also: Colonialism; Spanish Empire

References

Alcina Franch, José. "El Indianismo de Fray Bartolomé de Las Casas." In *Indianismo e Indigenismo en América,* edited by José Alcina Franch. Madrid: Alianza Editorial, 1990.

Bataillon, Marcel. *Estudios sobre Bartolomé de Las Casas.* Translated by J. Coderch and J. A. Martínez Schrem. Barcelona: Edicions 62, 1976.

Borges, Pedro. *Quién era Bartolomé De Las Casas.* Madrid: Ediciones Rialp, 1990.

CASTAS PAINTINGS

Castas paintings depicted and classified the different class, ethnic, and racial mixtures in colonial Mexico, particularly those of African lineage. Referring to Spanish America, and particularly Mexico, in the late 1700s, Margarita Orellana affirms, "It was in this society, where almost everyone mixed with everyone else, in a New Spain whose novelty was precisely this mixture, that *castas* paintings arose" (1990, p. 85). Primarily a late-eighteenth-century phenomenon, the materialization of the *castas* paintings can be attributed to the preoccupation and anxiety of the predominant white ruling class, which, influenced by the classificatory and categorically defined Age of Enlightenment, attempt to control and regulate the then-emerging intermediate racial entities resulting from widespread miscegenation. Orellana points out that the exoticism and festive spirit which characterized the literary Other during the previous century was replaced by science and rationalism in painting.

Edward J. Sullivan explains the anatomy of a typical *castas* painting: "Castas were always created in a series. Each picture usually contains a couple and at least one child. At times more than one child and even other figures may be illustrated. At the bottom or top of the picture there is an inscription that explains the racial mix shown" (1990, p. 86). Orellana adds, "There is no hint of social conflict between castes in this painting. It simply provides

Castas painting were used to identify classes of people based on specific racial or ethnic heritages. (Schalkwijk/Art Resource, NY)

a catalogue of what New Spain has to offer: castes, fruit, ways of dress, etc." (p. 85).

This ordering of races extended from the realm of the social functions they performed to the dress codes they were forced to espouse. For example, while Spanish, Indian, and Mestizo men were allowed to practice the skill of weaving, blacks were prohibited from pursuing the trade. Similarly, Thomas Gage, a seventeenth-century Dominican friar, describes the curious relationship between women of African descent and the clothes they donned: "The dress and accessories of the *negras* and *mulatas* is so scandalous, and their behavior and attitude so intoxicating, that there are many Spaniards, even those from the upper class, who leave their wives to be with them" (Castelló Yturbide, 1990, p. 54). The caste system was a way to bring order

to this hybrid New World and probably signified a welcome implementation for the Spaniards who resided there and were accustomed to their hierarchically designed Iberian society, which already had a long-standing tradition regarding the issue of blood purity.

Some fifty-three different *castas* are identified by Nicholas León, many of which stand out for their pejorative associations or prejudicial implications. Of those fifty-three, approximately thirty, more than half, refer to racial mixtures that include sanguineal ties to African peoples: Albarasado, Albino, Barzino, Cambujo, Campa mulato, Cuarterón, Cuarterón de mulata, Cuarterón de Chino, Chino, Genízaro, Galfarro, Gente blanca, Gíbaro, Grifo, Jarocho, Lobo, Morisco, Mulato, Mulato obscuro, No te entiendo, Puchuela de negro, Quinterón, Requinterón de mulata, Saltatras, Saltatras cuarterón, Saltatras quinterón, Tente en el aire, Tercerón, Zambo, and Zambo prieto. Many of these words are untranslatable but several, including Saltatrás (jump back) and Lobo (wolf), reveal the discriminatory bearing on a person's racial composition the farther away their particular mixture was from "pure" castes.

While the paintings were considered by many as aesthetically inferior precisely because of their unorthodox subject matter (the principal supporters of art—the Church and the State—. . . tended to patronize those artists who were able to create images similar or at least reminiscent of works by the great masters), this opinion has gradually shifted (Sullivan, 1990, p. 86). As their cultural value is now more recognized and appreciated, the *castas* paintings are seen as being ocular artifacts that depict a society in only the way a brush upon canvas can: "These visual descriptions of more or less swarthy races that mingle to produce other castes, in pictures that are frequently as beautiful as they are intriguing, provide endless material for the historian" (Orellana, 1990, p. 84). Moreover, they reveal as much about the Spanish and Creole mindset as they do about the people they depict. In the summer of 2004, the Los Angeles County Museum of Art held the first ever major exhibition of these *castas* paintings. Titled "Inventing Race through Art," it showcased the intersection of race, class, and gender for twenty-first century spectators.

The majority of the *castas* paintings were exported to Spain where, purchased as souvenirs, they were considered novelties for their ability to convey class, race, and social structures. Artists associated with their production include José de Paéz, Miguel Cabrera, Vicente Albán, and José Joaquin Magón. Magali Carrera's book *Imagining Identity in New Spain: Race, Lineage, and the Colonial Body in Portraiture and Casta Paintings* (2003) attributes the end of their production to the emerging spirit of independence and an incipient Mexican national identity.

Bonnie L. Gasior

See also: Mexico; Mexico (Afro-Mexican Identity)

References

Carrera, Magali. *Imagining Identity in New Spain: Race, Lineage, and the Colonial Body in Portraiture and Casta Paintings.* Austin: University of Texas Press, 2003.

Castelló Yturbide, Teresa. "Modes of Dress among the Mestizo Castes." *Artes de Mexico: La Pintura de Castas* 8 (1990): 87–88.

León, Nicolás. *Las castas del México colonial o Nueva España: Noticias etno-antropológicas.* Mexico City: Talleres gráficos del Museo Nacional de Arqueología, Historia y Etnografía, 1924.

Orellana, Margarita. "The Fever of the Image in *Castas* Painting." *Artes de Mexico: La Pintura de Castas* 8 (1990): 84–85.

Sullivan, Edward J. "A Visual Phenomenon of the Americas." *Artes de Mexico: La Pintura de Castas* 8 (1990): 85–86.

CASTRO RUZ, FIDEL (1926–)

Fidel Castro is a Cuban revolutionary and prime minister and president of Cuba who is known for his Marxist and revolutionary involvement in African and Caribbean nations. He is the longest-serving leader of any country in the world.

Fidel Castro was born in Biran, Cuba, on August 13, 1926, one of nine children. His family was successful in business. After Fidel attended public schools with less than stellar results, his father, Angel Castro, felt that Fidel needed a more disciplined environment. He was sent to private Catholic schools in Santiago and Havana and in 1944 was presented with the best athlete award in school. In 1945 Castro began his studies in law at the University of Havana. While he was a student at the university, his already-existing political aspirations became more defined, and he became a member of the Ortodoxo Party in 1947, a nationalist and reformist party formed in response to governmental corruption. Castro also became a member of the Caribbean League, made up of political exiles who resided in Cuba. The Caribbean League's plan was to overthrow Rafael Trujillo, the dictator of the Dominican Republic, an effort that proved unsuccessful.

When Castro started practicing law, he became aware of the economic and social inequality of Cuba's social classes. Castro's social consciousness was raised in part when he began to read José Martí. Immersing himself in all of Martí's writings, he

Cuban leader Fidel Castro in 1961, reading a newspaper. In 1959, Castro led the revolution that overthrew dictator Fulgencio Batista. (Library of Congress)

came to understand the latter's thinking and strategies. After Fulgencio Batista's 1952 coup, Castro created the 26th of July Movement to overthrow him. In 1953 an attack to depose Batista and his government failed miserably, and Castro and his brother Raul were imprisoned. At the trial, Castro defended his reasoning for the attack with his now famous "History Will Absolve Me" speech. It was at this trial that Castro and the others were sentenced to fifteen years in prison. However, Castro and his brother were given amnesty by Batista in 1955. At this time Castro, his brother, and others headed to Mexico to train for yet another revolution. Here, in Mexico, Castro was introduced to another revolutionary, Che Guevera, who, like Castro,

believed that social injustice and governmental oppression must not be tolerated. Together, they set out to dismantle Batista's dictatorship. The new revolution evolved in the Sierra Maestra mountains and produced the Sierra Manifesto. It was with the implementation of this manifesto that Batista's dictatorship was slowly dismantled. Castro's determination to overthrow Batista was fulfilled in December 1958, when Che Guevera's forces attacked Santa Clara. Castro's rebel army rode into Havana in January 1959, sending the United States–backed dictator into exile. Arriving in the capital with its tanks, the rebel army was enthusiastically welcomed. When Castro took over as leader and began to make his celebratory speech, a white dove landed on his shoulder, which in the audience's mind signified the coming of peace.

His recognition of social inequality was the catalyst for Castro's resentment of the upper classes and of Americans with businesses in Cuba. He despised the Cuban leaders of the time who, he felt, were merely puppets of the U.S. government. A failed invasion in 1961 of Southwest Cuba planned by the United States using Cuban exiles, known as the Bay of Pigs, further worsened Cuban-American relations.

The Cuban Missile Crisis of 1962 resulted in an agreement between the Soviet Union and the United States: Khrushchev would remove his missiles if the United States would never attack Cuba. Despite this guarantee, Castro's anger at being a pawn in a game played by other countries led him to reinforce his solidarity with revolutionaries in the developing world.

Castro felt that his mutual alliance with the Soviet Union would make his country stronger. When Cuba began suffering economically, Russia stepped in to offer financial support. Russia's subsidies of Cuba were also a political gesture that helped Cuba regain some economic stability and allowed Castro the opportunity to show the United States that his friendship with the USSR would allow him to remain free of U.S. interference.

Castro sought additional support by courting the favor of third world countries, mainly Africa, focusing on Ghana, Algeria, and Angola. His visits to third world countries won him allies as he pointed out the racism in capitalist countries, especially the United States. Castro denounced a situation in which some countries went without the basic essentials while other countries squandered their resources. The third

world nations admired Castro's audacity and tenacity in fighting the rich countries. Castro implored the people in the third world to use their inner strength to face adversity and survive without help from the wealthier countries.

After 1975 Castro launched Operation Carlota, sending Cuban troops to Angola to defend the Marxist government against an insurrection backed by South African troops. Once the soldiers were in place, he sent relief supplies to the Angolans with the message that he was offering safety and security to the oppressed.

Castro's reasoning for protecting and defending third world countries was his identification with Afro-Cubans and their origins as slaves. In addition, Operation Carlota helped confirm Castro as a leader in the eyes of Cuba and African nations such as Angola. When Somalia and Ethiopia became entangled in a war in 1978, Castro sent troops to defend Ethiopia. Castro's influence was rapidly gaining strength and he became the leader of the Non-Aligned Movement.

The more involved Castro became with Africa and other third world countries, the more disdain the United States and other developed countries showed toward Cuba. In Cuba, however, Afro-Cubans have been great supporters of Castro because they identified with his championing of the Cuban culture and admired his Marxist advocacy of total equality for everyone. When the Soviet Union collapsed in 1991, Cuba again faced an uncertain economic future, and Castro had to rely on foreign currencies including the U.S. dollar. Cuba has recovered from the worst deprivations of what Castro called the "special period" that followed the Soviet Union's demise. Still, in the first decade of the twenty-first century, Cuba is an impoverished nation. It is also a nation lacking in human rights and free elections. Opposition to him, however, remains weak. At the same time, Castro has created a society where professionals such as doctors, military officers, and government officials have been able to advance without discrimination on the basis of racial identity or class background. For black Cubans, who make up 70 percent of the population, racial discrimination has declined sharply, although it still exists in various forms. Castro has also taken pride in strengthening the country's educational and medical systems.

Karen E. Holleran

See also: Cuba; Voice of America

References

Castro, Fidel. *CHE: A Memoir by Fidel Castro*. Melbourne: Ocean Press, 1994.

Cawthorne, Nigel. "Fidel Castro." In *Tyrants: History's 100 Most Evil Despots & Dictators*. New York: Barnes and Noble, 2005.

Coltman, Leycester. *The Real Fidel Castro*. New Haven, CT: Yale University Press, 2003.

Fernandez, Alina. *Castro's Daughter: An Exile's Memoir of Cuba*. New York: St. Martin's Griffin, 1997.

Fontova, Humberto E. *Fidel: Hollywood's Favorite Tyrant*. Washington, DC: Regnery Publishing, 2005.

Latell, Brian. *After Fidel: The Inside Story of Castro's Regime and Cuba's Next Leader*. New York: Palgrave Macmillan, 2005.

Montaner, Carlos Alberto. *Cuba, Castro and the Caribbeans: The Cuban Revolution and the Crisis in Western Conscience*. New Brunswick, NJ: Transaction Books, 1985.

Oppenheimer, Andres. *Castro's Final Hour: The Secret Story behind the Coming Downfall of Communist Cuba*. New York: Touchstone, 1992.

Quirk, Robert E. *Fidel Castro*. New York: Norton, 1993.

Skierka, Volker. *Fidel Castro: A Biography*. Malden, MA: Polity Press, 2004.

Sweig, Julia E. *Inside the Cuban Revolution: Fidel Castro and the Urban Underground*. Cambridge, MA: Harvard University Press, 2002.

Szulc, Tad. *Fidel: A Critical Portrait*. New York: Perennial, 1986.

CATHOLICISM

Catholics have represented a significant population in Africa since the first century CE, and Catholicism has a significant historical and contemporary presence in the Americas. As Philip Jenkins thoroughly documents in his book *The Next Christendom: The Coming of Global Christianity* (2002), the Christian faith rose in the Middle East and developed predominantly in Africa and the Middle East until about 1400, when Europe and Europeanized North America became the hearts of world Christianity. Ironically, many Eurocentric historians have erroneously considered Christianity a religion rooted in the West. Some postcolonialists and other postmodernists have also made the mistake of associating Christianity exclusively with Western colonialism and imperialism.

Alongside Syria, Mesopotamia, and other Near Eastern countries, Africa was an abundant missionary field in the first century CE. A number of Christian communities and learning centers were located in Egypt and North Africa in the first and second centuries; many works of Christian fine art, music, and literature also originated in these areas. Christian monasticism, which for Westerners immediately recalls medieval Europe, originated in Egypt, where St. Anthony the Abbot and others established communities for hermits in the deserts in the third and fourth centuries. North Africa was the home to renowned Church fathers and founders of

Christian Latin literature. Carthage—in present-day Tunisia—was the birthplace of Tertullian (c. 160–220), one of the earliest Christian apologists; St. Cyprian (190–258), Tertullian's disciple and bishop; and St. Augustine (354–430), a doctor of the church and author of the Catholic masterpieces *Confessions* and *The City of God.* The continent of Africa has also produced such black Catholic saints as St. Benedict the Moor (1524–1589) and St. Martin de Porres (1579–1639).

The population of Catholic Africans has steadily grown. In the 1200s, considered the zenith of medieval Christian civilization in Europe, Africa had the largest Christian population in the world. In 1914 Africa had seven million baptized Catholics and an additional million catechumens; these numbers had doubled by 1938. As of 1955, Roman Catholicism claimed to have sixteen million believers in Africa; today, there are 120 million African Catholics, and the number is projected to increase to 230 million by 2025. The leading churches in Africa today include the Catholic, Anglican, and Methodist. Despite much publicity about the recent ascendancy of Independent congregations, Africa remains a predominantly Roman Catholic and Anglican continent. Indeed, Africa's Roman Catholic population outnumbers that of Independents by more than three to one.

Compared to its Protestant counterpart, the Catholic population among African Americans is still modest; as of 2006, the total number was estimated at approximately three million. However, there were black Catholic communities even before the American Revolution in the United States—mostly in Baltimore. Later, black Catholic communities were established in such places as Charleston and

New Orleans. In 1886 the first African American Catholic newspaper appeared, and Augustus Tolton became the first African American to be ordained a Catholic priest. Currently active black Catholic organizations include the Mother Theresa Maxis Duchemin, the National Black Catholic Evangelization Forum/Project Reach Out, the Sisters of the Blessed Sacrament, and the Society of St. Joseph of the Sacred Heart. Xavier University of Louisiana is the only Catholic and historically black institution of higher learning in the United States.

Catholicism arrived in Latin America with the Spanish and Portuguese conquests in the sixteenth century. Although millions of Catholics have converted to evangelical and Pentecostal denominations since the 1980s, Catholicism remains the predominant religion on the continent. Currently there are a total of 424 million Catholics—approximately 42 percent of the world's Catholic population—in Latin America; 105.9 millions of this figure are of African descent. Latin American countries with the largest numbers of black Catholics include Brazil (65 million), Colombia (20 million), and Mexico (12 million). The Caribbean is the home of 18 million Catholics of African descent; the Dominican Republic accounts for 8 million black Catholics, Haiti 6 million, and Cuba 4 million, respectively.

Catholicism plays a significant social and political role in Latin American life. Liberation theology—a school of left-wing theology emphasizing political, economic, racial, and social justice—arose in Latin America in the 1960s. Among its leading exponents were Gustavo Gutierrez (Peru), Leonardo Boff (Brazil), and Juan Luis Segundo (Uruguay), who considered Jesus mainly a liberator of the oppressed.

Although liberation theology has been condemned by the Vatican since the 1980s as a Marxist-inspired ideology incompatible with orthodox Catholicism, its global influence has been significant; many theologians in the third world have developed their own versions of liberation theology.

John J. Han

See also: Bakhita, Josephine, Saint; Brazilian Culture; Chikaba; Christianity (African American); Colombia; Mexico; Religion (Africa)

References

Gillis, Chester. *Roman Catholicism in America.* New York: Columbia University Press, 1999.

Hastings, Adrian, ed. *A World History of Christianity.* Grand Rapids, MI: Eerdmans, 2000.

Isichei, Elizabeth. *A History of Christianity in Africa: From Antiquity to the Present.* Grand Rapids, MI: Eerdmans, 1995.

Jenkins, Philip. *The Next Christendom: The Coming of Global Christianity.* New York: Oxford University Press, 2002.

Sanneh, Lamin. *Whose Religion Is Christianity?: The Gospel beyond the West.* Grand Rapids, MI: Eerdmans, 2003.

CEDDO

Ceddo is an Afro-British collective for film and television production addressing minority issues and people. Channel 4 of the British Broadcasting Company (BBC) went on the air in 1982, with the mission of representing groups who had not been represented on the main BBC channels and of commissioning British films addressing minority issues. One of the means to address these goals was the creation and partial funding of several Afro-British collectives, including the Ceddo Film and Video Workshop. Several founders of Ceddo were already experienced in television production, including Menelik Shabazz, Milton Bryan, and Imruh Bakari Caesar, a fact

that distinguished Ceddo from some of the other collectives formed at the same time. Ceddo's first film produced for Channel 4, *The People's Account* (1985), was not shown on British television due to objections from the Independent Broadcasting Authority over descriptions of the police as racist. Ceddo produced a number of documentaries, including Glenn Ujebe Masokoane's *We Are the Elephant* (1987), which depicted the struggle against apartheid in South Africa; Valerie Thomas's *The Flame of the Soul* (1990), about sickle cell anemia; and John Akomfrah's *Blue Notes and Exiled Voices,* about protest music. Akomfrah's *Handsworth Songs* (1986) combined documentary film shot during the riots of 1985 with newsreel and archival material to present a view of the causes of racial unrest in Great Britain. Menlik Shabazz, a founding member of Ceddo, also founded *Black Filmmaker Magazine* and the *Black Filmmaker Magazine* International Film Festival in 1998; the latter is presented annually and showcases African-themed films from all over the world.

Sarah Boslaugh

See also: Britain: People of African Origin and Descent

References

Lay, Samantha. *British Social Realism: From Documentary to Brit-grit.* London: Wallflower, 2002.

Ogidi, Ann. "Ceddo." http://www .screenonline.org.uk/people/id/569785.

CENTRAL AFRICAN REPUBLIC

The landlocked Central African Republic, just south of the equator, has an estimated population of 4,369,038 as of July 2007. Sixty-four percent of the land is forested, and much of the rest is savannah. It was originally a French colony administered as the colony of Ubangi-Shari. The first governor of Ubangi-Shari and Chad (the two colonies were joined together administratively from 1906 until 1920) was Émile Merwart, who later moved to the West Indies as governor of Guadeloupe in 1913–1917. One of the most well-known French officials in Ubangi-Shari was also connected with the Caribbean. René Maran's family was from the West Indies, Maran's father moving to Africa to serve in the colonial administration. René Maran wrote a novel *Batouala* (1921), partly about a chief, which was advertised as "a novel about negroes, seen from inside, written by a negro," and was a best-seller, winning the Prix Goncourt in the same year it was published. It was the inspiration for French writer André Gide, who subsequently wrote *Journey to the Congo* (1927). Maran himself was sacked from the colonial government, returning to France in 1925 and writing against the French colonial system. At around the same time, U.S. missionaries became active in Ubangi-Shari, with the Baptist Mid-Missions sending in missionaries from 1920, the National Brethren of Fellowship Churches from 1921, Africa Inland Mission from 1924, and the Evangelical Lutheran Church from 1930.

From early on Westerners were interested in Ubangi-Shari's mineral deposits, including diamonds, with the Baltimore Museum of Art and the Commercial Museum of Philadelphia having significant collections of early specimens. This interest increased in 1950 after two French companies started mining diamonds in the country, subcontracting their work to deliver diamonds to the U.S. government.

The country gained its independence from France on August 13, 1960, and David Dacko became the first president of the Central African Republic. The United States opened an embassy in Bangui, the nation's capital and one of only two cities in the country. W. Wendell Blancké was its first ambassador. He had served in Buenos Aires, Argentina, during World War II and after his time in West Africa became U.S. consul general in Mexico. Canada's ambassadors to Cameroon were also accredited to the Central African Republic. In 1962 G. Mennen Williams, the U.S. assistant secretary of state, visited Bangui. John H. Burns was U.S. ambassador from 1961 until 1963.

In 1966 Dacko's cousin, Jean-Bédel Bokassa, took over in a military coup d'état. Bokassa had been the head of the armed forces, having served with the French in Vietnam. His government was at first extremely idiosyncratic, and accusations of insanity were later leveled against him in U.S. and Canadian newspapers. This occurred mainly after December 1977, when he crowned himself as the emperor of the Central African Empire, spending lavishly on his coronation. In spite of invitations to, among others, President Jimmy Carter of the United States, President Jorge Rafael Videla of Argentina, and President Ernesto Geisel of Brazil, no foreign leader turned up at the enthronement, which was said to have cost U.S.$20 million. The aim, Bokassa said, was to ensure that everybody in the world would know about the country, and to that extent he achieved his aim.

However, very soon afterwards Bokassa was to gain much bad publicity following the arrest of two U.S. correspondents, one working for the Associated Press and the other with the *Washington Post*. The Associated Press had reported that Bokassa occasionally "served up" regime critics and political opponents at state banquets, and that diners at the coronation banquet may have unknowingly eaten human flesh. Relations were strained and the U.S. ambassador, Anthony Cecil Eden Quainton told Bokassa that given the money spent on the coronation, his government would cancel foreign aid to the country, although it would honor its pledges of $800,000 in 1977 and $475,000 in 1978.

Relations were normalized in 1978 but became strained again in early 1979 when demonstrations by school children against the Bokassa regime were ruthlessly suppressed. On September 9, 1979, the United States suspended all aid to Bokassa. Twelve days later, in another coup d'état, David Dacko returned to power and Bokassa fled into exile. Two years later Arthur H. Woodruff became U.S. ambassador to the country, and relations were normalized. The Central African Republic's air force has used Lockheed 60 utility transport aircraft made in Georgia in the United States. Not many researchers have entered the republic, especially aside from Americans and the French, although Mexico's Centro de Estudios de Asia y Africa at El Colegio de México has generated some serious studies of the country.

Justin Corfield

References

Kalck, Pierre. *Historical Dictionary of the Central African Republic.* Lanham, MD: Scarecrow Press, 2005.

Titley, Brian. *Dark Age: The Political Dynasty of Emperor Bokassa.* Montreal, QC: McGill-Queen's University Press, 1997.

CENTRAL INTELLIGENCE AGENCY

Between 1948 and 1980, as sweeping political changes took place throughout Latin America and Africa, sometimes through wars of national liberation and revolutionary political movements, the Central Intelligence Agency (CIA) of the United States was tasked with observing and influencing those developing regions of the world with the stated goal of furthering U.S. national interests. Among the CIA's priorities was promoting outcomes in times of political turmoil that would favor the United States over the Soviet Union during the cold war.

President Harry S. Truman created the CIA and the office of the director of Central Intelligence when he signed the National Security Act in 1947. The most fundamental task of the CIA during much of the cold war was to keep a vigilant eye on the Soviet Union's local activities as well as in other countries around the world. Much of U.S. cold war policy was formed around the idea of containing and rolling back the spread of Communism throughout the world. Thus, wars of national liberation and political upheavals in which far-left parties or groups rose to power or threatened to take control of governments became a primary focus for policy makers in Washington. They believed that wherever socialist or Communist movements were gaining strength, the Soviet Union was principally involved. Thus, many of the revolutionary movements in the developing world, including Latin America and Africa, were the subject of intense CIA observation and activity.

Political movements of interest to the CIA in Latin America were located in Guatemala, Cuba, and Chile, among other countries. In 1954 Operation Success (also known as Operation PBPSUCCESS) in Guatemala was a highly covert operation conducted by the CIA aimed at overthrowing the populist Jacobo Arbenz, who had been democratically elected in 1950. The operation, which was successful, consisted of forming and training a rebel liberation army in Nicaragua as well as conducting a propaganda campaign with the hope of weakening the Arbenz government prior to the liberation army's invasion.

Fidel Castro's rise to power in Cuba in 1959 led the United States, through the CIA, to make attempts to remove the Communist leader from power. The first attempt, codenamed Operation Pluto, was similar to the Guatemala plan in that it involved training a liberation army made up of Cuban exiles. This army would serve as an invasion force and land on the beaches of Cuba, fighting its way to Havana to liberate the Caribbean nation. The result is known today as the Bay of Pigs invasion of 1961 in which the invaders were routed.

The CIA did not stop trying to oust Castro. After the Bay of Pigs disaster, the CIA engaged in another covert operation, code-named Operation Mongoose. This prolonged operation included assassination attempts, in some cases with exploding cigars; sabotaging shipments of sugar from Cuba and shipments of machinery to Cuba; and commando raids on railroads, factories, and oil and sugar refineries. The goal of this operation was to incite a successful revolt against the Communist regime, which never occurred.

In Chile, the election of Salvador Allende to the presidency in 1970 posed problems for Washington. President Richard Nixon as well as many others in Washington felt that Allende was a radical Marxist and would become another Castro. Thus, Nixon and his national security adviser, Henry Kissinger, approved a plan, called Track II, to oust Allende from power. The operation involved infiltrating the Chilean military and encouraging soldiers

to overthrow the Allende government. Not all of the military forces went along with the plan. However, after Allende loyalist General Carlos Prats resigned in 1973, General Augusto Pinochet became the leader of the coup attempt, and it was subsequently successful in wrestling power from President Allende in 1973.

In Africa, movements for national independence began to take shape as nations sought to rid themselves of their colonial powers. Wars of national liberation were of interest to the United States as well as the Soviet Union as each vied for dominance in the developing world. Thus, the CIA was very active in Africa, particularly in the former Belgian Congo and Angola.

In 1960 the Congo gained its independence from Belgium with a government headed by the militant nationalist Patrice Lumumba. Fear of his ties with the Soviet Union prompted the CIA to begin operations within the Congo aimed at overthrowing the government and assassinating top officials. General Mobutu Sese Seko helped launch a coup d'état in 1965 and named himself president. Thus, the new role of the CIA in Zaire, as Mobutu renamed the Congo, was to aid the new ruler in fending off Lumumbist rebels who were being backed by the Soviet Union and China.

As nationalism began to take hold in Angola around the same time, Portugal, Angola's colonial overseer, struck down every uprising. The United States was caught in a balancing act, encouraging independence movements in Angola and persuading Portugal to speed the transition of the African country toward independence; but it was not willing to risk giving up strategic air bases that were located in the Azores, a Portuguese territory. CIA activity was more covert than in the case of Zaire and included mostly the provision of money and arms to pro-Western nationalist groups in Angola. Secrecy was necessary so as to not alert Portugal.

When the newly independent nation broke into civil war in 1975, the United States continued to back the pro-Western forces fighting against the Soviet-backed Popular Movement for the Liberation of Angola (MPLA). The MPLA, backed not only by the Soviet Union but also by Cuba, increased its military capability to the extent that South Africa, aided by the United States and the CIA, was secretly enlisted to help fend off the Soviet-backed group. Remarkably, the MPLA was a formidable opponent and was able to defeat many attempts to crush it. Angola remained in a state of civil war for sixteen years.

Both Angola and Zaire witnessed covert operations by the CIA that consisted of propaganda, manipulation of labor unions, assassination attempts, and sales of arms and other military equipment. Many of these operations mirrored in many ways operations that took place in Guatemala and Chile.

Mark Freeman

See also: Cold War; Congolese Independence; Decolonization, African; Socialism

References

Jeffreys-Jones, Rhodri. *The CIA and American Democracy.* New Haven, CT: Yale University Press, 1989.

Kelly, Sean. *America's Tyrant: The CIA and Mobutu of Zaire.* Washington, DC: American University Press, 1993.

Prados, John. *Presidents' Secret Wars: CIA and Pentagon Covert Operations from World War II through the Persian Gulf.* Chicago: Ivan R. Dee, 1996.

Reebel, Patrick A. *The CIA: Current Issues and Background.* New York: Nova Science Publishers, 2003.

Weissman, Stephen. "The CIA and U.S. Policy in Zaire and Angola." In *Dirty Work 2: The CIA in Africa,* edited by Ellen Ray, William Schaap, Karl Van Meter, and Louis Wolf. Secaucus, NJ: Lyle Stuart, 1979.

CÉSAIRE, AIMÉ (1913–)

Aimé Césaire was a major Martinican poet, dramatist, and politician and key theorist of Négritude. His writing posits the relationship between Africa and the Caribbean, mediated by Europe.

As a leading theorist of Négritude, and co-founder in 1947 and publisher of the Paris-based journal of African and Caribbean affairs, *Présence Africaine,* Césaire's credentials as an Atlantic figure are impeccable. (He was also Frantz Fanon's schoolteacher for a time). Négritude was a political and cultural movement and theory of black solidarity and antiracism, first developed in the 1930s and 1940s, that attempted to unite all black peoples in the world subjugated by European colonialism and Western racism. But it insisted on the centrality of Africa in determining black pride. Inspired by the Harlem Renaissance and expressed often via poetry, it was known for its lack of a coherent and agreed definition. It is, however, a crucial component in the black Atlantic World, given the diasporic communities created by the slave trade. Indeed, Césaire was quick to acknowledge his double, Atlanticist, heritage: "I am," he declared in 1975, "at the juncture of two traditions: American by geography, African by history" (Ngal, 1994, p. 13). Césaire underlines the paradox of being from Africa and yet not from Africa when he states that it is "part of my internal geography."

Négritude's poetic manifesto is undoubtedly Césaire's *Cahier d'un retour au pays natal* (1939; Notebook of a return to the homeland). Having met Césaire in 1942, the French surrealist André Breton described this epic poem as "the greatest lyric monument of our time." Mixing Caribbean, African, and European poetic traditions into a multivoiced and troubling narrative, the *Cahier* is a now a classic of Francophone Caribbean literature, still taught across the Atlantic in Africa. Inspiration for the poem was his return to Martinique in 1935 to find a downtrodden people who, by discovering their African roots and history of slave revolts, are shown to stand up and demand dignity and freedom. Césaire's Atlantic is conceived as resolutely triangular. Educated in France in the 1930s and a member of France's parliament (elected in 1945 to represent Martinique in the new Constituent Assembly in Paris), in the same decade he also cofounded the Parisian journal *L'Etudiant noir* (The black student). As a student in France's elite educational system, he assimilated the greats of French literature—Baudelaire, Rimbaud, Mallarmé. His 1950 speech, "Discours sur le colonialisme," was an indictment of European colonialism and a Communist tirade against American imperialism. (He later left the Communist Party over the 1956 invasion of Hungary). His main focus is, nevertheless, Africa and the Caribbean and the history of the antislavery movement. Having immortalized the Haitian antislavery leader Toussaint Louverture in the *Cahier,* describing the cell in which Napoléon had imprisoned Toussaint near the Swiss border (that is, as Napoléon said, as far away from the Atlantic as possible), Césaire wrote a biography of the Haitian revolutionary in 1961. In the aftermath of African independence he wrote a series of plays, the most famous

of which—*Une saison au Congo* (1967; A season in the Congo)—deals with the rebel Congolese leader Patrice Lumumba, assassinated in 1961 by the CIA and Belgian intelligence after he was delivered to them by a certain Colonel Mobutu, the maverick who became the longtime brutal leader of Zaire (now the Democratic Republic of the Congo). In his play Césaire calls this perfidious African character Mokutu. Indeed, though not a regular visitor to Africa, Césaire's work is saturated with references to it and with its echoes across the Atlantic, in both the Caribbean and France.

However, if the Caribbean, Africa, and Europe play out in Césaire's work a "circuit triangulaire," to borrow an expression of Martin Munro, it is not a straightforward arrangement. Munro shows how critics tend to see the Caribbean figure Césaire in dialogue with, and in search of, his African roots while underestimating the European dimension. Munro points not only to Césaire's education and erudition in the European tradition (especially the French tradition), but also to the very mix of European culture at the heart of the meeting between Carib and Arawak indigenous cultures (or what was left of it post-Columbus) and African exiled culture. Munro's citation of rhythms in Césaire's poetry shows how European religious singing mixed with indigenous and exilic song in a miscegenation of cultural forms that Césaire has embraced. It is all too easy, he suggests, to see rhythm in Césaire's *Cahier* as a purely African phenomenon that has simply traveled across the Atlantic. Munro's emphasis on the "circuit"—on the movement of cultural forms and practices in all directions—requires, then, complex negotiation and navigation. There is perhaps "no return to roots" in Caribbean consciousness; put another way, the complex tradition-modernity debate that exists in Africa does not pertain to the other side of the Atlantic; or, rather, perhaps it is all the more complex for the hybrid Caribbean experience. It is here that theories of *créolité* (creoleness) come into their own.

More recently, Césaire's Africanist approach has been criticized by theorists of *créolité* such as Confiant in his *Aimé Césaire* (1993); this coincided with stark criticism of Césaire's political achievements as deputy mayor of Fort-de-France in Martinique. Though Césaire brought about significant social and environmental improvements, he also helped draft the law in 1946 that "departmentalized" Martinique as part of French territory. This so-called postcolonial arrangement was in fact soon out of step with the newly independent African states, leaving Césaire politically isolated on the other side of the Atlantic and open to challenges from those looking for true independence for the French Caribbean. That said, Césaire has also been considered as both the "ante-créole" and the "anti-créole" in that, though never championing (or really ever speaking) creole language, his poetry has been celebrated by those creole theorists wishing to downplay the influence of slavery and Atlantic culture as a precursor to the liberation and flourishing of the creole language as a distinct (if interconnected, or "relational," to use Edouard Glissant's word) form of literary and cultural identity.

Andrew Stafford

References

Confiant, Raphaël. *Aimé Césaire: Une traversée paradoxale du siècle.* Paris: Stock, 1993.

Munro, Martin. *Shaping and Reshaping the Caribbean: The Work of Aimé Césaire and René Depestre.* Leeds, UK: MHRA/Maney, 2000.

Ngal, Georges. *Aimé Césaire: Un homme à la recherche d'une patrie.* Paris: Présence Africaine, 1994.

Rosello, Mireille. "One More Sea to Cross: Exile and Intertextuality in Aimé Césaire's *Cahier d'un retour au pays natal.*" Yale French Studies 2, no. 83 (1993): 176–195.

CHAD

The Republic of Chad has a population of approximately 9,539,000 (2004), drawn from 200 ethnic groups. The French controlled the landlocked area that they called Tchad. From 1906 until 1920 it was administered together with Ubangi-Shari (now the Central African Republic), and in 1920 it became a separate colony within French Equatorial Africa. In 1958 Chad voted in a referendum to be an autonomous state within the French Community. Chad gained its independence two years later.

Although Chad was geographically distant from the Americas, there were some connections between it and the Western Hemisphere as early as the 1860s. In 1863 an Austrian archduke, Maximilian, was offered the throne of Mexico and accepted, going to Mexico to become its emperor. Backing him, the French government sent contingents of soldiers, one of which included soldiers recruited from Sudan and Chad. The French later pulled out its soldiers and the regime collapsed, with Maximilian being executed soon afterward.

A number of French civil servants in Chad worked in the Caribbean before or after their African service. In 1906, when Chad was joined, administratively, with Ubangi-Shari, the first lieutenant governor was Émile Merwart, who served until 1911. He later moved to the Caribbean as governor of Guadeloupe in 1913–1917.

From 1910 until 1917 the governor of French Equatorial Africa, which included Chad, was Martial-Henri Merlin, who had previously served in Guadeloupe from 1901–1903. And the French governor of Chad from 1939 until 1941, Adolphe Félix Sylvestre Eboué, had previously been governor of Martinique from 1933 to 1934 and of Guadeloupe in 1936–1939.

U.S. missionaries have been working in Chad for many years, the Baptist Mid-Mission from 1925 and the Brethren Church from 1965. After independence, Wilton Wendell Blancké was U.S. ambassador to Congo (Brazzaville) from 1960 to 1963 while also accredited to Chad, and the U.S. Peace Corps was active in Chad from 1966 until 1979.

As Chad moved to independence, its most important politician was Gabriel Lisette, the leader of the Progressive Party in Chad. He had originally come from the French West Indies, a fact used against him by his political enemies. Lisette was prime minister of Chad until he was ousted as party leader on March 24, 1959, by N'Garta Tombalbaye, who led the country to independence, which was achieved on August 11, 1960. Tombalbaye became the first president of the country, which he ran until his assassination during a successful military coup d'état in April 1975. The new ruler, Noël Odingar, stood down after two days, and Félix Malloum became president for the next four years. In March 1979 he was overthrown in an insurgency led by Goukouni Oueddei, whose unstable rule lasted until June 1982.

Until Goukouni Oueddei took over the presidency, the United States had shown little interest in Chad, but it worried about Oueddei's close links to Libya. With France anxious not to antagonize Libya's leader

Muammar al-Qaddafi, the United States organized covert support for rival politician Hissène Habré. Civil war ensued, with the Libyans backing Oueddei and the CIA providing support for Habré, who came to power in 1982 and won some major military victories over the Libyans in 1987. Habré was overthrown, however, in 1990.

In 2006 Donald Yamamoto, the U.S. deputy assistant secretary of state for African affairs, visited Chad in connection with the petroleum pipeline from Cameroon, which moves 170,000 barrels per day for Exxon Mobil and ChevronTexaco.

Because of regional instability, wars, and poverty, few tourists have visited the country. Transatlantic aid has come in a variety of forms. Aid workers from the United States and Canada have been active helping Sudanese refugees in Chad.

Justin Corfield

See also: Humanitarian Assistance

References

Burr, Millard, and Robert O. Collins. *Africa's Thirty Years War: Libya, Chad, and the Sudan, 1963–1993.* Boulder, CO: Westview Press, 1999.

Decalo, Samuel. *Historical Dictionary of Chad.* Lanham, MD: Scarecrow Press, 1997.

Kirk, R. "The Sudanese in Mexico." *Sudan Notes and Records* 24 (1941): 113–140.

CHAMOISEAU, PATRICK (1953–)

Martinican novelist, essayist, and theorist of *créolité*, Patrick Chamoiseau is the first-ever winner from the French Caribbean of France's prestigious Goncourt Prize for literature, with his 1992 novel *Texaco*.

Chamoiseau (or Oiseau de Cham) writes in a French that owes much to his native creole language. He is deeply concerned with history and stories, especially in their oral deployment. As one of a set of creole theorists (with Jean Bernabé and Raphaël Confiant), he has promoted the distinctiveness of Caribbean culture and literature to the perceived detriment of African influence on the region. The history that his literary work investigates is that of a Caribbean, which has only the faintest vestiges of its African and slave-trade links. However, his most sustained essay on the writing of literature considers the problematic situation of writing in a country under another country's control. Considering not only the Caribbean, but also Africa, he provides an answer to his own question of how to write in a "dominated country" by deploying his highly creolized French to discuss the issue. The essay is a sustained debate with Edouard Glissant (and involves his other famous compatriot, Aimé Césaire, as well as Haitian creole writer Frankétienne), but it also engages with other (mainly French) poets and writers such as Saint-John Perse, Paul Valéry, Marcel Proust, and Victor Segalen. With Raphaël Confiant, he coined the neologism "diversality" to describe creole culture as both specific and universal, with its multiple ethnic determinants.

Yet Chamoiseau's work is deeply Atlantic in its preoccupations. *Texaco* describes the "drive," the endless *errance* (wandering), that Caribbean people, as rootless descendants of slaves, have to confront within their cultural identity. His 1997 novel, *L'esclave vieil homme et le molosse*—involving Glissant's choruslike interjections—is a vivid portrayal of an old slave who becomes a Maroon and is saved from a hunting dog by a rock. Indeed in *Le Roman Marron*, Richard D. E. Burton (1997) has shown how Chamoiseau, more than any other French Caribbean writer, represents and replays the

marooning spirit. His impressive photo-essay on "memory-traces," (1994), alongside photographs by Rodolphe Hammadi of the prison islands off French Guyana (where Henri "Papillon" Charriere was imprisoned), displays a deeply Atlanticist understanding of the region's past, making links between the (largely white) internees and those blacks who threw themselves into the sea to escape slavery. However, Chamoiseau's memory-traces—material objects such as rocks, prisons, and the ocean itself—are claimed as elements in a distinct Caribbean identity. It is the tension in his work between refinding a distinctly Caribbean history and acknowledging the (perhaps unquantifiable) slave influences on it, rather than any direct engagement with Africa (or France), that makes Chamoiseau an important Atlanticist writer.

Andrew Stafford

References

Chamoiseau, Patrick, and Raphaël Confiant. *Lettres créoles: Tracées antillaises et continentales de la littérature: Haïti, Guadeloupe, Martinique, Guyane, 1635–1975*. Paris: Gallimard, 1999.

Chancé, Dominique. *L'auteur en souffrance: Essai sur la position et la représentation de l'auteur dans le roman antillais contemporain, 1981–1992*. Paris: PUF, 2000.

Morel, Lise. "In Praise of Creoleness?" In *An Introduction to Caribbean Francophone Writing*, edited by Sam Haigh. Oxford: Berg, 1999.

CHIKABA (VENERABLE THERESE JULIANA OF SAINT DOMINIC) (1676–1748)

Chikaba was a Ghanaian-born woman who became enslaved, but her life differed from the lives of other slaves because she entered a convent, spent fifty-five years as a second-class nun, and is now in the process of being canonized. Her biography, written by her confessor a few years after Chikaba's death, can be read both as a religious slave narrative, a hagiography, or both.

It is believed that Chikaba was born around 1676, in the Elmina area of today's Ghana, to a respected and wealthy family. She grew up with a father (name unknown) mother (Abar), and three brothers (Juachípiter, Ensú, and Joaquín). Chikaba's father was a tribal chief. When she was about ten years of age, she was captured by a Spanish slave ship. Following the traditional maritime route, the ship stopped at the isle of São Tomé, where Chikaba was baptized and given a Christian name, Therese. The slave ship resumed the voyage, sailing first toward Lisbon and then Seville. Once in Spain, and following imperial custom, Chikaba was presented to the king, Charles II, who, in turn, offered her as a gift to the marquis and marquise of Mancera, aristocrats who lived in Madrid. Chikaba was a house slave but, we are told, she was treated by the Manceras more as a daughter than as a slave. Accordingly, the Manceras provided Chikaba with an elite education: she was taught how to read and write; she was instructed in the Catholic religion; and she was even allowed to sit at the Manceras' table for meals.

When Chikaba was about twenty-five years of age, she decided to enter the convent. The Manceras's petition was rejected on several occasions, and Chikaba was rejected in all the convents in Madrid and Avila for the sole reason of being black. It was thanks to the Manceras's family connections that she was finally accepted at the Convent of the Dominican Sisters of Saint Mary Magdalene, popularly known as the Convent of Penance, in Salamanca, where Chikaba arrived in 1703. Chikaba finally took her vows on June 29, 1704, receiving the name of Therese Juliana of Saint Dominic. Chikaba's conventual life was exemplary. Commonly known as "la negrita" (the little black girl), she devoted her life to working for her religious congregation, ignored those who looked at her with scorn or suspicion because of her skin color, and excelled in her piety, charity, and humility. At the convent Chikaba was relegated to doing the household chores (such as cooking, washing, and cleaning) and the sacristy, and she also worked as the doorkeeper. Due to her poor health, she died on December 6, 1748. Her relics are kept at the Dominican Sisters in Salamanca, popularly known as Las Dueñas.

The canonization process of Chikaba has already started, and she has recently been named Venerable. If canonized, Chikaba will become, together with St. Josephine Bakhita from Sudan, among the few freed female African slaves who are saints.

Chikaba's story is known thanks to her last confessor, the Reverend P. Juan Carlos Pan y Agua, who wrote *Compendio de la vida ejemplar de la Venerable Madre Sor Teresa Juliana de Santo Domingo* (Compendium of the exemplary life of the venerable Sr. Therese Juliana of Saint Dominic) in 1752. Following the tradition of hagiographies, or the recording of the lives of saints, Pan y Agua's religious biography emphasizes Chikaba's precocious wisdom, her long-lived search for God, her noble origin, and her death, which was accompanied and immediately followed by many kinds of supernatural events. Unfortunately, the biography of Chikaba provides very little information on her African childhood. Given the early age at which Chikaba was captured, the names, locations, and vicissitudes associated with her childhood are hard to verify. Chikaba's convent life, however, is documented in detail by Pan y Agua's work, which offers a day-to-day account of her religious life.

Maria Frias

See also: Bakhita, Josephine, Saint; Catholicism; Slave Narratives

Reference

Fra-Molinero, Baltasar. "La primera escritora afrohispánica: Chikaba o Sor Teresa Juliana de Santo Domingo." http://www.bates. edu/bframoli/pagina/chicaba.html.

CHILE

Chile has a history of involvement in slavery and the slave trade and has political relations with Africa as well as cultural and artistic connections. Chile is a country located on the western coast of South America. It occupies a narrow region running from north to south, from the Andean region to the southern tip of South America. It is bordered by dry land in the north, by the Antarctic in the south, by the Andean highlands in the east, and by the Pacific Ocean in the west. Chile was a colony of Spain from the time that Diego de Almagro claimed the region for the Spanish crown in 1536 to the time it achieved its independence in 1818.

Chile is considered the "whitest" country of Latin America, and the legacy of African slaves in Chilean history and society is not acknowledged. However, this does not mean that there were no Africans in Chile, only that the African presence in the country has faded away through centuries of miscegenation.

The first blacks to arrive in Chile came with Diego de Almagro in 1536. The importation of slaves began mostly as a way to supplement the indigenous labor force. Chile was of minor importance to the Spanish crown because it was a poor colony. The importation of African slaves, then, was not significant nor it was a priority for the crown.

Slaves were initially introduced to Chile to provide a workforce for the colony's mining industry. In fact, in the Spanish colonies of South America, it was only in Chile and Peru that African slaves worked in mines alongside native people. Slave labor in Chile was also used in agriculture and in urban centers as servants, skilled artisans, shoemakers, tailors, carpenters, and so on.

Slaves were brought to Chile by two routes, the Pacific and the Atlantic. The Pacific route began in the Atlantic on the coast of Africa, continued to the northern coast of South America (especially Cartagena and Panama), and proceeded overland to the Pacific and then to Chile. The Atlantic route also began on the coast of Africa but took slave ships to Argentina, more particularly to the port of Buenos Aires. From there, slaves were taken on foot across the Pampa region and the Andes to Chile. Both routes were extremely difficult, and the mortality rate could reach as much as 50 percent or even more.

The order of the Jesuits was the biggest owner of slaves in Chile, with perhaps as many as 2,000. The Jesuits employed slaves in all kinds of occupations, including agricultural and household work. When the Jesuits were expelled from Chile in 1767, they sold their slaves mostly in Peru. The slave population in Chile was never very large. For instance, it is estimated that the slave population in the late eighteenth century was around 12,000. One interesting aspect of the black population in Chile is that the number of blacks declined while the number of mulattos increased throughout the colonial period. For example, in the late sixteenth century there were about 10,000 blacks and no significant number of mulattos. However, by the mid-eighteenth century, there were about 3,000 blacks and almost 20,000 mulattos, and by the early nineteenth century, the numbers were around 1,500 blacks and almost 30,000 mulattos.

The proportion of Spaniards to Africans also changed throughout the colonial period in Chile. From the early sixteenth to the early seventeenth century, blacks outnumbered the Spaniards, but between the mid-seventeenth and the early nineteenth century, this picture changed drastically. For instance, in 1570 there were about 7,000 Spaniards in the country and 10,000 blacks. In 1620 there were 15,000 Spaniards and 22,500 blacks. Finally, by the late eighteenth century Spaniards began outnumbering blacks: in 1777 there were around 120,000 Spaniards and around 3,000 blacks and 20,000 mulattos. By 1813 the proportion was around 281,000 Spaniards to around 1,500 blacks and 30,000 mulattos.

In 1823 Chile freed all of its slaves, the first Spanish American republic to do so. Even though the African presence in Chile has been lost because of miscegenation, it is still present in the ethnic composition of the country. Africans did not disappear; they mixed with whites and natives, and in this way their legacy still exists. Evidence of their contribution to Chile is found in the country's official national dance, the *cueca,* which is believed to have African origins that were mixed with Spanish ones.

Still, the African presence in Chile has been ignored by both the authorities and scholars. In fact, many different governments, and especially the military regime of Augusto Pinochet, have attempted to affirm Chile as a European country. This effort has included making it difficult for Africans to immigrate and ignoring the presence and contributions made by descendants of Africans. As a consequence of the return of democracy, an organization called Oro Negro ("Black Gold") was formed in 2001 with the specific objective of lobbying for the recognition of the African presence in Chile and the rescue of the nation's African cultural roots.

Rosana Barbosa and Rosa Barbosa Nune

See also: Colonialism; Slavery (History)

References

Dominguez, Jorge I. *Race and Ethnicity in Latin America.* New York: Garland, 1994.

Fagerstrom, René Peri. *La Raza Negra en Chile: Una presencia Negada.* Santiago, Chile: Editora Hilda López Aguilar, 1999.

Klein, Herbert. *African Slavery in Latin America and the Caribbean.* New York: Oxford University Press, 1986.

Mellafe, Rolando. *Negro Slavery in Latin America.* Berkeley: University of California Press, 1975.

Sater, William F. "The Black Experience in Chile." In *Slavery and Race Relations in Latin America,* edited by Robert Brent Toplin. Westport, CT: Greenwood Press, 1974.

CHRISTIANITY (AFRICAN AMERICAN)

African American Christianity has shaped the religious practices and culture of Christianity and has also influenced African American cultural practices and political life. Since the early years of their arrival in the United States, the vast majority of African Americans have participated in some variation of Christianity. Enslaved Africans were denied the right to practice their African faiths in America; they were also excluded from Christian worship with white Americans and sometimes forbidden from Christian worship altogether. The roots of the African American Christian tradition are, consequently, a specifically African adaptation to the Christian faith, especially in the minimization of abstract doctrine and the maximization of physical and oral expression. Beliefs similar to Christian doctrine had been common in Africa, including notions of a supreme deity, good and evil spirits, the afterlife, worship services, and water baptism. Antebellum Protestant clerics were divided in their views on black slavery, while after the Civil War most white churches rejected black parishioners. Consequently, after 1865, black people were finally able to worship in a formal setting, and specifically black church communities formed, becoming a foundation of black cultural identity and political culture. In the 1950s and 1960s, many of these churches were at the forefront of the Civil Rights Movement. The five Christian faiths with the most African American adherents today are, in descending order, the Baptist, Methodist, Holiness-Pentecostal-Apostolic, Catholic, and Jehovah's Witnesses. The church history of these five is rife with conflict over black slavery. For instance, there was a schism between white and black Baptist churches over slavery that has not even now been repaired and which has spawned seven major African American Baptist churches. As a group, African Americans have associated themselves strongly with Christianity in modern times.

Alana Trumpy

See also: African Methodist Episcopal Church; Diaspora; Pentecostalism

References

Lincoln, C. Eric, and Lawrence Mamiya. *The Black Church in the African American Experience.* Durham, NC: Duke University Press, 2000

McMickle, Marvin Andrew. *An Encyclopaedia of African American Christian Heritage.* Valley Forge, PA: Judson Press, 2002.

Wilmore, Gayraud. *Black Religion and Black Radicalism: An Interpretation of the Religious History of African Americans.* Maryknoll, NY: Orbis, 1998.

CHRISTOPHE, HENRI (1767?–1820)

After playing a prominent military role in Haiti's war of independence (1791–1804), Henri Christophe became the president (1807–1811) and king (1811–1820) of Haiti's North. Christophe was born a slave in Grenada on or around October 6, 1767. After Haitian slaves revolted against their French masters in August 1791, Christophe joined the fighting, becoming one of Toussaint Louverture's, then Jean-Jacques Dessalines's, most famous subordinates. Among his most renowned revolutionary acts was the burning of Cap Haïtien (then known as Cap Français) in February 1802 before the city was taken by Napoléon's troops. (Christophe later collaborated with, then turned against, the French expeditionary force.)

A signer of the January 1804 Haitian Declaration of Independence, Christophe opposed Dessalines's massacre of the white population in Haiti. He then participated in the 1805 invasion of Santo Domingo (present-day Dominican Republic). Christophe took part in the revolt that overthrew Dessalines on October 17, 1806.

Under an agreement with mulatto leader Alexandre Pétion, Christophe was to become president, ruling the country jointly with Pétion, the president of the Senate. The relationship between the two quickly degenerated into a civil war. On February 17, 1807, Christophe established a separate state in northern Haiti, with himself as sole president. (Pétion declared himself president of the southern and western part of the country on March 9, 1807.) Though Christophe quickly established complete control over his half of the country, his repeated attempts to oust Pétion proved inconclusive.

On March 26, 1811, Christophe proclaimed himself King Henri I of the North. He then proceeded to create a nobility, then to organize a magnificent coronation ceremony held on June 2, 1811. Christophe ruled with an iron hand, creating a 4,000-strong police force known as the Royal Corps of Dahomey. Thieves, stragglers, and idle peasants were severely punished. Even though slavery had been abolished during the War of Independence, Christophe continued Louverture's and Dessalines's policy of *fermage*. Under this policy, peasants were forced to remain as workers on the plantations on which they had once been slaves in exchange for a 25 percent share of the crop and food, clothes, and housing (with the right to tend their own gardens on Saturdays).

Christophe's rule was brutal, but in comparison with Pétion's South, where a policy of land distribution had led to subsistence farming and plummeting exports of sugar, the North flourished economically. Christophe used some of the proceeds to build magnificent mansions, including Sans Souci palace in Milot, and the nearby citadel of La Ferrière (also known as Citadelle Christophe), a massive, 200-gun fortress surrounded by precipitous cliffs. Left paralyzed by a debilitating stroke on August 15, 1820, Christophe quickly found himself faced with an armed rebellion. He killed himself (allegedly with a silver bullet) on October 8, 1820. His wife, Marie-Louise Christophe, and their two daughters, Améthyste and Athenaire, fled into exile.

Philippe R. Girard

See also: Dessalines, Jean Jacq ues; Haiti; Louverture, Toussaint Bréda; Pétion, Alexandre Sabès

References

Cole, Hubert. *Christophe, King of Haiti.* New York: Viking Press, 1967.

Vandercook, John W. *Black Majesty: The Life of Christophe, King of Haiti.* New York: Harper and Brothers, 1980.

CITIES

According to some common definitions, human settlements may be considered cities when they reach the following conditions: a population of more than 5,000, diversity in jobs and services, a relatively high density of people per square unit of land, and a specialized economy of nonagricultural activities. In many cases, also, cities are more than just a locus of economic activities, and the design of cities in Africa and Latin America have often followed urban planning programs intended to consolidate emerging national identities as well as to establish urban centers as focal points for national development. Historically, the colonial administrations on both continents were highly centralized, and this centralization contributed to the concentration of national and metropolitan power, whether in the hands of colonial administrators or in the hands of local elites. In Latin America as well as in Africa, an historical trend to occupy peripheral land near the coastlines was strong, except in the case of urbanization in Colombia and Mexico, where it occurred primarily on the highlands.

The growth of cities in Latin America during the nineteenth century reflected the growing economic dependence of less industrialized countries upon industrialized nations. At the turn of the twentieth century, French planning exerted a huge influence in several capital cities of the world. Inspired by Georges-Eugéne Haussmann's interventions in Paris, planners and politicians undertook the urban renovation of Buenos Aires, Caracas, and Mexico City. These capitals were given monumental architecture, grand boulevards, and symbolic landmarks. However, the fast expansion of cities after World War II exceeded government capacities to extend basic services to the new districts in the outskirts of major urban centers. At the time, government agencies took charge of the construction and administration of basic services, and many municipalities faced financial crises when the accumulated debt escalated, mostly due to inadequate tax-collection systems.

With the nascent industrialization of the 1930s and 1940s, urban planners embraced modern ideas from Europe and North America, characterized by industrialized construction methods, large-scale highway construction to connect urban centers, public housing developments built along elite enclaves, and laissez-faire urban policies that produced distinctive spatial patterns of irregular settlements along the urban periphery. The great physical expansion of major cities in Latin America occurred in the 1930s, when Buenos Aires approached 3,000,000 inhabitants, Mexico City had 1,229,576, Sao Paolo was close to 1,000,000, Santiago de Chile had 712,533, and Havana rose to 655,823.

During this time, when Latin America already had twenty-eight cities with more than 100,000 people, that figure was surpassed by only three cities in Africa: Ibadan and Lagos in Nigeria and Omdurman in Anglo-Egyptian Sudan. Kano and Addis Ababa had around 80,000 inhabitants, while Dakar, Accra, Luanda, and Mombasa rose to 50,000 people. However, substantial urban growth occurred in Africa during the 1950s and 1960s, when cities like Ibadan and Kinshasa reached a million people each. The rapid urban expansion of both Latin American and African cities escalated in the 1960s, when irregular settlements expanded on the urban periphery and slowly but steadily were incorporated into the formal city.

The African continent in general, and sub-Saharan Africa in particular, are urbanizing fast. Africa has a long tradition of urbanism predating the colonial period. During the colonial era, however, major changes were introduced that led to the rapid expansion of cities. Within urban areas, colonial policy distorted land markets by adopting racially segregated land-use patterns as well as by taking steps to exclude Africans or limit their access to urban land. Nevertheless, the recognition of traditional tenure as a parallel system of accessing land was meant to transfer the control and management of land in these areas to reflect the indigenous social systems. Rapid urbanization in Africa has been associated with the failure of public authorities to provide sufficient land to meet the needs of the burgeoning population.

After independence and with the support of the World Bank, a number of countries undertook upgrading projects in the 1960s and 1970s, the purpose of which was to address irregular urban development by providing serviced sites for construction as well as improving their general environmental and tenurial conditions in unplanned areas. However, these scattered projects did not have a major impact on the development of irregular areas, in which by the 1980s a large proportion of the urban population in African cities lived. As the World Bank noted in the case of Conakry, Guinea, illegal settlements represented the most frequent form of urban land occupancy and resulted from informal and unregistered financial arrangements with customary occupants. Although in the past, irregular land was stigmatized as constituting neglected, dangerous, and illegal areas of the city, recent evidence suggests a more complex situation, with middle- and high-income households, as well as civil servants and prominent entrepreneurs, showing a sizable presence in these areas. In both Dar es Salaam and Nairobi, high-income households are seen to be developing high-rise or otherwise expensive buildings in irregular areas such as Manzese and Mathare. African cities continue to grow in physical size without expanding the capacity of their limited existing infrastructure and services. This has resulted in poor housing, rundown infrastructure, and environmental decay.

In Africa, cities maintain a significant role as centers of economic development, but this has led to the decline of rural regions due to the high migration rates to metropolitan areas. The concentration of facilities and opportunities in a very limited number of cities has given rise to dismayingly sharp differentials in urban and rural incomes and to growing social and geographical inequalities.

In both Latin America and Africa, the high concentration of migrants moving away from poor conditions in rural areas and townships has put unparalleled pressure on urban resources, infrastructures, transportation, and environments. Levels of poverty, unemployment, overcrowding, and informal settlement formation have been exacerbated. This has led to a severe crisis of maintenance and to the deterioration in urban services and quality of life in African and Latin American cities.

The rapid growth of cities and the migration of the rural poor has led to housing shortages that have not been dealt with by urban planners. What is often referred to as a vast "informal" sector in African and Latin American cities is in fact a working-class majority that survives at the level of subsistence. While building the formal city, public officials have always referred to housing construction as their main goal since the number of low-income housing units produced has been the key to their political success. However, public housing usually meets only one-tenth of the social housing demand, which means that the other 90 percent of the population must meet its needs through self-help housing.

A strategy widely promoted by international aid organizations, self-help practices were conceived as a substitute for government-sponsored initiatives. The strategy consisted in financing local groups and organizations that spontaneously emerged to deal with miserable urban conditions. The World Bank's Sites and Services program was inspired by self-help strategies, involving credit and "cost recovery," or liability, and were aimed at creating an incipient real estate market for the stable-income consumer. However, this approach ultimately could not solve the housing needs of the impoverished majority. Even when self-help strategies can serve as a positive instrument of development, a constant among the strongest and most influential self-help groups has been the demand for a stronger government role and a more equitable economic and political system.

Many housing policies call for the reduction of the government's share of the housing burden while incorporating the poor in the provision of their own housing. Under this policy of the "enabling approach" to housing, the government concentrates its efforts on those functions that nongovernmental sectors cannot undertake effectively, in particular, security of tenure, infrastructure and public services, community facilities, construction credit, and a viable legislative framework. This strategy, promoted by agencies such as the World Bank, are initiatives intended to mobilize resources from the formal and informal private sector, community-based and nongovernmental organizations, and individual households. However, asking the poor to access housing through the market presents substantial difficulties where unemployment and poverty rates continue to be very high, as in Africa. Alternative strategies may include enabling access to land at costs affordable to the poor, vigorously pursuing job creation through informal-sector programs that can promote income generation, and availing affordable credit to the poor to allow them to improve their housing incrementally.

Alfonso Valenzuela-Aguilera

See also: Colonialism; Urbanization

References

Becker, Charles M., Andrew M. Hamer, and Andrew R. Morrison. *Beyond Urban Bias in Africa: Urbanization in an Era of Structural Adjustment.* Portsmouth, NH: Heinemann, 1994.

Morse, Richard M., and Jorge Hardoy. *Rethinking the Latin American City.* Washington, DC; Baltimore; and London: The Woodrow Wilson Center Press and The John Hopkins University Press, 1992.

O'Connor, Anthony. *The African City.* London: Hutchinson, 1983.

Salau, A. T. "Urbanization and Spatial Strategies in West Africa." In *Cities and Development in the Third World,* edited by R. B. Potter and A. T. Salau. London: Mansell, 1990.

Simon, D. *Cities, Capital, and Development: African Cities in the World Economy.* London: Belhaven, 1992.

Stren, Richard E. *African Cities in Crisis: Managing Rapid Growth.* Boulder, CO: Westview Press, 1989.

CIVIL RIGHTS MOVEMENT

The Civil Rights Movement was the struggle to obtain equal rights for African Americans in the 1950s and 1960s, challenging racial segregation and disenfranchisement through peaceful means. The movement marked a time in America when the African American struggle for equality was brought to national and international attention. It was built on a long history of struggle for freedom and against oppression. As early as the 1940s, the Congress of Racial Equality was challenging racial segregation through sit-ins and other forms of peaceful protest. A critical turn for the African American community was the *Brown v. Board of Education* decision of the U.S. Supreme Court in 1954, which declared school segregation unconstitutional, effectively overturning *Plessy v. Ferguson* (1896). This was a crucial victory for the NAACP and lawyer Thurgood Marshall. *Brown vs. Board of Education* initiated a direct challenge to the "separate but equal" doctrine that had been sanctioned by *Plessy vs. Ferguson.* Unfortunately, school integration did not come easily, despite the Court's ruling. In fact, during 1957 President Dwight Eisenhower was forced to send U.S. troops into Little Rock,

Arkansas, to implement the desegregation of the high school there. Likewise when James Meredith became the first African American to enroll in the University of Mississippi in 1962, he was escorted by U.S. marshals.

The modern Civil Rights Movement began in 1955 with Rosa Parks and the Montgomery Bus Boycott. Parks was a member of the local chapter of the NAACP. The laws of that time required African Americans to sit at the back of city busses; in fact, a line was painted aboard each bus establishing the segregation of the races. On December 1, 1955, Rosa Parks was arrested when she refused to give up her seat in the front to a white male. Parks's arrest led to the Montgomery Boycott, a communitywide boycott of the bus company. The Montgomery Boycott proved instrumental, as it initiated similar movements across the South. The Montgomery Boycott was organized by the Montgomery Improvement Association and its newly elected president, Dr. Martin Luther King Jr. Dr. King was instrumental in bringing national attention to the boycott, and later to the broader movement, by utilizing television to focus national awareness on the struggles of the African American community. The Montgomery Bus Boycott lasted for one year and came to a close when the Supreme Court ruled that segregation in public transportation violated the U.S. Constitution.

The Montgomery Bus Boycott was instrumental in bringing Dr. King to the forefront of the Civil Rights Movement. In 1957 King, along with Charles Steele and Fred Shuttlesworth, established the Southern Christian Leadership Conference (SCLC), which took on an organizing role in the movement. King was very much

Dorothy Geraldine Counts walks to enroll at the previously all-white Harding High School in Charlotte, North Carolina, on September 4, 1957. White communities often strongly opposed desegregation, and white youths taunted her on her way to school. (Library of Congress)

influenced by the pacifist Mahatma Gandhi and supported the philosophy of peaceful resistance. This philosophy would be reflected in the marches, sit-ins, and other forms of protest that marked the movement. King preached as well as practiced a nonviolent philosophy. During his tenure as leader of the Civil Rights Movement, Dr. King was arrested numerous times. On April 16, 1963, King wrote "Letter from a Birmingham Jail," asserting the moral obligation of individuals to disobey unjust laws. In his most famous address, the "I Have a Dream" speech given on August 28, 1963, at the Lincoln Memorial in Washington, D.C., King professed his belief in nonviolent resistance and his desire to win racial equality in all aspects of American life. This speech was the highlight of the historical March on Washington, where more than 200,000 people joined together to protest the status of African Americans in America. The march was organized by a joint effort of civil rights leaders, leaders of the labor movement, and liberal politicians. The march had six official goals: the establishment of federal work programs; equal employment rights; equal housing rights; voting rights for African Americans; and integrated education, with the overall aim of the passage of civil rights laws. Following the march, Dr. King and other civil rights leaders met with President John F. Kennedy to discuss civil rights legislation. In 1964 Dr. Martin Luther King Jr. was awarded the Nobel Peace Prize in Stockholm, Sweden, in recognition for his work in the Civil Rights Movement. King was the third person of African descent to receive the award.

While he spoke about and lived a life of nonviolent resistance, Dr. King's death was marked by violence. He was assassinated on April 4, 1968, while in Memphis, Tennessee, to support striking city sanitation workers. King's death came the day after he had given his famous "I've Been to the Mountaintop" speech. Riots broke out across America in the days following King's death, which brought global attention to the experience of African Americans. Around the world King was recognized for his desire for equality and for his nonviolent pursuit of that dream, and his death, occurring in such a violent manner, helped bring to light the often-ignored discrepancy of life, citizenship, and rights for black people in American society. The world saw a divided image of the United States in which African Americans struggled to gain freedom while members of mainstream society sought to maintain a system of segregation. The Supreme Court's decision in *Brown v. Board of Education* initiated change across America, and nowhere was this more evident than in Little Rock, Arkansas, where the school board, in support of *Brown,* voted in 1957 to integrate the school system. Controversy erupted when the governor, Orval Faubus, called on the National Guard to prevent nine students from entering Little Rock's Central High School. In response, President Dwight Eisenhower federalized the National Guard and issued an order for it to retreat. The "Little Rock Nine," the African American children who sought to attend the school, were able to enter the building, but from the onset they were subject to physical and verbal abuse from their white peers. Several African American reporters who where there to mark the integration of Central High School were beaten severely by the mob that had gathered around the school in an attempt to keep the students out. By the middle of the first day, the "Little Rock Nine" had to be escorted from the school facility after city officials lost control of the angry mob outside. President Eisenhower then sent in the 101st Airborne Division to escort the Arkansas nine into the school. The troops patrolled outside the school and escorted the "Little Rock Nine" around the school each day. Eventually, the 101st was pulled out and in May of 1957 Ernest Green became the first African American to graduate from Central High School. Green was the only black student in the class of 602 graduates.

As in the case of King's death, much of the news of the Civil Rights Movement that circulated around the world involved violence that beleaguered it. Perhaps one of the most well-remembered moments of the movement occurred in Birmingham, Alabama, in an area known as Dynamite Hill. Churches, a long-established core of the African American community, played a significant role during the Civil Rights Movement. They served as meeting places for the African American community, and often marches, sit-ins, and other forms of nonviolent protest were conceived in churches, which were also frequently the starting point of demonstrations. As a center of the African American community and of the movement, churches came to represent a threat to those against integration and equal rights for all Americans. Church burnings thus became a common occurrence throughout the South. The Ku Klux Klan, in particular, was known not only to burn churches but to set crosses afire in front of them as well as the homes of African Americans. On September 15, 1963, in Birmingham, Alabama, an explosion occurred at the Sixteenth Street Baptist Church, a central meeting place of civil rights leaders. The bombing resulted in the deaths of four little girls: Denise McNair, Cynthia Wesley, Carole Robertson, and Addie Mae Collins. This event shocked the African American community in Alabama, in the South, in America, and in many places around the world and highlighted the level of racist violence in the United States. The death of these innocent girls also brought global attention to the Civil Rights Movement. Critics across the globe cast a critical eye on American society, reexamining the nation's ideology of freedom in light of the actual treatment of African Americans.

The death of King and these four little girls, coupled with other significant losses—Emmett Till, a fourteen-year-old who was kidnapped, tortured, and murdered in Mississippi in 1955; civil rights leader Medgar Evers, murdered in front of his home in Jackson, Mississippi in 1963;

civil rights workers James Chaney, Michael Schwerner, and Andrew Goodman, murdered in Philadelphia, Mississippi, in 1964; and Malcolm X, shot dead in New York City in 1965—presented an image of American society that was fractured, an impression in contrast to how the United States wanted to be seen. These deaths were unnecessary sacrifices that opened the eyes of Americans and individuals throughout the world to the marginalized status that African Americans continued to hold in American society. These losses challenged the image of America as the core of global freedom.

The success of the Civil Rights Movement was due to the efforts of many. In February 1960 the Greensboro Four, four African American students from North Carolina Agricultural and Technical College, initiated a sit-in at a Woolworth's counter after they were refused service. Throughout the South other youths followed them, gathering at lunch counters to protest the refusal of establishments to desegregate. Individuals who participated in sit-ins were instructed to dress well and sit quietly, following the nonviolent path that King had established for the movement. They left empty seats between them, encouraging white patrons to join them in their struggle.

The Congress of Racial Equality (CORE) played a crucial role in providing leadership, along with the Southern Christian Leadership Conference and the Student Nonviolent Coordinating Committee (SNCC), founded in 1960 at Shaw University. In 1961 CORE began sending student volunteers on bus trips into the South, testing a 1960 U.S. Supreme Court decision that prohibited segregation in interstate travel facilities. These Freedom Riders traveled into the Deep South in an attempt to desegregate bus company terminals. The Freedom Riders encountered violence: buses were firebombed and attacked by members of the Ku Klux Klan. Some riders were arrested and subjected to inhumane treatment.

The Council of Federated Organizations (COFO), a group of civil rights organizations that included CORE and SNCC, initiated the registration of black voters during the Freedom Summer, a 1964 campaign that included both black and white college students from the North and South. It was during this campaign that three civil rights activists, James Chaney, Andrew Goodman, and Michael Schwerner, were murdered by the Ku Klux Klan, bringing both national and international attention to Mississippi. The FBI was brought in to investigate the brutal deaths. The murders were a factor in the passing of the Civil Rights Act of 1964, which barred discrimination in public accommodations, employment, and education.

In 1965 SNCC and SCLC began an aggressive voting initiative in Selma, Alabama. On March 7, supporters set out on a fifty-four-mile march from Selma to Montgomery, the state capital. Six blocks into the march, at Edmund Pettus Bridge, the demonstrators were attacked by state troopers and local law enforcement. Footage of the peaceful demonstrators being brutalized by law enforcers were seen around the country and the world. President Johnson delivered a televised address to Congress eight days after the march, giving support to the voting rights bill that was before Congress at that time. On August 6, Johnson signed the Voting Rights Act of 1965, suspending poll taxes and literacy and other voter tests as well as authorizing federal supervision of voter registration.

Also active during this time were the NAACP and the Urban League. The NAACP Legal Defense and Education Fund provided the legal personnel for the Civil Rights Movement and played a key role in *Brown v. Board of Education*. The Fund was instrumental in helping James Meredith become the first African American student to attend the University of Mississippi in 1962.

As a consequence of the movement's successes, blacks began to move into positions of power in the United States. Most noteworthy, on October 2, 1967, Thurgood Marshall, who had been an instrumental figure in the *Brown v. the Board of Education* case, became the first African American U.S. Supreme Court justice. There are a growing number of African Americans in Congress and the Presidential Cabinet, and Barack Obama is currently the first nationally recognized candidate for the U.S. Presidency.

J. A. Brown-Rose

See also: King Jr., Martin Luther; Malcolm X

References

Carson, Clayborne, David J. Garrow, Darlene Clark Hine et al., eds. *Eyes on the Prize: Civil Rights Reader—Documents, Speeches, and Firsthand Accounts from the Black Freedom Struggle, 1954–1990.* New York: Penguin Group, 1991.

Collier-Thomas, Bettye, and V. P. Franklin. *Sisters in the Struggle: African American Women in the Civil Rights-Black Power Movement.* New York: New York University Press, 2001.

Lewis, John, and Michael D'Orso. *Walking in the Wind: A Memoir of the Movement.* San Diego: Harcourt Brace, 1999.

Parks, Rosa, with James Haskins. *Rosa Parks: My Story.* New York: Penguin Young Readers Group, 1999.

McWhorter, Diane. *A Dream of Freedom: The Civil Rights Movement from 1954 to 1968.* New York: Scholastic, 2004.

Williams, Juan. *Eyes on the Prize: America's Civil Rights Years, 1954–1965.* New York: Penguin Group, 1987.

CIVIL WAR, AMERICAN

The American Civil War began on April 12, 1861, when Confederate troops attacked Fort Sumter in South Carolina. Although complex economic and social forces motivated Southerners to secede and ultimately take up arms, the war was fought over the union of the United States, threatened by the issue of whether or not slavery would continue in the United States. Despite the popular myth that African Americans were simply the subjects of this debate, blacks were involved in and affected by nearly every aspect of the war. At the onset of the conflict, more than 4.5 million people of African descent lived in the United States, and 3.5 million of these men, women, and children lived as slaves in the South. (Blacks comprised nearly one-third of the overall population south of the Mason-Dixon Line.)

The Civil War came as the culmination of decades of heated political debate. The 1857 *Dred Scott* decision of the U.S. Supreme Court, which categorized enslaved African Americans as property and and declared that African Americans had no political rights, followed important laws that shaped the national conversation about slavery. The Compromise of 1850, a series of five laws, allowed the admission of California to the Union as a free state while declaring that future states carved from territory taken in the war with Mexico would be allowed to determine for themselves whether or not slavery would be permitted within their borders The Fugitive Slave Law, a part of the compromise, required

northern states to return runaway slaves. However, many citizens in the North refused to obey, and free blacks and abolitionists began to see war as inevitable. In 1859 antislavery advocate John Brown led a raid on a federal arsenal with the hope of eventually freeing slaves in the South, and in 1861 the Republican Party, which was formed by antislavery activists, gained control of the White House when Abraham Lincoln became president.

Before Lincoln was even inaugurated, South Carolina seceded from the Union, and by June 1861, ten other southern states had followed suit. Once the fighting began in April, African Americans heeded Frederick Douglass's call for "black men just now to take up arms in behalf of their country" (Hargrove, 1988, p. 2). Thousands of African Americans volunteered to join the Union Army; yet Lincoln initially objected to their participation, arguing that the chief goal of the conflict was to reunite the country, rather than abolish the system of slavery. As a result, many Northern blacks contributed to the war effort in non-military capacities by working in hospitals and factories. Others enlisted in the U.S. Navy, which allowed African Americans to serve as sailors.

With Northern forces moving deeper into Confederate territory, Union soldiers were approached by hundreds of escaped slaves who sought their protection. Following Lincoln's official policy, some U.S. generals immediately returned these men and women to their masters. Other generals considered runaway slaves to be contraband and held them in Union camps, where they proved to be an additional source of labor. More rarely, black men were allowed to fight as Union soldiers, and the first all–African American unit of the

The 4th U.S. Colored Infantry at Fort Lincoln during the Civil War, part of the defenses of Washington, D.C. (Library of Congress)

war was the First South Carolina Volunteer Regiment, recruited by General David Hunter in May 1862. (The U.S. Department of War quickly disbanded this unit and reprimanded Hunter for taking such action.) For those blacks who remained on the plantations, life during the war became increasingly difficult. Like whites in the South, African Americans experienced a scarcity of food, increased sickness, and a lack of access to Northern products. Finances became leaner for their owners, and slaves tended to be bought and sold with greater frequency, as their masters needed money.

Furthermore, African Americans were expected to support the Southern economy while their owners went off to fight. Nearly 80 percent of military-age white southern males participated in the war, and blacks were left to help build fortifications, deliver supplies, serve as blacksmiths and laundresses, and provide medical care for troops.

On July 17, 1862, the U.S. Congress had passed two acts that allowed for the enlistment of African Americans in the Union army. On January 1, 1863, Lincoln issued the Emancipation Proclamation, which granted freedom to all slaves in Confederate-held territory. Blacks came to comprise about 10 percent of the overall Union Army, and by August 1863 the army featured fourteen black regiments. Over the course of the next two years, African Americans steadily proved their value to skeptical U.S. commanders. In May 1863 blacks fought valiantly at the

Battle of Port Hudson in Louisiana, and in July the Fifty-fourth Massachusetts volunteered to lead a charge against Confederates at Fort Wagner, South Carolina. Despite their courage and skill as soldiers, African Americans were still considered to be fugitive slaves by opposing Confederate troops, who targeted blacks on the battlefield. In 1864 a force of more than 2,500 Southern men attacked Fort Pillow in Tennessee, which was manned by no more than 600 Union troops. The Confederate soldiers took the fort with little trouble, and of the 292 African American soldiers stationed there, only 62 survived the punishment that Southern soldiers sought to render. Confederates murdered blacks who attempted to surrender, and African American bodies were nailed to logs and lit on fire. By the end of the war, over 179,000 blacks had served in the Union Army and Navy, with 3,000 dying of wounds suffered in battle and 33,000 perishing from disease.

With the exception of Sherman's campaign through Georgia, African American soldiers served in every major battle of the war's last two years. Still, blacks in the Union Army experienced much discrimination, and it was not until near the end of the Civil War that Congress authorized equal salaries for African American soldiers. As a result of their courage, sixteen black soldiers were ultimately awarded the Medal of Honor, and Martin Delany, a doctor and writer, became the first black field officer when Lincoln commissioned him as a major of infantry in 1865.

On January 31, 1865, Congress ratified the Thirteenth Amendment, which banned slavery in the United States and its territories. Although this came as a relief to those who believed that the United States might revert to its former ways following the war, conditions for African Americans did not radically improve in the South. Many former slaves remained on the land of their previous owners, who became notorious for undercompensating these newly freed men and women. Other blacks relocated to urban areas, where education and work were often more available, or to Northern states, where the lure of starting a new life was attractive.

Clark Barwick

References
Hargrove, Hondon B. *Black Union Soldiers in the Civil War*. Jefferson, NC: McFarland, 1988.
Quarles, Benjamin. *The Negro in the Civil War*. New York: Da Capo Press, 1989.
Ramold, Steven J. *Slaves, Sailors, Citizens: African Americans in the Union Navy*. DeKalb: Northern Illinois University Press, 2002.
Trudeau, Noah Andre. *Like Men of War: Black Troops of the Civil War, 1862–1865*. Boston: Little, Brown, 1998.

CLEMENTE WALKER, ROBERTO (1934–1972)

Roberto Clemente was a Puerto Rican baseball player and humanitarian. As a baseball player, Clemente is considered one of the best right fielders ever to play the game. He was nicknamed "The Great One." Clemente's accomplishments include four National League batting championships, twelve Gold Glove Awards, the Most Valuable Player (MVP) award in 1966, and the World Series MVP in 1971.

Roberto Clemente was born on August 18, 1934 in Carolina, Puerto Rico, to Don Melchor Clemente and Dona Luisa Clemente. He was the youngest of seven children (six boys and one girl). His sister Rosa called him "Momen," which was the family nickname for Roberto. Americans would nickname him "Bob" or "Bobby," which he found to be insulting. He wanted everyone to know his name and his heritage.

Growing up, Clemente's love was for baseball. When Roberto was a young boy, he played with the Santurce Crabbers, a Puerto Rican winter league team comprised of Latinos, Negro League, and other Major League players. In 1954 he signed with the minor league Montreal Royals, and later that same year Clyde Sukeforth, a scout for the Pittsburgh Pirates, signed him with the Pirates.

Clemente's athletic abilities were his ticket to professional baseball; however, he was subjected to racism his whole life. Not only was racism prevalent in the mainland United States, it existed in Puerto Rico as well; in Montreal it was not as prevalent. One of the problems he faced in the United States was racial segregation, which became a serious problem when the Pirates were in Fort Myers, Florida, for spring training. There, he was labeled a "Puerto Rican hot dog" by the media (Markusen, 2001, p. 38). Clemente resented this label and decided that prejudice toward African Americans and Latinos needed to be addressed and resolved.

Clemente had to endure not only racial slights, but cultural differences as well. One major challenge that Clemente had to overcome was his use of the English language. He spoke broken English and some reporters typing up Clemente's comments would spell them phonetically for the readers. Doing this reflected the public's stereotypic picture of Latinos as lazy and awkward when it came to speaking the English language. Clemente realized he had been represented by the press as an uneducated Latino, a stereotype to which other ball players were subjected. He argued that Latino players were treated harshly and unfairly by umpires and the media. When reporters began attaching the words "Latin American" when identifying Clemente, he expressed disdain for the media. Another instance of discrimination occurred when Clemente and his wife went to a furniture store. When they entered the building, they were told that they had to go to another floor. As soon as Clemente was recognized, the store owner apologized and explained that he reacted the way he did because he thought Clemente might have been one of "those" Puerto Ricans, implying the stereotype of criminality. Because of his experiences, Clemente's campaign to address and get rid of discrimination was directed not just toward the game of baseball, but to societies as a whole.

Clemente was not just a baseball player who helped the Pirates to become a successful ball team; he was also a hero to the people of Puerto Rico. He returned to Puerto Rico every year and taught the children the game of baseball.

On December 31, 1972, Roberto Clemente and four other people boarded a plane to offer their assistance to the people of Nicaragua by taking relief supplies to Managua following a devastating earthquake. The plane crashed in the Caribbean Sea and Clemente's body was never found.

On August 8, 1973, Roberto Clemente was the first Hispanic player to be inducted into National Hall of Fame. That year the Roberto Clemente Award was created for athletes who not only excel in baseball, but who donate their time to the betterment of communities.

Clemente was an athlete, but first and foremost he was a humanitarian. His dream of having an athlete training facility for minorities has become a reality—the Ciudad Deportiva Roberto Clemente (the Roberto Clemente Training Center) located in Carolina, Puerto Rico. San Rico, Puerto Rico, named its coliseum Coliseo Roberto Clemente in honor of the "Great One." To honor the memory of Clemente, the Pittsburgh Pirates retired the uniform number 21. Monuments and memorials are found worldwide and include scholarships, schools, streets, bridges, postage stamps, and ballparks in Clemente's name. Clemente's legacy embodies the following quote from Clemente himself: "Any time you have the opportunity to accomplish something for somebody who comes behind you and you don't do it, you are wasting your time on this earth" (Walker 1988, p. 140).

Karen E. Holleran

References

Dunham, Montrew. *Roberto Clemente: Young Ball Player.* New York: Aladdin Paperback, 1997.

Engel, Trudie. *We'll Never Forget You, Roberto Clemente.* New York: Scholastic, 1999.

Greene, Carol. *Roberto Clemente: Baseball Superstar.* New York: Scholastic, 1991.

Musick, Phil. *Who Was Roberto? A Biography of Roberto Clemente.* New York: Doubleday, 1974.

Walker, Paul Robert. *Pride of Puerto Rico: The Life of Roberto Clemente.* San Diego: Harcourt Brace, 1988.

CLIFF, MICHELLE (1940–)

Michelle Cliff is a Jamaican American novelist, essayist, and educator. Author of several books, including *Free Enterprise* (1993), Michelle Cliff's creative works discuss the intersection of gender, race, and sexuality. She was born in the English-colonized Jamaica on November 2, 1946. Three years later her family moved to a Caribbean neighborhood in New York. At the age of ten, Cliff returned to Jamaica to attend school. She earned a BA in 1969 and from Wagner College in London. She completed an MPhil in the Italian Renaissance at the Warburg Institute of the University of London in 1974. Cliff worked in teaching and publishing for several years and did not begin writing until she was in her late thirties. She is the author of poetry collections, novels, short stories collections, and academic articles. Cliff has received many awards and fellowships, including National Endowment for the Arts fellowships in 1982 and 1989, a fellowship from MacDowell College in 1982, and a fellowship from Artists Foundation of Massachusetts in 1984. She was an Eli Kantor Fellow at the artists' community, Yaddo, in 1984; the Allan K. Smith Professor of English Languages and Literatures at Trinity College from 1993 to 1999; a Fulbright Distinguished Scholar in New Zealand; the Martin Luther King Jr., Cesar Chavez, and Rosa Parks Visiting Professor at the University of Michigan; a visiting professor at Johannes Gutenberg University; and a visiting writer at the Vermont Studio Center.

Being a light-skinned or white creole, a lesbian, and a Jamaican enable Cliff to speak within a transatlantic context on race, gender, class, language, history, and sexuality. Her fictional characters experience external and internalized racism, sexism, and homophobia. Her first two novels, *Abeng* (1984) and *No Telephone to Heaven* (1987), are considered autobiographical. In *Abeng,* Clare Savage is the light-skinned daughter of Boy Savage, a light-skinned descendant of a slave owner, and Kitty Savage, a dark-skinned descendant of the Maroons. The novel centers on the process by which Clare comes to terms with the implications of skin tone and race in Jamaica's history of slavery and colonialism. Clare is also the main character in *No Telephone to Heaven*. After studying in the United States and the United Kingdom, Clare returns to Jamaica. Cliff's third novel, *Free Enterprise* (1993), focuses on the imagined activist Mary Ellen Pleasant. The only historical record of such a person was a note signed by M.E.P. on the dead body of the U.S. abolitionist John Brown. In the novel, Mary Ellen Pleasant and the young Jamaican Annie Christmas join John Brown in the raid on Harpers Ferry. In *Free Enterprise* Cliff recreates a network of activism and resistance under oppressive English colonialism to explore the gaps in the history of Jamaican people.

Cliff's other works include the poetry collections *Claiming an Identity They Taught me to Despise* (1980) and *The Land of Look Behind* (1985) and the short story collections *Bodies of Water* (1990) and *The Store of a Million Items* (1998). The latter was chosen by the *Village Voice* in New York as one of the best books of 1998. Her story "Transactions" appeared in *Best American Short Stories 1997* (1998). Forthcoming by Cliff is a collection of essays called *Apocalypso*. Cliff currently lives in Hartford, Connecticut, and Santa Cruz, California.

Laura Madeline Wiseman

See also: Caribbean Literature; Feminism and Women's Equality Movements, Transatlantic; Feminism and Women's Equality Movements, U.S.

References

Cliff, Michelle. *Bodies of Water.* New York: Dutton, 1990.
Cliff, Michelle. "History as Fiction, Fiction as History." *Ploughshares* 20, nos. 2 and 3 (1994): 196–202.
Cliff, Michelle. *The Store of a Million Items: Stories.* New York: Houghton Mifflin, 1998.
Gifford, William Tell. *Narrative and the Nature of Worldview in the Clara Savage Novels of Michelle Cliff.* New York: Peter Lang, 2003.
MacDonald-Smythe, Antonia. *Making Homes in the West/Indies: Constructions of Subjectivity in the Writings of Michelle Cliff and Jamaica Kincaid.* New York: Routledge, 2001.

CODE NOIR

The Code Noir (black code) is the seventeenth- and eighteenth-century French legal code addressing the treatment of slaves that was applied to France's American colonies. (By extension, many refer to all the laws regulating slavery in the French colonies as Code Noir). The Code Noir was promulgated by French king Louis XIV (r. 1643–1715) in March 1685. Its sixty articles established legal precepts on how slaves should be treated. Secretary of the Navy Jean-Baptiste Colbert (1619–1683), conceived of the Code, which Charles de Courbon and Jean-Baptiste Patoulet wrote. The Code was applicable in France's American colonies, primarily Saint Domingue (Haiti), along with Guadeloupe, Martinique, St. Martin, Sainte-Croix, French Guyana, Quebec, Acadia, and St. Barthelemy. It was extended to the island of Réunion in 1723 and to Louisiana in 1724. France abolished slavery in 1794 (1793 for Haiti), then reestablished it in 1802; the Code was added to Napoléon Bonaparte's Code Civil in 1803 and remained valid until the slaves' final emancipation in 1848. The Code Noir contained clauses designed to ensure slave obedience and reduce the likelihood of slave revolts. Many of the Code's provisions protecting slaves, considered benign for its time, were never enforced.

Slaves were to be taught Catholicism and baptized (article 2); slaves practicing other religions, or owners allowing them to do so, were liable to punishment (article 3). The Code also expelled all Jews from French colonies (article 1) and protected Catholic slaves from religious discrimination on the part of their Protestant owners (article 5).

No slave was to work, or be auctioned, on Sundays (articles 6, 7). Slave owners could not sexually abuse any of their female slaves; if they did so, the only way to avoid being fined and having the slave confiscated was to marry her and to grant freedom to the slave and her offspring (article 9). Slaves could not be married without their owner's consent—but not against the slaves' will either (articles 10, 11). Slavery followed the maternal line: children of free women were free, while those of slave women were slaves, regardless of the father's status (article 13).

Owners were required to feed and clothe their slaves properly, even when they grew old; the Code even set a procedure for slaves to sue their owner for mistreatment (articles 22–27). Aside from this procedure, slaves could not sign contracts, sue in court, or act as witnesses; they could, however, still be prosecuted (article 28–31). Masters were financially responsible for their slaves' exactions against others (article 37).

Slaves could not own weapons and could not hold large gatherings (articles 15, 16). They could endure the death penalty for hitting their master or stealing a large animal (articles 33–35). Escaping was also punishable by death, starting with the third attempt (article 38). Such penalties were enforceable by courts only; masters, aside from lashes, could not single-handedly resort to torture or capital punishment against their own slaves (article 42).

Slaves were to be treated as property, with a few exceptions. They had to be shared equally among the master's heirs at a time when primogeniture remained customary in France (article 44). Slave families could not be separated (article 47). The Code established a simple procedure for freeing slaves and stipulated that freed Africans were to be treated as full citizens (articles 57, 59).

The Code, on paper, was an enlightened piece of legislation considering that few whites enjoyed due process in metropolitan France, where torture and cruel forms of capital punishment were legal. The gap between the law and reality was wide, however. Article 9 notwithstanding, masters often took one or more of their female slaves as mistresses. Despite article 47, families were frequently split up at auction, with children as young as six sold separately. Numerous anecdotes in travelers' accounts from colonial times recount cruel treatments (including death) unilaterally imposed by masters upon their slaves even though article 42 forbade such things; masters were rarely prosecuted for these crimes. Masters, despite the Code's clear prohibition in article 24, frequently ordered their slaves to supplement their diet by gardening in their spare time. (The practice, known as Samedi-Nègre, or Black Saturday, was legalized in 1786). In the late eighteenth century, free persons of African ancestry suffered from increasing racial discrimination, in clear violation of articles 57 and 59. Racial discrimination in French colonies continued after the abolition of slavery. Until 1946 French law distinguished between colonial "citizens" and "subjects," the latter (black Africans) being granted few legal and political rights.

Philippe R. Girard

See also: Haiti; Louverture, Toussaint Bréda; Slavery (History)

References

Klein, Herbert. *African Slavery in Latin America and the Caribbean.* New York: Oxford University Press, 1986.

Louis XIV. *L'Edit du Roi sur la police de l'Amérique Françoise.* Versailles, France, March 1685.

"The Black Code: Edict of the King Governing the Enforcement of Order in the French American Islands from the Month of March 1685, Registered at the Sovereign Council of Saint-Domingue, May 6, 1687." In *Le Code Noir ou recueil des reglements rendus jusqu'a present,* trans. John Garragus. Paris: Prault, 1767 [1980 rpt., Societe d'Histoire de la Guadeloupe].

Roach, Joseph. "Body of Law: The Sun King and the Code Noir." In *From the Royal to the Republican Body,* edited by Sarah Melzer and Kathryn Norbber. Berkeley: University of California Press, 1998.

South African novelist John Maxwell Coetzee, winner of the 2003 Nobel Prize for Literature. (AFP/Getty Images)

COETZEE, JOHN MAXWELL (1940–)

The winner of the 2003 Nobel Prize for Literature, John Maxwell (J. M.) Coetzee, was born in Cape Town, South Africa, in 1940. His work has circulated widely throughout the Americas, and he is considered an innovator of the postcolonial novel. He lived for a while in England before moving to the United States to take his doctorate degree in literature at the University of Texas at Austin, where he wrote his dissertation on Samuel Beckett's writing style. After having been denied U.S. citizenship in the early 1970s, Coetzee returned to South Africa to teach and write. In March 2006 Coetzee became an Australian citizen and he lives and continues to write there. A published author by age thirty-four, Coetzee's present international reputation is a product of his captivating works as well as his influence over the years as a teacher and writer at universities in the United States, England, and South Africa. More recently, he has served on the Committee on Social Thought and taught one term per year at the University of Chicago. The transnational flair inherent in Coetzee's life and writing leads Graham Huggan and Stephan Watson to observe in *Critical Perspectives on J. M. Coetzee,* "Essentially, he is a first-world novelist writing out of a South African context, from within a culture which is as bizarre and conflicted an amalgam of first- and third-world elements as any on this planet" (1996, p. 1). His novels are read around the globe and have been translated into multiple languages. Additionally, he has received several literary prizes aside from his Nobel, notably the CNA prize, South Africa's top literary award, for *In the Heart of the Country* (1976) and the Booker Prize for *Life and Times of Michael K* (1983) and again for *Disgrace* (1999).

Coetzee's novels often deal, in inventive ways and formats, with the highly polemical issues of the times in which they were written. For example, his 1974 novel, *Dusklands,* critiques the countries of Vietnam and South Africa in terms of spaces of invasion through the monologues of two fictional individuals who participate, each in his own right, in projects of colonization. In his "Literature and Politics" (1998), Michael Vaughn notes that "the juxtaposition of these two sections enables Coetzee to develop his overriding theme—Western man as colonizer—in terms of a dialectical opposition. The two sections negate and reinforce each other in their dialectical juxtaposition: the historically primary image of the explorer-colonizer is both reinforced and negated by the historically secondary image . . . of the hopelessly incorporated intellectual" (p. 55). Coetzee's style indeed was something new, at least from a South African novelist, and many literary critics (Michael Vaughn, Derek Attridge, David Attwell, and others) have noted that his early writing was characterized by recent literary aesthetics, modernism or postmodernism, already featured in European and North American fiction.

Coetzee's second novel, *In the Heart of the Country,* was followed by *Waiting for the Barbarians* in 1980, and it was this third novel that propelled the author to worldwide fame. In *Coetzee and the Ethics of Reading* (2004), Derek Attridge reveals that "the popularity of *Barbarians* led to the first-time publication of *Dusklands* in Great Britain in 1982 and in the US in 1985" (p. ix). Establishing Coetzee's place on the international literary map, the allegorical *Waiting for the Barbarians* recounts the story of an unnamed magistrate in an unnamed Empire who must deal in an unspecified time period with an evil Colonel Joll. Joll, responding to rumors of attack to be led by the "barbarians" who live at the edges of the Empire, sets off on a campaign to explore their land and to capture some of the "barbarians." He eventually brings several of them to the magistrate's town, where they are tortured and some are killed. The magistrate himself eventually becomes directly involved when he seeks to help an injured "barbarian" girl make her way home. Many of the incidents in the novel mirror in full or part specific historical incidents, such as Stephen Biko's death, that had taken place in Coetzee's native country. Attridge argues that "the novel was able to have its cake and eat it too: a powerful posing of the question of torture and of the responsibilities of those in power in the places where it is allowed to happen, it could be read both as an indictment of the atrocities that were keeping apartheid in place at the time of its publication and as a universally relevant, time- and place-transcending narrative of human suffering and moral choice" (ibid., p. 42). Thus, the force of this novel is evident in the multifarious levels of interpretation and analysis it demands. Consequently, critics insist on the relevance of the text to the political interactions of many nations and they categorize it as allegory, while Attridge adds that much in the novel evades such simple classification. Like *Barbarians,* Coetzee's *Life and Times of Michael K,* written in 1983, has also been classified as an allegory by some critics because its action takes place in an unspecified future time.

Life and Times of Michael K, winner of the 1983 Booker Prize, traces the path of a protagonist who faces the difficulties of living in a place made chaotic by civil war.

Coetzee's narrative experimentation is elaborated through Michael, who remains silent in the face of catastrophic events taking place around him. Michael is ironically able to "fight back" through his silence, which Michael Marais calls, in "The Hermeneutics of Empire" (1996), "a potent political tool through which the other escapes and challenges [imperial cultures]" (p. 75). In the end, Michael remains unaffected by the uprisings around him as Coetzee implies that those who, on the surface at least, appear as other, as the disenfranchised, can truly find agency to challenge "the fixity of dominant power structures and positions" (ibid., p. 75). While *Michael K* offers glimpses of stability despite the upheaval and turmoil caused by the South African civil war, one of Coetzee's latest novels, *Disgrace* (1999), also a winner of the Booker Prize, presents perspectives of interpersonal interactions within a postapartheid context.

Disgrace tackles the political and social vexations of postapartheid South Africa by following the dismissal of David Lurie from his university position. Lurie has been accused of sexual encounters with a student and is forced to leave his job. With no prospects, Lurie moves in with his daughter Lucy. They live their lives in complete disagreement and under great strain. After an incident in which three black males come onto their property to pillage, burn, and rape, Lurie blames all of society's ills on postapartheid disruptions of the status quo. Attridge observes that, from this white professor's perspective, all of which was perceived at one point in time as stable and good has been upended. He adds that rules and regulations no longer apply as they once did, and that nothing is in place to check and balance the actions and misdeeds of criminals and politicians. Finally, and most damaging for Lurie, the white man no longer controls the power; he is now "exposed and vulnerable" to the new rules and workings of government (2004, p. 170). Coetzee's evaluation of postapartheid South Africa through the course of *Disgrace* reveals sad deficiencies and shortcomings in a society that, since 1994, had anticipated great change for the benefit of all citizens.

Finally, it is imperative to note that Coetzee's contributions extend well beyond creative writing. His scholarship more than holds its own in the critical world while contributing to both literary and sociocultural arenas. Two examples, *White Writing: On the Culture of Letters in South Africa* (1988) and *Doubling the Point: Essays and Interviews* (2005), treat the intertwining issues of culture and literature within a South African and international context. Huggan and Watson offer two important points regarding Coetzee's writing and influence in *Critical Perspectives on J. M. Coetzee*. First, they note that the author's writing situates itself both inside and outside South Africa. That is to say, his work is both location specific and universal at the same time in terms of its subject matter and application. Second, they suggest that Coetzee is the prototypical creative author and socioliterary critic joined into one writer who realizes both with equal skill and expertise. His experiences living for periods of time in various countries around the world have served him well, as his work is as intriguing and germane for university students in cities in Europe and North America as it is for those reading from their locales in Pietersburg or Queenstown, South Africa.

Walt Collins

References

Attridge, Derek. *J. M. Coetzee and the Ethics of Reading: Literature in the Event.* Chicago: University of Chicago Press, 2004.

Attwell, David. *J. M. Coetzee: South Africa and the Politics of Writing.* Berkeley: University of California Press, 1993.

Huggan, Graham, and Stephen Watson, eds.. *Critical Perspectives on J. M. Coetzee.* London: Macmillan, 1996.

Marais, Michael. "The Hermeneutics of Empire: Coetzee's Post-colonial Metafiction." In *Critical Perspectives on J. M. Coetzee,* Graham Huggan and Stephen Watson, eds. London: Macmillan, 1996.

Vaughn, Michael. "Literature and Politics: Currents in South African Writing in the Seventies." In *Critical Essays on J. M. Coetzee,* edited by Sue Kossew. New York: G. K. Hall, 1998.

COFFEE

Coffee has been an international commodity from the sixteenth century to the present. It is one of the leading internationally traded commodities today. *Arabica* and *robusta* are the two major types of coffee that are grown and marketed worldwide. Coffee was first cultivated in Yemen around the sixth century. The Dutch brought it from Yemen to their colonies in Africa in the sixteenth century. Coffee crossed the Atlantic early in the eighteenth century when the Dutch brought it to Suriname. As the demand for coffee grew, so did slavery, which until abolition was the major form of labor used for its cultivation. In Brazil, for example, where the economy rested on coffee trade, approximately 2 million slaves imported from Africa labored on plantations until the late nineteenth century.

Today, the world's leading coffee producers and exporters are two Latin American countries. Brazil, which produces about 30 percent of the world's coffee, is followed by Colombia, whose share is about 10 percent. The crop is grown in Africa, Asia, and Oceania, too. In terms of their share in worldwide coffee production, the countries following Colombia are Vietnam, Indonesia, Côte d'Ivoire, Mexico, Guatemala, India, Uganda, Ethiopia, Honduras, Costa Rica, El Salvador, Peru, Ecuador, Thailand, Kenya, Cameroon, Venezuela, Papua New Guinea, and Nicaragua. The largest coffee importer today is the United States. It is followed by Western European countries such as Germany, France, and Italy. The remaining major importers are Eastern European countries and Japan. In terms of coffee consumption, the top three countries today are the United States, Brazil, and Germany. The exporters and importers are linked by transnational corporations (TNCs). Coffee enters the importing countries largely in the form of green coffee. It is processed and marketed by TNCs whose headquarters are in importing countries.

Elif Oztabak-Avci

See also: Agriculture; Cameroon; Colombia; Colonialism; Dutch Empire; Nicaragua; Peru

References

Graaff, de J. *The Economics of Coffee.* Wageningen, Netherlands: Pudoc, 1986.

Lucier, Richard L. *The International Political Economy of Coffee.* New York: Praeger, 1988.

COLD WAR

Tension and hostility between the United States and the Soviet Union (USSR) was evident across the globe from the late 1940s through the early 1990s. Their rivalry, known as the cold war, expressed itself in Africa through U.S. and Soviet involvement in regional African conflicts and in economic and military aid granted to African states by both superpowers. The transatlantic connections between the Americas and Africa during the cold war are clearly seen in activities such as Cuba's involvement in Angola's civil war and its provision of aid to other African states; the involvement of the United States in the Congo and other areas; and the ideological importance of Africa to the American Civil Rights Movement.

The early years of the cold war coincided with the onset of decolonization in the late 1940s and extending through the early 1960s. Newly independent states were increasingly pressured to align themselves with one superpower or the other. Some states chose to remain formally uncommitted to alignment with the United States or the Soviet Union. As nonaligned nations, these states could become ideological battlegrounds for the superpowers, yet official neutrality also allowed nonaligned countries the opportunity to manipulate the superpowers to achieve their own objectives of domestic security and economic development.

For example, in the 1960s, Ghana, under the leadership of President Kwame N'Krumah, was able to exploit superpower rivalry to obtain economic aid from both the United States and the Soviet Union. N'Krumah was one of the leading African members of the Nonaligned Movement and was deeply involved in Pan-Africanism and the formation of the Organization of African Unity. Under N'Krumah's leadership, Ghana received aid from the United States Agency for International Development (USAID) to build the Akosombo (Volta) Dam to generate electrical power for the area. Ghana also received aid from the Soviet Union to develop technical

schools, airstrips, hospitals, and state-run farms. By the mid-1960s Ghana was increasingly dependent on Soviet aid, causing some (including the Ghanaian military) to consider Ghana to be a client state of the Soviet Union and leading to N'Krumah's deposition by military coup in 1966.

Throughout the era of the cold war some African nations, such as Julius Nyerere's Tanzania, experimented with "African" versions of socialism, while other countries followed a more Marxist model. The Soviet Union and Cuba both wished to increase the number of Communist nations around the world, and Cuba was particularly concerned with encouraging revolutionary movements leading to Communist states.

In a speech before the United Nations (UN) General Assembly in September 1960, Cuban leader Fidel Castro drew parallels between Cuba and the Congo as states that had been ruled by racially discriminatory elites and emphasized Cuba's support for the Congo's leader, Patrice Lumumba, and for African self-governance across the continent. Cuba then supported this rhetoric with aid. In 1963 Cuba sent medical and military assistance to newly independent Algeria, and in 1965 a small Cuban force under the leadership of Che Guevara was sent to the Congo. In the mid-1960s Cuba also provided military and medical aid to Guinea-Bissau.

Cuba's intervention in Africa increased in the 1970s. In its support for revolutionary movements in Latin American countries, Cuba was often acting against legal governments and attracting the censure of the United States. In its actions in Africa, Cuba was generally supporting African anticolonial movements or assisting new states, as in Angola.

Civil war broke out in Angola during 1975 over which of three rebel groups would lead Angola at independence: the Popular Movement for the Liberation of Angola (MPLA), the National Front for the Liberation of Angola (FNLA), or the National Union for the Total Independence of Angola (UNITA). The MPLA received aid from Cuba and the Soviet Union, while the United States, through the Central Intelligence Agency (CIA), supported the FNLA and UNITA. South Africa supported UNITA as well. By 1976, with Cuban training and troops, the MPLA had gained the upper hand and formed a Marxist government. Because of continued guerilla warfare by the FNLA and UNITA, Cuba sent over 50,000 troops to Angola to support the government, and Cuban forces remained in Angola until the late 1980s. Cuba was also involved in cold war conflicts in the Horn of Africa (the area that is now Djibouti, Eritrea, Ethiopia, and Somalia). The Horn became a surrogate battlefield for the United States and the Soviet Union in the 1960s. Eritreans formed the Marxist group, the Eritrean People's Liberation Front, to fight for Eritrea's independence from Ethiopia, and Somalia wished to create a "Greater Somalia" including parts of Kenya, Ethiopia, and Djibouti. The USSR helped Somalia build up its arms, and the United States responded by providing economic and military aid to Ethiopia. In 1974 Ethiopian emperor Haile Selassie was removed from power by the military, and the ensuing military coordinating committee declared Ethiopia a socialist state. The Soviet Union replaced the United States as the primary cold war power in Ethiopia. In 1977 Somalia invaded Ethiopia. Cuba, acting in concert with the Soviet Union, sent approximately 15,000 troops to aid Ethiopia. Somalia then asked the United States for aid, and reversal in the Horn's cold war alignments was complete, with the Soviet Union and Cuba now dominant in Ethiopia and the United States prominent in Somalia through the 1980s.

In the 1980s over 10 percent of Cuba's annual budget went to maintaining a military presence in various African states, and by 1988 Cuba was beginning to withdraw Cuban troops from Angola and Ethiopia. Cuban interest in Africa did not cease, however, with the end of the cold war.

Throughout the cold war Cuba's stated goal was to support African states in their fight for freedom from colonial and racist governments. Since the conclusion of the cold war, aid to African states has continued in the form of educational and medical assistance. The Cuban government offers scholarships for African students to study in Cuba and sends Cuban medical personnel to African countries.

The involvement of the United States in Africa during the cold war was apparent not only in the Horn of Africa and Angola, but in the Congo as well. The civil war in the Congo from 1960 to 1965 was the first cold war conflict in Africa. Belgian colonial rule ended on June 30, 1960, and on July 1 Patrice Lumumba became prime minister of the independent nation of the Congo. Within two weeks of taking office, Lumumba was faced with a mutiny by the army, the secession from the Congo of the wealthy Katanga province, and the reentry of Belgian troops into the Congo. Lumumba requested United Nations assistance in recovering Katanga and Soviet assistance in removing the Belgians.

The Soviet Union viewed involvement in the Congo crisis as a way to establish its influence in newly independent Africa. The USSR sent equipment and over 100 military advisers to assist Lumumba. His turn to the Soviet Union for help discomfited the United States, however, and the CIA developed several unsuccessful plots to assassinate Lumumba. Because of its concerns about Lumumba's Soviet ties, the United States (through the CIA) backed Joseph Mobutu (later known as Mobutu Sese Seko) as an alternative leader of the Congo. After Lumumba's assassination in January 1961, power shifted to Mobutu. He acceded to power through a coup in November 1965 and imposed authoritarian rule for more than thirty years.

In 1965 Latin American resistance fighter Che Guevara and around 100 Cubans arrived in the Congo to provide assistance to former Lumumba supporter Laurent Kabila and his forces. Guevara's plan was to teach guerilla fighting and Communist ideology to the Congolese. Guevara found the Africans to be superstitious, ineffective fighters for whom classic Marxist reasons for revolution had little appeal. Seven months later Che and his troops left, their attempt at internationalizing the Communist revolution unsuccessful.

For much of the cold war, the United States also supported states in southern Africa as apparent bulwarks against Communism. South Africa portrayed itself as a leader in the global struggle against Communism, calling the African National Congress (ANC) a Communist organization and asserting that Communists were behind the uprisings in 1960 in Sharpeville and in 1970 in Soweto. South Africa passed laws such as the Suppression of Communism Act (1950) that outlawed perceived Communist activities, thus enabling the state to prosecute individuals involved in

antiapartheid groups such as the ANC. The United States valued South Africa for its strategic mineral resources, such as uranium, that were indispensable in the Cold War era of potential nuclear warfare, and the United States was willing to overlook South Africa's discriminatory policies in the name of anti-Communism. The United States refused until the mid-1980s to impose economic sanctions on South Africa for its policy of apartheid. Similarly, some Americans supported Rhodesia from its unilateral declaration of independence to its final independence as Zimbabwe in 1980. During this period the United States disregarded UN sanctions against Rhodesia by buying chrome from that country (to avoid getting it from the Soviet Union, the world's other major producer), and Vietnam veterans enlisted in the Rhodesian armed forces as mercenaries.

Although much of the cold war was fought by third world proxies, it was also an ideological conflict between democracy and Communism, with both sides touting the supremacy of their moral and philosophical systems. After World War II, the existence of Jim Crow laws separating African Americans and whites in the United States undermined claims the United States made to moral superiority over the Soviet Union. The Soviet Union and other Communist states pointed to racial discrimination in the United States as proof that American democracy was neither just nor fair. In 1960 Cuban leader Fidel Castro and his entourage stayed in a Harlem hotel while attending a session of the United Nations, improving Cuba's image among African Americans, Afro-Cubans, and Africans.

Before the civil rights legislation of the 1960s, African dignitaries and diplomats visiting the United States might be harassed because of their color, leading to increased tension with newly decolonized nations. During the cold war the United States passed civil rights laws in part to cultivate a global image as a bastion of equality and democracy and thereby, as one of the consequences, to win over newly independent states. The Voice of America transmitted news of the U.S. Supreme Court's decision in the *Brown v. Board of Education* (1954) case in thirty-four languages, and African newspapers published news on American race relations. From 1956 to 1978, the U.S. State Department sponsored tours of jazz and gospel musicians to the Soviet bloc and to developing countries such as the Congo in an effort to promote democracy and present jazz as the music of freedom. One Communist counter to American actions was education. For example, Cuba educated orphans of Algeria's war for independence, and in 1960 the Soviet Union founded a university in Moscow for students from Africa, Latin America, and Asia, enrolling over 500 students in its first year. In 1961 the university was renamed the Patrice Lumumba Peoples' Friendship University to emphasize its anticolonial sentiments, and it bore Lumumba's name until 1992.

Patricia G. Clark

See also: Castro Ruz, Fidel; Cuba; Selassie I, Haile; Socialism; South Africa, History and Politics

References

Borstelmann, Thomas. *The Cold War and the Color Line: American Race Relations in the Global Arena.* Cambridge, MA: Harvard University Press, 2001.

Dudziak, Mary L. *Cold War Civil Rights: Race and the Image of American Democracy.* Princeton, NJ: Princeton University Press, 2000.

Gleijeses, Piero. *Conflicting Missions: Havana, Washington, and Africa, 1959–1976.* Chapel Hill: University of North Carolina Press, 2002.

Guevara, Ernesto Che. *The African Dream: The Diaries of the Revolutionary War in the Congo.* Translated by Patrick Camiller. New York: Grove Press, 2001.

Horne, Gerald. *From the Barrel of a Gun: The United States and the War against Zimbabwe, 1965–1980.* Chapel Hill: University of North Carolina Press, 2001.

Von Eschen, Penny M. *Satchmo Blows Up the World: Jazz Ambassadors Play the Cold War.* Cambridge, MA: Harvard University Press, 2004.

COLOMBIA

Colombia is a country of northwest South America with coastlines on the Pacific and the Caribbean. Involved with the transatlantic slave trade and slavery, Colombia's modern and contemporary black communities of the twentieth and twenty-first century have faced unique social and political struggles. Enslaved Africans entered New Granada, or present-day Colombia, starting in the sixteenth century with the rise of the slave trade in the Atlantic. New Granadian elites imported slaves mostly for mining. The most important port of trade for African slaves was Cartagena, on the Caribbean coast. Many Maroon communities developed in the viceroyalty, like those of San Basilio in the Atlantic region and Patía in the southwest, in which runaway slaves settled. During the independence wars between 1810 and 1821, slaves and free blacks were utilized by royalist and patriot armies alike. Final abolition came in 1851, after long struggles by slaves and strong resistance by slave owners. In republican Colombia, national identity was based on the ideal of *mestizaje,* which praised race mixture. Hence, during the nineteenth and early twentieth centuries black communities in Colombia either pursued cultural adaptation or remained spatially bounded to their inherited, isolated territories. In the late twentieth century, along with indigenous movements, black communities organized and have pushed ethnic rights to the center of contemporary multicultural Colombian politics and the nation's constitution.

Colonial Colombia was organized into economic regions according to the extractive and productive needs of the Spanish Empire. In the northern Caribbean emerged Cartagena, the most important port city, controlling commerce and slave traffic. It was one of the only two ports of the empire authorized to receive slave imports. The city was an early center of an important point of encounter for newly arrived African slaves and domestic servants. Enslaved Africans were imported through Cartagena and taken inland to the Atlantic provinces, Antioquia, the southwestern mining regions, and further to the south into Quito. In the eighteenth century the economic use of slaves diversified to include production of sugar and its derivatives, cattle raising, craftwork, and domestic work.

The southwestern province of Cauca, with its center in Popayán, constituted an important location for slave labor in Colombia. Given the decimation of the indigenous population and the discovery of gold mines on the Pacific coast, slaves became the most common source of labor. Barbacoas was an important mining center in the seventeenth century, although its production receded early in the next century. By that time, however, new mines had been discovered in the northern Pacific coast in Chocó, where slave owners rushed to extract gold. Communities of free blacks formed near the gold-mining centers of Chocó, transforming race relations in the region. Free blacks became important sources of labor—they sometimes even owned mines—progressively affecting the notion of how black productivity was defined in the region.

Eighteenth-century Colombian slave society saw an important transformation with the advent of Bourbon rule and reform in the eighteenth century. Slavery was regulated by law for the first time in the Spanish Empire, and the enlightened tone and ideals of the new laws gave slaves a reason to turn eagerly to judicial courts to claim their new rights. These rights included being well fed and clothed and being instructed in the Catholic religion. Emphasis was placed on the care of slaves and the reduction of punishment. Southwestern slave owners reacted negatively to the pretensions of the Spanish crown to reduce their sovereignty over slaves, an attitude that foreshadowed their resistance to abolitionist thought in the nineteenth century.

Along with Bourbon reform the Atlantic slave traffic grew, but in Colombian territory by the late eighteenth century a stable homegrown slave population was already in place, and hence slave imports decreased. Also, especially in Chocó and Antioquia, free blacks and *mulatos* were becoming an alternative workforce.

Slave resistance took many forms. Legal strategies were customary from the seventeenth century. Slaves denounced their masters' cruelty and pleaded for their natural right to good care as Christians. Such strategies became more frequent in the enlightened context of eighteenth-century Bourbon legislation. Rebellion, on the other hand, was not always a safe path, as colonial authorities and slave owners applied strong measures to insubordinate slaves, such as mutilation or even death. However, New Granada saw many rebellions from the arrival of enslaved Africans in the early sixteenth century. A better alternative for slaves was to run away and form free communities, or *palenques*. The most important were San Basilio, west of the Magdalena River, and El Castigo, near the Patía River in the south near Popayán. San Basilio was formed by groups of Kongo, Angola, Arará, Mina, and Karabalí runaway slaves from haciendas around Cartagena, who defended their freedom under the leadership of a captain. In the seventeenth century the colonial government gave up on its project to subdue them and recognized them as autonomous black communities. The *palenque* of Patía congregated runaway slaves from the haciendas near Popayán and Valle del Cauca and from the mines in Barbacoas, Panamá, and Chocó. In constant tension with colonial society, the Maroons represented a menace to slave owners and an example of rebellion against domination for those who remained enslaved. Interestingly, their antagonistic position would be transformed when they participated in the independence wars on the royalist side.

Abolitionist ideas in Colombia were at first a by-product of the independence crisis. It was the royalists who first offered freedom to those slaves who joined their armies to fight the American rebels. This offer was an important source for destabilization of the slave regime, as slaves revolted. Royalist slaves enlisted to fight patriots because most Creole patriot elites were slave owners. An important royalist militia was in the Maroon community in Patía, which joined General José Maria Obando and the Spanish Army, which were combating southwestern patriots. Slaves and free blacks also joined patriot armies and became important symbols of slave liberation. Especially in Cartagena, where nearby Caribbean struggles such as that of Haiti had set an example, liberty and equality, including abolition, became the goals of independence. In 1820 Simón Bolívar ordered that 3,000 slaves be recruited for the liberation army and that they be offered their freedom in exchange. Hence, military participation became a crucial strategy for slaves who wanted to fight for their freedom.

After independence in 1821 the Congress of Cúcuta established as a national goal the incorporation of black slaves and Indians into the republic as citizens through the process of gradual manumission. By the mid-1840s the slave population was in decline, the product of an accelerated pace in manumissions, since in the context of Liberal government, antislavery ideas were on the rise. Finally, in 1851, while General José Hilario López was president, Congress decreed the abolition of slavery as law beginning in January 1852.

In the nineteenth century most Afro-Colombians were Liberals. Even if they had never been slaves, their politics were linked to erasing all the legacies of slavery, which included questions of land, rights, and citizenship. The entrance of blacks into national politics profoundly shook social dynamics. In the southwest it was the Liberal Party that embraced black populations, paving the way for democratizing Colombian political discourse.

A new phase of politics in Colombia's black communities began in the 1970s when, following the example of North America's black rights movements,

Afro-Colombians organized their own movements, especially in urban areas. Besides advocating for civil rights and a voice in the political process, these organizations emphasized the resistance of Afro-Colombians to their historic exploitation since their arrival as slaves. First, the goal was to integrate into the national society. More recently, the emphasis has shifted to a struggle for the recognition of cultural difference. This national political reform resulted from the new Constitution of 1991. That document challenged the previous national project, which was based on promoting a homogeneous "mixed" race; put forth a notion of a multicultural and pluri-ethnic society; and gave unprecedented rights to ethnic and religious minorities. This context made possible the emergence of new indigenous and black movements in line with the cultural and political precepts of the new legal framework.

The most important project and product of black organization in the 1990s was Law 70, which aimed to demarcate collective territories for black communities. The many black groups in Colombia defend general political rights for blacks such as their right to their own identity, to have a territory and political autonomy, and to build their own vision of the future based on their traditional forms of production and social organization. They also claim solidarity with the struggle of black people around the world in their search for an alternative vision of development. The communities have emphasized territory as a fundamental element of a vision of their future and a guarantee of their reproduction as cultures. Such notion of territory is different from the notion of land characteristic of peasant struggles in Latin America. It reflects the new nature of the political practice of black communities, profoundly embedded in postmodern notions of development. Colombia's black communities also share the struggle to build a collective identity with other contemporary social movements that are facing the challenge of cultural politics, namely, to provide an alternative to the state's global interests regarding development and environmental issues.

Marcela Echeverri

See also: Coffee; Diaspora; Quilombo; Slavery (History); Slave Revolts/Maronnage

References

Escalante, Aquiles. *El negro en Colombia.* Bogota, Colombia: Universidad Nacional de Colombia, 1964.

Escobar, Arturo. *Encountering Development: The Making and Unmaking of the Third World.* Princeton, NJ: Princeton University Press, 1995.

Friedemann, Nina S. *De sol a sol: Génesis, transformación, y presencia de los negros en Colombia.* Bogota, Colombia: Editorial Planeta, 1986.

Helg, Aline. *Liberty and Equality in Caribbean Colombia, 1770–1835.* Chapel Hill: University of North Carolina Press, 2004.

Jaramillo Uribe, Jaime. *Ensayos de historia social.* Bogota, Colombia: Ceso-Banco de la República-ICANH-Colciencias-Alfaomega, 2001.

Romero, Mario Diego. *Poblamiento y sociedad en el Pacífico colombiano, siglos XVI al XVIII.* Cali, Colombia: Editorial Universidad del Valle, 1995.

Safford, Frank, and Marco Palacios. *Colombia: Fragmented Land, Divided Society.* Oxford: Oxford University Press, 2002.

Sanders, James. *Contentious Republicans: Popular Politics, Race, and Class in Nineteenth-Century Colombia.* Durham, NC: Duke University Press, 2004.

Wade, Peter. *Blackness and Race Mixture: The Dynamics of Racial Identity in Colombia.* Baltimore, MD: Johns Hopkins University Press, 1993.

COLONIAL ARMIES IN AFRICA

Africa has a history of conscripted army service in which colonial powers used local populations. These armed forces are known as colonial armies in Africa. Colonial powers relied heavily on locally recruited colonial armies to secure territory, guard frontiers, and maintain law and order. The earliest such armies were recruited in the Americas and were composed of slaves: for example, the West India Regiment, formed in 1795, employed to police Britain's West Indian possessions but also used in recently acquired areas of West Africa. The Spanish also had a sizable black army in Cuba during the nineteenth century. These patterns and practices were transferred to Africa in the nineteenth century. Other powers in Africa, for example the Ottoman-Egyptian state under Muhammad Ali, recruited African slaves as soldiers for the armies that fought in the Sudan and the Levant. The largest colonial army in the world was the Indian Army. From 1858 to 1946, Indian troops were used in imperial campaigns in Asia, Africa, and Europe, thus reducing the need to employ African troops overseas.

Colonial armies were essentially mercenary forces. In the early days, most were composed of runaway slaves. However, for regular recruitment Europeans began to identify as martial races ethnic groups living on the periphery of a colony and even outside its borders. Thus Hausa and Bambara men were recruited by the British, French, and Germans in West Africa. The martial race idea was a myth, but it served the interests of colonial recruiters. Soldiers were loyal aliens who transferred their allegiance from African rulers to white officers and who could be used to police people different in language and culture. Soldiers' allegiance to the colonial order was cemented by their acquisition of arms, a uniform, regular wages, and welfare and fiscal benefits. In the twentieth century many former soldiers were employed as policemen and in other security roles. As agents of the colonial system, African soldiers were regarded with considerable hostility by most subject peoples. The allegiance of colonial armies could not be taken for granted by the colonial authorities, which kept a watchful eye on their "loyal aliens" to prevent excesses in policing, desertion, and mutiny. Serious mutinies did occur, for example, in the Congo Free State in the late 1890s, in the Sudan Defence Force in 1924, in British Somaliland (1937) and the Belgian Congo (1895), and in Dakar in 1944. However, mutinies were rare. Most were little more than strikes by soldiers over pay and conditions of service and thus easily contained.

Colonial armies were commanded by white officers and had a leaven of strategically placed European noncommissioned officers. Before 1940 only the French were prepared to give Africans, or black men, a commissioned rank. By the 1930s 10 percent of the officers in the French colonial army were black. In the British colonial forces the highest rank an African could achieve was warrant officer. Policy changed in 1940, and by the end of the war three Africans had become officers in the West African Frontier Force. By the end of the colonial period, Africanization was accepted policy, although it was slowly implemented. The Belgians failed to promote Africans to commissioned rank in the Force Publique, one of the causes for the mutiny by the army at independence in 1960. Ironically, in the 1970s and 1980s, the armies of the remaining white-run regimes in southern Africa—the

Portuguese colonies, Rhodesia, and South Africa—had a growing percentage of Africans in their total forces and a growing number of African junior officers.

Most colonial powers in Africa recruited soldiers for use within the colony. For example, in South Africa, African regiments, commanded by Europeans, fought in the frequent frontier wars of the nineteenth century. Although the World Wars changed these colonial policies of restricted employment, from the outset the French used colonial troops in overseas campaigns. In the 1850s Louis Faidherbe in Senegal recruited *tirailleurs* to conquer the French Sudan, and they were later used to fight colonial wars in Indochina and Madagascar and to serve as garrison troops in North Africa. With the partition of Africa in the late nineteenth century, all the colonial powers began to recruit armies. Most were small in size, numbering no more than a few thousand men, infantry forces of lightly armed gendarmeries commanded by white officers. The French colonial army was the largest. General Charles Mangin envisaged *la force noire,* recruited in West Africa, as a contingent that would relieve French troops in North Africa in the event of a war with Germany. When World War I came in 1914–1918, French West Africa contributed 160,000 men, many of whom died on the western front. There were also sizable North African contingents fighting in France. The *Force Publique,* used to conquer and police the vast area of the Congo Free State (Belgian Congo after 1908), was also relatively large, with 18,000 men in 1914–1918. So also was the Italian colonial army in Eritrea, where men were recruited to fight a disastrous war with neighboring Ethiopia in 1896, against the Senussi in Libya, and then in the invasion of Ethiopia

in the 1930s. Mussolini's fascist regime in the 1930s claimed to have a colonial army of over 200,000, but this proved to be chimerical when Italy went to war with Britain and France in 1940.

The two World Wars forced the belligerent colonial powers to recruit larger colonial armies and to employ them in new roles. In 1914–1918 the French conscripted West African soldiers for the war in Europe, a policy that led to serious rebellions in the Sudan. In the same conflict British colonial armies soon defeated the small forces of Schutztruppe ("Protection Force") in the German colonies of Togoland and Kamerun. However, the campaign to control German East Africa started badly for British and Indian troops. From 1916 onward the bulk of the fighting was left to colonial troops, including men from West and southern Africa, who were deemed more expendable as well as better suited to tropical conditions. During the war French colonial troops fought in various European theatres; after the war, in 1919, they were used, in the face of much German and international opposition, to occupy the Rhineland and as part of French military intervention in Russia.

Selective conscription was used by the French in West Africa during the interwar years, and when war with Germany broke out in 1939, a sizable force of colonial troops was in France, deployed to defend the country. With France's defeat in mid-1940, the bulk of General Charles de Gaulle's Free French force consisted of African colonial troops in Chad, located in central Africa. Colonial troops fought for both the Vichy and Free French in the conflicts in Africa, Syria, and Madagascar. Colonial soldiers, invading from the south, helped to liberate France in 1944. Britain's policy not to use Africans in European wars was questioned in times of acute manpower shortages, especially in 1918 and 1940. In 1918 the war ended, but in 1940–1941 African colonial troops from West and East Africa fought against the Italians in the Horn of Africa. Having proved their worth, military commanders decided to use them in North Africa, the Levant, and also in Italy. Many African soldiers were recruited as noncombatant labor. South African policy in both World Wars was that black troops should be used only as labor, although battlefield circumstances moderated this policy slightly.

The commonly held view that the British did not use conscription in Africa during World War II is not borne out by the evidence. Conscription was selectively used to recruit certain groups of soldiers and also to secure labor for use both within and without the colony. As with French conscription policy in both World Wars, forcible enlistment in British colonies was widely resisted, although it did not lead to rebellion. People fled at the approach of recruiting parties and whole villages crossed nearby borders to the relative safety of foreign territory.

When Japan invaded Southeast Asia and Burma and threatened India in 1941–1942, the British decided that African troops should be used as garrison troops in India and Ceylon and also against the Japanese. By 1943 East and West African troops were fighting in Burma. They acquitted themselves well because of their skills in forest fighting and also because they were able to operate flexibly in rugged terrain with supply lines worked by porters. When the war ended, African troops were slowly repatriated and demobilized, a process not completed until 1947.

Lack of work, shortages of goods, and inflation in the postwar colonies led to unrest among veterans. A few were involved in protests, the most notable being the demonstration in Accra, Gold Coast, in February 1948, when armed police killed three former soldiers. In Kenya and South Africa a small number of veterans were prominent in nationalist politics. However, contrary to what is argued by the nationalist-focused literature of the 1960s, former soldiers were no more active politically than any other occupational grouping. The vast majority of soldiers recruited during World War II came from the traditional recruiting areas. They were illiterate peasants who on demobilization returned to their rural homes. Of course, wartime service helped to broaden soldiers' horizons and gave them new cultural experiences; some learned to speak other languages, but this was rarely translated into political activity.

All tropical campaigns, especially those fought in tsetse fly–infested areas where cattle and horses could not be used, required large numbers of porters or carriers. Carriers were recruited, often by force; in some colonial armies they constituted a regular part of the army. For example, the operations against the Asante in 1873–1874 involved 20,000 carriers drawn from different parts of West Africa. The campaigns of World War I required large numbers of laborers, mainly men but some women, many arbitrarily rounded up and conscripted. A brass disk bearing a number was commonly their only form of identification. In the long-drawn-out military operations in East Africa from1914 to 1918, as many as one million porters were recruited. Up to 10 percent of the porters died from disease, malnutrition, and harsh treatment. In Egypt, the British also recruited several hundred thousand *fellahin* ("peasant") laborers for use in the operations against the Ottoman forces in Sinai, and smaller contingents of African laborers were employed in other theaters. The South African Native Labour Contingent was sent to Europe in 1916, 20,000 unarmed but uniformed laborers who in France were lodged in closed compounds similar to those used for African labor in the South African mines. In World War II, a large part of the British colonial army was composed of noncombatants. Men from the Indian Ocean islands, organized in a military labor corps, continued to be employed by the British in the Middle East until the early 1950s.

After 1945 African colonial armies continued to be used in imperial campaigns. The French employed West African troops in their wars in Indochina and Algeria between 1945 and 1960. In 1952 detachments of the King's African Rifles, recruited in East and Central Africa, went to fight in Malaya at the same time as battalions at home were being deployed to combat the Mau Mau rebellion in Kenya. As nationalist agitation increased throughout Africa in the 1950s, so colonial armies were increased in size and better trained to deal with internal unrest. However, military forces were rarely used except in those colonies of white settlement where there was strong resistance to a transfer of power. At independence most African armies for a brief period continued to be led by white officers. This changed, but enlistment patterns for many decades continued to be largely determined by the recruitment patterns of the colonial period; the majority of the rank and file came from specific ethnic groups, while officers were drawn from a small educated elite from another area of the country. This led to instability and rivalry within the armies of many African states and was a major cause of repeated coup attempts within military regimes.

David Killingray

See also: Colonialism; Hausa; South Africa, History and Politics

References
Echenberg, Myron. *Colonial Conscripts: The Tirailleurs Sénégalaise in French West Africa, 1857–1960*. Portsmouth, NH: Heinemann, 1991.
Hodges, Geoffrey. *The Carrier Corps: Military Labor in the East African Campaign, 1914–1918*. Westport, CT: Greenwood Press, 1986.
Killingray, David, and David Omissi, eds. *Guardians of Empire*. Manchester, UK: Manchester University Press, 1999.
Killingray, David, and Richard Rathbone, eds. *Africa and the Second World War*. Basingstoke, UK: Macmillan, 1986.
Lawler, Nancy Ellen. *Soldiers of Misfortune. Ivorian Tirailleurs of World War II*. Athens: Ohio University Press, 1992.
Lunn, Joe. *Memoirs of the Maelstrom: A Senegalese Oral History of the First World War*. Portsmouth, NH: Heinemann, 1999.
Parsons, Timothy H. *The African Rank-and-File: Social Implications of Colonial Military Service in the King's African Rifles, 1902–1964*. Portsmouth, NH: Heinemann, 1999.

COLONIALISM

Colonialism is the expansion of one country's control over another territory, resulting in the effective occupation of that territory and its peoples. The aim of colonialism is to dominate another region's resources, labor, and markets to ensure economic security and supremacy. Colonialism also refers to the set of beliefs used to legitimize the occupation. From the ancient Romans to Europe's occupation of the Americas, great empires have benefited from the resources of their colonies. Countries such as the United States, Canada, and Australia all had their beginnings as colonies. While there are examples of colonialism that date back to the ancient world, and while colonial empires in the Western Hemisphere played an integral part in Europe's economic development from the fifteenth through eighteenth centuries, the term "colonialism" in reference to Africa is generally used to refer to the expansion of European power and influence in the late nineteenth century, during a time often referred to as the Age of Imperialism. The demands of the industrial revolution placed increased pressures on European nations to secure sources of raw materials, markets for manufactured goods, and new opportunities for investment. European nations looked outside their borders to secure what they needed for continued prosperity.

European nations had a long history of contact with African kingdoms. During the ancient era, Africa interacted with Europe via the extensive Mediterranean and trans-Saharan trade systems. In the fifteenth century, the Portuguese made their way down the western coast of the continent on route to Asia, establishing trading posts along the way. The first time European colonialism was felt in Africa was through its incorporation into the emerging Atlantic World via the transatlantic slave trade. But even with the onset of the slave trade, economic relations between Europeans and Africans were conducted as equal partners. Europeans had to recognize sovereign African kingdoms and negotiate trade agreements. But once Europe industrialized, the balance of power shifted and the relationship changed. With the abolition

of the transatlantic slave trade in 1807, Europeans demanded that African kingdoms develop "legitimate trade" focusing on agricultural commodities such as cocoa, peanuts, and palm oil. This transition was not easy for many African states. However, despite the economic dislocation caused by the abolition of the slave trade, Africans showed great resourcefulness and adaptability, so that by 1880 the mainstays of Africa's external trade economy were ivory, gum, cloves, beeswax, honey, wild coffee, peanuts, cotton, and rubber. Africans proved themselves interested in and eager to gain the knowledge of a technologically advanced Europe.

But while Europeans were increasingly interested in what Africans could offer their newly industrialized economies, African rulers were not always amenable to European demands. Europeans became aware of the economic potential of Africa's natural wealth at a time when industrialization was creating competition between European powers over access to and control over such resources. European interstate rivalry was exacerbated by French and British expeditions into the African continent. As a result of industrialization, European nations were no longer interested in negotiating with sovereign African states but rather sought to exert direct political and economic control of resources and markets. And by the end of the nineteenth century, industrialization had also given European nations the military means they needed to ensure their interests were served in Africa. Breech-loading rifles and the Maxim gun ensured supremacy over African armies armed at best with muzzle-loading muskets or flint rifles. The last barrier to European expansion into Africa fell in the 1850s when European medical advances decreased the impact of malaria. However, by 1880 there were no real indications of Africa's susceptibility to European power. An overwhelming majority of Africans enjoyed a sovereign existence, and so what happened in the next twenty years was in many ways surprising and sudden. Between 1880 and 1900, 90 percent of Africa was occupied by Britain, France, Germany, Belgium, Portugal, Spain, and Italy; only Ethiopia escaped colonization. While the demands of continued industrialization were clearly at work behind Europe's expansion into Africa, there were also powerful political and social forces behind the establishment of colonialism there.

Nineteenth-century Europe was characterized not only by the profound economic transformation caused by the industrial revolution but also by the development of nationalism often expressed in an exaggerated promotion of a country's prestige. European nations sought not only economic and political security but also recognition, and overseas colonies became status symbols for their influence. The influence of nationalism cannot be underestimated in the expansion of the colonial system. Colonies not only ensured necessary elements for continued economic development but also determined status within Europe's community of nations.

The other element in Europe's new relationship with Africa centered on the moral justification for colonialism—the civilizing and Christianizing mission, the so-called "White Man's Burden." The moral justification centered on the belief that colonialism elevated the colonized, that European control of Africa would provide the economic, political, and social infrastructure necessary for the development and modernization of the continent and its peoples. Such attitudes exhibited the overt ethnocentrism that is inherent in colonialism. But if the social and religious justifications for European colonial control over Africa were insufficient, the words of French poet Hilaire Belloc illustrate the European attitude toward Africa on the eve of colonization: "Whatever happens we have got; the Maxim gun and they have not."

As European states sought to extend their presence in Africa, concern arose among the European powers of the potential for conflict that the "Scramble for Africa" could cause. So to decrease the potential for clashes, representatives of all major European powers met at the Berlin West Africa Conference in November 1884 to determine the "rules of the game." There were no African representatives in attendance. In January 1885 the participants called for free commerce on the Niger and Congo rivers and the continued effort to eradicate the slave trade and the four main rules of European colonial expansion: before a European power could claim an area in Africa, it had to inform other European powers of its intent to do so; claims had to be followed by formal annexation of the region and effective occupation; European nations had to respect the sovereignty of any treaties signed between other European powers and African rulers; and each European power had the right to extend its coastal presence inland to establish a sphere of influence that could later be claimed, annexed, and occupied. These four rules were set up to avoid European conflicts, to facilitate the carving up of that "magnificent cake" of Africa, and to establish a process for the advance of colonialism throughout the world. The race for colonies in Africa was actually part of a worldwide phenomenon of European expansion.

With the rules of the game established, European nations pushed into the continent via three mechanisms. European nations and African rulers signed protectorate treaties in which Africans gained protection of the European nation in return for exclusive trading rights; however, many of these treaties caused African rulers to unwittingly give up their sovereignty. European nations also signed bilateral treaties between themselves, defining their spheres of influence without any input from African rulers. The final stage to the Scramble was the effective occupation of a region by a European power that often came through military conquest and occupation. The Africans' reaction to the loss of their sovereignty was varied. In some cases, African rulers submitted to European powers, recognizing that resistance would be futile or hoping that cooperation could result in benefits. Others sought alliances and tried to play off one European power against the other, not aware of the cooperation among European powers engendered by the Berlin Conference. Some rulers attempted diplomacy and others attempted military resistance. But armed resistance proved futile against the industrial and military strength of the Europeans. Some kingdoms, like the Asante in West Africa and the Zulu in the Cape, fought bitter battles to prevent colonial control. Other groups like the Magi Magi in Madaba and the Matumbi Hills in present day Tanzania, armed with only traditional charms and magic water believed to make them impervious to bullets, fell quickly to the advanced weaponry of the Germans. Europeans had the technological edge as African armies had outmoded weapons and limited economic resources to

sustain protracted conflict. Europeans also continued to use the "divide and conquer" strategy—promoting old conflicts and rivalries—that had served them well for centuries in Africa. In two decades, Africa's complex system of independent states was replaced by approximately forty artificially created colonies controlled by European powers.

The Berlin Conference proved effective in keeping European conflict to a minimum during the era of colonial expansion, but now the practical questions of how to oversee the new colonies quickly emerged. Generally, two systems, indirect and direct rule, were established to administer the colonies. No matter which system was implemented, all colonial powers were concerned about the cost of colonization and all used a combination of the two systems.

The British implemented the policy of indirect rule, developed by F. J. D. Lugard, high commissioner of the British Protectorate of Northern Nigeria. Britain ruled through existing tribal authorities where possible. These authorities continued to oversee the population using traditional systems and customary laws; the British simply administered from above. This system required the least effort and cost and preserved African political traditions, thus having moral benefits as well as practical ones. In areas where strong, highly centralized states existed, indirect rule preserved traditional tribal community structures, but in areas where cultural identities were more complex and fluid, the British had to create authority structures where none were thought to exist. As a result, colonial powers created artificial communities and authority structures that necessitated rigid ethnic identities and sowed the seeds for future conflict. Generally, however, the system of indirect rule left indigenous customs and practices undisturbed—although the activities and demands of Christian missionary organizations did not. Where there were no obvious indigenous political elites, the British created them, and where local elites proved uncooperative, the British removed and replaced them.

Those local elites who cooperated were rewarded, as the British confirmed their authority and often unwittingly removed restrictions on a chief's power by abolishing traditional systems of checks and balances. Local authorities were expected to maintain order, collect taxes, and organize labor and military drafts. They were under the supervision of British district officers who served as intermediaries between local authorities and the central colonial administration. While the British system of indirect rule appeared to function with little disruption of traditional authority, in actuality, local authorities often found their legitimacy challenged as they were seen as simply implementing and enforcing British desires and as being complicit in the maintenance of a colonial system that denied opportunities to the African population.

Most other European powers initially used direct rule, a model of governance most associated with the French. Using the model established in France, the French divided up their colonies into districts, assigned a French commissioner to oversee them, and appointed a governor-general to administer all the districts in a single colony. Colonial administrative boundaries were often established to divide up powerful tribes to weaken their resistance to French policy, and powerful African leaders were undermined or replaced with more cooperative figures. The French commissioners were responsible for tax collection,

labor and military drafts, overseeing public and social works, acting as a local judiciary, and enforcing the decisions of the governor-general. Africans had access to positions in the lower levels of the French bureaucracy but generally had to be considered assimilated into French culture and fluent in the French language. The French generally had two policies for the African population, assimilation and association, and they vacillated between the two throughout the colonial era. Assimilation of the African was the stated goal of French colonial policy as they sought to transform the African in the Western image. This policy rested on the assumption of the superiority of French culture above all others and to a certain extent on the legacy of the Enlightenment's ideals of the universality of man. For those not capable of assimilation, the French established association, a kind of collaboration with locals. As the colonial era wore on, the French increasingly embraced elements of indirect rule. Direct rule was too costly, required too much manpower, and was not as effective in dealing with local customs and communities.

After World War I most colonial powers implemented elements of indirect rule, although the timing varied throughout the continent and was often determined by the nature of the colonies' populations. The colonial system was expanded as administration extended into rural areas usually under the direction of a district official and small native army under European command. Colonial policy matured, and while the development of natural resources continued to be a focal point of the system, colonial authorities attempted to extend social services and opened up some limited mobility to Africans within the colonial bureaucracies as a growing Westernized and educated African class emerged. In some colonies the expanded opportunities for Africans within the system were met with segregation and increased race consciousness among the European settler elite. But ultimately the impact of the two World Wars resulted in the transformation of the colonial system into a type of "sacred trust" that was to be managed by Europeans until Africans were capable of self-government. Labor unions and young political activists in Africa, influenced by socialism, began pressuring the colonial systems to change. By the late 1940s colonial occupation was seen as costly and was increasingly criticized; by the 1950s African nationalist movements started sweeping the continent. In some regions of Africa the colonial era transitioned into the post-independence era with relative ease, but in other regions independence came at a great cost and often with violence and conflict.

There has been great debate about the impact of colonialism on Africa. In the grand scheme of the continent's history, the colonial era lasted a short time—less than a century. Most early accounts of the colonial period were written by Eurocentric scholars who emphasized the positive impact of colonization by focusing on the civilizing mission, the introduction of new technology and medical advances, and the onset of modernity. But the era of African nationalism resulted in the emergence of Afrocentric and Marxist analyses of the colonial era that were hardly sympathetic to the European point of view. Generally, these studies concluded that the colonial era interrupted Africa's natural development and condemned the continent to stagnation and continued exploitation. It is clear that African nations emerged as artificial creations of colonial powers with populations often burdened with rigid, artificially created ethnic identities. While European political institutions were established with the intent to develop forms of representative democracy, the lack of African participation and access to those institutions during the colonial era undermined their legitimacy even after the colonial system was dismantled and Africans took control of the executive, legislative, and judicial branches of government.

Some scholars blame colonialism for a kind of political immaturity in Africa. While Africa was integrated into a world economic system, it was accomplished through exploitative relationships. Politically, Africans were isolated from the rest of the world, for as colonies they could not exercise independent diplomacy or foreign relations. Some critics refer to a kind of "colonial mentality" exhibited in the belief that public property and finance belong not to the people but to the colonial government and could and therefore should be taken advantage of at the least opportunity. This belief continued, they say, into the national era, resulting in high levels of government corruption. Still others blame colonialism for Africa's chronic political instability because of the powerful and interventionist militaries established in that era, arguing that the colonizers used black soldiers against their own peoples and manipulated ethnic differences within the armies against the general population. This, the critics claim, set a dangerous precedent for postcolonial military intervention in the political processes of African nations.

Economically speaking, colonialism fostered the construction of economic infrastructure—roads, telegraph, railroads, and ports—but again critics point out that these facilities were built to extract Africa's resources for the benefit of the colonial power and not for the future development of Africa's peoples. The nature of economic activities promoted during the colonial period caused the spread of cash crop agriculture, which in some cases allowed Africans to acquire wealth and raise their standard of living. But while these new market opportunities benefited some, they often eroded traditional standards of wealth and status in communities and thereby increased tensions among the population. The purposeful emphasis on cash crop agriculture impeded industrial development in Africa: European nations did not want industrial competition. Also, Africa's integration into a world economy resulted in a system that encouraged Africans to produce what they could not consume and consume what they did not produce, creating national economies extremely susceptible to economic crisis.

In the arena of social impacts, those who promote the benefits of colonialism often refer to the introduction of modern medicine and the new economic opportunities and modern amenities provided by urbanization. Such arguments are often countered by the criticism that these benefits were limited in number and access. Other critics comment on the negative impact of colonialism on women, who often found themselves pushed into domestic activities and out of traditional economic activities and social roles. But the topic most debate on the social and cultural legacies of colonialism is that of the impact of Christianity. The introduction of Christianity and its adoption by some Africans introduced new social tensions into African society. Converts adopted European behaviors and dress, gained access to modern medicine and European education, and as a result abandoned traditional practices. African societies split into two groups: a small, Christian European-educated Africa elite and a larger traditional, predominantly rural and illiterate group. The adoption of Christianity meant undergoing Westernization and resulted in many Africans being alienated from both cultures. They were no longer traditional, and in fact often openly condemned anything traditional, but neither were they allowed, despite their dress, education, and behavior, to be European. It was in this transformation that the seeds of colonialism's dismantling were planted. For it was out of the Westernized, European-educated African elite that movements for Africa's independence would grow. The colonial era came to an end with the emergence of independence movements in Africa. The century of European domination and colonialism was an extremely important era in Africa's history, one whose legacy continues to impact and direct the continent's present and future.

Heather Thiessen-Reily

See also: Africa, Precolonial; Afrocentrism; American Missionary Association; Berlin West Africa Conference; British Empire; Brussels Act; Columbian Exchange; Decolonization, African; Neocolonialism; Pre-Columbian America; Portuguese Empire; Spanish Empire

References
Achebe, Chinua. *Things Fall Apart.* New York: Anchor Books, 1994.
Adu Boahen, A. *African Perspectives on Colonialism.* Baltimore, MD: John Hopkins University Press, 1989.
Adu Boahen, A. *Africa under Colonial Domination 1880–1935. Vol. VII. General History of Africa.* Abridged ed. Berkeley: University of California Press, 1990.
Falola, Toyin, ed. *Africa.* Vol. 3, *Colonial Africa 1885–1939.* Durham, NC: Carolina Academic Press, 2001.

Oliver, Roland. *Africa since 1800.* Cambridge: Cambridge University Press, 2005.

Packenham, Thomas. *Scramble for Africa.* New York: Harper Perennial, 1992.

Robinson, Ronald, and John Gallagher. *Africa and the Victorians.* New York: St. Martin's Press, 1967.

COLORED FARMERS NATIONAL ALLIANCE

The Colored Farmers National Alliance was formed to address unfair practices in labor and economy for black farmers in postemancipation America. Faced with racial segregation, escalating interest rates, and decreasing commodity prices, all farmers sought relief during the mid-1880s. On December 11, 1886, sixteen black farmers and one white farmer organized the Colored Farmers National Alliance and Cooperative Union in Houston County, Texas. Unable to gain membership in the white-controlled Northern and Southern Alliance, black farmers envisioned their Alliance as a mechanism to confront unfair practices. The lone white member, R. M. Humphrey, viewed the organization as a method for gaining black political support in Reconstruction-era Southern politics. Humphrey assumed leadership as superintendent and J. J. Shuffer was named president.

The Alliance worked to organize poor, uneducated, and landless black farmers. Fearing retaliation from white supremacists, organizers worked quietly behind the scenes. Adopting many populist ideas, the group promoted railroad regulation, an increased money supply, and fair taxation policies. A fraternal organization, the group formed banks and insurance agencies. In 1890 the group merged with the National Colored Alliance. The following year, the new organization claimed over one million members in twelve states.

Despite impressive growth, the organization could not escape the tentacles of white supremacy. Unconvinced that the growing Populist Party, which supported the Alliance, could sustain political clout, black Republicans were reluctant to desert their well-established party. Other blacks, fearing increased white power in the Democratic Party, rejected the perceived radicalism of the Alliance. Yet despite pressure from black Republicans, assaults from white supremacists, and politically divided black laborers, the Colored Farmers National Alliance paved the way for subsequent labor and political organizations.

Janice E. Fowler

References

Goodwyn, Lawrence. *The Populist Moment: A Short History of the Agrarian Revolt in America.* New York: Oxford University Press, 1978.

Woodward, C. Vann. *Origins of the New South: 1877–1913.* Baton Rouge: Louisiana State University Press, 1971.

Handbook of Texas Online. "Colored Farmers' Alliance." http://www.tsha.utexas.edu/handbook/online/articles/CC/aac1.html.

COLORED METHODIST EPISCOPAL CHURCH

The Colored Methodist Episcopal Church is an African American church body in the Methodist tradition, formed after the Civil War. In 1865, during the final days of the American Civil War, thousands of former African American slaves sought to form a church body affiliated with the historic Methodist tradition yet separate and independent from the predominantly white Methodist Episcopal Church, South. These men and women did not want to attend churches comprised of former slave owners, nor did they desire to join the historically free black churches of the North, such as the African Methodist Episcopal Church. In 1870, during Reconstruction in the U.S. South, a group of over forty black ministers and church leaders met at Jackson, Tennessee, to form the Colored Methodist Episcopal Church in America (CMEC).

Once the organizational structure of the CMEC was in place, the leaders created nine separate conferences composed of various church congregations throughout the southern United States. The church also started a printing house and published a newspaper, *The Christian Index,* for church members interested in the latest church reports and news from around the country. The CMEC was the first national organization composed of former slaves, and it elected two African American ministers, William H. Miles and Richard H. Vanderhorst, as bishops to guide the church into the future. In the years following, the CMEC forged its own religious identity and provided a safe refuge for black membership experiencing racial discrimination in the post–Civil War United States.

During the twentieth century the CMEC was very active in the American Civil Rights Movement, particularly within the National Association for the Advancement of Colored People and the Southern Christian Leadership Conference, led by Dr. Martin Luther King Jr. In 1954 the leadership of the Colored Methodist Episcopal Church changed the name of the denomination to the Christian Methodist Episcopal Church. The name change reflected the desire of many within the church to emphasize inclusiveness and racial diversity. Today, the national headquarters of the Christian Methodist Episcopal Church is located in Memphis, Tennessee. The church sanctions five institutions of higher education and remains active in social and political concerns throughout the world.

Christopher J. Anderson

See also: Christianity (African American); Civil Rights Movement

References

Dvorak, Katharine L. *An African-American Exodus: The Segregation of the Southern Churches.* Brooklyn, NY: Carlson Publishing, 1991.

Lakey, Othal Hawthorne. *The History of the CME Church.* Memphis, TN: CME Publishing House, 1985.

Sommerville, Raymond R. *An Ex-Colored Church: Social Activism in the CME Church, 1870–1970.* Macon, GA: Mercer University Press, 2004.

COLUMBIAN EXCHANGE

Following Christopher Columbus's first voyage to the Americas in 1492, a dramatic biological, cultural, and human exchange known as the Columbian Exchange took place between Africa, Europe, and the Americas.

Prior to Europeans' arrival in the Americas, the Western Hemisphere's north-south orientation, combined with high mountain ranges and geographical isolation, had resulted in limited biological diversity, particularly for large mammals and germs. When the Spanish, Portuguese, Dutch, English, and French explored and then settled areas previously occupied by Amerindians, and as millions of African slaves were brought to the Americas, a vast exchange of germs, crops, animals, and humans took place across the Atlantic Ocean.

The number of germs brought back to Europe from the Americas was limited.

Columbus's crew may have brought back venereal syphilis to Spain in 1493. Animals imported from the Americas were equally small in number (guinea pigs, llamas, cochineals). On the other hand, the Americas contributed many new crops such as varieties of beans, cacao, corn, manioc, peanuts, chili peppers, pineapples, sweet potatoes, white potatoes, squash, tobacco, tomatoes, and vanilla. Such crops as potatoes, which allowed a high yield per acre, and tomatoes, which provided much-needed vitamins, improved Europeans' diet and resulted in a dramatic increase in Europe's (as well as China's) population.

Europeans introduced a wide variety of germs to the Americas, including whooping cough, diphtheria, influenza, measles, the bubonic plague, smallpox, and typhus. The Native American population, estimated at 50 to 100 million prior to Columbus's arrival, dropped 50 to 90 percent in the following century, in large part because Amerindians had no immunity to these diseases. Tainos and Caribs disappeared from most Caribbean islands entirely; Mexica and Quechua Indians (in present-day Mexico and Peru, respectively) fared slightly better. Aside from the demographic impact, smallpox facilitated Spanish conquest, as in Tenochtitlán (Mexico City), where an epidemic broke out during Hernán Cortés's conquest of the Aztec Empire (1519–1521), and Peru, where the Inca emperor Huayna Capac and his heir both succumbed to smallpox, sparking a bloody civil war before and during Francisco Pizarro's conquest (1531–1533).

Europeans contributed animals, such as cows, large dogs, horses, sheep, goats, pigs, and rats. Mediterranean crops introduced by the Spaniards (figs, grape vines, lemons, olives, onions, oranges, chick peas,

wheat) were not always suited for the Americas; other plants that they introduced, such as sugarcane (of Middle Eastern origin), coffee bushes (from Ethiopia), and banana trees (originally from Southeast Asia) radically transformed the agricultural economy of the American tropics.

Africans' presence in the Americas was a direct consequence of the Columbian Exchange. Following the introduction of lucrative tropical crops in the Caribbean and Brazil, and as the native population there was limited (Brazil) or dwindled into oblivion (the Caribbean), the need for imported labor grew more acute. An estimated 10 million African slaves were forcibly transported to plantation colonies (mostly in Brazil and the Caribbean). Tropical diseases the slaves brought along, most notably yellow fever and malaria, further increased reliance on African labor, since Africans were less vulnerable to these diseases than were Europeans and Amerindians. Internecine warfare in Africa, aimed at seizing slaves for the American market, destabilized several African kingdoms, including the Kongo.

The Americas today remain deeply marked by the Columbian Exchange, particularly on a human level. Population exchanges have created remarkable racial diversity, including large groups of mixed racial background, such as the mestizos (Caucasian-Amerindians), mulattos (African-Caucasians), and *zambos* (African-Amerindians). Religious syncretism (Haiti's voodoo, for example) and a blending of languages (creoles) are other, more indirect consequences of the Columbian Exchange.

Philippe R. Girard

See also: Agriculture; Atlantic World; Brazil; Colombia; Creole/Criollo; Diaspora; Haiti; Jamaica; Mexico; Peru; Voodoo

References

Cook, Noble David. *Born to Die: Disease and New World Conquest, 1492–1650.* Cambridge: Cambridge University Press, 1997.

Diamond, Jared. *Guns, Germs, and Steel: The Fate of Human Societies.* New York: Norton, 1997.

COLUMBUS, CHRISTOPHER (1451–1506)

Christopher Columbus was a Genoese sailor and merchant often credited with the "discovery" of the Americas by Europeans. Although Columbus cannot be held directly responsible for the institution of slavery in the New World, his position regarding the mistreatment and enslavement of indigenous peoples, which Queen Isabel herself openly opposed, sparked a larger debate about slavery that ultimately justified the use of African slave labor in the Americas. (For more information see the exchange between Bartolomé De las Casas and Juan Ginés de Sepúlveda). It is also important to note that with Columbus's arrival, many European diseases were introduced into the New World, thus decimating a large percentage of native populations and contributing to the search for alternative labor sources elsewhere.

Columbus, seeking to establish a Western trade route from Europe to Asia via the Atlantic Ocean, first approached the Portuguese king João II for patronage and financial support, but he refused to honor Columbus's request. Columbus later appealed to the Spanish king and queen, Fernando de Aragón and Isabel de Castilla y León, also known as the Catholic Monarchs, who finally agreed to back what became known as "the enterprise of the Indies" following the expulsion of the Moors from southern Spain, which marked the end of the 700-year-long Spanish Reconquest. Throughout the fifteenth century, the Spanish and the Portuguese competed for control over African trade routes along the Atlantic coast. This conflict eventually resulted in the signing of a treaty in which Spain agreed to relinquish its claims on West African gold markets as well as cede control over the eastern route to India to the Portuguese.

Due to large debts incurred during the Reconquest, the Catholic Monarchs eventually agreed to support Columbus on his voyage, with hopes that he would find the much-desired gold needed to replenish the royal treasury. Likewise, conversion of people to Christianity also became a primary goal for Columbus in an attempt to expand the holdings of the Spanish Empire, both geographically and spiritually. In exchange for discovering new lands for Spain and converting its inhabitants to Christianity, Queen Isabel granted Columbus the "Admiralty of the Ocean Sea" and governing rights over the lands that he would discover, in addition to a small percentage of the profits, based on the amount of gold that he would find.

On October 12, 1492, Columbus and his men accidentally landed their ships, the Niña, the Pinta, and the Santa María, on what he thought was the Indies. Beginning with his first voyage (1492) and ending with his fourth and last voyage (1504), Columbus succeeded in claiming a large portion of the New World for the Spanish crown, namely Central America, many Caribbean islands, and the mouth of the Orinoco River in present-day Venezuela. However, Columbus failed to find an adequate amount of gold to cover his costs, let alone a surplus, and spent most of his life trying to claim the money and recognition that had been promised him.

The information that we gather about Columbus comes primarily from his journals documenting his voyages. His writing style is often described as an awkward Castillian Spanish, strongly influenced by Portuguese. Interestingly enough, as his text *Libro de Profecías* ("Book of Prophecies") suggests, Columbus was heavily influenced by millenarian philosophies, whose goals included worldwide conversion of people to Christianity and the restoration of Christian control over Jerusalem, which was under Muslim jurisdiction, in order to prepare the way for the second coming of Jesus Christ.

Nicole L. Sparling and María Luján Tubio

References

Davidson, Miles. *Columbus Then and Now: A Life Reexamined.* Norman: University of Oklahoma Press, 1997.

Garganigo, John F., et al., eds. *Huellas de las literaturas hispanoamericanas.* 2nd ed. Upper Saddle River, NJ: Prentice Hall, 2002.

Kadir, Djelal. *Columbus and the Ends of the Earth: Europe's Prophetic Rhetoric as Conquering Ideology.* Berkeley: University of California Press, 1992.

Phillips, William, and Carla Rahn Phillips. *The Worlds of Christopher Columbus.* Cambridge: Cambridge University Press, 1992.

COMOROS

A nation in the Indian Ocean, the Union of the Comoros has a population of about 812,000 concentrated on three small main islands. Located off of Africa's eastern coast, northwest of Madagascar, the Comoros Islands have been important transit points for traders and sailors. Consequently, starting in the sixteenth century, the islands saw the simultaneous arrival of both Arab and Portuguese traders. French influence grew rapidly across the eighteenth and nineteenth centuries. In 1908 Comoros became an official French colony. The islands gained independence in 1975.

Like other African island nations, Comoros is historically connected to the Americas primarily through transoceanic trade and through its strategic geopolitical and military location. Prior to the opening of the Suez Canal in 1869, Comoros served as a major transshipment point for trade in spices across the Indian Ocean to the Americas. Because of this role, Comoros has historically contained a diverse mix of people of Arab, European, African, and Asian, particularly Malaysian and Indonesian, descent.

Although the opening of the Suez Canal changed shipping patterns for the region, the islands rose in geopolitical importance as European powers such as France, Britain, and Russia vied for economic and political dominance in the Indian Ocean. Later, as World War II drew near, Japan and the United States would also enter the region seeking to expand their influence.

During and after World War II, the defeat of British naval forces in the Indian Ocean weakened British regional influence and, in the postwar era, the major powers in the area would be the United States and the Soviet Union. France, Comoros's colonial power, would also retain a large naval force in the Indian Ocean, with bases in the Comoros. In effect, these small islands found themselves part of the larger geopolitical maneuverings of the cold war. Like Madagascar, Comoros was a focus of U.S. cold war strategic interest because of its location in the Indian Ocean. Since the end of the cold war, attention has shifted to Comoros as a transfer point for narcotics coming to the United States across the Indian Ocean.

Independence in 1975 was followed by thirty years of political instability. In those decades, the nation experienced more than eighteen coups. Two of the larger islands, Anjouan and Moheli, violently seceded in 1997. They rejoined the Union in 2001 only after being given autonomy.

Comoros held its first peaceful elections in early 2006. Although U.S. relations with Comoros have been friendly, the latter's political instability has made the United States reluctant to send economic aid to the nation, despite its general poverty and indebtedness. In 2000, Comoros was one of thirty-four African nations regarded as too unstable to be included in the trade liberalization policy announced by U.S. president Bill Clinton, aimed at improving African access to U.S. markets. In 2006, as the elections approached, the African Union (AU) sent troops to the country in an effort to bolster stability. Comoros has become one test of the AU's ability to create stability in the region.

Comoros has also received international attention as one of Africa's most biologically unique regions. Because of its location, Comoros and the surrounding waters have many rare animals and plants. Three species are internationally famous: the Livingstone fruit bat, the ylang ylang, and the coelancanth. Comoros has a diverse range of African fruit bats, and the giant Livingstone fruit bat, among the largest of its kind, is unique to the islands. Endangered fruit bats have been the focus of considerable scientific study and conservation efforts. Ylang ylang is a plant producing an essential oil commonly used in perfumes. Comoros is the source of 80 percent of the world's supply of ylang ylang.

The coelancanth is a rare ancient fish of significant scientific value. From 66 to at least 400 million years old, the species was formerly thought extinct until it was recognized that fishermen from Comoros had been catching them for some years. Because of its biodiversity, Comoros and its surrounding waters have become, over the last decade, the focus of conservation efforts through the United Nations and U.S. agencies and nongovernmental organizations.

Richard Juang

See also: African Union; Environmentalism

Reference
Newitt, Malyn. "The Perils of Being a Micro State: São Tomé and the Comoros Islands Since Independence." In *The Political Economy of Small Tropical Islands: The Importance of Being Small,* edited by H. M Hintjens and M. D. D. Newitt. Exeter, UK: University of Exeter Press, 1992.

COMPANY OF MERCHANTS TRADING TO AFRICA

The Company of Merchants Trading to Africa was created in England during 1750 to facilitate the coastal slave trade in West Africa. The company's trade rapidly increased the number of slaves carried across the Atlantic while developing England's relationship with the Fante.

The late-seventeenth-century decision by Parliament to expand England's African trade by allowing "free traders"—traders representing individual, rather than national, interests—to buy slaves set the foundations for the decline of the Royal African Company (RAC), which had formerly monopolized the slave trade, and the expansion of England's slave trade. While the RAC continued to operate during the first half of the eighteenth century, Parliament finally decided to replace it in 1750 with a new company. The Company of Merchants Trading to Africa embodied the growing belief that free trade allowed anyone willing to pay the forty-shilling fee to join the company. While the company embraced free trade, Parliament believed that England's African trade could only be successful by maintaining a state-sponsored coastal presence. The company's creation allowed England to maintain its numerous coastal structures, and the continued English presence in turn continued the already-existing relations with various coastal peoples. In the act that created the company, Parliament agreed to provide it with a yearly grant to maintain this coastal infrastructure. This was vital because while the company's servants were allowed to trade in slaves, the corporate entity was not. Therefore, the company possessed no way to raise a revenue. This yearly parliamentary grant was given to the company's London-based African Committee, consisting of three members who were from London, Liverpool, and Bristol. They used the money to purchase commodities to send to Cape Coast Castle, the company's administrative headquarters in West Africa, where they would then be distributed to the various other forts. (The company was not allowed to send currency to West Africa.) Large quantities of commodities were sent from England on the yearly supply ships.

For these shipments to be useful, the Africa Committee members needed to know what was desired along the Gold Coast; thus, the governor of Cape Coast Castle continually informed them of what was in demand. This knowledge added to the servants' success as slave traders. Once these goods arrived in West Africa, the company utilized them in a variety of ways.

One was to pay the wages of the company's European servants, who then used the goods to buy and sell slaves. The servants paid their free and unfree African laborers; kept members of the coastal elite in their pay; paid a series of ground rents and customs to the local peoples where their forts stood; and used the goods to settle local disputes. From its establishment in 1750 to its decline after the abolition of the slave trade in 1807, the company proved successful in maintaining this coastal infrastructure. It did so by preserving old coastal relations while developing new ones, by building new trade enclaves, especially at Annamaboe, and by challenging the French and Dutch along the Gold Coast.

Ty M. Reese

See also: Cape Coast Castle; Royal African Company

References
Martin, Eveline C. *The British West African Settlement, 1750–1821: A Study in Local Administration.* 1927. Reprint, Westport, CT: Negro Universities Press, 1970.
Priestly, Margaret. *West African Trade & Coast Society: A Family Study.* Oxford: Oxford University Press, 1969.

CONDÉ, MARYSE (1937–)

Maryse Condé is a novelist, essayist, and educator from Guadeloupe who publishes her works in French. She was born on February 11, 1937, in Pointe-à-Pitre, Guadeloupe, the eighth child in her family. Before writing her first novel, Maryse Condé experimented with drama, producing several plays, including *Le Morne de Massabielle (The Hills of Massabielle)* (1974) and *The Tropical Breeze Hotel* (1988), staged respectively in 1991 and 1998 at the Ubu Repertory Theatre in

New York. Her play, *An Tan Revolisyon (In the Time of the Revolution)* (1989), was commissioned for the bicentennial of the French Revolution and performed at the University of Georgia at Athens. In addition to being a renowned writer and award-winning novelist, Condé has taught at Harvard, the University of Virginia, and the University of California at Berkeley. She has also held several prestigious and distinguished appointments, including the chair of the Center for French and Francophone Studies at Columbia University. Additionally, Condé was elected an honorary member of the Académie des letters du Québec in 1998 and president of the Comité Mémoire in Paris in 2002. The author of numerous novels, Condé has gained not only national but also international recognition—many of her novels have been translated into English, German, Dutch, Italian, Spanish, Portuguese, and Japanese. Condé lived in Africa for several years, namely in Ghana, Senegal, and Guinea, where she worked in the capacity of instructor-schoolteacher at various secondary schools.

Condé's personal experiences in Africa have shaped her writings, as her first two novels testify. Disillusioned with her mother's land, Guadeloupe, like her protagonists in her semi-autobiographical novels *Heremakhonon* (1988) and *Une Sason à Rihata (A Season in Rihata)* (1981), Condé migrated to Africa. The exact geographic locations are skewed in Condé's first two novels, but *Segou: Les Murailles de terre* (1984), awarded the Prix Liberatur (Germany, 1988), is set in the eighteenth-century African kingdom of Segu, a town on the Niger River in present-day Mali. Condé details the transformations—cultural, political, and geographical—of this African

tribal society, changes that were forged by religion, specifically the rise of Islam, and the slave trade. The Bambara tribal beliefs and customs were challenged and obfuscated by the intervention of New World culture and religion. Condé's fourth novel, *Segou: La Terre en Miettes (The Children of Segu)* (1985), a sequel to *Segu,* further depicts the theme of the spread of Islam and French colonialism, detailing the invasion of the French and the subsequent fall of the once great Bambara Empire at the hands of the French colonial army.

In *Moi, Tituba, Sorciere Noire de Salem (I, Tituba, Black Witch of Salem)* (1986), the winner of La Grand Prix Littéraire de la Femme, Africa is no longer a designated home site; instead the Caribbean is reclaimed as the "true" native land. Condé traverses the Caribbean through her eponymous heroine, Tituba, giving her voice and visibility and according her agency. Tituba is the embodiment of an African soothsayer and healer, for in her reside the voices of the novel's ancestors, her surrogate mother Mama Yaya and her biological mother Abena. Tituba's legendary status is also linked to Nanny, the famous Jamaican Maroon, a figure of empowerment and resistance, responsible for not only staging a revolution but also saving her people from a life of servitude and bondage.

La vie Scelerate (Tree of Life) (1987), awarded the Prix de L'Academie Française in 1988, details the impoverished life of a Guadeloupean family that battles not only poverty but also racism and discrimination yet manages eventually to escape its impoverished state, while *Traversee de la Mangrove (Crossing the Mangrove)* (1989) also invokes the past as important to the needs of the present. *Windward Heights* (1998) is Condé's rewriting of Emily

Bronte's *Wuthering Heights,* providing a Caribbean sensibility and geography as the events of the novel take place in Guadeloupe, her homeland, Cuba, and Dominica. Condé returns to the theme of lack, absence, secrecy, and loss in *Desirada* (1997), winner of the Prix Carbet de la Caraibe.

In her memoir, *Le Coeur à rire et à pleurer, contes vrais de mon enfance (Tales from the Heart: True Stories from My Childhood)* (1999), which won the Prix Yourcenar 1999 for excellence in French writing, Condé offers an autobiographical account of her childhood, providing rich details of her pains, her joys, and her relationships with her parents and her brother and confidant. She documents the racial and class struggles that affect the Guadeloupean populace, including her parents, who identified more with the French colonials than with the native people. Condé details her dismay, lack of identity, and alienation in this coming-of-age story.

Simone A. James Alexander

See also: Caribbean Literature; Colonialism; Nanny

References

Alexander, Simone A. James. *Mother Imagery in the Novels of Afro-Caribbean Women.* Columbia: University of Missouri Press, 2001.

Condé, Maryse. "Pan-Africanism, Feminism, and Culture." In *Imagining Home: Class, Culture, and Nationalism in the African Diaspora,* edited by Sidney J. Lemelle and Robin D. G. Kelly. New York: Verso, 1994.

Condé, Maryse. *Tales from the Heart: True Stories from My Childhood.* Translated by Richard Philcox. New York: Soho Press, 2001.

CONGO (BRAZZAVILLE)

Located in west-central Africa, the Republic of Congo is often distinguished by its capital as Congo (Brazzaville) from the Democratic Republic of Congo, or Congo (Kinshasa). Congo (Brazzaville) has ties to the Americas dating back to the precolonial era. The kingdom of the Kongo traded with the Portuguese in the late fifteenth century and its coast was heavily involved in the transatlantic slave trade. The kingdom of the Kongo exported approximately 13,000 slaves a year. Connections also existed in the other direction as well: maize, manioc, tobacco, groundnuts, and other New World plants were introduced into the kingdom. These crops from the New World transformed Kongo's agriculture in the seventeenth century by increasing yields and providing better nutrition and health.

In the nineteenth and twentieth centuries, Congo was a French colony. Congo gained its independence in 1960. The new nation faced several years of recurrent civil war, followed by a quarter century of experimentation with Marxism and some forms of multiparty democracy. In the 1970s and 1980s, Congo was a socialist nation with strong educational, economic, and military ties to the Soviet Union, East Germany, and Cuba. With the waning of the cold war, the late 1980s saw a warming of Congolese relations with the West. When Communism fell in 1991, Congo adopted multiparty democracy, improving its relations with the United States. The United States gave substantial support to Congolese democratization efforts, helping to fund elections.

Democratization and free-market economic reforms have led to American and Canadian interest and support. Starting in the 1990s, the United States made African democratization a central priority of its foreign policy toward the continent, and the United States Agency for International Development (USAID) began to oversee the implementation of U.S. assistance programs in Congo, focusing on its central objectives: economic development, improved health, protection of basic human rights, the development of communications technology, women's education, government accountability, and environmental protection.

Congo's economy is based primarily on petroleum, by far the country's major revenue source, although its abundant mineral and natural resources (timber, lead, zinc, uranium, phosphates, natural gas, plywood, sugar, cocoa, coffee, and diamonds) has attracted American investments. Though the Congolese oil sector is dominated by the French oil company TotalFinaElf, American oil companies, including Amoco, Conoco, Chevron, and Texaco, are active in petroleum exploration and production. In June 1997 Congo and the United States signed a treaty designed to facilitate and protect foreign investment.

Philip A. Ojo

See also: French Empire; United States Agency for International Development

References

Gibbs, David N. *The Political Economy of Third World Intervention: Mines, Money, and U.S. Policy in the Congo Crisis.* Chicago: University of Chicago Press, 1991.

Harbeson, John W. "Externally Assisted Democratization." In *Africa in World Politics: The African State System in Flux,* edited by John W. Harbeson and Donald Rothchild. 3rd ed. Boulder, CO: Westview, 2000.

Rotberg, Robert I., ed. *Africa in the 1990s and Beyond: U.S. Policy Opportunities and Choices.* Algonac, MI: Reference Publications, 1988.

Vansina, J. "The Kongo Kingdom and its Neighbours." In *UNESCO General History of Africa.* Vol. V, *Africa from the Sixteenth to the Eighteenth Century,* edited by B. A. Ogot. London and Berkeley: Heinemann Educational Books and University of California Press, 1992.

CONGO (KINSHASA), DEMOCRATIC REPUBLIC OF THE

The Democratic Republic of Congo (DRC), formerly known as Zaire, is a republic of west-central Africa that achieved independence from colonial rule in 1960 and is known for its role in world politics in both the colonial and independence eras. The DRC, with a vast wealth of mineral resources, is potentially one of the richest countries in Africa. This same mineral wealth has proven attractive to foreign governments and corporations seeking riches to plunder. From the brutalities of Belgian colonialists and their Western backers to the trespasses of neighboring governments in Uganda and Rwanda, Congo has been made a killing floor of exploitation. In Congo, various national armies and local militias, proxies of imperialist powers, have fought or are fighting over control of some of the world's largest and richest deposits of gold, diamonds, cobalt, and coltan.

The death toll from the ongoing war in the DRC, which began in 1998, is higher than in any other military conflict since World War II, with an estimated 4.7 million killed in the last four years alone. The International Rescue Committee, an aid agency based in New York, reports that the mortality rate in Congo is higher than the United Nations rates for any other country.

The war in Congo began in August 1998, when an uprising against the Kinshasa government of Laurent Kabila was launched in the east, backed by forces of the Ugandan and Rwandan governments (which received their main support from the governments of the United States and Britain). The Ugandan government claimed it was defending its western borders against rebels based in Rwanda, while the Rwandan forces claimed to be defending themselves against Hutu militias on the Congo border. Apparently, this border protection required Rwandan forces to occupy the diamond-rich town of Kisangani, 700 miles inside Congo.

Militias were also funded by neighboring governments hostile to the Congolese government. The conflict in Congo has over its course seen involvement from the governments and rebels of Angola, Uganda, Rwanda, Burundi, and South Africa. This has led some commentators to refer to the conflict as "Africa's World War." Along the way there has been evidence of involvement by mercenary companies including MPRI of the United States, Sandline of Britain, and Executive Outcomes of South Africa.

Throughout the tumultuous post-independence era, Congo has remained subjected to the forces of imperialism and neocolonialism. Imperialist interests pursuing private gain have always played a significant and sinister part in the ongoing Congo tragedy.

Congo has been geopolitically significant for a number of reasons. It is the second largest African country in terms of area, bordering nine other countries in the center of the continent. The country is a link between the states of the Indian and the Atlantic oceans. DRC is home to the world's largest deposits of copper, cobalt, cadmium, and coltan.

For many Westerners, Congo "has long been a symbol of Africa. The very word 'Congo' has resonance for the many Americans who never heard of most of the African states which quietly reached independence and unobtrusively went about their business" (Ferkiss, 1966, p. 169). In few areas have Western colonialism and

imperialism been so vicious and destructive as in Congo. In his "Congo: The Western Heart of Darkness" (2001), Asad Ismi notes that genocide and plunder have been central to Western policy toward mineral-rich Congo since the Berlin West Africa Conference of 1884–1885 assigned Congo as the personal property of Belgium's King Leopold II.

Congo suffered under 115 years of Belgian colonialism and neocolonialism. More than ten million Congolese were killed in those years, halving the population. Under brutal Belgian rule, millions of Congolese were subjected to torture, slavery, and forced labor as the colonizers pursued the maximum exploitation of ivory and rubber. Workers' hands were severed for not working hard enough, and women were kidnapped to force their husbands to collect rubber sap. The regimes of primitive capitalist accumulation imposed by the Belgian colonialists were so horrific that George Washington Williams, an African American human rights activist who worked to end the atrocities in Congo, coined the term "crimes against humanity" in 1890 to describe what he had seen upon a visit to the country. As an eerie precursor to the present-day exploitation of Congo to serve the needs of the information age, Leopold's brutal predations in the Congo were driven by the newly emerging appetites of the auto age, notably, the growing need for rubber for pneumatic tires.

As V. C. Ferkiss has noted in *Africa's Search for Identity* (1966), "the ghost of a Congo political entity which was a mask for foreign economic exploitation of Africans was born at the Free State's demise" (p. 170). Since independence, governance in the Congo has followed this same pattern.

Congo fell within the U.S. sphere of influence in 1960–1961, after a CIA-sponsored coup that saw the murder of Patrice Lumumba, leader of the country's first elected government. The U.S. government feared that Lumumba would take Congo into the pro-Soviet camp, and President Dwight Eisenhower himself approved of Lumumba's assassination.

Western political machinations were responsible for finally installing the CIA's paid agent, Mobutu Sese Seko, in power in 1965. Under his dictatorship, which received ongoing U.S. backing, Congo suffered another thirty-seven years of terror and looting similar to what had been imposed under Belgian rule.

In the years following independence in 1960, much of Congo's turmoil centered on the mineral-rich Katanga Province and its Western-backed secessionist government. Two major invasions of Katanga Province by opposition forces of the Front de la Libération Nationale Congolaise (FNLC; Congolese National Liberation Front) were met by interventions from outside forces in support of Mobutu: Moroccan forces in 1977 and French forces in 1978. Indeed, outside forces were instrumental in defending the Mobutu regime from popular uprisings.

Between 1965 and 1991, Mobutu's regime received more than $1.5 billion in military and economic aid from the United States. At the same time, U.S. multinational corporations were granted increased access to Zaire's mineral wealth.

As a Western ally, Mobutu also played a part in cold war geopolitics. As an imperialist foothold, Zaire was used by the United States as a base to launch campaigns against the nominally socialist government in Angola from its assumption of power in 1975 until Mobutu's ouster in 1997.

Eventually, Mobutu's personal pillaging of Zaire, which saw as much as 95 percent of the country's budget reserved for his own "discretionary spending," led the United States to seek alternatives in the country that might allow even greater access for Western corporations. Especially unacceptable to imperialist interests were Mobutu's attempts to maintain state control over mining operations.

Since the removal of Mobutu, outside forces have maintained a steady hold on the successor regimes, continuing to shape the political economy of Central Africa. The manner in which imperialist forces have maintained their grip on the post-Mobutu Congo is crucial for any understanding of the political economy of contemporary Central Africa.

The struggles that led to the replacement of Mobutu by Kabila in some ways had the character of classical imperialist battles between competing states as described by Lenin. Laurent Kabila's rise to power came with considerable backing from North American interests. U.S. backing of Kabila provided the opportunity "of playing the modernising card in opposition to the neo-colonial manipulation of the European powers" (Biel, 2003, p. 84).

Once in power, Kabila surprised his former allies by refusing to hand over control of Congo's mineral wealth. Kabila also retracted several mining contracts signed with U.S. and European companies during the period of his alliance with Uganda and Rwanda, including a US$1 billion contract with American Mineral Fields International (AMFI), a mining company based in former U.S. president Bill Clinton's hometown of Hope, Arkansas. He also refused to pay the huge debt to the International Monetary Fund (IMF) and World Bank run up under Mobutu. Kabila began to nationalize resources and allowed mining concessions to China and North Korea. International capital grew so frustrated with Kabila's dishonoring of contracts that he had signed with foreign businesses that some companies offered him $200 million to leave the Congo. There is even reasonable speculation that Kabila was assassinated because he refused to cede outright control over the country's enormous mineral deposits, including some of the world's most significant deposits of gold, diamonds, cobalt, manganese, uranium, copper, zinc, and, increasingly important, coltan, a key component in cell phones and computers.

The new president, Kabila's son Joseph, has openly embraced neoliberal capitalist policy. One of his first acts as president was to fly to the United States to give back mining concessions to companies whose rights had been revoked under his father's rule. In trips to Paris, Brussels, Washington, and New York, he has held many private sessions with top European and American business leaders. Additionally, he publicly pledged during a trip to the United States to deregulate the Congolese economy, privatize major state-run companies, and introduce neoliberal investment codes in line with IMF demands.

Jeff Shantz

References

Biel, Robert. "Imperialism and International Governance: The Case of U.S. Policy toward Africa." *Review of African Political Economy* 95 (2003): 77–88.

Ferkiss, Victor. C. *Africa's Search for Identity.* Cleveland, OH: Meridian Books, 1966.

Griswold, Dierdre, and Johnnie Stevens. "Bush, Clinton in the Web: Behind the Assassination of Kabila." http://www.iacenter.org, 2001.

Taylor, Ian. "Conflict in Central Africa: Clandestine Networks and Regional/Global Configurations." *Review of African Political Economy* 95 (2003): 45–55.

CONGOLESE INDEPENDENCE

The crucial importance of Congolese raw materials to the U.S. economy and the determination to resist any expansionist drives of the Soviet Union led to U.S. intervention in the 1960s in what is now the Democratic Republic of the Congo. As part of its economic and cold war interests, the United States supported the overthrow of Congo's first president, Patrice Lumumba, in 1960 and supported the subsequent regime of Mobutu Seso Seko.

The rich mineral deposits in the Katanga area made the former Belgian Congo one of the most highly developed regions of the African continent. Congo's vast resources also attracted American interests. Although Western interests in Congo were predominantly Belgian at the time of independence in 1960, the United States perceived the central African country to be an untapped source of wealth, including valuable mineral resources (gold, copper, cobalt, diamonds, and uranium), and a place with potential investment opportunities. This perception influenced American conduct in Congo. The U.S. government also sought to protect American business interests in Central Africa more generally, which included important investments through American Mineral Fields Incorporated (AMF), a gold and diamond mining corporation; American Metal Climax (AMAX), a mining company with extensive African holdings; Morgan Guaranty Trust; Standard Oil; Mobil Oil; Read and Company; and Dillon. Specifically, the

United States sought to reduce Belgian influence in Congo, both politically and economically, and to increase its own influence. By late 1965 the United States had emerged as the dominant power. By 1970, when a Tempelsman-led consortium gained control of the largest copper seams in the Congo, at Tenke Fungurume, American investors, especially contractors and commercial lenders, had largely displaced Belgian influences.

The dominant position of the United States emerged in the context of post-independence turmoil. Between late 1959 and early 1960, internal tribal and regional differences developed into what was known as the Congo crisis of 1960, in which the United Nations (UN) intervened in the newly independent nation. The United States seized the opportunity for vigorous involvement in African affairs while working under the auspices of the UN. In the wake of the political and social instability of the early years of Congolese independence, the most distinctive feature of U.S. policy was the deep hostility toward the then prime minister of Congo, Patrice Lumumba, who was suspected by the U.S. government of serving the interests of the former Soviet Union and accepting Soviet military and technical assistance. There was no evidence that the Soviets actually sought to take control of the Congo, and Lumumba's actions as prime minister did not suggest a predilection for Communism. The United States was acting primarily to preclude Soviet expansionism and Communist influence and to protect Western security, and to defend its economic interests. The CIA-sponsored coup d'état resulting in Patrice Lumumba's assassination in 1961 would lead to the profoundly corrupt and violent government of Mobutu Sese Seko. Mobutu received large amounts of U.S. aid to sustain Congo as an anti-Soviet sphere of influence and protect U.S. economic interests in the Central African nation's mineral wealth.

Philip A. Ojo

See also: Congo (Kinshasa), Democratic Republic of the; Lumumba, Patrice

References

Arkhurst, Frederick S. *U.S. Policy toward Africa.* New York: Praeger, 1975.

Gibbs, David N. *The Political Economy of Third World Intervention: Mines, Money, and U.S. Policy in the Congo Crisis.* Chicago: University of Chicago Press, 1991.

Whitaker, Jennifer Seymour. "Introduction: Africa and U.S. Interests." In *Africa and the United States—Vital Interests,* edited by Jennifer Seymour Whitaker. New York: New York University Press, 1978.

CÔTE D'IVOIRE

Located in West Africa, the Republic of Côte d'Ivoire has ties to both its former colonial ruler, France, and has had connections with the Americas beginning with the transatlantic slave trade in the fifteenth century. Precolonial Côte d'Ivoire's coastal towns of Assinie, Grand Bassam, and San Pedro were collection points for slaves. After abolition, some slave trading continued along the Ivorian coast.

American missionaries arrived in Assinie, Grand Bassam, and San Pedro in 1840, relocating there after local hostility drove them away from a settlement on the Gabon River. Today, Adventist and Baptist missions from the United States have a significant presence in the country.

Côte d'Ivoire's first president, Felix Houphouët Boigny, who led the country to independence from France in 1960, spoke of the importance of promoting international cooperation between Côte d'Ivoire and the Americas. During his 1962 visit to the United States, he requested and received aid. Further contacts with American businessmen led to private investments in Côte d'Ivoire. In December 1999, the nation experienced political turmoil and a military coup. Because of its substantial involvement in Côte d'Ivoire, the United States supported UN intervention.

Cultural influences from the Americas have been substantial. This has particularly been the case in music. Côte d'Ivoire's Alpha Blondy, the African Rasta, who creates Jah-centered anthems, became the first African star of reggae with the recording *Jah Glory* (1983). More recently, hip-hop has been taken up by Ivoirian youth. Dozens of rap groups have emerged, including *Parlement supreme posse, Negromuffin, Big Daddy Kane, Gangstarr, Alasko Deejay,* and *Ras Goody Brown.* These groups claim as their influences Bob Marley, Michael Jackson, and other American pop musicians. The groups rhyme in Dioula, Baoule, French, and English.

Philip A. Ojo

See also: French Empire; Popular Music, American Influences on African

References
Collins, Edmund John. "Musical Feedback: African America's Music in Africa." *A Journal of Opinion* 24, no. 2 (1996): 26–27.
Harbeson, John W. "Externally Assisted Democratization." In *Africa in World Politics: The African State System in Flux,* edited by John W. Harbeson and Donald Rothchild. 3rd ed. Boulder, CO: Westview, 2000.
Whitaker, Jennifer Seymour. "Introduction: Africa and U.S. Interests." In *Africa and the United States— Vital Interests,* edited by Jennifer Seymour Whitaker. New York: New York University Press, 1978.
Woronoff, Jon. *West African Wager: Houphouët versus Nkrumah.* Metuchen, NJ: Scarecrow Press, 1972.

CREOLE REVOLT

The Creole Revolt was a rebellion of U.S. slaves that sparked a jurisdictional debate over the international slave trade. In November 1841 slaves being transported from Virginia to Louisiana staged a revolt on board the *Creole*. Expecting a smooth voyage, the harsh captain, Robert Ensor, did not shackle or otherwise restrain the slaves. The ship's cook, Madison Washington, led the rebellion and, along with eighteen other men, stabbed Ensor and captured other men on board. However, they did not injure other passengers, including Ensor's family. The rebels forced William Merritt, the ship's overseer, to sail to the British port of Nassau in the Bahamas. Though British officials initially arrested the rebels, they subsequently freed them, ruling that since the revolt had occurred in their territory, the British Emancipation Act of 1833 applied to the American slaves. Americans had different responses to this sequence of events that illustrated the nation's internal conflict over the issue of slavery and the slave trade. While the South responded with fury over British interference in what they considered to be legal trade, the northern abolitionists praised the rebels and called Madison Washington a hero. Out of the dispute came the Webster-Ashburton Treaty of 1842, signed by Secretary of State Daniel Webster and British representative Lord Ashburton. Agreeing that the slaves on the *Creole* should not be tried by American laws, Webster nonetheless used the revolt as an opportunity to negotiate America's Northeast boundary disputes with Britain. To compensate the slaveholders who lost capital in the *Creole* affair, the British government paid them $110,330. The British ceased interference with American ships carrying slaves but worked with the U.S. Navy to encourage a unanimous enforcement of the prohibition of the Atlantic slave trade.

Merinda Simmons Dickens

See also: Amistad Case, The; Slavery (History)

References

Hendrick, George, and Willene Hendrick. *The Creole Mutiny: A Tale of Revolt Aboard a Slave Ship.* Chicago: Ivan R. Dee, 2003.

Harrold, Stanley. "Romanticizing Slave Revolt: Madison Washington, the *Creole* Mutiny, and Abolitionist Celebration of Violent Means." In *Antislavery Violence: Sectional, Racial, and Cultural Conflict in Antebellum America,* edited by John R. McKivigan and Stanley Harrold. Knoxville: University of Tennessee Press, 1999.

Sale, Maggie Montesinos. *The Slumbering Volcano: American Slave Ship Revolts and the Production of Rebellious Masculinity.* Durham, NC: Duke University Press, 1997.

CREOLE/CRIOLLO

"Creole" (or *criollo*) is a term referring to mixture or something created through cultural convergence. One of the most misunderstood and most frequently misused words in American English, "Creole" derives its etymology from the Latin *creare*—"to beget" or "create." The term "Creole," whether used as a noun or an adjective, generally refers to a mixture of sorts—something created through cultural convergence. Although used in similar ways throughout the world, neither the definition nor application of the term is absolute or universal.

The widespread use of "Creole" as an identifying term emerged mainly in the context of European colonization, when millions of Africans were enslaved and forcibly shipped across the Atlantic Ocean to the Americas. France, Spain, Britain, and Portugal were the principal agents in colonial expansion and as such their cultures, and particularly their languages, became ideologically dominant throughout the colonies. It is no wonder that the term finds its origin in Portuguese as *crioulo,* meaning a New World slave of African descent. The first Europeans to instigate the colonization and enslavement of African people, Portuguese merchants and settlers started to "mix" with African women almost immediately and to such an extent that miscegenation was a given in Portuguese colonies—which explains the large population of Creoles of Portuguese descent throughout the world. When borrowed by the Spanish, the term *criollo,* meaning a person native to a locality, identifies any person of mixed ancestry born in a Spanish colony. Likewise, the culture (music, food, language, etc.) of those people of mixed ancestry born into a colony is identified as Creole.

In the United States, "Creole" refers almost exclusively to the people and culture of southeastern Louisiana, where African, Spanish, and French influences were deeply rooted throughout Louisiana history. Louisiana Creoles are a people of multiracial and multicultural heritage, usually any combination of African, French, and Spanish ancestries. While Creole culture is inclusive of language, music, and dance, Creoles are certainly best known for their food, which gains its popularity from its signature blending of West African, Caribbean, French, and Spanish cuisines.

Because it is associated with colonialism throughout the African diaspora, however, "Creole" takes on variable meanings as the constituent elements of the cultural blend change according to particular location. More often, the term identifies a particular language that, although native to a specific locality, represents the multiple, layered languages that have existed in the history of that locality. In Senegal, the Creole language reflects a fusion of the native Wolof with the languages of European colonizers, specifically, the Portuguese and French; but in Cape Verde, each of the eleven islands with its own local language or languages, has its own distinct Creole, each influenced by centuries of Portuguese domination. While both the Senegalese and the Cape Verdean Creoles maintain linguistic vestiges of Portuguese, they are not mutually comprehensible, though some speakers may be able to understand each other fairly well.

Because they emerged within the constraints of colonization and enslavement, Creole languages have been long stigmatized throughout history, often regarded as "primitive" and not worthy of academic consideration. However, current linguistic research shows that Creoles are languages of the same caliber as their African and European constituents and reflect linguistic properties common to most other languages.

Yaba Amgborale Blay

See also: Colonialism; Columbian Exchange; Diaspora; English, African American Vernacular

References

Dormon, James. H. *Creoles of Color of the Gulf South.* Knoxville: University of Tennessee Press, 1996.

Hall, Gwendolyn. M. *Africans in Colonial Louisiana: The Development of Afro-Creole Culture in the Eighteenth Century.* Baton Rouge: Louisiana State University Press, 1992.

Kein, Sybil, ed. *Creole: The History and Legacy of Louisiana's Free People of Color.* Baton Rouge: Louisiana State University Press, 2000.

CRISIS, THE

The Crisis is the official journal of the National Association for the Advancement of Colored People (NAACP). Originally subtitled "A Record of the Darker Races," it was founded in 1910 by the organization's new director of publicity and research, William Edward Burghardt Du Bois, who served as its editor until 1934, when Roy Wilkins succeeded him as its editor. *The Crisis* was more than simply "a record"; it became a powerful venue for relentless and biting criticism of racial injustice and race relations in the United States. *The Crisis* also sought to be mindful of global concerns, advocating suffrage for women and encouraging readers to learn about current events in other countries.

The Crisis has also been notable for its support of African American writers and visual artists. Jessie Redmon Fauset joined the staff as literary editor in 1919 and was instrumental in encouraging many young writers featured in the journal, including Langston Hughes, Zora Neale Hurston, and Countee Cullen. *The Crisis* also awarded annual literary prizes for a number of years. Work of painters Aaron Douglas and Romare Bearden also was featured in the journal. Du Bois was particularly interested in the possibility of black art serving as propaganda in the struggle for racial justice, and literature and art from unknown as well as established artists has been featured.

Now nearing one hundred years old, *The Crisis* remains committed to exploring issues of particular interest to minority populations in the United States. It is still the official organ for the NAACP but is currently produced by The Crisis

Publishing Company, Inc., a separate organization.

Kristina D. Bobo

See also: Civil Rights Movement; Du Bois, William Edward Burghardt; Harlem Renaissance; Hughes, Langston; Hurston, Zora Neale; Schomburg, Arthur Alfonso

References

Lewis, David Levering. *W. E. B. Du Bois: Biography of a Race, 1868–1919.* New York: Henry Holt, 1993.

Lewis, David Levering. "Du Bois and the Challenge of the Black Press." *The Crisis Magazine On-Line: History.* 2005. *The Crisis* Magazine On-line. http://www.thecrisismagazine.com.

Moon, Henry Lee. "History of *The Crisis.*" *The Crisis Magazine On-Line: History.* 2005. *The Crisis* Magazine On-Line. http://www.thecrisismagazine.com.

Cuban singer and songwriter Celia Cruz in 1962. (Library of Congress)

CRUZ, CELIA (1924–2003)

Celia Cruz was a Grammy-winning, Afro-Cuban female vocalist. Blessed with a powerful contralto voice, a winning smile, and a radiant stage presence, Cruz rightfully earned the title Queen of Salsa. Born to poverty in Havana, Cuba, Cruz won amateur singing competitions that led to a career in music. Her first major break came with La Sonora Matancera (Mantacera Sound) in 1950, with whom she performed and recorded for over a decade. In the 1950s she traveled widely, and songs like "Yerbero Moderno," "Sopita en Botella," "Caramelo," and "Burundanga" became known throughout all of Latin America. The latter song earned Cruz her first gold record in 1957 and her first trip to the United States. Cruz and La Sonora Matancera went on tour to Mexico after 1960 and stayed, expressing public disagreement with Fidel Castro's revolution. She never returned to Cuba and was particularly bitter at Castro's regime for denying her entry to attend her mother's funeral in 1962. In that same year she married Pedro Knight, a trumpeter with La Sonora Matancera, who would become her most trusted adviser, manager, and companion until her death. Her anti-Castro politics probably cost her some support in the radical 1960s, but to view Cruz as a right-wing ideologue with a magnificent voice would be a gross simplification. Cruz was proud of her Afro-Cuban heritage, which she defended (and sang about) publicly, along with the rights of women and the need to preserve Latino-Latina culture in the United States, including the right to speak Spanish.

Although Cruz teamed up with Tito Puente in 1966, their several recorded albums were not a huge commercial success. Cruz's career renewed itself in the 1970s while working with New York–based salsa musicians, singing with the Fania All Stars in Zaire for the Foreman-Ali fight. She recorded several hit albums with bandleader and flutist Johnny Pacheco, then worked with Willie Colón, Ray Barreto, and Papo Lucca and his Sonora Ponceña. She was named best female vocalist by *Billboard* magazine in 1978. By then Cruz was able to sell out Madison Square Garden, as happened at a 1982 tribute concert to her career. In 1983 she won another gold record for *Tremendo Trío* (Tremendous Trio). In the mid-1980s Cruz frenetically recorded and toured, sometimes performing music based on Yoruba chants. In the 1990s she appeared in the feature films *Mambo Kings* and *The Pérez Family* and continued to tour Europe, Japan, Africa, and Latin America as the international icon of Latin music. By 2002, stricken with cancer, Cruz struggled to record her last album, *Regalo del alma* (A gift from my soul), a moving finale to her career that was released in 2003, just months before her death. Cruz won six Grammies and two Latin Grammies and has a star on the Hollywood street of fame. Also, Eighth Street in Miami's Little Havana is now called Celia Cruz Way.

Alan West-Durán

See also: Cuban Music, African Influence in

References

Fernández, Raúl. "Arte y autonomía de Celia Cruz." *Encuentro de la Cultura Cubana* 12, no.13 (Spring–Summer 1999): 45–51.

Valverde, Umberto. *Celia Cruz, Reina Rumba.* 2nd ed. Bogotá, Columbia: Arango Editores, 1995.

CUBA

Cuba is an island republic of the Caribbean, located south of Florida, that has been involved with slavery, abolition, and world politics and has helped to shape the culturally and politically significant concept of Afro-Cuban heritage. On October 27, 1492, Christopher Columbus landed on the island of Cuba and originally named it Juana. In 1511 Diego Velásquez conquered Cuba, where he fought the Ciboney tribe, one of several indigenous people on the island. In 1513 four African slaves were brought to Cuba. Two years later Valásquez founded the city of Havana. Cuba was the home of many successful business ventures at the expense of the original inhabitants, who succumbed to the horrific treatment of their conquerors to the point of extinction; in 1520, the Spanish began the importation of more slaves to continue the economic development of the island.

Spain maintained a firm hold on Cuba until 1763, when Havana was captured by the British, held as a bargaining tool, and returned to Spain in exchange for Florida. At this time, slaves were brought into Havana. Loosening its control of Cuba in the late eighteenth and early nineteen centuries, Spain deregulated the trade of tobacco, permitting it to be traded throughout the world in 1818.

Black slaves were now the majority population and they managed to conduct numerous rebellions between 1823 and 1838, reacting to the repressive actions of Captain-General Miguel de Tacon. The rebellions for independence included not only blacks, but Creole participants as well. After one of the largest rebellions by slaves was quelled, a Ten-Year War (1868–1878) started against Spain. Led by the revolutionary Carlos Manuel de Cespedes, independence was the focus. Independence for Cuba, however, was seen as a threat to the United States, which blocked all moves for the island's liberation from Spain.

Between the years 1837 and 1839, 25,000 Africans were transported into Cuba, in violation of the 1817 treaty between Spain and Great Britain, which declared that it was illegal to transport slaves into Spanish colonies. The Spanish vessel *La Amistad,* which set sail from Havana for Puerto Principe loaded with slaves and gold, was one such vessel. The slaves—led by one of their number, named Cinque—staged a mutiny in July 1839 that left them in charge of the *Amistad.* They saved two of the crew, Ruiz and Montez, while killing Captain Ferrer, and demanded that the ship return to Africa. The slaves' demand was not met; instead, the *Amistad* sailed to the United States, where the ship was apprehended by the USS *Washington* and remanded to stay in Connecticut for a trial concerning the property and territory rights of the enslaved Africans, the Spanish, and the American waters into which they had sailed. The slaves won their freedom in 1841 and returned to West Africa, while Spain continued to demand compensation for the loss of their property until 1860.

In 1843 a black slave named Carlota was responsible for an uprising of slaves at a Matanzas sugar mill. A subsequent uprising in South Africa—the Battle of Crito Cuanavale—was named "Black Carlota" after her. In 1878 the Cubans and the Spaniards ended their war in a stalemate: both parties signed the treaty of Zanjon, which designated slaves who fought on either side as free, but slavery was not abolished and Cuba continued to be under Spanish rule. In 1886 slavery in Cuba was abolished by royal decree. Despite the abolition of slavery, blacks still suffered from racism and desired political independence from Spanish rule and the growing threat of Cuba's annexation by the United States. In the push toward Cuban independence, the Partido Revolucionario Cubano (the Cuban Revolutionary Party), started by José Martí, was formed, which sought freedom for all, with total equality. A third party was formed after Independence, called Independientaes de Color (Independents of Color), which was led by Evaristo Estenoz. This party promoted a hierarchical approach to gaining equality based on color and caste and claimed to represent the interests of other minority groups in Cuba as well as blacks.

Cubans expelled Spain with the signing of the Treaty of Paris on December 10, 1898, but the United States effectively controlled Cuba before and after their independence, which was formally declared on May 20, 1902. Estenoz, who lobbied for the recognition of political and economic shares due black Cubans and other minority groups, was murdered when he ignored the warning of the United States that he would suffer consequences for promoting such agitation against Cuba. The Cuban army carried out a massacre of black Cubans, known as the Little Black War of 1912, in which it is estimated that between 3,000 and 6,000 were murdered, including Estenoz. This incident caused irreversible damage to the black population, from which it has never fully recovered. This race war is rarely mentioned in Cuban histories.

In 1925 another party was created: the Partido Socialista Popular, better known as the first Communist Party. With the establishment of this party, blacks felt that they now had a chance for equality.

Unfortunately, U.S. dominance in Cuba delayed the fruits of independence. Gerardo Machado y Morales (1871–1939) brought hope to the country in 1924 when he was elected president of Cuba. During Machado's time in office, many Afro-Cubans became members of the Cuban Communist Party. The party's founder, Julio Antonio Mella, was assassinated in 1929 by several agents of Machado. With Machado's presidency failing on all fronts, he was exiled in 1933. Miguel Mariano Gomez (1889–1950) succeeded Machado, but he was soon impeached. After Gomez, Ramon Grau San Martin (1887–1969) ruled Cuba for a total of 120 days from 1933 to 1934. During his presidency, he gave women voting rights and advocated the eight-hour work day, among other programs. In 1940 Fulgencio Bastista y Zalvidar (1901–1973) won the presidential election and became Cuba's official leader. Batista, a mulatto, was Cuba's fourteenth president, and in 1943 he recognized and legalized the Communist Party. In May 1947 the Ortoxodos, or the Cuban People's Party, was formed. In March 1952 the United States committed itself to giving financial support to Batista's government. In 1959 the revolution led by Fidel Castro violently overthrew the government, forcing Batista to flee Cuba.

Through all of these changes of government and upheavals, Afro-Cubans continue to struggle for full equality. Afro-Cubans comprise 80 percent of the Cuban population, including mulattos. Despite being the majority, they are still held back by racism and discrimination. Economically, they are and have been the lowest paid members of society. Despite living in poverty, Afro-Cubans have attempted to preserve their dignity by maintaining they are successful and productive members of society. Afro-Cuban religion is based on Santeria, which has been practiced since the sixteenth century. It is considered the street religion of Cuba. Today, Castro recognizes Santeria as an accepted religion.

In response to the oppressions and hypocrisies in today's Cuba, a number of the Afro-Cubans have attempted to leave for America, where, they have heard, a better life beckons. Some Afro-Cubans participated in the Mariel boat lift (April 15–October 31, 1980), but they experienced in the United States the same types of racism and discrimination as in their homeland.

Despite their demonstrated talents in sports, especially baseball, Cuban athletes still have to endure racism. Rafael Almeida, Adolfo Luque, Roger Hernandez, and Esteben Bellan are some examples of Cuban baseball players who have experienced these problems.

Prominent writers on the Afro-Cuban experience include Lydia Cabrera, who wrote *El Monte* (The hill) (1983); José Martí; and Nicolás Guillén, the poet. Music has been an essential element of Cuban tradition. Machito, the father of Afro-Cuban jazz; Jose Silvestra White, the Afro-Cuban composer and violinist; Tito Puente, referred to as the "Mambo King" or "El Rey" (The King); the Afro-Cuban All Stars; Don Ruben Gonzalez, pianist with the Afro-Cuban All Stars; and the Buena Vista Social Club have contributed to bringing generations of skilled musicians together to introduce Cuban music to the world. Dance combines with the music to express the Afro-Cuban experience. One popular type of Cuban dance music involves the *son,* which is a primary source of the salsa. Another favorite is the *danzon,* or ballroom dance music. With roots in both Africa and Spain, this art form is a living physical representation of Afro-Cubans' heritage.

With their strong traditions and tenacious pursuit of social change, Afro-Cubans are able to achieve success and even fame. But despite their successes, all Afro-Cubans are obstructed by the long history of slavery, social persecution, and a reluctance to recognize the existence of social injustices based on race.

Karen E. Holleran

References

Amistad. VHS. Dreamworks, 1997.

Bardach, Ann Louise. *CUBA Confidential: Love and Vengeance in Miami and Havana.* New York: Vintage, 2002.

Cable, Mary. *Black Odyssey: The Case of the Slave Ship Amistad.* New York: Penguin, 1998.

Cameron, Sarah, and Ben Box, eds. *1994 Caribbean Islands Handbook.* 5th ed. Chicago: Passport Books, 1993.

Corbett, Ben. *This Is Cuba: An Outlaw Culture Survives.* Cambridge, MA: Perseus, 2004.

Gimbel, Wendy. *Havana Dreams: A Story of a Cuban Family.* New York: Vintage, 1998.

Gott, Richard. *Cuba: A New History.* New Haven, CT: Yale University Press, 2004.

Jones, Howard. *Mutiny on the Amistad: The Saga of a Slave Revolt and Its Impact on American Abolition, Law, and Diplomacy.* New York: Oxford University Press, 1997.

Oppenheimer, Andres. *Castro's Final Hour: An Eyewitness Account of the Disintegration of Castro's Cuba.* New York: Touchstone, 1992.

Paterson, Thomas G. *Contesting Castro: The United States and the Triumph of the Cuban Revolution.* New York: Oxford University Press, 1994.

CUBAN MUSIC, AFRICAN INFLUENCE IN

Cuban music demonstrates both African retention and the innovation of Cuban musical genres such as *son,* rumba, columbia, yambú, Latin Jazz, mambo, and the *cha-cha-chá.* For some, the term "Afro-Cuban music" is a redundancy, since virtually all of Cuba's music seems to incorporate some degree of African influence. Conversely, Cuba's African influences have been so intertwined with Europe's that the subsequent transculturation has made cultural purity exceedingly difficult to trace, if not suspect altogether. Music of African origins can be seen as a form of social and collective memory born of slavery, colonization, and neocolonial domination, as well as subtler forms of racism and discrimination that persist today, despite claims that differences of class, gender, and race have been eradicated. The powerful presence of African religions and music in Cuba has historical and demographic antecedents. First, more than three-quarters of all the slaves shipped to Cuba were brought in the nineteenth century, mostly due to the Haitian Revolution of 1791–1804 that created the first black republic of the Americas and made Cuba the Caribbean's major sugar producer. Second, Cuba was the last country in the hemisphere, excepting Brazil, to abolish slavery—in 1880 formally, in 1886 in practice.

From the ritual music of the Yoruba, Bantú-Congo, and Abakuá to *son,* rumba, Latin Jazz, and rap, Cuba's musical genres are one of the most creative and profound examples of Afrodiasporic dialogue in history. In the United States there have been many Cuban musicians and performers, both black (Mario Bauzá, Machito, Mongo Santamaría, Chano Pozo, Celia Cruz, Dámaso Pérez Prado) and white (Don Azpiazú, Desi Arnaz, Chico O'Farrill, Gloria Estefan, Arturo Sandoval) who have played or made significant contributions to Afro-Cuban music. Even non-Cubans have been great disseminators of this music, including Dizzy Gillespie, Al McKibbon, Cal Tjader, Stan Kenton, Xavier Cougat, Tito Puente, Johnny Pacheco, and Poncho Sánchez.

Cuban musical genres can be described through the increasing recognition and influence of Afro-Cuban forms and genres. The *danzón* was the first of these, and its public launching in 1879 is credited to Matanzas composer Miguel Faílde (1852–1921), though clearly *danzones* existed before that date. The *danzón's* origins lie in the English country dance, which crossed the Channel and became the French *contredanse,* played on piano, flute, and violin. This in turn became the Spanish *contradanza* and influenced the Cuban *habanera.* Brought to Cuba by "French blacks" as a result of the Haitian independence struggle (1791–1804), both Haitian and Afro-Cuban rhythms were incorporated into the *contradanza.* Although banned by Spanish colonial authorities during the Ten Years' War (1868–1878) as a blatant symbol of Cuban nationalism, the *danzón* quickly became the musical-cultural emblem of the country from 1879 to 1920, when it was surpassed by the *son.* The traditional *danzón* has a marchlike introduction (A), followed by a clarinet or flute section (B), a return to the introduction (A), then a slow, songlike part dominated by the violins (C), a return again to the introduction (A), and finally a rapid section (D), yielding an overall structure of ABACAD, which was later simplified to ABAD or ABD. *Danzones* have often been called sound collages, because in either the (B) or (C) sections show tunes, opera arias, *sones,* and jazz melodies have been inserted. *Danzones* were originally only instrumental, but sung versions, called the *danzonete,* emerged in 1929. In the twentieth century the (D) sections often incorporated *sones.* Some of the great *danzón* composers were Antonio María Romeu (1876–1955) and the brothers Orestes López (1908–) and Israel López (1918–), nicknamed

"Cachao," creators of the danzón-mambo, which eventually led to the *cha-cha-chá,* the mambo, and the *descarga* (jam sessions).

The Son

An Afro-European hybrid, the *son* gives more importance to the lyrics than does the *danzón* and was sometimes based on satirical *guarachas* of the nineteenth century and Congolese-derived rhythms. Although the *son* began in Oriente Province in the nineteenth century, it was not until it became popular in Havana (by the early 1920s) that it began to be considered the national musical genre. Originally, the *son* was played on guitar, *tres,* or both; *marímbula* (replaced by the bass); bongo; maracas; and claves (two wooden sticks). Trumpets were added in the 1920s and later other brass and piano. The *son* has an opening melodic part with fixed lyrics called the largo. The second section, called the *montuno,* has an improvising *sonero* (singer) answered by a chorus singing a repeated phrase. Four rhythmic planes characterize the *son:* (1) an ostinato and melody (played by the guitar, *tres,* or piano); (2) an improvisation section played by the bongos or congas; (3) a fixed pattern on clave and maracas; and (4) a syncopated figure (bass), which gives harmonic foundation for the vocal particle. The *son,* along with the rumba, are among the primary sources of salsa music. Some of the great *son* composers were Ignacio Piñero (1888–1969), Miguel Matamoros (1894–1971), and Arsenio Rodríguez (1911–1971).

The Rumba

Rumba, which grew out of the tenements of Matanzas and Havana, is considered the most African of the island's genres, yet it is in part derived from the rumba flamenca of

Spain. It is a secular music and performed only with percussion. It is played with three drums or *cajones* (boxes), *catá* (a wooden cylindrical instrument played with two sticks), and claves. Other percussion can be added, such as *chékeres* and shakers. The voices follow a call-and-response format. There are three principle rumba genres. The first, and the most popular, is guaguancó. It is a reenactment of courtship and sexuality, with the male dancer pursuing the female, seeking the *vacunao* (vaccination, or pelvic thrust) of the female at the opportune moment. It usually begins with the clave and the "la-le-leo" syllabifications, as if to announce the party is about to begin (*diana*). There are three drums: the *salidor,* which sustains the basic rhythm, an intermediate one called *los tres golpes* (three beats), and the *quinto,* which improvises.

The Columbia

The columbia is rurally derived and faster than the guaguancó rhythm. This variant is, for the most part, only danced by males. The movements are somewhat influenced by the *íremes* (little devils) of the Abakuá religion, but principally the columbia is defined by mimetic gestures of daily life: riding a bike, playing baseball, imitating a lame person, using a hat as a prop, and so on. It usually begins with rapid percussion; then the singing begins, with a lamentlike expression (*lloraos*).

The Yambú

The third form is the oldest, the yambú. Some date it to the beginning of the nineteenth century. There is no *vacunao* in the yambú, and it is the slowest of the three genres. It begins with onomatopoeic singing (*diana*). The movements often imitate those of older people, but still the

dancing is sensual. It seems to have steps from the Spanish *zapateo* and other "couples dancing" of Hispanic tradition, but also from the *calenda* and other African-based dances.

After 1959, the Cuban revolutionary government tried to make rumba the national dance for several reasons. Rumba was clearly associated with blacks; therefore, it was a way of affirming blackness within a nationalist and revolutionary project, but with the understanding that said blackness would not detract from social unity. Even though it was an African-based music, it was not religious, which was important since the Cuban government was building an atheist state. Rumba's practitioners had a clear class background, since most blacks were poor, and rumba expressed a collective spirit, one of social solidarity. It was also a beautiful entertainment spectacle, lending itself to folkloric presentation and having a strong appeal to tourists. While rumba is widespread (the verb "rumbear" is synonymous with partying), it is difficult to dance to, making other dance forms (*casino,* salsa, *timba*) more popular.

Latin Jazz

The 1940s and 1950s also saw new, hybrid genres emerge: Latin Jazz (Afro-Cuban jazz), the mambo and the *cha-cha-chá.* Afro-Cuban jazz drew from Afro-Cuban rhythms (rumba, *son,* ritual music) and U.S. jazz. The two major creative sources were Frank Grillo, or "Machito" (1909–1984), and his Afro-Cubans and the fortuitous collaboration between Dizzy Gillespie (1917–1993) and legendary percussionist-composer Luciano "Chano" Pozo (1915–1948). Machito's trumpeter-arranger was Mario Bauzá, the creator of "Tanga" (1943), a seventeen-minute suite that features several genres from the mambo and the bolero to the rumba and is considered the first Latin Jazz composition. The Gillespie-Pozo partnership produced memorable work like "Manteca" and "Cubana Be/Cubana Bop." Arturo "Chico" O'Farrill (1921–2001) was the other major Cuban composer-arranger who advanced Afro-Cuban jazz to new levels of sophistication. These traditions have been built upon since the 1970s by the likes of the group Irakere, Chucho Valdés, Gonzalo Rubalcaba, Paquito D'Rivera, and Arturo Sandoval.

Mambo

Though the word "mambo" had currency—and existed as a dance—before the 1950s, it was Dámaso Pérez Prado (1916–1989) who made mambo a worldwide craze. The López brothers (Orestes and Cachao) had written *danzones* with a new rhythm called *danzón-mambo,* but Pérez Prado took these new rhythms, added a second set of percussionists and an array of jabbing horn writing, and interesting piano riffs, not to mention his trademark grunts, and created a sound that was unmistakably his. In Cuba, however, the mambo was never as popular as it was abroad: the 1950s was dominated by the *cha-cha-chá.*

Cha-Cha-Chá

The genre *cha-cha-chá* grew out of the *danzón* and *danzón-mambo* and was also influenced by the French *charanga* groups (flute, violin, piano, and percussion). Its creator was Enrique Jorrín (1926–1997), and the gentle tempo (compared to the furious and sometimes difficult mambo) and lack of syncopation (compared to the *son*) made it an easier genre for dancing.

Although not at its ruling reign of the 1950s, the *cha-cha-chá* is still a popular genre kept alive by groups like Orquesta Aragón and Melodías del 40.

Since the Revolution in 1959 that brought Fidel Castro to power, Afro-Cuban music has continued to thrive, although in its initial years the new government made greater efforts to support classical music and Nueva Trova, the New Song Movement, which offered ballads with a social message. Cuban dance music, still based on the *son,* rumba, and salsa, is now called *timba,* which has incorporated more aggressive horns, more jagged rhythms, and a singing style that has slight rap inflections and ever greater erotic and audacious dance moves.

The Buena Vista Social Club craze of the late 1990s sparked world interest in Afro-Cuban music, music of a bygone era. Often ignored was the fact that excellent Cuban music was still being created by composers who are under eighty years old and by *timba* groups like Los Van Van, NG La Banda, and Charanga Habanera, as well as Cuban rappers.

Cuban classical composers have also used Afro-Cuban rhythms and themes. Amadeo Roldán (1900–1939) and Alejandro García Caturla (1906–1940) often used the poetry of Afro-Cuban poet Nicolás Guillén. Also, Ernesto Lecuona (1895–1963) wrote exquisite piano pieces that reveal an intimate view of Afro-Cuban roots.

In contrast to the United States, Cuba's African heritage of music is central to defining Cuba's national and cultural identity. This was not always so, but it certainly has been since 1920 as a result of the rise and consolidation of the *son.* Even so, in that period *comparsas* (which feature the conga rhythms and dances) were banned during carnival (from 1914 to 1936.) In the eastern part of Cuba the *tumba francesa* and the *tajona,* brought over by French-Haitian Mestizos, were important aspects of Afro-Haitian cultural contact with Afro-Cuban traditions. Equally significant is the fact that 1936 was the year in which the *batá* drums used in the sacred music of Regla de Ocha were first exhibited publicly in Cuba in a nonritual setting. Much has changed since then, and Afro-Cuban music, both ritual and secular, is now considered quintessentially Cuban.

Alan West-Durán

See also: Bauzá, Mario; Cruz, Celia; Cuban Ritual Music, African Influence in; Hip-Hop, Cuban; Music (African); O'Farrill, Arturo "Chico"; Transculturation

References

Daniel, Yvonne. *Rumba, Dance, and Social Change in Contemporary Cuba.* Bloomington: University of Indiana Press, 1995.

Evora, Tony. *Orígenes de la música cubana.* Madrid: Alianza Editorial, 1997.

Fernández, Raúl. *Latin Jazz.* San Francisco: Chronicle Books and the Smithsonian, 2002.

Moore, Robin. *Nationalizing Blackness: Afrocubanismo and Artistic Revolution in Havana, 1920–1940.* Pittsburgh, PA: University of Pittsburgh Press, 1997.

Ortiz, Fernando. *La africanía de la música folklórica de Cuba.* Havana, Cuba: Editorial Letras Cubanas, 1993.

CUBAN RITUAL MUSIC, AFRICAN INFLUENCE IN

Afro-Cuban ritual music falls broadly into three types: those of Yoruba, Bantu-Congo, and Abakuá origins, each corresponding demographically speaking to the three largest cultures of Africans brought to Cuba as slaves.

Yoruba

From the area of what is known today as Nigeria and Benin, the Yoruba are the most numerous and influential, both musically and religiously. Their religion, Regla de Ocha, is also known as Santeria because of its syncretisms with Catholic saints over the centuries. Music and singing usually accompany different types of ceremonies, which range from giving thanks to the orishas (deities or guardian spirits), to commemorating an anniversary or the feast of a saint, and to an initiation or a tribute to an orisha that has requested it. The main instruments for liturgical purposes are the three double-sided *batá* drums, which are played on both sides, placed on the drummer's lap. The *iyá* is the largest and mother drum, with the deepest tone. Its spoken rhythm is highly figurative, with a great variety of strokes, and it recreates the inflections of spoken Yoruba. The medium drum, or *itótele,* creates reiterative patterns that pertain to each orisha following the *iyá*'s lead, and the smallest, with the most acute sound, is the *okónkolo,* which performs the basic rhythmic pattern. Other percussion can be added, such as shakers, whistles, rattles, bells, and buzzing instruments. The *batá* drums in ritual ceremonies must be blessed and the drummers (males only) must be initiates as well. The batás hold a secret (*añá*), also considered to be an orisha, and therefore the drums must be propitiated. The *batás* are central to ceremonies in which *orichas* come down and can mount a believer or initiate.

Singing is performed by a soloist (*akpwón*), male or female, who can often begin without musical accompaniment by singing, praying, or both, but most often it proceeds in a call-and-response format, with the chorus echoing the soloist or repeating short phrases. Yoruba music of Cuba has been described as the building of two sonorous planes that sometimes intersect, but not always. One could view the music as a concatenation of motifs—but not necessarily one that is "resolved" in a typically Western musical fashion)— that builds in astonishingly layered ebbs and flows.

The *iyesá* drums are played by Yoruba peoples from the Oyo region of southwestern Nigeria, near Benin. There are four sacred drums: the *caja* (the tallest); two drums of equal size called *segundo* (second) and *tercero* (third); and a fourth drum that was added in Cuba called the *bajo* (bass). Much smaller than the *batás* and barrel-shaped, they are also double-sided, but only one side is played at any particular time. The drums are played with a stick, except the *bajo,* which is played with the hands. Two *agogos,* bell-like instruments played with a stick, add a timbre that is characteristic of *iyesá* music, and the *güiro* (a scraper) rounds out the ensemble. Like the *batás,* the *iyesá* drums need to be consecrated. They have the *añá* (secret) within and must be played by drummers who are also initiates.

The *bembé* is a drumming party for the orishas. The drums can be of a different size, but they are not *batá* drums, rather, stave-barreled ones. The *bembé* is not a religious ceremony, strictly speaking, and the word has passed into the Cuban vernacular as a synonym of "to party" (as has the word rumba).

Bantu-Congo Music

Compared to Yoruba music, Bantu music is based on briefer motifs, and melodic shifts are based on fixed sounds that end or signal an end. It is tied to various religious manifestations known as Regla de Palo Mayombe, Regla de Palo Briyumba, and Regla Kimbisa. *Palo* (stick) musical genres employ wooden percussive instruments like the *guaguá* or the *catá.* The music often begins with the wooden percussion, followed by the drums, called the *ngoma,* now known as conga drums. In addition, other metallic instruments, such as the plow, the hoe, and the cowbell are played.

In remote rural areas *yuka* drums are used, made from the wood of fruit trees and ox hide (instead of the usual goat skin) for the head. The largest is the *caja*; the medium-sized drum is the *mula,* called so because its constant rhythm is reminiscent of a mule's trot; and the smallest is the *cachimbo.* As in Yoruba music, the largest drum executes the widest variation of figures, while the two smaller ones maintain steadier or constant rhythms. The *yuka* were used for the *maní* dance, which is no longer practiced. A highly pugilistic dance, it had movements similar to Brazilian *capoeira,* with two dancers battling within a circle. Different plantations organized teams to compete with each other and bet heavily. Although for the most part a male activity, there were well-known women *maniseras* as well.

Makuta drums, of which there are two, are rarely made anymore. The larger drum is called the *caja,* the smaller is the *kimbandu.* (In the past, three drums were often used.) The *makuta* is also a couples dance, with a key moment of pelvic contact among the dancers.

The *toque de garabatos* substituted for the drums. The *garabato* is a branch from a tree in the form of a large check mark, with the shorter part used as a kind of hook to pick up small plants, which are then cut with a machete. When made from plants associated with magical powers they become a ritual symbol, and beating them on the ground becomes a way of attracting those powers. Several *garabato* players work in tandem to produce the rhythmic planes necessary for creating a song. The *toques de garabatos* have associations with death and are often used during funeral ceremonies.

The *kinfuiti,* another drum used by the Congos, is played by applying internal friction. A string is played from within the drum. It is usually accompanied by three small drums. *Kinfuiti* drums are kept covered and played behind the curtain, and along with the *makuta* drums, they are the only drums used in ceremonies in which animal blood is offered in sacrifice. The *kinfuiti* is used to call the spirits of the dead (*ndoki*) that inhabit the *nganga,* an iron cauldron where sticks and ritual objects reside that house a spirit. The drummers for the *kinfuiti* and the *makuta* drums must be initiates (as with the *batá* and *iyesá*). Drummers moisten their hands with holy water before playing.

Ritual songs are called *cantos de fundamento* and can be prayers to begin a ceremony, prayers to make the *nganga* work; events that can stimulate spirit possession; and *managuas* or *makagua,* which are satirical chants, often funny, or chants that describe incongruent or enigmatic situations. Soloist and chorus function in similar ways to singing in Yoruba music. The soloist is called *gallo* or *insunsu,* and the chorus *vasallo* or *muana.* Different from the Yoruba, the rhythmic structures remain the same for the different powers or divinities being invoked. Variation occurs in the words and intent of the song or chant.

Abakuá Music

The Abakuá come from the Calabar region of southeastern Nigeria, near the Cross River, and are also known as *carabalí* in Cuba (Ejagham peoples help to form the larger Abakuá group, along with the Efut and Efik). The Abakuá society is an all-male secret society and has been described as a "confraternity and magical-religious esoteric society." Their elaborate ritual and ceremonies, called *plantes,* have been compared to a religious drama, with processions, drumming, singing, mystical drawings on the ground (*firmas*), and the dancing of the *íremes,* an intriguing figure who represents a soul that has reincarnated (or a supernatural being) who assists with ceremonies.

The Abakuá have two orders of drums, one that is symbolic and silent, and others that are played to accompanying songs and dances (*biankomeko*). The four symbolic drums are the *empegó* (a signal to come to order, pay attention, and be alert), the *ekueñón* (for matters related to sacrifice), the *enkríkamo* (to call and dominate the *íremes*), and the *seseribó* (to direct processions and marches). They are struck with a few symbolic strokes, but not played. The fundamental drum is the *ekué,* which is kept behind a curtain and is played by using friction; its sound imitates the magic voice Tanze (a sacred fish), central to Abakuá mythology.

The second order of drums accompanies the songs and dances of the *íremes.* The *biankomeko* are also made up of four drums: the *bonkó-enchemillá* (the largest), the *biankomé,* the *obí-apá,* and the *kuchiyeremá.* Other percussion includes two percussive sticks (*itones*), a cowbell (*ekón*), and two *sonajas* (*erí-kundí*), a shaker-type instrument. The drums have feathers. The *bonkó-enchemillá* produces the talking rhythm, created by a wide variety of drumming techniques.

Different rhythms are not played for different functions. There are two types of *toque* (beats), distinguished by the names of the two tribes divided by the Oddán River (Cross River). The Efó had the secret and so the stories tell of the struggles between them and the Efí for the voice of Tanze. The Efí, however, were the owners of the drum, of music. Efí drumming is faster, filled with figures, while Efó drumming is slower.

The singing always alternates between a soloist and chorus. They tell the stories (or comment on them) that originated in Africa. They are passed on orally, but some old practitioners have written them down in notebooks. Many chants or songs are without musical accompaniment. The choral sections seem more isolated, and there is much that is sung without dance, since it is done among the initiates.

Since the number of people who participate in the Abakuá ceremonies is severely circumscribed and since the religion functions with a strict hierarchy of officials, one could say that Abakuá music is carefully chosen and executed. The same people tend always to be the soloists and the chorus, with less being left to improvisation or for people to join in, as often happens in a *toque* of Regla de Ocha or Regla de Palo.

Cuba has also been influenced significantly by the Arará (Fon) culture and music from Benin, mostly in the province of Matanzas. Arará religion is within the West African vodoun tradition. Finally, due to the presence of Haitians in Cuba, there are *radá* and *gagá* drums and music, linked to the Afro-Haitian religious practices.

Alan West-Durán

See also: Cuban Music, African Influence in; Kongo; Music (African); Nigeria; Religion (Africa); Yoruba

References

Eli Rodriguez, Victoria and Casanova, Ana Victoria Olivia, eds. *Instrumentos de la música folclórico-popular de Cuba.* 2 vols. Havana, Cuba: Editorial Ciencias Sociales, 1997.

León, Argeliers. *Del canto y el tiempo.* Havana, Cuba: Editorial Letras Cubanas, 1984.

Ortiz, Fernando. *La africanía de la música folklórica de Cuba.* Havana, Cuba: Editorial Letras Cubanas, 1993.

Ortiz, Fernando. *Los instrumentos de la música afrocubana.* 2nd ed. 2 vols. Madrid: Editorial Música Mundana, 1996.

CUDJOE

One of the greatest resistance leaders in African Jamaican history, Cudjoe (also spelled Cudjo and Cujo) was the leader of the Leeward Maroons. Undoubtedly Kromanti, his name represents the transliteration and anglicization of Kojo, meaning a male child born on Monday, consistent with the Akan practice of naming children according to the day of the week they were born. Cudjoe relied upon Akan spiritual practices (Obeah) and traditional Ashanti methods of warfare to help orchestrate the first Maroon War (1720–1738). With the assistance of his brothers, Johnny and Accompong (on the Leeward coast), and his "captains," Queen Nanny, Quao, and Cuffee (on the Windward coast), Cudjoe's army held the British at bay for over twenty years, defeating them on every occasion. Realizing defeat, British colonial leaders reportedly sought out Cudjoe and offered a peace treaty granting the Leeward Maroons sovereignty. Not only did the contract proffer their autonomy, but it also granted the Maroons 1,500 acres of land and freedom from taxation. In exchange, the Maroons agreed to end all resistance, decline refuge to escaped Africans and return them to their owners, and provide the British assistance in any future insurrections. Before signing the treaty, Cudjoe is said to have demanded that both sides, Maroon and British, drink a mixture of rum and blood drawn from the opposing leaders in order to seal the agreement. Today, a monument commemorating his life and victories stands in Accompong Town, home to hundreds of Maroon descendants, where each year, on January 6, they celebrate Cudjoe Day.

Yaba Amgborale Blay

See also: Akan; Jamaica; Obeah; Nanny; Slave
    Revolts/Maronnage

Reference
Campbell, M. C. *The Maroons of Jamaica:
    1655–1796.* Granby, MA: Bergin &
    Garvey, 1988.

*Silhouette head-and-shoulders portrait of Paul Cuffe,
a prosperous businessman and sea captain most
commonly known for his work in helping free blacks
immigrate to Sierra Leone with the help of his shipping
company. (Library of Congress)*

CUFFE, CAPTAIN PAUL (1759–1817)

Captain Paul Cuffe was a sailor, sea captain, shipowner, wealthy merchant, and a key figure of the Pan-African world. He was born on Cuttyhunk, one of the Elizabeth Islands, off the coast of Massachusetts. Cuffe visited Africa on whaling voyages as a teenager. He saw firsthand how Africans lived and began to understand the ways diasporic Africans were interconnected across geographical distances and national boundaries. Through his shrewd business acumen, Cuffe was able to build a trading network that earned him a large personal fortune and allowed him to travel to several West African nations, forming business partnerships as he went. This experience convinced Cuffe that diasporic Africans might have a better future in Africa than they did in the Americas, and that establishing economic connections around the black Atlantic could provide diasporic Africans with a homeland where they might have room to gain the cultural and economic influence necessary for them to free themselves from slavery and racism. After establishing many of these cultural and economic connections himself, Cuffe proposed the first ever black-led back-to-Africa movement. Unfortunately, after he secured permission from England to repatriate Africans to Sierra Leone, his efforts were stalled by the War of 1812. Following the war, however, in 1816, Captain Paul Cuffe sailed his ship the *Traveller* to Sierra

Leone with thirty-eight African Americans who were determined to make a new home in Africa.

Matthew D. Brown

References

Harris, Sheldon. *Paul Cuffe: Black American and the African Returns.* New York: Simon & Schuster, 1972.

Salvador, George. *Paul Cuffe, the Black Yankee.* New Bedford, MA: Reynolds-DeWalt Printing, 1969.

Thomas, Lamont. *Rise to Be a People: A Biography of Paul Cuffe.* Urbana: University of Illinois Press, 1986.

CUSH KINGDOM

Cush Kingdom was an ancient African kingdom, located in present-day Egypt, that lasted two thousand years. The Kingdom of Cush (Kush, Nubia) lay along the Nile River roughly between the first cataract above Aswan to the sixth cataract near the confluence of the Blue and White Nile Rivers at Khartoum.

The Kingdom of Cush began around four thousand years ago. The first kingdom, dominated by Egypt, was centered near the second cataract. Biblical references to Cush are often to this first kingdom.

However, power shifted to Napata, near the fourth cataract, as the capital of the Napatan (Cush) Kingdom. At the height of its power, Cush conquered Egypt. The kings of the period became the pharaohs of the Twenty-fifth Dynasty. This period lasted a brief hundred years, ending with the conquest of Egypt by the Assyrians.

When the Cush Dynasty ended, Napatan was abandoned for a new center up the Nile at Meroe, about halfway between the confluence of the Atbara River and the Nile and the sixth cataract. There an iron forging and trading center with connections to the Red Sea was developed.

The Meroite Kingdom of Cush went into permanent decline after it suffered military defeat at the hands of King Ezana of Axum (ancient Abyssinia) about 1,650 years ago. Ruins of magnificent pyramids, temples, public buildings, ironworks, and homes are located at Jebal Barkal and at many other places.

Andrew J. Waskey

See also: Egypt

Reference

Welsby, Derek A. *The Kingdom of Kush: The Napatan and Merotic Empires.* Princeton, NJ: Markus Wiener, 1998.

D

DABYDEEN, DAVID (1956–)

David Dabydeen is a British-Guyanese poet and novelist of East Indian descent. Born on a sugar plantation in Guyana, Dabydeen immigrated to England as a teenager and was educated at the University of Cambridge. His first volume of poetry, *Slave Song* (1984), awarded the Commonwealth Poetry Prize, consists of a series of creole monologues remarkable for extending the boundaries of poetic expression, through their use of a creole idiom and what he describes as savage lyricism. Dabydeen's next book of verse, *Coolie Odyssey* (1988), charts, as the title suggests, the odyssey that is the Indian Diaspora, the transportation of East Indian coolies to the plantations of Guyana and the Caribbean islands and subsequent migration to the British "Mother Land." Here, Dabydeen continues his exploration of the psychosexual dimensions of slavery and colonialism in his redeployment of the archetypal figures of Miranda and Caliban, and in doing so he contributes to the many Caribbean reappropriations of Shakespeare's New World play, *The Tempest*.

His third collection of verse, *Turner: New and Selected Poems* (1994), prefaces a selection from his earlier books with the long poem-sequence *Turner,* an extended meditation upon J. M. W. Turner's painting, *Slavers Throwing Overboard the Dead and the Dying, Typhoon Coming On* (1840), popularly known as *The Slave Ship*. In his preface to the poem, Dabydeen explains that *Turner* focuses upon the submerged head of the African in the foreground of the painting, and he defines his own response to the picture against that of John Ruskin, who consigned the subject of the artwork, the shackling and drowning of African slaves, to a brief footnote that "reads like an afterthought, something tossed overboard" (p. ix). The submerged African is symbolic, for Dabydeen, of the Western erasure or relegation to a footnote of black life and history and, by extension, black culture.

Turner, then, is a poem of retrieval, and as such complements the other ways in which Dabydeen has sought to bring a black subtext to British cultural history to the surface of inquiry in his capacity as professor of British and Comparative Literature at the University of Warwick and in texts such as *Hogarth's Blacks* (1985) and *Black Writers in Britain 1760–1890* (1991), co-edited with Paul Edwards. One of the black writers represented in the latter text is the former slave and author Olaudah Equiano, a figure with whom Dabydeen feels a close and even psychic kinship and whose presence is palpable in his 1999 novel, *A Harlot's Progress*. This text, a reinvention of William Hogarth's prints of 1732, revisits in the medium of fiction Dabydeen's earlier academic analysis of Hogarth and the representation of race at the same time that it returns to and develops the themes of Africa, the Middle Passage, and fabulation that are central to *Turner*. Dabydeen's rewriting of *Turner* as fiction is indicative of that transition from poetry to the novel that characterizes the careers of many writers from the Caribbean region, such as George Lamming and Wilson Harris. Dabydeen's three earlier novels are *The Intended* (1991), in which various aspects of the Indian Diaspora are explored through the theme of adolescence; *Disappearance* (1993), Dabydeen's "condition of England" novel; and *The Counting House* (1996), an imaginative exploration of Indian indentureship.

Lee M. Jenkins

See also: Caribbean Literature; Equiano, Olaudah

References
Dabydeen, David. "On Not Being Milton: Nigger Talk in England Today." In *The State of the Language,* edited by Christopher Ricks and Leonard Michaels. London: Faber and Faber, 1990.
Dabydeen, David. *Turner: New and Selected Poems.* London: Jonathan Cape, 1994.
Dabydeen, David. *A Harlot's Progress.* London: Jonathan Cape, 1999.
Grant, Kevin, ed. *The Art of David Dabydeen.* Leeds, UK: Peepal Tree, 1997.
Jenkins, Lee M. "On Not Being Tony Harrison: Tradition and the Individual Talent of David Dabydeen." *Ariel* 32, no. 2 (2001): 69–88.

DADIÉ, BERNARD BINLIN (1916–)

Bernard Binlin Dadié is a playwright, novelist, poet, journalist, and administrator who is regarded as the father and founder of Ivorian literature and modern African theater, being the first to propose a new concept of African theater inspired by traditional oral forms. Born in 1916 in Assinie, Côte d'Ivoire, he became, in the 1930s, the colony's most prominent writer while pursuing a successful career as a journalist and a politician. His works include several volumes of poetry, traditional tales and legends, novels, and plays.

Dadié received his higher education in Senegal where, in 1934, he entered the William Ponty School in Gorée, a center that prepared the black elite for careers in teaching and administration. He qualified as a civil servant in 1939 and then worked at Dakar's Institut Fondamental d'Afrique Noire (Foundational Institute of Black Africa) until 1947 before returning to his country and taking part in the independence movement. He had started writing as a journalist as early as 1928 and subsequently contributed under his own name and several pseudonyms to a number of newspapers, including *The Young Senegal, Dakar-Jeunes, La Communauté, Le Réveil,* and *Le Démocrate*. Dadié's adult literary career began with the play, *Assemien Dehylé, roi du Sanwi* (1935), performed in 1936 in Dakar by fellow students and at the Colonial Exposition in Paris of 1937. Subsequently, for more than a decade, Dadié tried his hand at different genres: theater, tales, poetry, and short stories, using literature as both an informational tool to reach his audiences and as a powerful weapon to fight social injustice and promote human rights. Literary recognition came with

Afrique debout (1950; *Africa Upright*), followed by the autobiographical novel *Climbié* (1956), listed in February 2002 as one of the hundred best African books of the twentieth century. In 1955 he reached an international audience with the publication of his first collection of African tales, *Le pagne noir (Black Cloth)*. His novel *Patron de New York* (1964)—translated as *One Way: Bernard Dadié Observes America* in 1994—which was awarded the Grand Prix Littéraire d'Afrique Noire, looks at black communities and culture in the United States. While his father, himself a political activist, influenced Dadié's nationalism and inspired his fight for social justice, the writer drew his inspiration from his traditional background, his appreciation of oral genres, and his vast literary culture in addition to his observation of the political scene. In particular, his personal witness of events like the 1938 Dakar-Niger strike and its subsequent repression and his prison experience as a political dissident in 1949–1950 left a mark on his writing.

While he continued writing, Dadié pursued an administrative and political career, becoming one of the founding members of the Rassemblement democratique africain (RDA; Democratic African rally) in October 1946. He worked in UNESCO from 1964 to 1972 and served as Ivorian minister of culture from 1977 until his retirement in 1986.

Dadié's works have been translated into many languages. Today he is acclaimed, in the United States, as well as Africa, as a model writer who draws from African tradition to offer a critical viewpoint on a generation that came of age during the era of colonial and national struggle.

Francoise Parent Ugochukwu

References

Mayes, Janice. *Critical Perspectives on Bernard Dadié*. Boulder, CO: Lynne Rienner Publishers, 1995.

Edebiri, Unionmwan, ed. *Bernard Dadié: Hommages et etudes*. Ivry-sur-Seine, France: Nouvelles du Sud, 1992.

D'AGUIAR, FRED (1960–)

Fred D'Aguiar is a British Guyanese author of drama, poetry, and fiction. He was born and, as a teenager, grew up in London, yet he spent most of his childhood in Guyana in a small village near Georgetown. For D'Aguiar, therefore, there are three fundamental points of biographical reference, and seemingly incompatible ones: the openness of Guyana's landscapes with its immeasurable sea, savannahs, and skies standing against London's ordered, encroaching urbanity; the modulated rhythms of Guyanese English clashing with the received or less received dialects of the "center"; and, not least, the literary tradition of writers like Martin Carter and, above all, Wilson Harris confronting an English legacy from Wordsworth to Eliot. D'Aguiar's work is often seen as a complex synthesis of voices driven by a quest for a crosscultural, and transethnic, understanding.

Even though D'Aguiar also wrote dramatic texts for the stage (*An Irish Airman Foresees His Death* [1995]) as well as for the BBC, he is mainly known for his poetry and fiction. His volumes of poetry so far comprise *Mama Dot* (1985), *Airy Hall* (1989), *British Subjects* (1993), *Bill of Rights* (1998), *Bloodlines* (2000), and *An English Sampler* (2001). The epic, book-length poem *Bloodlines* may serve as a representative example to illustrate D'Aguiar's negotiation of traditions. It lyrically evokes two love stories: that of two elderly fugitive slaves on their way to Canada and the relationship of a young slave with the son of a plantation owner. D'Aguiar celebrates a crosscultural dialogue both thematically and structurally; he combines the rigid formal requirements of the *ottava rima* (a verse form famously employed by Lord Byron in his *Don Juan*) with calypsonian rhythms through the poem's speaker.

D'Aguiar has also written four highly acclaimed novels. *The Longest Memory* (1994) is set on a North American plantation in the nineteenth century; sacrificing a singular narrative authority, it revolves around an instance of black and white romance in a polyphonic composition of many different voices. The memory of slavery is further pursued in *Feeding the Ghosts* (1997). It fictionalizes the historical incidences on the slave ship *Zong* in 1781, when 132 living slaves were thrown into the sea to secure the insurance money for "lost freight." One slave, however, managed to climb back on board again. In his novel D'Aguiar gives her a name, a history, and a voice to tell her story.

The novels *Dear Future* (1996) and *Bethany Bettany* (2003) are set in contemporary Guyana. D'Aguiar is very careful to note that his work on Atlantic slavery inevitably feeds into these narratives, in that the legacy of history has fundamental reverberations on the current political and social realities in the Caribbean. In both novels, these realities are largely filtered through the eyes of children. Through such an innovative perspective, uncommon in Anglo-Caribbean writing, D'Aguiar seeks to combine aesthetic innovation with a sensitivity to the common humanity of the people about whom he writes.

Lars Eckstein

See also: Britain: People of African Origin and Descent; Caribbean Literature

References

D'Aguiar, Fred. *Bloodlines.* London: Chatto and Windus, 2000.

D'Aguiar, Fred. "Home Is Always Elsewhere: Individual and Communal Regenerative Capacities of Loss." In *Black British Culture and Society,* edited by Kwesi Owusu. London and New York: Routledge, 2000.

Ledent, Bénédicte. "Remembering Slavery: History as Roots in the Fiction of Caryl Phillips and Fred D'Aguiar." In *The Contact and the Culmination: Essays in Honour of Hena Maes-Jelinek,* edited by Marc Delrez and Bénédicte Ledent. Liège, Belgium: L3, 1997.

DAN FODIO, UTHMAN (1754–1817)

Uthman Dan Fodio was an Islamic writer, scholar, teacher, and reformer of present-day Nigeria. As the first Sokoto Caliph, he successfully led the Fulani jihad (1804–1810) against the Hausa kingdoms. He built the largest empire in Africa until it fell to European colonization in 1903. Uthman is considered the most important figure in revitalizing Islamic faith in West Africa during the nineteenth century.

Uthman was born in Maratta, Gobir, Hausaland, but moved with his family to Degel in his childhood. He learned the Qur'an from his father and Islamic sciences from various teachers. Under the influence of Jibril ibn Umar, Uthman became a Sufi Muslim and conceived the idea of establishing an ideal society based on Islamic principles. He earned the title of shaykh and, with the approval of Bawa, the sultan of Gobir, built a religious community in Degel. Bawa's successor Yunfa, however, revoked the autonomy of Uthman's community and sought to kill him. In 1804

Uthman and his jihadists fled to the Fulani, where they allied with the Fulani nomads and Hausa peasants and launched attacks on oppressive Hausa rulers. After swiftly toppling the Hausa federation, Uthman founded the Fulani Empire and ruled it until 1815, when his son Muhammad Bello inherited the caliphate.

John J. Han

See also: Fulani; Hausa; Islam, African American; Sokoto Caliphate

References

Balogun, Ismail A. B. *The Life and Works of Uthman dan Fodio: The Muslim Reformer of West Africa.* Lagos, Nigeria: Islamic Publications Bureau, 1975.

Last, Murray. *The Sokoto Caliphate.* New York: Humanities Press, 1967.

DANGAREMBGA, TSITSI (1959–)

Tsitsi Dangarembga, author of the widely renowned Anglophone postcolonial African novel *Nervous Conditions* (1988), was born in Rhodesia (Zimbabwe in 1980, at full independence from Britain) in 1959, the year the United Nations denounced apartheid in Africa. Born around the time most African countries sought and received their independence from the British and the French, Dangarembga is preoccupied in her writing with not only the myriad of ways in which colonization impacted Africans, but also the degree to which postindependence Africans struggled to stabilize their newly liberated countries. While her novel *Nervous Conditions* generally receives the greatest amount of attention in terms of scholarly analysis, Dangarembga had published a play, *She No Longer Weeps* (1987), and had written other dramas for presentation by a university theater troupe as well as several short stories before the novel appeared. Later, one of her stories inspired the film *Neria,* which was released in 1992, and she directed and wrote the screenplay for her own film, *Everybody's Child,* released in 1996.

In their introduction to *Negotiating the Postcolonial* (2002), a collection of critical essays, Ann Elizabeth Willey and Jeanette Treiber situate the author's works in terms of reception and influence and update readers specifically about the emerging success of her novel. They note that for many years, American students studying literature, history, or anthropology read Chinua Achebe's *Things Fall Apart* (1958), an early standard of African literature in English, to get a glimpse of what life and culture in Africa were like. Willey and Treiber contend, however, that starting in the early 1990s, students read Dangarembga's novel with increasing frequency instead of Achebe's classic. To support their observation, they point to the variety of themes and issues the novel addresses—from women's issues and the influence of the community on an individual's life to the roles of education and colonization in the development of selfhood. Likewise, Willey and Treiber note that the novel was first published not in Zimbabwe but in England, where the author likely encountered sexism in the publishing arena.

The first novel by a black Zimbabwean female to reach readers' hands would not have done so if not for the British-run Women's Press. In an interview with Jane Wilkinson published in *Talking with African Writers* (1992), Dangarembga states that at the time the manuscript was turned down, she remembers wondering if the rejection had more to do with her writing ability or with the content of the work, which most probably was construed by male publishers as negative criticism. In her article "Debunking Patriarchy" (1995), Pauline Ada Uwakweh reminds us that "patriarchal subordination of the female is reflected in the male domination of the literary arena" as well, which likely accounts for the initial rejection of Dangarembga's text for publication and undoubtedly is responsible for so many skewed and unrealistic representations of females in African literature by males (p. 75). Testament to her influence not only on European readers but also on their American counterparts, Dangarembga's text was published first by Seal Press in the United States in 1988, and remains in print today, with tens of thousands of copies sold.

With *Nervous Conditions* alone, Dangarembga has contributed enormously to helping the world understand the cultural convolutions, crises of identity, and power struggles that are set into motion when one country decides to colonize another. Yet her multifaceted influence in Africa and the United States continues far beyond the novel as well, given her work in other literary genres of drama, short prose, and film.

Walt Collins

References

Uwakweh, Pauline Ada. "Debunking Patriarchy: The Liberational Quality of Voicing in Tsitsi Dangarembga's *Nervous Conditions.*" *Research in African Literatures* 26, no. 1 (1995): 75–84.

Wilkinson, Jane. *Talking with African Writers: Interviews with African Poets, Playwrights, and Novelists.* London: James Currey, 1992.

Willey, Ann Elizabeth, and Jeanette Treiber. *Negotiating the Postcolonial: Emerging Perspectives on Tsitsi Dangarembga.* Trenton, NJ: Africa World Press, 2002.

DANISH EMPIRE

The kingdom of Denmark became involved in West African trade during the early seventeenth century and established settlements in what is now Ghana from 1658. In 1671 Danes occupied the island of St. Thomas in the Caribbean and expanded their possessions in the region to include St. John in 1717 and St. Croix in 1733. Initially, these three Caribbean islands were owned by the Danish West India Company, but in 1754 the three islands were sold to the king of Denmark and became Danish colonies. They were occupied by the British in 1801 and again during 1807–1815. The Danes sold the last of their forts in West Africa to the British in 1852. In 1916 the Danish West Indies were sold to the American government, and Danish rule ended in 1917. These then became the U.S. Virgin Islands.

In West Africa, the Danes expelled the Swedes from parts of the Gold Coast (modern-day Ghana) that the latter had controlled, located around their fort of Osu, near Accra, which had been built in 1661. The Danes renamed the post Christiansborg and used it as the center of their trading activities along the West African coast. They built or took over other posts at Ada (Fort Konigstein), Keta (Fort Prinzenstein), Ningo (Fort Friedensborg), and Teshi (Fort Augustaborg). Most of these quickly became centers for the slave trade, with Keta being enlarged in 1785. In 1792 the Danes announced the abolition of the slave trade at the end of 1802; there was a massive increase in slaves being shipped in the interim ten years, after which the bases had little purpose. In 1839, when Christian VIII became king, plans were drawn up to sell the Danish Gold Coast bases to the British. This took place in 1850, and the Danish possessions became parts of the British colony of the Gold Coast. Remains of some of the forts survive.

By contrast, when the Danes decided to establish a colonial empire in the West Indies, many of the islands were already occupied by other European powers, and as a result, Denmark was only able to occupy two islands that were not already colonized: St. Thomas in 1671 and St. John in 1717. Both were important in the production of sugar, and the early Danish settlers planned for a large number of Danes, with a mix of free settlers and indentured servants and similar numbers of slaves. Certainly, in 1688 the numbers on St. Thomas were approaching parity: 317 whites and 422 African slaves. Some of these slaves came from Danish bases in West Africa, while others were acquired elsewhere in Africa or in the Caribbean. However in a census three years later, while the white population had risen to 389, there were 547 slaves. The numbers were even more disparate in 1715, when there were 555 whites as against 3,042 slaves.

There were many reasons why only small numbers of Danes were keen to move to the West Indies. During that period the population of Denmark was less than 500,000, with a population density only half that in England, France, or the Netherlands. Gradually, other Europeans came to settle on the St. Thomas, and also on St. John, which was occupied by the Danes in 1733 by a total of 208 white settlers and indentured servants and 1,087 slaves. In that year there was a slave rebellion, and although it was put down, its occurrence was a discouragement to white settlement. Nevertheless, Danes tried to work out schemes to

persuade more whites to move to the Danish Caribbean. The life of an indentured laborer, however, did not seem very promising, and one contemporary, J. L. Carstens, compared their treatment to that of the slaves. The indentured labor system was abandoned in the early eighteenth century. A plan to send convicts to the island was also shelved after a few shiploads of prisoners were transported because the authorities on St. John became terrified of a convict rebellion.

With few Danes wanting to move to St. Thomas, other Europeans were welcomed, so that by 1715 the white population was largely non-Danish. Before the Danes occupied St. Thomas, it had been occupied by Prussians, and to boost the non-slave population, the Danish administrators encouraged Dutch settlers. Gradually, however, the white population of St. Thomas fell as the number of slaves rose to a peak of 2,302 in 1770.

In 1733 the Danish West India Company bought the island of St. Croix from the French. It was much larger than the other two islands and in 1755 had a population of 1,303 whites and freedpersons and 8,897 slaves. The topography of this island lent itself far more easily to plantation agriculture, and there was a well-established elite of some fifty English families who had settled during the French period and were encouraged by the Danes to remain. The importance of the English population was reflected in the fact that when the first regular newspaper, the *Royal Danish American Gazette,* appeared in 1770 it was largely in English, except for government proclamations, which appeared in Danish. Under the Danes, the sugar industry on St. Croix expanded, and by 1770 the number of slaves had risen massively, to 18,884, as opposed to 1,515 whites.

During the Napoleonic Wars, Denmark initially remained neutral. However, it was gradually brought into alliance with the French. On March 30, 1801, British ships appeared off the island of St. Croix, which quickly surrendered to the power of the Royal Navy. The authorities on the island, worried about a slave rebellion, were keen that the transfer of authority go smoothly. No Danish fleet was present to protect the islands, and on April 2, 1801, the British destroyed the Danish fleet at the First Battle of Copenhagen. The islands were, however, returned by the Treaty of Amiens in 1802. But in 1807 the British again seized the islands after the Second Battle of Copenhagen, and they held it until the end of the Napoleonic Wars in 1815. Two years earlier the Danish state was declared bankrupt, and by a treaty of January 14, 1814, Denmark ceded Norway to Sweden.

Since settlement began in the seventeenth century and as families prospered, property ownership in the Danish West Indies became more and more concentrated in a relatively small number of hands. In 1841 St. Croix was divided into 101 estates, 16 owned by the state, 60 by foreign creditors, and the remainder held by 25 proprietors. At the same time, the political and economic situation in Europe remained full of conflict. In 1848 Denmark abolished slavery and—being on the point of selling the Danish Gold Coast to the British—also considered selling the Danish West Indies to the United States. A treaty of sale was drawn up in 1867 but the U.S. Senate did not ratify it. The Danes remained in possession of the Danish West Indies until 1916. As American economic and political influence grew dramatically,

however, it became clear that the US would remain the dominant force in the Western Hemisphere. In 1916 the islands were finally sold to the U.S. government for $25 million, with the official transfer taking place on March 31, 1917. Now known as the U.S. Virgin Islands, the Danish West Indies became an outlying territory of the United States.

Justin Corfield

See also: British Empire

References

Hall, Neville A. T. *Slave Society in the Danish West Indies.* Baltimore, MD: Johns Hopkins University Press, 1992.

Larsen, Kay. *De Danske i Guinea.* Copenhagen: Nordiske forfatteres forlag, 1918.

Nørregard, Georg. *Danish Settlements in West Africa, 1658–1850.* Boston: Boston University Press, 1966.

Reindorf, Joe. *Scandinavians in Africa: Guide to Materials Relating to Ghana in the Danish National Archives.* Oslo, Norway: Universitetsforlaget, 1980.

Westergaard, Waldemar. *The Danish West Indies under Company Rule, 1671–1754.* New York: Macmillan, 1917.

DANTICAT, EDWIDGE (1969–)

Edwidge Danticat's long list of publications makes her, perhaps, the most prolific Haitian writer of international stature. The first Haitian writer to be widely published in English (she, like many others in the African Diaspora, learned English as a second language), Danticat has earned widespread critical acclaim by academics and general audiences. Danticat's work offers a complex portrait of the African Diaspora, particularly the journey of African culture to Haiti and then her own journey from Haiti to the United States. While her writings fittingly take much of their inspiration from the author's experiences in her native

Port-au-Prince, Haiti, and by extension from her African ancestry, she refuses to be seen as the mouthpiece of her people, especially of Haitian Americans. In an interview with David Barsamian in the fall of 2003, she acknowledged that she has fought against that task: "I think I've been assigned that role [Haiti's oracle], but I don't really see myself as the voice of the Haitian American experience. . . . There are many; I'm just one" (Barsamian, 2004, p. 1). Much of her writing, though, processes her personal experiences with great insight and originality. And these experiences not only detail her Haitian upbringing, but recall larger experiences, influenced by African culture and traditions, of communal and extended family cohabitation and interaction, of myths and legends passed down orally through the generations, and of tension and conflict between Western and developing countries and between developing countries themselves.

Danticat's first novel, *Breath, Eyes, Memory,* published in 1994, relays the semi-veiled memories of the author's childhood transformed for fictional protagonist Sophie Caco. Four years after its release, the novel was chosen for Oprah Winfrey's book club. This debut novel topped the *Publishers Weekly* paperback best-seller list, and Vintage Publishers increased its print run to 600,000. Focused on a troubled mother-daughter relationship and the pressure of the past on the present, the novel explores themes central to literature written across the African Diaspora.

While her first novel reveals personal circumstances of the author, *The Farming of Bones* (1998), her third major project, depicts a key event in Haitian history. Winner of the American Book Award, *The Farming of Bones* chronicles the massacre of Haitian-born harvesters of sugar cane (bones) at the hands of the violently anti-immigration movement of Dominican leader Rafael Trujillo Molina. For decades, Haitians found good work in the neighboring Dominican Republic, but in 1937 thousands of immigrant workers were killed. The story is told through Amabelle Desir, a Haitian working as a maid on a Dominican plantation who tries to escape as the violence erupts. She is injured, her lover killed. In *Allegories of Desire* (2004), M. M. Adjarian contends that "the writer's concern for Haitian peasant women gives way to a more generalized concern for the peasant underclass . . . , by expanding the narrative focus to include consideration of both the women and the men of the dispossessed classes, the writer aligns herself with another Haitian literary tradition: that of the *roman paysan,* or peasant novel" (pp. 101–102).

Recently, Danticat's focus has shifted from texts based loosely on her own experiences to those embracing issues and events of greater Haitian interest. Since *The Farming of Bones,* Danticat has written *After the Dance: A Walk through Carnival in Jacmel* (2002), a nonfiction work of travel writing, and *The Dew Breaker* (2004), short stories that track a certain torturer's wickedness under Duvalier.

As her writing shifted its focus from personal experiences to tribulations facing the greater Haitian community, Danticat became more personally involved in facilitating gatherings of youth groups of Caribbean immigrants in New York. She also participated in the National Coalition for Haitian Rights. After spending years in New York, Edwidge Danticat currently lives in Florida, where she has taught creative writing at the University of Miami and continues to offer her perspective on the joys and hardships of life lived in the United States as well as in Haiti, and ultimately of life lived in the greater African community.

Walt Collins

See also: Caribbean Literature; Haiti

References

Adjarian, M. M. *Allegories of Desire: Body, Nation, and Empire in Modern Caribbean Literature by Women.* Westport, CT: Praeger, 2004.

Barsamian, David. *Louder Than Bombs: Interviews from "The Progressive Magazine."* Cambridge, MA: South End Press, 2004.

DASH, JULIE (1952–)

Julie Dash is an African American producer, writer, and director. She was born and raised in New York City. She studied at Studio Museum of Harlem, the City College of New York, and the Center for Advanced Film and Television Studies of the American Film Institute. She earned a BA degree from the Leonard Davis Center for the Performing Arts in the David Picker Film Institute and a MFA degree at the University of California, Los Angeles. She produced the film *Diary of an African Nun* (1977) and directed the music video "Give Me One Reason" (1996), by Tracy Chapman. Dash has received many accolades, including the Jury Prize for *Illusions* (1989), Sundance Film Festival's Best Cinematography for *Daughters of the Dust* (1990), and the NAACP Image Award for *The Rosa Parks Story* (2003). *Illusions,* a thirty-four-minute film, tells the story of two African American women struggling in the Hollywood film industry in the 1940s. *Daughters of the Dust* tells the story of an African American family living on the Sea Islands off the coast of South Carolina at the beginning of the twentieth century, exploring themes of family, heritage, and oral tradition. The Gullah people on those islands and their distinctive language, formed in isolation from the mainland, are seen in the film through a family that maintains a distinctive African culture half a century after the end of the transatlantic slave trade.

Laura Madeline Wiseman

See also: Film (Atlantic); Film (North America); Georgia's Sea Islands; Gullah

References

Brouwer, Joel R. "Repositioning: Center and Margin in Julie Dash's *Daughters of the Dust.*" *African American Review* 29, no. 1 (Spring 1995): 5–16.

Dash, Julie, director. *Daughters of the Dust.* New York: Kino International, 1992. Film.

Dollar, Steve. "'*Daughters of the Dust*' Dances with the Dialect of Women's Tales." *Atlanta Journal-Constitution,* October 6, 1991.

DEBT CANCELLATION

Debt cancellation refers to the movement to eliminate the massive governmental debt of African countries. Massive loans were made to African nations by international institutions such as the International Monetary Fund and the World Bank during the postcolonial period. Such large debts, and the poor prospects of their repayment, were caused by the financial mismanagement of Africa's postcolonial leaders. Many African states also had a disadvantaged start because the decolonialization process often neglected long-term economic consequences. While colonial powers focused on maximizing their financial take in their withdrawals, revolutionary and independent forces were more focused on obtaining political autonomy regardless of the long-term costs. Most African states experienced considerable economic disadvantages because of their lack of infrastructure, educational and medical systems, general governmental services, cohesive national identity, and virtually every requirement and condition deemed necessary by economists to produce favorable economic development results. African debt cancellation is portrayed by some as a necessary step to push economic development forward. Some argue that interest paid to non-African banks represents funding that could be redirected to domestic social causes such as human development projects involving education, medicine, food, clean water, and housing.

At independence, most significant existing private industries were foreign-controlled export operations. For example, in Ghana, railroad lines were constructed for the sole purpose of transporting cocoa beans from an interior collection center to a coastal port designed for export. The export-driven infrastructure focused primarily on extracting resources rather than developing local economies. In the decades following African state independence, foreign-controlled industries maintained a minimal infrastructure to service their extraction-based operations.

Africa's debt crisis has multiple historical and political roots. Areas outside of direct foreign investment interests were neglected, ignored, and poorly managed by municipal and regional leaders who often lacked appropriate training to perform their responsibilities. Local infrastructure frequently lurked at preindustrial levels, retaining equipment and facilities dating to pre–World War II levels of technology. After colonial withdrawal, many places appeared abandoned by the forces of modernization. Geography heavily influenced the degree of abandonment. Some regions, such as the Mediterranean, the Horn of Africa, and South Africa benefited from pre-independence trade routes to Europe, Asia, and the Americas. Africa's noncoastal regions experienced significant disadvantages due to their geographic isolation. Such insulation hindered their ability to acquire independent capital resources or to secure development-oriented investments for their own welfare.

Exploitive private interests and leaders who placed their own financial welfare ahead of their people compounded this discrepancy between more successful coastal regions and the less-connected landlocked states. Tribal warfare and unstable political factions heightened many African leaders' sense of self-preservation; many seized much of their government's borrowed money to maintain their power or to enrich themselves enough to live a wealthy life in retirement. The fact that many former African presidents and leaders reside in Europe or the Middle East on stolen funds untouched and unlikely to be extradited by their host governments is seen by many as a continued collusion between former colonial powers and former African leaders.

Africa's debt crisis exists because impoverished states have, in a sense, financed their former leaders' retirement and paid the maintenance costs for longer-term political dictatorships rather than incur unstable and short-lived governmental regimes. African debt has been a means of keeping intact states with artificial boundaries drawn during colonialism and decolonization. After guaranteeing a stable business environment, the retiring or exiled former African leaders experience a close relationship with their European and other former colonial business interests while residing outside of Africa. In that regard, African debt represents continued economic imperialism or a variation of neocolonialism. Existing African states endure a heavy cost to cover past financial indiscrepencies and effectively continue to support those that mismanaged their funds and resources.

Newly formed African states faced the challenge of nation building, of settling their own domestic and external disputes while simultaneously abiding by strict United Nations (UN) border guidelines and UN and African oversight. This awkward situation resulted in a shaky foundation that led foreign interests to intervene on their own behalf and to influence African leaders as they saw fit. Foreign pledges of military aid and logistical support manipulated Africa's warring factions because they provided the means to obtain or maintain power. The need for assistance created an environment of dependence and indecisiveness in which successive governments were fixated on self-preservation and the destruction of opposition forces. Many investments intended to build African nations never found their intended target, but instead were lost in military conflicts or by various forms of embezzlement.

The complex nature of African black market economies and the high cost of governmental stability, which is often reliant on military forces, means that borrowed money from the International Monetary Fund, the African Development Fund, and the World Bank typically fails to be used for building commercial, industrial, or municipal resources. Mixed with rising interest rates, African debt substantially inhibits domestic developmental projects. Stable governments must, in turn, endure the hardship of overcoming massive debt inherited from previous wasteful regimes.

The desire to cancel debt arises from the argument African nations would be freed from debt repayment responsibilities to devote more financial resources to civil investments. In Africa there is considerable anger and frustration at having to contribute so much of present budgets to service debt owed to external parties, debt often produced by opposition forces previously in power. It is believed that canceling debt will allow more loans to develop a sustainable economy. People discouraged by the lack of current developmental progress hope that eradicating debt will remove Africa from a kind of debtor's prison. Debt relief, some believe, would promote greater political stability.

In the 1990s debt-relief groups, after failing to make progress on their own, found powerful public relation allies through supporters such as Bono of the Irish rock group U2. As Africa's resources in food, labor, health, education, housing, and basic utilities failed to meet national needs, debt-canceling bodies argued that new revenues should only be spent on sustainable economic development and not on government salaries or military forces.

However, Africa's situation may be more difficult than suggested by debt-relief groups. Recent evidence indicates that eight of the twenty recipients of debt cancellation returned to indebted status within one year. Furthermore, a depressed African market is less appealing to investors than markets in other developing nations and regions, such as China, India and Eastern Europe. The effects of communicable diseases, such as AIDS/HIV, have also wreaked havoc on Africa's social fabric and workforce. In some places the median age has fallen to under twenty, which has a chilling effect on the economy. Extreme poverty, plus the migration of the better educated to developed nations, further depletes the human resources of the already-taxed societies and economies. Violent crime, unchecked by corrupt police forces, poses a continuing problem. Eliminating the problem of African debt is not likely to be a sufficient solution for a continent under a multitude of stresses.

Josiah Baker

See also: Decolonization, African; Democracy, African; Health, Public; International Monetary Fund; Human Immunodeficiency Virus and Prevention; Neocolonialism; United Nations; World Bank

References

Blomstrom, Magnus, and Mats Lundahl, eds. *Economic Crisis in Africa*. London: Routledge, 1993.

Herbst, Jeffrey. *U.S. Economic Policy Toward Africa*. New York: Council on Foreign Relations, 1993.

Lancaster, Carol. *African Economic Reform*. Washington, DC: Institute for International Economics, 1991.

Leonard, David K. *Africa's Stalled Development*. Boulder, CO: Lynne Rienner Publishers, 2003.

Nafziger, E. Wayne. *Economic Development*. Cambridge: Cambridge University Press, 2005.

Organization for Economic Co-operation and Development. *African Economic Outlook 2005/2006*. Paris: Organization for Economic Co-operation and Development, 2006.

Reno, William. *Warlord Politics and African States*. Boulder, CO: Lynne Rienner Publishers, 1999.

Whiteside, Alan. *The Political Economy of AIDS in Africa*. Aldershot, UK: Ashgate Publishing, 2004.

DECOLONIZATION, AFRICAN

African decolonization refers to the process by which formerly colonized African nations became independent of European rule, from approximately 1920 to 1975. It marks one of the most important transformations of the modern world.

Three explanations are typically given for why African decolonization occurred: that it was a deliberate imperial policy of the colonizing European nations; that it was the result of pressures imposed by African nationalism; and that it was the result of a post–World War II international situation of powerful empires in rivalry with each other (predating and also including the cold war). The study of specific former colonies reveals a complex interaction among all three of these forces in the process of decolonization. In addition, differences in decolonization existed among the different regions of Africa—southern, northern, and sub-Saharan—as well as differences based on the colonial administration of each colony (French distinct from British, for example) and its interaction with the government of the metropole (Senegal with France, Nigeria with Britain, for example).

During World War II, Africans fought on behalf of their colonial power's interests, and the continent's colonies provided key resources in raw goods. The stability of the world's European colonial empires concluded with the close of World War II. Despite growing unrest in the colonies and a growing awareness at home of the unjustifiability of the Western imperial model, however, the major European empires of Britain and France, and also Portugal, held onto their colonies past 1945. The war had demonstrated the economic value and potential of Africa, and industries in African colonies entered an economic boom in which exports and revenue increased tremendously. Shaped by the Atlantic Charter, a 1941 agreement between Great Britain and the United States to avoid territorial conflict and to collaborate on international security and economic growth, and the concept of the United Nations, colonizing powers held onto their territories and devised ambitious development schemes for social and economic advancement through both education and crop production.

At the same time, African national liberation movements had become influential after World War I and gained influence through the transnational meeting of leaders at the Pan-African Conference of 1945, attended by George Padmore, Kwame N'krumah, and Jomo Kenyatta, and the All-African Peoples' Conference of 1958, held in Accra, Ghana, which was attended by delegates of the nationalist movements of twenty-eight African colonies and independent nations. This latter meeting demonstrated that decolonization in Africa, rather than being a phenomenon locally specific to the region surrounding Ghana, which had won independence the year before, would spread from West Africa to the rest of the continent.

Influential African nationalists, including Kwame N'krumah (Ghana), Jomo Kenyatta (Kenya), and Leopold Senghor (Senegal), shaped anticolonial sentiment into a platform of political, aesthetic, and economic ideals addressing the needs of colonized peoples. These leaders presented themselves primarily as intellectuals and secondarily as politicians, shaping a position of intellectual and moral respectability from which to tackle colonial domination. Senghor, for example, as a poet helped to found the Négritude movement. These leaders addressed Europeans as much as they did Africans, in part to garner support for their ideas in Europe. They also forged a connection with the intellectual legacy of African American and West Indian scholars and activists such as W. E. B. Du Bois and Marcus Garvey.

African nationalist ideas directed independence movements in Ghana, Kenya, Senegal, Côte D'Ivoire, and elsewhere. Plans for an African-centered economy sometimes worked in tandem with socialist ideals (in Congo (Kinshasa), Tanzania, and Angola, for example). In the case of Tanzania, Julius Nyerere's plan for African Unity (Umoja) was based on his unique vision of African socialism (Ujamaa). The socialist agendas and Soviet involvement behind some of the socialist movements inevitably prompted the interest of nations not formally involved in African colonization, namely the United States and Cuba.

Through the Central Intelligence Agency (CIA), the United States funded and provided arms to rebel groups that were selected often for their opposition to Communism. After the first wave of African decolonization in the 1950s, the United States established an embassy in every independent African nation.

Cuba became involved with the independence movements of seventeen African colonies. Under the direction of Fidel Castro, Cuban interventions included aid to Algeria when it was under the leadership of Ahmed Ben Bella, to Amilcar Cabral in Guinea-Bissau, and to Laurent Kabila in Congo. Cuba's largest engagement was with Angola. In 1975 troops from Cuba and Angola fought on behalf of the Marxist Popular Movement for the Liberation of Angola (MMPLA) against what was later revealed as Operation Savanna—a secret invasion of Angola using the combined forces of South African troops and Angola's two local, anti-Communist groups, the National Union for the Total Independence of Angola (UNITA) and the U.S.-backed

National Front for the Liberation of Angola (FNLA). U.S. and South African involvement in Angola followed the ascendancy of the MMPLA after Portugal's departure from its former colony. This covert invasion, occurring just one month before the formal date of decolonization, attempted to divert the Marxist quest for power. Significantly, Cuba acted independently in sending Cuban troops—special forces and artillery—to intervene in Angola, neglecting to consult first with the Soviet Union and demonstrating that in this decisive action, Cuba was not merely the puppet of the Soviets. The defeat of the CIA- and South African–backed operation may have influenced and empowered the anticolonial, anti-apartheid African National Congress of South Africa.

Some scholars argue that decolonization has given way to the continued Western domination and exploitation of Africa through the continent's dependency on global markets, international capital, and corporations based in developed nations, a situation often called neocolonialism. Financial institutions for development such as the World Bank and the International Monetary Fund, which exert a powerful influence on the domestic economy and international relations of African nations, are pointed to as signs of the continued economic and political domination of Africa by Western powers. In terms of a historical understanding of present-day realities, then, the study of decolonization allows one to understand the relations of Europe and North and South America to African nations, the transformation of imperial power in the twentieth century, and the way in which a global, transnational black intellectual heritage has been shaped by colonialism.

Noelle Morrissette

See also: Cabral, Amilcar; Castro Ruz, Fidel; Central Intelligence Agency; Cold War; Colonialism; Congolese Independence; Du Bois, William Edward Burghardt; Garvey, Marcus; International Monetary Fund; N'krumah, Kwame; Négritude; Neocolonialism; Pan-Africanism; Senghor, Leopold Sedar; United Nations; World War II

References
Gleijeses, Piero. *Conflicting Missions: Havana, Washington, and Africa, 1959–1976.* Chapel Hill: University of North Carolina Press, 2002.
Oliver, Roland, and J. D. Fage. *A Short History of Africa.* New York: Penguin, 1990.
Wilson, Henry S. *African Decolonization.* London: Oxford University Press, 1994.

DELANY, MARTIN ROBINSON (1812–1885)

Martin Robinson Delany had a remarkable life as a political writer, physician, soldier, judge, businessman, husband, and father of eleven children. Throughout his life he lobbied for the resettlement of African Americans to Africa and for the formation of an independent national identity.

Delany was born free in Charlestown, Virginia (now in West Virginia), on May 6, 1812. When he was ten years old, his mother moved the family to Chambersburg, Pennsylvania, and the father joined them after having bought his freedom. In 1831 Martin Delany moved to Pittsburgh, where he attended the Bethel African Methodist Church School, assisted a local physician, and offered paramedical services as a "cupper and lecher."

In 1843 Delany turned temporarily to journalism, first as the editor of his own abolitionist newsletter, *The Mystery,* then in 1847–1849 as co-editor of Frederick Douglass's *North Star.* His attempt to study medicine at Harvard was thwarted when he

Martin Robinson Delany, a physician, social reformer, and soldier, served as a surgeon with the 54th Massachusetts Volunteers in the Civil War. Delany was the first African American to be commissioned (Major) in the U.S. Army. (Getty Images)

was dismissed for racist reasons; he became a school principal instead and started writing *Blake, or, The Huts of America* (1862), an novel of early nationalist aspirations in opposition to the conciliatory tenor of Harriet Beecher Stowe's *Uncle Tom's Cabin* (1852). Earlier, in 1852, Delany published a treatise titled *The Condition, Elevation, Emigration, and Destiny of the Colored People of the United States, Politically Considered,* which focused on the possibility of an African American nation outside the United States. He strongly advocated the flight of slaves to Canada and Mexico and discussed re-migration to African countries, favoring East Africa over the West African coast. He held in deep contempt the American Colonization Society and its efforts to resettle free African Americans,

calling the supposedly independent republic of Liberia "a burlesque on a government." Leading a National Emigration Convention in 1854, Delany addressed the delegates as representatives of a "Broken Nation." He headed a commission that in 1859–1860 visited the Yoruba country on the lower Niger River to explore the viability of a settlement project in negotiations with the local rulers. However, the agreement reached in Abeokuta, and Delany's hopes of return to his ancestral homeland, never materialized.

Instead, Delany helped to recruit volunteers for the Union cause during the Civil War, and on February 26, 1865, he was appointed major in the 104th U.S. Colored Troops, making him the first African American staff officer in the U.S. Army. After the war, Delany worked for the Freedmen's Bureau in South Carolina and ran for lieutenant governor in 1874. In the violent election campaign of 1876, Delany supported the Democratic candidate and former Confederate general Wade Hampton. Despite his earlier criticism of Liberia, he supported the Liberian Exodus Joint Stock Steamship Company in 1878 but returned to his initial vocation as a physician when that project failed and his political base in South Carolina eroded. On January 24, 1885, Delany, whom Abraham Lincoln had called "this most extraordinary and intelligent black man," died in Ohio.

Wolfgang Hochbruck

See also: Abolitionism; American Colonization Society; Liberia

References

Levine, Robert S. *Martin R. Delany: A Documentary Reader.* Chapel Hill: University of North Carolina Press, 2003.

Ullman, Victor. *Martin R. Delany: The Beginnings of Black Nationalism.* Boston: Beacon Press, 1971.

DEMOCRACY, AFRICAN

In contrast to most Latin American nations, which experienced political independence in the nineteenth century, African political autonomy and the democratization process arrived relatively late in the twentieth century. Democracy in much of Africa remains in its infancy. In the decades after obtaining independence, many African countries constructed democratic facades that did not long hide their regimes' autocratic nature or that collapsed due to internal power struggles or the inefficient use of resources.

African democratic movements are both beneficiaries and victims of the postcolonial era. That era, which began in the 1950s, is within the living population's memory. Almost all of Africa, with the exception of a northwestern area called Western Sahara—which is in dispute between Morocco, Mauritania, and scattered tribal groups—is in the postcolonial era. In almost all cases, independence from European powers meant formal democracy, though few have created a long-term, viable democratic government.

Africa's preexisting political, historical, economic, and social structures harmed and delayed its democratic development. Most notably, the Berlin West Africa Conference of 1884–1885 shaped Africa's modern political boundaries, European colonialization claims, and African trade. The conference, hosted by a recently independent and unified Germany under its first chancellor, Otto von Bismarck (1815–1898), carved Africa into areas of control for mostly European imperial powers. Bismarck, who organized the event to promote German Central African trade interests, effectively supervised Europe's formal acquisition of Africa. Only Ethiopia

and Liberia were spared from European political annexation. Since Liberia was a colony of freed African American slaves and their descendants, who voluntarily returned to Africa, the United States had a special interest to ensure its independence. In Berlin, Europeans drew Africa's modern political boundaries by creating states largely without any consideration of ethnic composition, historical tribal boundaries, or ongoing tribal hostilities. These decisions were based primarily on European security and political needs and the distribution of African resources.

Later, when African states obtained independence one at a time, a realignment of political borders appeared impractical. In almost all cases, these newly formed African states were identical in size and ethnic composition to the colonial states. In the past, the colonial powers had interceded and imposed their own will in almost all sizable tribal disputes. After imperial policing ended with independence, widespread violent tribalism erupted. The artificial political states inherited from the European colonial era aggravated tribal animosities. By default, enemies were frequently forced into cooperating in a fledgling political environment that lacked any genuine cultural or social unity.

Multiple political complications hindered the solidification of national identity, including the unwillingness to forego tribalism in favor of national interests. In many cases, aside from the effort to expel a colonial power, there was no common political goal or interest to unify competing tribal groups. Inevitably, any credible democratic political order disintegrated under such enormous internal pressure. Often the strongest, most vicious tribal leader would emerge as the national leader. Those within the dominant tribe or tribes would benefit tremendously. For example, during Mobutu Sese Seko's corrupt (often labeled "kleptocratic") presidency in Zaire (now the Democratic Republic of the Congo), members of his tribe frequently drove their new Mercedes sedans around the capital city of Kinshasa while villagers in rival ethnic groups languished in extreme poverty, were imprisoned, and were periodically killed. In Uganda, Idi Amin (1924–2003), the president of Uganda in 1971–1979, seized control in a coup and became infamous for his atrocities, including the torture and murder of 300,000 to 500,000 Ugandans, targeting, among others, the Acholi, Lango, Indians, and Christians.

Although many African political movements had used the idea of democracy as a battle cry to mobilize their independence movements, the term would later be used toward highly antidemocratic ends. The concept of democracy provided a moral justification for eradicating the nondemocratic, nonrepresentative, imperialistic institutions of the past. However, either by design, through perceived necessity, or by the unadulterated seduction of power, many postcolonial African political leaders emerged as "Big Men" or as possessed of a "Big Man Syndrome," terms that refer to their corrupt and autocratic personal rule. These African Big Men often labeled their actions as democratic to justify their means of enforcing and consolidating their personal political power. Instead of exhibiting the behavior of elected presidents, these Big Men acted more as tribal chiefs or African monarchs. During the cold war years (1945–1991), the United States and its allies tolerated many autocratic African and Latin American presidents because they guaranteed government stability and assured foreign commercial interests access to cheap natural resources. For Africa and Latin America, the cold war meant an ongoing struggle between pro-Soviet and pro-American factions. Most civil wars and other forms of unrest served as proxy battles between the superpowers as they wrestled to control the regions for their own geopolitical interests.

International community leaders overlooked the many human atrocities committed by African presidents, fearing that calls for political reform would contribute to further regional destabilization. Since Marxist and Communist dialogue during the cold war decades focused on the conspicuous economic inequities throughout Africa, leftists argued that economic equality was as important as political equality; this became a central point of their rhetoric as they sought to spark revolutionary change. American and pro-American political interests suppressed most seemingly socialist projects of income and wealth redistribution in order to prevent Africa as a continent from falling under the Soviet sphere of control.

Africa and Latin America share a common political history in that during these cold war decades, the desire of American and pro-American forces to keep these countries non-Communist by means of brutal nondemocratic dictators superseded noble political goals. Allowing fully functional representative democracies to emerge carried a very likely possibility that the disenchanted masses would elect a pro-Communist or leftist leader. Illiteracy, poor communications, human rights violations by pro-Soviet groups, and concerns over the consequences of people's desperation were common justifications for the United States and pro-U.S. groups to avoid the active advocacy of democracy.

After the end of the cold war, pressures from Havana and Moscow on both Latin America and Africa lessened. With Soviet influence having vanished and Cuba's minimized, non-Communist factions no longer had pressing reasons to interfere with left-leaning governments or to tolerate brutal nondemocratic regimes. For example, the cold war provided a political environment that tolerated South African apartheid, the government's official system of racial segregation from 1948 to 1991. With the end of the cold war, the U.S. government's willingness to tolerate apartheid ceased. In many cases, the cold war's end positively contributed to African democracy. The end of the cold war also led to Namibia's independence. South Africa had occupied its northwestern neighbor during the cold war to defend it from Communist insurgent activities and hostilities originating from its northern neighbor, Angola. As the cold war came to a close, Namibia received its independence in 1990.

During the 1990s some dictatorships became rapidly unstable and were stricken by both internal and external power struggles. Weakened, many dictators were forced to resign and in some cases go into exile. A key example is the "Big Man" of Central Africa, Mobutu Sese Seko (1930–1997). The president of Zaire (now the Democratic Republic of the Congo) from 1965 to 1997, he rose to power by overthrowing Patrice Lumumba, the elected president. However, after the CIA withdrew active support in the early 1990s, his power steadily eroded. In 1997 he lost control of his country and shortly after died in exile.

By the beginning of the twenty-first century, nearly a decade after cold war geopolitical issues had vanished, African states were poised to seek more independent political paths. No longer caught between competing imperial or cold war interests, for the first time in centuries, democracy in Africa has blossomed in recent years. Of Africa's fifty-two sovereign nations, excluding Western Sahara, forty-five governments have some republican or democratic elements. All claim to have some manner of separation between the chief of state, a legislative body, and a judicial body. Nearly half of Africa's nations possess a truly functional separation of this sort.

However, beyond these, twenty-two countries have had leadership succession via coup, assassination, outright election fraud, voting irregularities, or other coercive means. Africa also still has examples of the Big Man phenomenon. Robert Mugabe (1924–) has been Zimbabwe's head of government since 1980. Idriss Deby (1952–), president of Chad and the self-proclaimed head of the Patriotic Salvation Movement, represents an ethnocentric Zaghawa Islamist government and has a private presidential army formed from the Zaghawa. Lieutenant General Teodoro Obiang Nguema Mbasogo (1942–) has been president of Equatorial Guinea since 1979, when his 600 mercenaries killed his uncle, the former leader. Prior to becoming president, Obiang was head of the infamous Black Beach prison and leader of the National Guard. Umar Hassan Ahmad Al-Bashir, the field marshal and president of Sudan, came to power after a 1989 military coup that overthrew the democratically elected prime minister, Sadeq al-Mahdi; he immediately banned all political parties, cracked down on the press, and dissolved Parliament upon assuming absolute control of the nation. He remains Sudan's Big Man as the chairman of the Revolutionary Command Council for National Salvation and as the de facto leader for all posts.

Africa's process of democratization is still in its early stages as African states have a mean constitutional age of seventeen years and an average tenure for chiefs of state of ten years. Excluding the Sudan and barring future troubles in Central Africa in such countries as Rwanda, Burundi, Uganda, and the Democratic Republic of the Congo or in the previously troubled West African states of Liberia, Sierre Leone, and Guinea, Africa in 2007 has had fewer violent armed conflicts than the Africa of previous decades. Hopefully, Robert Mugabe and similar figures will be Africa's last Big Men.

While constitutional and state reform has progressed somewhat in recent years, many hurdles remain. The vast majority of sub-Saharan Africa lacks an infrastructure appropriate for sustenance, let alone economic growth. Governmental oversight of the capital invested in infrastructure remains weak. Because of inadequate infrastructure, foreign investment remains limited, except for the purchase and exploitation of minerals and other natural resources. The consequent persistence of a poor quality of life is likely to lead to the cyclical toppling of governments.

The widespread presence of human immunodeficiency virus (HIV) represents another tremendous obstacle to Africa's economic development and social stability. HIV and its consequent acquired immunodeficiency syndrome (AIDS) is poised to cripple the workforce of African nations and their leaderships by creating a glut of independent minors, often called AIDS orphans, in an already distressed economic environment.

Religious forces in Africa, in particular the clash between Islamic and non-Islamic factions, are a substantial obstacle to democratization. Though much of Africa's Islamic influence is indigenous—along the northern and eastern parts of Africa, Islam has been a part of the cultural fabric for many centuries—some foreign Islamic incursions have added to conflicts. Islam does not threaten political development so much as the cultural and political conflicts that embroil Islamic and non-Islamic leaders. In Uganda, Sudan, Egypt, and Algeria, Islam has often been used as a rallying point against a target political opposition, sometimes leading to violence. An example of a culturally embattled region is Darfur (which means "home of the fur" in Arabic) in western Sudan, where Islamic and non-Islamic forces regularly clash. Religious leadership has a sizable role in making political decisions in Africa. African parties sympathetic to Iran or to Osama bin Laden are attracted to the common culture that Islam offers. Islam offers authenticity to a way of life and counters the state of confusion, powerlessness, and alienation that is widespread in Africa. For many, it appears to offer a way to unify African states that without it lack a common culture.

Determining the effectiveness and validity of many African democracies is difficult. Africa's tainted history of Big Men and numerous developmental issues cloud the credibility of current governments. Future democratic reform is dependent upon continual and substantial economic and social development.

Josiah Baker

See also: Berlin West Africa Conference; Cold War; Congo (Kinshasa), Democratic Republic of the; Congolese Independence; Decolonization, African; Democracy, Latin American; Human Immunodeficiency Virus and Prevention; Lumumba, Patrice; South Africa, History and Politics; Uganda

References

Ake, Claude. *Democracy and Development in Africa.* Washington, DC: Brookings Institution, 1996.

Berman, Bruce, Will Kymlicka, and Dickson Eyoh. *Ethnicity and Democracy in Africa.* Oxford: James Currey Publishers, 2004.

Buijtenhuijs, Rob, and Celine Thiriot. *Democratisation in Sub-Saharan Africa.* Leiden, Netherlands: Africa Studies Centre, 1995.

CASS Monograph. *Democratisation of Disempowerment in Africa.* Port Harcourt, Nigeria: Malthouse, 1994.

Laidi, Zaki. *The Superpowers and Africa: The Constraints of a Rivalry, 1960–1990.* Chicago: University of Chicago Press, 1990.

Marte, Fred. *Political Cycles in International Relations: The Cold War and Africa, 1945–1990.* Amsterdam: VU University Press, 1994.

Ndegwa, Stephen N. *A Decade of Democracy in Africa.* Leiden, Netherlands: Koninklijke Brill NV, 2001.

DEMOCRACY, LATIN AMERICAN

In the first decade of the twenty-first century, democratization has become a challenge and high priority for the diverse peoples and governments of Latin America. Although the majority of the region's governments are formal democracies today, the process of democratization, in terms of democratic consolidation and deepening, continues. Citizens throughout the hemisphere, not unlike citizens across the Atlantic in Africa, are demanding greater accountability; transparency; civil, political, and human rights; community control and local participation; and socioeconomic reforms. The meaning of democracy has expanded from a narrow structural and institutional emphasis on elections, even free, fair, and competitive elections, or electoral democracy, to broad grassroots participation and empowerment, or fully participatory democracy. Democracy has become integrally linked with legitimacy, or the belief that the majority of citizens hold that their political system and government has the right to function on their behalf.

Various theories, such as the popular wave theory of Samuel P. Huntington, explain the worldwide diffusion of democracy as a historical process of ebb and flow. Generally, the period between 1828 and 1926 represents a "long wave" of democratic development, followed by the "reverse wave" of nondemocratic rule from 1922 to 1942. A "short wave" of progress between 1943 and 1962 is followed by another "reverse wave" spanning 1958 to 1975. The years 1974 to 1990 culminate in an advanced, or "third wave" of democratization. The wave theory remains a matter of continuing scholarly debate; critics of it observe that the wave theory applies more readily to Latin America, where independence from colonial rule occurred in the nineteenth century, than to Africa, where decolonization began a century later, after World War II.

Historically, the authoritarian, elitist, and racist colonial legacy of Latin America—problems similar, in some respects, to those of Africa—impeded the process of democratization. From 1828, after most Latin American countries had achieved independence, the region suffered a half century of caudillo politics, or rule by ruthless and corrupt military dictators and strongmen. With the notable exceptions of Brazil, which remained under monarchical rule until 1889, and Cuba, Panama, and Puerto Rico, which did not achieve full independence or home rule until the early and mid-twentieth century, oligarchic republicanism characterized Latin American regimes between 1880 and 1939.

The restricted suffrage of oligarchic regimes gave way by the 1930s as more voters, especially those of the laboring classes, were enfranchised and mobilized into politics. Populist, charismatic leaders, often with military backgrounds who initially seized power by military coup, like Argentina's Juan Perón or Brazil's Getulio Vargas, used mass electoral politics and nationalistic and populist agendas to legitimize their "semi-democratic" rule. Some populist military reformers who headed military coups, like David Toro, Germán Busch, and Gualberto Villarroel in Bolivia, never held elections and ran nondemocratic, although not overtly repressive, regimes.

During these years most leaders, like Fulgencio Batista in Cuba, Rafael Trujillo in the Dominican Republic, and Marcos Pérez Jímenez in Venezuela became entrenched, brutal dictators. In Latin America, as in Africa, oligarchical rule and dictatorship bred revolution. In 1952 the Bolivian National Revolution overthrew the civilian oligarchy and instituted major social and economic reforms. A universal suffrage law permitted the first free, fair, competitive, and participatory elections in the country's history. In contrast, the Cuban Revolution of 1959 overthrew one dictatorship for another. The new socialist state was dominated by the authoritarian and personalistic rule (a type of rule often termed "sultanistic") of Fidel Castro and his Cuban Communist Party, founded in 1965. Although the Cuban Revolution achieved a degree of socioeconomic equality, it did so at the expense of development and democracy.

The Nicaraguan Revolution of 1979 was both inspired and cautioned by the Cuban Revolution. A decade-long guerrilla struggle overthrew the dictatorship of Anastasio Somoza Debayle, the third ruler of a family dynasty that had dominated Nicaragua since 1933. Revolutionary struggles in El Salvador and Guatemala against repressive oligarchical and military regimes in the 1980s cost many lives but ended in stalemate. In the 1990s both countries achieved a gradual transition to civilian, semi- or full electoral democracy.

In Haiti, the first independent black republic in the Americas, a revolution in 1986 successfully overthrew the dictatorial "Papa Doc" François Duvalier and "Baby Doc" Jean-Claude Duvalier dynasty. After some chaos and a series of military juntas, the country finally held its first democratic election in 1990. Despite a campaign of intimidation and terror, the populist reformer and Catholic priest, Father Jean-Bertrand Aristide, was elected president by a large majority. However, in less than a year Aristide, who was unpopular among some circles of the U.S. government, was overthrown by a military coup. Haiti soon disintegrated into internecine bloodshed and civil war. Only after a U.S. and a UN embargo, humanitarian intervention, and lengthy peacekeeping mission did Haiti finally achieve a fragile electoral stability in 2006.

The role of the United States during the cold war decades (1945–1991) did not advance democratization in Latin America (or Africa). In the interests of regional stability and national security, U.S. administrations actively and tacitly supported the region's friendly dictators. President John F. Kennedy, who advanced the Alliance for Progress and gradual socioeconomic development in the region as the best way to forestall radical revolution, believed that although the goal of U.S. policy should be democracy, dictatorship might be necessary to prevent Communist regimes from coming to power. In this era, covert action and intervention were employed to secure U.S. national security interests. Also, increased U.S. military assistance strengthened ties with the region's militaries and helped establish national security states in the region, ostensibly to defend democracy against internal and external subversion.

By the 1990s, however, U.S. policy was reoriented toward the aggressive promotion of democracy in Latin America and democratic enlargement globally. In Central America and the Caribbean, the post–cold war shift in U.S. foreign policy and post-conflict reconstruction brought about a tentative and gradual transition to civilian and semidemocratic rule. Thus, by the 1990s, with the notable exception of Cuba, the majority of Latin American governments, which had been nondemocratic or authoritarian in previous decades, had established forms of electoral democracy. Nevertheless, across much of the region, comprehensive, participatory democratization remained an ongoing process despite some setbacks, as in Haiti, for example. The civil wars, drug wars, and guerrilla insurgencies, which had undermined democracy in the previous decades, had dissipated in Central America and Peru and were contained in Colombia with the re-election of President Alvaro Uribe in 2006. At the same time, fully representative and participatory democracy had not been achieved in most Latin American countries.

In Guatemala, El Salvador, Chile, Argentina, Peru, and Brazil, the "dirty wars" and "counterinsurgency wars" waged by military authoritarians against insurgents, indigenous peoples, leftists, and social activists had given way to truth and reconciliation commissions similar to those in South Africa and Rwanda. As in much of Africa, the majority of human rights violators and perpetrators of genocide in Latin America received amnesty or remained sheltered by civilian governments. In many countries democracy was still new and fragile, and governments (Argentina, Chile, Peru, Uruguay, El Salvador, and Guatemala) feared that revisiting the horrors of the past would antagonize the military, invite political destabilization, and impede reconciliation. Still, across the region many egregious crimes came to light and were denounced as torture and genocide by publics at home and abroad. And although the armed forces remained influential across Central America and the Andes, the governments of both Argentina and Chile made significant strides in reducing the military's role in politics. In Venezuela, however, the Bolivarian, populist revolution of Hugo Chávez, who was twice democratically elected, followed a distinct path of semidemocratic (or in the view of some, semiauthoritarian) rule, heavily reliant on a loyal military cadre and peoples' militias.

Since 2000, vigorous and effective grassroots activism has represented a significant development in the region's progress toward comprehensive democratization. Popular social movements, assisted by European and North American nongovernmental organizations (NGOs), have organized successful campaigns to expand socioeconomic, civil, and citizenship rights across the hemisphere. A stronger civil society has been able to challenge unpopular state policies, such as privatization and neoliberal reforms, and revitalize state-directed socioeconomic development and welfare programs.

There have been impressive milestones in empowering indigenous peoples and women as well. In Ecuador a national indigenous movement—the strongest in Latin America—and its powerful indigenous-based political party mobilized some 80 percent of the country's indigenous citizens to help elect a president in 2002 and win seats for indigenous party activists in the cabinet. In 2005 an unprecedented indigenous ascent to national power occurred in Bolivia, a change arguably akin to the historic election of Nelson Mandela in postapartheid South Africa. Bolivian voters elected the country's and the Andean region's first president of Indian heritage, Evo Morales Aima, in an overwhelming mandate for democratic reform and inclusion. In 2006, Chileans elected socialist Michelle Bachelet, their first woman president—a historical first, paralleling the election of Ellen Johnson Sirleaf in Liberia, the first woman president in all of Africa. Both women, who shared a legacy of bloodshed and oppression, had become symbols of national reconciliation and democratization. In Chile and Liberia, voters seemed to believe that a woman as president could best help heal the wounds of years of violence and dictatorship. Because these leaders represented underprivileged, subordinated, and marginalized groups, their elections advanced democratic participation at home and promised greater political and social inclusiveness in the region as a whole.

Constitutional reforms and decentralization and municipalization laws, which were enacted in a number of countries across the region in the 1990s, have been indispensable to the ability of marginalized groups, especially in Ecuador and Bolivia, both to run candidates in local and national elections and to win office and cabinet seats. Decentralization has allowed financially limited political actors, such as women and indigenous organizations, to compete at the local and regional levels. In many cases new electoral laws facilitated the electoral participation of social movements and indigenous communities that were not official political parties and simplified the registration of those that were. Moreover, in many countries electoral reforms proportioned seats along ethnic and gender lines, guaranteeing a more diversified representation for the citizenry.

Although the rise of indigenous movements in Latin America began in the 1970s and 1980s, only recently has indigenous identity been politicized and utilized to form political parties, win elections, and advance an indigenous rights agenda. Ethnic parties in Latin America are changing the face of democracy. Further political decentralization in the region will continue to challenge, redefine, and expand the meaning and practice of democratic citizenship. In turn, the steady empowerment of the underprivileged and subordinated groups of Latin America has served to make national and regional struggles for democracy and justice globally visible.

The devolution of power to local and regional government and the reform of the central state's relations with civil society, especially below the national level, continues to be important to the expansion of democratic governance in Latin America as well as a focus of contention. Proponents believe that decentralization will make government more accountable; equalize access to citizenship rights; increase citizen engagement in the political process; and reverse the traditional exclusion of women, minorities, and ethnic groups. However, decentralization can also undermine democratic governance by increasing the influence of regional elites, fragmenting the national political community, and introducing new inequalities in the distribution of revenues and resources.

Today, the majority of Latin American countries have achieved minimal or partial civil liberties. A greater number of governments than in the past now guarantee extensive civil liberties or freedom from exploitation, social coercion, and violence, particularly from paramilitary groups and organized crime.

The persistence and longevity of democratic governments have also increased in Latin America, in contrast to the African experience. None of the nineteen governments that were electoral democracies in 2000 have reverted to authoritarian rule. Of the region's four older democracies—Costa Rica, Colombia, the Dominican Republic, and Venezuela—only Venezuela, in 1999, became a semidemocracy. In the more recent democracies—Argentina, Bolivia, Brazil, Chile, Mexico, Peru, and Uruguay—respect for human rights and civil liberties have increased and more participatory elections have taken hold. However one defines democracy, there is more of it in Latin America today than there was two decades ago.

As a region, Latin America's peoples have embraced democracy and the majority of governments have continued along the challenging path of democratization. Elections, especially of populist, left-leaning, and socialist candidates across the region, have helped to diffuse some of the growing popular discontent and frustration at the lack of economic development and chronic poverty. In some countries—Argentina in 2001 and Bolivia in 2003 and 2004—various forms of "street" democracy and

"direct" democracy, such as mass demonstrations, protests, strikes, and roadblocks, have erupted into civil violence and brought down presidents. Generally, however, the frustration has been directed not at incumbent leaders alone, but at political parties, legislatures, political systems, and unpopular social and economic policies.

Ironically, the expansion of democracy in the region, which has rapidly mobilized more groups into politics, has also increased the danger of political and social instability in the short term. Democratization also brought with it demands for greater national sovereignty and autonomy from external influences and pressures, primarily the United States and the International Monetary Fund. Indeed, as Latin America matures and develops a stronger and deeper democratic tradition, it becomes more likely that its relations with the United States will be contentious.

Waltraud Q. Morales

See also: Aristide, Jean-Bertrand; Bolivia; Cold War; Castro Ruz, Fidel; Cuba; Democracy, African; Duvalier, François; Duvalier, Jean-Claude; Ethnicity; Haiti; Insurgency and Counterinsurgency; International Monetary Fund; Mandela, Nelson; Socialism; Truth and Reconciliation Commissions

References
Blake, Charles H. *Politics in Latin America: The Quest for Development, Liberty, and Governance.* New York: Houghton Mifflin, 2005.
Huntington, Samuel P. *The Third Wave: Democratization in the Late Twentieth Century.* Norman: University of Oklahoma Press, 1991.
Polgreen, Lydia, and Larry Rohter. "Where Political Clout Demands a Maternal Touch." *New York Times,* January 22, 2006.
Smith, Peter H. *Democracy in Latin America: Political Change in Comparative Perspective.* New York: Oxford University Press, 2005.

Tulchin, Joseph S., and Andrew Selee, eds. *Decentralization and Democratic Governance in Latin America.* Washington, DC: Woodrow Wilson Center for Scholars, 2004.

Van Cott, Donna Lee. *From Movements to Parties in Latin America: The Evolution of Ethnic Politics.* New York: Cambridge University Press, 2005.

Yashar, Deborah J. *Contesting Citizenship in Latin America: The Rise of Indigenous Movements and the Postliberal Challenge.* New York: Cambridge University Press, 2005.

DENVER AFRICAN EXPEDITION

The Denver African Expedition was an early-twentieth-century anthropological safari traveling from South Africa to the Mandated Territory of South West Africa to study the Bushmen. This 1925 expedition was typical of an emerging genre of "popular anthropology" safari expeditions. It traveled from Cape Town up to South West Africa. Inspired by the discovery of the 500,000-year-old Taung skull, the expedition planned to find the "missing link" and to "capture" some wild Bushmen and bring them back to the United States but eventually settled for attempting to make a film and taking many photographs.

The expedition was organized by a self-styled "doctor," C. Ernest Cadle, a South African who had gone to the United States to become a clergyman but found that showmanship was more lucrative. In this regard he was emulating other white South Africans who marketed themselves as Africa experts, including Fritz Duquesne (who advised Teddy Roosevelt on his African safari). Sponsored by some sixteen businessmen and the *Denver Post,*

the expedition consisted of Cadle; Paul Hoefler, a cinematographer-journalist at the *Denver Post*; and Grant John, a wealthy Denver physician. In Cape Town they were joined by their guide, Donald Bain, and the pioneering professional archaeologist A. J. Goodwin, who accompanied them for the first part of their expedition.

From Windhoek they traveled to Kaokveld, which did not produce much of interest except for some good hunting. In the Etosha Game Reserve they spent a few months filming the so-called Heikum, or Hei-om Bushmen or San. They arranged what they maintained was the largest group of Bushmen ever to assemble. These people, they claimed, had never seen or been seen by Europeans. However, later research showed that all these ostensibly "wild" Bushmen had a long history of rural proletarianization by Europeans. Hoefler took a series of some 500 sepia-tinted photographs while working on a movie entitled *The Bushman,* which premiered in May 1926, less than a month after the return of the Safari participants to Denver. It was not a striking success, and the relationship among them dissolved in a rancor of bickering, largely about finances and control of the images. Most of the footage was overexposed, and the "talkies," sound film, had just made its appearance and had begun to replace the silent film market, which meant that Cadle had to resort to using the film on lecture tours.

The significance of this minor expedition, however, lies elsewhere. It provides important insights into the zeitgeist of the era, and its still photographs, ostensibly of "wild" Bushmen, were slickly and successfully marketed and incorporated in some of the most popular social studies textbooks used in the United States, thus contributing to the stereotype of "wild" Bushmen skilled at camouflage and hunting. While Cadle vanished into obscurity, Hoefler launched into a successful career as an "educational" filmmaker, producing propaganda films for the South African regime. Bain achieved prominence in 1936, when he brought a troupe of the last surviving South Africa Bushmen to the Empire Exhibition in Johannesburg. The Bushmen had been expelled from their domicile with the declaration of their land as a game reserve. His purpose was to focus attention on their plight and to move the public and government to support them. Regrettably, he failed.

Robert Gordon

See also: Exploration and Explorers, Africa; South Africa, History and Politics

Reference

Gordon, Robert J. *Picturing Bushmen: The Denver African Expedition of 1925.* Athens: Ohio University Press, 1997.

DESSALINES, JEAN JACQUES (1758–1806)

Jean Jacques Dessalines was a participant in the Haitian Revolution and the first emperor of independent Haiti's South. On January 1, 1804, he declared Saint Domingue independent of French rule and gave it the indigenous name Haiti. Dessalines was a complicated figure, historically both revered and reviled. He was born a slave in 1758 in Cormiers, Grande-Rivière-du-Nord, and fought under Toussaint Louverture; following the latter's imprisonment by the French, Dessalines and the mulatto leader André Rigaud together secured independence. As Emperor Jacques I, the semi-illiterate Dessalines set about establishing

Marble bust of Jean Jacques Dessalines, one of the leaders of the Haitian Revolution and the first ruler of an independent Haiti. (Library of Congress)

a new state: he instituted forced agricultural labor, forbade whites from owning property, taxed highly, and expropriated land from free blacks and the fleeing French. Dessalines soon undertook a systematic massacre of the French but spared a Polish regiment that had fought for independence as well as French priests, doctors, and artisans. These stayed on, sheltered by the 1805 constitution's unprecedented step of proclaiming all Haitians black, regardless of skin color.

Dessalines valued relations with other nations, both economic and political. He opened commerce with Britain, Jamaica, and the United States and, cognizant of Haiti's example to other enslaved peoples, offered money to divert U.S.-bound slaves to his state. He invaded the neighboring Santo Domingo in 1805 to abolish slavery and voiced hope that "a spark" from Haiti would leap to nearby Martinique. Dessalines's influence was felt in Cuba, too, where paintings of "Salinas" (Dessalines) circulated. However, fearing invasion, Dessalines warned Haitians against propagandizing abroad. Ultimately, his harsh rule and high taxes alienated many, especially southern mulattos, and en route to quash an 1806 insurrection, Dessalines was ambushed at Pont-Rouge and assassinated.

Rachel Price

See also: Christophe, Henri; Haiti; Louverture, Toussaint Bréda

References

Fischer, Sibylle. *Modernity Disavowed: Haiti and the Cultures of Slavery in the Age of Revolution.* Durham, NC: Duke University Press, 2004.

Gaspar, David Barry, and David Patrick Geggus. *A Turbulent Time: The French Revolution and the Greater Caribbean.* Bloomington: Indiana University Press, 1997.

James, C. L. R. *The Black Jacobins: Toussaint L'Ouverture and the San Domingo Revolution.* 2nd ed. New York: Vintage Books, 1963.

Pascal-Trouillot, Ertha, and Ernst Trouillot. *Encyclopédie Biographique d'Haïti.* Montreal, QC: Editions SEMIS, 2001.

DIAMONDS

Valued both as gemstones and for their industrial uses, including as drill bits, diamonds have long been mined and traded in Africa. When they are bought and sold in order to purchase arms and fund internal violent conflicts, such as civil wars in Sierra Leone and Libera, these diamonds have become known as "conflict diamonds."

Until the discovery of diamonds in Minas Gerais, Brazil (1720s), most diamonds had come from alluvial deposits in India and Kalimantan (Borneo). Brazil's diamonds were discovered by the *bandeirantes* (explorers). The discovery changed Brazil, as people and economic power shifted away from the coast and to the southern and central parts of the country. African slaves were quickly put to work in diamond mining for the Portuguese government's royal monopoly. The slaves who survived added an African flavor to Brazilian music, religion, and culture. From 1730 until 1870 Brazil supplied the world with gemstone quality diamonds. In the late 1800s diamonds were found in Venezuela and Guyana.

Diamonds were found in 1867 in the Cape Colony of southern Africa. At first the diamonds were taken from alluvial deposits. However, they soon were mined from blue kimberlite, found in ancient volcanic pipes located near the mining town of Kimberly. In 1888 Cecil John Rhodes formed De Beers Consolidated Mines Ltd. to control the vast production flowing from the African diamond fields.

During the late nineteenth and early twentieth centuries, the growing supply of diamonds interacted with the rising prosperity of both Europe and the United States to stimulate the demand for diamonds both for industrial uses and for gemstones as gifts. The hunt for diamonds led to numerous discoveries across Africa. Diamonds were found in 1908 in the German colony of Kolmanskop (later South West Africa, now Namibia) and in the 1930s in Sierra Leone. Today the world's richest diamond mine is in Botswana at the the Jwaneng mine. Major diamond-producing countries on the African continent are the Democratic Republic of the Congo (formerly Zaire), Botswana, South Africa, Angola, Namibia,

Miners pan for diamonds near Koidu in northeastern Sierra Leone in 2004. During the country's 1991–2001 civil war, civilians were used as slaves to mine the diamonds that funded the rebels' wartime efforts. Even with the end of the civil war in 2001, the diamond industry continues to struggle toward reducing the number of so-called conflict diamonds that enter the foreign market. (AP/Wide World Photos)

Ghana, Central African Republic, Guinea, Sierra Leone, and Zimbabwe.

The instability and ethnic violence in Africa after the end of colonialism led, by the 1990s, to trafficking in conflict diamonds taken from mines, a trade dominated by criminal gangs and terrorist groups. Many innocent people in diamond-mining areas were killed or deliberately mutilated. The armed bands entered a diamond-producing area and deliberately chopped off a hand or a foot of men, women, and children to brutalize the people of the area so they would be psychologically as well as physically unable to resist or even to flee. The diamonds produced in these areas became blood or conflict diamonds. In Sierra Leone, the so-called Revolutionary United Front (RUF) was able to control much of the diamond-producing area, purchasing weapons with its diamond profits.

Terrorist groups, including Al Qaeda, became financially involved in the diamond trade. Great profits were made from rough diamonds transported by terrorists to diamond centers for cutting and polishing before emerging into legitimate market streams. The U.S. government, although aware of the fact of Islamic terrorist trafficking in conflict diamonds, did little about it until after the terrorist attacks of September 11, 2001.

In November 2002 a global movement among nongovernmental organizations (NGOs) and other activists pressured the diamond industry and the governments of diamond-producing countries to take action on conflict diamonds. After a meeting in Kimberly, South Africa, the Kimberley Certification Process Scheme was adopted. In August 2003 the Kimberly Process, a joint government, international diamond industry, and civil society initiative for stemming the flow of conflict diamonds, was instituted.

The Kimberly Process has forty-three participants—including the European Community, Canada, Russia, and the African diamond producers. The participants in the Kimberly Process control an estimated 99.8 percent of the global production of rough diamonds. Part of the process is the development of a certification by diamond sellers that their diamonds are not conflict diamonds.

Many NGOs charge that the Kimberly Process is not working because it depends too much upon self-regulation. By 2006 nearly four million Africans in Sierra Leone, Liberia, Angola, and the Democratic Republic of the Congo had been killed because of conflict diamonds. The International Criminal Court is seeking to prosecute war lords, gunrunners, and corporate executives selling conflict diamonds as war criminals and purchasers with involvement in genocide.

Andrew J. Waskey

See also: Brazil; Ghana; Kongo; Sierra Leone; South Africa, History and Politics; Zimbabwe

References

Bernstein, Harry. *The Brazilian Diamond in Contracts, Contraband, and Capital.* Lanham, MD: University Press of America, 1986.

Campbell, Greg. *Blood Diamonds: Tracing the Deadly Path of the World's Most Precious Stones.* Cambridge, MA: Westview Press, 2004.

Farah, Douglas. *Blood from Stones: The Secret Financial Network of Terror.* New York: Broadway Books, 2004.

Fry, Carolyn. "Conflict Diamonds." *Times Educational Supplement.* May 27, 2005.

Kanfer, Stefan. *Last Empire: De Beers, Diamonds, and the World.* New York: Farrar, Straus, Giroux, 1993.

DIASPORA

"Diaspora" is a term describing mass migrations of people, forced and voluntary. Africa and the Americas have each been defined by such mass migrations of both kinds. Both regions host as well as generate diasporas. Yet it is important to distinguish diasporas from other waves of migration. The original Greek term meant dispersion and described mainly voluntary colonization. However, it soon came to refer particularly to the scattering of Jews following exile from Babylon; only in the past century has "diaspora" been used to refer to a wider variety of dispersed populations. For centuries connoting forcible, even catastrophic exile, diaspora more recently has come to denote sizable communities of a given people outside their "homeland"; reasons for such emigration include not only political or religious persecution but also trade or labor demands and imperial expansions. Whatever the impetus for displacement, diasporas, as opposed to other forms of migration, tend to share the following characteristics: a sense of group identity, often reinforced by exclusion from, or inability to assimilate into, the host culture; a collective memory of the group's past, particularly acute when dispersion follows a traumatic event; a desire to transmit the group's identity and traditions; and, perhaps most crucially, a myth about a homeland, to which the diaspora maintains a connection and, frequently, an expectation of return.

Diasporas often enjoy a vexed but crucial relation to their respective homelands. Committed to an abstract and often nostalgic idea or ideal of such a homeland, diasporic politics can be conservative, seeking to maintain a "pure," unchanging, or archaic culture in their homeland, often to the dismay of those who still live there. Sometimes, too, as a reaction against discrimination, fears of assimilation, or the general struggles of adapting to a new culture, cultural practices felt to be traditional are emphasized in the diaspora to a degree they would not be in the homeland itself.

Historical instances abound of diasporas aiding their homeland in times of crisis. But with the advent of globalization and augmented communication and travel between diasporic locales and homeland, diasporas increasingly wield significant and ongoing influence upon peoples and politics in the sending nations. Many sending nations respond accordingly, formally recognizing diasporas as having political and legal claims on the homeland as well. For instance, Mexico has passed several laws designed to facilitate the participation of U.S.-based Mexicans in Mexican politics. A number of nations allow for dual citizenship to facilitate participation by mobile members of their communities. Such legal and political responses are due in no small part to the role economically driven diasporas often play in sustaining the economies of the sending nations, where diasporic remittances (money sent back) in certain cases constitute the largest source of income for the homeland.

Historically, numerous diasporic communities have settled in Africa and the Americas, from South Asians in Africa to Chinese in the Americas. The region has hosted diasporas of a both classic and more recent cast. For example, already diasporic Jews, banished from Spain in 1492, found a more tolerant climate in North Africa under the caliphate. A sizable number were also among the first colonists in both North and South America. Substantial Jewish communities were later established, particularly in Argentina, Uruguay, the United States, and Canada.

Differing markedly in character, the forced migration of Africans to the Americas during the slave trade has bequeathed entire new communities of African Americans throughout the Caribbean and the Americas, but some debate exists as to whether these discrete communities together constitute a common, shared diaspora. The slave trade violently yoked together Africans from numerous ethnic groups, religions, and languages who would not have felt part of a single community, much less have identified "Africa" as their homeland (though the continent has represented a mythic homeland for twentieth-century American movements such as Pan-Africanism or Ethiopianism). In fact, multiple African diasporas exist. They began with a slave trade and forced migration across the Sahara and into the Persian Gulf area under Islamic rule in the seventh and eighth centuries. Later came the Atlantic slave trade, and today there is a more cosmopolitan, economically driven emigration to Europe and the Americas. Further, descendants of African slaves have historically engaged in little of the typically diasporic shuttling back and forth between homeland and host country, but instead have integrated, however uncomfortably, into the latter. Still, a shared history and the common experience of slavery and its aftermath in racialized cultures has generated what many scholars argue may indeed be considered a diaspora boasting certain shared cultural attributes.

As slavery was abolished throughout the Atlantic, various groups of Asians and South Asians were recruited to labor in the place of African or African American slaves. In the second half of the nineteenth century, for example, some 800,000 Chinese are estimated to have migrated to the United States, the Commonwealth nations, the West Indies, and Latin America. Much of this emigration was organized in a manner akin to indentured servitude, based on contracts stipulating that workers reimburse the price of their tickets. Some of these subsequent American communities have, with time, lost their diasporic character and been assimilated into the respective national cultures. Japanese and Indians, however, are two examples of groups that made their way to the New World (principally to Brazil and the West Indies, respectively) and that have since maintained ethnic enclaves that preserve, to some degree, language and cultural practices, as well as ties with Japan and India. The late nineteenth and first half of the twentieth century also saw massive waves of European migrants settling in the Americas, some of whom viewed themselves as members of a diasporic community; thus, one may find, for example, communities of Italian or German speakers today in Latin America. A majority, however, simply understood their transatlantic move as emigration and sought neither return to a homeland nor the upholding of religion, language, or customs, but instead assimilation to a new land.

The second half of the twentieth century witnessed catastrophes of increasing magnitude that spawned newer diasporas, many with sizable communities in the Americas. Indeed, the bulk of recent diaspora scholarship has focused on these increased movements of peoples in the post-1945 era. Like earlier immigration spurred by natural or economic disaster, today's immigrants may not exhibit all the classic criteria for diasporas but do underscore the increasing flexibility of the term.

While clinging to myths of homeland, diasporas necessarily go beyond the confines of nation-states and invite a similarly changing definition.

Rachel Price

See also: Atlantic World; Diaspora, Demography of; Falasha (Beta Israel); Pan-Africanism; Slavery (History)

References

Chaliand, Gérard, and Jean Pierre Rageau. *Penguin Atlas of Diasporas.* Translated by A. M. Berrett. New York: Penguin, 1997.

Cohen, Robert. *Global Diasporas: An Introduction.* Seattle: University of Washington Press, 1997.

Evans Braziel, Jana Mannur, and Anita Mannur, eds. *Theorizing Diaspora: A Reader.* Malden, MA: Blackwell Publishing, 2003.

Harris, Joseph E., ed. *Global Dimensions of the African Diaspora.* Washington, DC: Howard University Press, 1993.

DIASPORA, DEMOGRAPHY OF

The demography of diaspora deals with the human conditions of the African Diaspora in context. Understanding the contemporary lives of Africans and people of African descent around the Atlantic requires a detailed understanding of the demographic complexity of the African Diaspora. Overall, Africans in Africa have the lowest average life expectancy in the world and the highest death rates. However, there are some regions and countries on the continent, such as North Africa and Indian Ocean nations, that have relatively high life expectancy and low death rates. People of African descent in the Americas, on the other hand, have average life expectancy rates significantly higher than not only Africans in Africa, but also the world average. Their average death rates are also not only substantially lower than those in Africa, but also significantly lower than the world average or even the rates in developed nations. Among the many factors contributing to the low rates in life expectancy and high death rates in Africa are diseases, civil wars, hunger or famine, and lack of adequate education. As a result, the demographic data below show that geographic location might have contributed in influencing the different human conditions or well-being of the same group or race of people.

Life Expectancy and Death Rates in Africa

Africa as a whole, on average, has the lowest life expectancy and the highest death rates in the world. However, there are regional and country variations, with certain parts or countries of the continent having relatively high rates of life expectancy and low death rates.

As of 2005, out of fifty-six nations or territories in Africa, the average life expectancy at birth was 52.62 years, the lowest rate in the world. The world average in that same year was 64.33 years (males, 62.73 years, and females, 66.04 years). Of the five regions of the continent, Northern Africa had the highest rates of life expectancy, 70.77 years (68.85 years for males and 72.78 years for females), followed by Western Africa, with 52.09 years (50.51 for males and 53.73 for females); Eastern Africa, with 51.56 years (50.10 for males and 53.05 for females); 50.00 years for Middle Africa (48.59 years for males and 51.46 years for females); and Southern Africa, with 38.68 years (39.22 for males and 38.12 for females).

Nine countries had average life expectancy rates of 70 years or more, with five of them being island nations. Twelve countries had average life expectancy rates of 60 years or more, with eight of them being island nations (Cape Verde, Comoros, Mauritius, Mayottee, Reunion, Saint Helena, Sao Tome and Principe, and Seychelles). Thirty countries had life expectancy rates lower than 50 years.

The ten African nations with the highest life expectancy rates in 2005 were Saint Helena (77.76 years), Libya (76.5 years), Tunisia (74.89 years), Reunion (73.95 years), Algeria (73 years), Mauritius (72.38 years), Egypt (71 years), Morocco (70.66 years), Cape Verde (70.45 years), and Sao Tome and Principe (66.99 years).

The African nations with the lowest life expectancy rates in 2005 were Botswana (33.89 years), Swaziland (35.65 years), Angola (36:61 years), Zimbabwe (36.67 years), Lesotho (36.68 years), and Malawi (36.97 years).

There are significant differences in death rates among the regions and nations in Africa. For example, the average death rate in Africa as of 2005 was 14.76 per 1,000. The average for Northern Africa was 5.54; 14.47 for Western Africa; 14.64 for Eastern Africa; 15.29 for Middle Africa; and 23.87 for Southern Africa. The world average in 2005 was 8.78.

Of the fifty-six African nations, the life expectancy rate for females in 2005 was 75 years or more in seven of them. For another seven nations, the life expectancy rates for females were lower than 40 years.

Of the fifty-six African nations, twelve had twenty deaths or more per every 1,000. Thirteen nations had lower than ten deaths per every 1,000. The six nations with the highest death rates were Botswana (29.36), Angola (25.90), Swaziland (25.26); Lesotho (25.03); Zimbabwe (24.66); and Malawi (23.39). The six nations in Africa with the lowest death rates in 2005 were Libya (3.48), Algeria (4.6), Tunisia (5.09), Egypt (5.26), Reunion (5.48), and Morocco (5.64).

Life Expectancy and Death Rates in the Caribbean

Life expectancy rates are relatively higher in the twenty-four nations of the Caribbean than in African nations, while death rates there are relatively lower than in African nations, the world average, and a significant number of developed nations. For example, the average life expectancy in the Caribbean as of 2005 was 73.54 years (70.77 years for males and 76.04 years for females). Of the twenty-four nations in the Caribbean, only one country, Haiti, had life expectancy rates lower than 60 years (52.9 years). Twenty-two nations had life expectancy rates of 70 years or more.

The six countries with the highest average rates of life expectancy in the Caribbean in 2005 were Cayman Islands (79.95 years), Aruba (79.14 years), Martinique (79.04 years), U.S. Virgin Islands (78.91 years), Montserrat (78.71 years), and Guadeloupe (77.9 years).

In twelve of the nations in the Caribbean, the average life expectancy rates for females were 75 years or more. Seven nations had average life expectancy rates for females of 80 years or more, with one nation having average life expectancy rate of 79.65 years.

The average death rate for the twenty-four nations of the Caribbean in 2005 was 6.85 per 1,000. Only one nation, Haiti, had death rates in double figures (12.34). Sixteen nations had death rates below 7.2. Three nations had death rates below 5 deaths per 1,000. The nations with the seven lowest death rates in the Caribbean in 2005 were Turks and Caicos

Islands (4.28), British Virgin Islands (4.42), Cayman Islands (4.81), Saint Lucia (5.12), Jamaica (5.37), Anguilla (5.43), and Antigua and Barbuda (5.44).

Life Expectancy and Death Rates in Latin America

The specific life expectancy and death rates for people of black African descent for each Latin American nation are not presented separately. Still, it is worth presenting the general figures for the nations in the region.

The average life expectancy in the twenty-two nations that comprise Latin America was 71.80 years as of 2005 (69.10 years for males and 74.63 for females). Each of the countries in the region had an average life expectancy rate of at least 60 years in 2005. Seven nations had life expectancy rates of 75 years or more, with one nation having a rate of almost 75 years (74.89). In no nation was the rate for males 75 years or more. For females, two nations had rates of 80 years or more and six nations had rates of at least 79 years.

Average death rates in Latin American countries are among the lowest in the world. In 2005 the average death rate for the twenty nations of Latin America was 6.08 per 1,000. No nation in the region had death rates in double figures. In fact, only five nations had death rates of 7 or more. Seven nations had death rates that were less than 5 deaths per 1,000.

Life Expectancy and Death Rates in North America

In 2005 Bermuda's population was estimated at 65,365. In 2000 blacks comprised 54.8 percent; whites, 34.1 percent; mixed, 6.4 percent; other, 4.3 percent; and those unspecified, 0.4 percent. The life expectancy in Bermuda in 2005 was 77.79 years (75.7 years for males and 79.91 years for females). The death rate in Bermuda in 2005 was 7.63 per 1,000.

In Canada, although specific figures for blacks are not presented, average life expectancy in 2005 was estimated at 80.1 years (76.73 years for males and 83.63 years for females). Its death rate in 2005 was 7.73 years.

In the United States, as of 2005, the average life expectancy for the general population was 77.71 years (74.89 years for males and 80.67 years for females). Its death rate in 2005 was 8.25 years.

As for a breakdown of the average life expectancy of blacks in the United States, in 2002 their average life expectancy was 72.3 years (68.8 years for males and 75.6 years for females). For white Americans it was 77.7 years (75.1 years for males and 80.3 years for females) in 2002.

The statistics on the life expectancy and death rates in the regions studied reveal that geographic location plays a crucial role in determining whether a person of black African descent has relatively high life expectancy or relatively low death rates. The data show that sub-Saharan Africa, especially on the mainland, has the lowest rates of life expectancy and high death rates. The data also show that the average death rates in the Caribbean, Latin America, and a number of African nations are actually lower than those of advanced nations such as the United States and Canada and, as well, France (9.08 deaths per 1,000); Germany (10.55); Japan (8.95); Italy (10.3); and the United Kingdom (10.18).

There are many factors responsible for the unusually low life expectancy and high death rates in Africa. These factors include famine, poverty, diseases, and civil wars. For example, by the beginning of the twenty-first century, scientists had found cures or medicines for many of the diseases that once killed millions of people all across the world. However, many of these same diseases that have been eradicated in developed nations are still taking away the lives of millions of Africans. For example, in Africa, malaria infects 1 in 2 people in Malawi; tuberculosis, 1 in 263 in Botswana; measles, 1 in 431 in Botswana; and leprosy, 1 in 6,481 in Malawi. From 1999 to 2005, HIV/AIDS has killed at least 2.2 million Africans a year. From 1990 to 2007, civil wars in sub-Saharan Africa killed millions of people from Sierra Leone to Liberia, from Rwanda to the Democratic Republic of the Congo. The diseases cited above also affect people of black African descent outside of sub-Saharan Africa (in the Americas), but not at such high rates as in Africa. So the data at least reveal that geography plays a crucial role in whether a black African has high life expectancy or low death rates.

Amadu Jacky Kaba

References

Central Intelligence Agency (CIA): World Factbook. Pittsburgh, PA: Global Support Imaging and Publishing Support, 2005.

Kochanek, Kenneth D., Sherry L. Murphy, Robert N. Anderson et al. "Deaths: Final Data for 2002." *National Vital Statistics Reports* 53 (2004): 1–116.

Pratt, Cornelius B., Louisa Ha, and Charlotte A. Pratt. "Setting the Public Health Agenda on Major Diseases in Sub-Saharan Africa: African Popular Magazines and Medical Journals, 1981–1997." *Journal of Communication* 52 (2002): 889–904.

DINKA

With a population estimated at about two million, the Dinka are the largest ethnic group in the Sudan, comprising between 10 percent and 15 percent of the total population. Primarily cattle herders, the Dinka have traditionally controlled almost 40,000 square miles along the White Nile in the southern Sudan. At the center of this territory are the Bahr el Ghazal marshlands.

The Dinka have never had a formal political structure. Instead, they have been organized into almost two dozen major clans defined by a complex system of kinship ties. This organization has served them well throughout most of their history. It has long enabled them to maintain their territories against the incursions of neighboring black African peoples, the Nuer and the Anuak, as well as those of the Nuba Arabic peoples that have dominated the northern Sudan. In the late nineteenth century, the Dinka fiercely resisted attempts by the Ottoman Turks to subjugate them as they had subjugated most of the rest of the Nile Valley.

Traditional Dinka religious beliefs center on a supreme being named Nhialac, involve a complex hierarchy of other gods, and emphasize communication with one's ancestors. The Dinka have resisted attempts to convert them to both Islam and Christianity, though Christian missionaries have made some inroads during the recent, extended civil war between the Dinka and the Sudanese government.

In 1982 John Garang led a Dinka uprising against the Muslim-dominated, increasingly fundamentalist federal government of the Sudan. Over the subsequent quarter century, the Sudanese military has massacred thousands of Dinka in its attempt to crush the rebel Sudanese Liberation Army. Large segments of the Dinka population have been forced from their homeland into neighboring regions, and the conflict has been further complicated by the attempts of the Nuer to seize Dinka territories by force.

Martin Kich

See also: Religion (Africa); Sudan (Darfur Region)

References
Deng, Francis Mading. *The Dinka of the Sudan.* New York: Holt, Rinehart, and Winston, 1972.
Deng, Francis Mading. *The Dinka and Their Songs.* Oxford: Clarendon, 1973.
Deng, Francis Mading. *Dinka Cosmology.* London: Ithaca, 1980.
Deng, Francis Mading. *Tradition and Modernization: A Challenge for Law among the Dinka of the Sudan.* 2nd ed. New Haven, CT: Yale University Press, 1987.
Ryle, John. *Warriors of the White Nile: The Dinka.* Amsterdam: Time-Life, 1982.

DIOP, CHEIKH ANTA (1923–1987)

Cheikh Anta Diop was born in Caytu, Senegal, on December 29, 1923. As a scholar, Diop sought to restore the importance of Africans in the origins of human civilization and to counter Eurocentric historiography. His intellectual efforts were foundational to subsequent Afrocentric thought in the United States.

In his early twenties Diop traveled to Paris, France, to study physics with Frederic Joliot-Curie at the College of France. After several years he became increasingly interested in the study of African culture, linguistics, and history. As a result he expanded his studies at the Sorbonne, focusing on the social sciences. For his doctorate of letters, he relied on Greek travel descriptions, historical analysis, and linguistic data to argue in his dissertation that ancient Egyptians were black. Further, he argued that Egyptians had a distinct, autonomous culture that was not part of a Eurasian identity but a Pan-African identity. In this and subsequent work, he would speak to the cultural exchange between Egypt and parts of sub-Saharan Africa. His steering committee did not support the validity of this thesis and rejected the work in 1951. Presence Africaine published his thesis under the title, *Nations, nègres, et cultures* (Negroes, nations, and cultures) in 1954.

While studying in Paris, Diop was also heavily involved in political and intellectual endeavors. Between 1950 and 1953, he was the secretary of the political party, Rassemblement Democratique Africain (RDA; African Democratic Rally). In 1956 he participated in the Conference of Negro Writers and Artists at the Sorbonne in Paris. In 1960, the year Senegal would become independent, he published two more books, *L'Unite Culturelle de l'Afrique Noire (Cultural Unity of Black Africa)* and *L'Afrique Noire Precoloniale (Precolonial Black Africa)*. That year he also established a center for radiocarbon testing at the Institut Fondamental d'Afrique Noire (IFAN; Foundational Institute of Black Africa) in Dakar, Senegal. At the radiocarbon laboratory, he self-developed a test to examine the level of melanin in Egyptian mummies. During the next decade he would publish several more books. In 1974, *Antériorité des Civilisations Nègres (African Origins of Civilization: Myth or Reality)* was published in English. In subsequent years, several of his works would be published in English. The expanded accessibility of Diop's writings increased his global visibility.

With English translations of his works available, Diop's audience expanded. The effort to restore blacks to African history and the intellectual and political importance of African-centered research attracted many new followers. In particular, one of his most fervent supporters is an African American scholar, Molefi Asante. Born Arthur Lee Smith in Georgia, Asante changed his name to reflect his African heritage. Asante, the former director of Temple University's African American Studies Program, instituted, at Temple, the first doctoral program in African American Studies in 1987. He has published dozens of monographs and edited collections that often cite Cheikh Anta Diop.

Cheikh Anta Diop died on February 7, 1987, but various components of his research agenda continue in the United States and Senegal. Other U.S. academic followers of Professor Diop are Runoko Rashidi, Leonard Jeffries, Ivan van Sertima, and Asa Hilliard. There is a Center for Diopian Inquiry and Research on Education as Culture Transmission (DIRECT Center) at Medgar Evers College in New York.

During his lifetime, Cheikh Anta Diop received a mixed reception in Senegal. He was respected for his work at IFAN's radiocarbon lab and some of his social science scholarship. He also attracted some enemies as a high-ranking member of an opposition political party. He maintained a local newspaper, printed in Wolof, which allowed him the opportunity to share some of his ideas with a larger audience. Soon after his death, the University of Dakar was renamed the University of Cheikh Anta Diop at Dakar.

Donna A. Patterson

See also: Afrocentrism

References

Diop, Cheikh Anta. *The African Origin of Civilization.* New York: Lawrence Hill Books, 1974.

Diop, Cheikh Anta. *Civilization or Barbarism: An Authentic Anthropology.* New York: Lawrence Hill Books, 1991.

Fauvelle-Aymar, François-Xavier, Jean-Pierre Chrétien, and Claude-Hélène Perrot. *Afrocentrismes: L'histoire des africains entre Egypte et Amérique.* Paris: Karthala, 2000.

Van Sertima, Ivan. *Great African Thinkers: Cheikh Anta Diop.* Somerset, NJ: Transaction Press, 1986.

D**JEBAR**, A**SSIA** (1936–)

A leading French francophone novelist, playwright, poet, essayist, filmmaker, university-trained historian, and journalist, Assia Djebar was born Fatima Zohra Imalayen on June 30, 1936, in Cherchell, Algeria. Born and raised in French colonial Algeria in an Arabic-speaking household with Berber ancestors, she attended French colonial school, a decisive factor for her subsequent literary and academic career. Interestingly, all of her published works are written in French rather than Arabic—the language of the colonizer, or the enemy, which she refers to as the *langue adverse* (adversary language)—a fact that is widely discussed by critics as well as by the author herself. Imbued with several cultures and languages (French, North African, oral and literary Arabic, Berber, and English) and shuttling back and forth between North Africa, France, and, later on in her life and literary career, the United States (as well as Germany, where she gives readings of her books on a regular basis), Djebar is acutely aware of cultural, religious, linguistic, and gender differences, diversity, and nuances as well as the importance of history, poetry, structural rigidity, and musicality—key factors that inform her writing. Consequently, her multifaceted, hybrid, exilic literary works address topics that transcend time as well as geographical and linguistic boundaries.

Clearly, Djebar's influence and recognition, as a scholar and internationally acclaimed writer who considers herself not so much a "exilic subject" as rather a francophone voice, spans both sides of the Atlantic. Today, her work is widely read, discussed, and critiqued on both sides of the Atlantic. Djebar left her mark in the United States, where she headed the Center for French and Francophone Studies at Louisiana State University in Baton Rouge from 1995 until 2001 before moving on to New York University, where she was appointed Silver Chair and Professor for French and Francophone Literature in 2002. In the United States alone, where her work is generally included in the corpus of postcolonial literature or postcolonial French francophone literatures, over thirty doctoral dissertations focus on her literary works, which are taught at French and francophone literature departments and have been incorporated into the literary canon. Among numerous other literary honors, Djebar was awarded the Peace Prize at the Frankfurt book fair in 2000 and elected a member of the prestigious Académie Française in 2005 in recognition of her literary work.

Her collection of essays, *Ces voix qui m'assiègent* (1999; *These Voices that Besiege Me*), stresses the importance of asserting and perpetuating a francophone voice in and outside of postcolonial Algeria and the need to ensure the survival and proliferation of French francophone literatures across the globe. Similarly, *Le Blanc de l'Algérie* (1995; *Algerian White: A Narrative*) represents not only a coming to terms with death—a homage to artists, writers, and intellectuals murdered by Algerian fundamentalists in the 1990s, many of whom were close friends of the author—but certainly also serves to raise international awareness of the rising insecurity, turmoil, and extreme violence in her native country. Similarly, the short stories in *Oran, Langue morte* (1997; *Oran, Dead Language*), set alternately in France or Algeria, are further testimony of violence in Algeria of the 1990s. After a decade of literary silence in the 1970s, which was spent filming *La Nouba des femmes du Mont Chenua* (1979; *The Spree of the Women of Mount Cenua*) and *La Zerda ou les chants de l'oubli* (1982; *Zerda, or the Songs of Forgetting*), she published *Femmes d'Alger dans leur appartement* (1980; *Women of Algiers in Their Apartment*), a collection of short stories that describe the multifaceted emancipatory struggles of Algerian women to make their voices heard in a rigidly patriarchal, highly devout Muslim society, a topic she also tackles in *Ombre Sultane* (1987; *A Sister to Scheherazade*). Her predilection to intertwine fiction, autobiography, and history shines through in *La Femme sans sépulture* (2002; *Unburied Woman*), which tells the story of a female freedom fighter during the Algerian War of Liberation (1954–1962), as well as in *Loin de Médine* (1991; *Far from Medina*), a fictional history surrounding the life and death of the prophet Mohammed.

Her early works, *La Soif* (1957; *The Mischief*) and *Les Impatients* (1958), focus on domestic issues and gender relationships, describing the coming of age of young, educated Algerian bourgeois women, as do her subsequent novels, *Les Enfants du nouveau monde* (1962; *Children of the New World: A Novel of the Algerian War*) and *Les Alouettes naïves* (1967; *Foolish Birds*) which describe women's coming of age during the War of Liberation. Djebar crosses geographical and cultural borders in *Les Nuits de Strasbourg* (1997; *Strasbourg Nights*), a love story about an Algerian

woman and a Frenchman. Her later, more important works foreground the impact of colonial history on her native Algeria, showing how history—in particular colonialism, then postcolonialism—language, and religion shape definitions of selfhood, and in particular definitions of womanhood. Her later works are increasingly autobiographical, in particular *Vaste est la prison* (1995; *So Vast the Prison: A Novel*) and her 1985 masterpiece, *L'Amour, la fantasia* (*Fantasia: An Algerian Calvacade*). *L'Amour* intermingles family history with colonial history and fiction by juxtaposing and alternating fragments taken from the author's personal life and family history with accounts of the 1830 conquest of Algiers by the French and episodes from the Algerian War of Liberation. These key historic episodes are resurrected, recounted, and to a certain extent reinvented from an indigenous and feminine point of view that calls into question and undermines the "official" historiography, which is essentially a legacy of the French colonizer. Exile and the crossing of space and time are topics of her latest novel, *La Disparition de la langue française* (2003; *The Disappearance of French*), an account of a man's return to his native Algeria in early the 1990s after twenty years spent in France.

Christa Jones

References

Callegruber, Mireille, ed. *Djebar, nomade entre les murs*. Paris: Maisonneuve et la Rose, 2005.

Donadey, Anne. *Recasting Postcolonialism: Women Writing between Worlds*. Portsmouth, NH: Heinemann, 2001.

Kelly, Debra. *Autobiography and Independence: Selfhood and Creativity in North African Postcolonial Writing in French*. Liverpool, UK: Liverpool University Press, 2005.

Mortimer, Mildred. *Assia Djebar*. Philadelphia, PA: Celfan Editions Monographs, 1988.

DJIBOUTI

Located on the east coast of Africa on the Red Sea, this small country of 9,000 square miles (23,310 square kilometers) has a population of about 467,000. The French acquired the territory in 1862 and occupied it twenty-two years later. Called Obock until 1892, it became Djibouti the following year and then became the Côte français des Somalis (French Somaliland) in 1902. In 1908 a Boston-born businessman and settler, William G. "Billy" Sewall, traveled through Djibouti on a reconnaissance safari with the aim of establishing U.S. business interests in the region. Not much trade with the United States, or indeed any other parts of the Americas, resulted, mainly because so much trade at the time went through the nearby port of Aden, controlled by the British. However, some French civil servants from Djibouti served in the West Indies. The most famous was Marie François Julien Pierre-Alype, who was governor of French Somaliland from 1937 until 1939 and was then posted to the Caribbean as governor of Guadeloupe from 1939 until 1940.

Strategically located at the southern end of the Red Sea, opposite Aden, it was also an important coal bunkering station; for these reasons, it was occupied by the British in World War II. Djibouti was the major French military base in the region after World War II, its port being the mainstay of the Djibouti's wealth. In a 1958 referendum, the people voted to become an overseas territory of the French Union rather than becoming autonomous. In 1967 it was named Territoire des Afars et Issas (Territory of Afars and Isas). It became independent as the Republic of Djibouti on June 27, 1977, taking its name after the city of Djibouti, the capital, where two-thirds of the population lived. The United States has recognized the country since independence, and its first ambassador was Jerrold Martin North, who was there from 1980 until 1982. Canada's ambassador to Ethiopia was also accredited to Djibouti.

Because of its very small size and its geographical position, the Republic of Djibouti has had few connections with the Americas. However, a number of Canadians and former U.S. residents, as well as a few others from Latin America and the Caribbean, have been based there as members of the French Foreign Legion.

Antigovernment riots broke out in 1989, when many locals protested the affluence enjoyed by the small European and American population, in contrast to the poverty in much of the country; as a result, some American residents left the country. In the following year Djibouti was again in the news when it concluded a military pact with Saddam Hussein several months before the Iraqi invasion of Kuwait. As Djibouti also had a military pact with France and had just received $1.7 million from the United States, its criticisms of the U.S.-led military buildup in the Gulf caused pressure to be put on the country by the U.S. and its allies. Eventually, Djibouti allowed its port to be used by U.S. and Italian warships during the Gulf War.

The situation had normalized by 2000, when Donald Yamamoto was appointed U.S. ambassador to Djibouti. Born in Seattle and of Japanese ancestry, he was a career foreign service employee and had been deputy director for East African affairs until his appointment to Djibouti. He was subsequently appointed deputy assistant secretary of state for African affairs under George W. Bush.

Justin Corfield

See also: Ethiopia; French Empire; World War II

Reference

Alwan, Daoud A., and Yohanis Mibrathu. *Historical Dictionary of Djibouti.* Lanham, MD: Scarecrow Press, 2000.

DOE, SAMUEL K. (1951?–1990)

Samuel Kanyon Doe was the president of Liberia from 1980 until his assassination in 1990. Born in Tuzon, a small town in southeastern Liberia on May 6, 1951 (possibly later changing the year to 1950 to meet the constitutional requirement that the president be thirty-five or older), Doe became a career soldier, eventually being promoted to master sergeant in the Liberian Army in 1979. On April 12, 1980, Doe seized power in a military coup, assassinated President William R. Tolbert Jr., and established military rule, for the first time in Liberia's history, through the People's Redemption Council. The Doe regime was marked by mass executions and political repression.

Doe, whose military experiences included training by the American Green Berets, developed a close connection with the U.S. government, especially during the Reagan administration. As a combative supporter of U.S. cold war foreign policy, Doe proved a temporarily useful ally for the United States and its interests in Africa. Liberian ports were opened to North American and European ships and Doe's government enjoyed substantial foreign investment from shipping firms keen to take advantage of Liberia's growing status as a tax haven. Despite the Doe government's atrocious human rights record, Liberia, during the decade of Doe's rule, received more political and military assistance than at any time previously in the country's history.

A career soldier who seized power in a bloody coup in 1980, Samuel Doe was president of Liberia until his murder in 1990 by rebel forces. He appears during a state visit to Washington in 1982. (U.S. Department of Defense)

With the thawing of the cold war in the late 1980s, the U.S. government began to view the blatantly corrupt Doe regime as a liability, eventually canceling the foreign aid that was so crucial for Doe's capacity to maintain his rule. Already facing mounting opposition from growing popular movements of dissent, the withdrawal of aid left Doe without a primary pillar of support in the battles to come.

On December 24, 1989, a former Doe ally, Charles Taylor, entered Liberia from Côte d'Ivoire to wage a guerilla war against the faltering government. The Liberian Army quickly lost ground, and within months Liberia was controlled by a variety of rebel factions.

In August 1990 the Economic Community of West African States (ECOWAS) sent a peacekeeping force of 4,000 to Liberia. On September 9, 1990, on a visit to the peacekeeping force's headquarters in Monrovia, Doe was captured, tortured, and killed by Prince Y. Johnson, the leader of the Independent National Patriotic Front of Liberia, which had previously split from Taylor's National Patriotic Front of Liberia.

Jeff Shantz

References

Brehun, Leonard. *Liberia: The War of Horror*. Accra, Ghana: Adwinsa Publications, 1991.

Ellis, Stephen. *The Mask of Anarchy: The Destruction of Liberia and the Religious Dimensions of an African Civil War*. New York: New York University Press, 1999.

Givens, Willie. *The Road to Democracy under the Leadership of Samuel Kenyon Doe: The Policies and Public Statements of Dr. Samuel K. Doe*. London: Bucks, 1986.

Wonkeryor, Edward L. *Liberia Military Dictatorship: A Fiasco Revolution*. Chicago: S.C.P. Third World Literature Publishing House, 1985.

DOMINICAN REPUBLIC, THE

The Dominican Republic shares the Caribbean island of Hispaniola with the neighboring nation of Haiti. Hispaniola was the site of the first European colony in the Western Hemisphere as well as the location of the first enslaved Africans in the Americas. While the majority of the current population is of mixed African and European ancestry, African cultural elements are often minimized or attributed to foreign influences in Dominican nationalist discourse.

After Christopher Columbus arrived on the Taino island of Ayti (also known as Quisqueya or Bohio) in 1492, he renamed it La Española (Hispaniola) in Spain's honor. The Spanish colony on the island was named Santo Domingo. In the early sixteenth century, the Spanish monarchs, King Ferdinand and Queen Isabella, authorized Fray Nicolás de Ovando, the Spanish governor of Santo Domingo, to import enslaved people of African descent. In 1502 the first large group of enslaved Africans arrived in Santo Domingo, and by 1503 a number of them had managed to escape slavery and were living outside the colonial borders as fugitives.

The majority of Africans brought to Santo Domingo came from Senegambia, Guinea, and Congo-Angolan (Bantu) areas. Escaped slaves often lived in self-sufficient Maroon communities called *manieles* or *palenques,* beyond the reach of Spanish authorities. The native Taino population had been essentially eliminated by the Spanish by 1513, and increasing numbers of enslaved Africans were forcibly transported to Santo Domingo to work in mines and later on sugar plantations.

In 1522 the first documented slave insurrection in the Americas occurred at the Nueva Isabela plantation owned by Columbus's brother Diego. By the end of the sixteenth century, gold and sugar production on the island had declined. While the plantation system that fueled the transatlantic slave trade spread to other areas in the hemisphere, Santo Domingo became a forgotten colony that depended on cattle and on contraband trade with the Dutch for economic subsistence. Many wealthy Spaniards left the island for the greener pastures of Mexico and Peru.

In an effort to consolidate power after this economic devastation, the small, outlying settlements were burned to the ground and the colonial population was forced to relocate near the capital of Santo Domingo on the southern coast in the early seventeenth century. This scorched-earth strategy of colonial reorganization resulted in further economic hardship and ushered in an era known to Dominican historians as the Century of Misery. During this century the French established a permanent colony on the western side of the island. It was not until 1777, however, that the Treaty of Aranjuez divided the island between the French colony of Saint Domingue on the western third of the island and the Spanish colony of Santo Domingo on the island's eastern twothirds.

While the French abolished slavery in Saint Domingue in 1793, it was not until 1801 that Haitian leader Toussaint Louverture abolished slavery in Santo Domingo. After the French exiled Louverture to France, slavery was reestablished on the eastern side on the island, which remained officially under French rule from 1795 to 1809. In 1809 Spain regained political control of Santo Domingo only to lose power in 1821 to a group of wealthy Dominican elites that wished to make Santo Domingo part of Simon Bolívar's Gran Colombia. After five weeks, a period known as the

Ephemeral Independence, Haitian leader Jean Pierre Boyer took control of Santo Domingo and again abolished slavery. A new independence movement named La Trinitaria and organized by Juan Pablo Duarte led to the establishment of the Dominican Republic as an independent nation on February 27, 1844. In 1861, however, the Dominican general Pedro Santana returned the country to its former colonial status by annexing it to Spain.

The Afro-Dominican patriot Francisco Sánchez, who had been a member of Duarte's independence movement, was executed in 1861 for rebelling against Santana. The Haitian government gave the Dominican rebels weapons, food, and other material support in their fight to reestablish Dominican independence and put an end to European rule on the island of Hispaniola. Unlike earlier independence movements, this struggle successfully mobilized popular support and Dominicans of all backgrounds joined forces to fight in what became known as the Restoration War (1863–1865). The most prominent figure of this period was the Afro-Dominican Gregorio Luperón, a poor man from the rural north who joined the military, defeated Santana, and later became a highly respected liberal politician.

The Restoration War did not result in economic independence for the country, however. The Afro-Dominican dictator Ulises Heureaux, known as Lilís, borrowed heavily from other countries to maintain control of the government from 1886 to 1899. In 1905 the United States assumed financial control of the Dominican Republic, and from 1916 to 1924, U.S. Marines occupied the entire country. During the occupation the messianic Afro-Dominican spiritual leader Liborio was killed. Forty years after Liborio's death in 1922, his followers regrouped as the Palma Sola Movement and were again violently repressed by military authorities. Following the departure of U.S. forces, General Rafael Leónidas Trujillo, a recruit trained by the U.S. Marines during their occupation, assumed military control of the country and maintained an authoritarian rule either directly or through puppet presidents from 1930 to 1961. In 1937 Trujillo ordered the ethnic cleansing of Haitians living in the border region of the Dominican Republic near Haiti in an effort to whiten the Dominican Republic and rid it of African influences. Thousands of Haitians and many black Dominicans were murdered in what became an international scandal. Censorship and repression under the Trujillo dictatorship prevented reliable information about the massacre from circulating within the Dominican Republic. Trujillo promoted an erroneous official version of events in which Dominican peasants supposedly murdered Haitians in spontaneous acts of anger directed at Haitians for illegally crossing into the Dominican Republic.

The racist campaign to whiten the nation and promote a Hispanic Dominican identity gave rise to the modern ideology of anti-Haitianism promoted by prominent Dominican intellectuals such as Joaquín Balaguer and Manuel Arturo Peña Batlle. After the assassination of Trujillo in 1961, Juan Bosch was elected president in the first democratic election held in decades. Seven months after his election, Bosch was forced into exile in a coup organized by a coalition of Dominican elites. A countercoup sought to bring him back to the presidency, but the U.S. military occupied the island in 1965, preventing Bosch from reassuming his position.

From 1966 to 1974 and then again from 1986 to 1996, the country was governed by President Joaquín Balaguer. Balaguer, who had been a puppet president under Trujillo, was also one of the chief ideologues of anti-Haitianism. In 1996 Balaguer formed the National Patriotic Front (FPN), joining with former political enemies to prevent the black politician Francisco Peña Gomez from winning the presidency. The National Patriotic Front promoted the idea that blackness was foreign to Dominican identity and that the only patriotic way of voting was to oppose the supposedly foreign elements represented by Peña Gomez. The beneficiary of Balaguer's Patriotic Front was the mixed race-candidate of the Dominican Liberation Party (PLD), Leonel Fernández; he held the presidency from 1996 to 2000 and was reelected in 2004 for the term ending in 2008.

Despite its troubled history of racial and ethnic prejudice, the Dominican Republic preserves considerable African influences. Musical instruments such as the *palos* and *atabales,* African rhythms, folklore, the syncretic religious practices of Dominican vodú (Voodoo), religious *cofradías* (brotherhoods), the *gagá* ceremonies in the *bateyes* (sugarcane settlements), and the creolization of language, cuisine, and musical styles all testify to a strongly African-influenced cultural heritage. Descendants of freed U.S. slaves, Haitians, and immigrants from English-speaking Caribbean islands have also contributed to African influences in the Dominican Republic, particularly on the eastern peninsula of Samaná.

It is telling that the grounds of the *Museo del Hombre Dominicano (Museum of the Dominican Man)* originally had only two statues to symbolize the nation's legacy of cultural encounter when the museum was established in 1973: a statue of the Spanish clergyman Bartolomé de las Casas and a statue of the Taino cacique, Enriquillo. Today, however, the museum also boasts a statue of the African leader of a slave insurrection, Sebastián Lemba. Heightened interest in Afro-Dominican history and its legacy is also visible in the work of contemporary scholars and artists. The writing of Afro-Dominican author Blas Jiménez and the music of Luis "Terror" Díaz and Xiomara Fortuna are examples of Dominican cultural production that incorporates Afro-Dominican elements.

El Movimiento de Mujeres Dominico-Hatiana (MUDHA; The Dominican-Haitian Women's Movement), a nongovernmental organization founded in 1995 and based in Santo Domingo, challenges ongoing racial, ethnic, and gender discrimination in the Dominican Republic. While the recent increase in attention to the rich legacy of African influences in the Dominican Republic bodes well for the future, this growing awareness of African contributions to Dominican history, culture, and society has not yet freed Dominican society of all prejudice.

Sara Armengot

References

Brandon, George. "African Religious Influences in Cuba, Puerto Rico, and Hispaniola." *Journal of Caribbean Studies* 7, nos. 2–3 (Winter 1989–Spring 1990): 201–231.

Davis, Martha Ellen. "Music and Black Ethnicity in the Dominican Republic." In *Music and Black Ethnicity: The Caribbean and South America,* edited by Gerard H. Béhague. New Brunswick, NJ: Transaction, 1994.

Howard, David John. *Coloring the Nation: Race and Ethnicity in the Dominican Republic.* Boulder, CO: Lynne Rienner Publishers, 2001.

Lipski, John M. "Creole-to-Creole Contacts in the Spanish Caribbean: The Genesis of Afro-Hispanic Language." *PALARA: Publication of the Afro-Latin/American Research Association* 3 (1999): 5–46.

Sagás, Ernesto. *Race and Politics in the Dominican Republic.* Gainesville: University Press of Florida, 2000.

Stinchcomb, Dawn F. *The Development of Literary Blackness in the Dominican Republic.* Gainesville: University Press of Florida, 2004.

Torres-Saillant, Silvio. "The Tribulations of Blackness: Stages in Dominican Racial Identity." *Callaloo* 23, no. 3 (2000): 1086–1111.

DONGALA, EMMANUEL BOUNDZEKI (1941–)

Congolese (Brazzaville) novelist, poet, and playwright, Chevalier des Arts et des Lettres, and leading chemistry scholar Emmanuel Boundzeki Dongala was born in Alindao on July 16, 1941. His father was a missionary-trained schoolteacher, and his mother was from the Central African Republic. Dongala went to study for a master of science degree at Oberlin College, Ohio, in the United States, with a Ford Foundation scholarship in 1959. There he discovered British and American literature and met the novelist Philip Roth. He later got a PhD degree from the University of Montpellier in France. In 1979 he returned to Congo, joined the staff of the University of Brazzaville, and was appointed head of the Chemistry Department in 1981, then dean of academic affairs in 1985. He founded the Théatre de l'éclair, one of the best-known theater companies in Congo, in 1981. In 1997 he left the country and relocated to the United States, where he is currently a professor of chemistry and francophone African literature at

Simon's Rock College of Bard in Great Barrington, Massachusetts.

Dongala belongs to a new generation of novelists speaking for a war-torn continent, and he won the prestigious Fonlon-Nichols Prize in 2003 for literary excellence in the defense of human rights. In 1999 he was awarded a Guggenheim Fellowship to begin work on his fourth novel. His novels and short stories have received numerous awards, in addition to the Fonlon-Nichols Prize: the Ladislas-Dormandi Prize; the Grand Prix Littéraire de l'Afrique Noire (1998); and the Prix RFI-Temoin du Monde (1999). His works have been translated into several languages, including Danish, Dutch, English, German, Hungarian, Norwegian, Portuguese, and Spanish.

Francoise Parent Ugochukwa

See also: Goyemide, Etienne; Kongo

References

Dongala, Emmanuel Boundzeki. *The Fires of Origins: A Novel.* Chicago: Lawrence Hill Books, 2003.

Thomas, Dominic. *Nation-Building, Propaganda, and Literature in Francophone Africa.* Bloomington: Indiana University Press, 2002.

DOUGLASS, FREDERICK (1818–1895)

Frederick Douglass was a leading African American abolitionist, orator, writer, and activist for women's and African American rights. He was also a newspaper editor and diplomat. A race leader, Frederick Douglass rejected pseudoscientific concepts of racial hierarchy and purity and worked tirelessly throughout his life to promote social justice in the United States. Douglass also lectured on social justice in the United Kingdom, France, Italy, Egypt, and Greece and held diplomatic positions in Haiti and the Dominican Republic.

Douglass was born Frederick Augustus Washington Bailey on a plantation in Tuckahoe, Maryland, to Harriet Bailey, a slave, and an unidentified white man. Douglass was raised by his maternal grandparents and had little contact with his mother. After her death Douglass was sent to Baltimore, Maryland, in 1826 where he lived for seven years and worked at a shipyard. In 1838, under the assumed name Frederick Johnson, Douglass escaped from Maryland by taking a train to New York City, where he was assisted by members of the Underground Railroad. In the North, Douglass married his fiancée Anna Murray, whom he had met in Baltimore previously and with whom he would have five children. They moved to New Bedford, Massachusetts, where he changed his surname from Bailey to Douglass.

In 1841 Douglass spoke for the Massachusetts Antislavery Society, beginning a long and illustrious career as an orator. His first autobiography, *Narrative of the Life of Frederick Douglass, An American Slave, Written by Himself* (1845), was an immediate success. Shortly after its publication, Douglass accepted an overseas speaking tour and began lecturing at abolitionist meetings in England, Ireland, Scotland, and Wales. After returning to the United States, Douglass moved to Rochester, New York, where he founded his weekly newspaper, *The North Star,* in 1847. Douglass's editorial efforts made his newspapers, including *The North Star* and later *Douglass' Monthly,* the most successful black newspapers of the period.

In 1854 Douglass argued in "Claims of the Negro Ethnologically Understood" that

European and American civilization is derived from that of ancient Egyptians who had the same skin color as the black population of the United States. In this essay Douglass powerfully refuted popular racist claims that Africa and blackness were connected to backwardness and lack of culture. Douglass's second autobiography, *My Bondage and My Freedom* (1855), again draws comparison between ancient Egyptians and black Americans. In this text, as well as in the first and second editions of his final autobiography, *The Life and Times of Frederick Douglass* (1881, 1892), he identifies the physiognomy of the ancient Egyptian pharaoh, Ramses II, with that of his mother.

In 1871 Douglass was named assistant secretary of the Santo Domingo Commission by President Ulysses S. Grant. He accompanied three commissioners on their tour of the Dominican Republic and approved Grant's plan to annex the Caribbean country before resigning his position later that year. After the death of his first wife and his subsequent marriage to Helen Pitts, Douglass toured England, France, Italy, Egypt, and Greece from 1886 to 1887. While his meeting with Haitian university students in Paris impressed him greatly, his autobiographies emphasize his experiences in Italy and Egypt. Through his travels he developed a narrative of the racially mixed origins of all civilizations and maintained the impossibility of adequately categorizing humanity into distinct biological races.

In 1889 Douglass was appointed U.S. minister to Haiti and American chargé d'affaires for the Dominican Republic. He was criticized by white U.S. politicians for failing to obtain a lease from Haiti to use Mole St. Nicolas as a U.S. Navy coaling station. Douglass resigned his diplomatic positions in 1891, but he denied the claims that his loyalties were with the black nation of Haiti rather than the United States, asserting only that he wanted the best for both nations. While Douglass never held another diplomatic post for the United States, the appreciation of the Haitian government was demonstrated in 1893, when he was named commissioner in charge of the Haitian Pavilion at the World's Fair in Chicago. Douglass died in 1895 of cardiac arrest.

While the time Douglass spent in Africa was brief, his written accounts of experiences in Europe and the Caribbean as well as in Egypt demonstrate the increasingly prominent position Africa came to hold in his writing. For Douglass, Africa was not a place of essential blackness or racial purity, but a dynamic crossroad of civilizations offering ample support for his lifelong struggle to promote the idea that all humanity belongs to a common race.

Sara Elizabeth Scott Armengot

See also: Abolitionism; Slave Narratives

References

Brantley, Daniel. "Black Diplomacy and Frederick Douglass' Caribbean Experiences, 1871 and 1889–1891: The Untold History." *Phlyon* 45, no. 3 (1984): 197–209.

Cheney, Michael A. "Picturing the Mother, Claiming Egypt: My Bondage and My Freedom as Auto (bio) ethnography." *African American Review* 35, no. 3 (2001): 391–408.

Levine, Robert S. "Road to Africa: Frederick Douglass's Rome." *African American Review* 34, no. 2 (2000): 217–231.

McFeely, William S. *Frederick Douglass.* New York: Norton, 1991.

Sundquist, Eric J., ed. *Frederick Douglass: New Literary and Historical Essays.* Cambridge: Cambridge University Press, 1991.

DRAMA, AFRICAN AMERICAN

African American drama incorporates social and literary practices that draw on the revaluation of African American identity and culture through racially defined cultural nationalism. The concept of Africanisms in African American art has evolved out of the pressing need for black artists to resist stereotypes and redefine artistic forms that would address the unique conditions and struggles of their people. The process emphasizes the celebration of black heroism and cultural values by tapping into ritual designs, musical and dance patterns, and themes influenced by an African worldview.

Africanisms derive from the disenchantment and deprivation that distinguish black American history from other subhistories within America. From the folk theater of the 1920s and 1930s through the revolutionary drama of the 1960s, African American dramatists have responded differently to their collective history of oppression. But they remain connected by a shared experience and heritage, with Africa providing an important cultural and artistic resource. In this regard, W. E. B. Du Bois's 1926 blueprint for black drama is timely, as it prescribed a genre that would be, "About us . . . By us . . . For us . . . Near us." (1926, p. 134). African American drama continues to evolve around the need for, means to, and implications of achieving a theater about, by, for, and near black people.

As far back as the 1800s, when black professional entertainers first appeared on the American stage, their curiosity about Africa was apparent. During this period slaves would gather in Congo Square, a large dusty space in New Orleans, where they sang, danced, and played African drums on Sundays and public holidays.

Reference to the Square as "Congo"—a region in central Africa—illustrates the connection the slaves established with their ancestry. Also, in the early 1900s, when African American performers began to respond to their century-old typecasting, suppression, and prostitution by Euro-American prejudice, they showed a fascination with African themes. For this reason, some early-twentieth-century black musicals, like *In Dahomey* (1902) and *Abyssinia* (1906), by Bert Williams and George Walker, have been described as "back-to-Africa" musicals.

When Euro-American playwrights displayed renewed interest in black themes from the end of World War I into World War II, they merely succeeded in reinscribing old stereotypes that depicted black characters as backward and ignorant. Prominent among plays that fall within this category are Ridgley Torrence's *Granny Maumee* (1914) and *The Rider of Dreams* (1917); Eugene O'Neill's *The Dreamy Kid* (1919), *The Emperor Jones* (1921), and *All God's Chillun Got Wings* (1920); and Ernest Culbertson's *Goat Alley* (1921). Others are DuBose and Dorothy Heyward's *Porgy* (1927), Jo Em Basshe's *Earth* (1927), Marc Connelly's *Green Pastures* (1930), and Paul Green's *In Abraham's Bosom* (1924). African American dramatists were subsequently stirred to negate these false images and, as in the past, they looked to Africa as a valuable counteractive resource, both culturally and artistically.

Africanisms in black drama have sometimes been realized in the re-creation of original African settings. Influenced by the revival and commemoration of African histories and traditions during the Harlem Renaissance of the 1920s, such direct delineations of Africa appeared in early pageants like Dorothy C. Guinn's *Out of the Dark* (1924) and Edward J. McCoo's *Ethiopia at the Bar of Justice* (1924), and in plays like Maud Cuney-Hare's *Antar of Araby* (1929) and Willis Richardson's *The Black Horseman* (1929). The pattern continued in the 1930s with plays like Shirley Graham's *Tom-Tom* (1932), Langston Hughes's *Emperor of Haiti* (1936), and pageants like Frances Gunner's *The Light of the Women* (1930). In later years the trend would be revisited in plays like William Branch's *A Wreath for Udomo* (1961), which is set in South Africa and focuses on the rise and fall of an African prime minister.

From pre– to post–civil rights eras (1950s to date), the increased participation of African Americans in all areas of America's socioeconomic, political, industrial, and intellectual life compelled black artists to raise new questions about the role of Africa in creativity and in the quest for identity and freedom. Inspired by civil rights struggles and the emergence of movements like the Black Arts and Black Aesthetics, African American playwrights redefined forms that not only exposed their pain and resistance, but also venerated their cultural and artistic roots. The reliance on and portrayal of African symbols became an important aesthetic weapon in the hands of a number of playwrights, such as Lorraine Hansberry (*A Raisin in the Sun* [1959], *Les Blancs* [1970]), Amiri Baraka (*Slave Ship* [1967]), and Joseph A. Walker (*Ododo* [1968]). During the 1970s, the direct exploitation of African images continued to emerge in plays like Baraka's *Bloodrites* (1971) and Ntozake Shange's *For Colored Girls . . .* (1975).

Significant to the presence of Africanisms in African American drama is the utilization of ritual prototypes. As in African ritual practice, this approach provides a cleansing and transformational role, uniting and strengthening African Americans in their struggles and solidarity. It is a trend that goes back to the early half of the twentieth century, when dramatists like Jean Toomer, Thelma Duncan, Frances Gunner, Dorothy Guinn, Hall Johnson, and W. E. B. Du Bois tapped into the concept of drama as ritual. Ritual has either been the main preserve of theater companies or has served as a fundamental aspect of plot development in traditional plays. Theater companies like Barbara Ann Teer's National Black Theatre (NBT)—founded in 1968—emphasized participatory rituals and the promotion of spirituality as a pathway to healing, and they celebrated black values through workshops in movement, dance, meditation, and spiritual release. At Brown University in the fall of 1970, George Bass and some students established a theater troupe, Rites and Reason, which was committed to performing ritual dramas. The New Lafayette Theatre, established in 1966 at the original site of the Lafayette Theatre (established in New York in 1913), also produced improvisational ritual dramas.

In black plays, ritual emerges as a sacrificial tool or as a basis for communal bonding, as is evident in the action of the freedom fighters in Hansberry's *Les Blancs,* the participatory folk song session in Hansberry's *Drinking Gourd* (1960), the women's unanimity in Shange's *For Colored Girls,* the illusionary musicians in Shange's *Boogie Woogie Landscapes* (1981), the militant soldiers in Baraka's *Experimental Death Unit #1* (1965), and the black chorus in Baraka's *Police* (1968). Similar group participation is nurtured in early pageants by Du Bois, Dorothy Guinn, and Frances Gunner and in the choral presence of religious devotees in plays by Hall Johnson, Langston Hughes, Ossie Davis, and James Baldwin.

The reinvention of black and pro-black heroes and heroines is also fundamental to the preservation of Africanisms in African American drama and becomes a foil to stereotypical black characters. Through a reaffirmation of their historic achievements, Frederick Douglas and John Brown are honored in William Branch's *In Splendid Error* (1953). Black heroes promoted in drama of the civil rights and post–civil rights periods compare with those extolled by Hughes, Randolph Edmonds, Theodore Browne, and May Miller as early as the 1930s. Such legitimate black heroes counteract characters like Othello—really a white hero in blackface—and replace submissive black characters like Uncle Tom in George Aiken's *Uncle Tom's Cabin* (1852), written shortly after Harriet Beecher Stowe's novel by the same name, and Emperor Brutus Jones in Eugene O'Neill's *The Emperor Jones* (1921). They also replace the various Coon, Sambo, Topsy, and Dandy stereotypes that were popularized by minstrel shows and which have been reshaped and reused over the years. The African freedom fighters in Hansberry's *Les Blancs* and Hannibal, the antislavery hero of Hansberry's *Drinking Gourd,* resemble Baraka's violent black revolutionaries of the 1960s, who are antiwhite, antiblack compliance, and antiblack bourgeoisie. They are also reminiscent of their forerunners: slaves who revolted on slave ships; Nat Turner, who carried out a bloody insurrection in 1831; and the slaves who took up arms with John Brown in 1859. Black heroines are portrayed in Mama in *A Raisin,* the woman dancer in *Les Blancs,* and several of Shange's

women. Symbolizing strength and defiance, like Ma Rainey in August Wilson's *Ma Rainey's Black Bottom* (1982), these women refuse to be overcome by racism and sexism.

Through Africanisms in African American drama, Africa becomes the cultural, geographical, and historical basis for the formulation of a theatrical genre that simultaneously belongs to and at the same time breaks away from mainstream American theater. Africanisms afford African American dramatists the opportunity to exemplify a commonality bound historically, culturally, and aesthetically to a shared history, myth, and theatrical legacy. They also provide a channel through which to enter into a theatrical heritage that exploits the richness of indigenous dance, song, music, history, myth, ritual, storytelling, and sermon traditions. But most of all, Africanisms allow African American dramatists to wage war against constraints imposed by European or Euro-American theatrical rules and models, which propose, define, and shape the values that are accepted as ideal and which fail to give sufficient attention to the cultural peculiarities and sociopolitical needs and concerns of African Americans.

Philip Effiong

References

Asante, Molefi Kete. *The Afrocentric Idea.* Philadelphia, PA: Temple University Press, 1987.

Baldwin, Joseph A. "African Self-Consciousness and the Mental Health of African Americans." *Journal of Black Studies* 15, no. 2 (December 1984): 177–194.

Du Bois, W. E. B. "Krigwa Players Little Negro Theatre: The Story of a Little Theatre Movement." *The Crisis,* July 1926.

Holloway, Joseph E., ed. *Africanisms in American Culture.* Bloomington: Indiana University Press, 1990.

Jahn, Janheinz. *Muntu: An Outline of Neo-African Culture.* Translated by Marjorie Grene. London: Faber and Faber, 1961.

Molette, Barbara J., and Carlton W. Molette. *Black Theatre: Premise and Presentation.* Bristol, IN: Windham Hall Press, 1986.

DRED SCOTT V. SANDFORD (1857)

Dred Scott v. Sandford was a U.S. Supreme Court case whose outcome in 1857 defined the legal status of blacks in antebellum America and challenged the role of Congress in restricting slavery in the American territories. The case was hotly disputed during the sectional crisis that led to the Civil War.

Dred Scott was a slave in Missouri who moved with his owner, Dr. John Emerson, to Illinois and then the northern territories in the 1830s. After Emerson died in 1843, Scott sued for freedom on the grounds of having lived in a free state and free territory. For the next eleven years, Scott's case bounced through the Missouri courts, where Scott won an appeal in 1850 only to have it overturned by the state supreme court in 1852. In 1854 Scott sued his new owner, the widow Emerson's brother, John Sanford, for freedom in a federal court but lost. The appeal went to the United States Supreme Court in 1856 (with Sanford's name misspelled due to a clerical error).

The case gained political significance in the dispute over slavery in the territories. The decision, issued by a 7 to 2 vote, ruled against Scott. Chief Justice Roger Taney's proslavery decision was far-reaching, as he wrote that Scott had no right to sue for freedom at all, since blacks were not, nor ever could be, U.S. citizens. Further, he ruled that Congress had no authority to prohibit slavery in the territories—overturning decades of legislative compromises,

Dred Scott v. Sandford *pamphlet advertisement. (Library of Congress)*

including the Missouri Compromise. The ruling sparked outrage among the many northerners who saw the decision as a great victory for proslavery interests. Far from settling the matter, the case increased the tension between proslavery and antislavery forces in the nation.

Ian M. Spurgeon

See also: Fugitive Slave Law

References

Fehrenbacher, Don E. *The Dred Scott Case: Its Significance in American Law and Politics.* New York: Oxford University Press, 1978.

Zarefsky, David. *Lincoln, Douglas, and Slavery: In the Crucible of Public Debate.* Chicago: University of Chicago Press, 1990.

DU BOIS, WILLIAM EDWARD BURGHARDT (1868–1963)

An African American scholar, civil rights activist, writer, and editor, W. E. B. Du Bois was a renowned intellectual and perhaps the most important civil rights figure in the United States in the first half of the twentieth century. He was a fervent advocate of the oppressed—not only African Americans but also all colored people in Africa, Asia, and Latin America. He is also regarded as the father of Pan-Africanism—a belief in the unity among blacks in and outside Africa as well as an anticolonial movement to solidify all blacks in their fight for liberty.

African American historian, W. E. B Du Bois was one of the leading intellectuals and civil rights figures of the twentieth century. His work examined the history and impact of slavery and race relations in the United States. (Library of Congress)

Du Bois was born in Great Barrington, Massachusetts, on February 23, 1868. He was valedictorian of his graduating class at—and the first black to graduate from—Great Barrington High School. Upon graduation from Fisk University as valedictorian with a BA degree in 1888, he earned a BA degree in philosophy, an MA degree in history, and a PhD degree in history at Harvard University. He was affiliated with Wilberforce University (1894–1896) and the University of Pennsylvania (1896–1897) before joining the faculty of Atlanta University as a professor of economics and history in 1897.

From then onward he dedicated his life to the advancement of African Americans through his publications, speeches, and political activism. Du Bois's book *The Philadelphia Negro: A Social Study* (1899) was the pioneering sociological research study of an urban black community in the United States. He served as a leader of the first Pan-African Conference (1900), a transatlantic meeting designed to unify all blacks and discuss issues affecting their interests. The signers of the "Address to the Nations of the World by the Races Congress in London, 1900" included four leaders of the conference: Alexander Walters, president; Henry B. Brown, vice president; H. Sylvester Williams, general secretary; and W. E. B. Du Bois, chairman of the Committee on the Address.

In *The Souls of Black Folk: Essays and Sketches* (1903), Du Bois's most celebrated book, the author theorized the doubleness of the African American identity and openly challenged the American educator Booker T. Washington concerning the road to advancement for African Americans. While Washington promoted racial accommodation, hard work, and education in improving the standing of blacks, Du Bois advocated a sustained protest against racial injustice. In the book, Du Bois also stressed the role of college-educated blacks in the struggle for civil rights. In the 1900s Du Bois was instrumental in the creation of the Niagara Movement (1905–1910) and of the National Association for the Advancement of Colored People (NAACP; 1909–).

In 1910 Du Bois left Atlanta University to serve full time as the NAACP's director of publicity and research. In 1910–1934 he also edited the NAACP magazine, *The Crisis: A Record of the Darker Races,* which covered many Pan-African issues, recommending Africa-related books, announcing conferences on African studies, and condemning racial segregation in South Africa. As editor of *The Crisis,* Du Bois is credited with uncovering and promoting talented African American writers and artists. He advocated cultural nationalism for fellow blacks, encouraging the development of writing that is both uniquely African American and universally appealing.

The early 1910s saw the publication of three books by Du Bois: *The Quest of the Silver Fleece: A Novel* (1911), a work of fiction set in Tooms County, Alabama; *The Star of Ethiopia* (1913), a theatrical production intended to promote African American history and civil rights; and *The Negro* (1915), an examination of race as a social construct. In 1919 he organized another

Pan-African Congress held in Paris, France, intentionally to coincide with the Paris Peace Conference. The Pan-African Congress was part of the transatlantic movement to represent the political and economic interests of blacks in Africa, the Caribbean islands, and the Americas. (Du Bois was also the main organizer of the Pan-African Congresses in 1921, 1923, 1927, and 1945.)

In 1920 Du Bois published *Darkwater: Voices from within the Veil,* which blended multiple literary types, including biographical essays, sketches, fiction, and lyrical poems. The author stressed the kinship of all humans in the world: they were different in appearances only; they were alike in their deep souls and in their potential for unlimited development. His next work, *The Gift of Black Folk: The Negroes in the Making of America* (1924), highlighted the many contributions African Americans made toward the formation and development of the United States.

In 1934 Du Bois returned to Atlanta University, where he chaired the Sociology Department until 1944. During this period he edited the university's quarterly, *Phylon* and wrote three books: *Black Reconstruction: An Essay toward a History of the Part Which Black Folk Played in the Attempt to Reconstruct Democracy in America, 1860–1880* (1935), a Marxist approach to the Reconstruction Era; *Black Folk, Then and Now: An Essay in the History and Sociology of the Negro Race* (1939), a historical and sociological study of the exploitation of blacks by slave traders; and *Dusk of Dawn: An Essay toward an Autobiography of a Race Concept* (1940), an exploration of race as the central issue of the United States and of the world.

In 1944–1948, Du Bois directed the NAACP Department of Special Research. At the founding conference of the United Nations in 1945, he represented the NAACP in San Francisco, California. His book *Color and Democracy: Colonies and Peace,* in which he strongly denounced imperialism, appeared in 1945. Two years later Du Bois's *The World and Africa: An Inquiry into the Part Which Africa Has Played in World History* was issued.

Disillusioned with the conservative social positions of the NAACP and with the slow progress of race relations in the United States, Du Bois left the organization for the last time in 1948, embracing Communism as his central ideology. Du Bois's later writings included *In Battle for Peace: The Story of My 83rd Birthday* (1952), a memoir about his arraignment and trial involving the Peace Information Center, an antinuclear organization. The organization was, in 1950, labeled an agent of a foreign government by the U.S. Department of Justice and, in 1951, Du Bois was charged with being a Soviet agent. Although acquitted, Du Bois remained under suspicion by the U.S. government. *The Black Flame: A Trilogy* comprised three novels embodying his gradually more radical social philosophy: *The Ordeal of Mansart* (1957), *Mansart Builds a School* (1959), and *Worlds of Color* (1961).

In the fall of 1961, at age ninety-three, Du Bois officially joined the Communist Party U.S.A. Later that year he moved to Ghana to serve as director of the *Encyclopedia Africana,* a government-sponsored project. Two years later the U.S. government refused to reissue a passport for him, alleging his Communist activities as the reason; he and his wife, Shirley Graham, renounced their American citizenship and became naturalized citizens of Ghana. Du Bois's health declined beginning in 1962; on August 27, 1963 he died in Accra, Ghana, at age ninety-five. Du Bois was given a state funeral at Christianborg Castle in Accra and was buried outside the Castle; the *Encyclopedia Africana* remained unfinished at his death.

In his lifetime, Du Bois regularly contributed essays to many periodicals, including the *Chicago Defender,* the *Pittsburgh Courier,* the *Atlantic Monthly,* the *New York Amsterdam News,* and the *San Francisco Chronicle.* His experimental creative works—such as the short story "The Coming of John" and the poem *The Song of the Smoke*—were published in the magazines he edited: the *Moon Illustrated Weekly* (1905) and the *Horizon* (1907–1910). *The Autobiography of W. E. B. Du Bois: A Soliloquy on Viewing My Life from the Last Decade of Its Final Century* came out posthumously in 1968, and *The Correspondence of W. E. B. Du Bois* was published in three volumes in 1976.

Du Bois received many honors and awards. In addition to the International Lenin Peace Prize awarded by the Soviet Union, he was awarded the Spingarn Medal from the NAACP, was made Knight Commander of the Liberian Humane Order of African Redemption, and had the rank of minister plenipotentiary and envoy extraordinary conferred upon him by President Calvin Coolidge. Du Bois was the first African American to be elected to the National Institute of Arts and Letters, and he served as a lifetime member and fellow of the American Association for the Advancement of Science.

John J. Han

See also: Crisis, The; Ghana; N'Krumah, Kwame; Niagara Movement; Pan-Africanism

References

Byerman, Keith E. *Seizing the Word: History, Art, and Self in the Work of W. E. B. Du Bois.* Athens: University of Georgia Press, 1994.

Horne, Gerald. *Black and Red: W. E. B. Du Bois and the Afro-American Response to the Cold War, 1944–1963.* Albany: State University of New York Press, 1986.

Lewis, David Levering. *W. E. B. Du Bois— Biography of a Race, 1868–1919.* New York: H. Holt, 1993.

Lewis, David Levering. *W. E. B. Du Bois: The Fight for Equality and the American Century, 1919–1963.* New York: H. Holt, 2000.

Marable, Manning. *W. E. B. DuBois, Black Radical Democrat.* Boston: Twayne, 1986.

Moore, Jack B. *W. E. B. Du Bois.* Boston: Twayne, 1981.

Rampersad, Arnold. *The Art and Imagination of W. E. B. Du Bois.* Cambridge, MA: Harvard University Press, 1976.

Reed, Adolph L., Jr. *W. E. B. Du Bois and American Political Thought: Fabianism and the Color Line.* New York: Oxford University Press, 1997.

Rudwick, Elliott M. *W. E. B. Du Bois: Propagandist of the Negro Protest.* 2nd ed. Philadelphia: University of Pennsylvania Press, 1968.

Smith, Shawn Michelle. *Photography on the Color Line: W. E. B. Du Bois, Race, and Visual Culture.* Durham, NC: Duke University Press, 2004.

DUTCH EMPIRE

The Dutch Empire spanned the globe and included New Netherlands, the Dutch Caribbean islands (currently the Dutch "overseas countries" of the Netherlands Antilles comprised of Curaçao, Bonaire, Saba, St. Eustatius, St. Maarten, and Aruba), Dutch Brazil and Suriname, the Dutch East Indies, Cape Coast in southern Africa, and parts of West Africa. Beginning in the seventeenth century, much of the Dutch colonial world was founded and governed under the monopolies of the Dutch East India Company in the Cape of Good Hope and the Pacific and the Dutch West India Company in the Americas and West Africa. Although acting on behalf of the Dutch government, these two companies exerted enormous influence over their colonial possessions. The history of the Dutch Empire is marked by its immersion in trade interests and competition with its Portuguese, Spanish, English, and other European colonial rivals over land, labor, resources, and power.

The Dutch Empire in Africa and the Americas

The Dutch Empire's links between Africa and the Americas consisted of varied historical, economic, political, and cultural connections. The Dutch presence on Cape Coast (in southern Africa) and the slave castles of the Gold Coast (now Ghana) and other parts of West Africa was evident from the sixteenth century. One of the enduring memories of the brutalities of the transatlantic slave trade rests in the ruins of the once Dutch-held Elmina slave castle on the Gold Coast. The Dutch colony of Cape Colony (at the Cape of Good Hope) was initially established in 1652 as a transshipment point en route to Asia and soon became of vital importance because of the growing Dutch trade in the East Indies. Although Cape Coast eventually fell into the hands of the British, some historians note that the introduction of slavery into the multinational Cape Colony was the first time a sizable black population was brought into the Dutch consciousness. New Netherlands (later New York), the Dutch North American colony, originally came into existence because the Englishman Henry Hudson stumbled into New York Bay in 1609 while seeking a route to Asia for the

Dutch East India Company. The West India Company purchased the island of Manhattan (New Amsterdam, within New Netherlands) from Native Americans for 60 guilders in 1626. The Dutch Caribbean islands of Curaçao and St. Eustatius initially were centers of legal and illegal trade and commerce that were used as transshipment points for African slaves to Dutch Brazil and elsewhere. Peter Stuyvesant departed from his garrison on Curaçao to become the governor of the Dutch colony of New Amsterdam in 1647. English naval superiority in the Americas resulted in the Breda Treaty of 1667, which formally granted the English possession of New Netherlands. In exchange, the Dutch took the colony of The Netherlands was among the first foreign powers to recognize the United States when it saluted the U.S. flag on St. Eustatius in 1776.

The Dutch Empire and the Transatlantic Slave Trade

The initial involvement of the Dutch in the slave trade in the late sixteenth century was unlawful under the Dutch legal norms of the day. Christian religious and secular humanist ideas prevalent in the Netherlands during this period initially made slavery an disfavored practice, but this changed over the years with increased competition amongthe European powers for economic, political, and military dominance. Although the initial activities of the Dutch were illicit because they did not have the *asiento,* or license, of the Spanish monarchy that allowed shipment of African slaves to the Americas, illegal Dutch involvement in the slave trade did not cease. When the supply of indigenous labor in the Americas proved inadequate, the West India Company solved its labor problems there with the importation of African slaves. Soon the company began to challenge Portuguese as well as Danish, Swedish, and English competitors on the West African coast for slaves. In 1637 Johan Maurits, the West India Company's governor in Dutch Brazil, captured Elmina, the Portuguese's slave castle, on the Gold Coast, and the Dutch capture of Portuguese settlements in present-day Angola and other areas of Africa soon ensued. The Dutch trading colonies stretched along some 200 miles of West African coastline and were known as Dutch Establishments on the Guinea Coast. The English ultimately ousted the Dutch from this area in 1872.

Major Dutch involvement in the slave trade began in the 1630s. The current Dutch Antillean islands of Curaçao and, later, St. Eustatius, became major slave depots for the entire Caribbean and the Americas. Most African captives in the Dutch slave trade originated from the Guinea Coast and the Bantu-speaking west-central coast of Africa and were bound for the main Dutch markets in Brazil and the Dutch Antilles. Although the Dutch lost control of their possessions in Brazil to the Portuguese in 1661, the Dutch competition with the Portuguese over sugar production had before that resulted in the West India Company's control over parts of Brazil and the mass importation of African slave labor for a period of time. The Dutch soon were also able to supply the Spanish and French with slaves for their colonies and in 1675 were able to obtain the *asiento* from Spain, although by this point it was largely unnecessary due to Spain's growing inability to control the flow of slaves into its empire. Although the Netherlands Antilles (then including Aruba) came under Dutch influence when placed under the direct authority of the West India Company in 1634, Dutch control of Suriname, as previously noted, was established with the Breda Treaty of 1667. Suriname would become the only real plantation economy under Dutch rule, with Curaçao as a main transshipment point for African slaves. Suriname and the Antilles, with the exception of Aruba, became actively involved in the slave trade. The Dutch are responsible for the transshipment of some 500,000 Africans to the Americas, approximately 5 percent of the total Atlantic slave trade. The Dutch slave trade waned and had virtually ended by 1780 because of English and French competition and lack of profitability. The final abolition of slavery was not enacted until the Emancipation of 1863, many years after abolition by Britain (1834) and France (1848) because of controversy over the compensation to be paid to former slave owners.

Dutch Colonial Administration in the Dutch Caribbean

After the Napoleonic Wars ended, the previous Republic of the Unified Netherlands was succeeded in 1815 by a Dutch kingdom, with the former republic's colonial possessions of Suriname and the Antilles in the Caribbean. Colonial rule came under the direct control of the first king, Willem I, who tried to make improvements over the previous Dutch colonial authority in the Caribbean, the West India Company. King Willem initiated a division of Dutch Caribbean colonial authority in which the Caribbean possessions were split into three divisions—Suriname, Curaçao, and the latter's dependencies—but this did not prove satisfactory, so in 1828 the Dutch colonies were reestablished in the form of a single administrative unit with a Suriname-based governor. As this did not prove effective due to the geographic distance between Suriname and the Dutch islands, in 1848 the islands of the Netherlands Antilles were separated from Suriname and, with this change, Curaçao became the administrative capital with the rest of the Dutch islands as its dependencies.

The Official End of Colonial Relations

The relations between the Netherlands and the Dutch Caribbean to the 1940s have been characterized as colonialism without a clear focus because the Dutch were primarily concerned with their prosperous colony of Indonesia in the Dutch East Indies. All Dutch colonial islands were ruled in a centralized manner up until 1951. As a consequence of a devastating colonial war resulting in the loss of Indonesia, its most prized colony, in 1949, and with the process of decolonization going on around the world, the Netherlands initiated a model decolonization process that would lead to greater autonomy for the Netherlands Antilles and Suriname.

The Charter for the Kingdom of the Netherlands of 1954 represented the official end of colonial relations. The charter of 1954 granted the Netherlands Antilles and Suriname the status of self-governing partners within the Dutch kingdom. Defense and foreign affairs remained the responsibility of the kingdom. These political arrangements have remained unchanged, except that Suriname achieved full independence in 1975, as a consequence of which, half of its population migrated to the Netherlands.

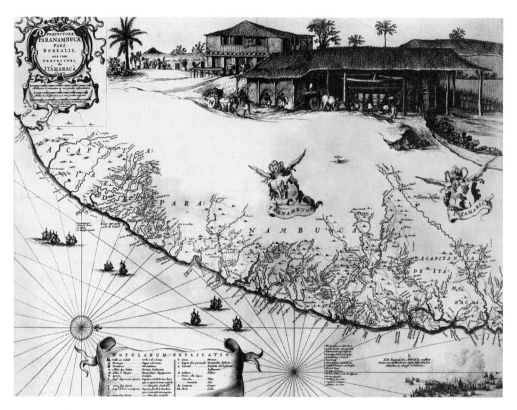

A seventeenth-century map of Pernambuco, Brazil, with a vignette of a sugar plantation. In 1630, the Dutch West India Company seized Pernambuco to control the lucrative sugar district. (Library of Congress)

The Contemporary Kingdom of the Netherlands

The remnants of the Dutch Empire with a legal connection to the Netherlands are Aruba and the Netherlands Antilles, which is a loose national construction of the five islands of Curaçao (the administrative capital), Bonaire, Saba, St. Eustatius, and St. Maarten. The Netherlands Antilles, Aruba, and the Netherlands comprise, in effect, a partnership that makes up the contemporary Kingdom of the Netherlands. The Netherlands Antilles and Aruba are Dutch overseas self-governing nations and their peoples have the right to Dutch nationality and citizenship. Defense and foreign affairs remain the kingdom's responsibility. Although Aruba was once a part of the Netherlands Antilles, it obtained *status aparte* in 1986, which granted it independence from the Netherlands Antilles. Aruba's scheduled full independence for 1996 was not implemented because a referendum in Aruba that year favored its remaining a part of the Dutch kingdom.

Oil in Aruba and Curaçao in the Twentieth Century

Oil refineries had a significant role in the economies of Aruba and Curaçao during the twentieth century. After the end of slavery, the Dutch island of Curaçao received little attention from the Dutch, and both Aruba and Curaçao received little favor for a period of time due to their limited agricultural capacities. Then, however, the discovery of oil in Lake Maracaibo, Venezuela, and the opening of the Panama Canal in the 1910s were the major catalysts for Aruba's and Curaçao's becoming economic successes. Both benefited from the establishment of oil refineries and tanker harbor installations. In the 1920s the Lago Oil Company (Esso/Exxon) and Isla Oil Company (Royal Dutch Shell) began to refine Venezuelan oil and ship it from Aruba and Curaçao to world markets. Aruba's and Curaçao's deep harbors, unlike the shallower harbors closer to the Venezuelan oil fields, were conducive to receiving large oil tankers. Additionally, the oil companies were concerned about the impact of the instability of several successive Venezuelan governments on the regional oil industry. This prompted the location of the oil refineries on the comparatively stable Dutch islands, where they were protected by the Dutch law and military. Aruba and Curaçao soon became areas of vital strategic importance.

By the 1930s, they had once again become important to the Netherlands because of the wealth produced by their oil industries. Native Dutch were sent from the Netherlands to the colonies, and, by 1936, Dutch had become the only language of instruction in the schools. As the Caribbean has been characterized by labor migration since the end of slavery, many came to take advantage of this economic opportunity. Exxon and Shell actively recruited foreign labor, including Surinamese, Colombians, Venezuelans, and persons from the Dutch and British Windward Islands, as well as Portuguese and native Dutch from the Netherlands. During World War II, Lago became a primary source for fuel and eventually the largest oil refinery in the world. Aruba and Curaçao's close proximity to Venezuelan oil and their connection to the Netherlands produced prosperity and economic emancipation.

The charter of 1954 coincided with the decline in the 1950s of the oil industry and the end of oil-sector expansion, which resulted in increasing unemployment in both Curaçao and Aruba. The majority black population of Curaçao regarded its racially segregated society and the government of the white, Protestant–led Democratic Party as a semi-dictatorship. This resulted in a revolt on May 30, 1969, in which the Netherlands intervened militarily under the terms of the charter. Although some view this as a labor revolt, others see it as a revolt against racism and oppression that resulted in Curaçao's having a black mayor and governor. Automation of the refineries and reduced employment opportunities initiated some migration from Curaçao and Aruba; then, the closing in 1985 of the oil refineries prompted a massive outmigration to the Netherlands. Subsequently, tourism was developed as a principal industry on many of the Dutch islands. In 2002 Queen Beatrix of the Netherlands made an unprecedented expression of deep regret and sorrow for the Antillean and Surinamese victims of the transatlantic slave trade at her commemoration of a national slavery monument in Oosterpark, Amsterdam. The irony is that, since authorities feared possible civil unrest or violence in the presence of the queen, only a select few people were allowed to participate in this historic event.

Michael Orlando Sharpe

See also: Caribbean Community and Common Market; Caribbean Literature; Colonialism; Oil; Slavery (History)

References

"Dit is Onze Bevrijdingsdag." *Algemeen Dagblad* (Caribbean ed., Willemstad, Curaçao), July 2, 2002.

Baker, Randall, ed. *Public Administration in Small and Island States.* West Hartford, CT: Kumarian Press, 1992.

Blakely, Allison. *Blacks in the Dutch World.* Bloomington and Indianapolis: Indiana University Press, 1993.

Koulen, Ingrid, and Gert Oostindie. *The Netherlands Antilles and Aruba: A Research Guide.* Dordrecht, Netherlands: Foris Publications Holland, 1987.

Oostindie, Gert, and Inge Klinkers. *Decolonising the Caribbean: Dutch Policies in a Comparative Perspective.* Amsterdam: Amsterdam University Press, 2003.

Postma, Johannes Menne. *The Dutch in the Atlantic Slave Trade, 1600–1815.* Cambridge: Cambridge University Press, 1990.

Sizoo, Koen. *The Netherlands and the United States: A Story of Old Friends.* Translated by Liz Berkhof. The Hague: Ministry of Foreign Affairs, 1997.

Van Hulst, Hans. "A Continuing Construction of Crisis: Antilleans, Especially Curacaoans, in the Netherlands." In *Immigrant Integration: The Dutch Case,* edited by Hans Vermeulen and Rinus Penninx. Amsterdam: Het Spinhuis, 2000.

DUTTY, BOUKMAN (?–1791)

Boukman Dutty, a Haitian slave, is best-known for taking part in the events that sparked the Haitian War of Independence (1791–1804). Boukman, a Voodoo priest born in Jamaica, lived in Saint Domingue (present-day Haiti) when the island was still a colony of France. In August 1791 Boukman took part in a Voodoo ceremony held at Bois Caïman (Alligator Wood) in northern Haiti. Aside from Boukman, participants included fellow slaves Georges Biassou, Jeannot Billet, Jean-François Papillon, and possibly Toussaint Bréda Louverture. Cécile Fatiman, a *mambo* (female Voodoo priest) and mulatto slave, supposedly slit the throat of a black pig and shared the warm blood with the other slaves. Boukman made everyone vow that they would fight against the white slave owners, exact vengeance for slavery, and accept Boukman's leadership. A tropical storm then broke out, and the participants dispersed.

Haitians usually relate the Bois Caïman ceremony as a historical event that started their war of independence, but modern scholarship suggests that details about the episode might owe more to myth than to reality. There probably was not one, but two slave gatherings, one held at the Normand de Mézy plantation in Morne Rouge on August 14, which the French uncovered by torturing slave participants, and another one in Bois Caïman held a week later, about which very little is known. According to Léon-François Hoffmann's *Haitian Fiction Revisited* (2000), details about the second meeting were invented by Antoine Dalmas in his *Histoire de la révolution de Saint-Domingue* (1793) in order to portray the slave gathering as a bloody, satanic assembly. This story was accepted unquestioningly by later historians. Some historians, with limited evidence, also argue that Boukman might have been a Muslim, not a Voodoo priest.

Following the Bois-Caïman ceremony, the slave revolt started on August 21, when most plantations surrounding Cap Français (present-day Cap Haïtien) were burnt and a thousand white Frenchmen killed. During the ensuing fighting, the French managed to capture Boukman, who was beheaded at Cap Français in November 1791. (The body was burned and the head placed on a pike.)

Philippe R. Girard

See also: Louverture, Toussaint Bréda

References

Dalmas, Antoine. *Histoire de la révolution de Saint-Domingue, depuis le commencement des troubles, jusqu'à la prise de Jérémie et du Môle St. Nicolas par les Anglais.* 2 vols. Paris: Mame Frères, 1814.

Hoffmann, Léon-François. *Haitian Fiction Revisited.* Pueblo, CO: Passeggiata Press, 2000.

James, C. L. R. *Black Jacobins: Toussaint l'Ouverture and the San Domingo Revolution.* New York: Random House, 1963.

As the president of Haiti for 14 years, François Duvalier stayed in power longer than any other Haitian president in history. He was an avid supporter of black nationalism and voodoo. (Hulton Archive/Getty Images)

DUVALIER, FRANÇOIS (1907–1971)

François Duvalier, nicknamed "Papa Doc" because he first served as a doctor, was dictator of Haiti from 1957 until his death in 1971. Duvalier was born on April 14, 1907, to a middle-class family in Port-au-Prince. His father, Duval Duvalier, was a teacher, justice of the peace, and journalist; his mother, Uritia Abraham, worked in a bakery. He attended the Lycée Pétion and then studied medicine in Haiti and at the University of Michigan. He served as assistant to the U.S. Army medical mission that worked to eliminate yaws from 1943 to 1946, then as director-general of the national public health service and as minister of health and labor under President Dumarsais Estimé.

Parallel to his medical career, Duvalier displayed growing interest in ethnology, Haitian culture, and Voodoo in particular. This reflected his and other black Haitian intellectuals' anger at the U.S. occupation of their country (1915–1934), which grew into *noirisme* (from the French *noir,* or black), a political and intellectual movement emphasizing racial pride, Haiti's African roots, and nationalism. During the 1930s he published articles on the question in the newspaper *Action Nationale* under the pen name Aberrahman. In 1938 he founded the *noiriste* review, *Les griots,* with ethnologist Jean Price-Mars and Professor Lorimer Denis.

Duvalier became politically active as well. In 1950 he denounced Paul Magloire's coup d'état and was forced into internal exile as a country doctor for the next few years. When Magloire's fall resulted in growing political instability—there were five separate governments in 1956–1957 alone—Duvalier came back into the public limelight. With the army's support, he was elected president of Haiti on September 22, 1957 and was inaugurated a month later.

The 1957 election, even though it was marked by various irregularities, was one of the most democratic in Haitian history, substantiating the claim that Duvalier enjoyed significant popular support during the early period of his tenure in office. His *noiriste* agenda had much to do with it, and Duvalier proceeded to name fellow black Haitians to prominent government jobs where mulattos had previously been over-represented. To symbolize the black under-class's new role, Duvalier changed the national flag's colors from blue and red to black and red in 1964.

Despite occasional protests over partic-ularly gruesome murders, the United States supported Duvalier's government for fear that his departure might spark a Commu-nist takeover. Although staunchly national-istic in theory, Duvalier welcomed U.S. support; a marine training mission was sent to Haiti in 1959, and Duvalier repeatedly offered to sell the country's best natural port, Mole St. Nicolas, to the U.S. Navy.

During his first few years in office, Duvalier encountered determined opposi-tion to his rule. Aerial bombing runs and terrorist attacks regularly spread panic in Haiti. In July 1958 a filibustering expedi-tion led by three Haitian exiles and five U.S. adventurers temporarily took over the capital's main army barracks. When Duvalier suffered a crippling heart attack on May 24, 1959, many surmised, wrongly as it turned out, that he would lose his grip on power. Cuban-trained Communists landed their own unsuccessful operation in August 1959. It took two months for the Haitian army to repulse a force of thirteen expatriates that landed near Jérémie in August 1964.

Always dressed in a conservative black suit and wearing bookish, thick-rimmed glasses, Duvalier was initially perceived as a weak, soft-spoken, timid country doctor. He emerged, however, as a resilient dictator

who ruled Haiti with an iron hand. Elected for a nonrenewable six-year term in 1957, he had himself reelected in a fraudulent 1961 election, then elected president-for-life in an equally fraudulent 1964 plebiscite. (His regime was the longest-lasting in Haiti at that point.)

Political repression increased following the succession of coup attempts in 1957–1959. Bypassing the Haitian army, Duvalier expanded his private security detail into a monstrous police force, nick-named Tontons Macoutes after the bogey-men of the Voodoo pantheon. These henchmen, who eventually elbowed out the Haitian army as the main enforcing arm of the government, enjoyed complete immunity as they arrested, tortured, and summarily executed Duvalier's opponents. One of the torture chambers was located next to Duvalier's private apartments, allowing him to oversee the proceedings through a hole pierced in one of the apart-ment's walls. Madame Max Adolphe, a "fillette Lalo" (female Macoute leader), made a gruesome reputation for herself as she designed inventive sexual tortures in the regime's main prison, Fort Dimanche.

An avid student of Voodoo and most likely a *houngan* (Voodoo priest) himself, Duvalier was rumored to hold supernatural powers and to rely on the regime's magical number, 22. Always clad in black, he re-minded Haitians of Baron Samedi, the Voodoo god (*loa*) in charge of guarding graves.

Political repression from 1957 onward sparked several waves of Haitian emigra-tion. In the subsequent decades, until the end of Duvalier's regime in 1971, an esti-mated 80 to 90 percent of Haiti's skilled citizens fled into exile to escape repression. As the regime focused on political control at the expense of economic development, the economy's downward spiral accelerated.

Duvalier died on April 21, 1971. Married on December 27, 1939, to Simone Ovide Faine, Duvalier had four children: Marie-Denise, Simone, Nicole, and Jean-Claude. Jean-Claude became dictator of Haiti upon his father's death and ruled until he was forced into exile in February 1986.

Philippe R. Girard

See also: Duvalier, Jean-Claude; Haiti; Noirisme; Voodoo

References

Abbott, Elizabeth. *Haiti: The Duvaliers and Their Legacy.* 1988. Reprint, New York: Simon & Schuster, 1991.

Diederich, Bernard, and Al Burt. *Papa Doc: Haiti and its Dictator.* 1969. Reprint, Maplewood, NJ: Waterfront Press, 1991.

DUVALIER, JEAN-CLAUDE (1951–)

Jean-Claude Duvalier, nicknamed "Bébé Doc" after his father, "Papa Doc," ruled as dictator of Haiti from 1971 to 1986. Duvalier was born on July 3, 1951, of dictator François Duvalier and Simone Ovide Faine. On January 22, 1971, sensing that his health was rapidly deteriorating, an aging François Duvalier announced that his son would replace him upon his death. (François Duvalier had been in power since October 1957.) The decision was ratified unanimously in a sham plebiscite, and Jean-Claude became president-for-life of Haiti when his father passed away on April 21, 1971.

When Jean-Claude Duvalier was inaugurated, many observers surmised that his tenure in office would be short—his forceful sister, Marie-Denise, seemed better equipped for the task. Duvalier had inherited little of his father's extreme cruelty and keen appetite for power. Young, overweight, round-faced, he seemed living proof that his popular nickname, Bébé (baby), was well suited. He boasted that he fell asleep every night with his textbooks, but the renowned professors whom François Duvalier had hired as private tutors for his son rectified such claims: Jean-Claude had little taste for learning and literally slept through his classes. His father had been an avid student of Haitian folklore and Voodoo. Cars, motorcycles, and women monopolized Jean-Claude's attention throughout his presidency.

Despite his personal shortcomings, Jean-Claude remained in power even longer than his father had. The police apparatus he inherited from his father, the Tontons Macoutes, remained in place, and various attempts to overthrow Jean-Claude ended in failure. A force of thirty-nine men led by exile Bernard Sansaricq failed to gain a foothold on the Haitian mainland during a January 1981 invasion; eight survivors isolated on the island of La Tortue were rounded up and executed.

By slightly lessening the political repression prevalent in his father's days, Jean-Claude was able to secure increased foreign aid, totaling $1 billion during the 1970s, much of it from the United States. Little economic growth ensued, however, for much of the aid was spirited away by the regime's top henchmen. By the late 1970s, emigration, mostly involving the skilled middle-class during François's rule, spread to the poorest segments of the population; from 1972 to 1981, the favorite destinations of the "boat people," as they were called, were Florida, Québec, the Bahamas, and the French West Indies. From May 1982 on, Haiti's pigs, central to Haiti's peasant economy, were slaughtered for fear that an epidemic of African swine fever might spread to pigs in the United States. Land erosion worsened as peasants cut down trees to sell as charcoal. An AIDS scare in the 1980s dramatically reduced tourism income. Foreign aid, representing 70 percent of the state's budget, finally declined in the 1980s because of corruption and human rights concerns. A March 1983 visit by Pope John Paul II backfired when he declared that "things have got to change here."

Initially seen as a congenial, compassionate alternative to François Duvalier, faithful to the father's popular slogans of nationalism and racial pride, Jean-Claude saw his popularity decline as the economic situation worsened and the regime displayed little sympathy for the population's woes. In 1982 Jean-Claude married Michèle Bennett in a sumptuous wedding ceremony. (Michèle, the mother of two children from a previous marriage, delivered Jean-Claude's son Nicolas on January 31, 1983.) Duvalier admirers complained that marrying a wealthy mulatto was a betrayal of the official black nationalist agenda. Since she was the daughter of one of François's enemies, Ernst Bennett, observers concluded that the regime had lost its iron touch. Most importantly, Michèle's taste for furs, diamonds, and million-dollar shopping sprees in Miami, Paris, and New York led her and her relatives to increase dramatically the size of the embezzlement schemes that had always characterized the regime. (Michèle's brother also dabbled in the cocaine trade.) The vast gap between impoverished peasants and slum dwellers and a spoiled elite that flaunted its wealth became offensive.

Strikes multiplied, while critics such as Jean-Bertrand Aristide, a popular priest, delivered disparaging sermons. The U.S. government, long supportive, curtailed aid, and Secretary of State George Shultz announced that a switch to a more democratic regime would be welcome. Bowing to internal and international pressures, Duvalier fled into exile on February 7, 1986. He first lived on the French Riviera. After his savings ran out and his wife divorced him, he moved to a less expensive abode in the Paris suburbs. There were rumors in the late 1990s that he was planning a return to power in a context of continued political instability in Haiti, but they proved unfounded.

Philippe R. Girard

See also: Aristide, Jean-Bertrand; Duvalier, François; Haiti

References
Abbott, Elizabeth. *Haiti: The Duvaliers and Their Legacy.* 1988. Reprint, New York: Simon & Schuster, 1991.
Wilentz, Amy. *The Rainy Season: Haiti since Duvalier.* New York: Simon & Schuster, 1989.